LIVERPOOL
A PICTORIAL HISTORY

LIVERPOOL
A PICTORIAL HISTORY

NEAL SIMPSON

EMPICS

BREEDON
BOOKS
SPORT

First published in Great Britain by
The Breedon Books Publishing Company Limited
44 Friar Gate, Derby DE1 1DA
1992

ISBN 1 873626 23 1

Printed and bound by The Bath Press Limited, Bath and London.
Jacket printed by BDC Printing Services Ltd of Derby.

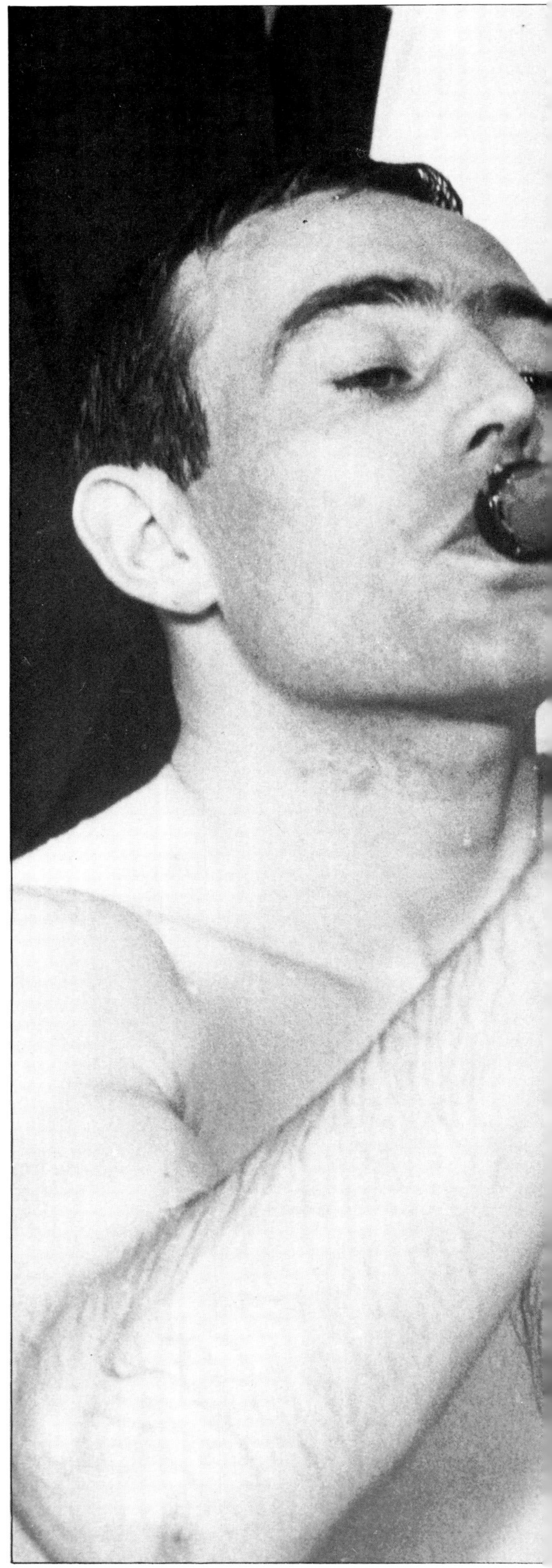

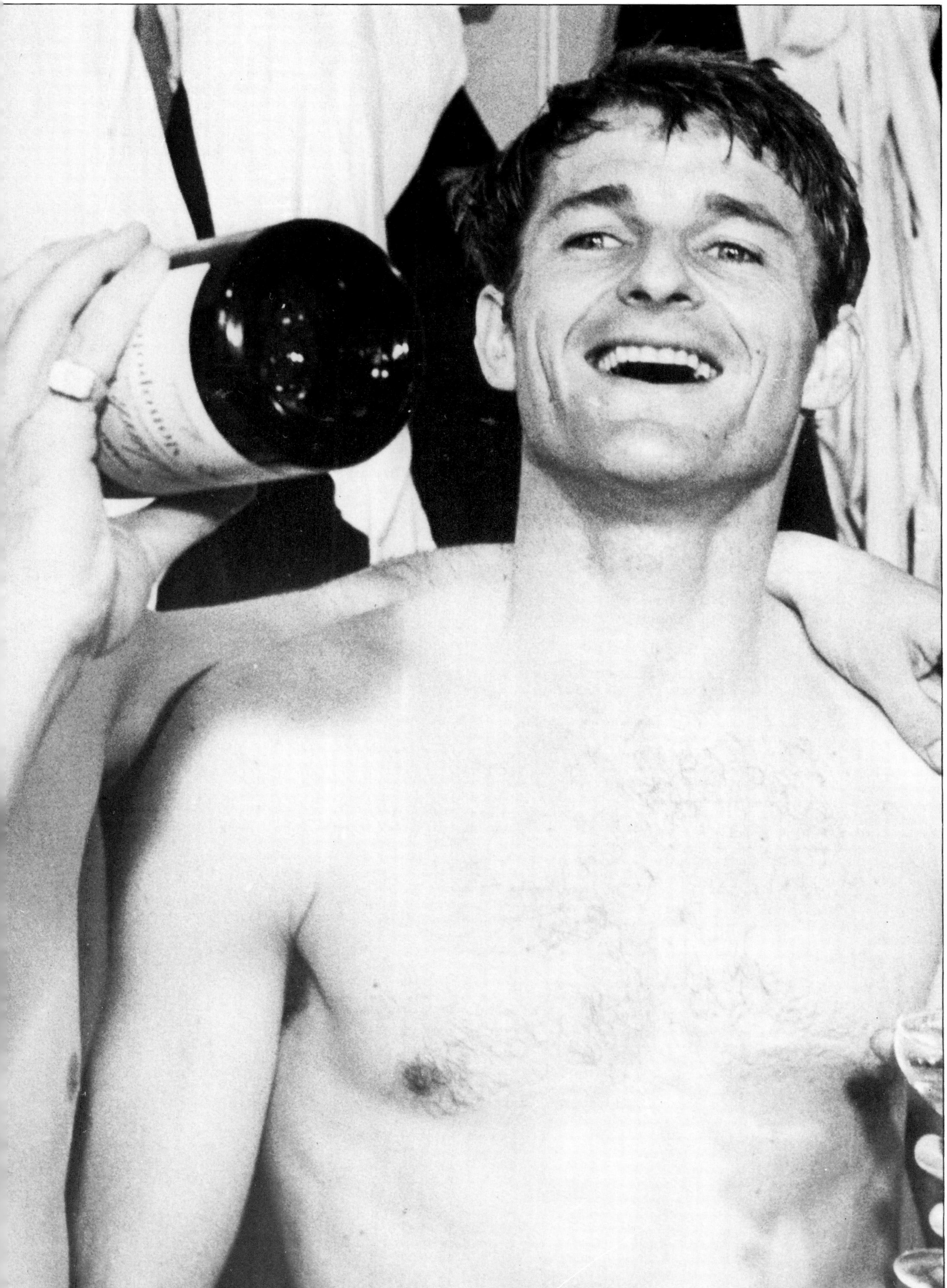

Introduction

THIS book is the second in what is planned to be a series of pictorial history titles of leading soccer clubs and it is wholly appropriate that Liverpool FC should be the subject of this pioneering new series, for the Reds of Anfield are, without doubt, one of the world's most famous clubs.

Winners of a record 18 Football League Championship titles, Liverpool have also lifted the European Cup four times, the FA Cup on five occasions, the most recent of which was in 1992, and were victorious in four successive League Cup Finals in the 1980s.

In times past the Reds have also written their name on numerous trophies, beginning with the Second Division title in 1893-4 — only their second year in existence and their first in the Football League — and before World War One they had taken the First Division title on two occasions. Consecutive titles followed in the 1920s and another in the first post-war season of 1946-7.

The arrival Bill Shankly heralded the start of an era which has just gone on and on, Liverpool winning trophy after trophy. This book chronicles those successes and the players who swept Liverpool to them. It uses some of the best photographic images available, many of them rarely seen, and is culled mostly from the files of the Hulton-Deutsch Collection and the Midlands-based agency, Empics, who also act for FIFA's official photographer Peter Robinson. Some other pictures first appeared in the Liverpool Echo. Some are from Syndication International.

The result is a pictorial parade through the history of a great club and it is hoped that the contents will both inform and entertain, bringing back memories distant and not so distant, of some great Merseyside football.

LIVERPOOL Football Club

Honours

Football League Champions
1900-01, 1905-06, 1921-22, 1922-23, 1946-47, 1963-64, 1965-66, 1972-73, 1975-76, 1976-77, 1978-79, 1979-80, 1981-82, 1982-83, 1983-84, 1985-86, 1987-88, 1989-90
Runners-up
1898-99, 1909-10, 1968-69, 1973-74, 1974-75, 1977-78, 1984-85, 1986-87, 1988-89, 1990-91

Second Division Champions
1893-94, 1895-96, 1904-05, 1961-62

FA Cup Winners
1964-65, 1973-74, 1985-86, 1988-89, 1991-92
Runners-up
1913-14, 1949-50, 1970-71, 1976-77, 1987-88

Football League Cup Winners
1980-81, 1981-82, 1982-83, 1983-84
Runners-up
1977-78, 1986-87

European Cup Winners
1976-77, 1977-78, 1980-81, 1983-84
Runners-up
1984-85

UEFA Cup Winners
1972-73, 1975-76

European Cup-winners' Cup Runners-up
1965-66

European Super Cup Winners
1977
Runners-up
1978, 1984

World Club Championship Runners-up
1981

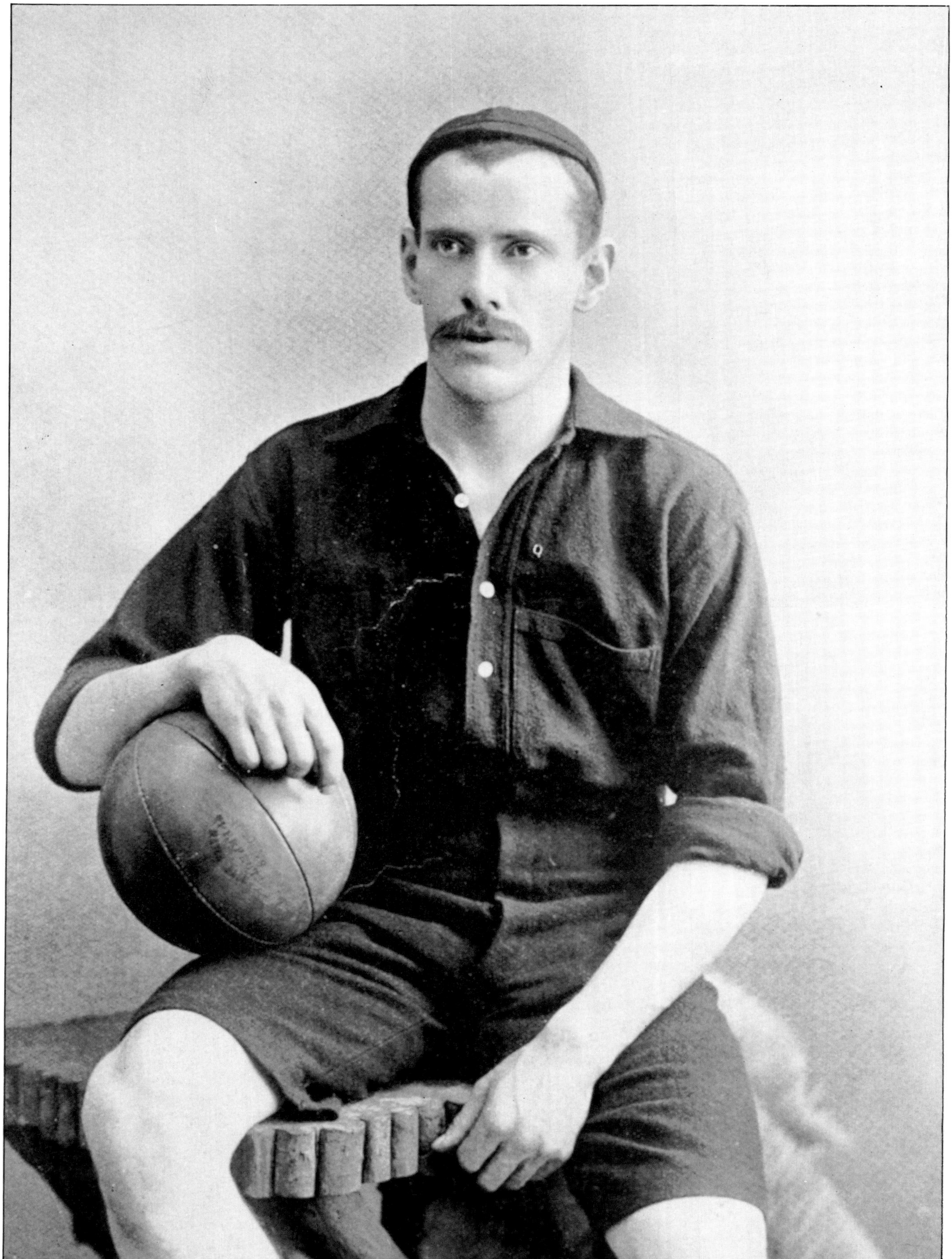

Goalkeeper Harry Storer made 121 League and FA Cup appearances for Liverpool after joining them from Woolwich Arsenal, for £75 in December 1895 after being suspended by Arsenal following a 'breach of discipline'. Storer won a Second Division championship medal with Liverpool in his first season with the club. He had played for the Football League in 1895. His son, also Harry, played soccer for England, managed Coventry City, Birmingham City and Derby County, and was in Derbyshire's 1936 County Cricket Championship-winning side. Harry senior's brother, William, kept wicket for England.

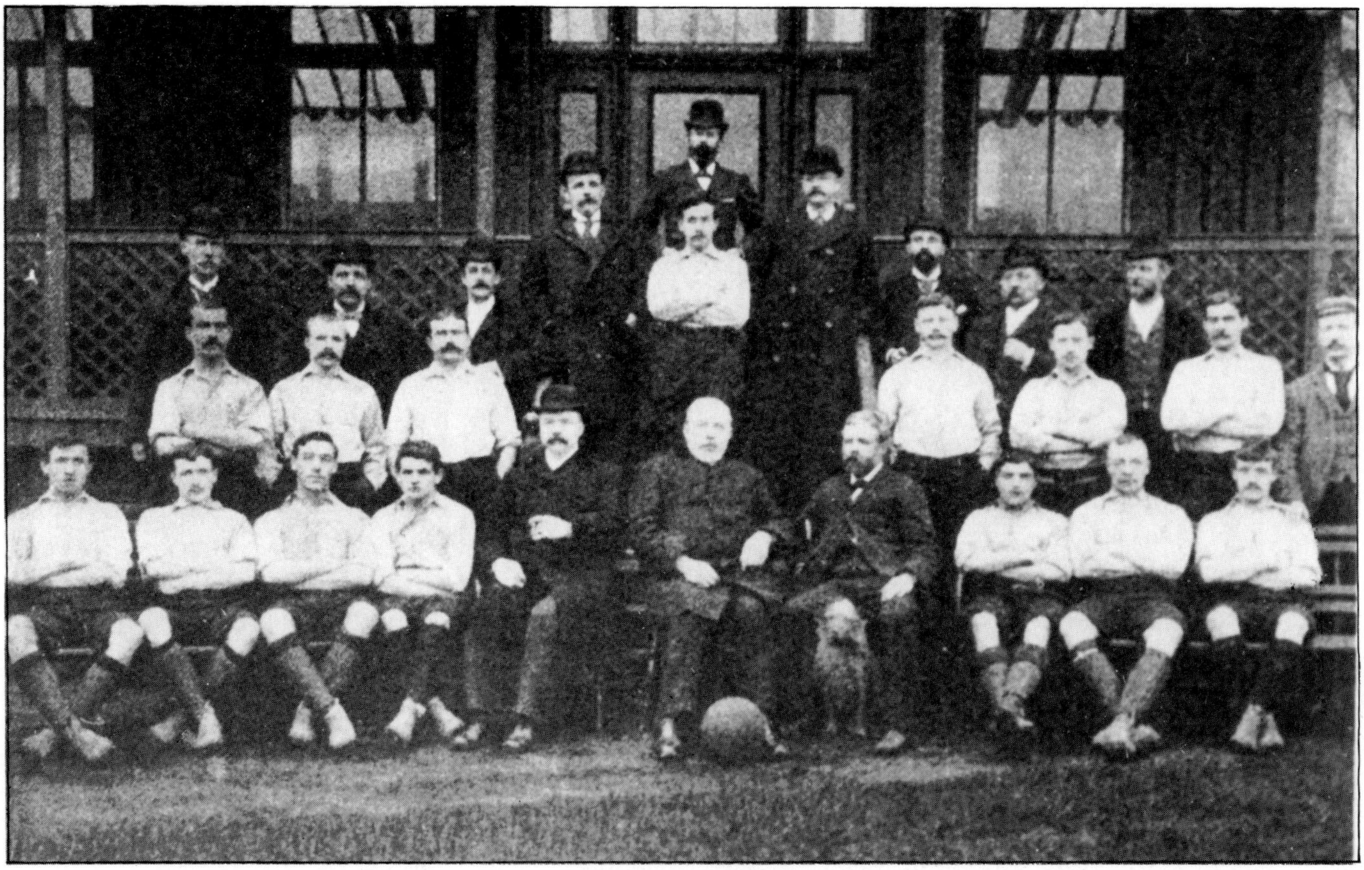

Liverpool, Second Division champions in 1893-4. Back row (left to right, players only): McCartney, M.McQueen, Hannah, McOwen, McLean, Dick, Henderson. Front row: Gordon, McVean, McQue, McBride, Bradshaw, Stott, H.McQueen.

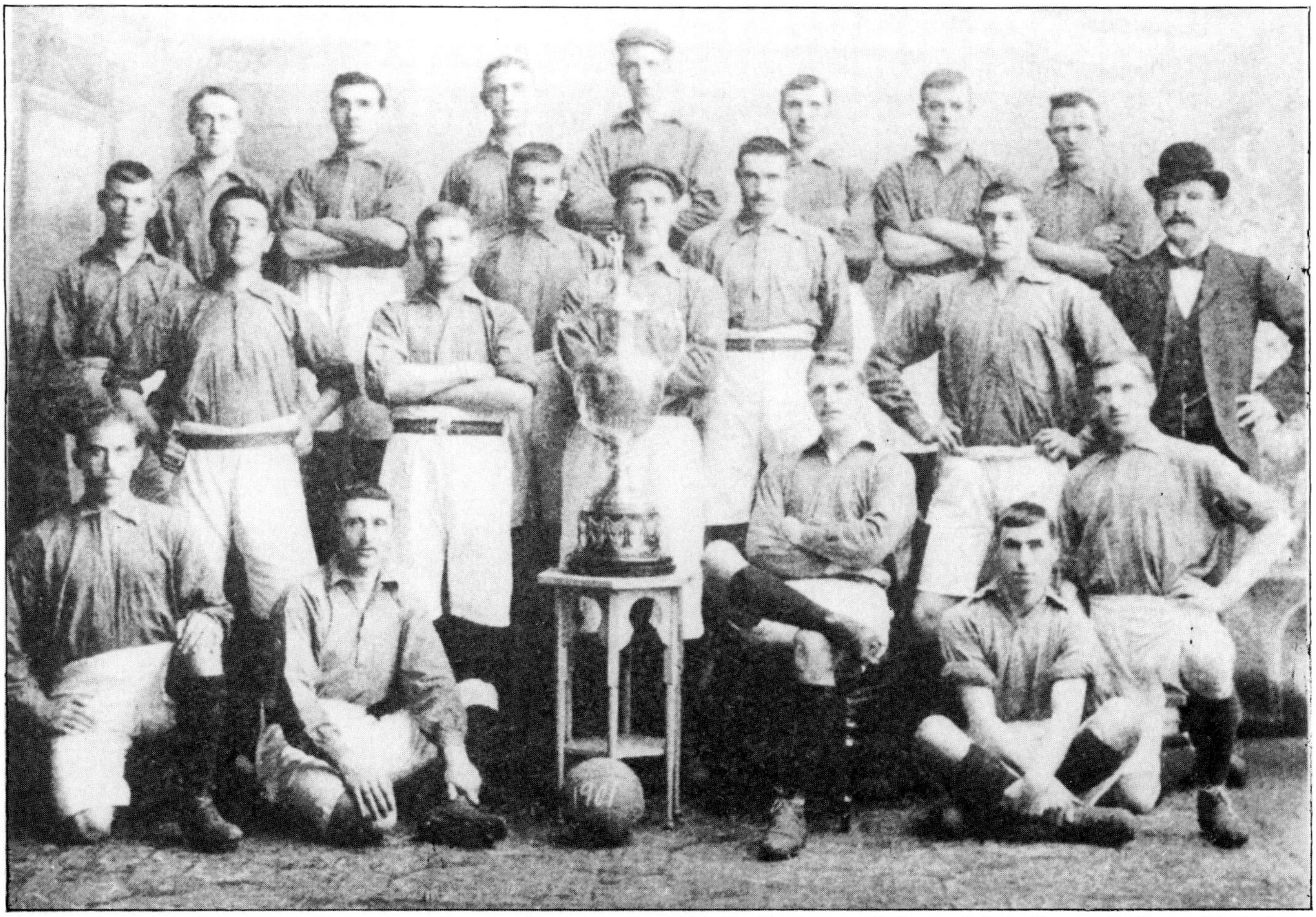

Liverpool, Football League Champions for the first time in 1900-01. Back row (left to right): Ottey, Goliver, McGuigan, Foster, S.Hunter, J.Hunter, Howell. Middle row (players only): Soulsby, Wilson, Raybould, J.Robertson, Perkins, Goldie, Parry. Front row: Walker, Dunlop, Raisbeck, Cox, T.Robertson.

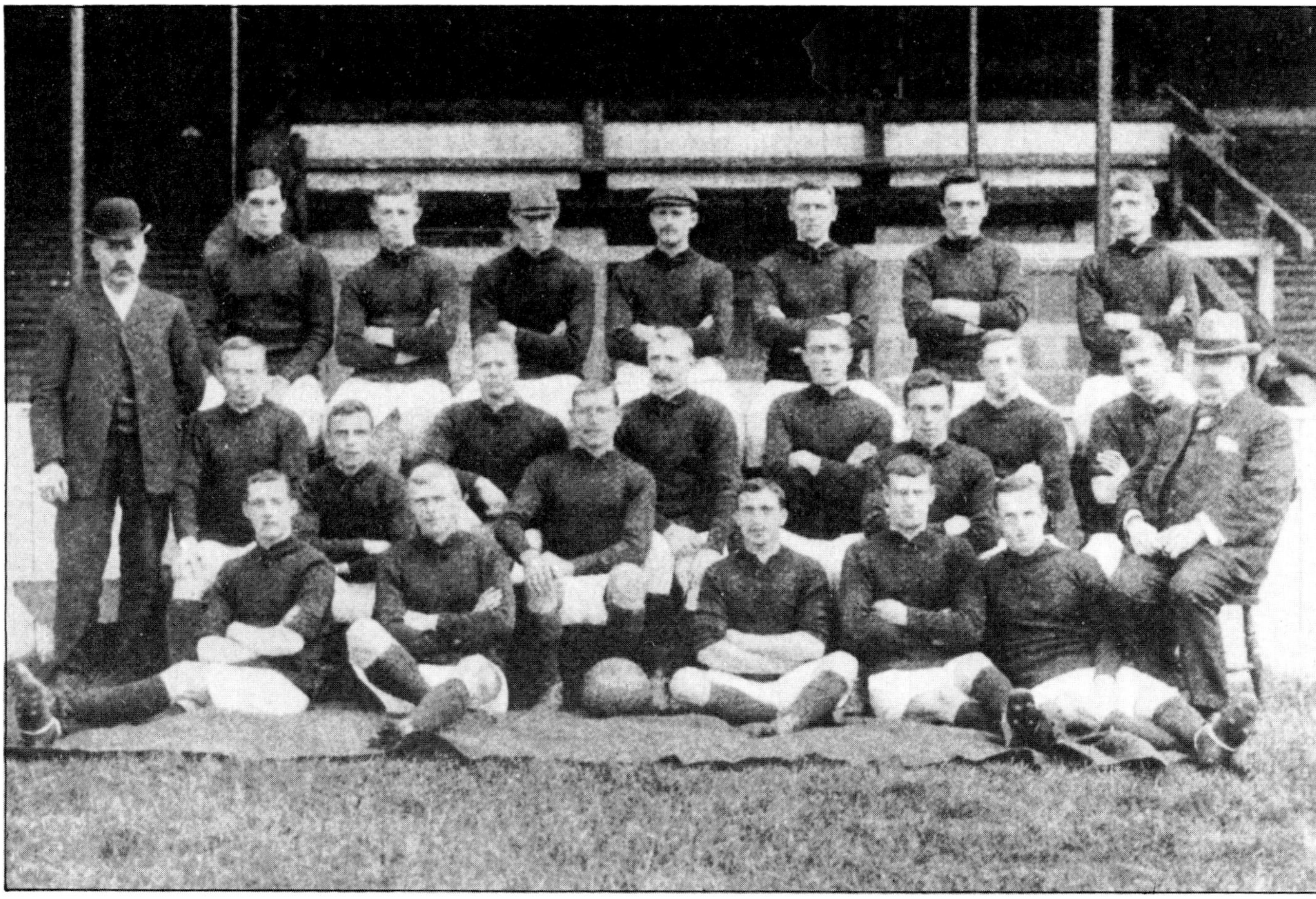

Liverpool, Second Division champions in 1904-05. Back row (left to right, players only): Parry, Murray, Platt, Doig, Dunlop, Wilson, Evans. Middle row: Fleming, Carling, Latham, Raybould, Raisbeck, Hughes, Parkinson, Chorlton, Cox. Front row: Goddard, Robinson, Morris, Hewitt, Garside.

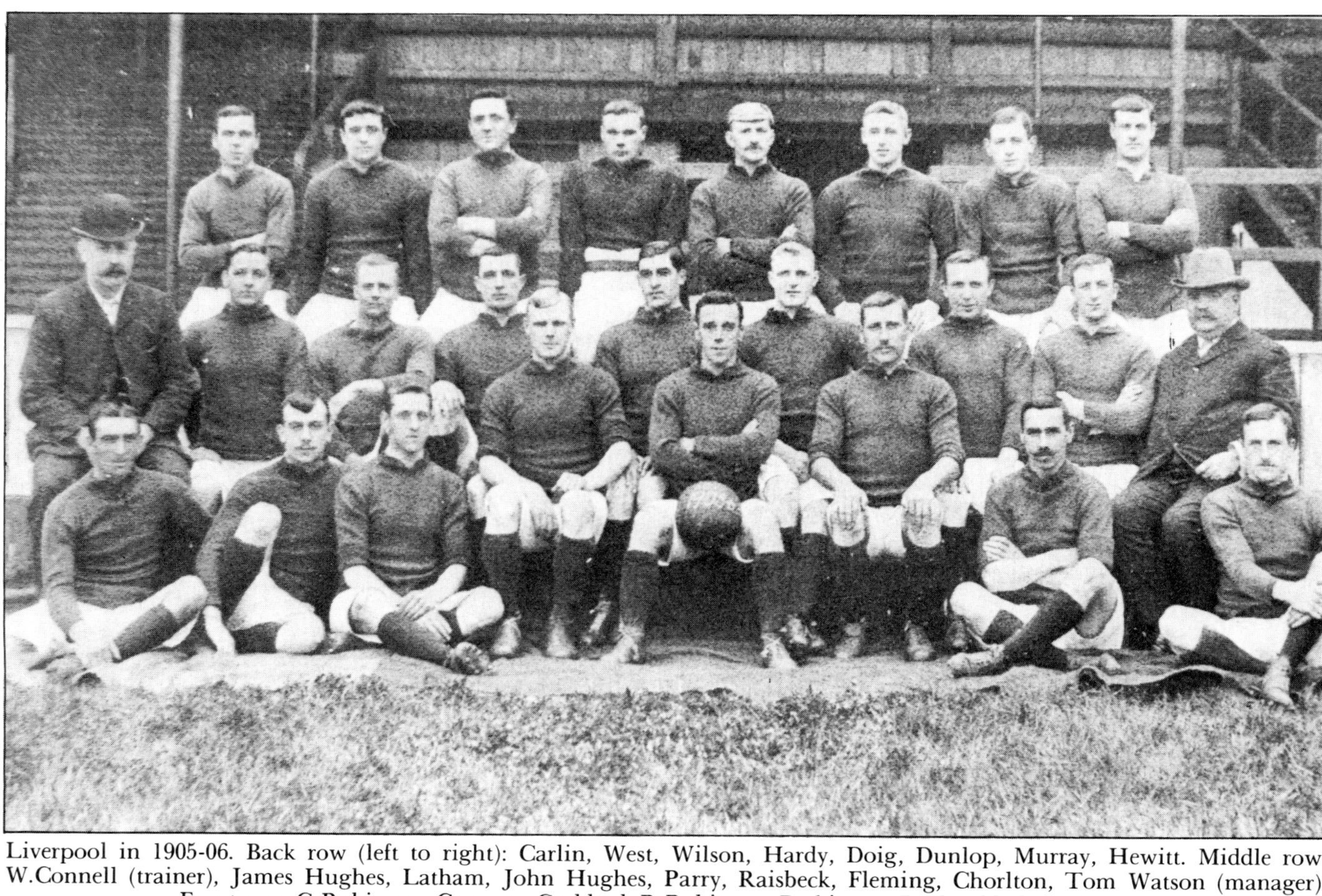

Liverpool in 1905-06. Back row (left to right): Carlin, West, Wilson, Hardy, Doig, Dunlop, Murray, Hewitt. Middle row: W.Connell (trainer), James Hughes, Latham, John Hughes, Parry, Raisbeck, Fleming, Chorlton, Tom Watson (manager). Front row: G.Robinson, Gorman, Goddard, R.Robinson, Parkinson, Raybould, Cox, Garside.

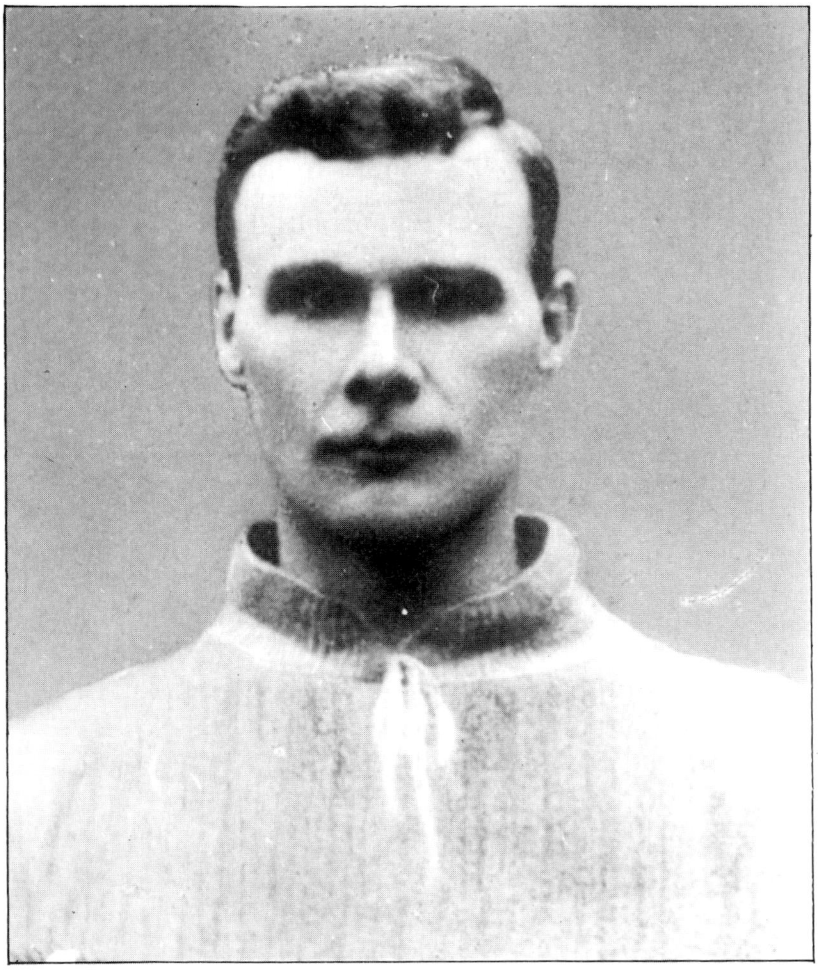

Sam Hardy was the first of a long line of truly great Liverpool goalkeepers. Hardy joined the Reds from Chesterfield in May 1905 and won England caps whilst at Anfield. After 239 League and FA Cup appearances, he was transferred to Aston Villa in May 1912.

Liverpool come under attack at Stamford Bridge in September 1912. The Merseysiders, though, went away with a 2-1 victory, thanks to second-half goals from Goddard and Gracie. A crowd of 25,000 watched the game. Liverpool ended the season in 12th place in Division One.

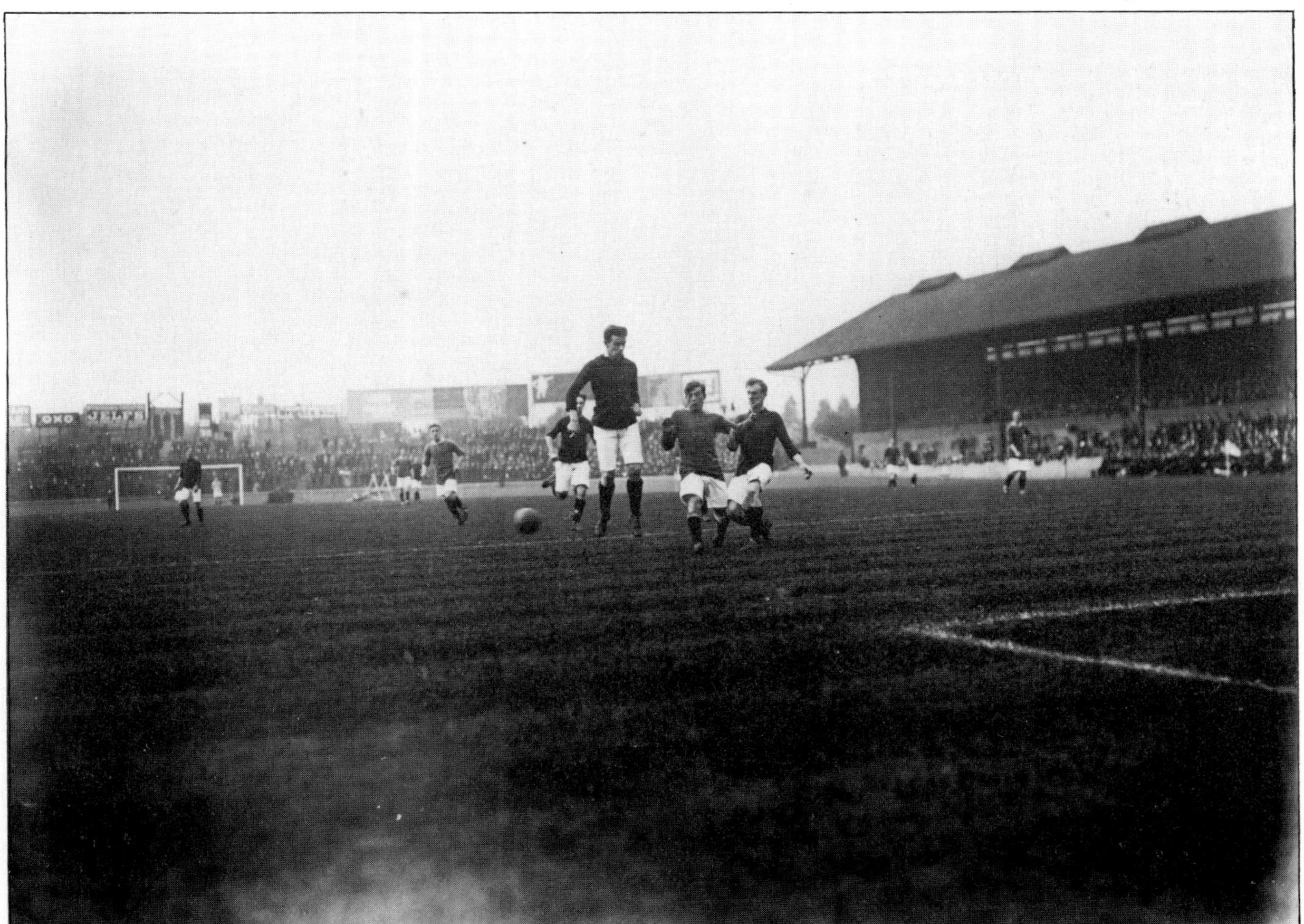

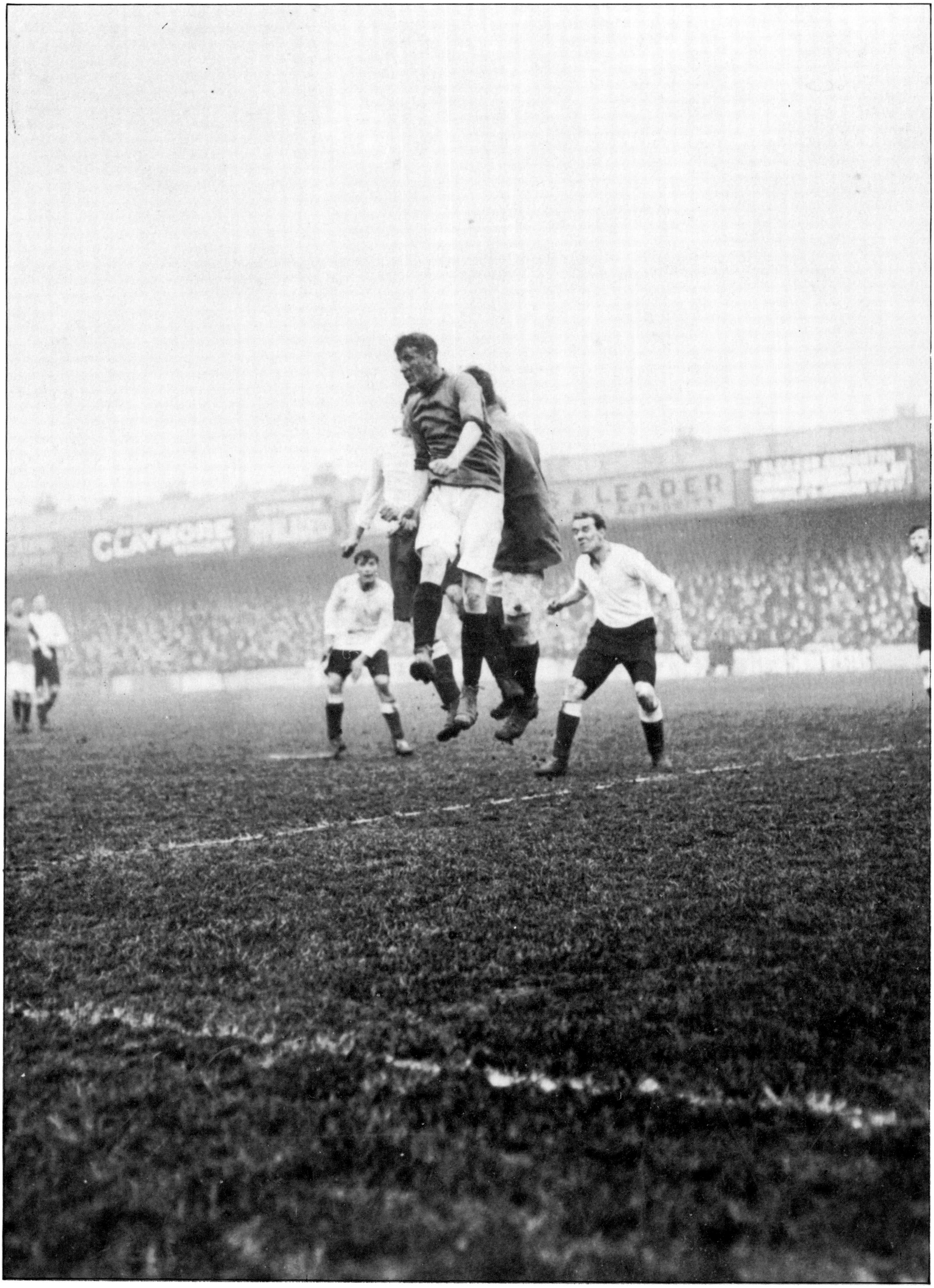

Liverpool are on the defensive here against Tottenham Hotspur at White Hart Lane in April 1914. They drew 0-0 with Tottenham Hotspur on their way to finishing 16th in Division One, although there was more than enough compensation when the Reds reached the FA Cup Final.

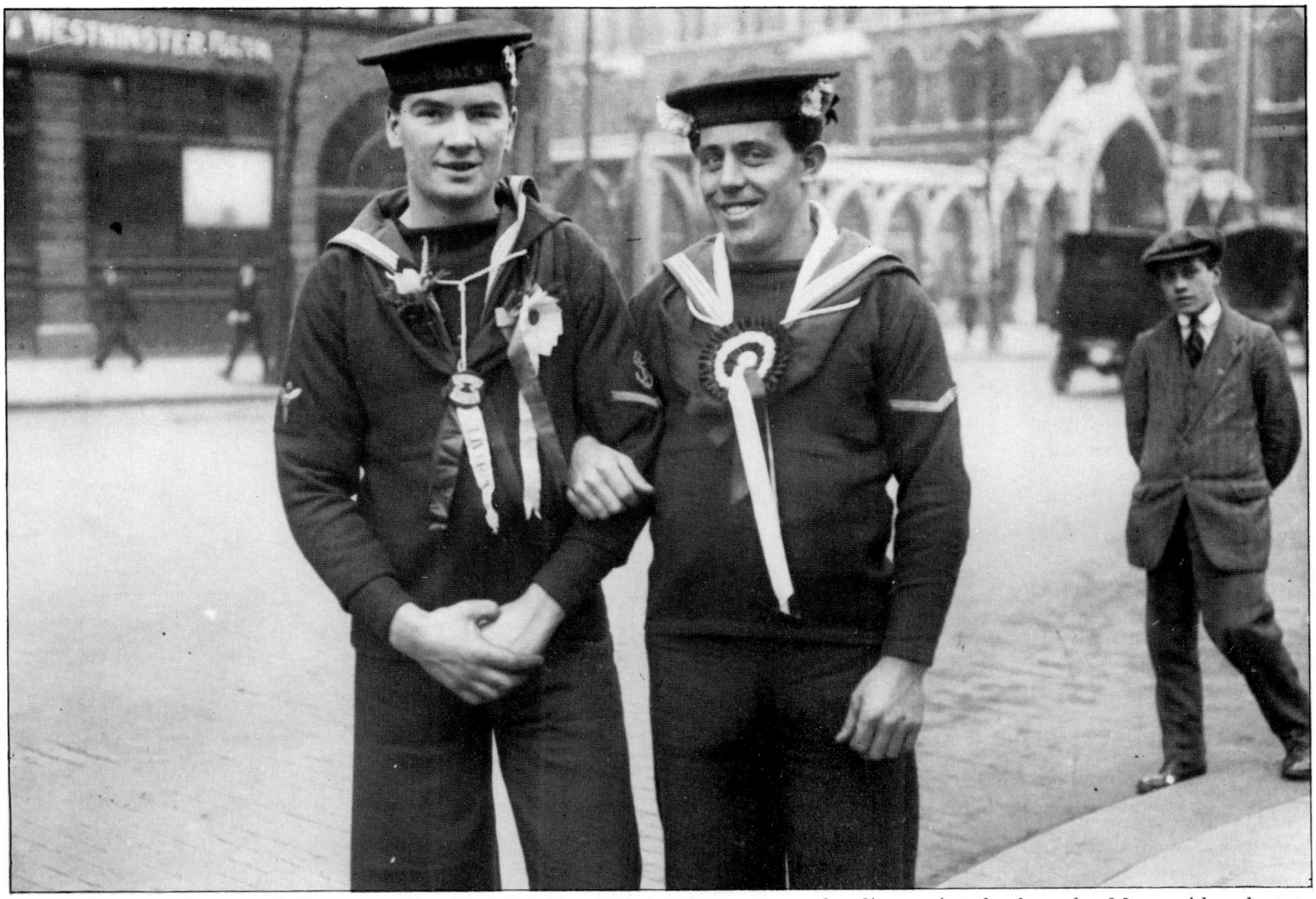

Two Liverpool fans on their way to the 1914 FA Cup Final. They were to be disappointed when the Merseysiders lost to Burnley by the only goal of the game.

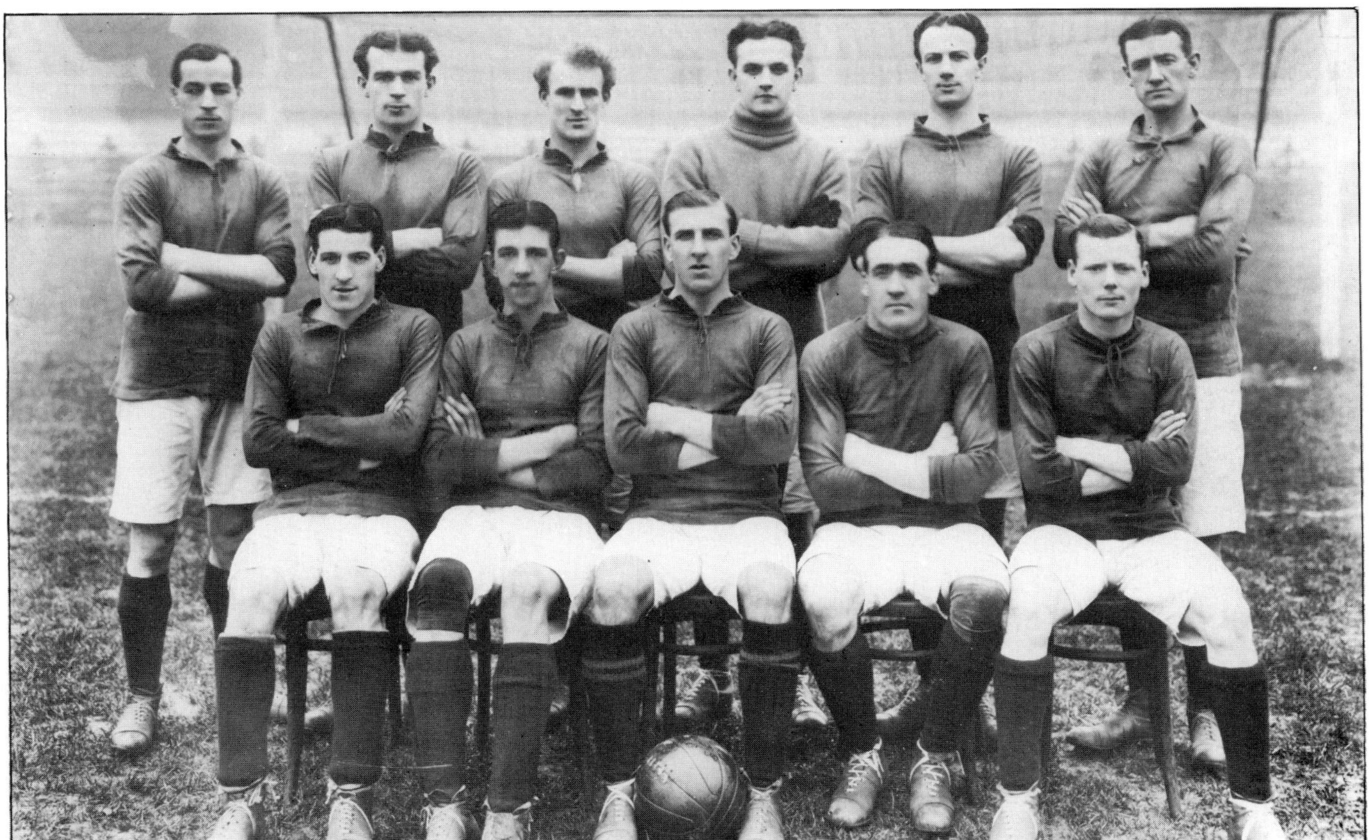

Liverpool in 1913-14. Back row (left to right): Fairfoul, Lowe, Longworth, Campbell, Pursell, Ferguson. Front row: MacKinlay, Dawson, Miller, Lacey, Sheldon. Nine of this side met Burnley in the FA Cup Final at the Crystal Palace, the absentees being Nicholl and Metcalfe. The Reds' leading scorer this season was Tom Miller, who joined them from Hamilton Academical in February 1912. He made his Scotland debut whilst at Anfield, scoring twice in a 5-4 defeat by England.

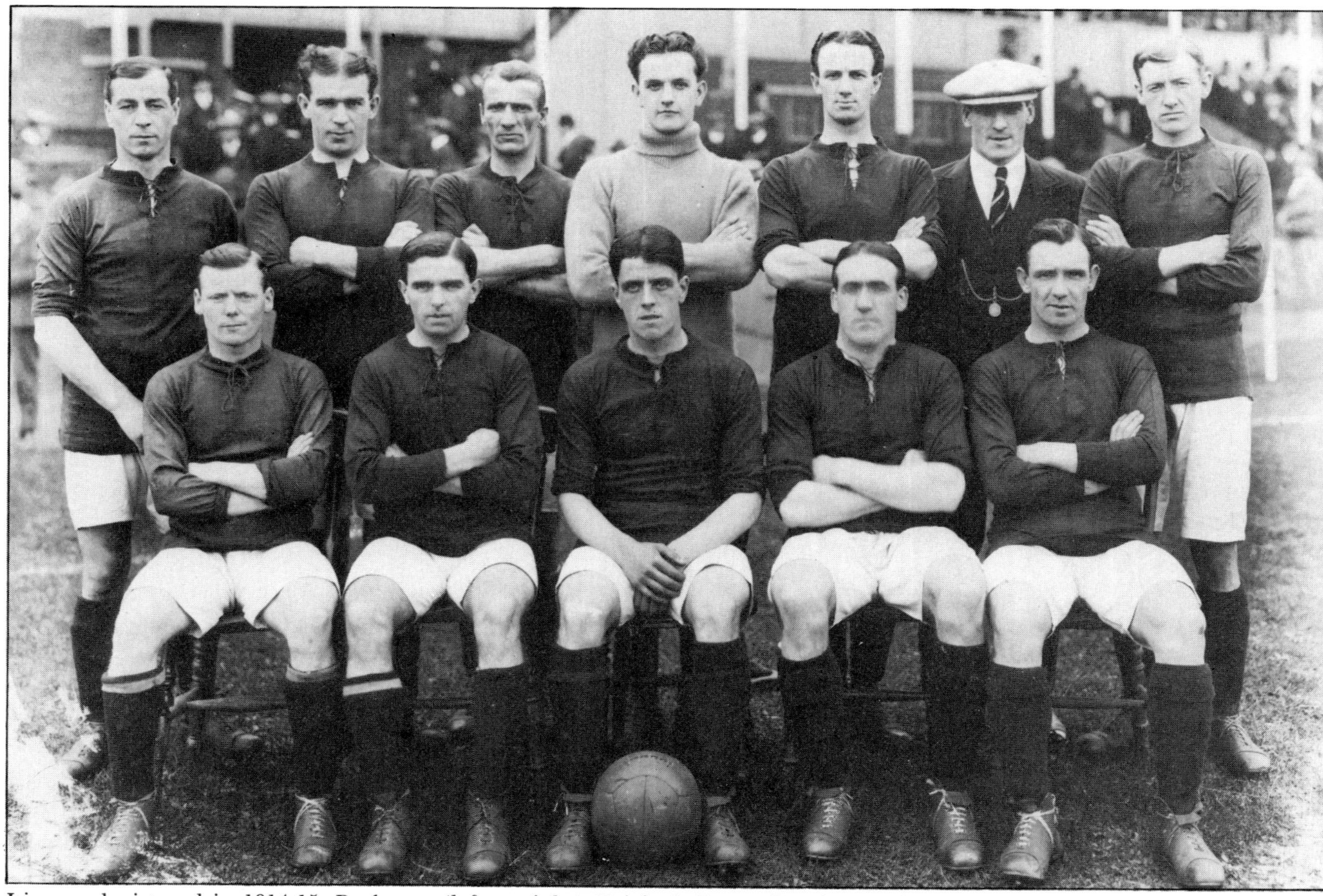

Liverpool pictured in 1914-15. Back row (left to right): Fairfoul, Lowe, Speakman, Campbell, Pursell, MacKinlay, Ferguson. Front row: Sheldon, Metcalfe, McDougall, Lacey, Nicholl. Jimmy Nicholl was the only ever-present this season as the Reds finished 14th in Division One.

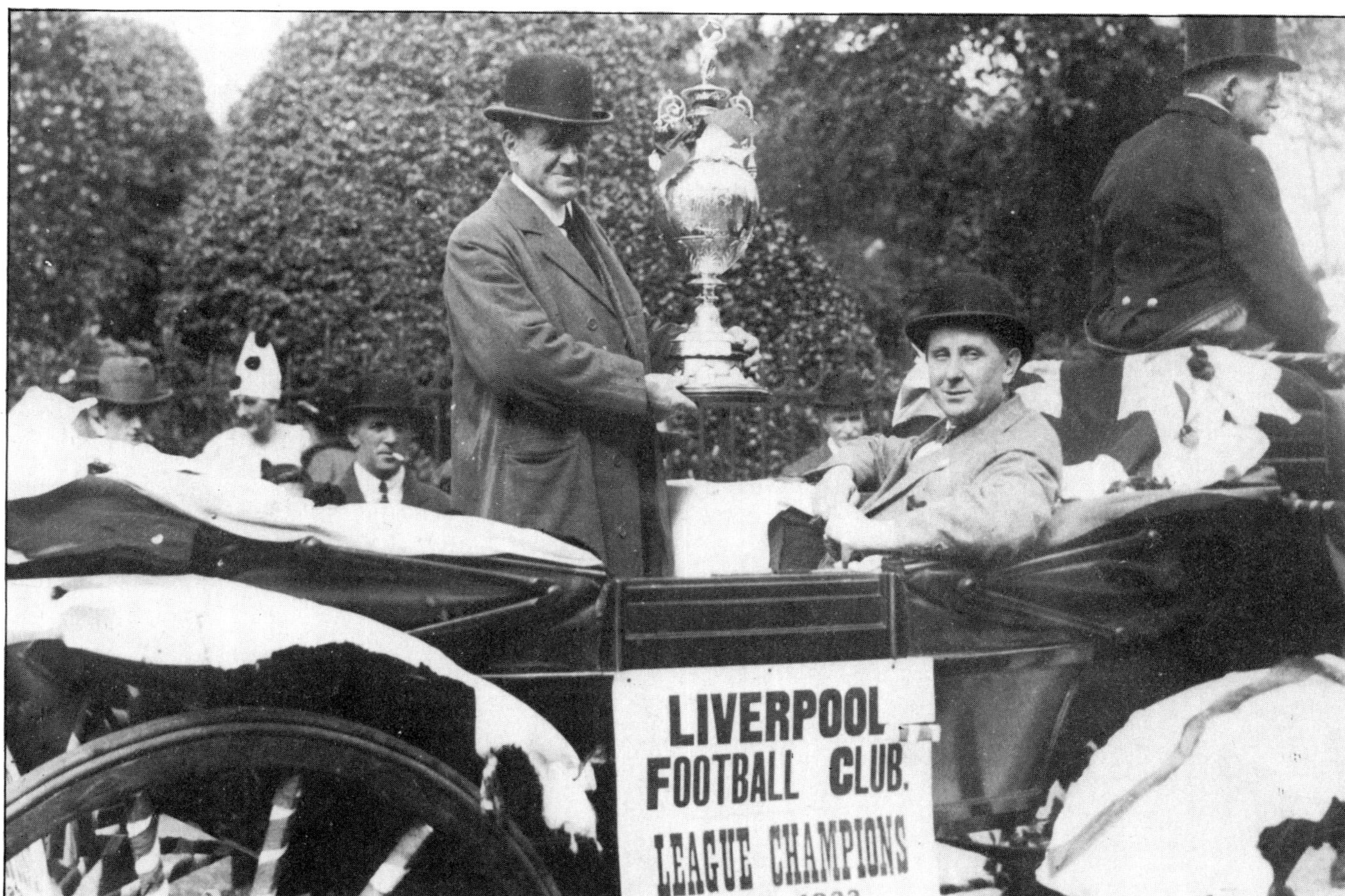

Liverpool are Football League Champions and trainer Charlie Wilson holds the trophy with Andy McGuigan seated in the carriage. Both played when the Reds first won the title in 1900-01. The following year the Reds retained the title.

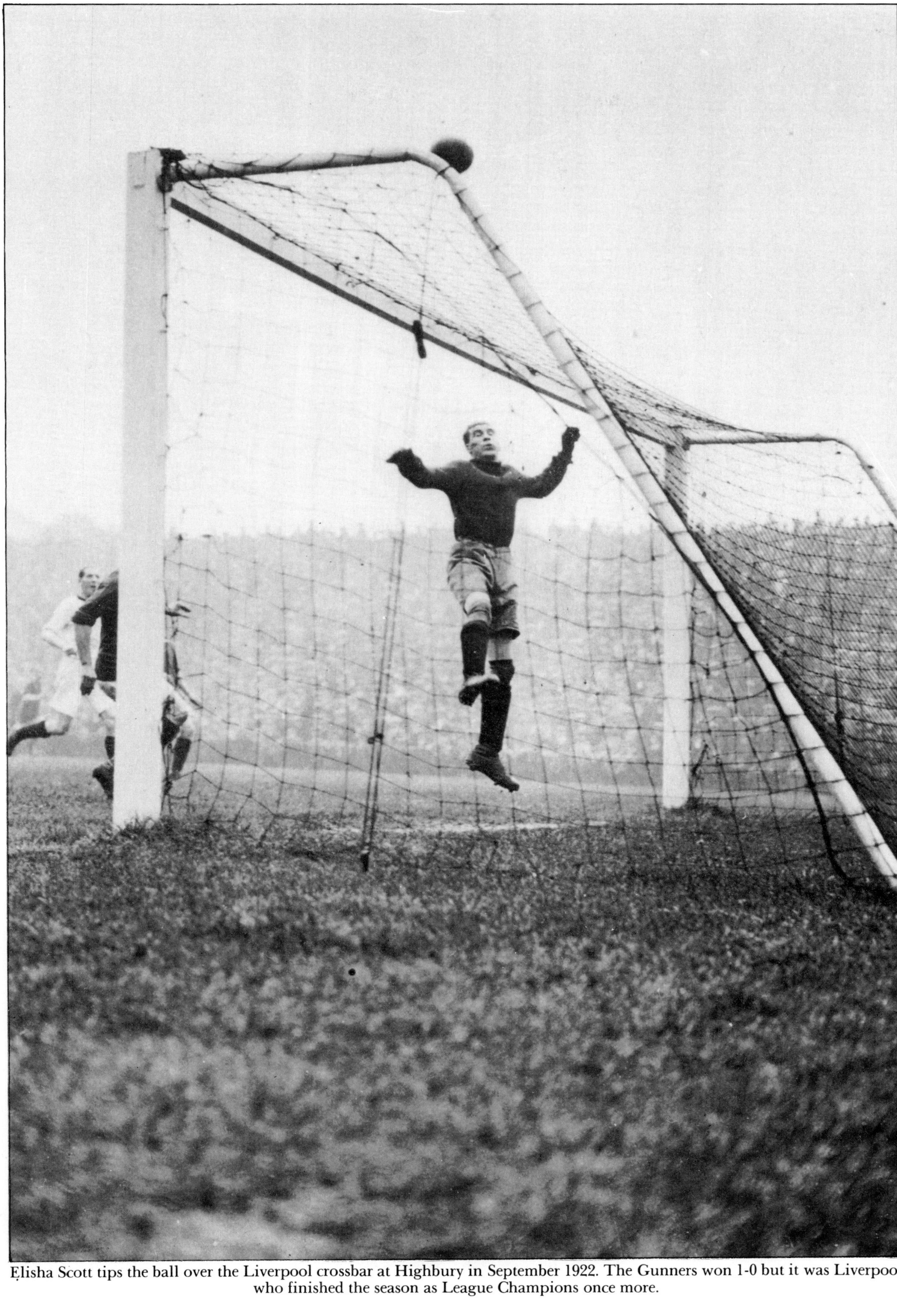

Elisha Scott tips the ball over the Liverpool crossbar at Highbury in September 1922. The Gunners won 1-0 but it was Liverpool who finished the season as League Champions once more.

Long-serving goalkeeper Elisha Scott joined Liverpool in 1912 and clocked up 467 senior appearances before becoming player-manager of Belfast Celtic in 1934. Scott, who was capped 31 times for Ireland, was one of the greatest footballers produced by the British game.

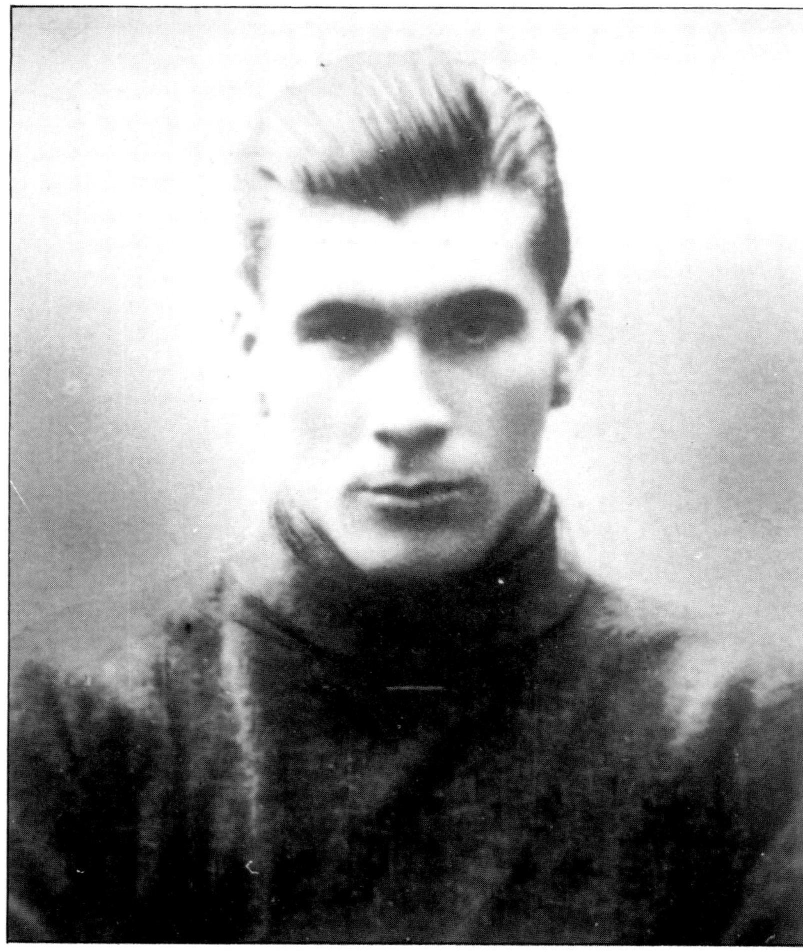

Scott snatches the ball away from a Tottenham Hotspur forward at White Hart Lane in November 1922. Liverpool won 4-2 before 45,000 fans.

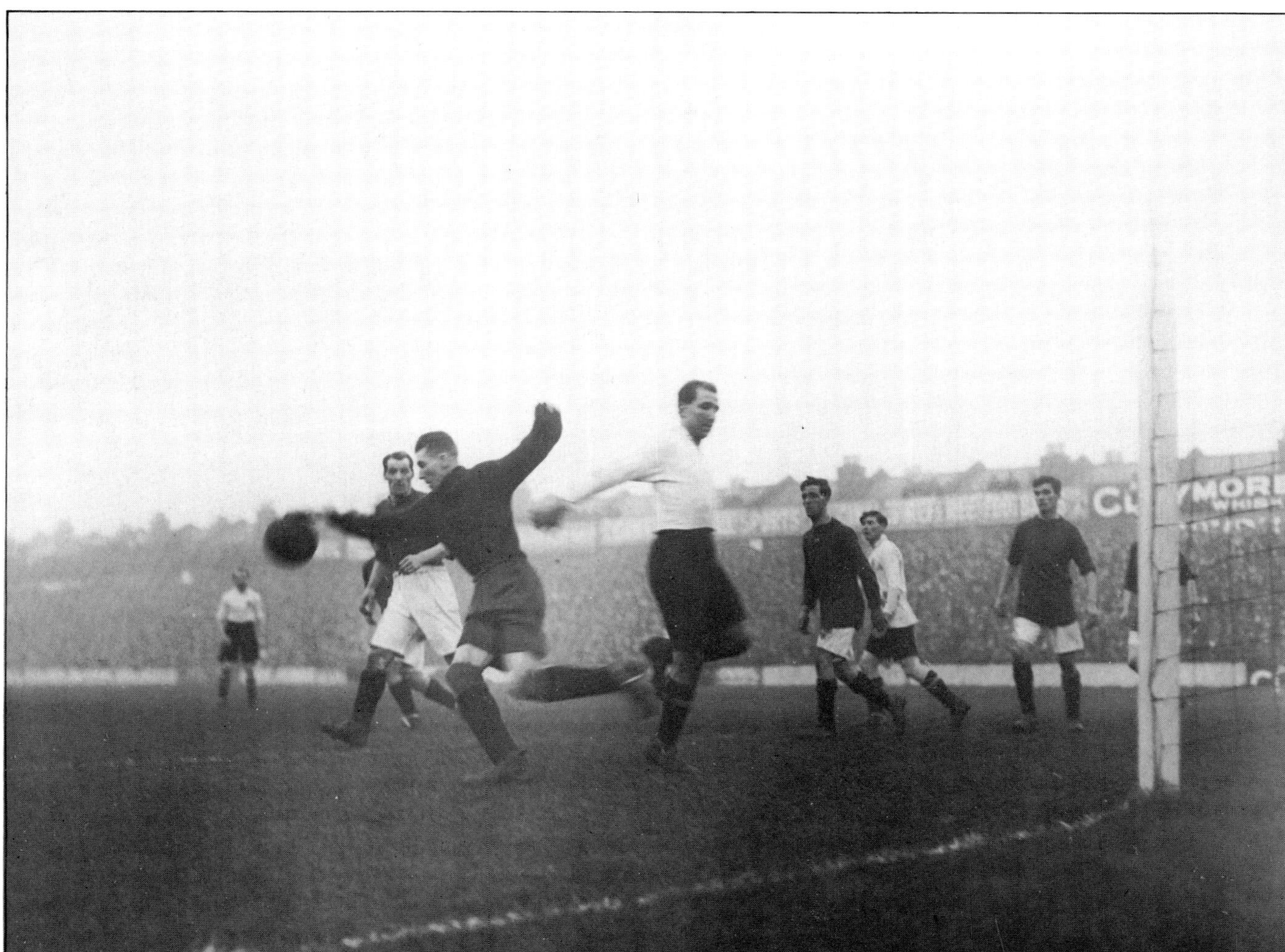

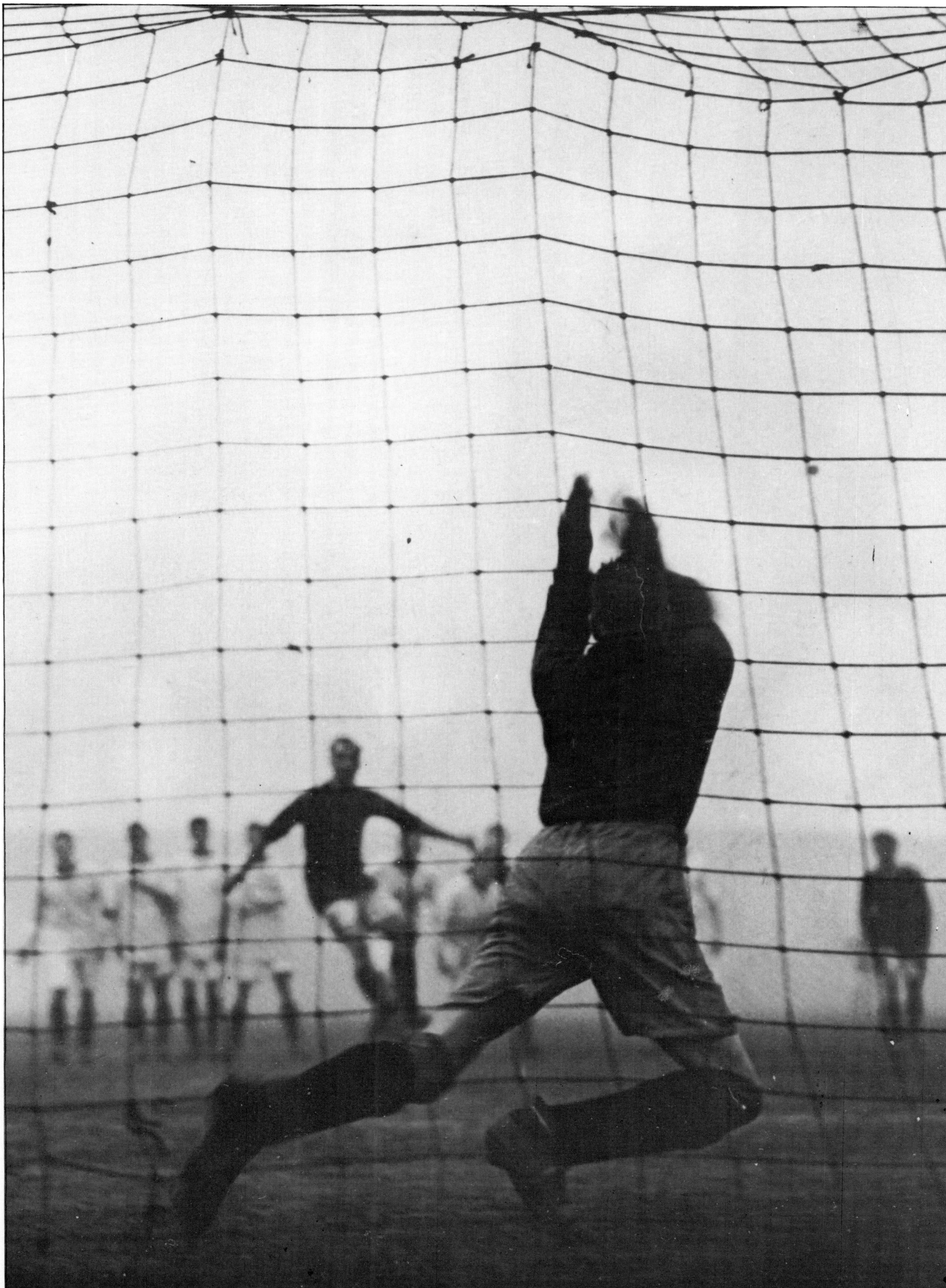

Scott in action at Highbury again, this time saving a penalty in the FA Cup first-round replay there in January 1923. After a goalless draw at Anfield, Liverpool beat the Gunners 4-1 and then won at Wolves before going out to Sheffield United at home in the third round.

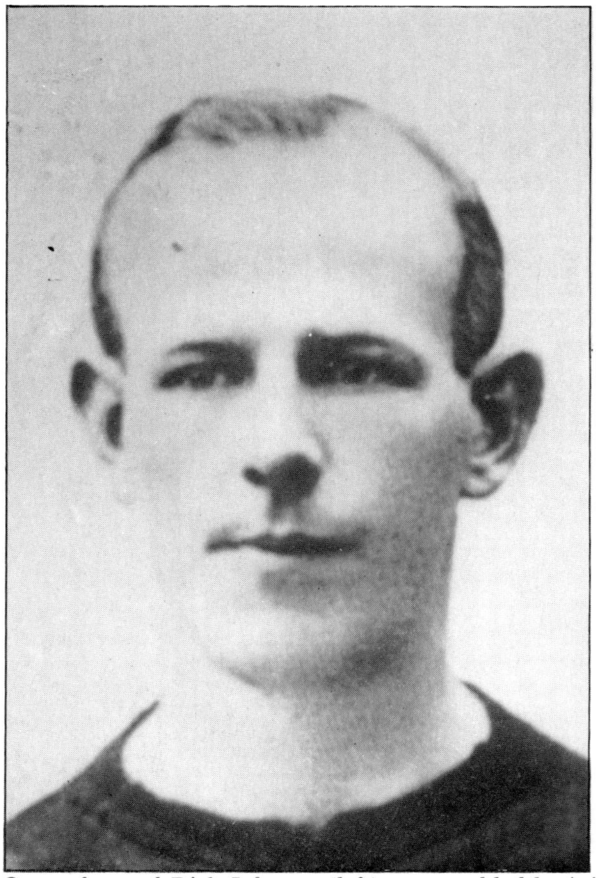

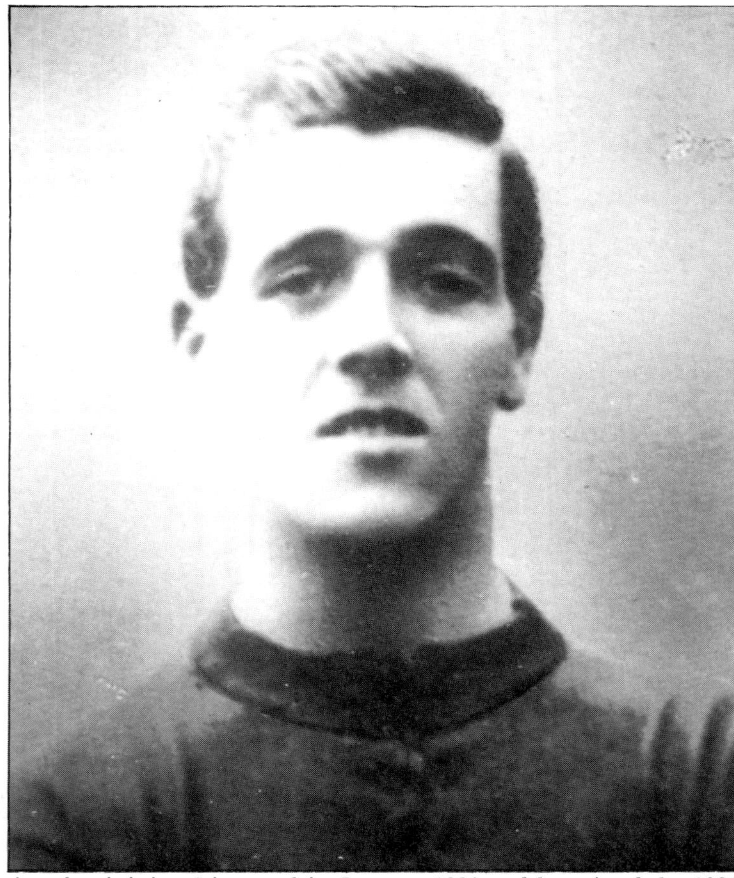

Centre-forward Dick Johnson (left) was troubled by injuries after joining Liverpool in January 1920 and he missed the 1921-2 Championship-winning season before returning to gain a medal the following campaign. He was transferred to Stoke in February 1925, after scoring 30 goals in 83 League and Cup appearances for the Reds, and won a Third Division North championship medal with the Potters in 1926-7. Wing-half Tommy Bromilow (right) joined Liverpool from local football in 1919. By the time he retired in 1930, Bromilow had been capped for England, played in two League Championship teams and altogether made 374 League and Cup appearances for the Reds.

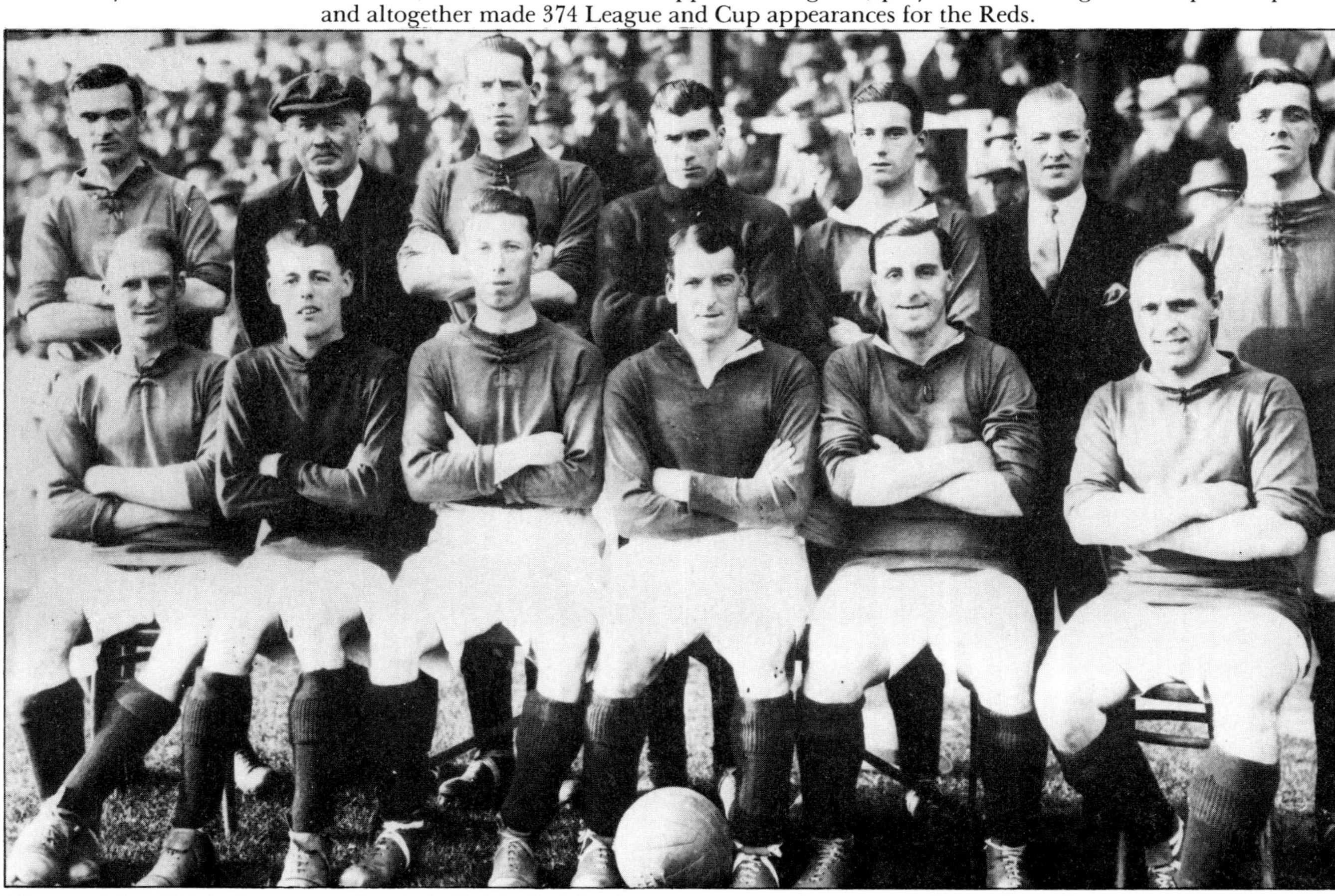

Liverpool in 1923-4, the season the Reds finished 12th after two consecutive League Championships. Back row: Wadsworth, Connell (trainer), McNab, Scott, Walsh, director, Bromilow. Front row: Longworth, Gilhespy, Forshaw, McKinlay (captain), Chambers, Hopkin.

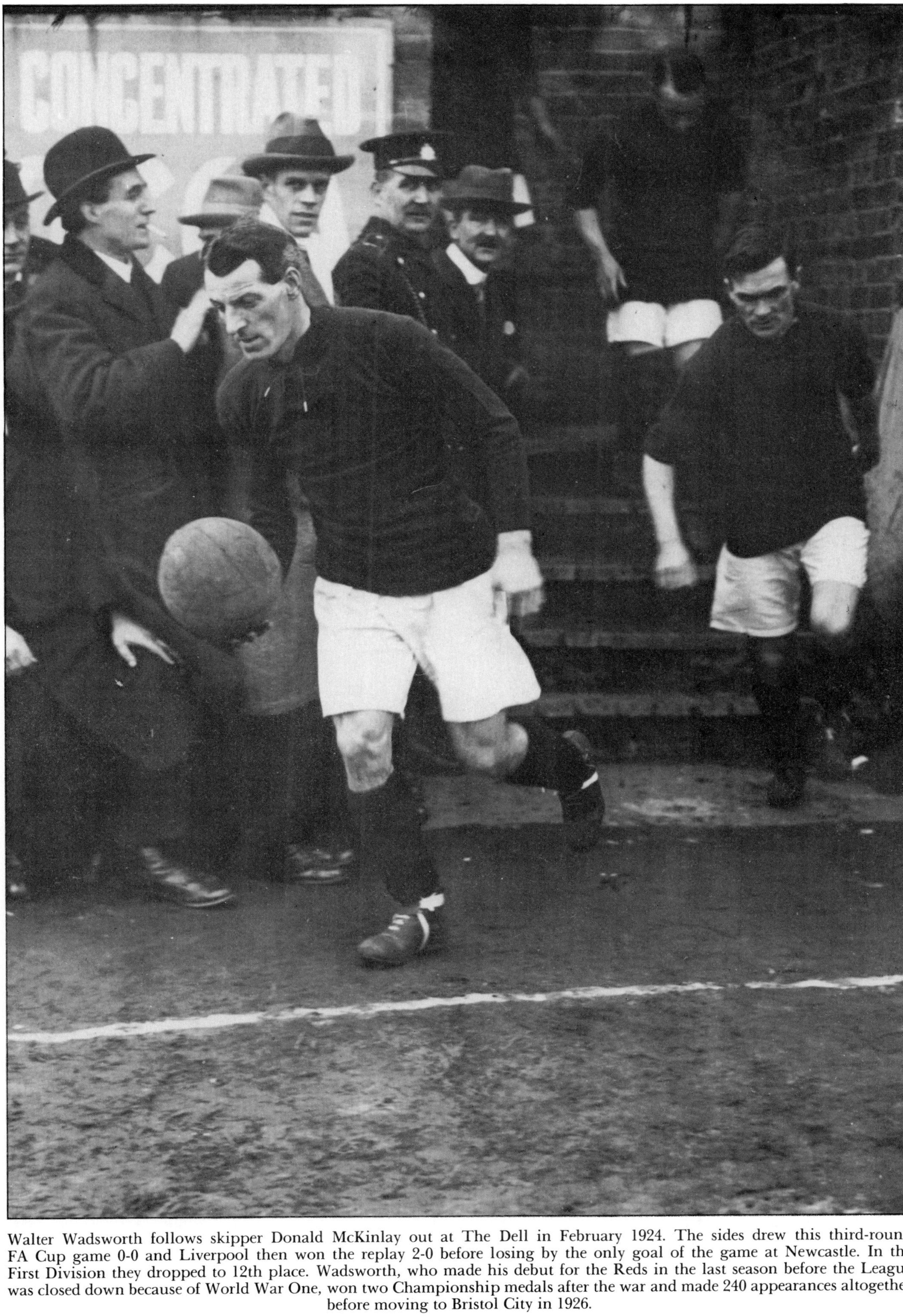

Walter Wadsworth follows skipper Donald McKinlay out at The Dell in February 1924. The sides drew this third-round FA Cup game 0-0 and Liverpool then won the replay 2-0 before losing by the only goal of the game at Newcastle. In the First Division they dropped to 12th place. Wadsworth, who made his debut for the Reds in the last season before the League was closed down because of World War One, won two Championship medals after the war and made 240 appearances altogether before moving to Bristol City in 1926.

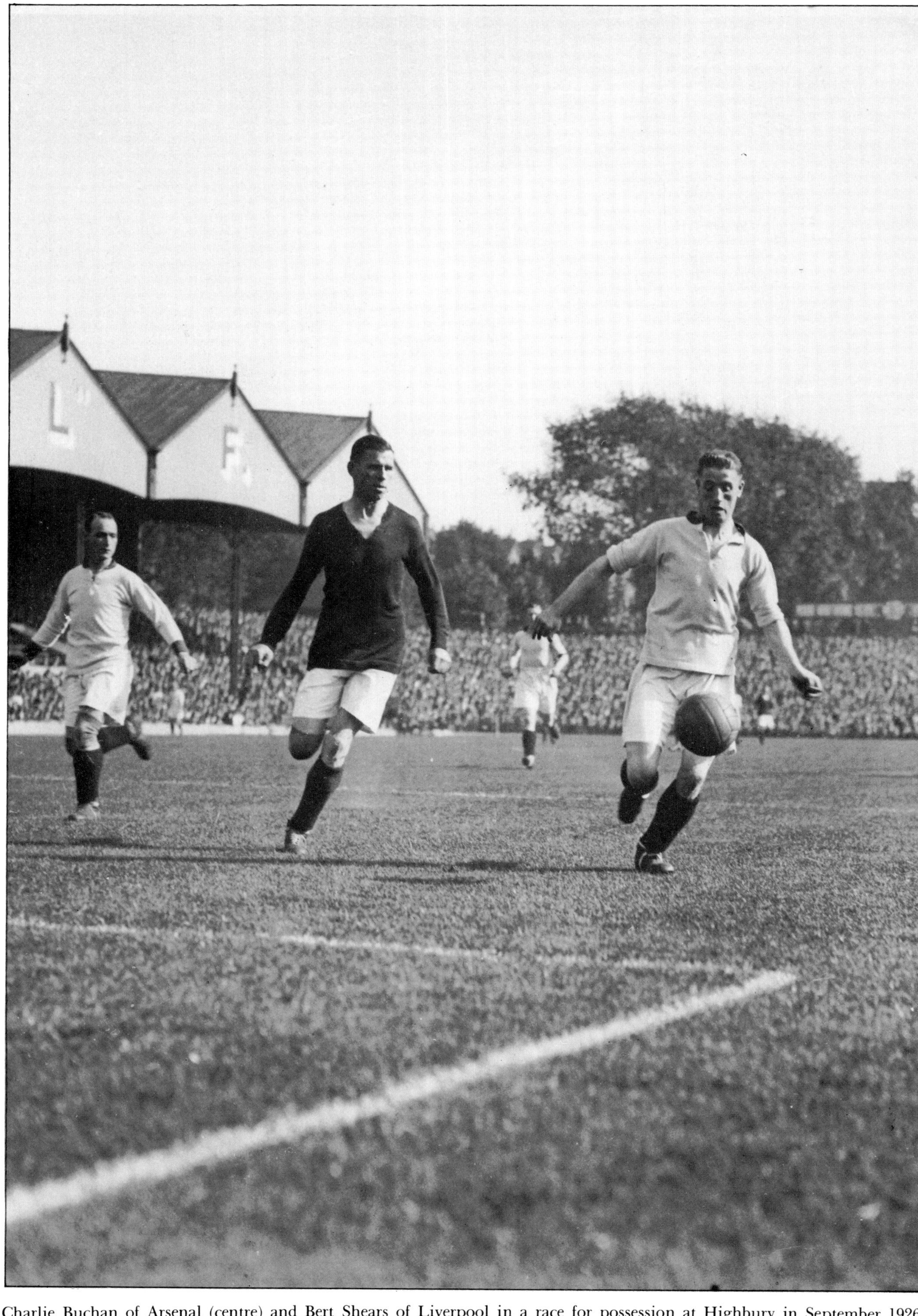

Charlie Buchan of Arsenal (centre) and Bert Shears of Liverpool in a race for possession at Highbury in September 1926, when the Merseysiders went down 2-0. They ended the season in ninth place.

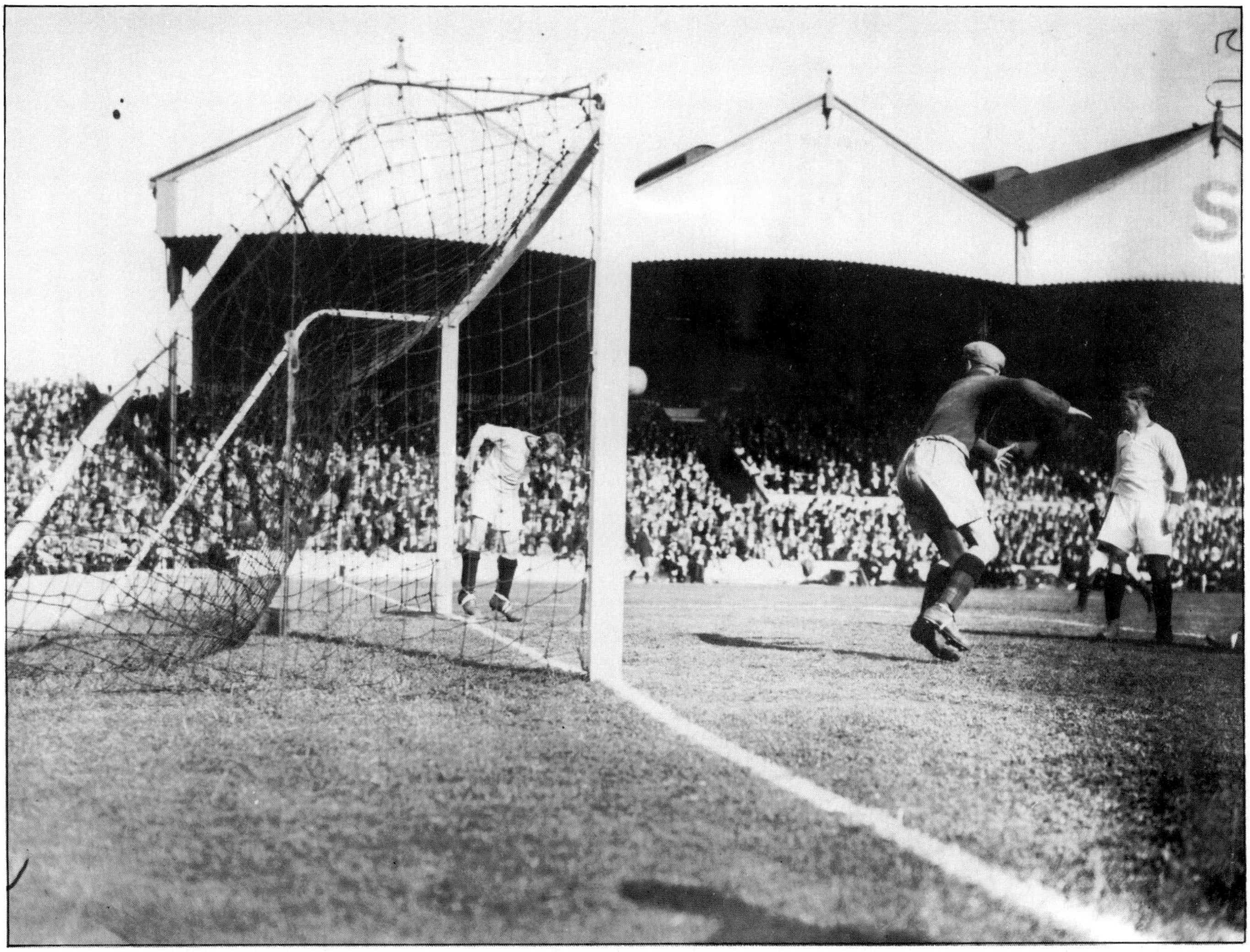

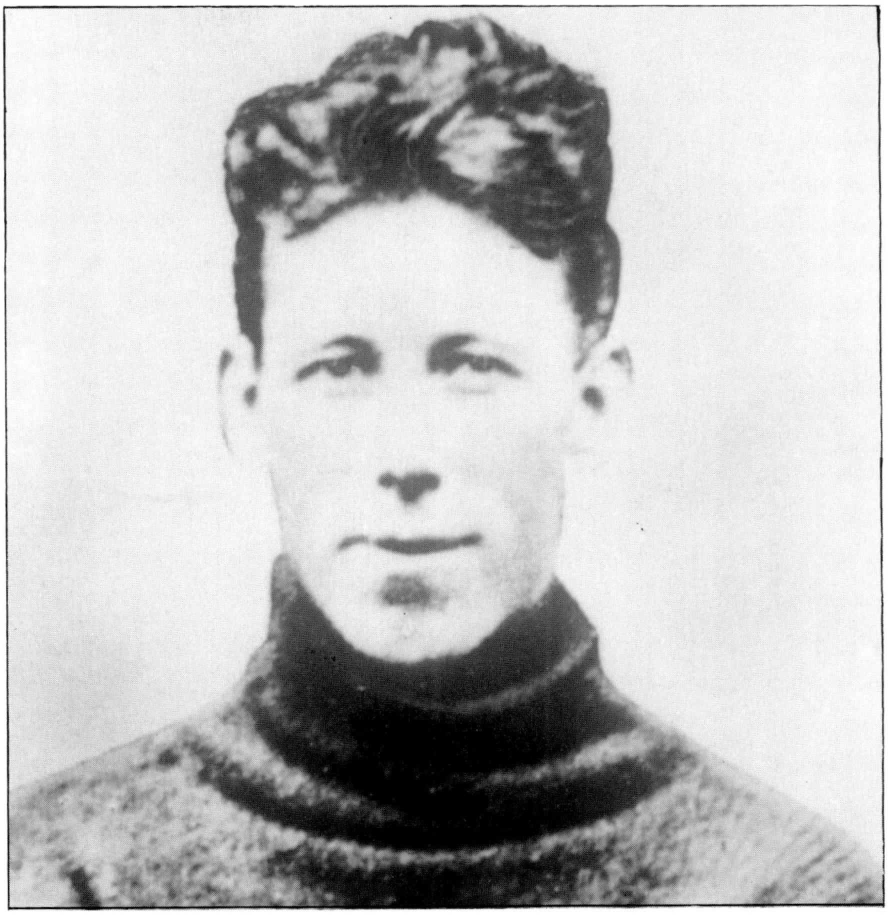

In the same game, Liverpool's South African amateur international goalkeeper Arthur Riley misses a shot from Arsenal's Jimmy Brain but full-back Eph Longworth heads off the goal-line.

Forward Dick Forshaw scored 124 goals in 287 League and FA Cup games for Liverpool after signing from non-League football in the close season of 1919. Ever-present in two Championship-winning seasons for Liverpool, he was transferred across Stanley Park to Everton in March 1927.

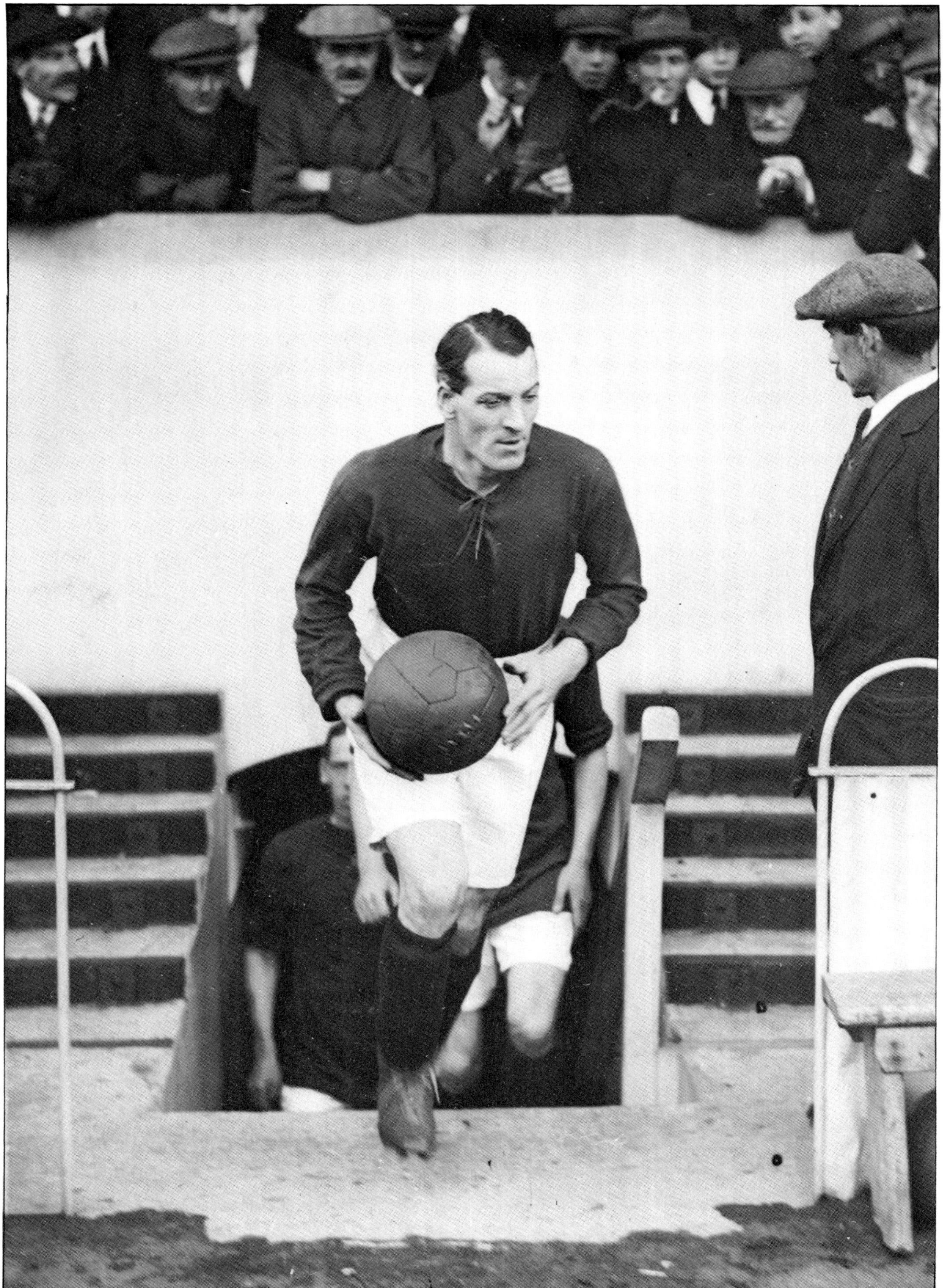

Donald McKinlay leads out Liverpool. McKinlay joined the Reds from Scottish junior football and his 19 years with the club is one of the longest career-spans for a Scottish footballer with one English club.

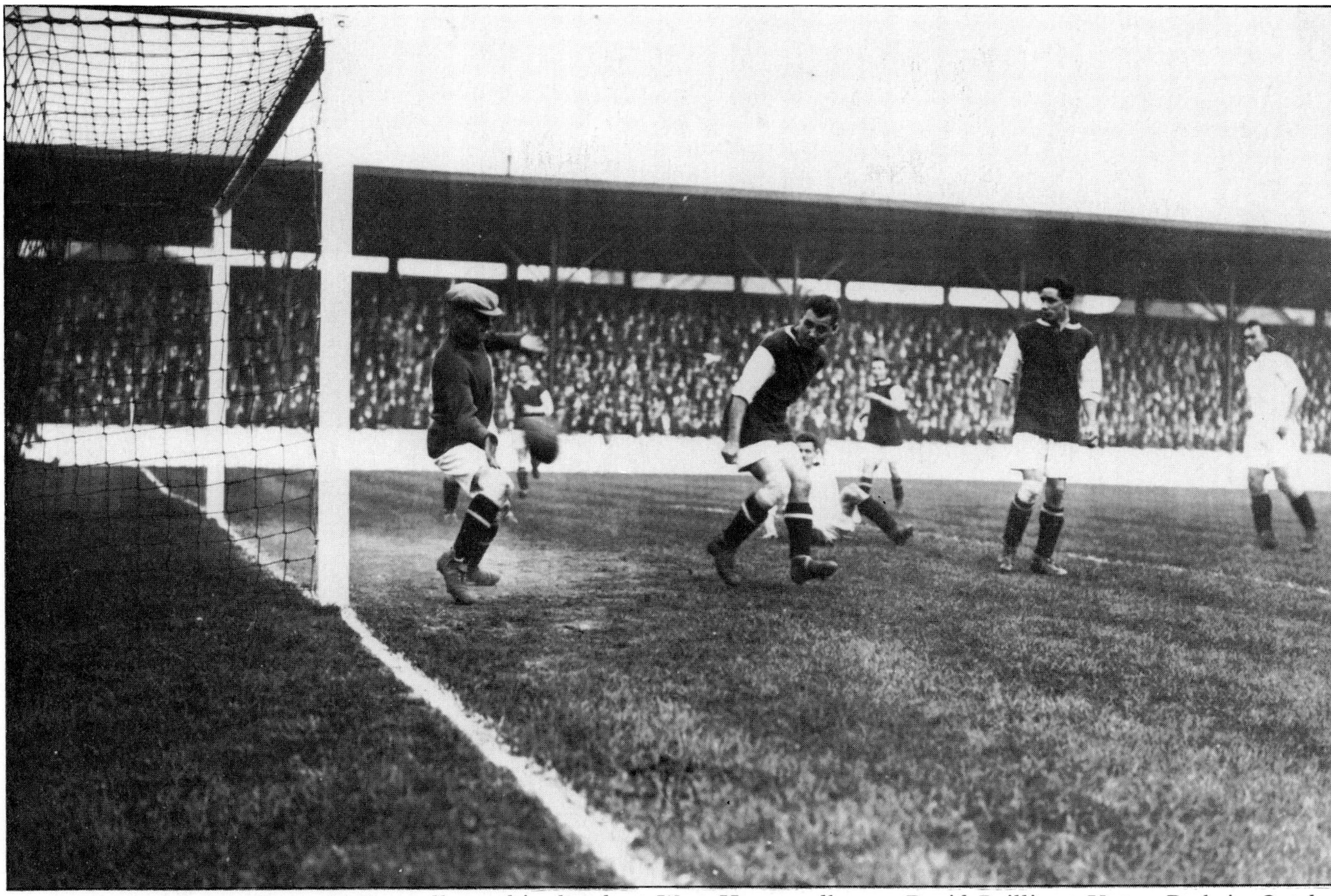

Scottish international Jimmy McDougall sees his shot beat West Ham goalkeeper David Baillie at Upton Park in October 1928. It helped Liverpool to a 1-1 draw.

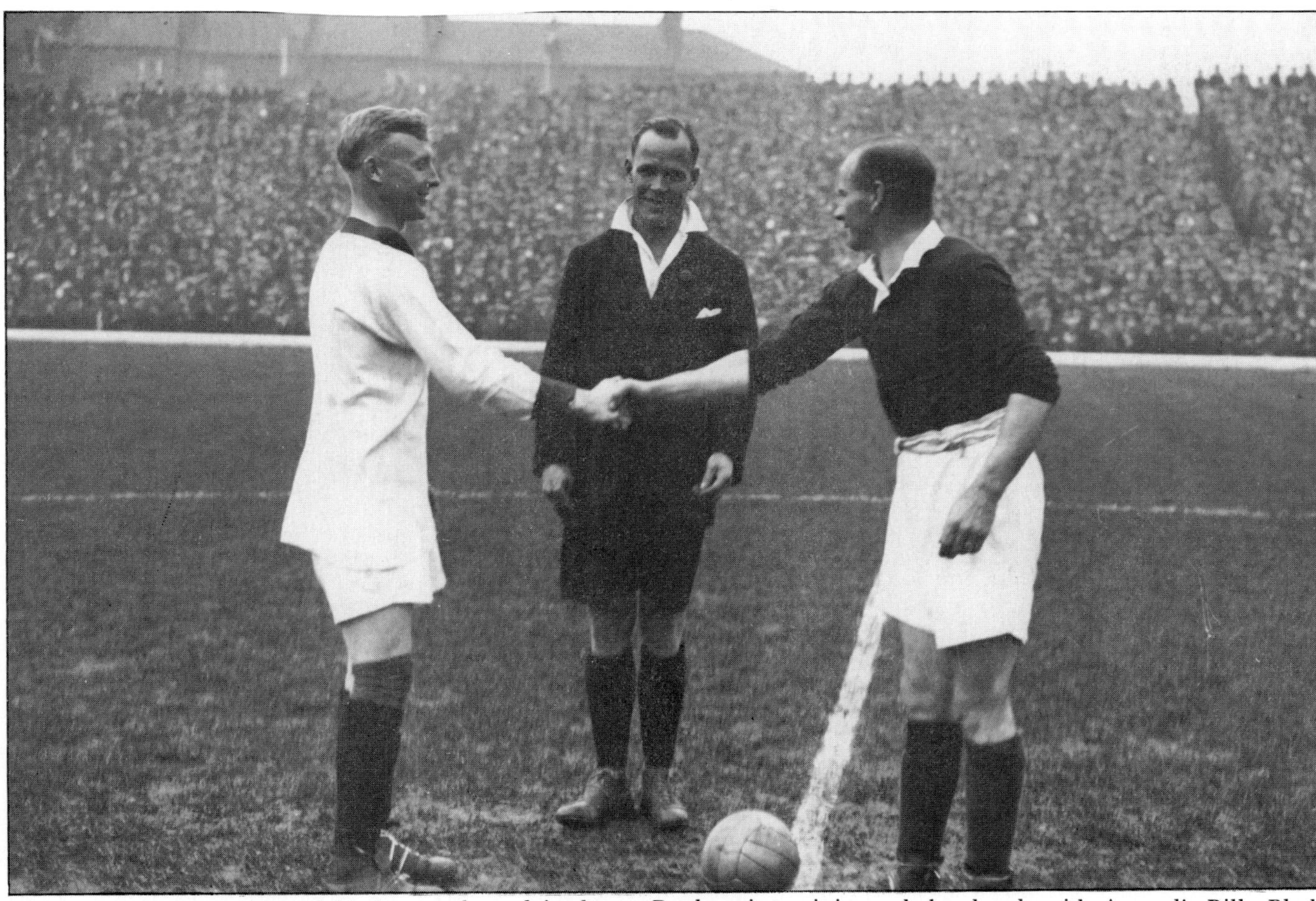

Liverpool's Jimmy Jackson (left), later to be ordained as a Presbyterian minister, shakes hands with Arsenal's Billy Blyth at Highbury in October 1928. Arsenal finished the season fifth in Division One. Jackson, who joined the Reds from Aberdeen, made 224 senior appearances, mostly at full-back although he also appeared in the half-back and forward lines. He retired in 1933.

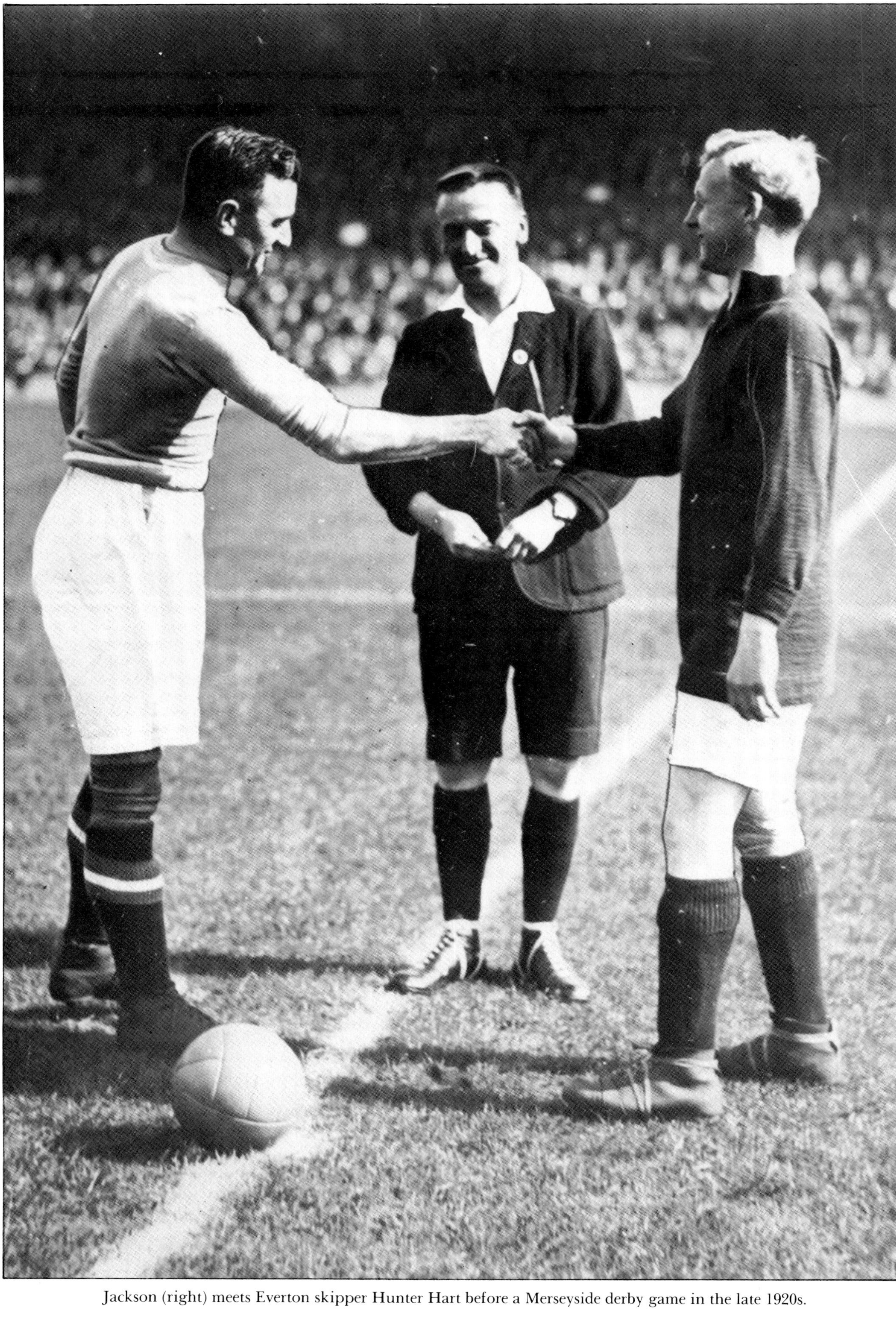

Jackson (right) meets Everton skipper Hunter Hart before a Merseyside derby game in the late 1920s.

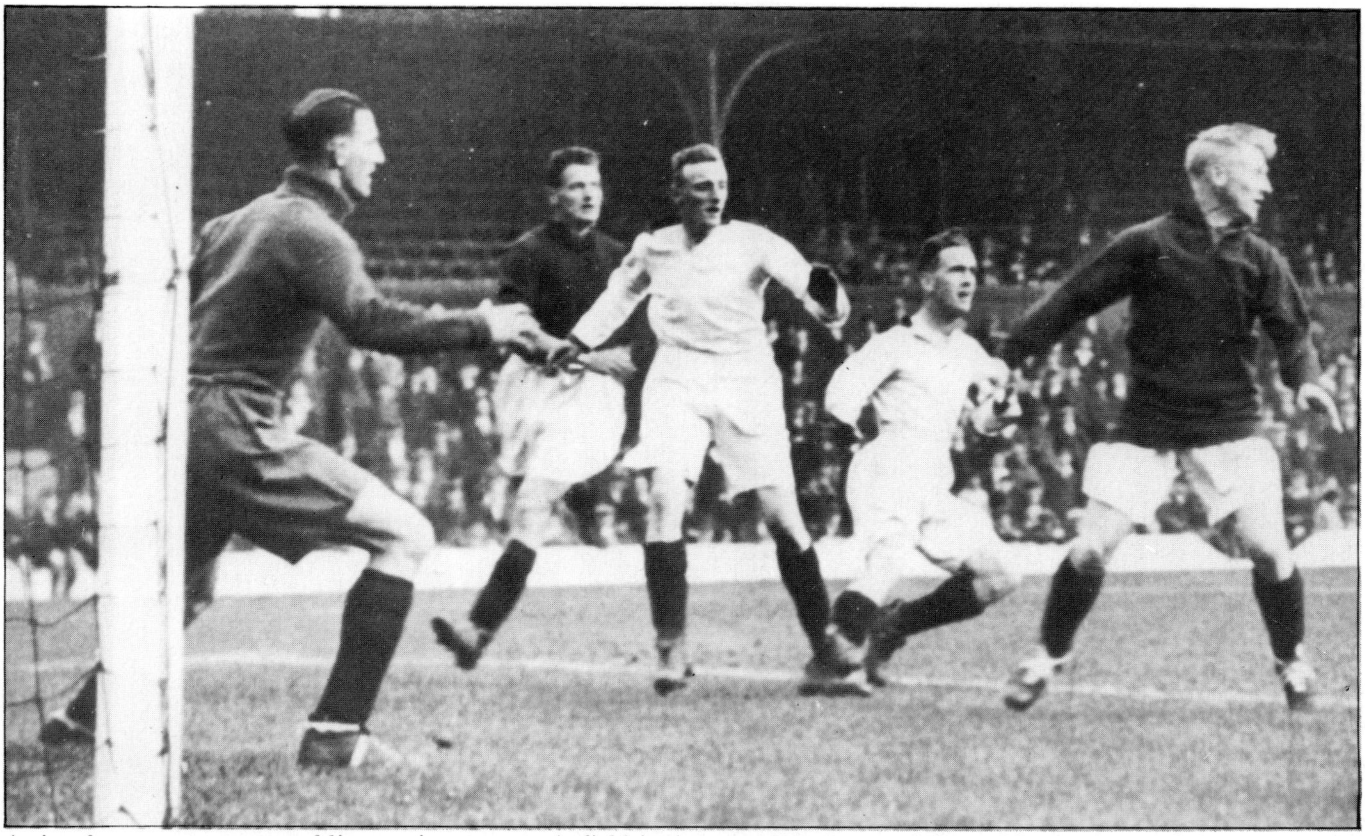

Action from a pre-season public practice game at Anfield in August 1929. One week later, Liverpool started the season with a 5-0 defeat at Middlesbrough and went on to end the season in 12th position in Division One.

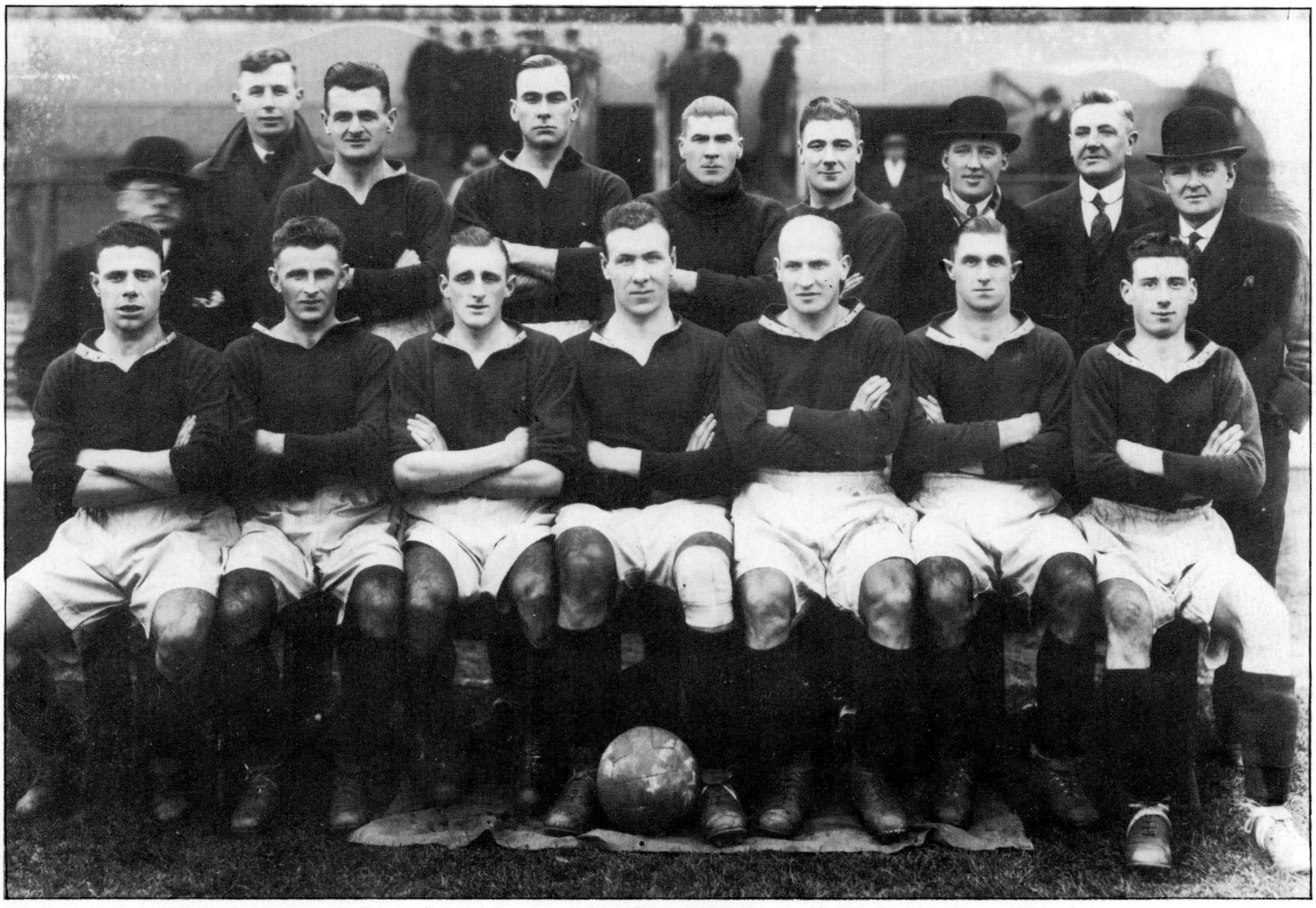

Liverpool in 1932-3. Back row (left to right, players only): James, McDougall, Hodgson, Scott, Morrison. Front row: Done, Steele, Barton, Bradshaw, Wright, Gunson, Roberts. Gordon Hodgson was leading scorer with 24 goals in a season when the Reds finished 14th in Division One.

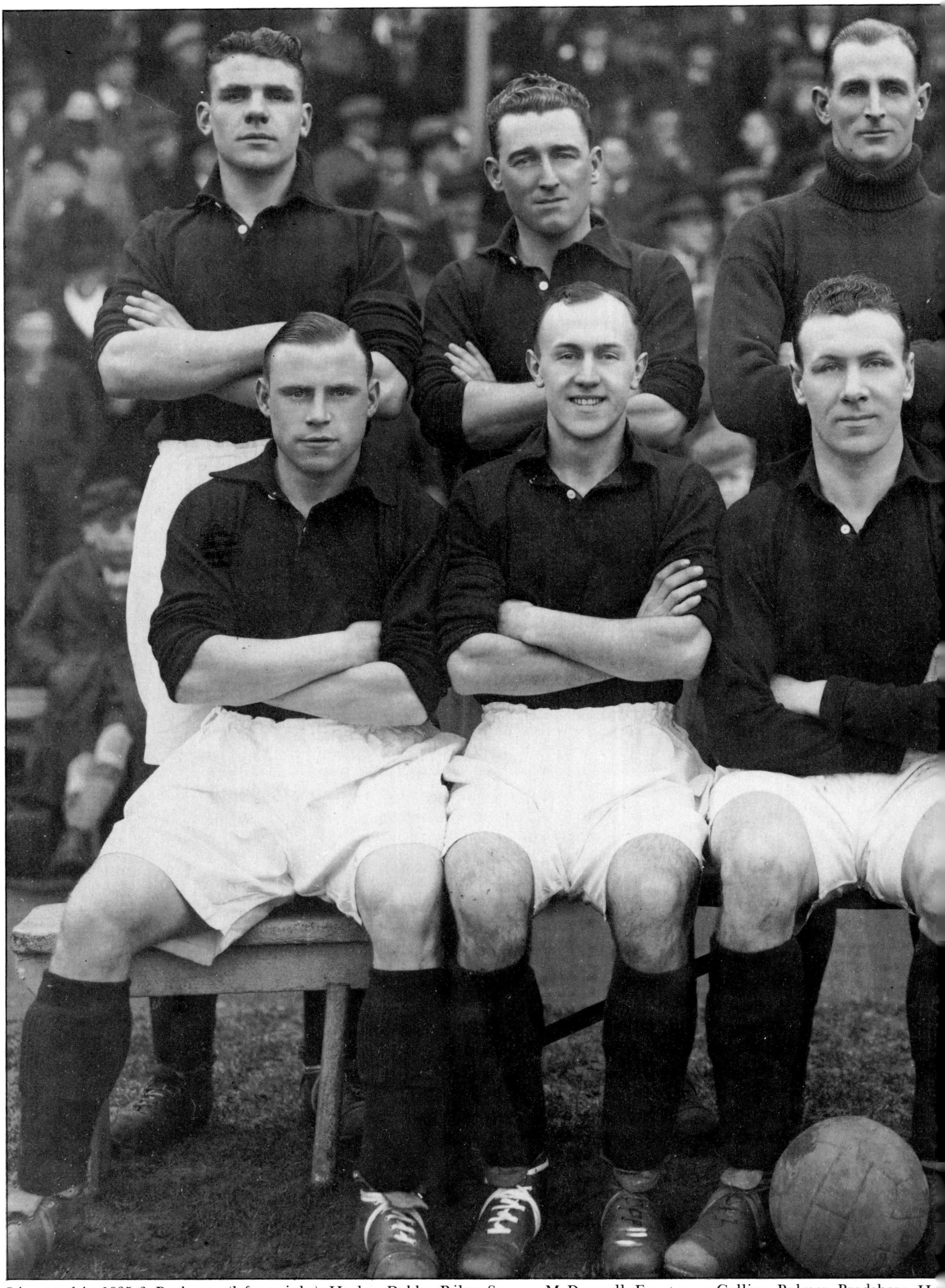

Liverpool in 1935-6. Back row (left to right): Harley, Dabbs, Riley, Savage, McDougall. Front row: Collins, Balmer, Bradshaw, Hc
Bury in 1930 for £8,000 and made 291 senior appearances for the Reds.

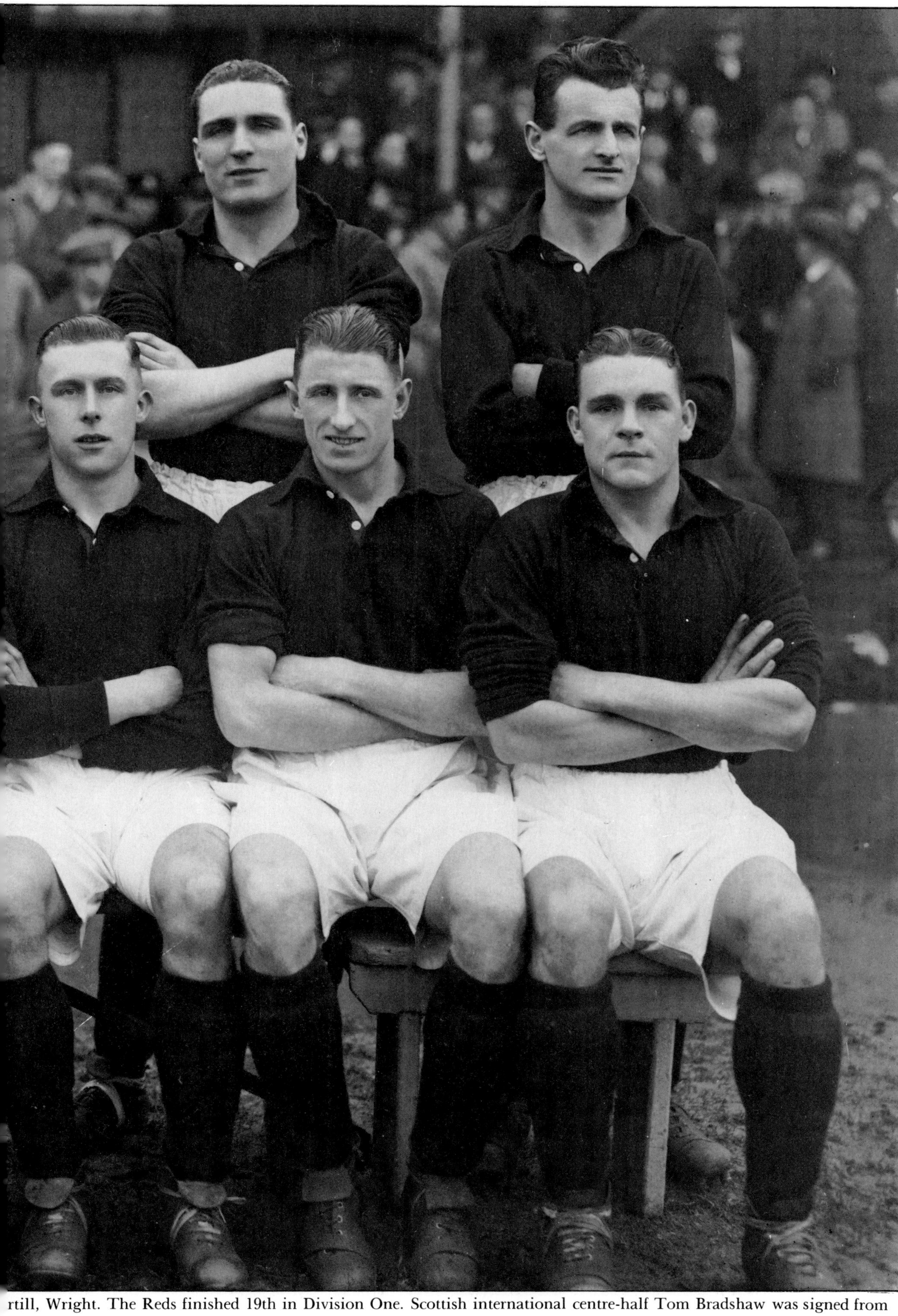

rtill, Wright. The Reds finished 19th in Division One. Scottish international centre-half Tom Bradshaw was signed from

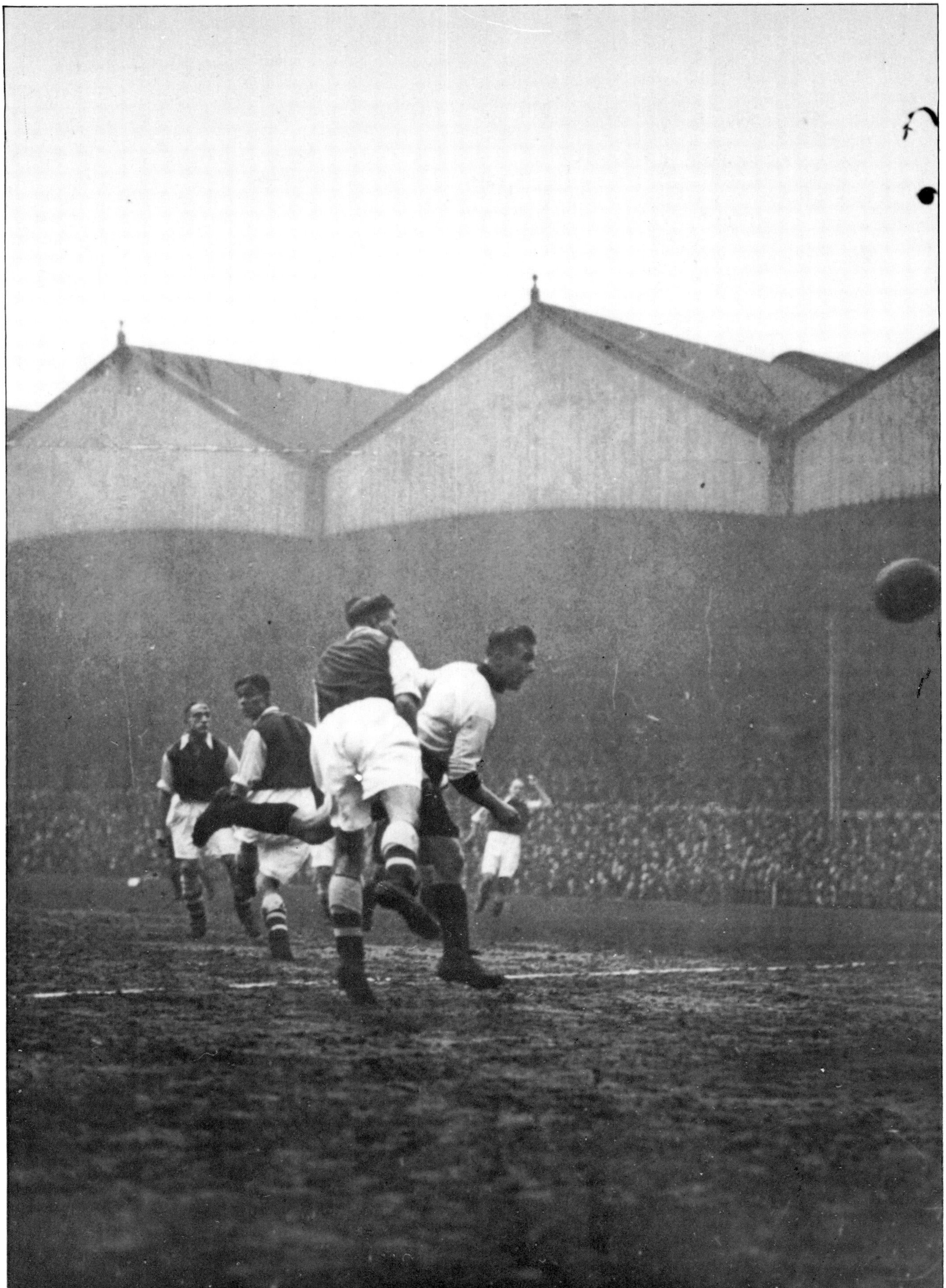

Liverpool's Vic Wright heads goalwards at Highbury on Boxing Day 1935. The Reds snatched a 2-1 win when Fred Howe netted the winner in the 80th minute. By now, Arsenal were the leading side in the country but Liverpool were still going strong, enjoying their 27th consecutive peacetime season of First Division football.

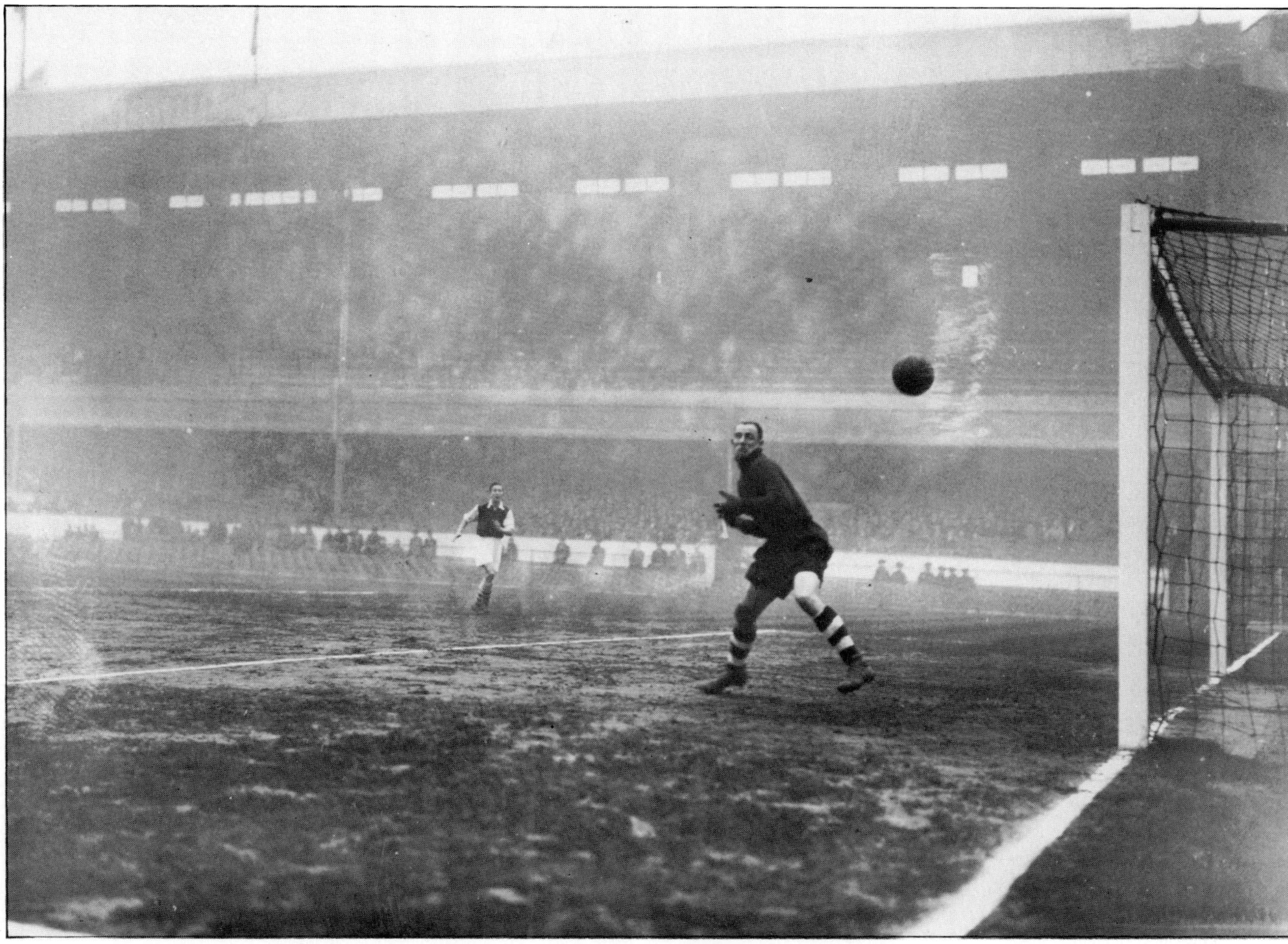

Arthur Riley fumbles a shot from Kirchen and Arsenal score their first goal in March 1937. It proved to be the winner and sent Liverpool further down the table, where they eventually finished in 18th position.

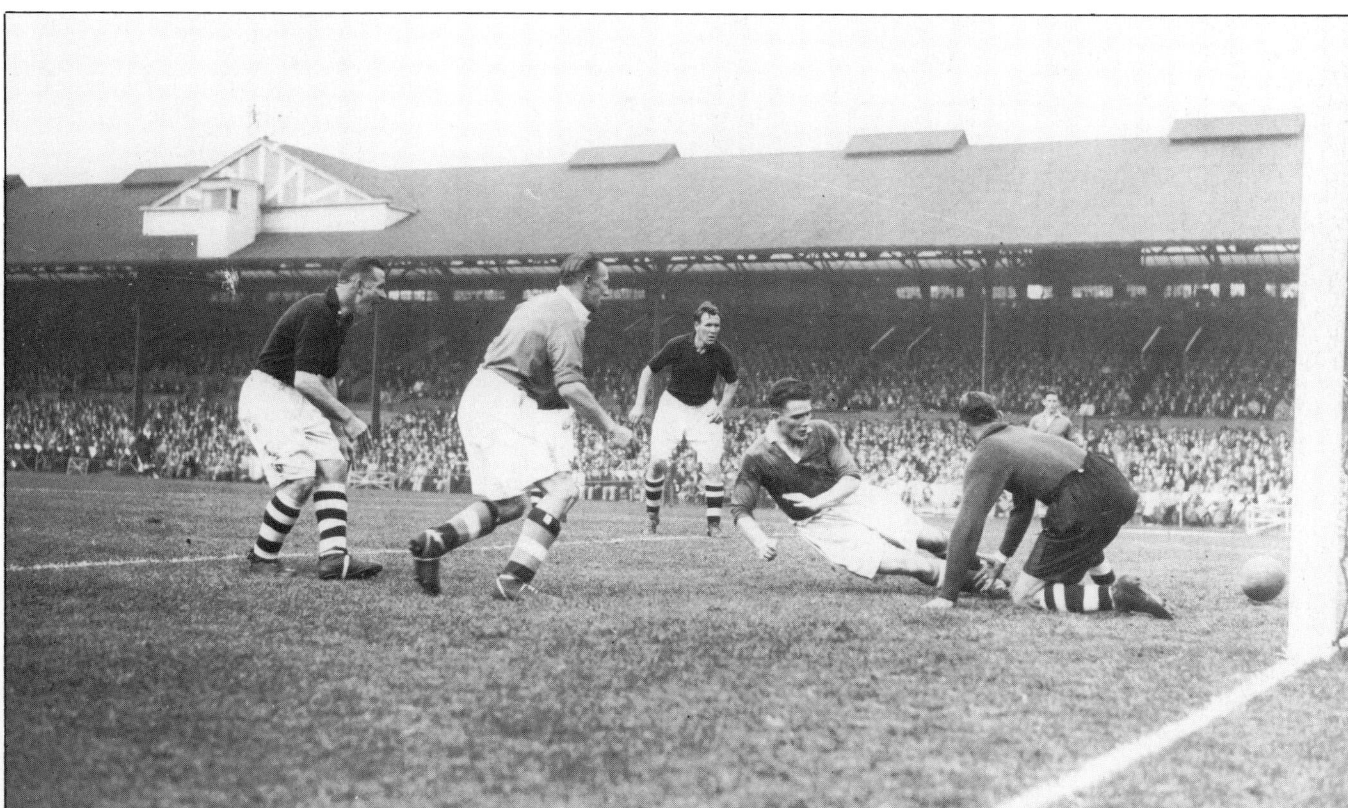

On the opening day of the 1937-8 season, Liverpool went down 6-1 at Stamford Bridge. This photograph shows the Pensioners' Harry Burgess scoring his side's last goal past Riley.

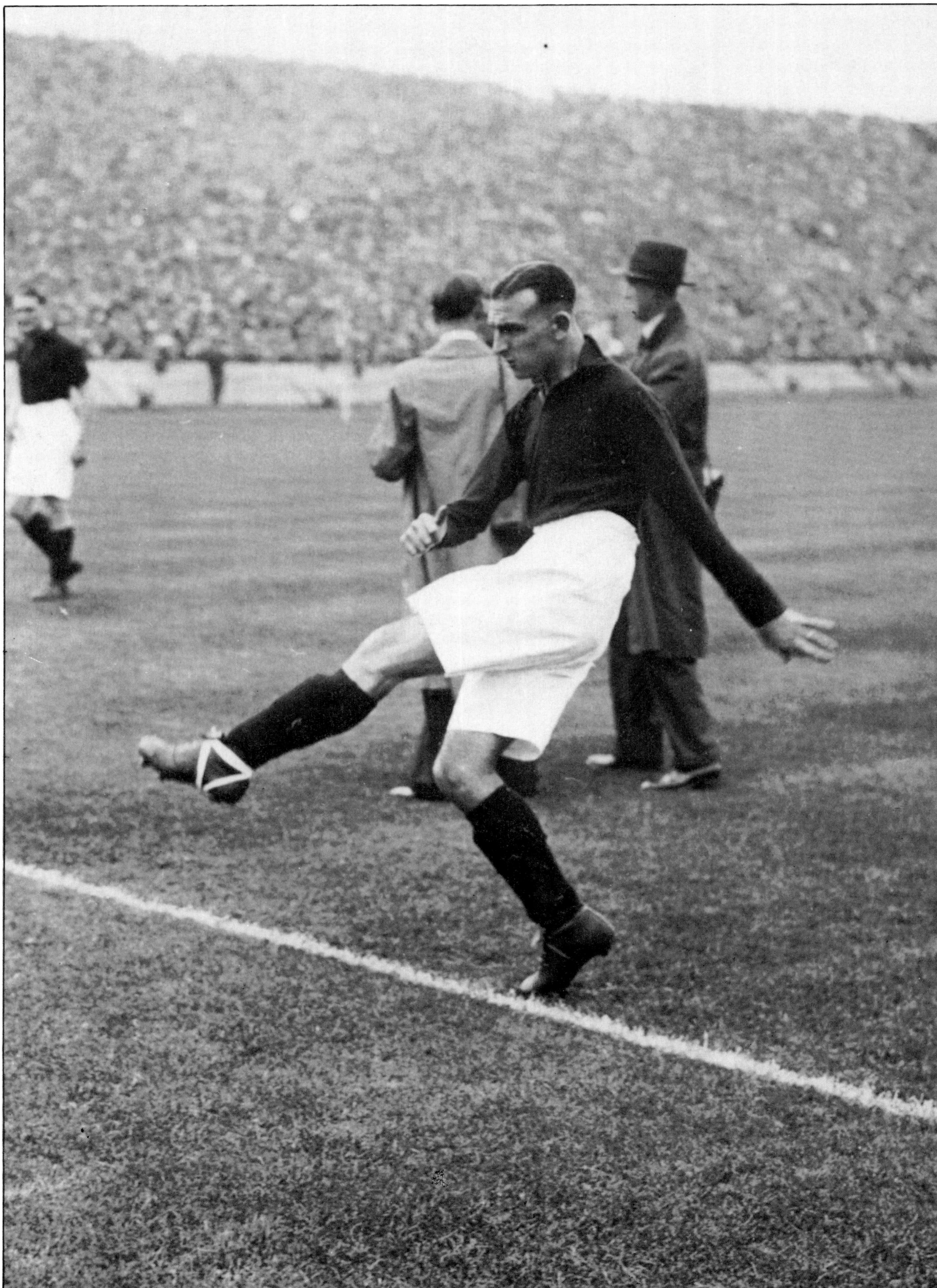

Liverpool outside-left Alf Hanson, a plumber by trade, who joined the Reds in November 1931, after being rejected by Everton. His speed and accuracy laid on plenty of goals for Berry Nieuwenhuys, who came in from the other wing, and his inside-forwards. His younger brother, Stan Hanson, kept goal for Bolton Wanderers from 1935 to 1956. Alf Hanson scored 52 goals in 177 senior appearances for the Reds before joining Chelsea in July 1938 for £7,500.

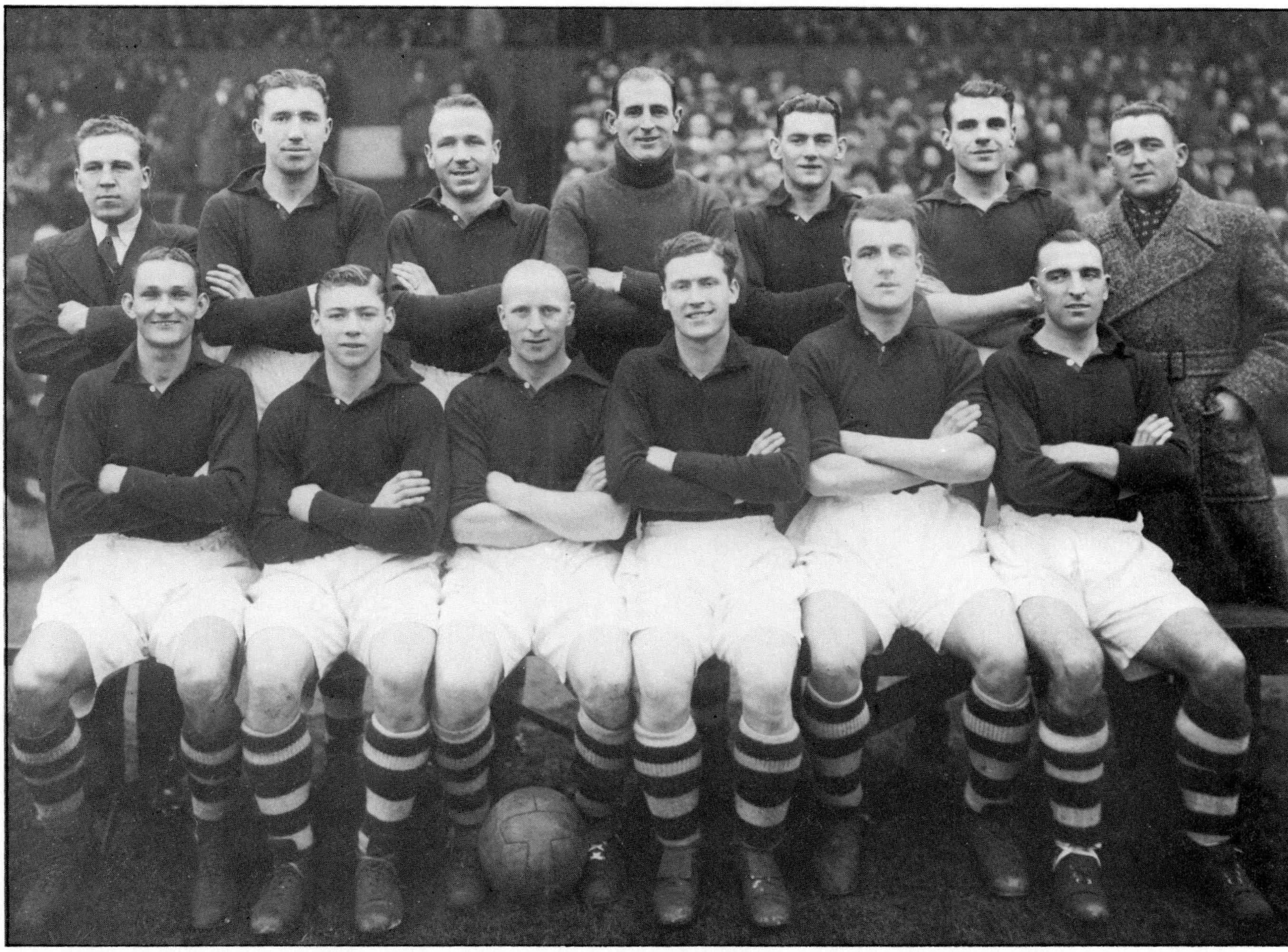

Liverpool in 1937-8. Back row (left to right): Browning, Bush, Busby, Riley, Taylor, Harley, Dabbs. Front row: Nieuwenhuys, Shafto, Cooper, Fagan, Rogers, Hanson. Matt Busby joined the Reds from Manchester City for £8,000 in February 1936 and, of course, after the war became a football legend as manager of Manchester United.

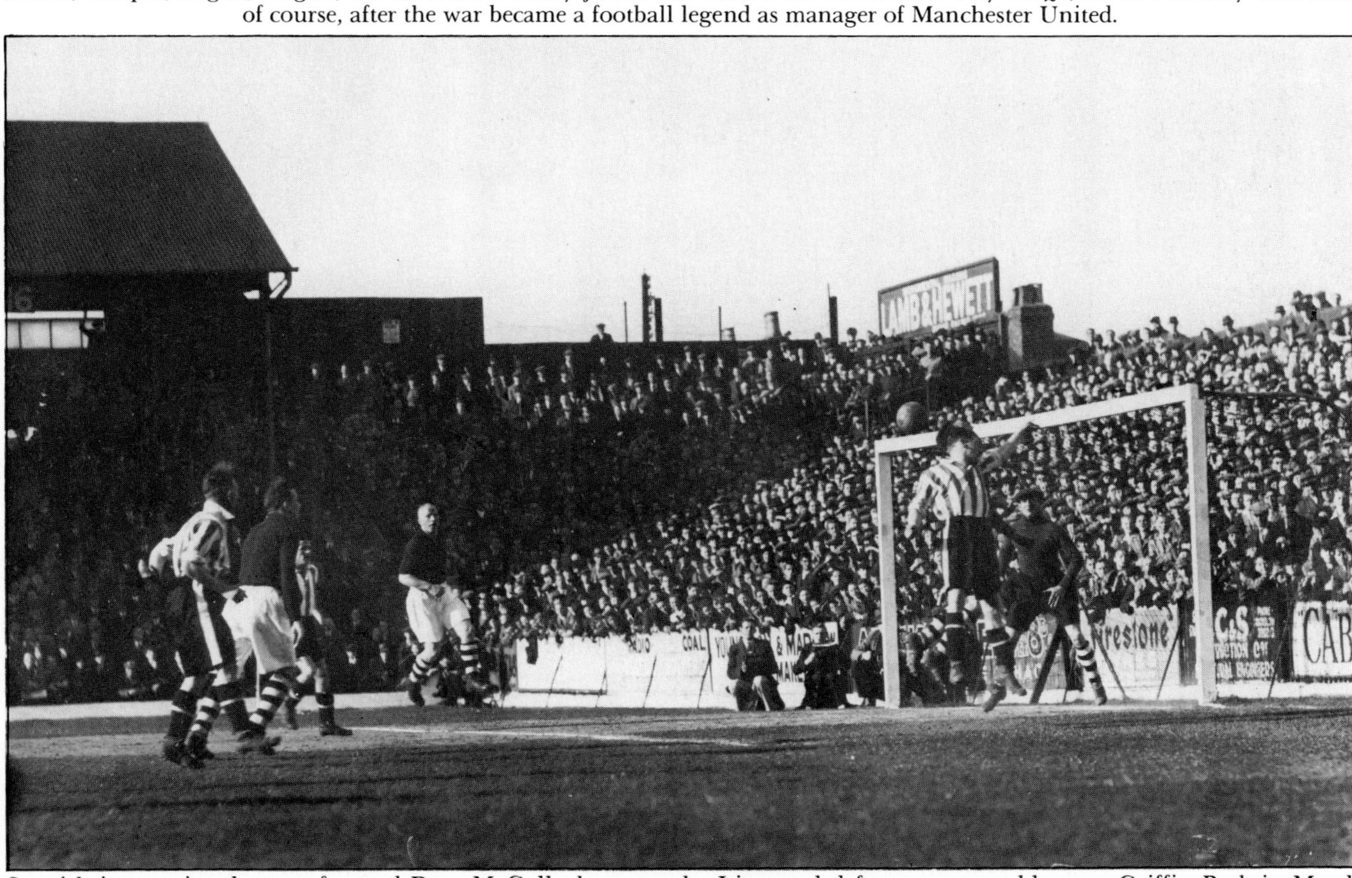

Scottish international centre-forward Dave McCulloch causes the Liverpool defence some problems at Griffin Park in March 1938, but the Reds beat Brentford 3-1. They recovered from that awful start to the season to finish 11th.

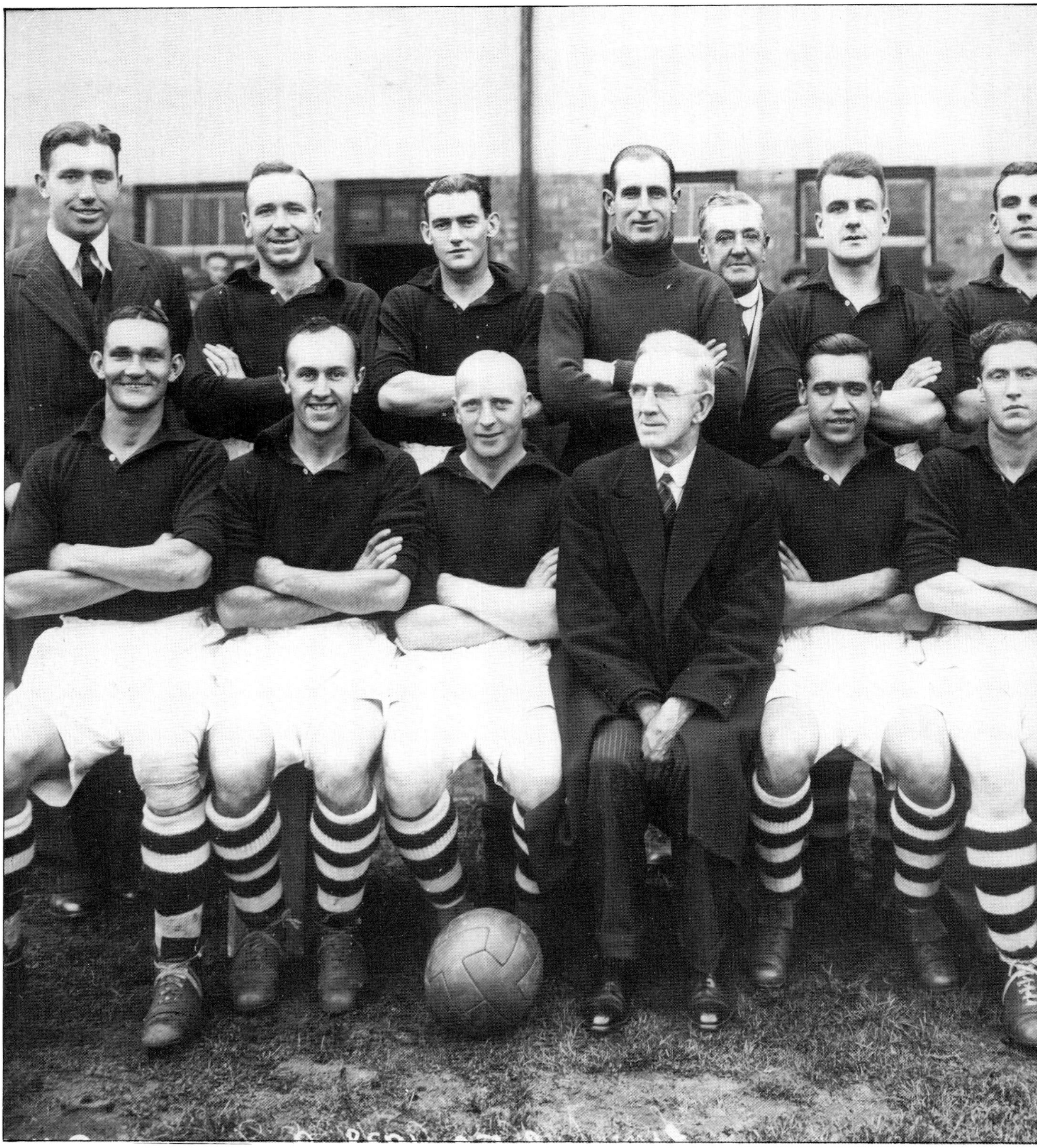

Liverpool in 1938-9, the last full season before World War Two. Back row (left to right): Bush, Busby, Taylor, Riley, C.Wilson (trainer), Rogers, Harley, G.H.Richards (director). Front row: Nieuwenhuys, Balmer, Cooper, W.J.Harropp (chairman), McInnes, Fagan, Van Den Berg.

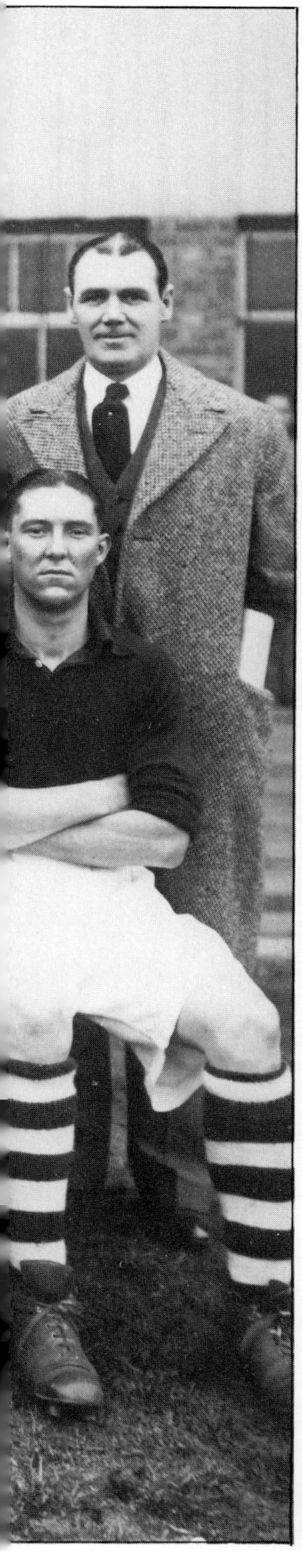

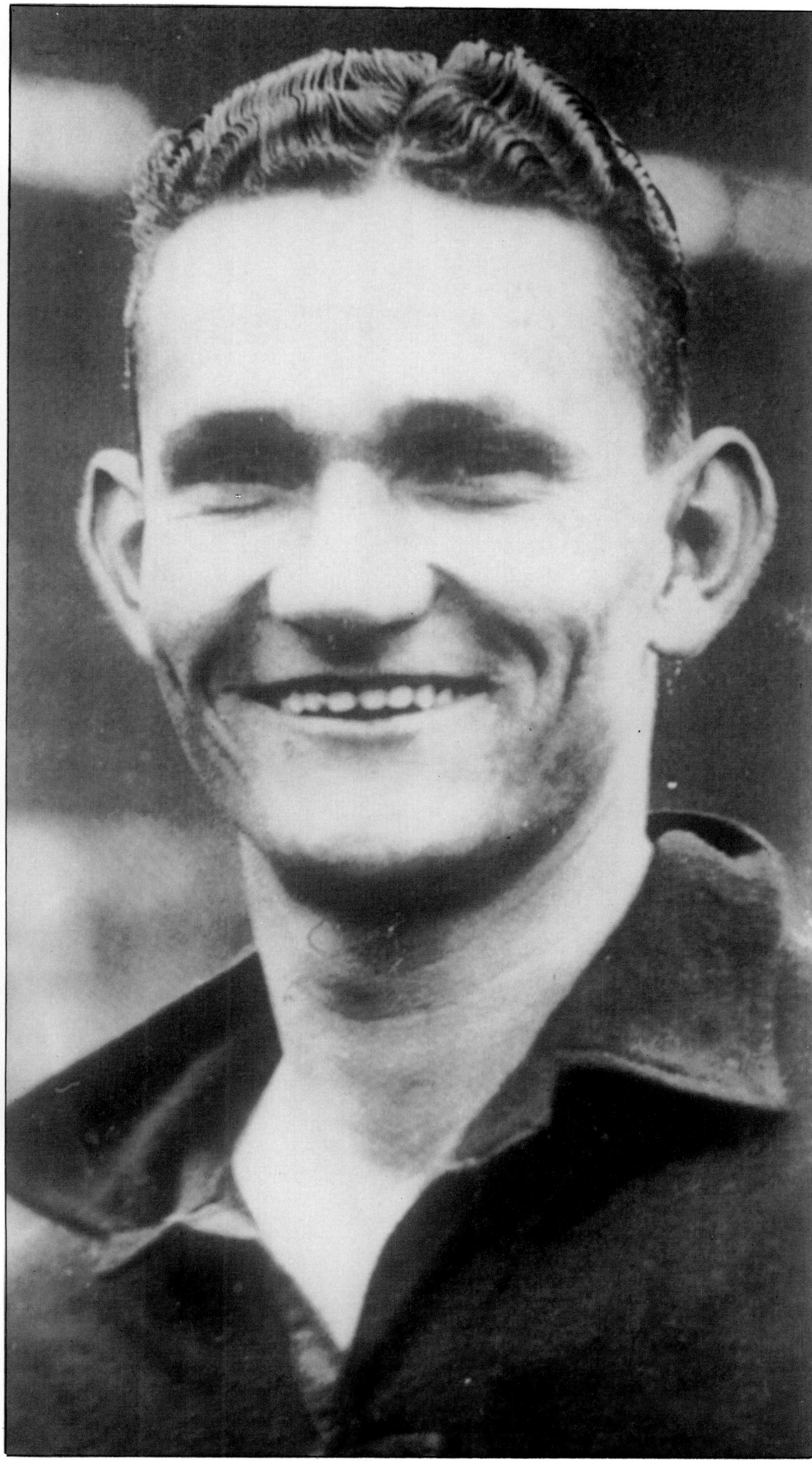

South African winger Berry Nieuwenhuys scored 79 goals in 239 senior appearances for Liverpool after joining the Reds in September 1933.

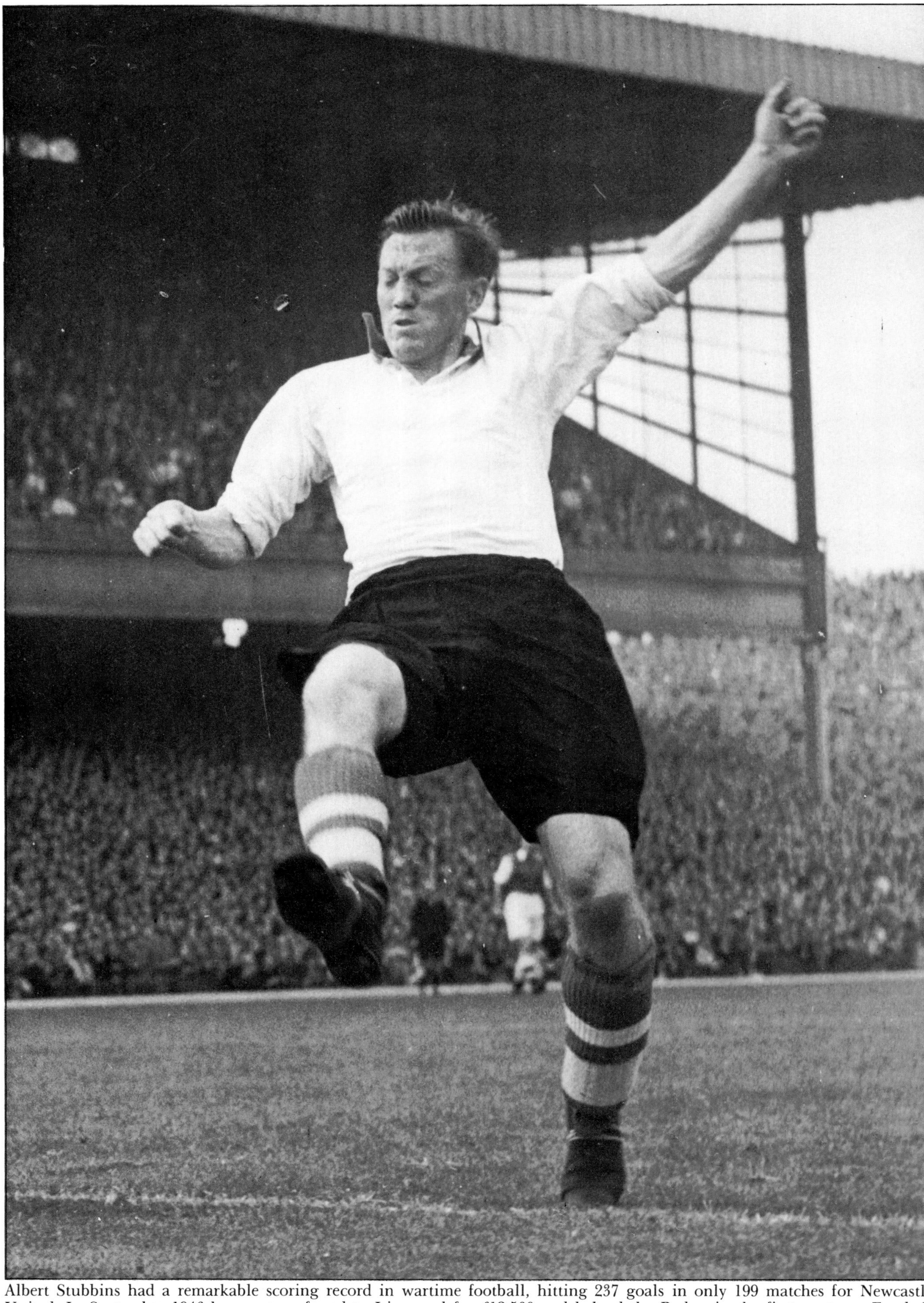

Albert Stubbins had a remarkable scoring record in wartime football, hitting 237 goals in only 199 matches for Newcastle United. In September 1946 he was transferred to Liverpool for £12,500 and helped the Reds win the first post-war Football League Championship. For Liverpool, Stubbins scored 83 goals in 183 games before going into non-League football with Ashington in September 1953. In 1960 he was the USA national soccer coach.

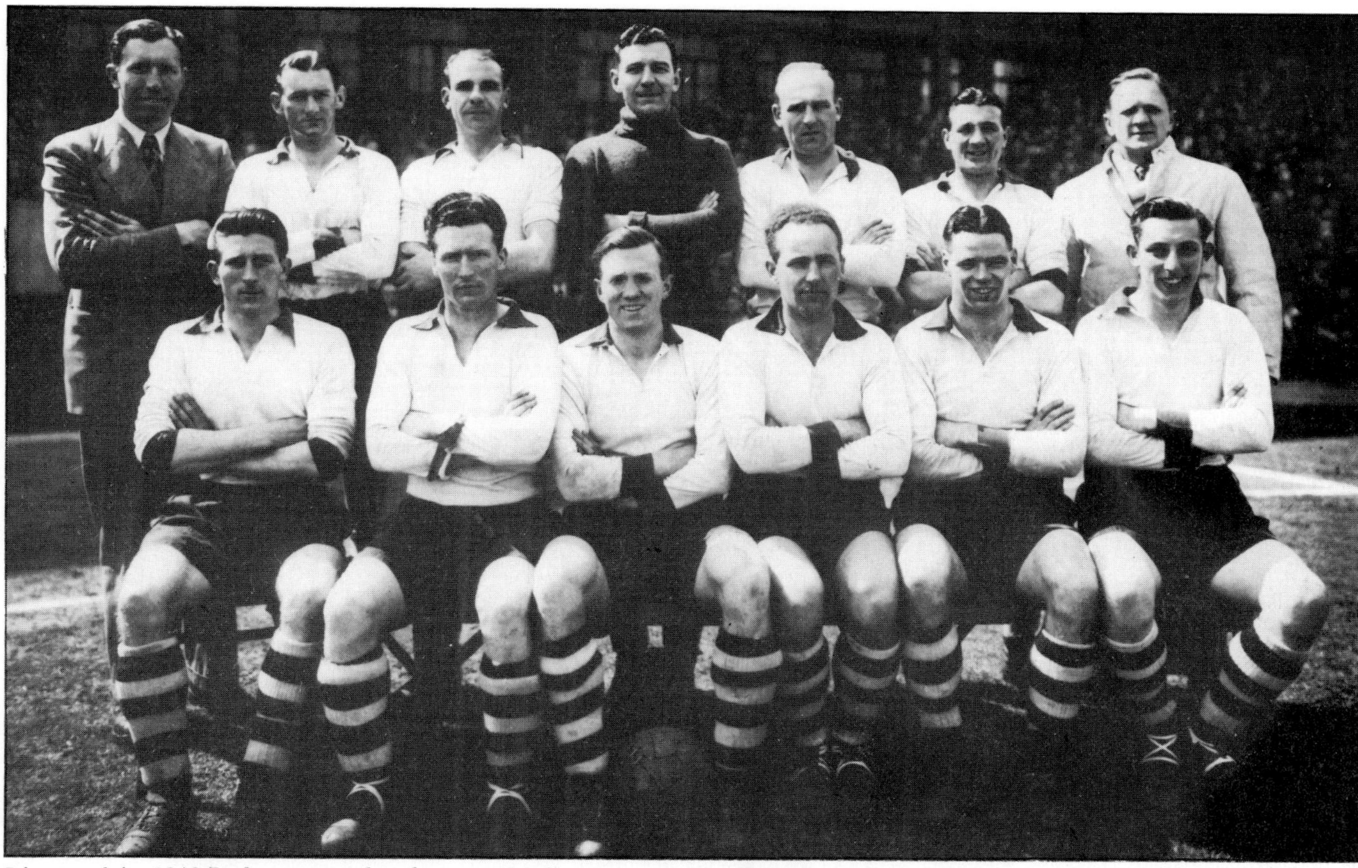

Liverpool in 1946-7, the season they became the first post-war Football League Champions. Back row (left to right): Bush, Taylor, Harley, Sidlow, Lambert, Paisley, A.Shelley (trainer). Front row: Watkinson, Fagan, Stubbins, Polk, Liddell, Hughes.

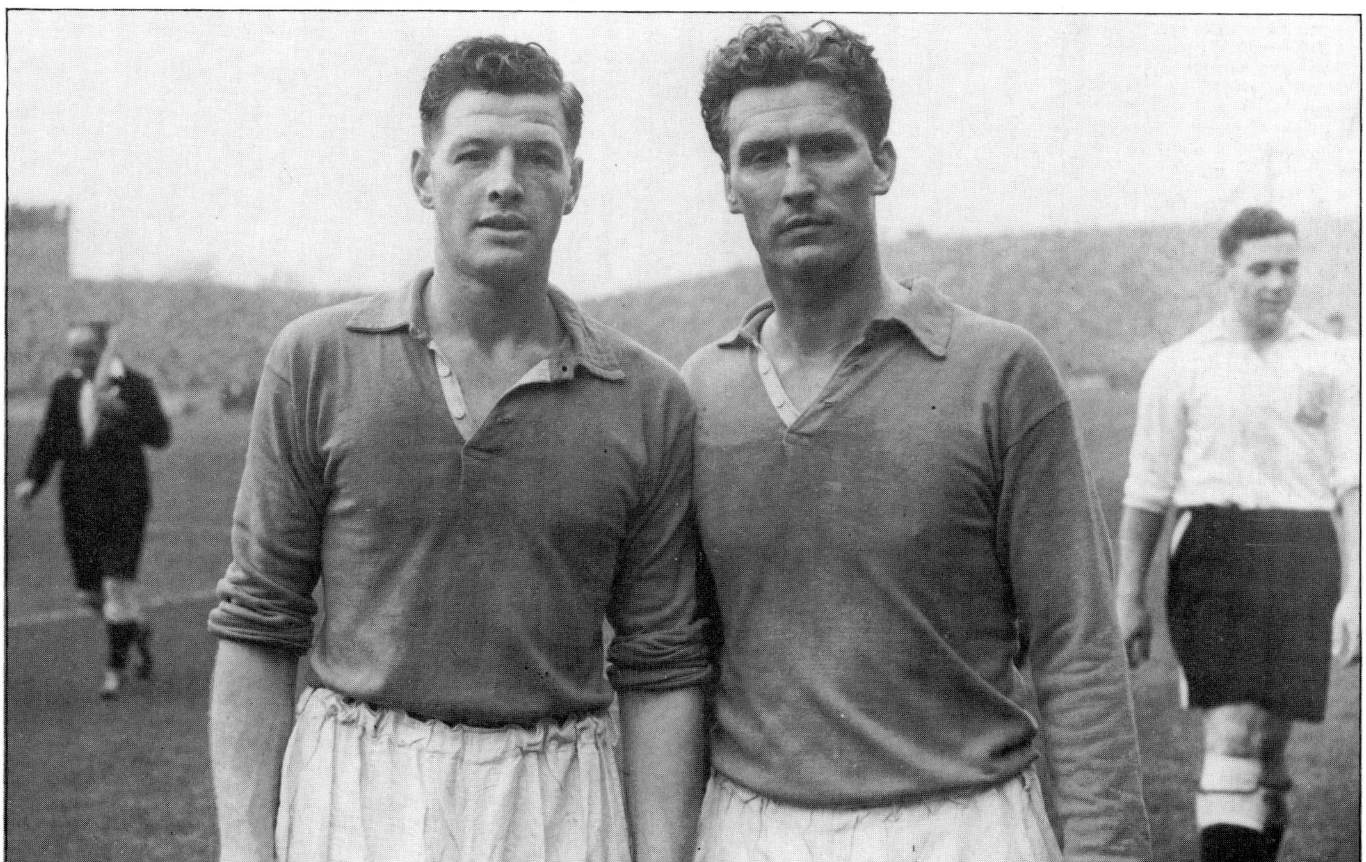

Liverpool-born Eddie Spicer signed for the Anfield club straight from local football in October 1939 and made his early appearances at wing-half before settling at full-back in 1949-50. He retired through injury in 1953, after making 168 senior appearances. Forward Willie Fagan (right) joined the Reds from Preston North End in October 1937 and appeared in wartime internationals for Scotland before helping Liverpool to the first post-war Championship. Fagan scored 57 goals in 185 League and Cup games before joining Belfast Distillery in January 1952.

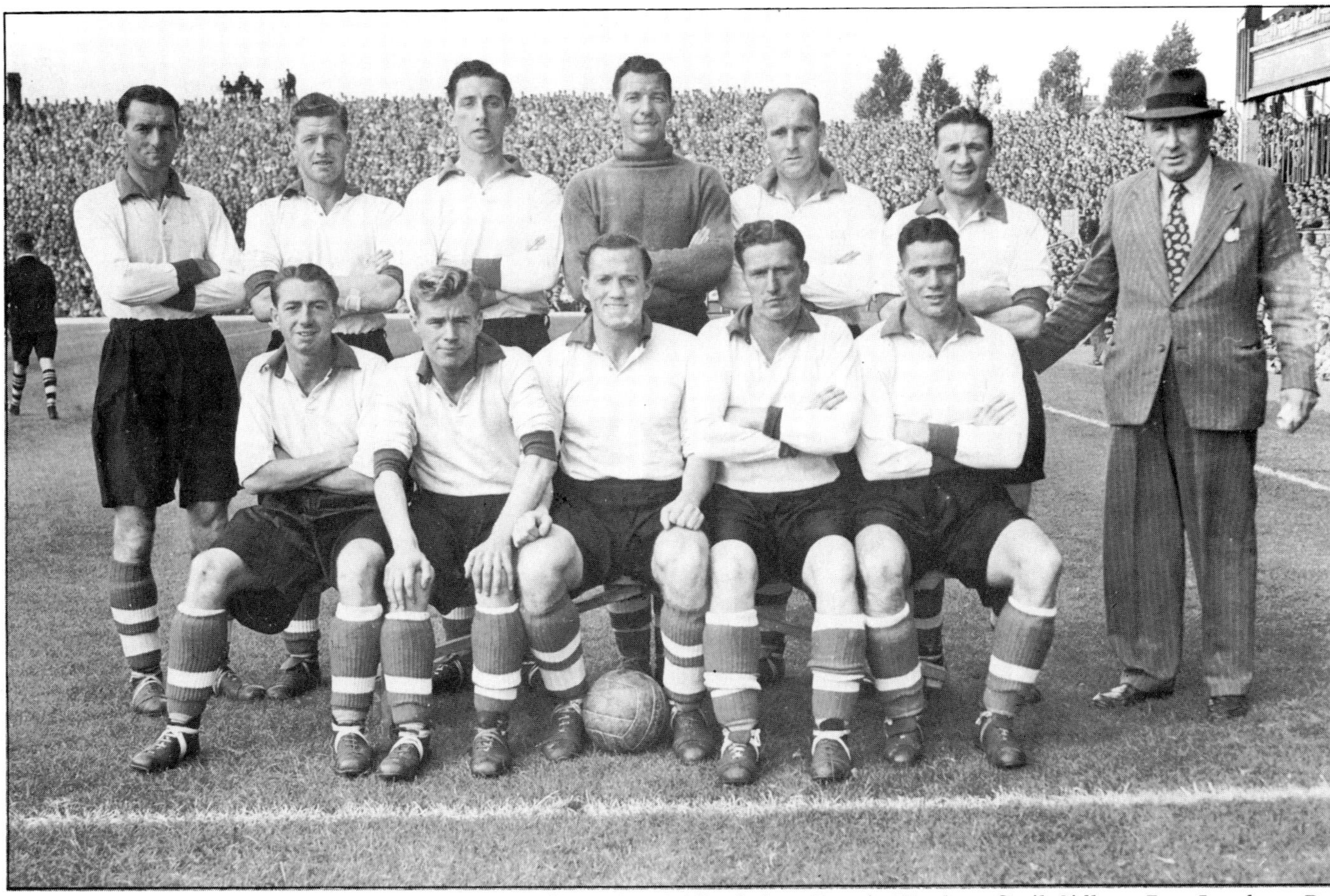

Liverpool in 1949-50. Back row (left to right): Phil Taylor, Eddie Spicer, Laurie Hughes, Cyril Sidlow, Ray Lambert, Bob Paisley, George Kay (manager). Front row: Jimmy Payne, Kevin Baron, Cyril Done, Willie Fagan, Billy Liddell.

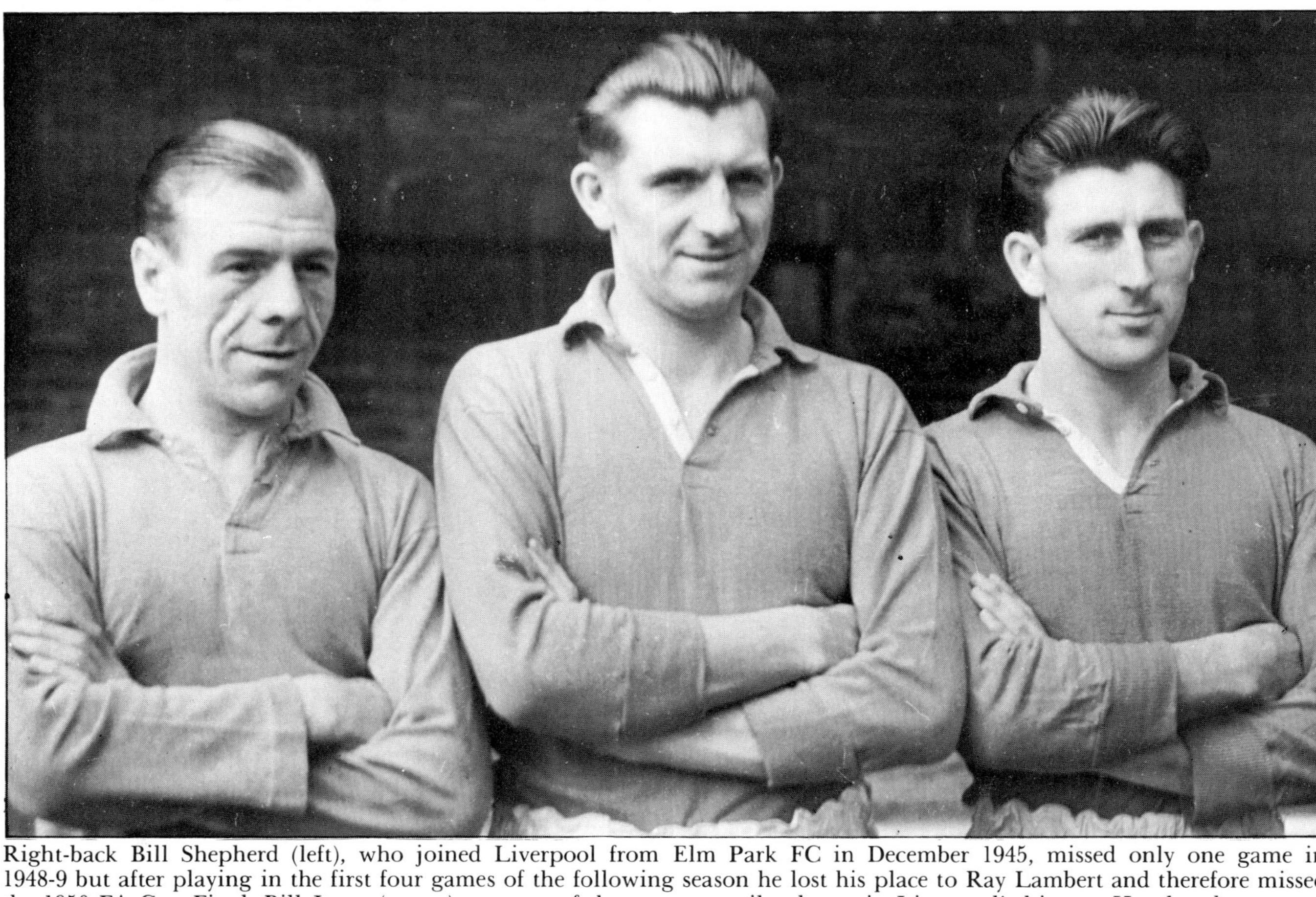

Right-back Bill Shepherd (left), who joined Liverpool from Elm Park FC in December 1945, missed only one game in 1948-9 but after playing in the first four games of the following season he lost his place to Ray Lambert and therefore missed the 1950 FA Cup Final. Bill Jones (centre) was one of the most versatile players in Liverpool's history. He played at centre-half for England and at full-back and in the forward line for Liverpool, appearing in six different positions in the 1946-7 Championship side. Billy Watkinson (right) was also an adaptable player, appearing at inside-left but mostly at outside-right. He had more success with Accrington Stanley and Halifax Town in the Third Division North.

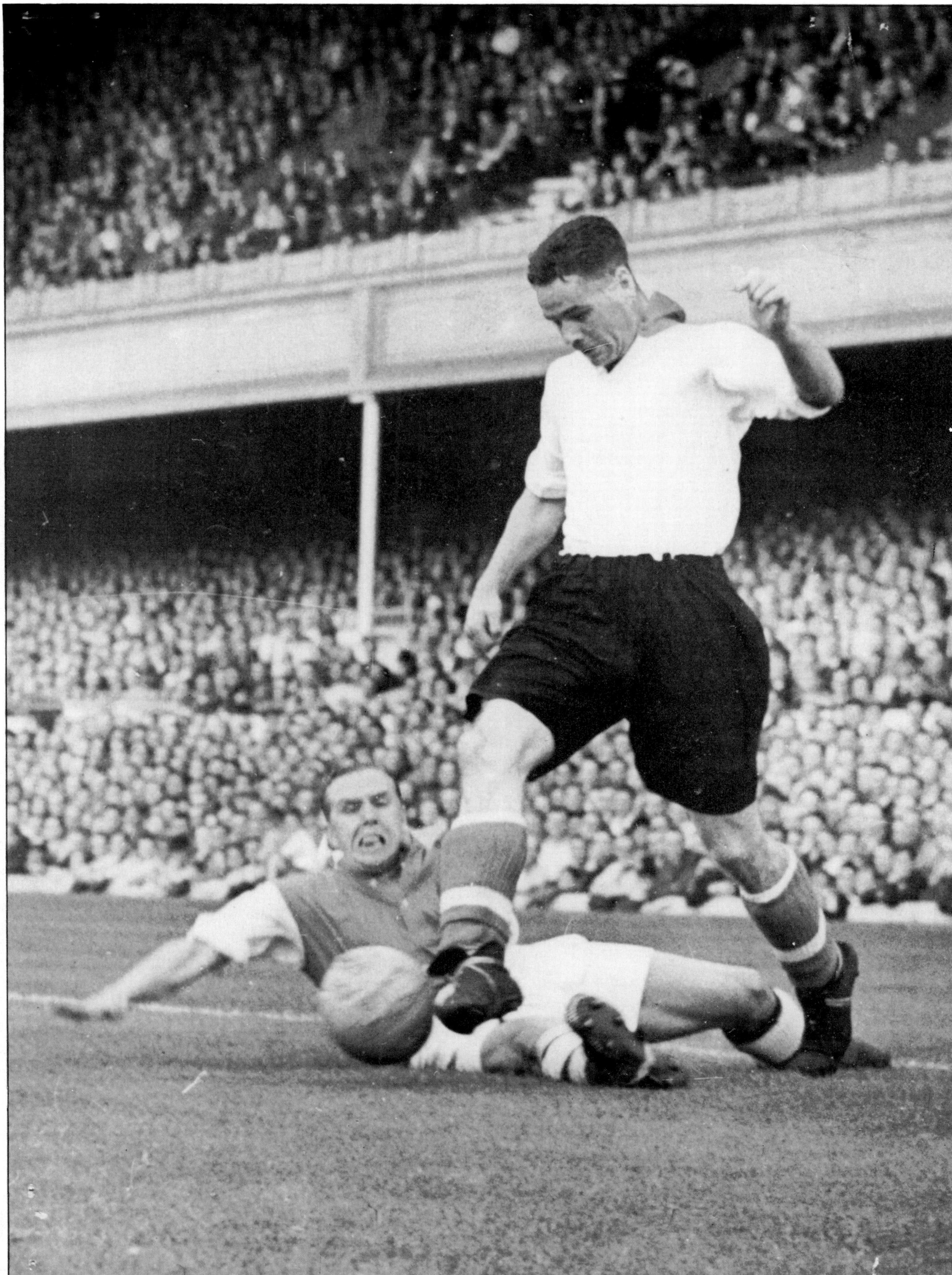

Billy Liddell, one of the truly great names in Liverpool's history. Although best remembered as a flying outside-left, Liddell also played with distinction on the other flank and at centre-forward. He joined the Reds before the war and played until he retired in May 1961. During that time, Liddell played for Scotland and Great Britain, won League Championship and FA Cup winners' medals and scored 216 goals in 495 League games for the Reds as well as playing a prominent part in the public life of Liverpool.

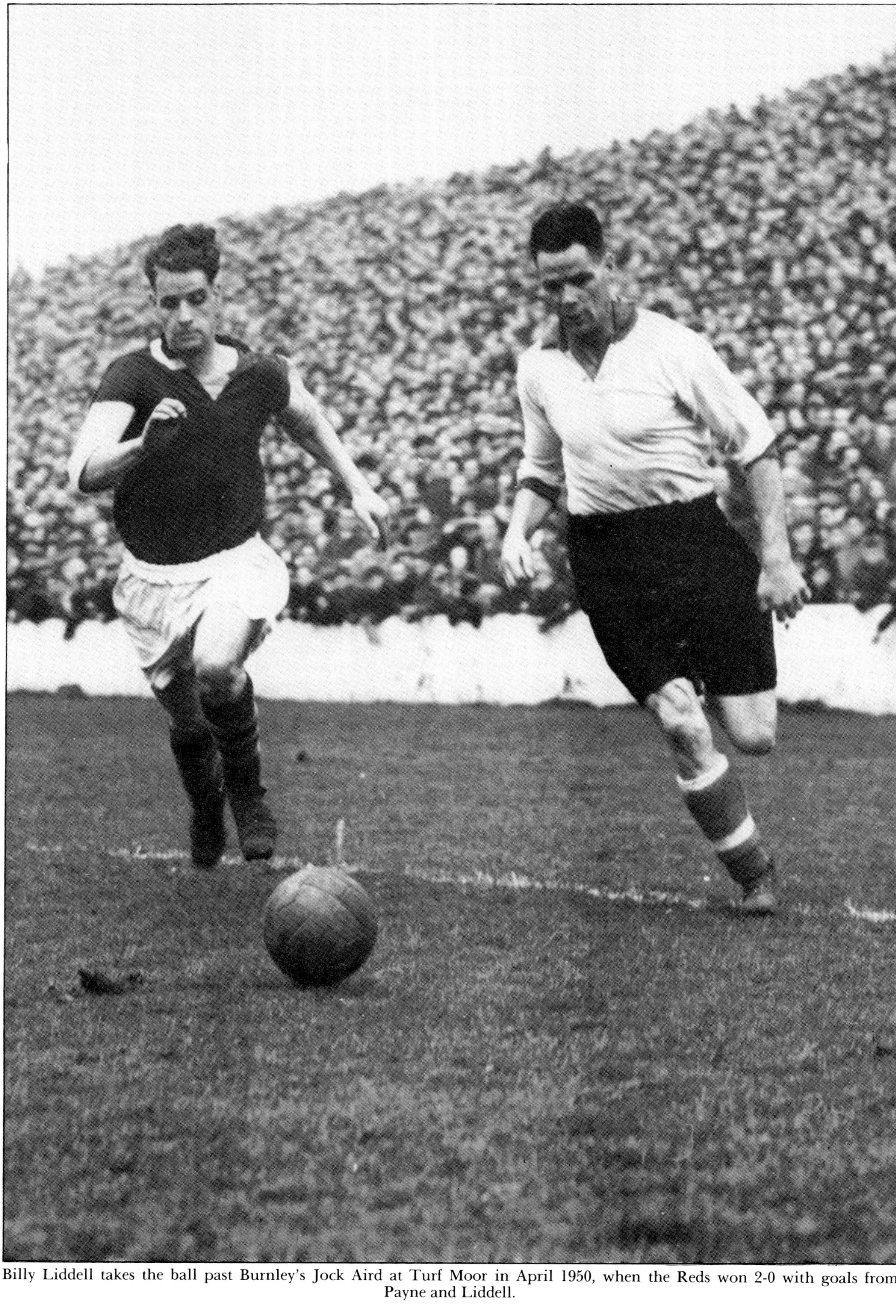

Billy Liddell takes the ball past Burnley's Jock Aird at Turf Moor in April 1950, when the Reds won 2-0 with goals from Payne and Liddell.

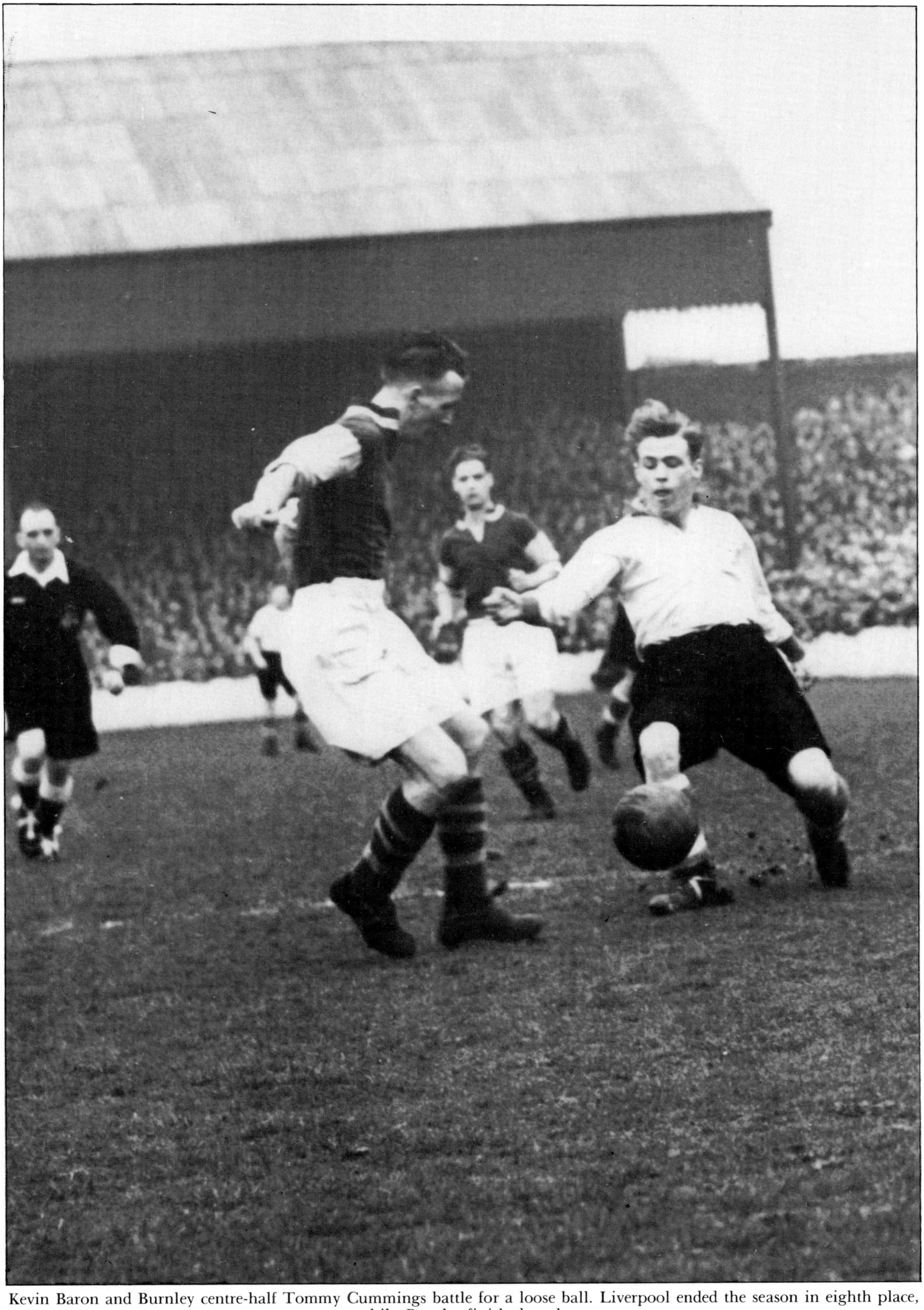

Kevin Baron and Burnley centre-half Tommy Cummings battle for a loose ball. Liverpool ended the season in eighth place, whilst Burnley finished tenth.

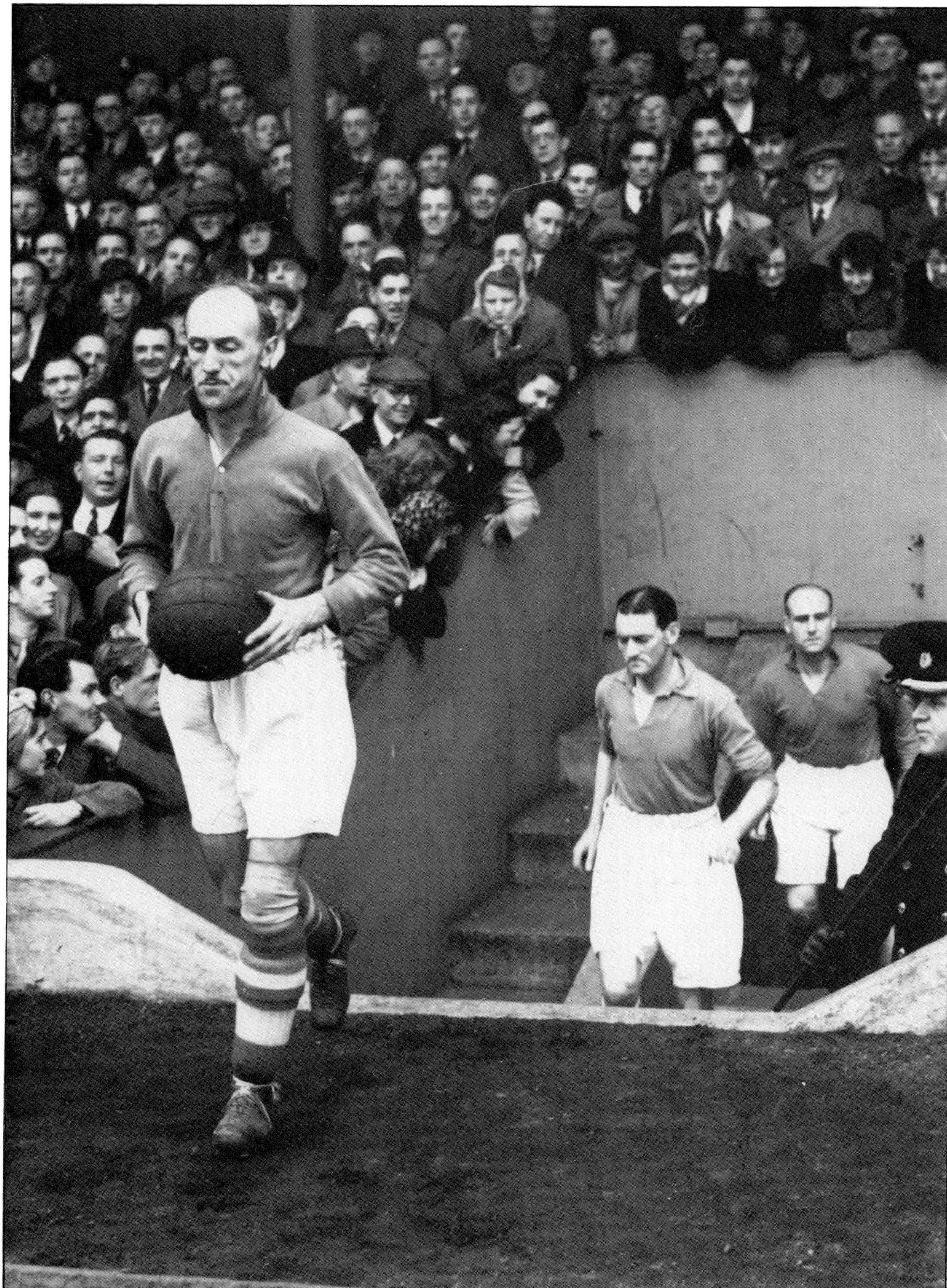

Jack Balmer leads out Liverpool at Anfield. Balmer, a nephew of two famous Everton full-backs of the early 1900s, joined the Reds in May 1935 after being an amateur at Goodison Park. He was a high-scoring centre-forward, who altogether hit 99 League goals for Liverpool. In 1946-7, when the Merseysiders won the League Championship, Balmer scored 15 goals in a seven-game spell, including three consecutive hat-tricks.

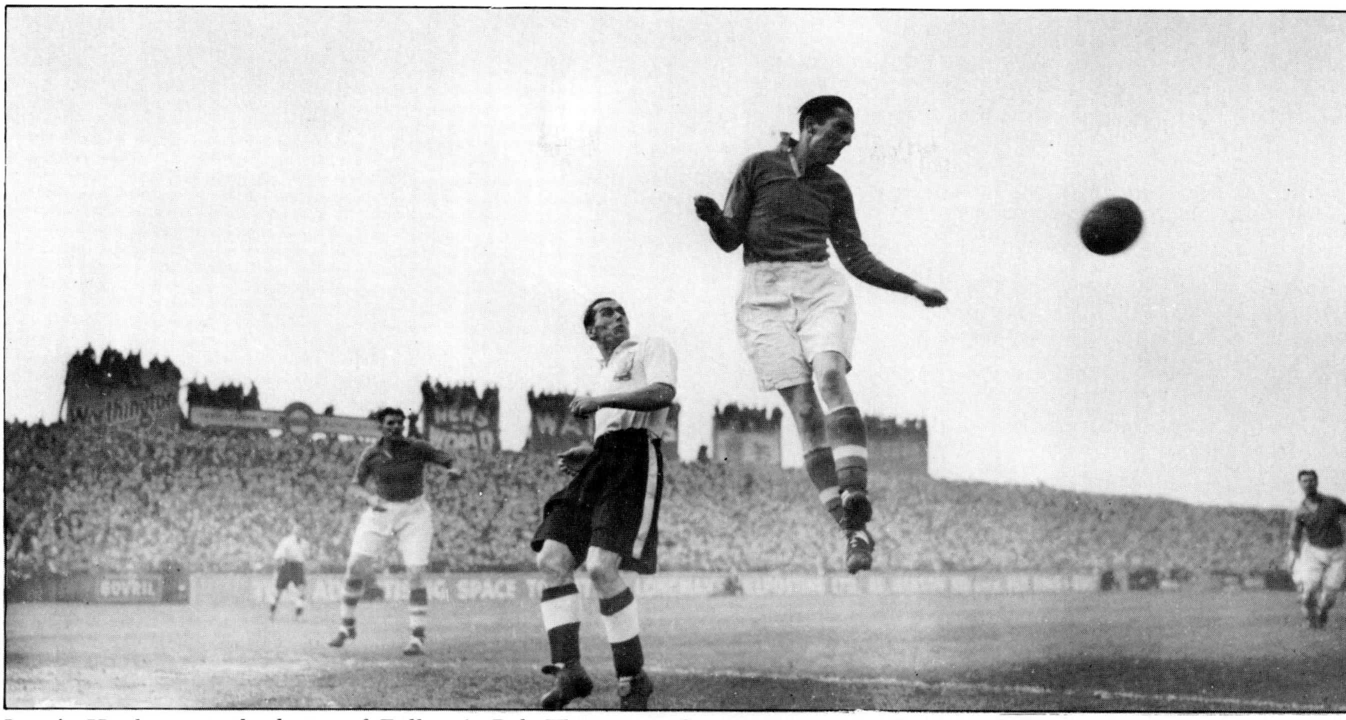

Laurie Hughes gets the better of Fulham's Bob Thomas at Craven Cottage in October 1949, when Liverpool won 1-0 in a First Division game.

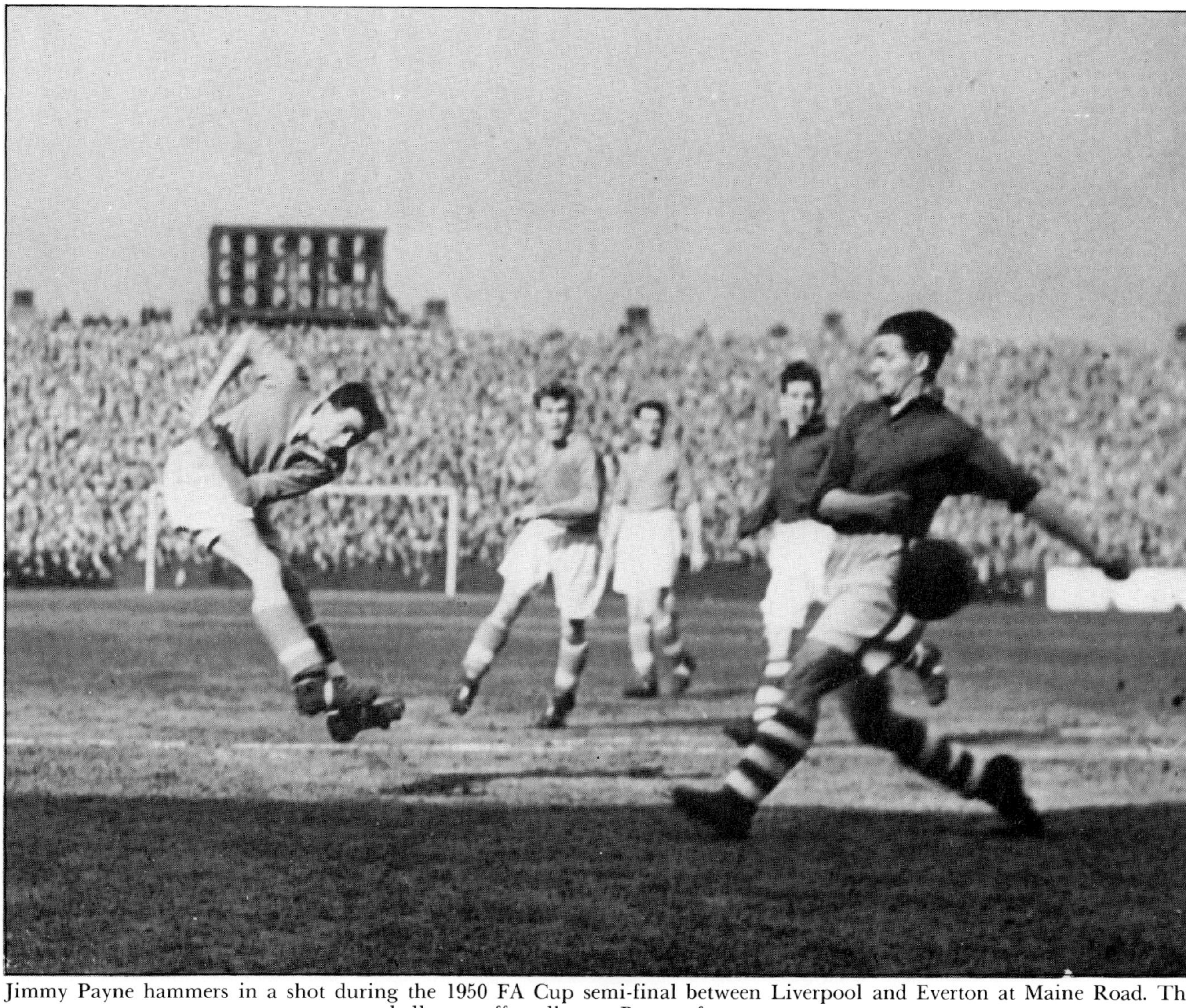
Jimmy Payne hammers in a shot during the 1950 FA Cup semi-final between Liverpool and Everton at Maine Road. The ball went off goalkeeper Burnett for a corner.

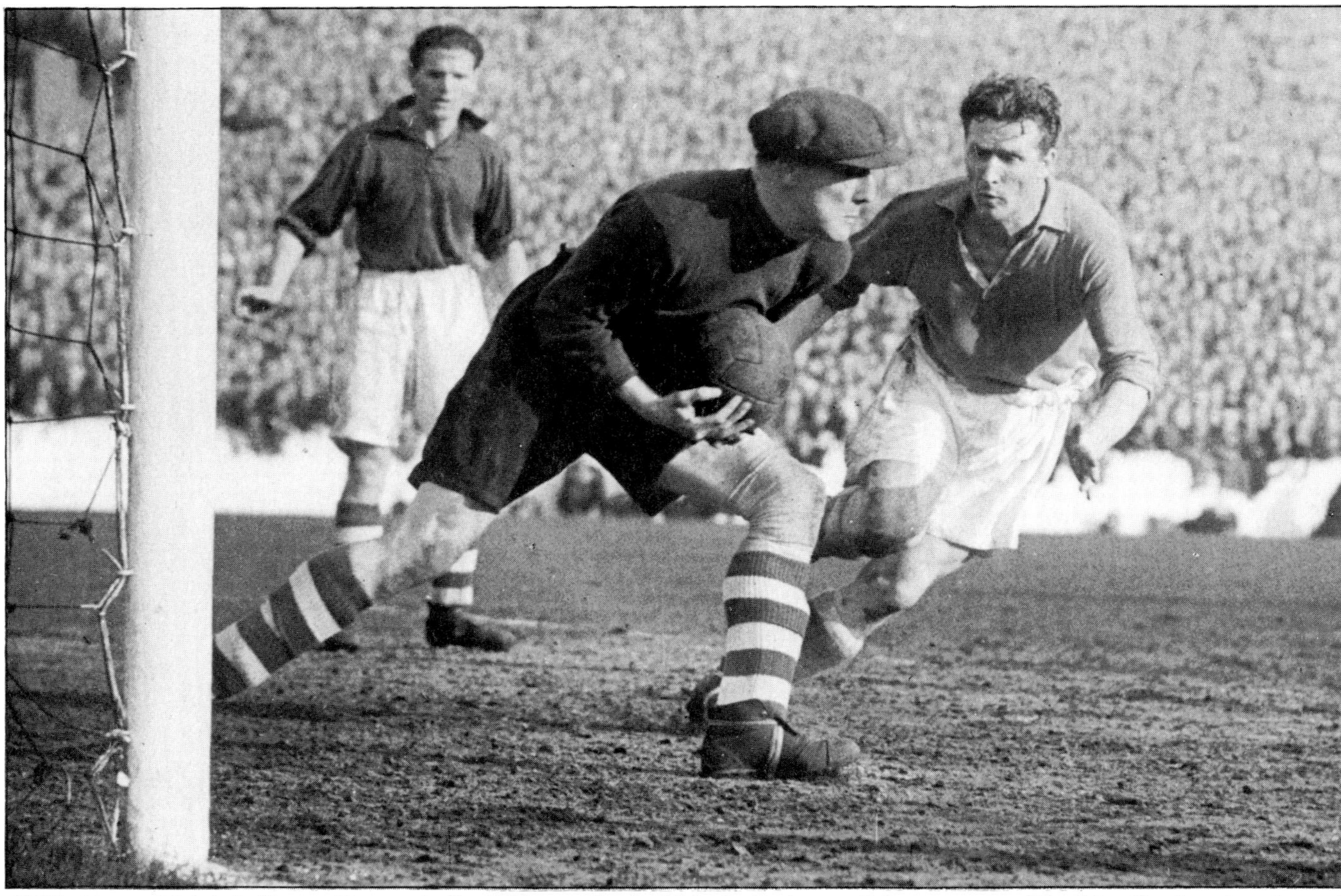

Willie Fagan (right) challenges Burnett in the 1950 semi-final which the Reds won 2-0 to move to a Wembley Final against Arsenal.

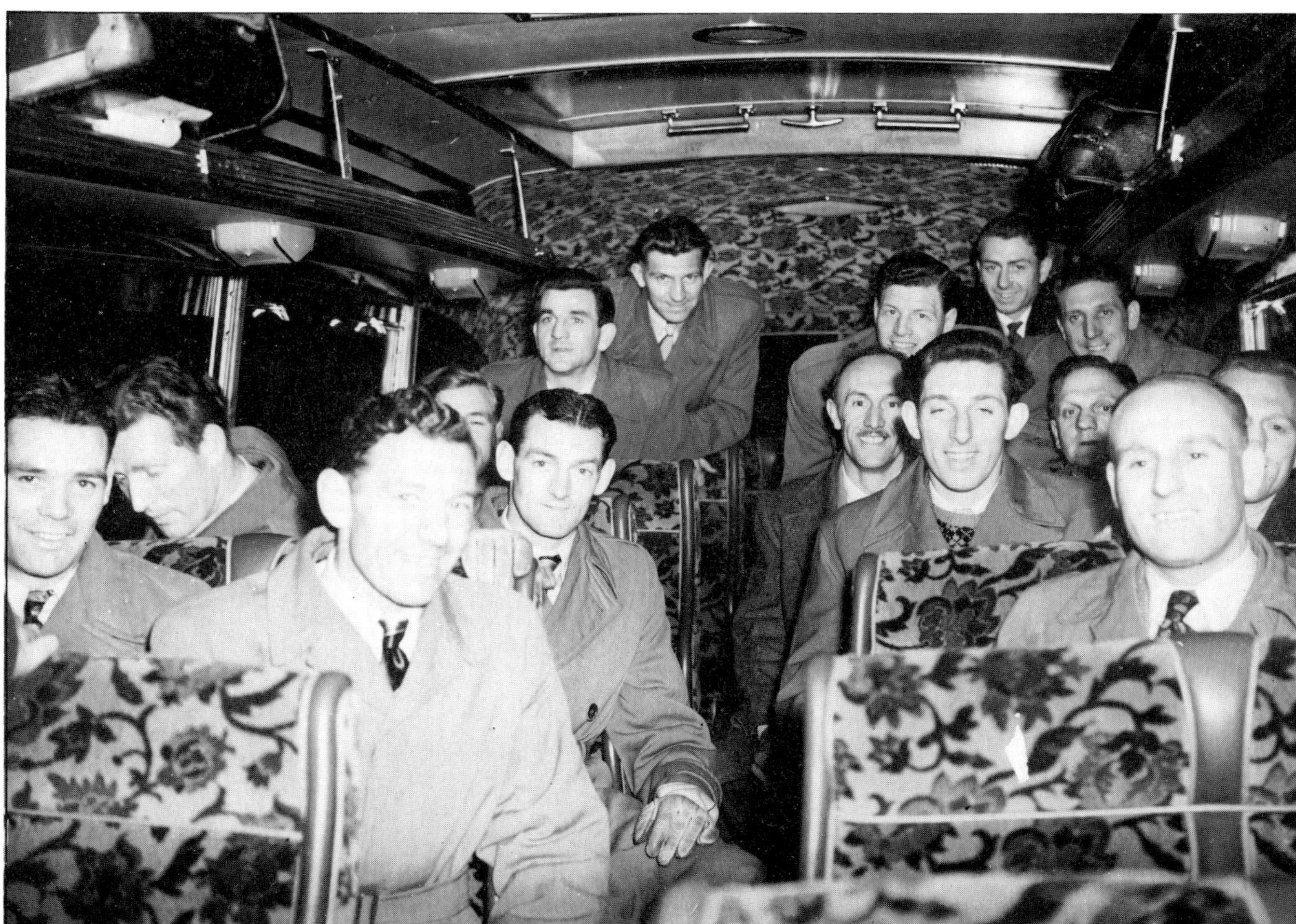

The Liverpool party on their way to their hotel after arriving at Euston station two days before their Wembley Final.

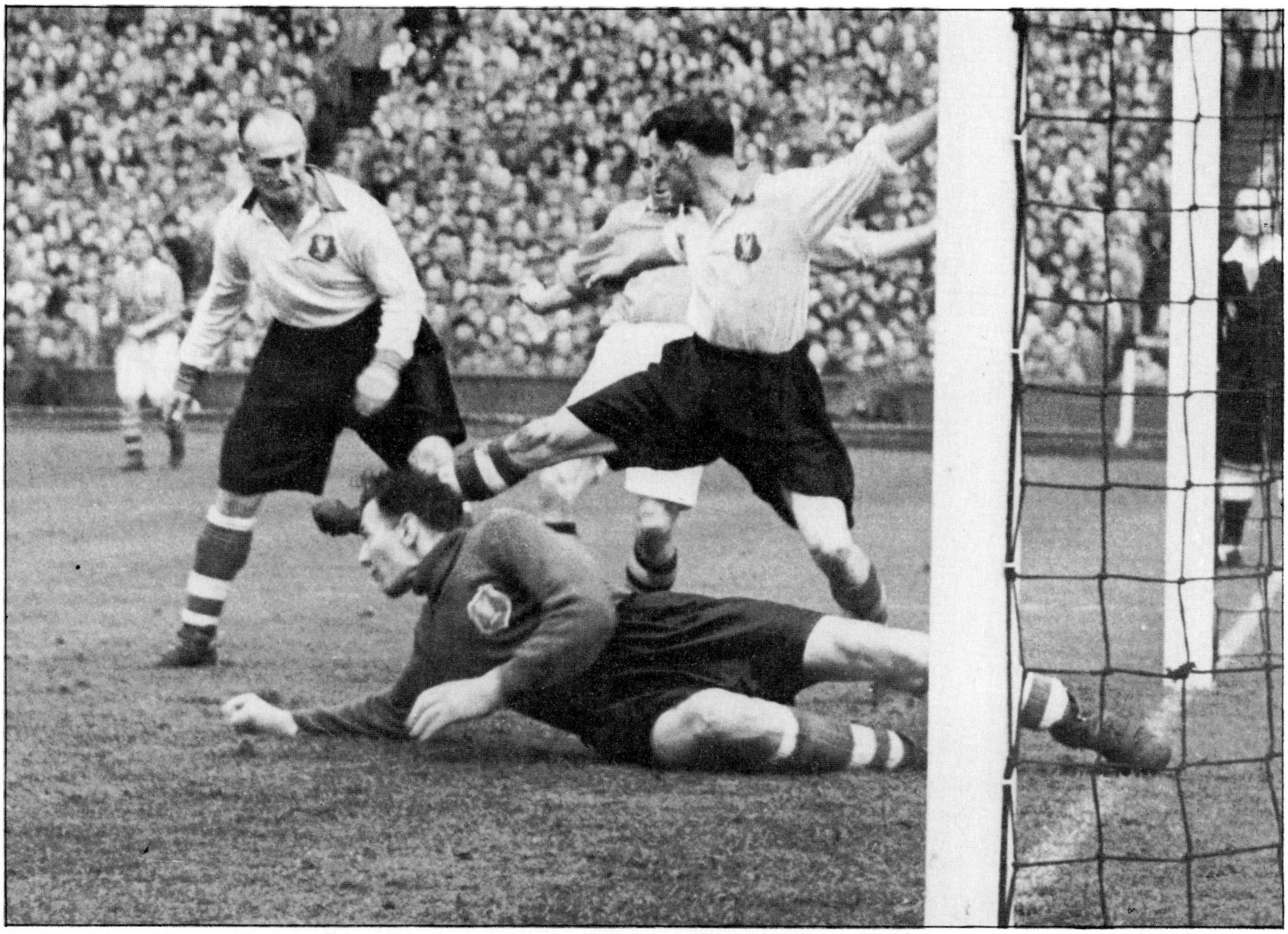

At Wembley, Liverpool went down 2-0 to goals from Reg Lewis. In this picture, Liverpool goalkeeper Cyril Sidlow and his fellow defenders try desperately to keep out the Gunners' threat.

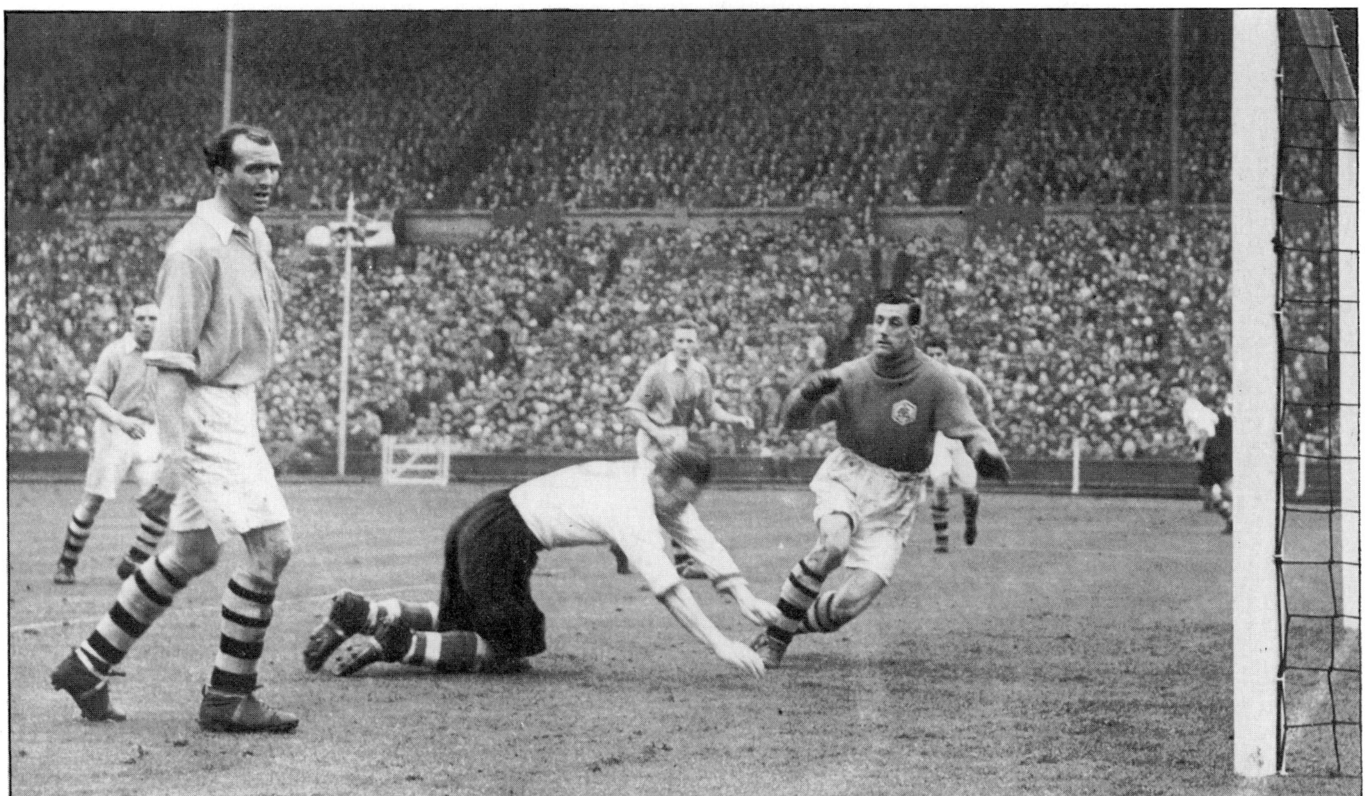

Albert Stubbins dives forward but the ball has flashed past the Arsenal post. Goalkeeper George Swindin and Welsh international full-back Walley Barnes look on.

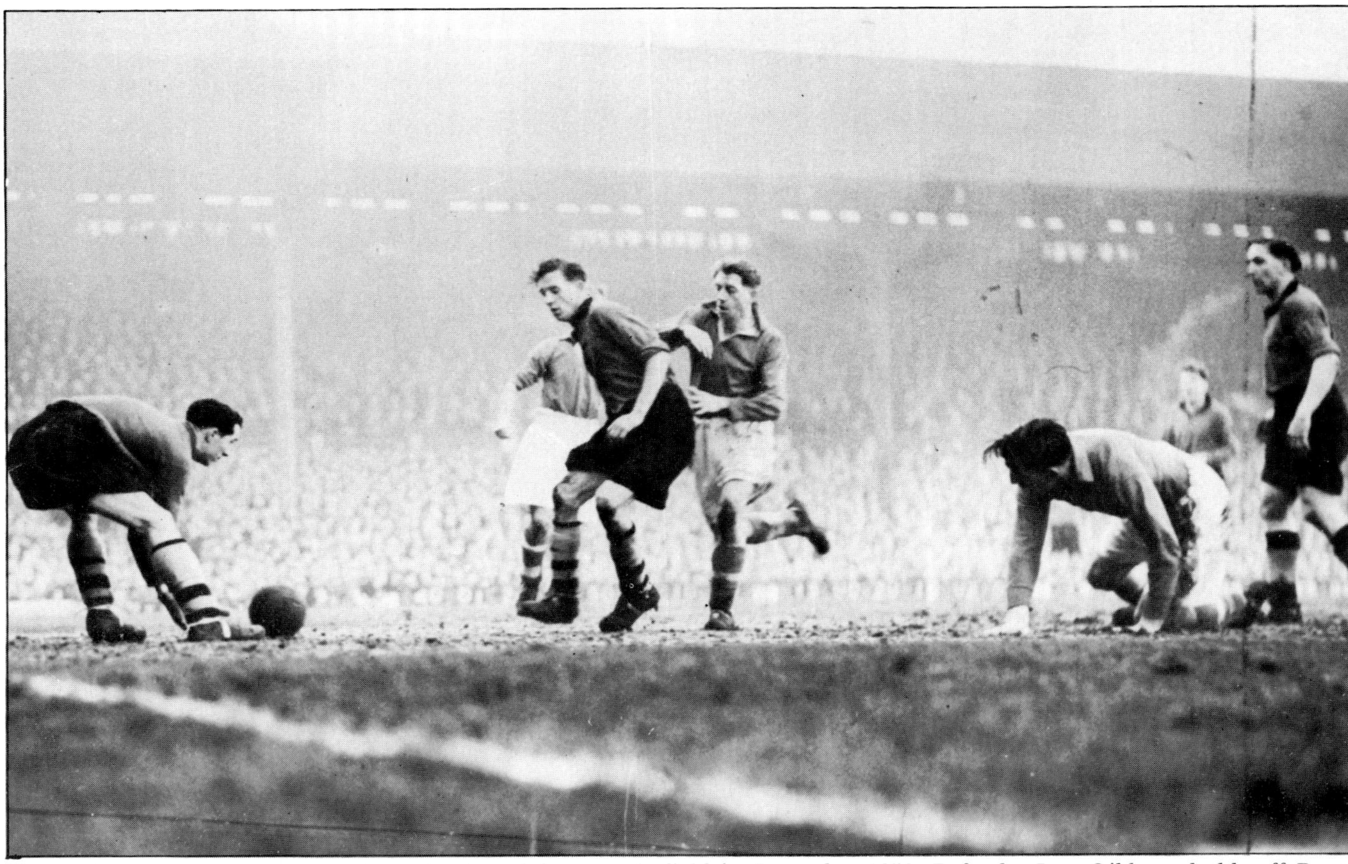

Jimmy Payne cannot get through the Wolves defence at Anfield in December 1950. Defender Len Gibbons holds off Payne as Dennis Parsons collects the ball. Liverpool went down 4-1 and finished ninth in Division One.

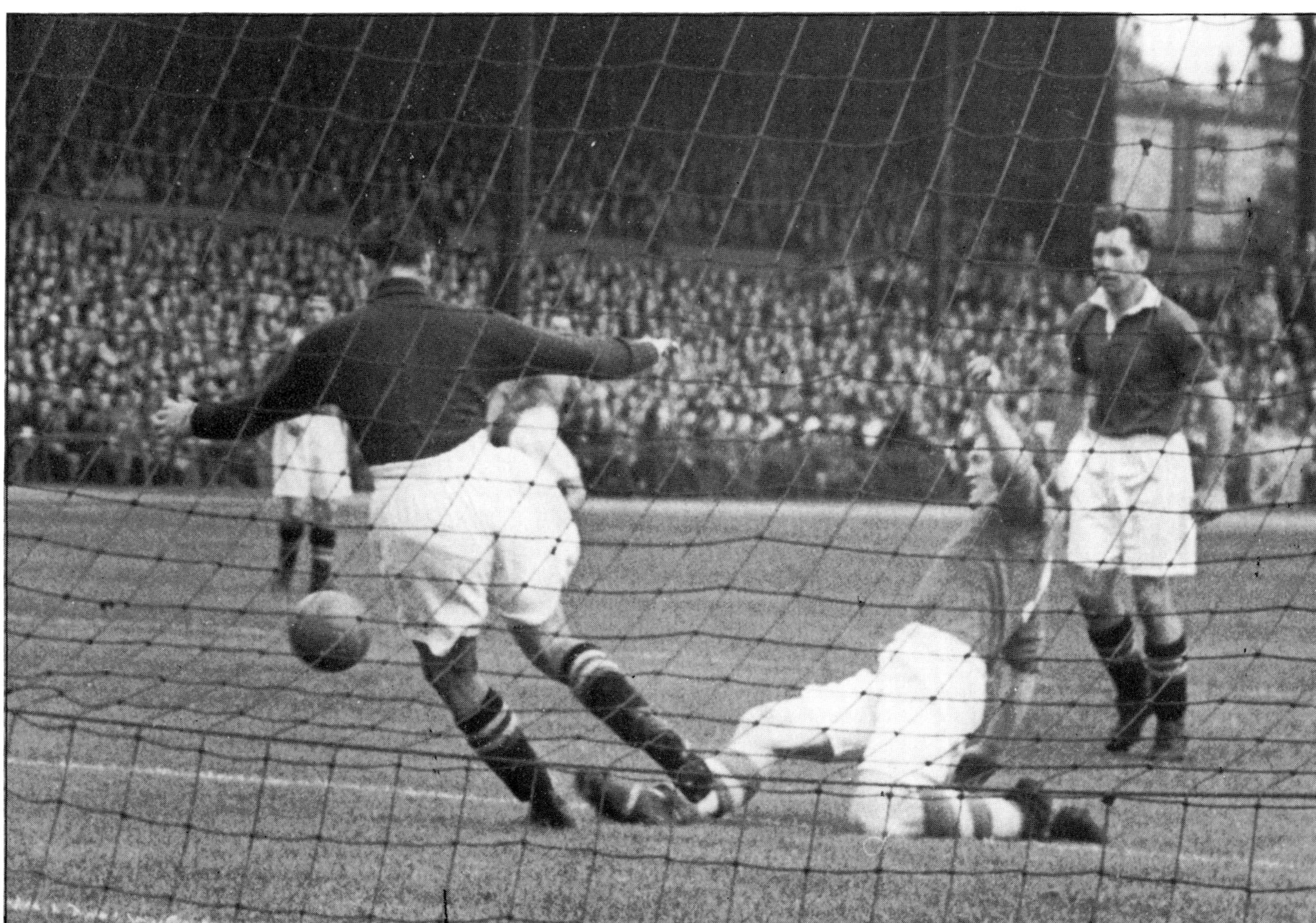

Stubbins gets his foot to the ball at Stamford Bridge in August 1951 but Bill Robertson, the Chelsea goalkeeper, watches it go wide. Liverpool won 3-1.

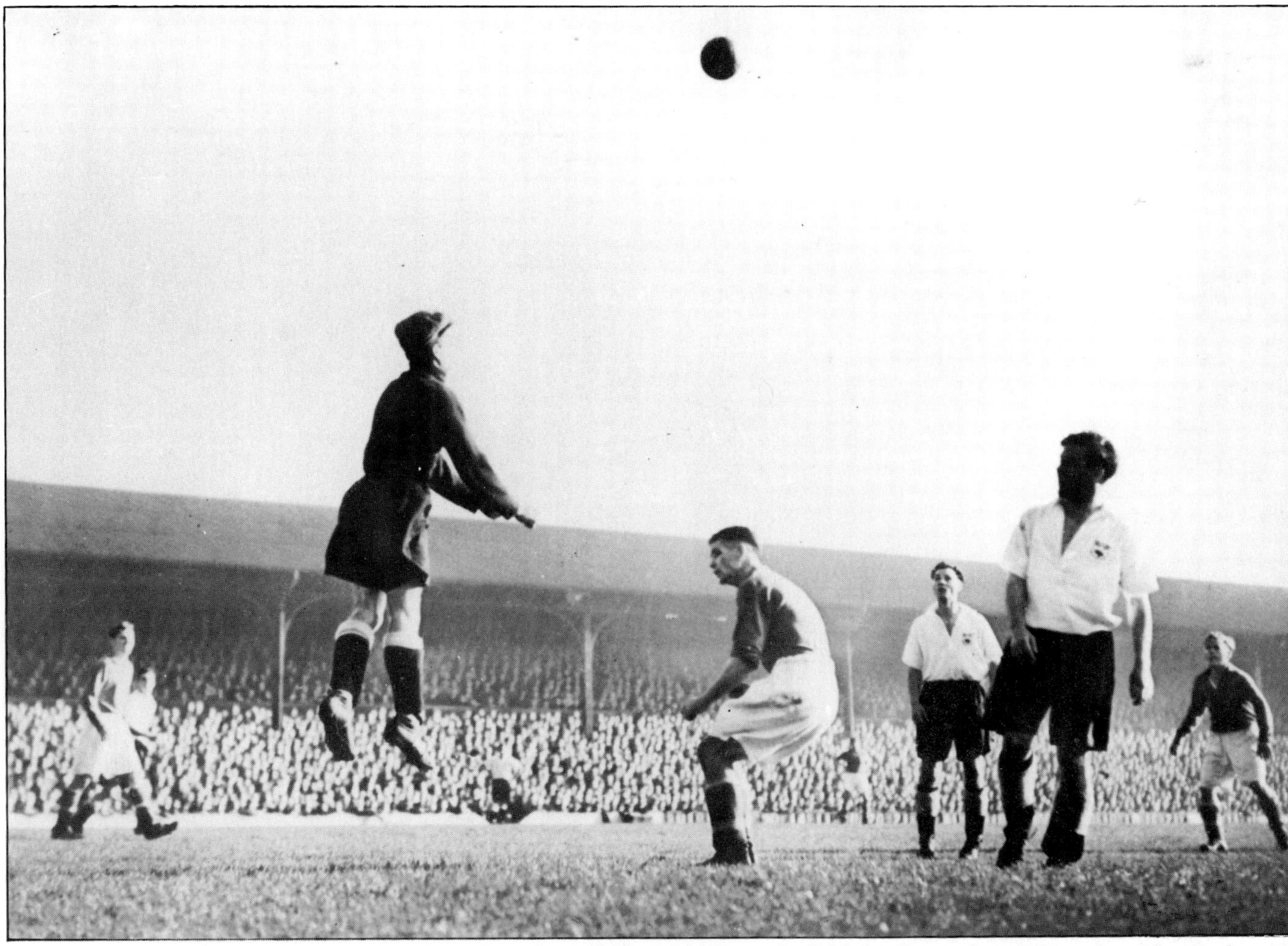

Derby goalkeeper Ray Middleton punches clear from Billy Liddell at Anfield in September 1951, when the Reds won 2-0. They finished 11th in Division One.

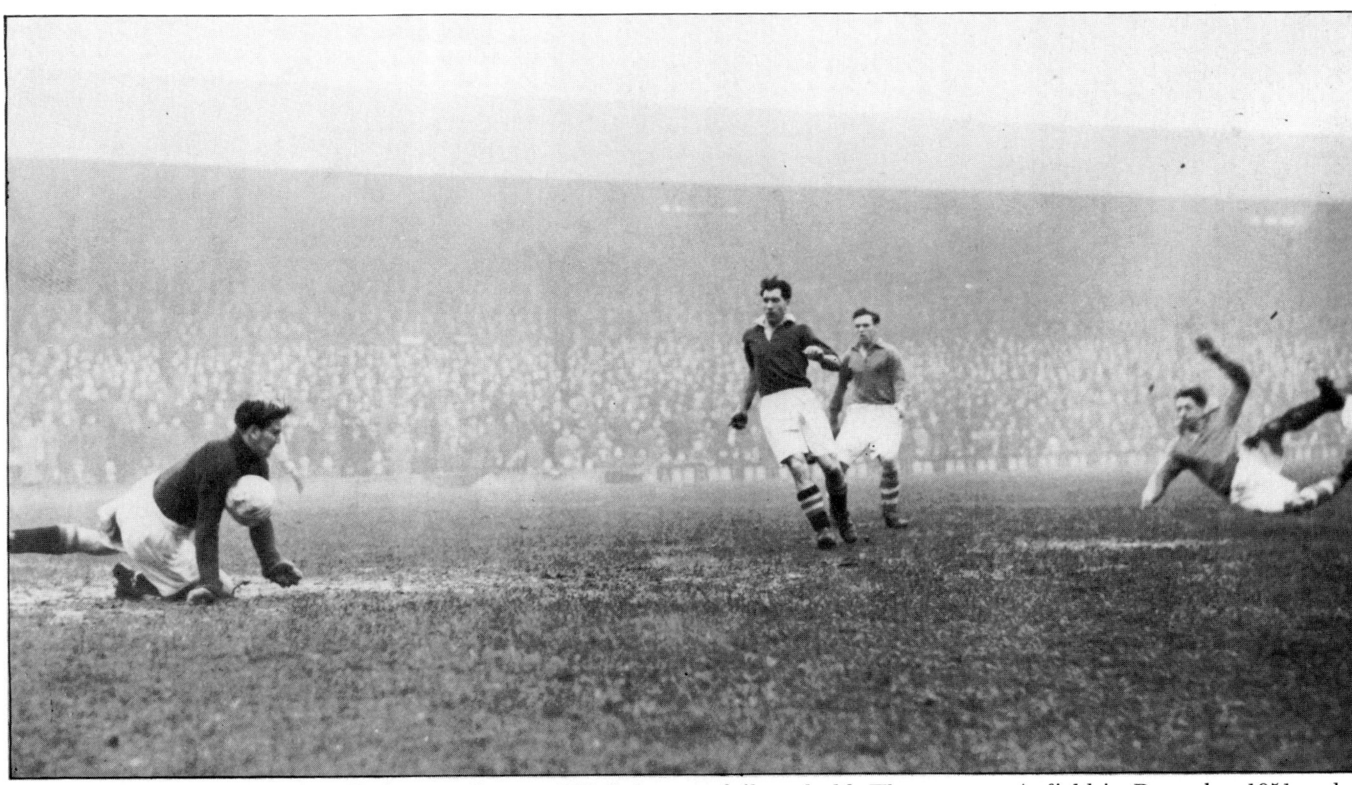

Jimmy Payne tries a shot that Chelsea goalkeeper Bill Robertson fails to hold. The game at Anfield in December 1951 ended in a 1-1 draw.

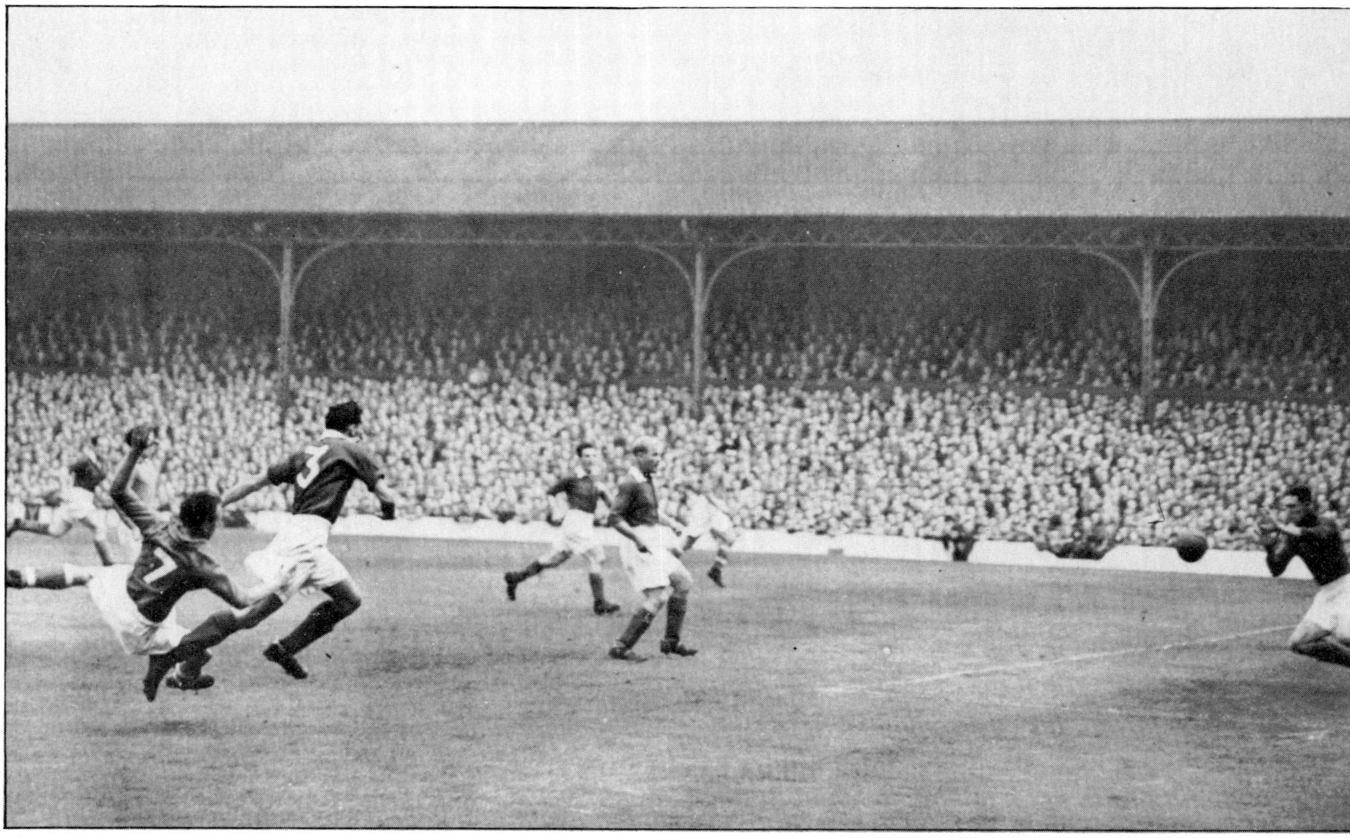

Jimmy Payne's shot is knocked down by Portsmouth goalkeeper Ernie Butler at Anfield in September 1952. The result was a 1-1 draw.

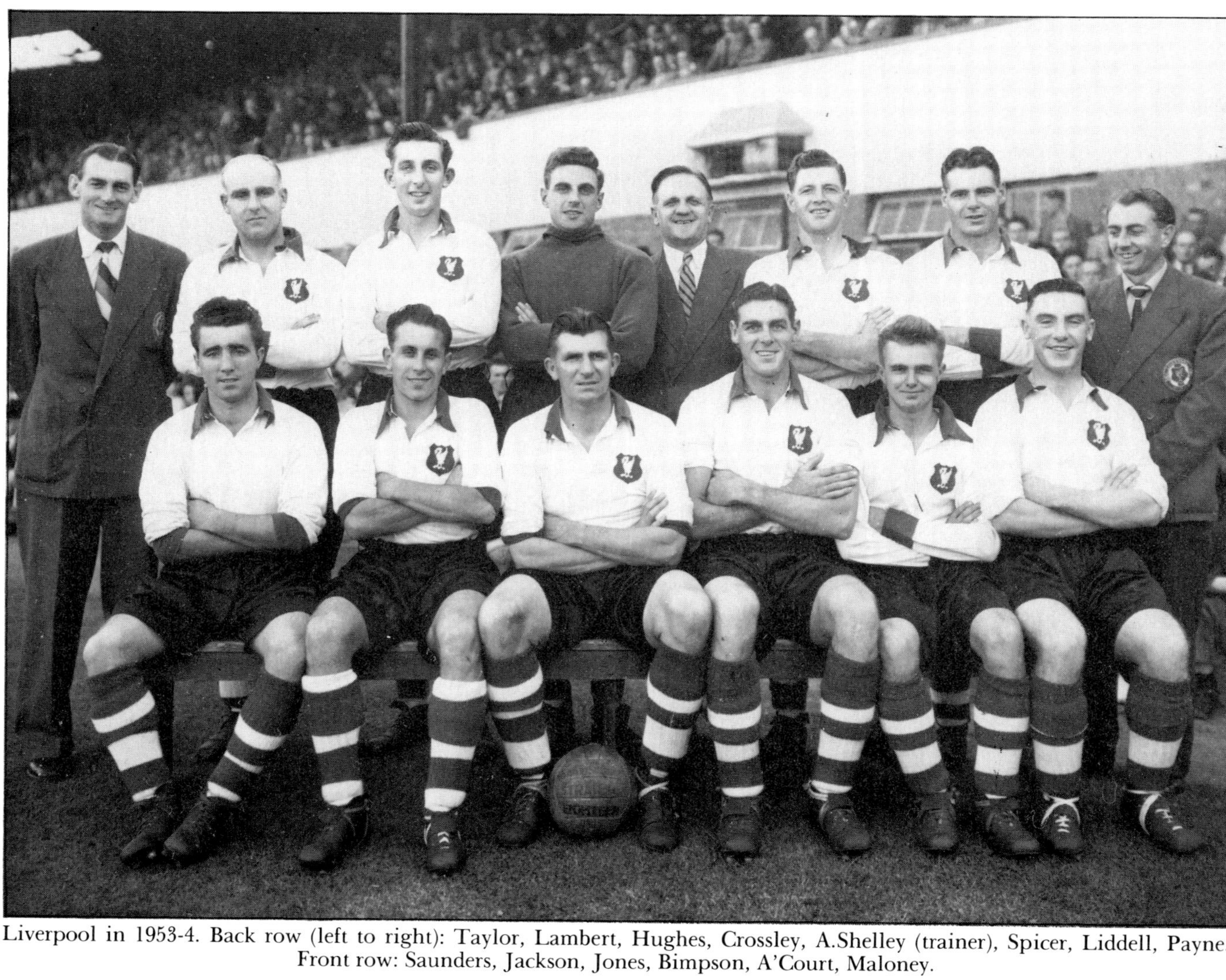

Liverpool in 1953-4. Back row (left to right): Taylor, Lambert, Hughes, Crossley, A.Shelley (trainer), Spicer, Liddell, Payne. Front row: Saunders, Jackson, Jones, Bimpson, A'Court, Maloney.

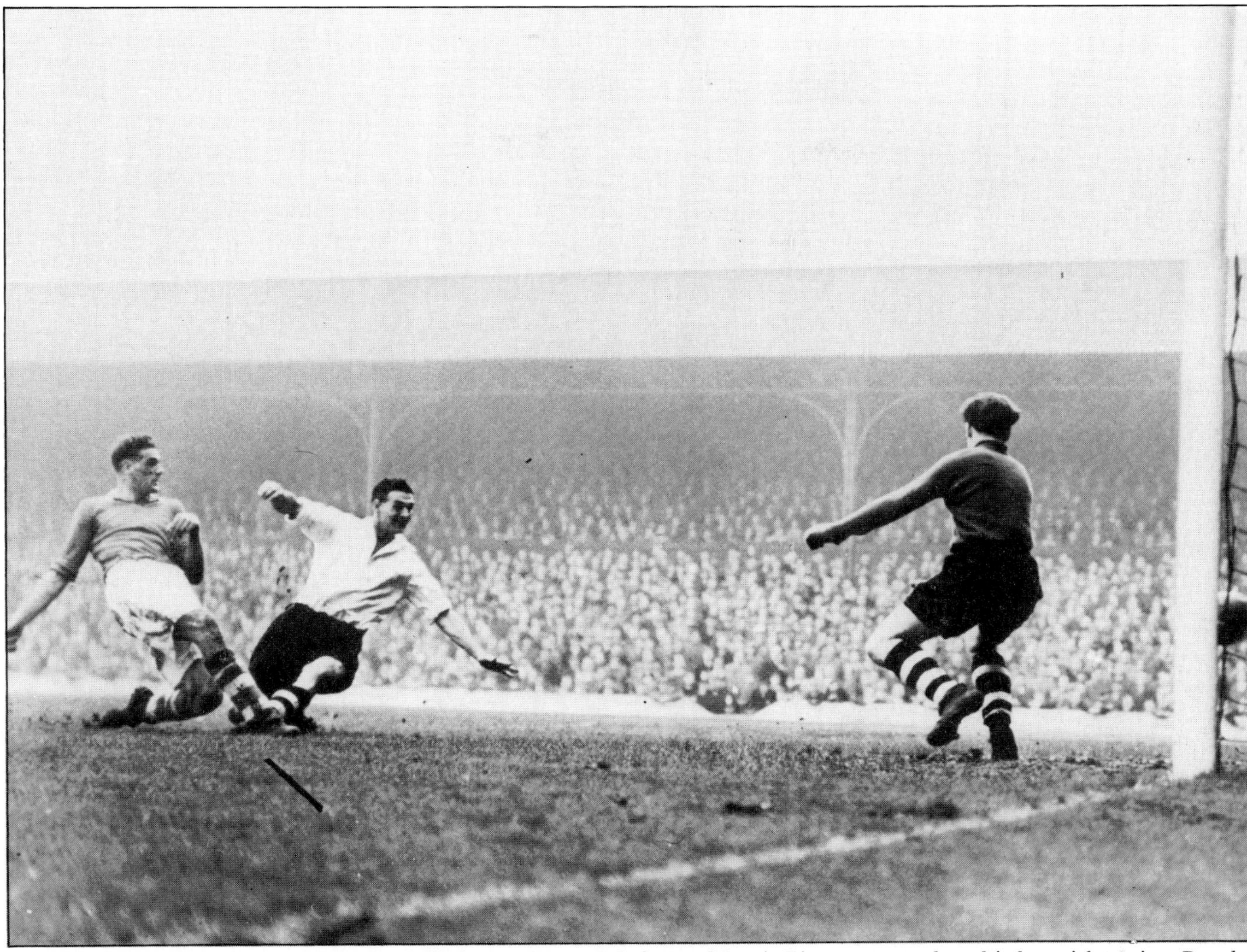

In only his second season of League football, former Burscough forward Louis Bimpson completes his hat-trick against Burnley at Anfield in September 1953. Liverpool went on to win 4-0 and Bimpson scored all their goals, ending the season as the Reds' leading scorer. In 100 senior games for Liverpool, Bimpson netted 40 times before joining Blackburn Rovers in November 1959.

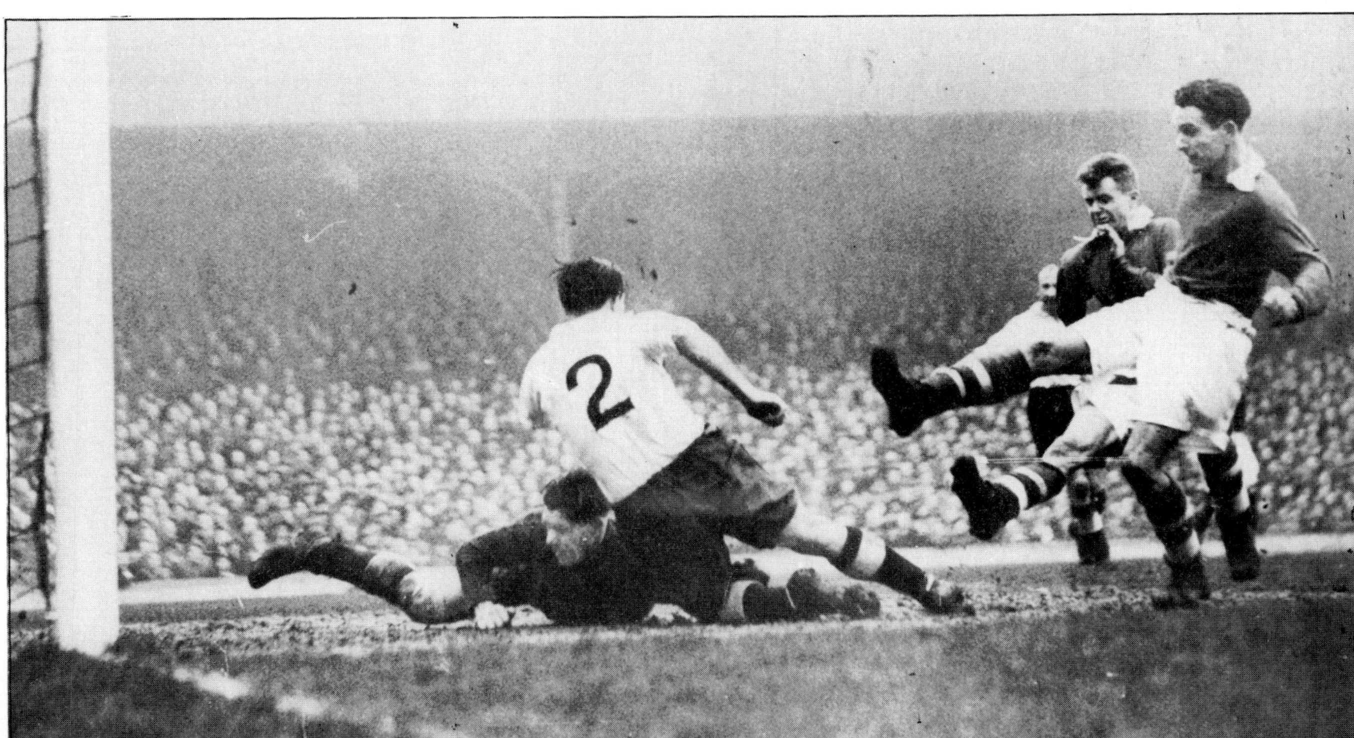

Tottenham's Ted Ditchburn and Alf Ramsey hold up Liverpool's Alan A'Court and Eric Anderson at Anfield in January 1954. The game ended in a 2-2 draw in what was Liverpool's last season in the First Division for eight years. They had enjoyed continuous membership of the top flight since being promoted in 1905.

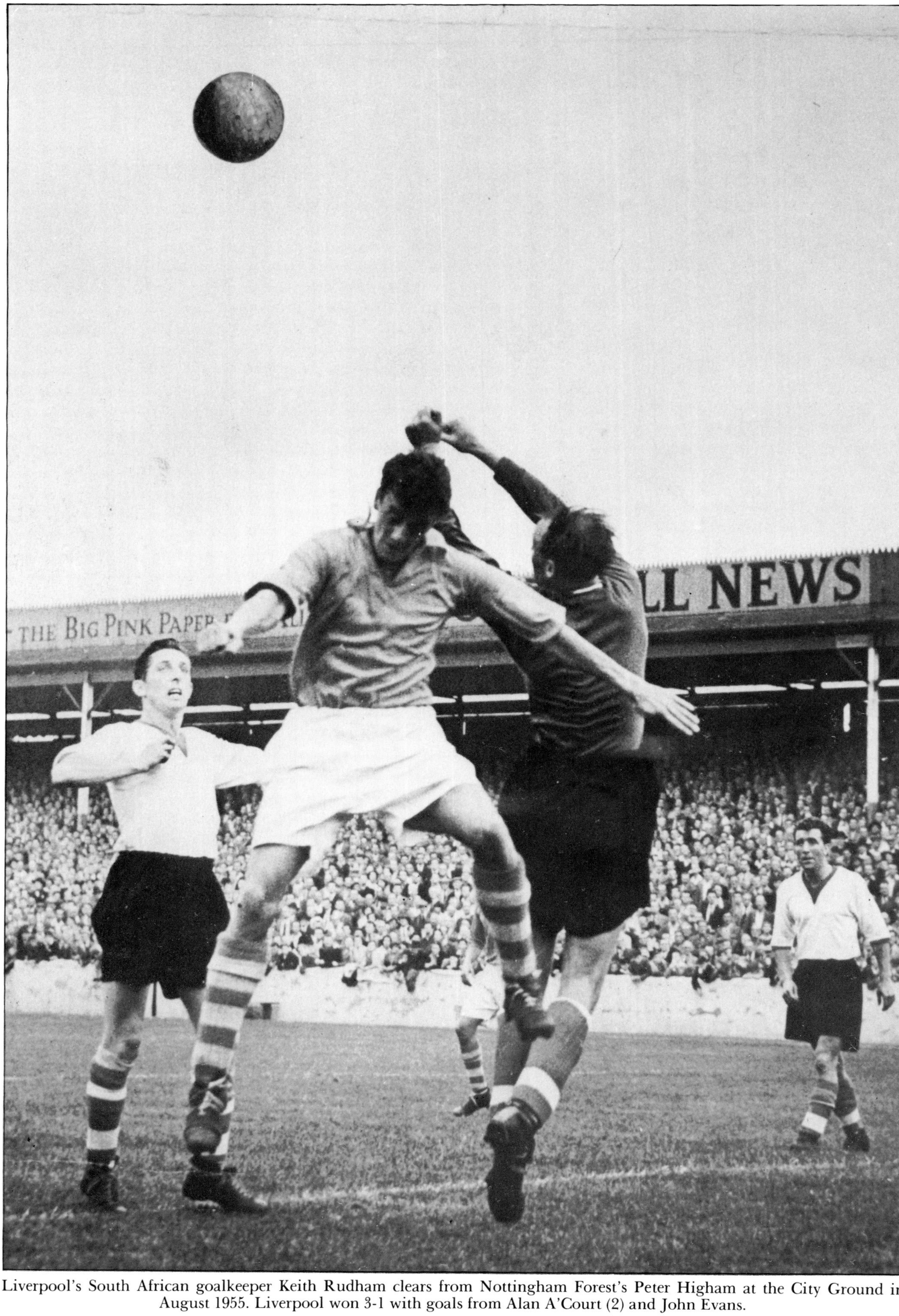

Liverpool's South African goalkeeper Keith Rudham clears from Nottingham Forest's Peter Higham at the City Ground in August 1955. Liverpool won 3-1 with goals from Alan A'Court (2) and John Evans.

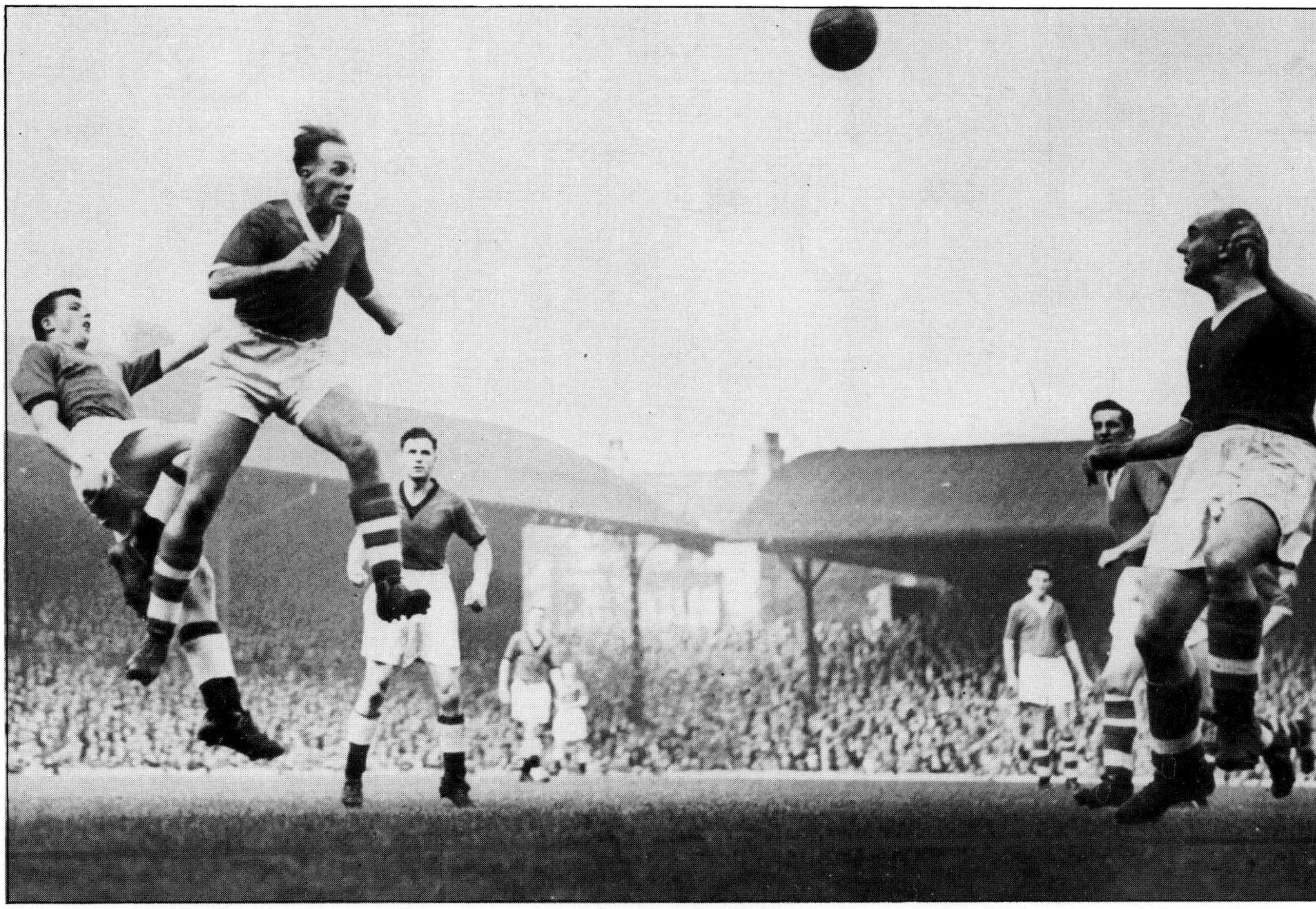

Ronnie Moran heads clear from a Plymouth Argyle attack at Anfield in September 1954. The game ended in a 3-3 draw and Liverpool ended their first season back in Division Two in 11th place.

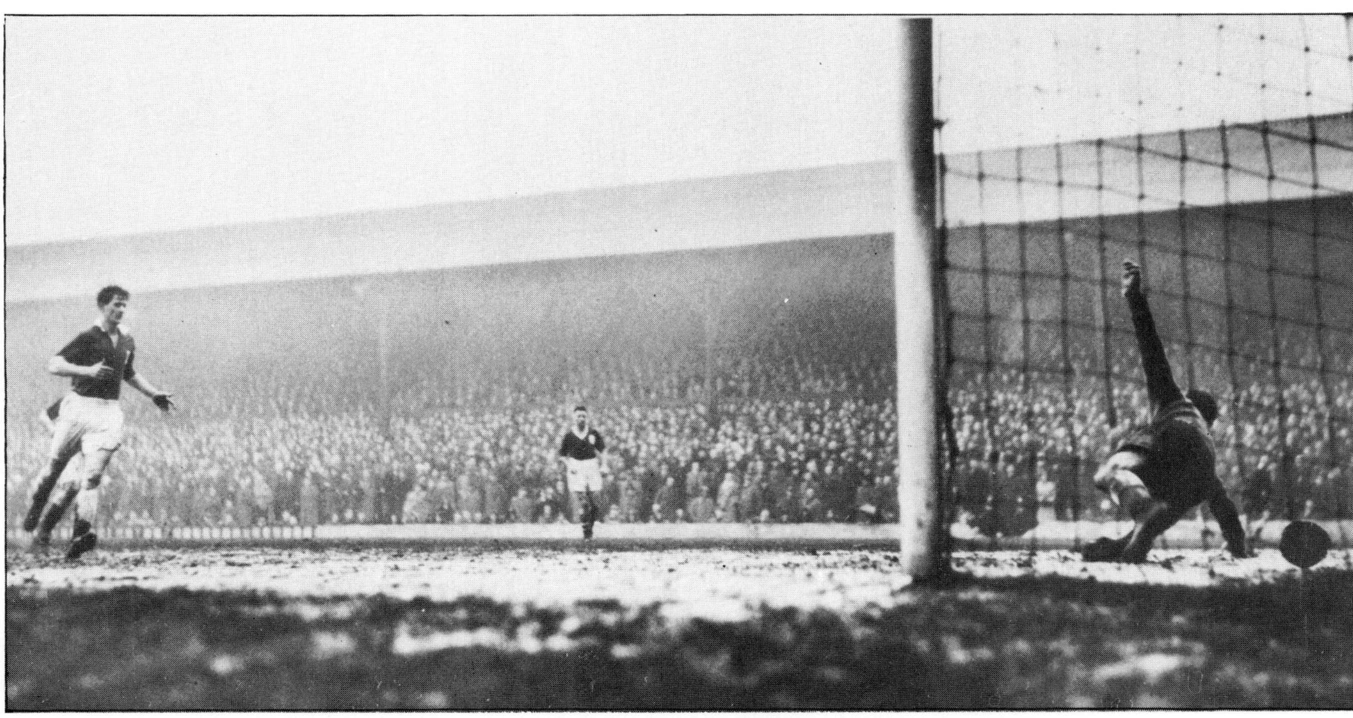

Alan Arnell scores Liverpool's second goal against Leicester City at Anfield in January 1956. Liddell scored twice in the Reds' 3-1 win.

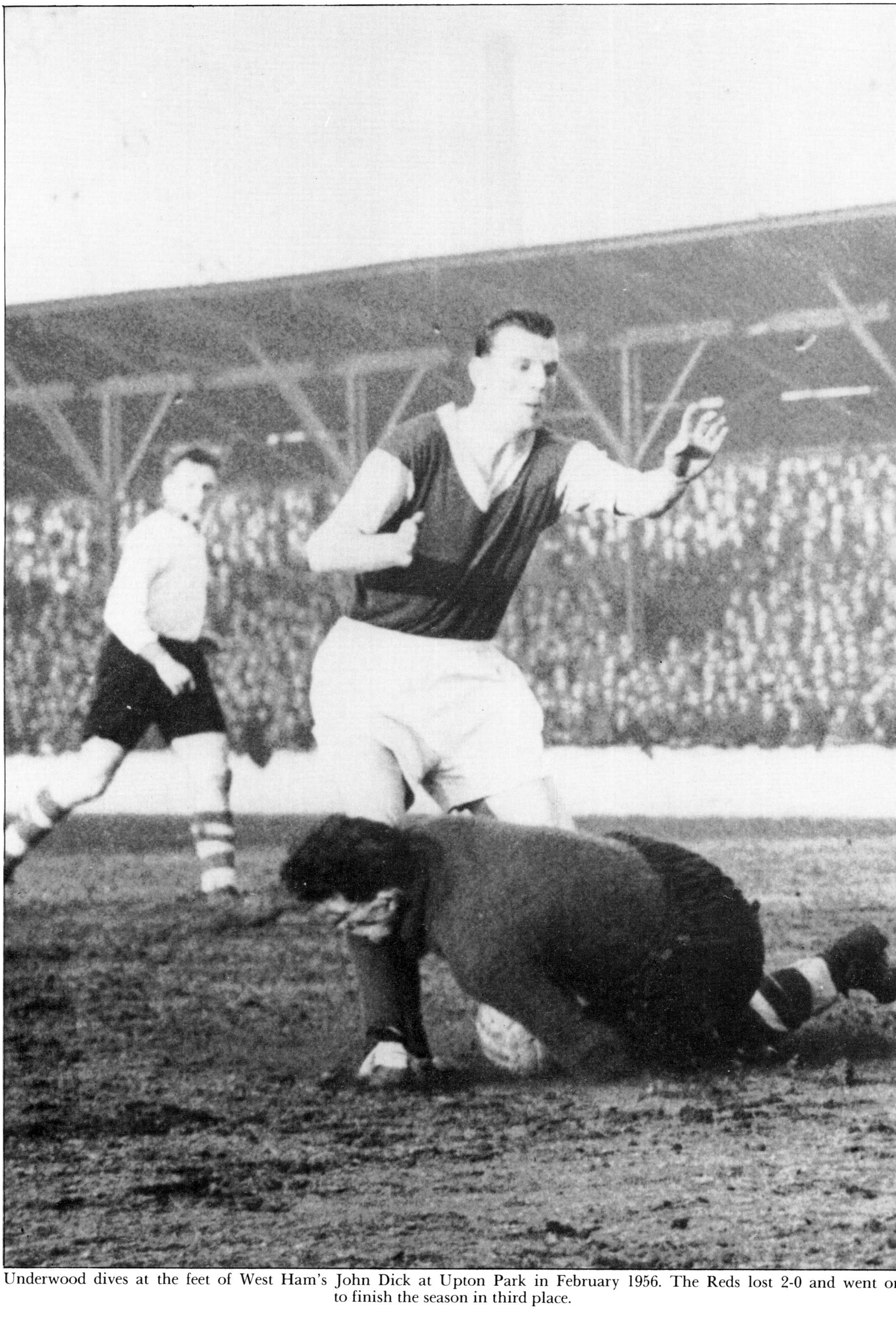

Underwood dives at the feet of West Ham's John Dick at Upton Park in February 1956. The Reds lost 2-0 and went on to finish the season in third place.

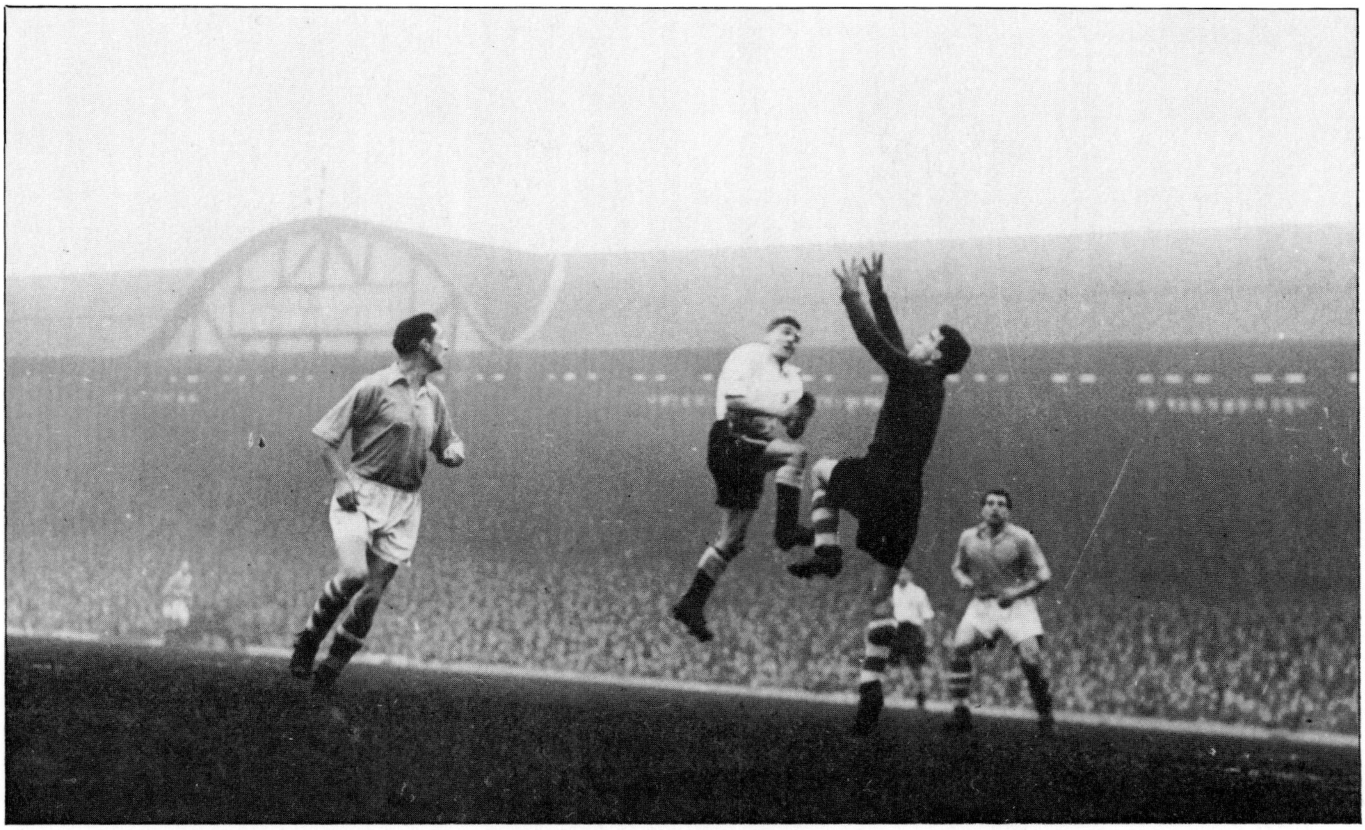

Liverpool goalkeeper Dave Underwood is challenged by an Accrington Stanley forward during the third-round FA Cup tie between the clubs at Anfield in January 1956, when a crowd of 48,385 saw the Third Division North side beaten 2-0. Liverpool then took two games to dispose of Scunthorpe United before losing to Manchester City after another replay.

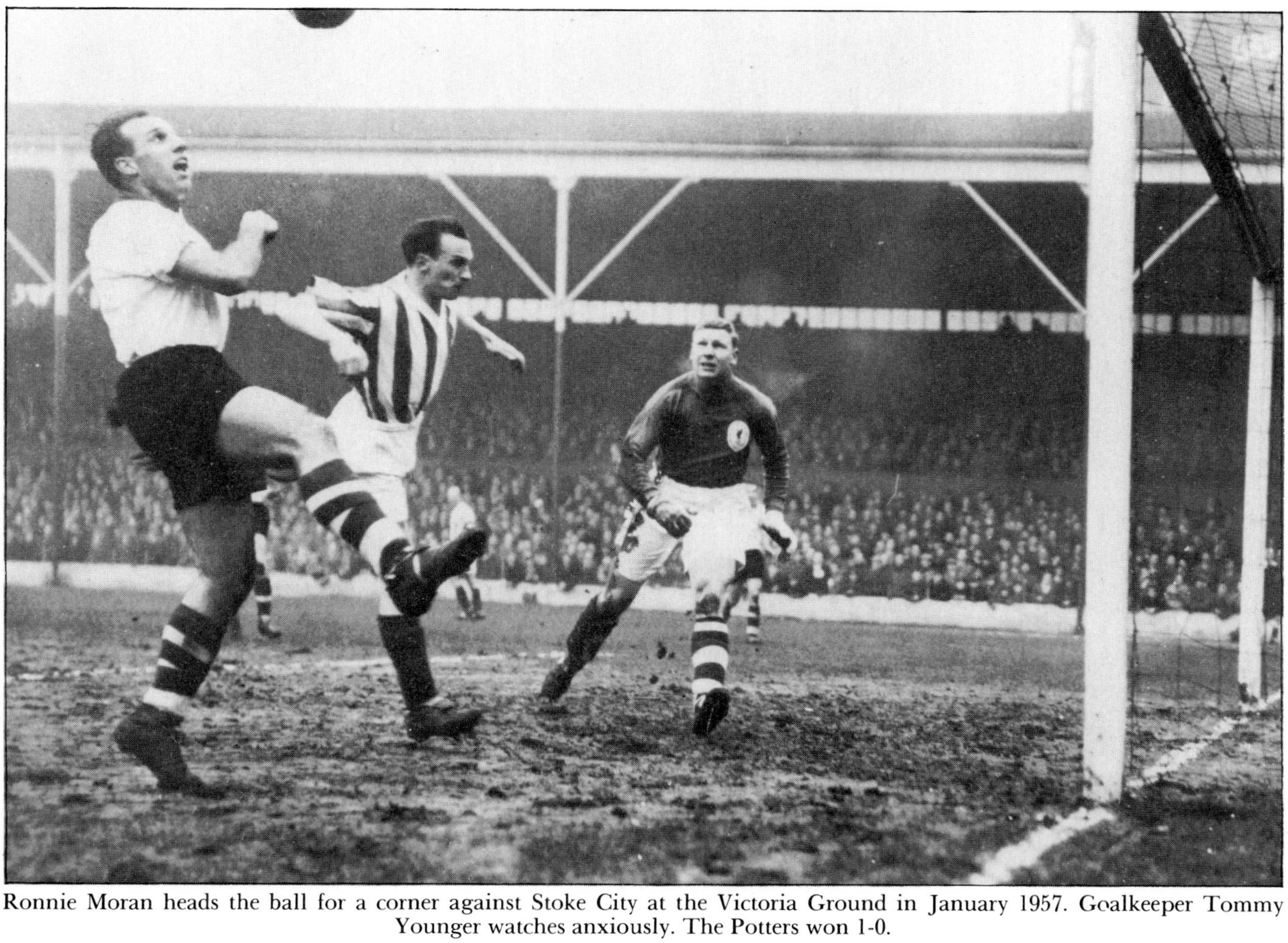

Ronnie Moran heads the ball for a corner against Stoke City at the Victoria Ground in January 1957. Goalkeeper Tommy Younger watches anxiously. The Potters won 1-0.

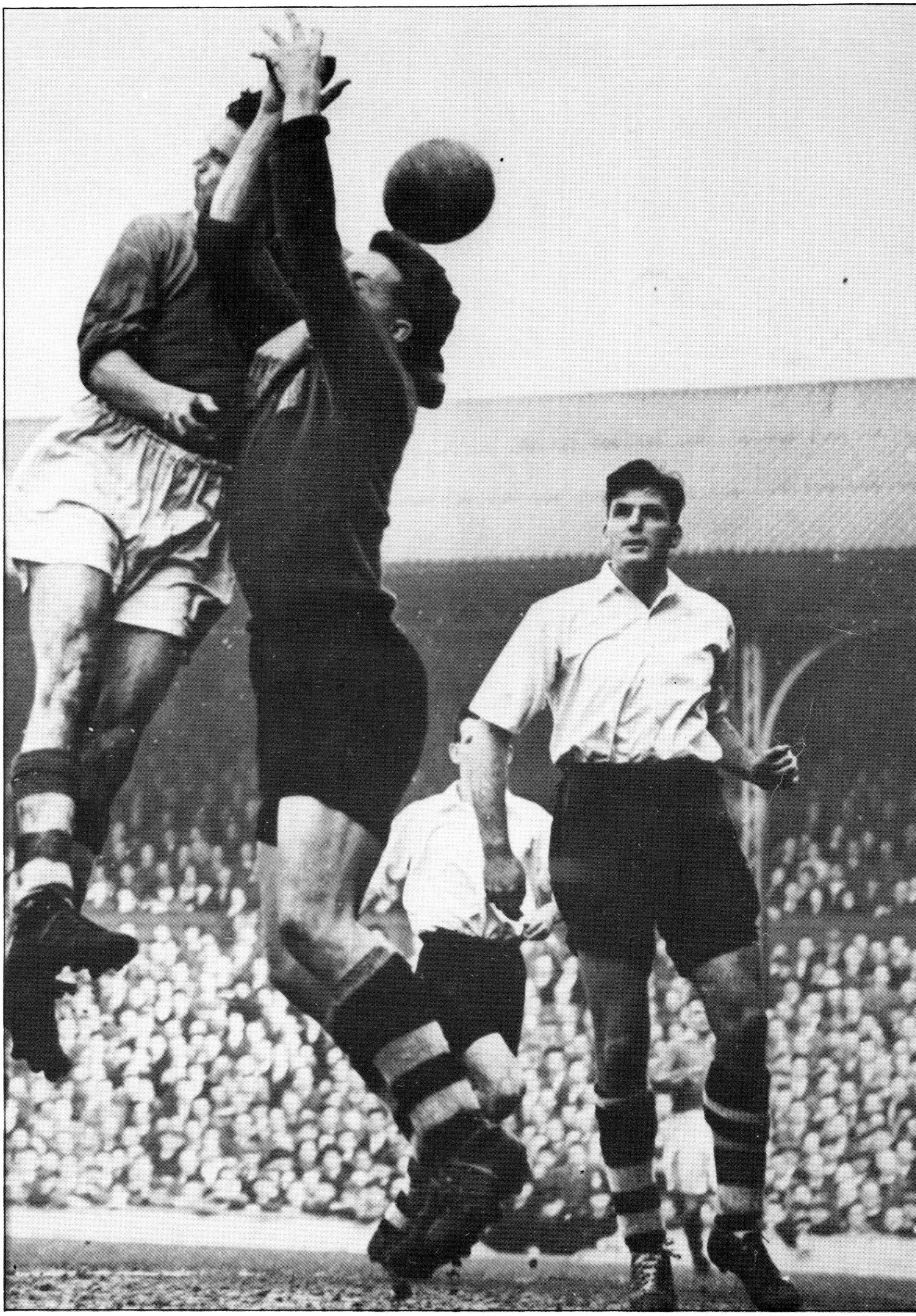

Rotherham United goalkeeper Roy Ironside misses the ball as Tony Rowley challenges him at Anfield in March 1957. Rowley was one of the scorers in Liverpool's 4-1 win.

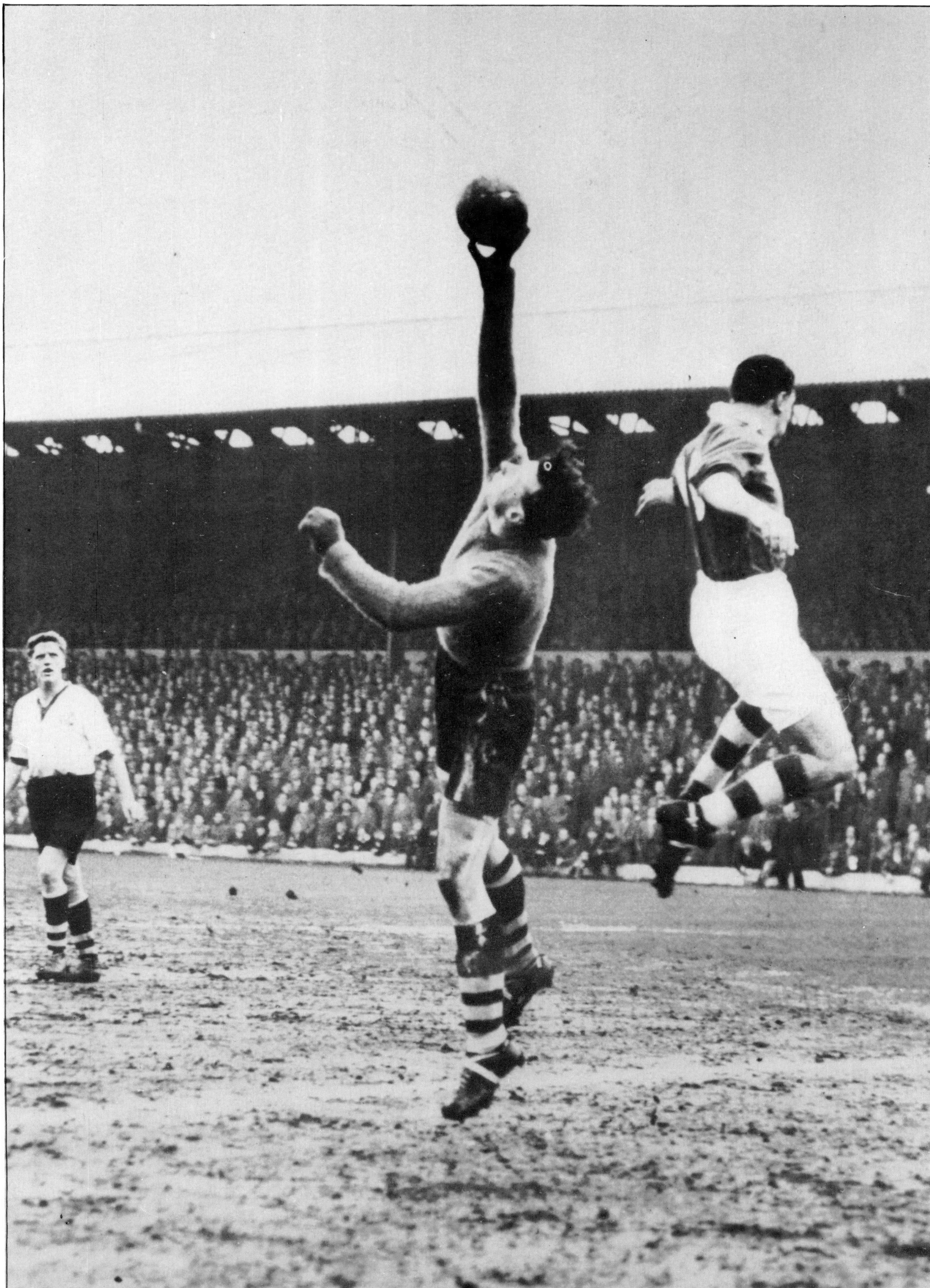

Port Vale goalkeeper Ray King gets his hand to the ball to thwart two-goal Tony Rowley at Vale Park during Liverpool's 2-1 victory there in March 1957. The Reds again finished the season in third place.

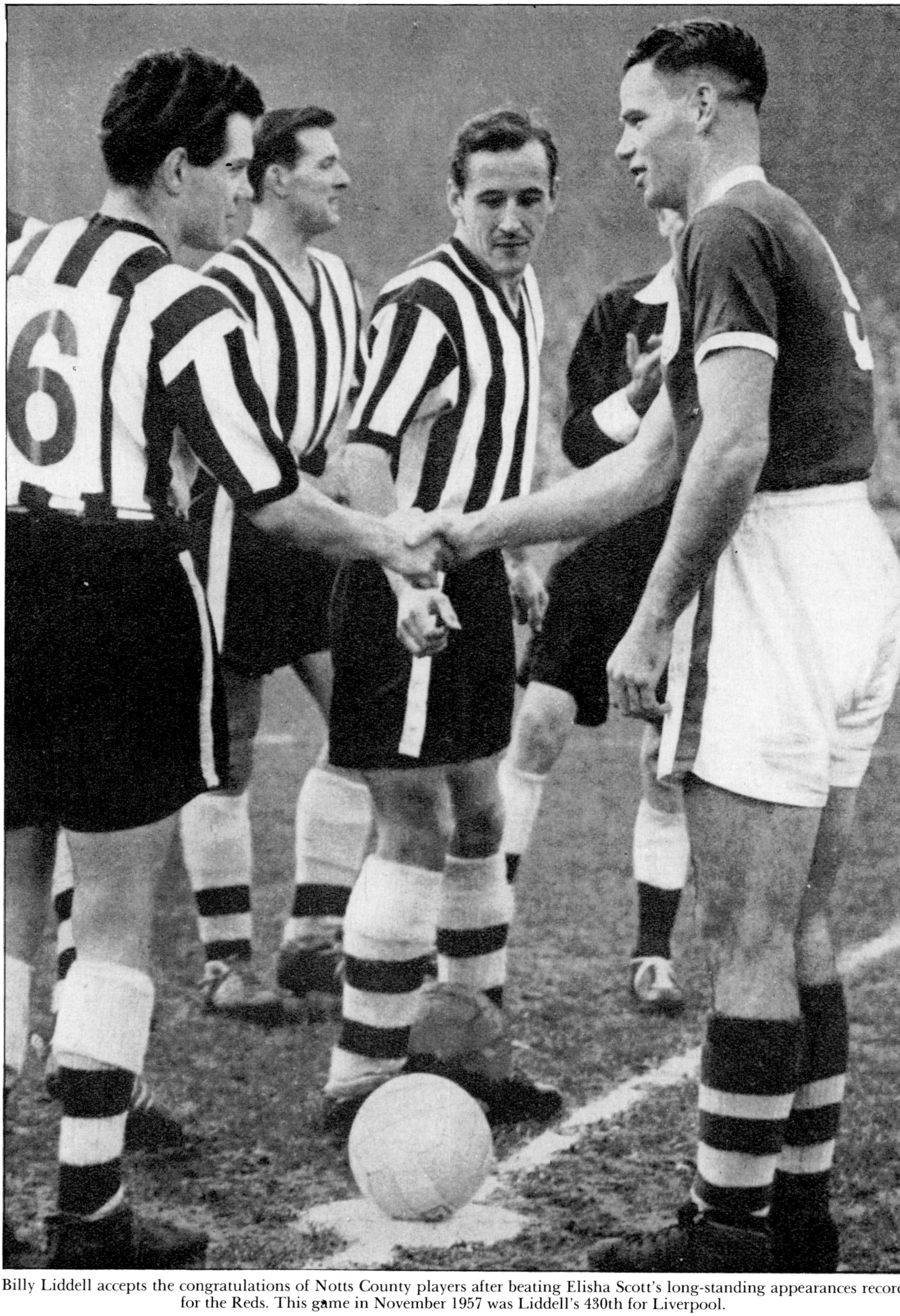

Billy Liddell accepts the congratulations of Notts County players after beating Elisha Scott's long-standing appearances record for the Reds. This game in November 1957 was Liddell's 430th for Liverpool.

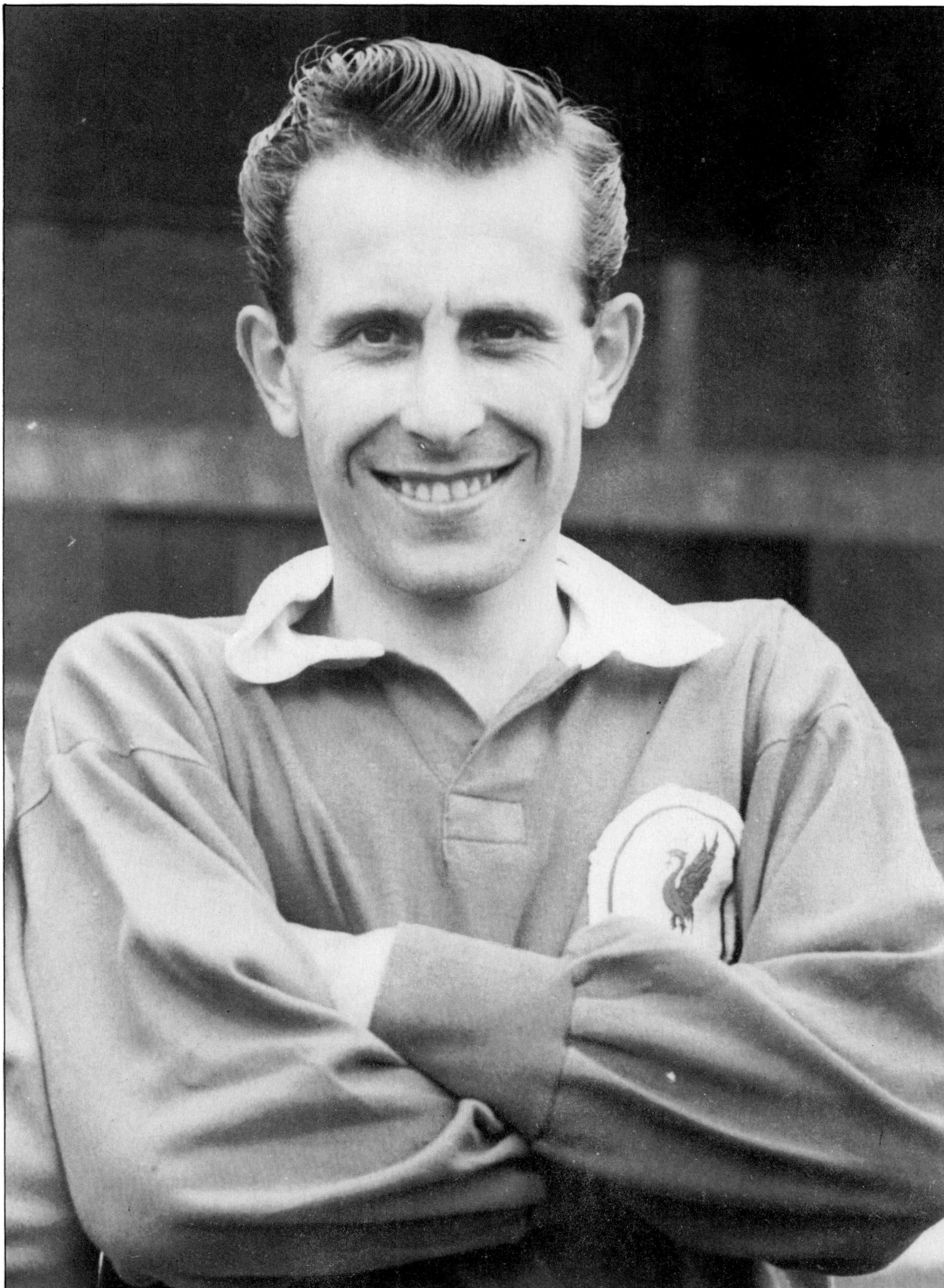

Brian Jackson played in his last game for Liverpool during the 1957-8 season. Jackson, who signed from Leyton Orient in November 1951 for a fee of £6,500 plus Donald Woan, made 131 League and FA Cup appearances before being transferred to Port Vale in June 1958 for £3,000. He won a Fourth Division championship medal with Vale in his first season with them.

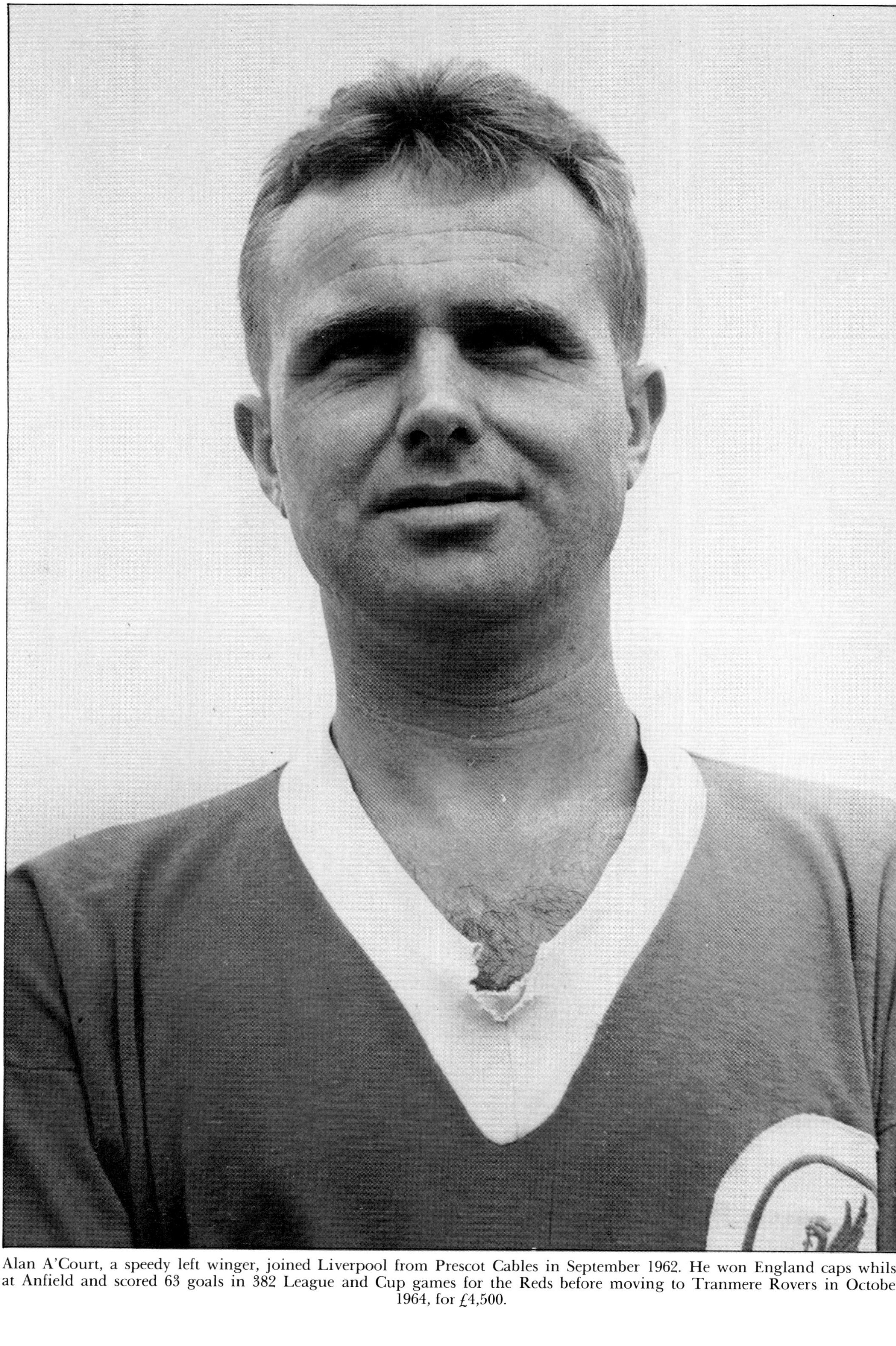

Alan A'Court, a speedy left winger, joined Liverpool from Prescot Cables in September 1962. He won England caps whilst at Anfield and scored 63 goals in 382 League and Cup games for the Reds before moving to Tranmere Rovers in October 1964, for £4,500.

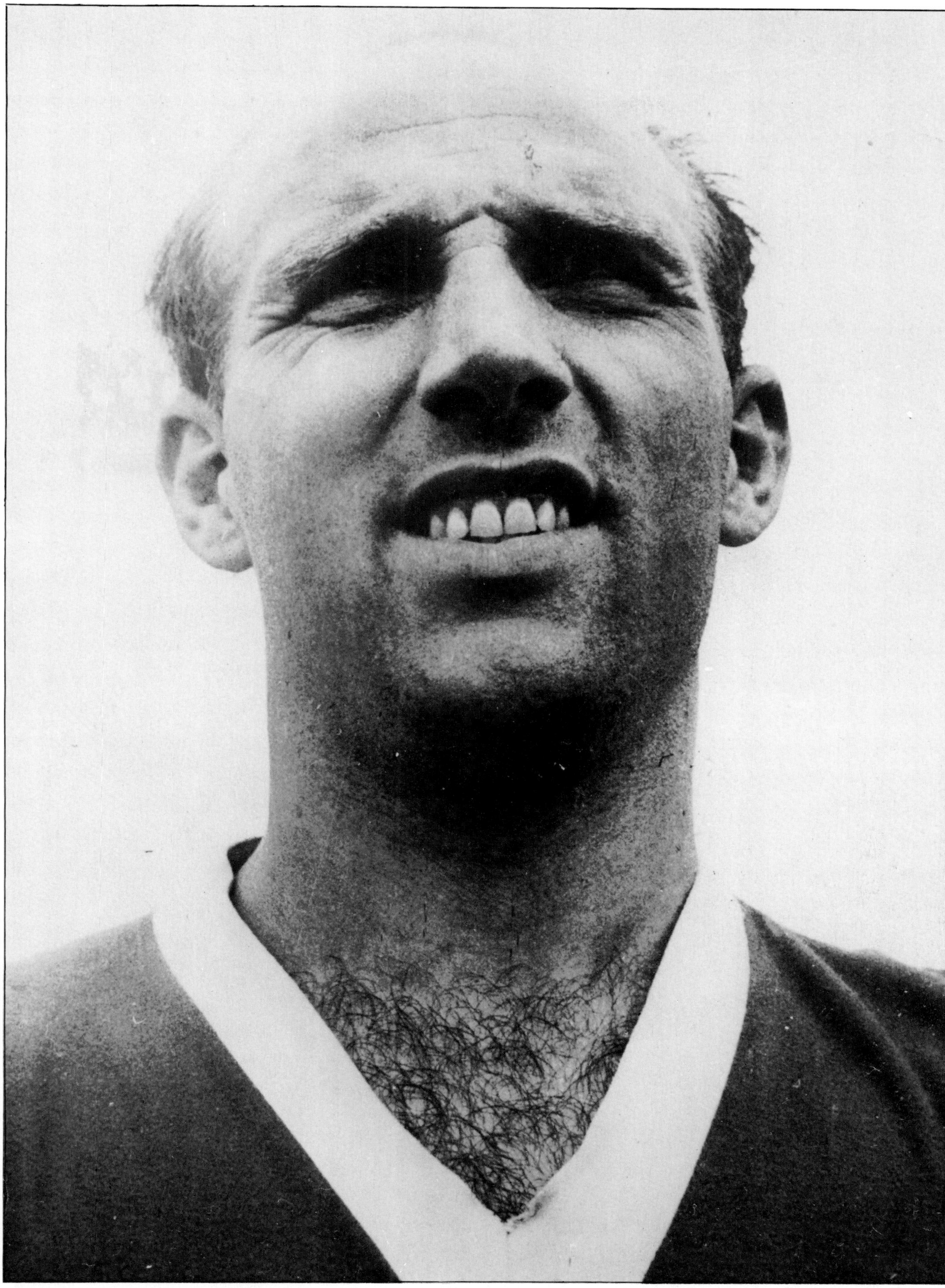

Full-back Ronnie Moran joined Liverpool from local football in January 1952 and ten years later was a key member of the side which won promotion from Division Two. In 1964 he won a League Championship medal and altogether proved a great Liverpool servant, making 379 League and FA Cup appearances before joining the club's training staff during the 1968-9 season. Moran stood in for manager Graeme Souness when the Reds reached Wembley in 1992 and Souness underwent a major heart operation.

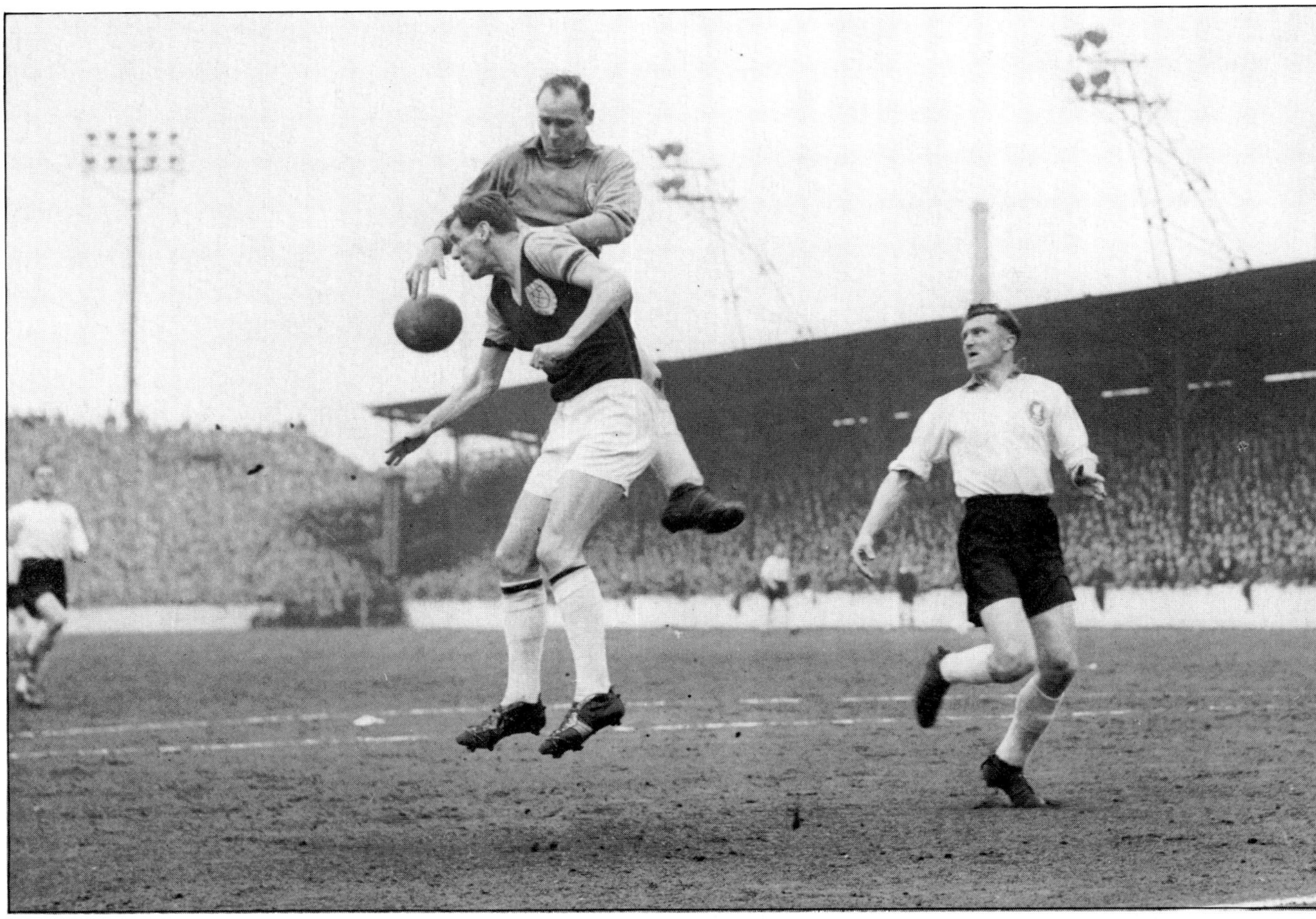

Liverpool goalkeeper Keith Rudham tangles with West Ham forward Vic Keeble at Upton Park in April 1958. Billy Liddell put the Reds ahead but the Hammers pulled back to draw. Liverpool could still not make the jump back into Division One, this season slipping back to fourth, a position they maintained 12 months later.

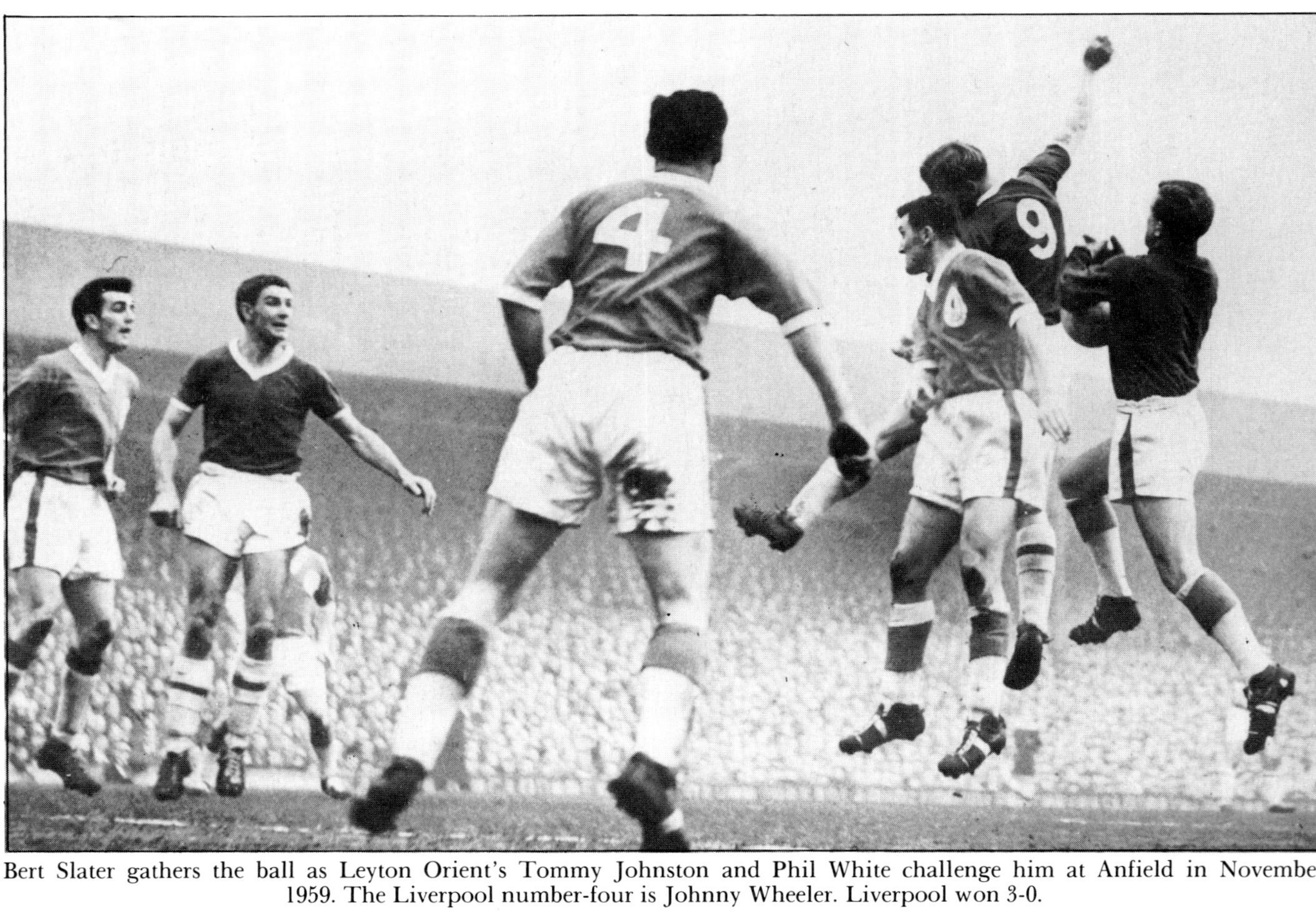

Bert Slater gathers the ball as Leyton Orient's Tommy Johnston and Phil White challenge him at Anfield in November 1959. The Liverpool number-four is Johnny Wheeler. Liverpool won 3-0.

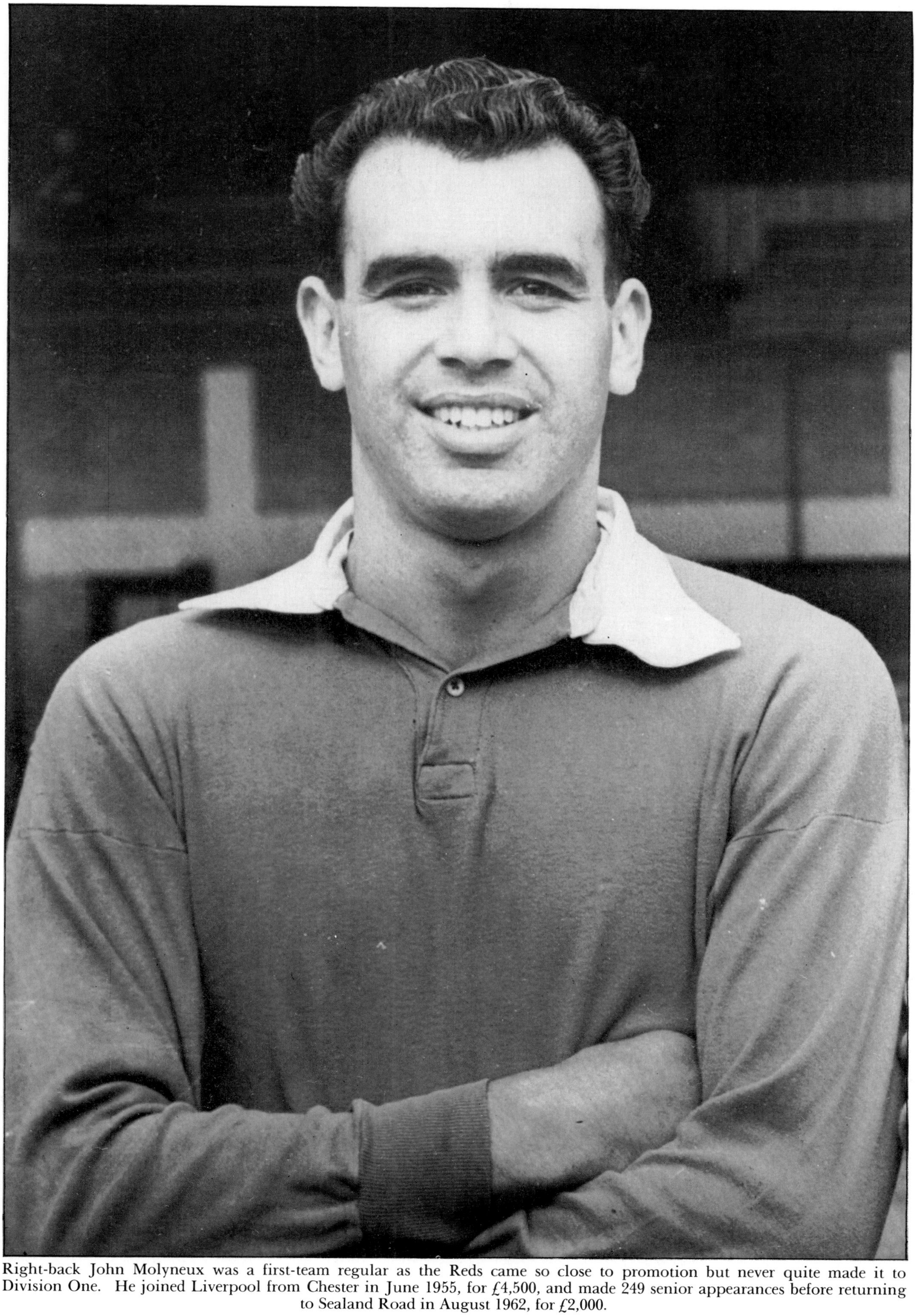

Right-back John Molyneux was a first-team regular as the Reds came so close to promotion but never quite made it to Division One. He joined Liverpool from Chester in June 1955, for £4,500, and made 249 senior appearances before returning to Sealand Road in August 1962, for £2,000.

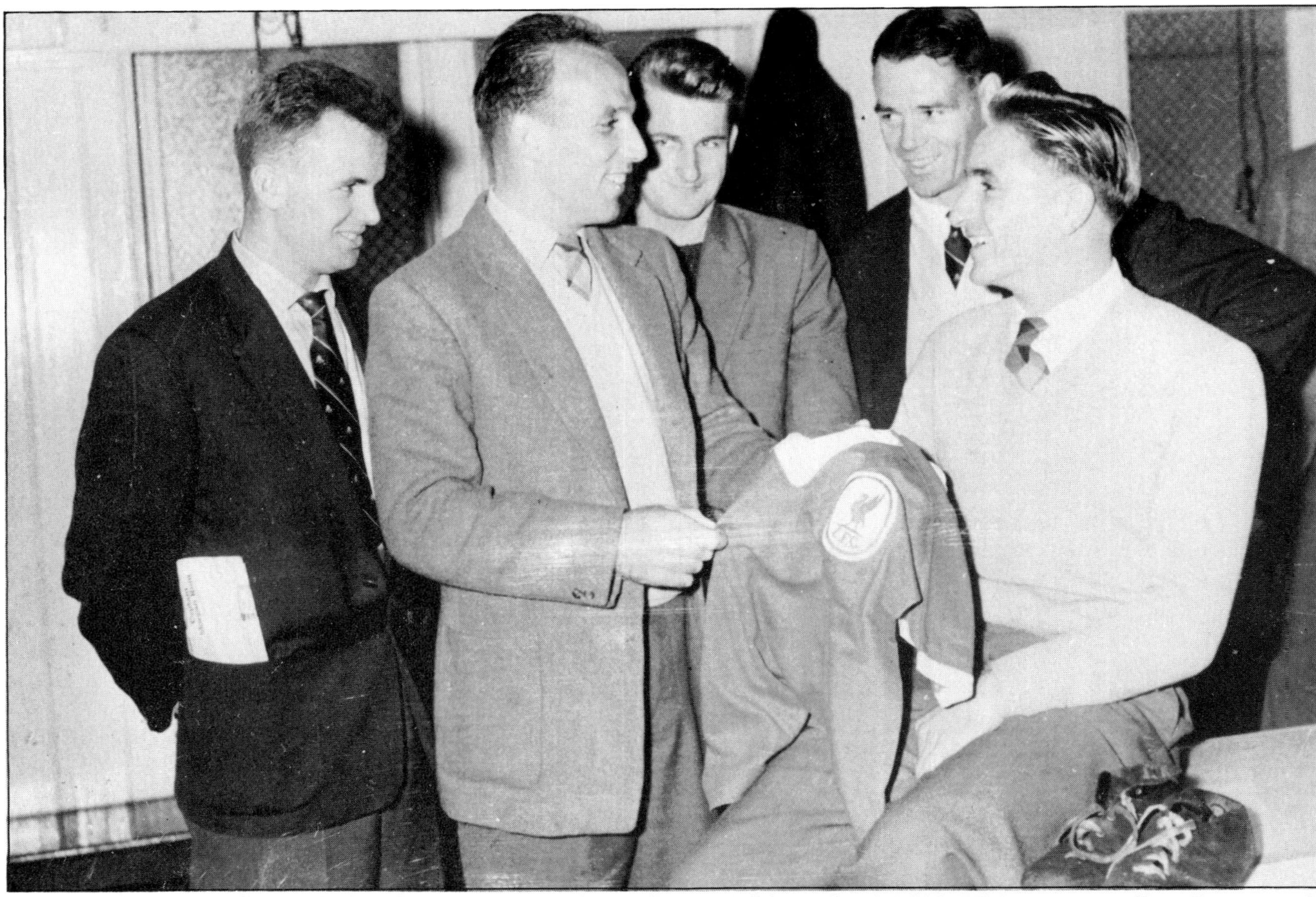

In November 1959, Liverpool signed Everton centre-forward Dave Hickson for £10,500. Hickson was a fiery figure on the field, if a gentle character off it. For the Reds he scored 37 goals in 60 appearances before being transferred to Cambridge City in July 1961. In this picture Hickson (right) is handed his Liverpool shirt by skipper Ronnie Moran. The other players (left to right) are Alan A'Court, Roger Hunt and Billy Liddell.

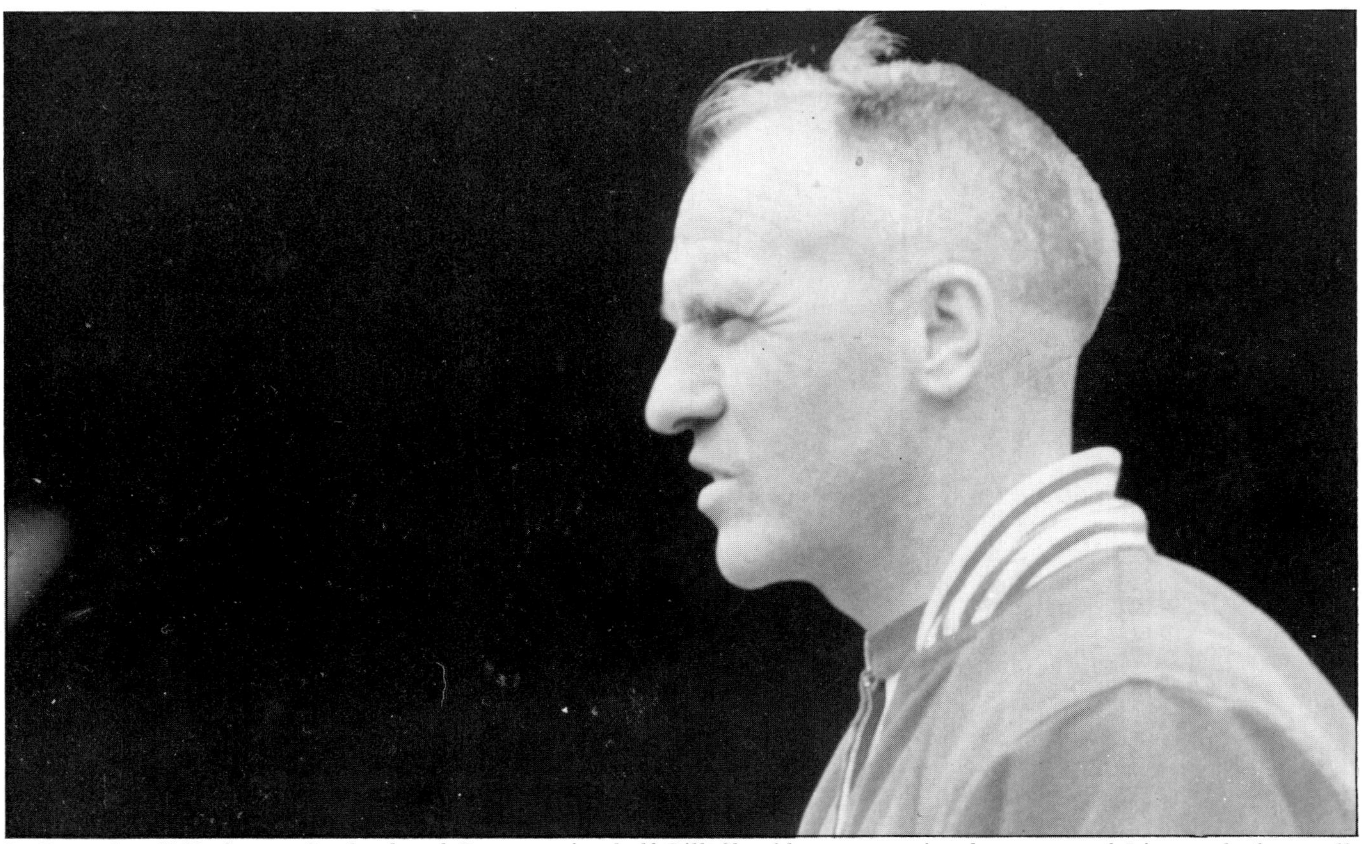

In December 1959, former Scotland and Preston wing-half Bill Shankly was appointed manager of Liverpool after spells at Carlisle United, Grimsby Town, Workington and Huddersfield Town. It was the start of a remarkable era and all of Liverpool's subsequent successes can be traced back to that day.

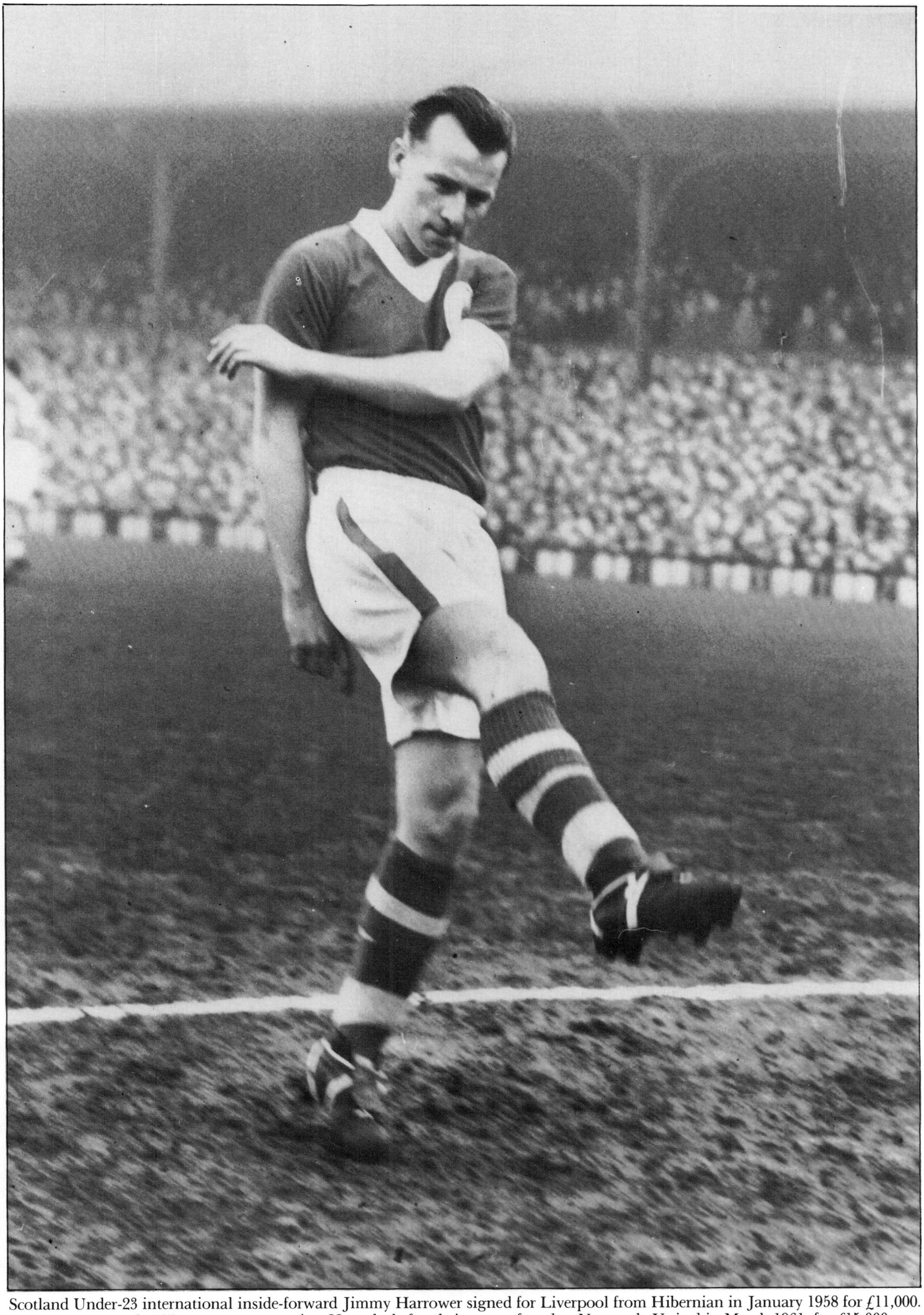

Scotland Under-23 international inside-forward Jimmy Harrower signed for Liverpool from Hibernian in January 1958 for £11,000. Harrower made 105 appearances, scoring 22 goals, before being transferred to Newcastle United in March 1961, for £15,000.

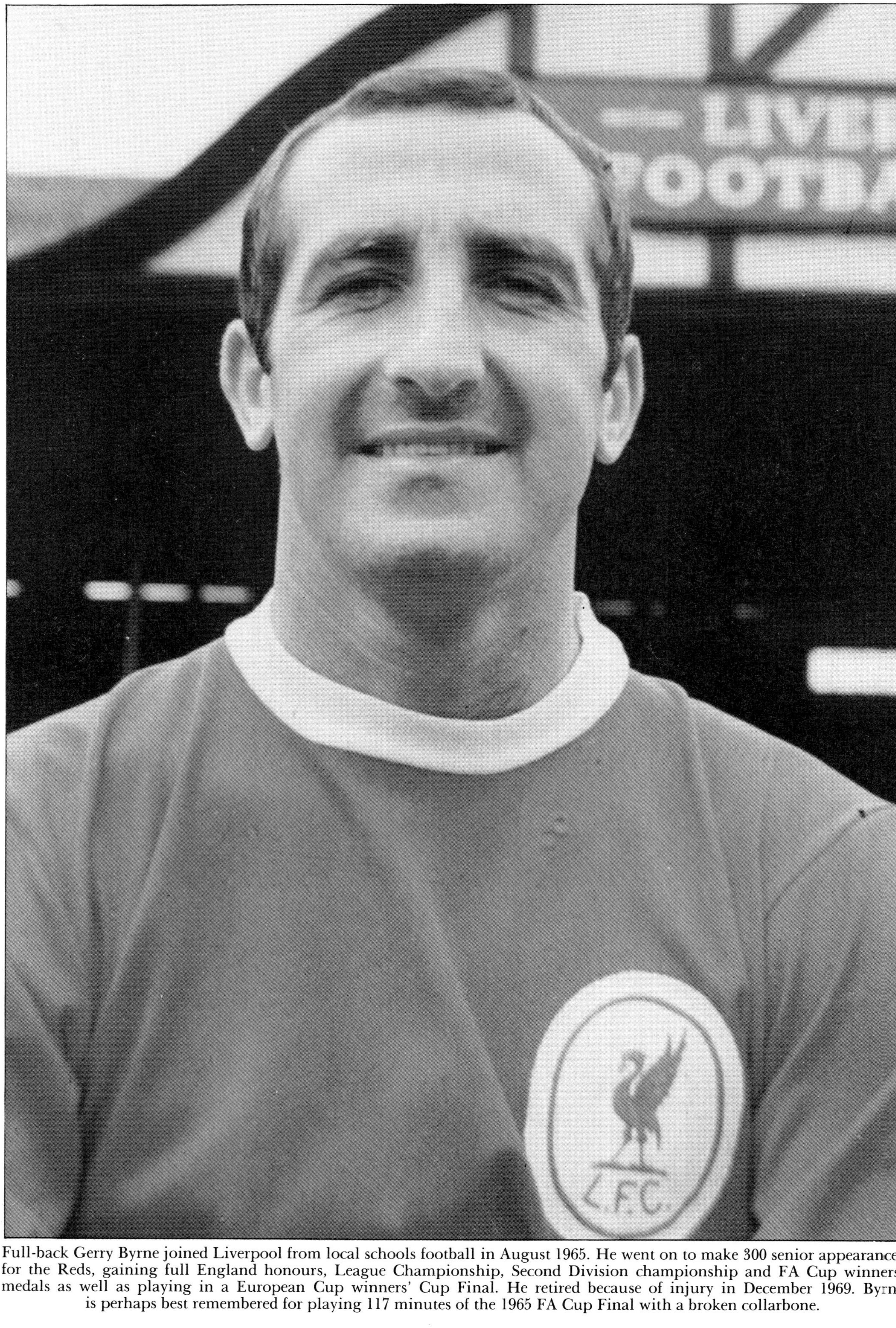

Full-back Gerry Byrne joined Liverpool from local schools football in August 1965. He went on to make 300 senior appearances for the Reds, gaining full England honours, League Championship, Second Division championship and FA Cup winners' medals as well as playing in a European Cup winners' Cup Final. He retired because of injury in December 1969. Byrne is perhaps best remembered for playing 117 minutes of the 1965 FA Cup Final with a broken collarbone.

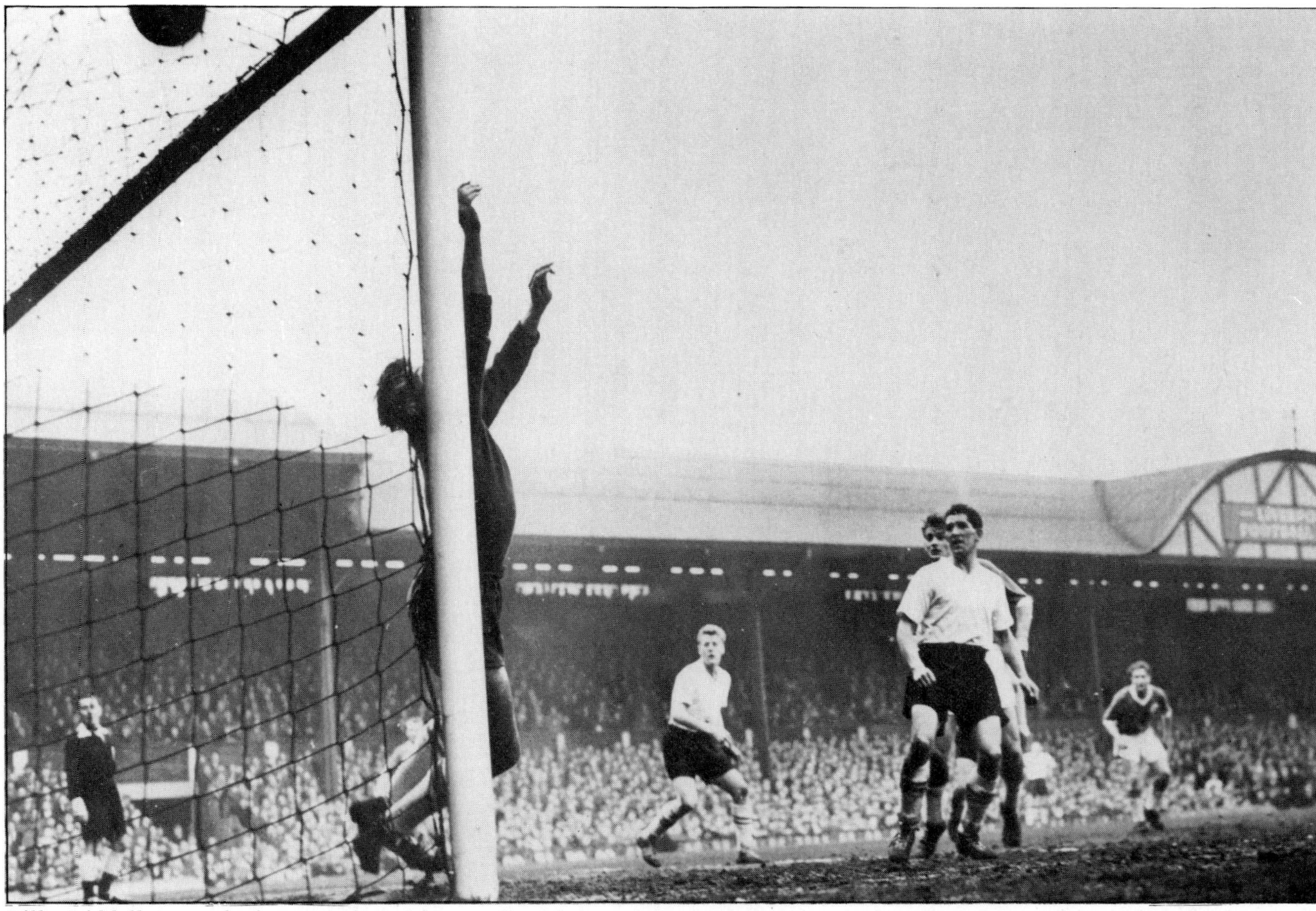

Billy Liddell (out of picture) scores Liverpool's third goal in their 5-1 victory over Stoke City at Anfield in March 1960. The Reds climbed back up to third place in Division Two but promotion was still tantalizingly out of reach.

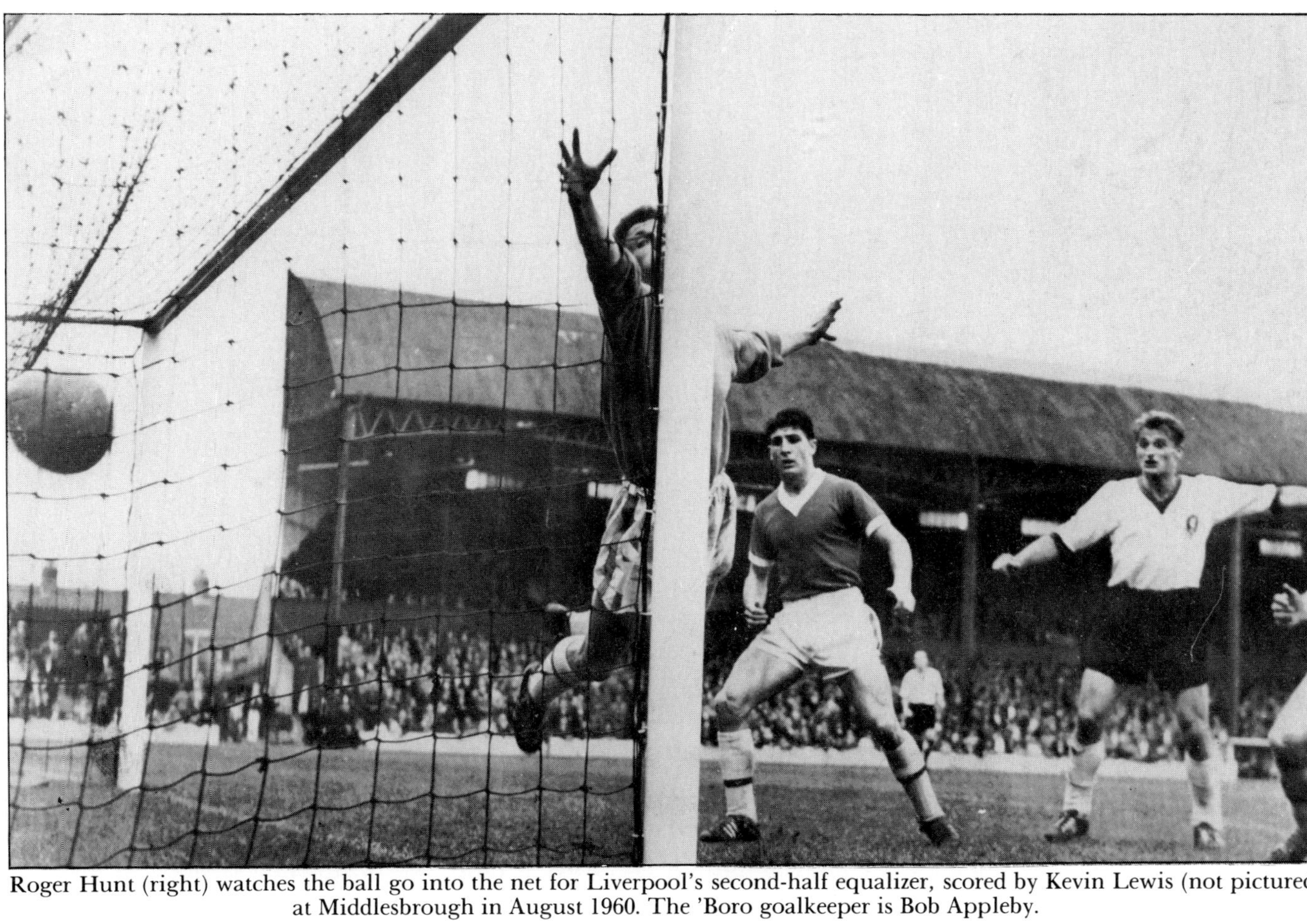

Roger Hunt (right) watches the ball go into the net for Liverpool's second-half equalizer, scored by Kevin Lewis (not pictured) at Middlesbrough in August 1960. The 'Boro goalkeeper is Bob Appleby.

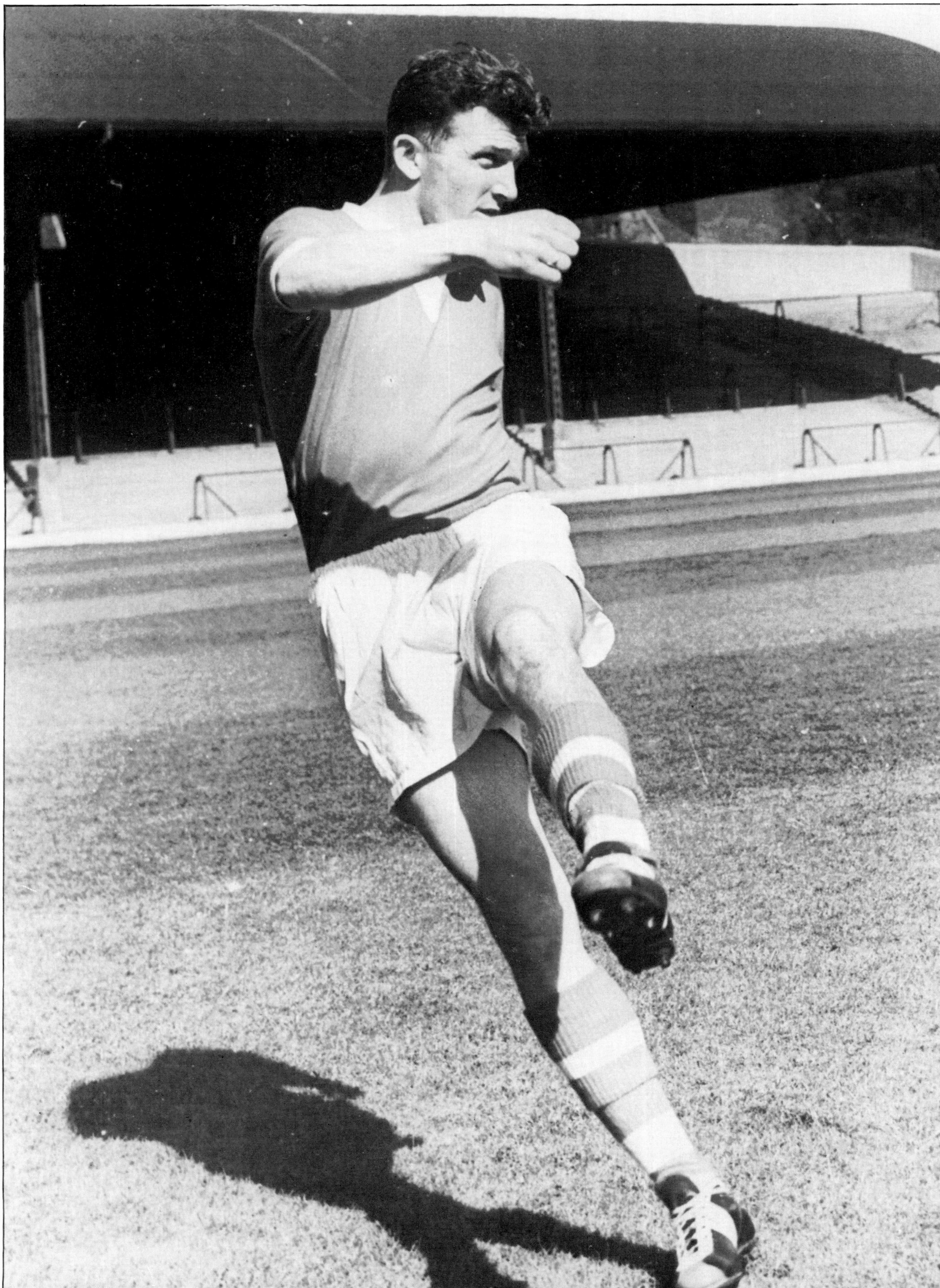

Centre-half Dick White made 216 League and Cup appearances for Liverpool after joining the Reds from Scunthorpe United in November 1955. He joined Scunthorpe in their Midland League days and helped them become established in Division Three North before settling quickly to a higher grade of football. White moved to Doncaster Rovers in May 1962 for £3,500.

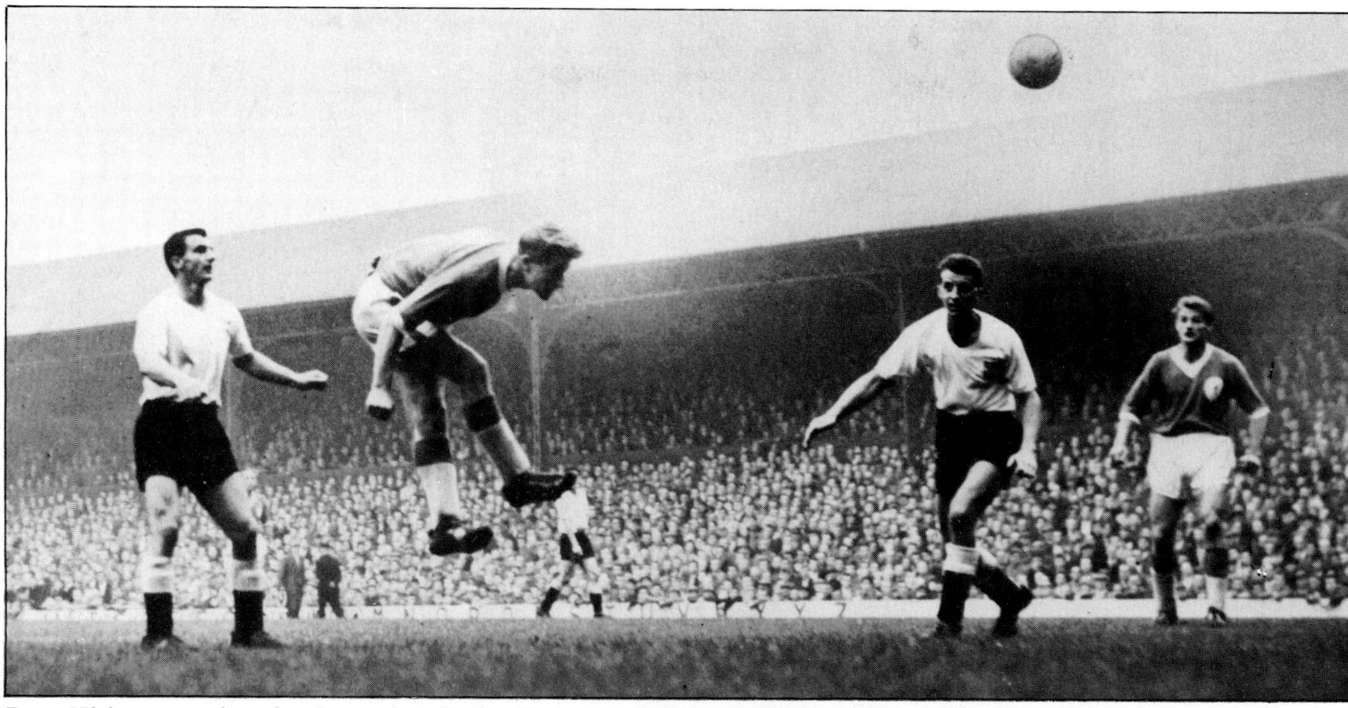

Dave Hickson gets in a header against Derby County at Anfield in October 1960. Johnny Wheeler scored the only goal of the game and eventually Liverpool ended the season in third place, narrowly missing promotion for the sixth consecutive season. Roger Hunt is the other Liverpool player, Jack Parry and Ray Young the Derby men.

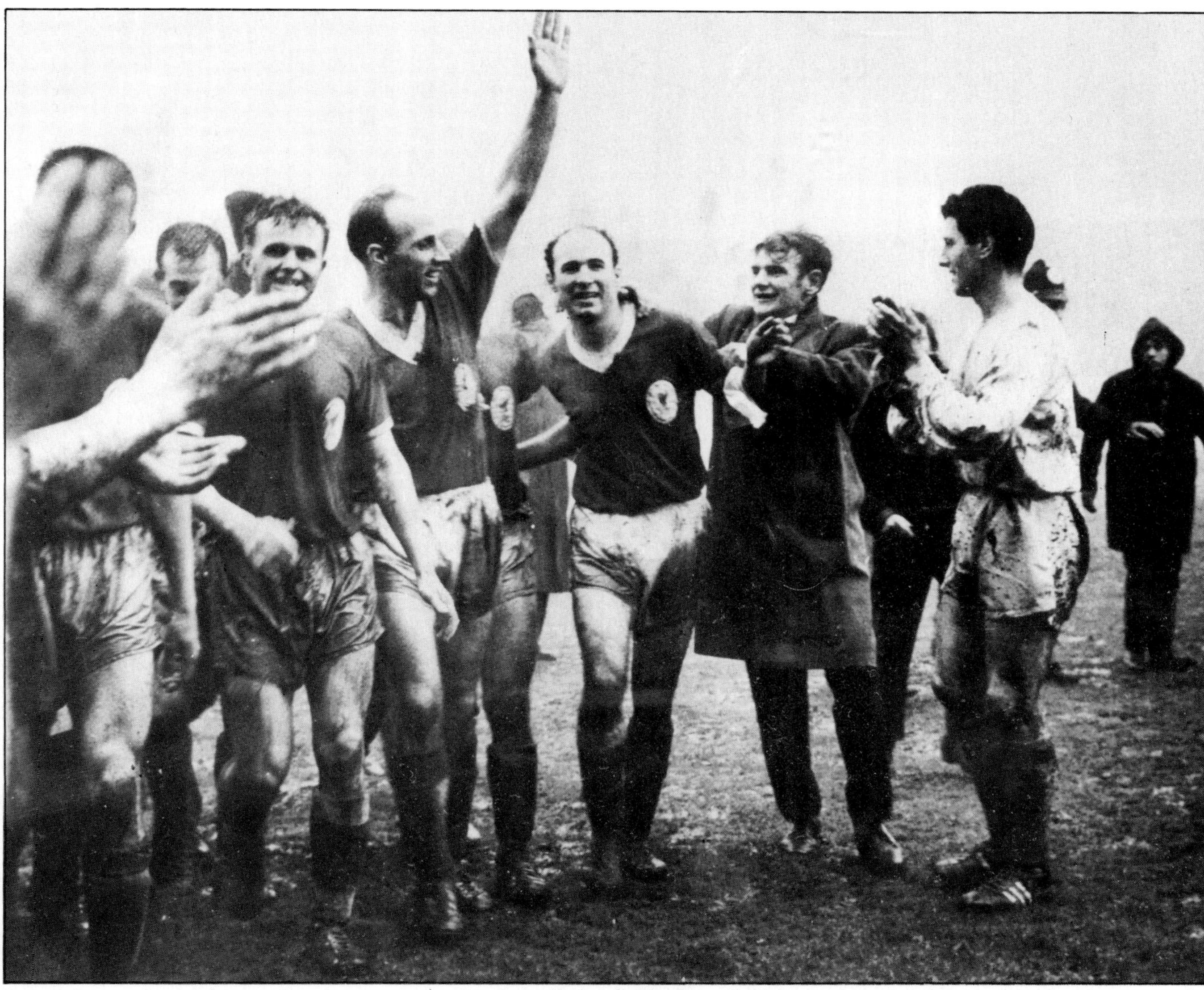

Promotion at last! Liverpool's players are applauded off the field after clinching promotion by beating Southampton 2-0 at Anfield in April 1962. Ronnie Moran acknowledges the crowd, Alan A'Court (left) and Jimmy Melia are the players either side of him. The Reds ended the season as Second Division champions, eight points ahead of runners-up Leyton Orient.

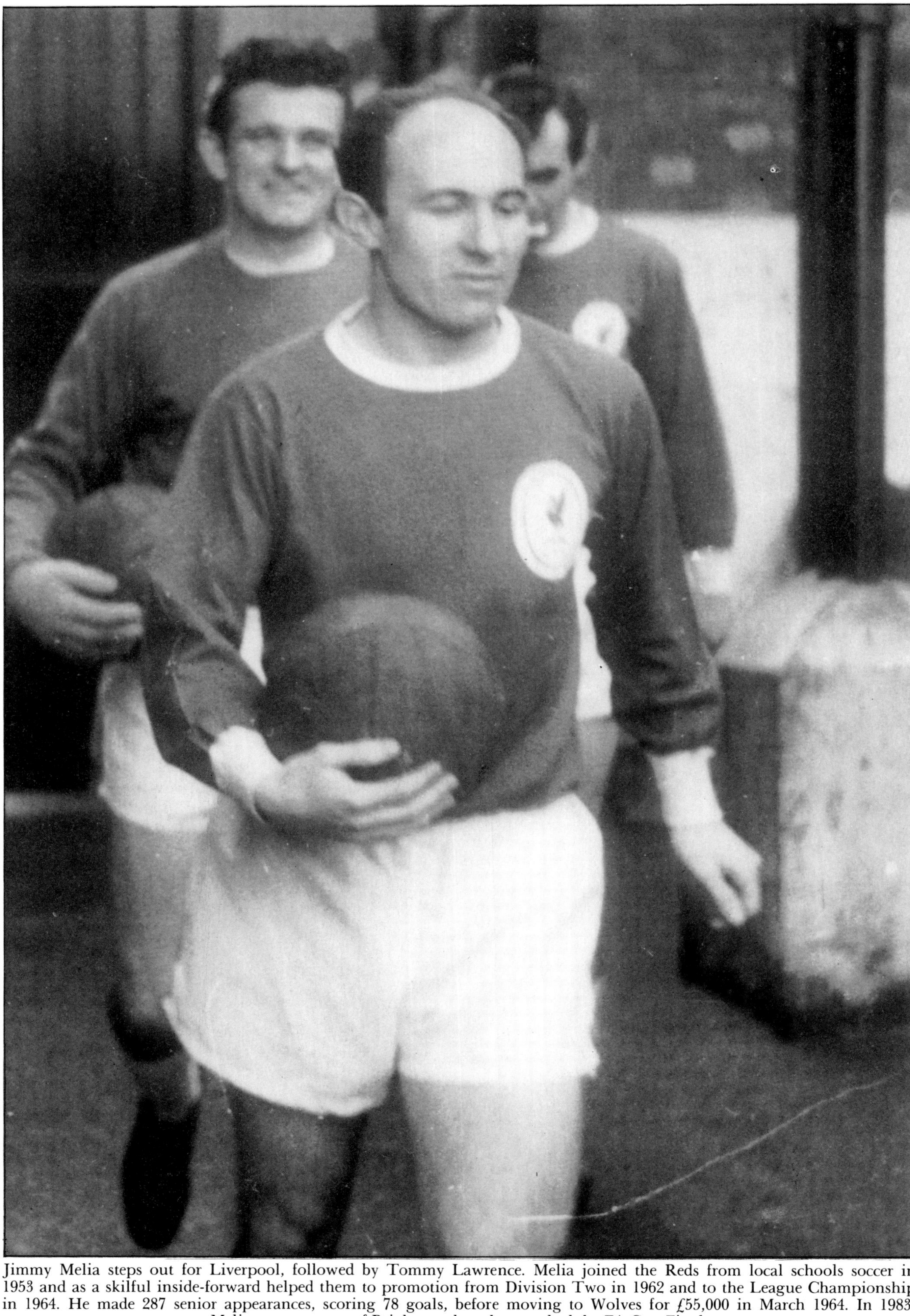

Jimmy Melia steps out for Liverpool, followed by Tommy Lawrence. Melia joined the Reds from local schools soccer in 1953 and as a skilful inside-forward helped them to promotion from Division Two in 1962 and to the League Championship in 1964. He made 287 senior appearances, scoring 78 goals, before moving to Wolves for £55,000 in March 1964. In 1983, Melia was manager of Brighton when they reached the FA Cup Final.

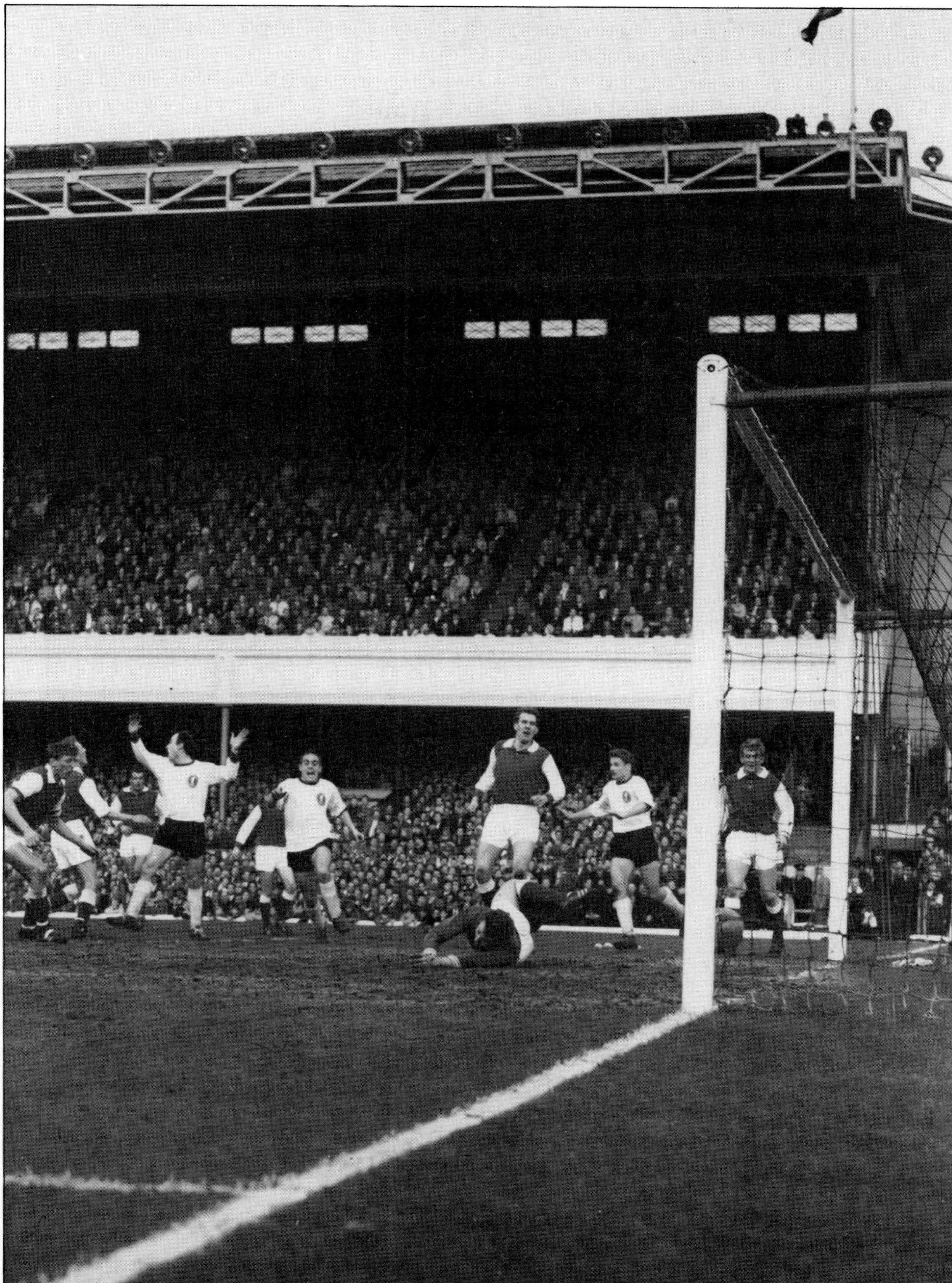

Roger Hunt turns away after scoring his side's second goal at Highbury in March 1963. Jimmy Melia is the player with his arms raised, Ian St John is the Liverpool player in the centre of the picture. The Merseysiders drew 2-2 after taking a two-goal lead in the 19th minute. Their first season back in Division One saw them finish eighth and they also reached the semi-final of the FA Cup, where they were beaten by Leicester City.

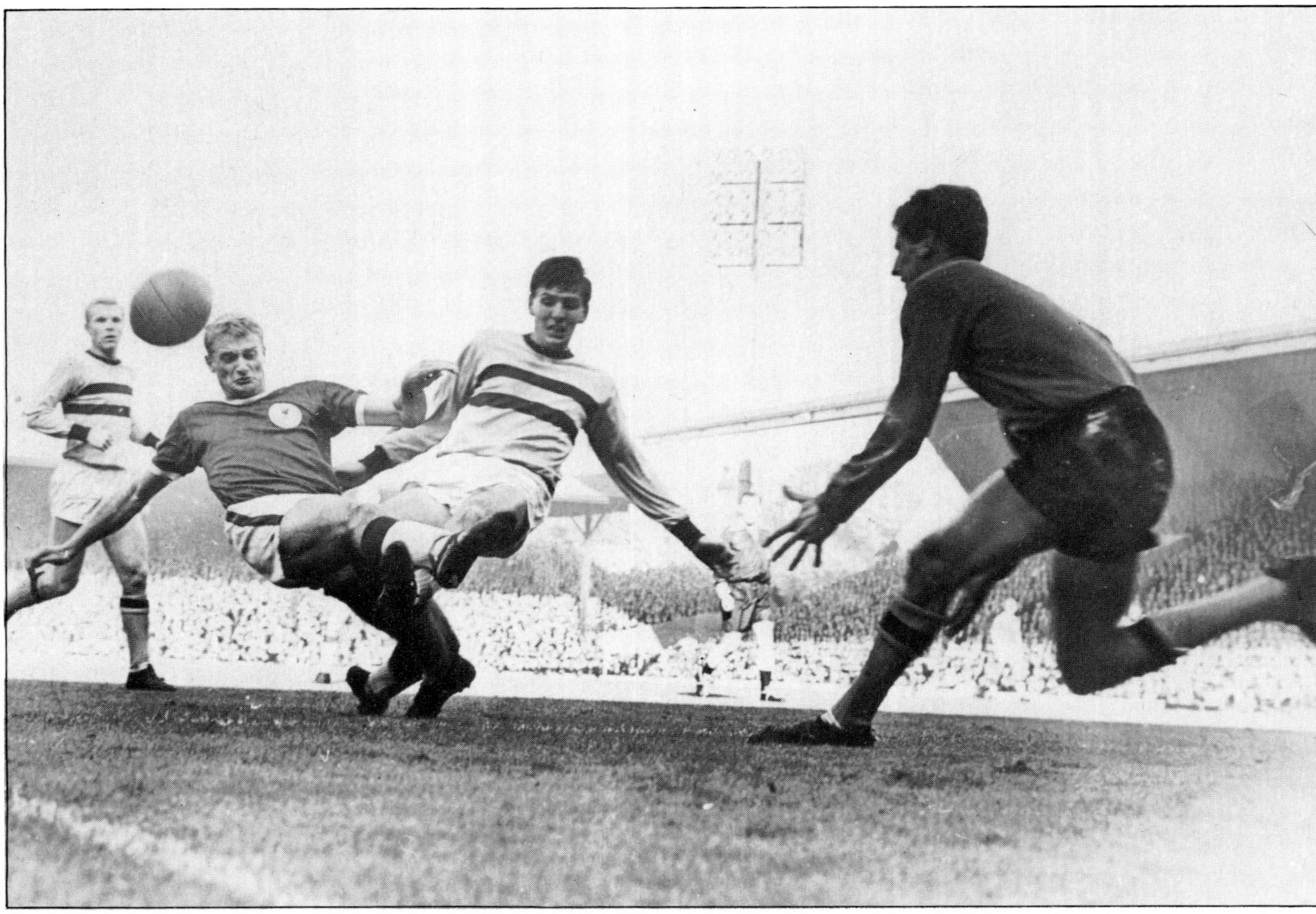

The following season of 1963-4, Liverpool won their first Football League Championship for 17 years. In September, though, they lost 2-1 at home to West Ham United. In this picture, Martin Peters hammers the ball away from Roger Hunt and out for a corner as the Hammers' goalkeeper Jim Standen rushes out.

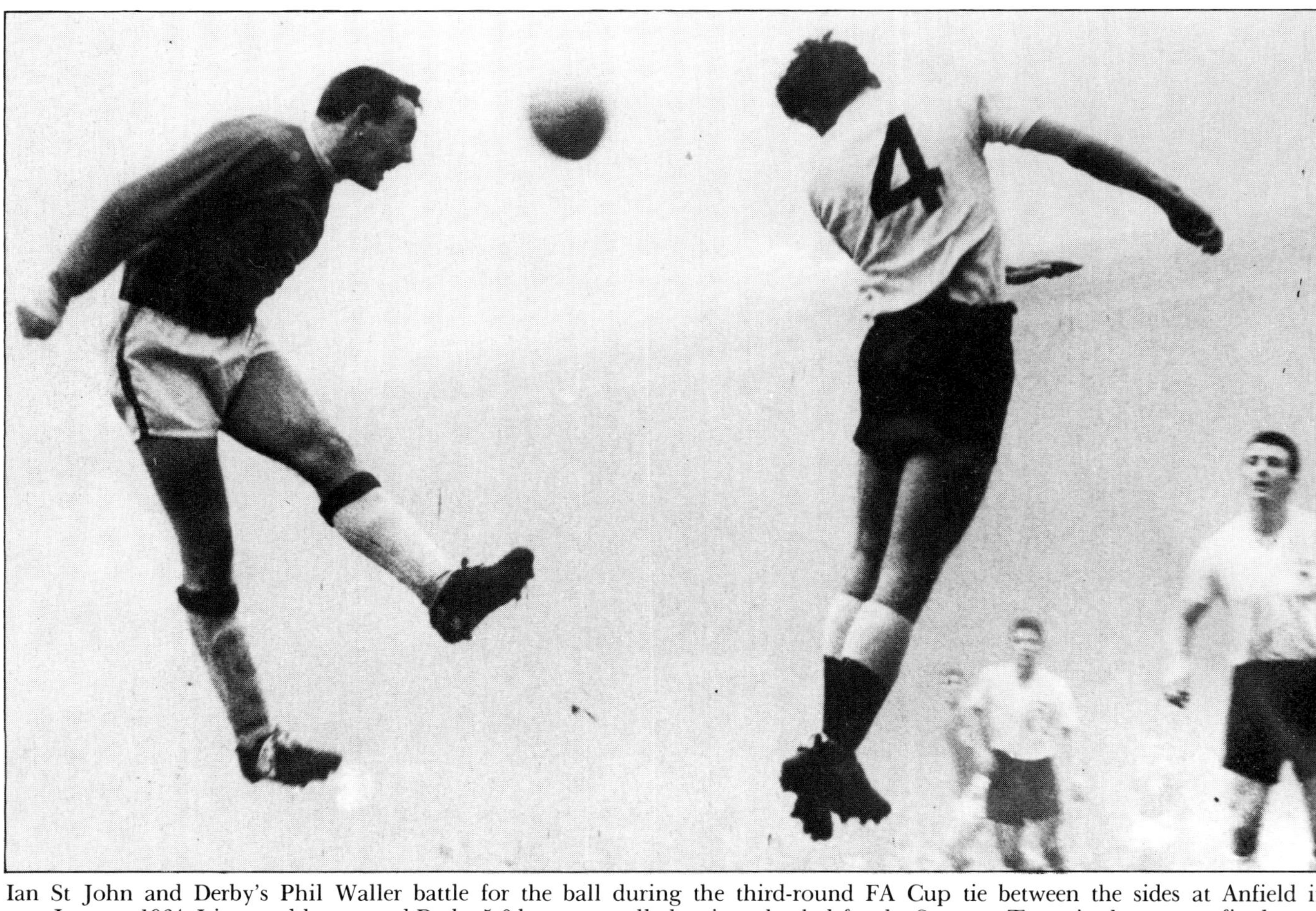

Ian St John and Derby's Phil Waller battle for the ball during the third-round FA Cup tie between the sides at Anfield in January 1964. Liverpool hammered Derby 5-0 but eventually lost in a shock defeat by Swansea Town in the quarter-finals.

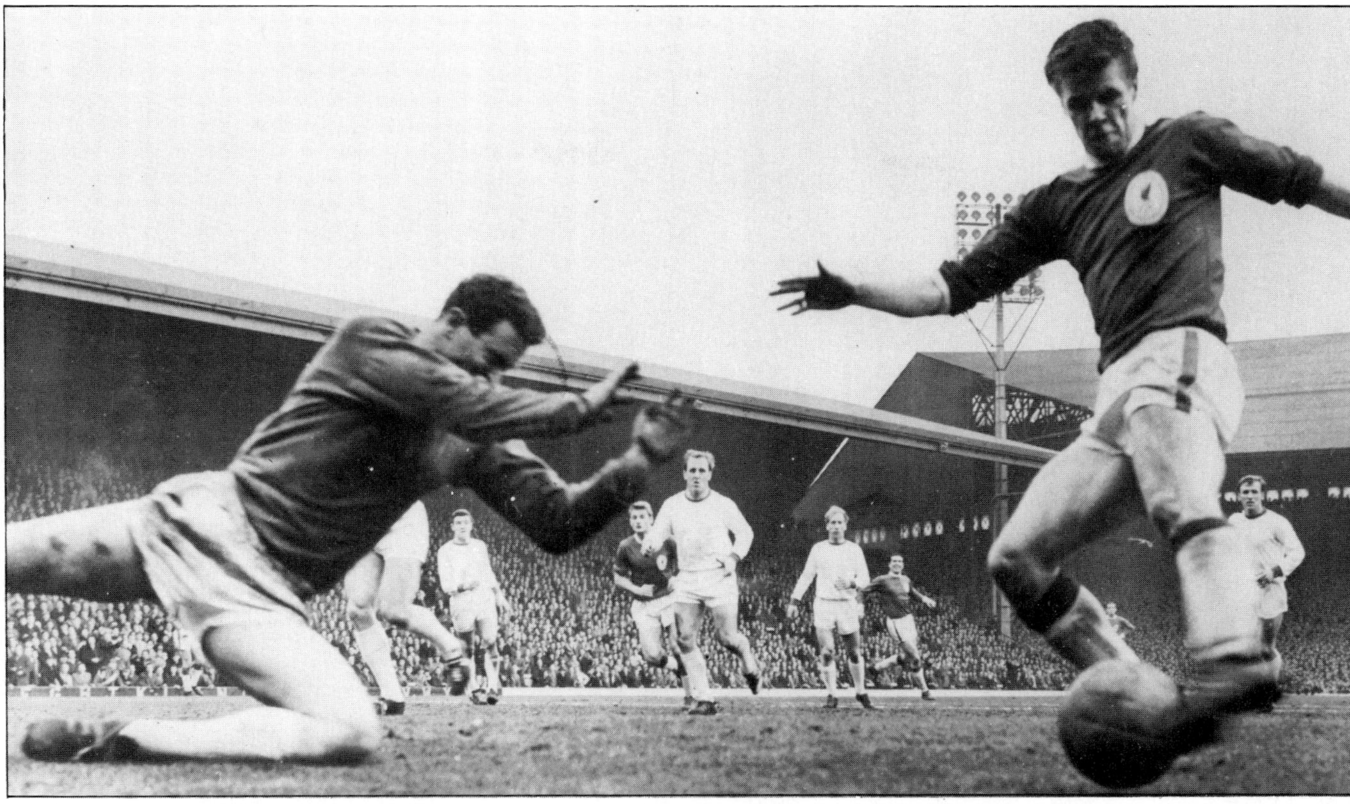

April 1964 and Liverpool are nearing the title. Alf Arrowsmith's shot is about to be smothered by Manchester United goalkeeper Harry Gregg. Arrowsmith scored twice as Liverpool won 3-0 and that victory left them two games from the Championship which they duly sealed with a 5-0 win over Arsenal at Anfield.

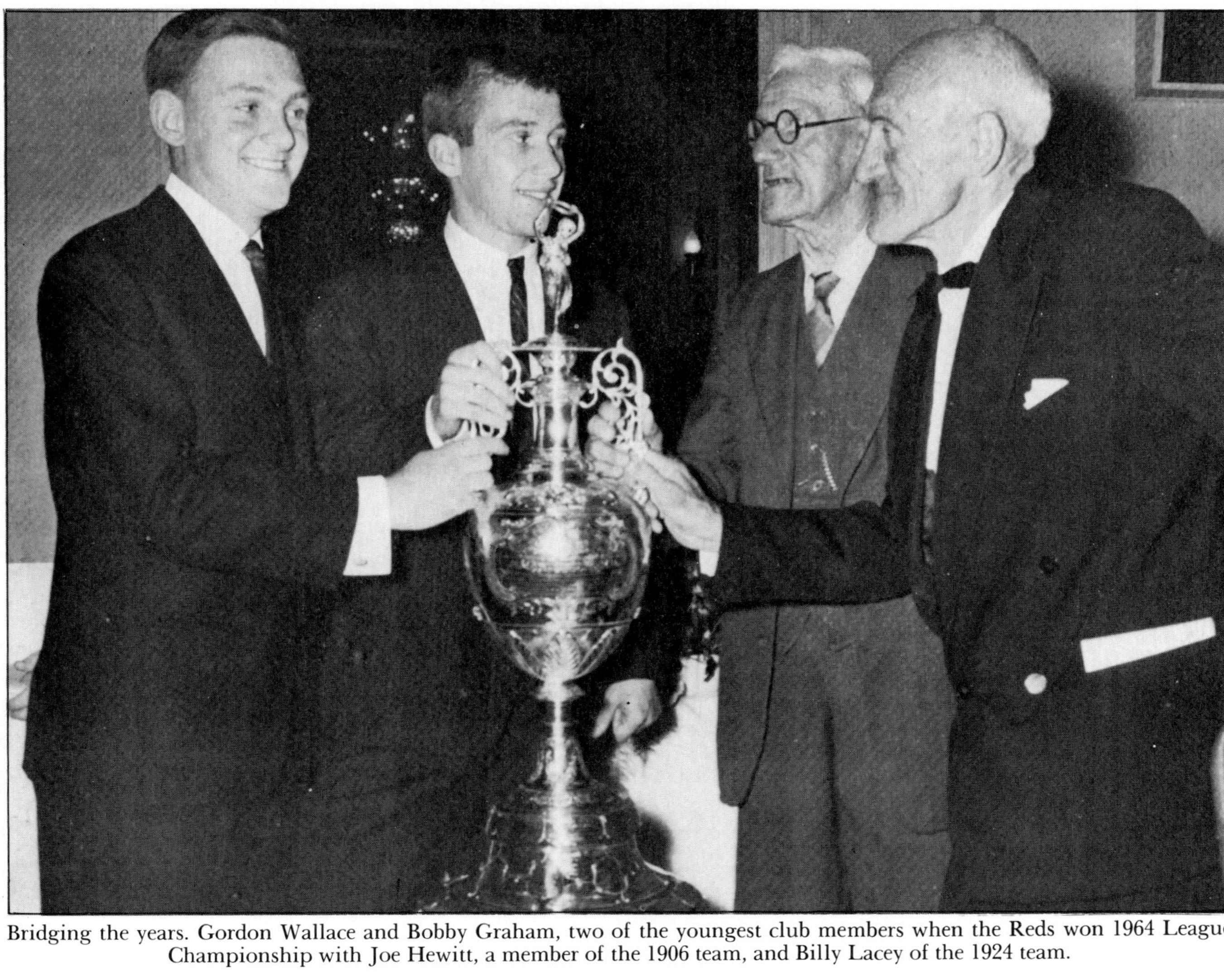

Bridging the years. Gordon Wallace and Bobby Graham, two of the youngest club members when the Reds won 1964 League Championship with Joe Hewitt, a member of the 1906 team, and Billy Lacey of the 1924 team.

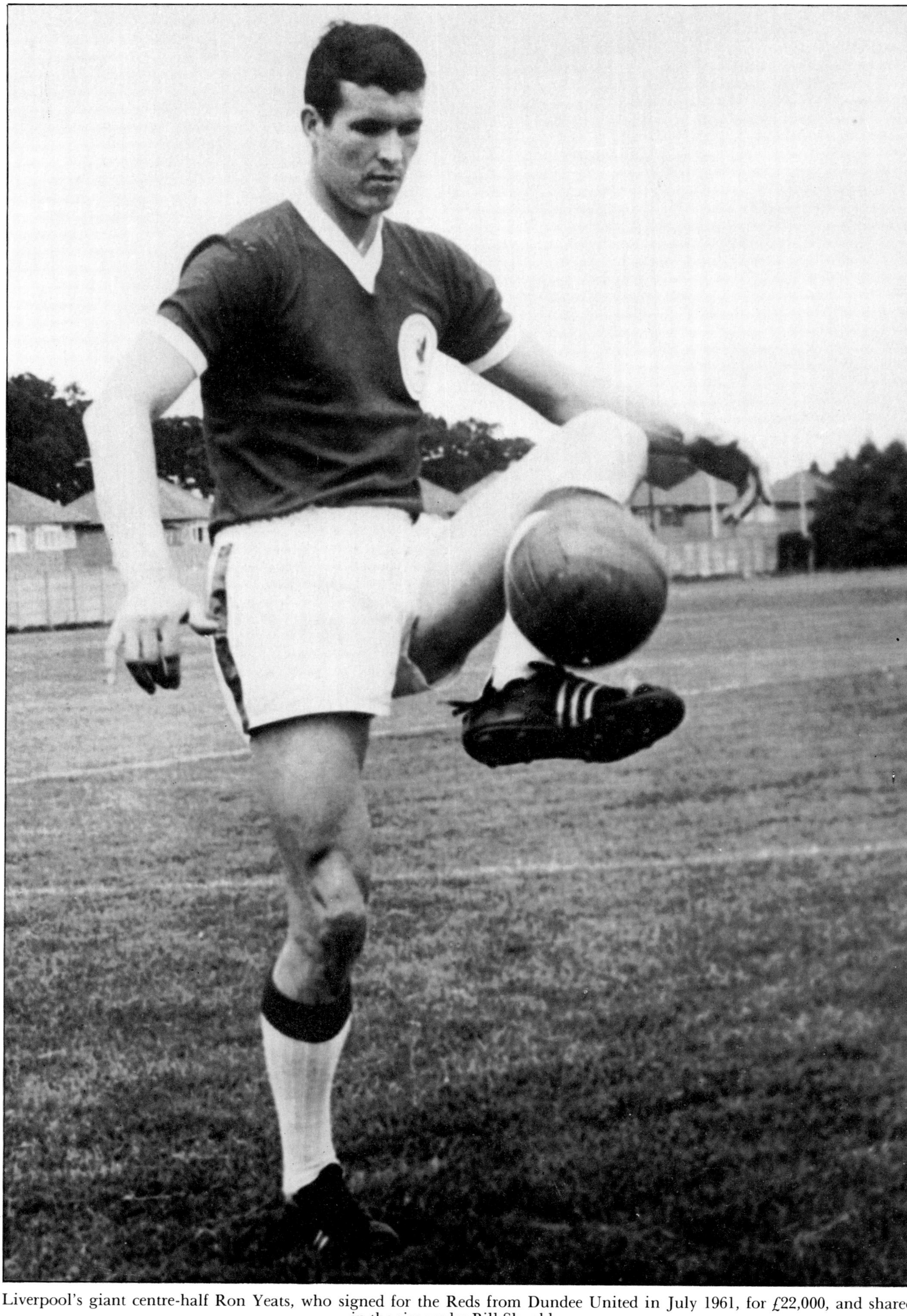

Liverpool's giant centre-half Ron Yeats, who signed for the Reds from Dundee United in July 1961, for £22,000, and shared in the rise under Bill Shankly.

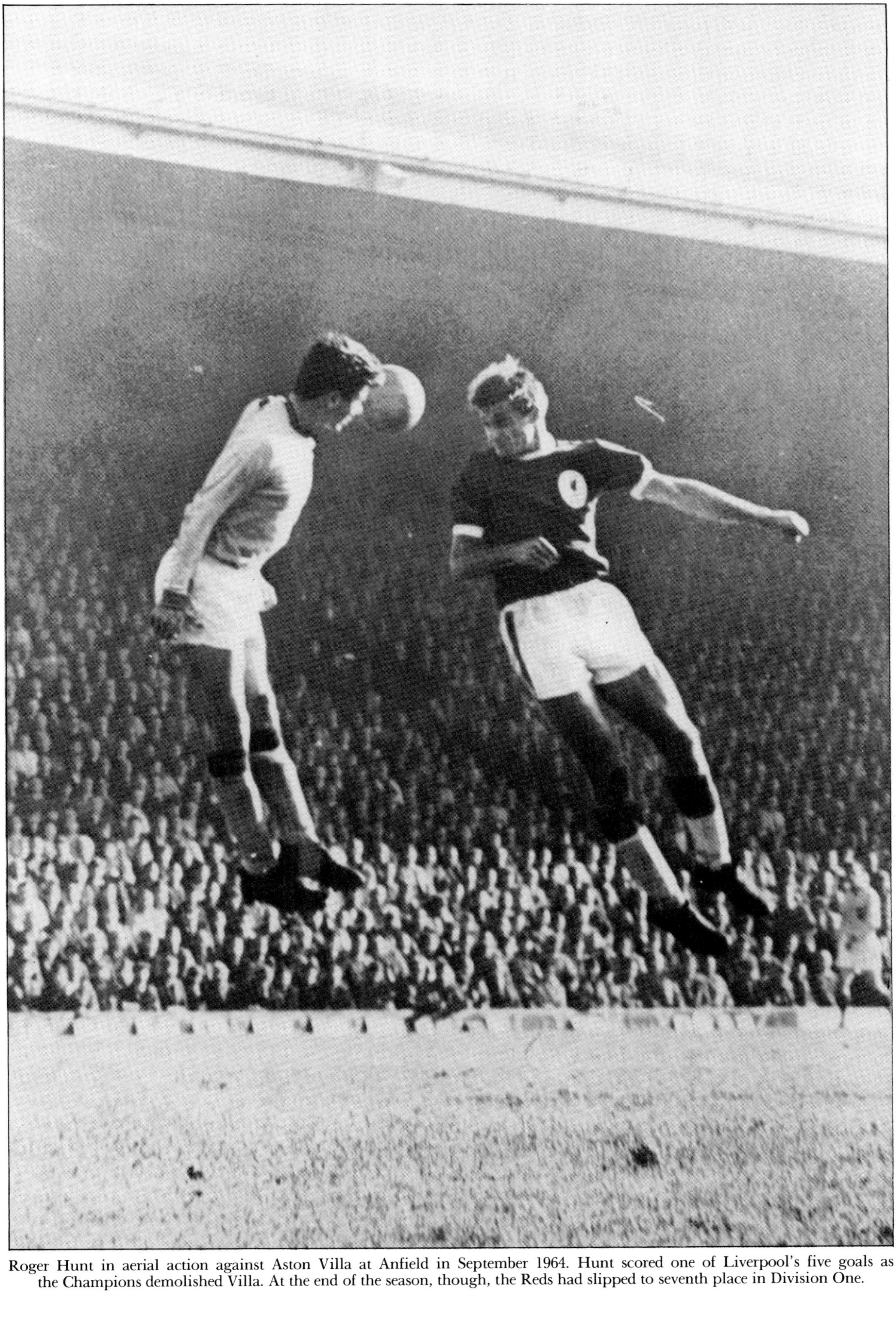

Roger Hunt in aerial action against Aston Villa at Anfield in September 1964. Hunt scored one of Liverpool's five goals as the Champions demolished Villa. At the end of the season, though, the Reds had slipped to seventh place in Division One.

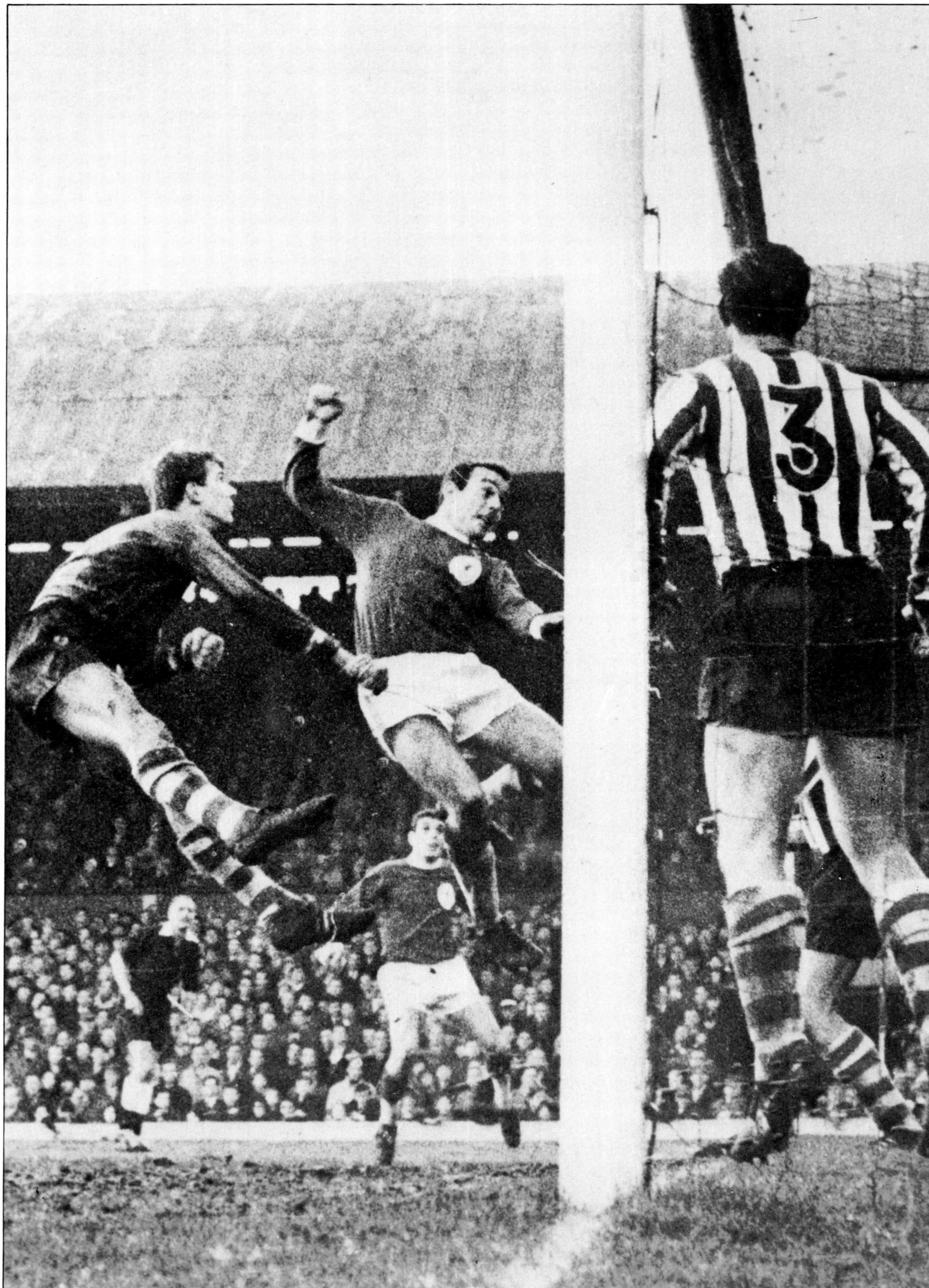

Ian St John scores Liverpool's fourth and last goal against Sheffield Wednesday in January 1965. Hunt (2) and Milne netted the others in front of a 42,000 crowd.

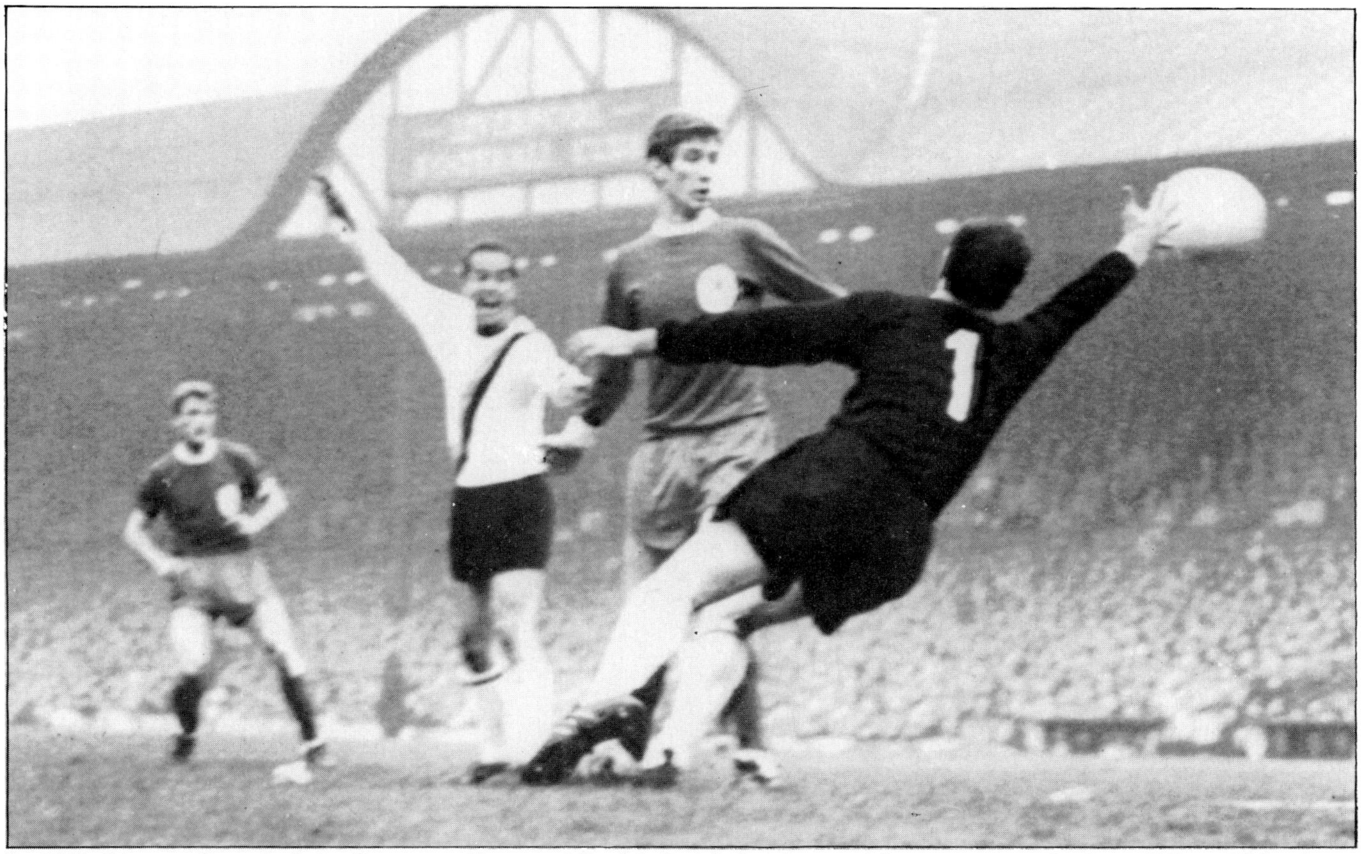

In 1965, Liverpool reached the European Cup semi-final before being beaten 4-3 on aggregate by Inter-Milan. This picture shows Chris Lawler's 'goal' which was disallowed in the first leg at Anfield. The Reds won that game 3-1 but went down 3-0 in Italy.

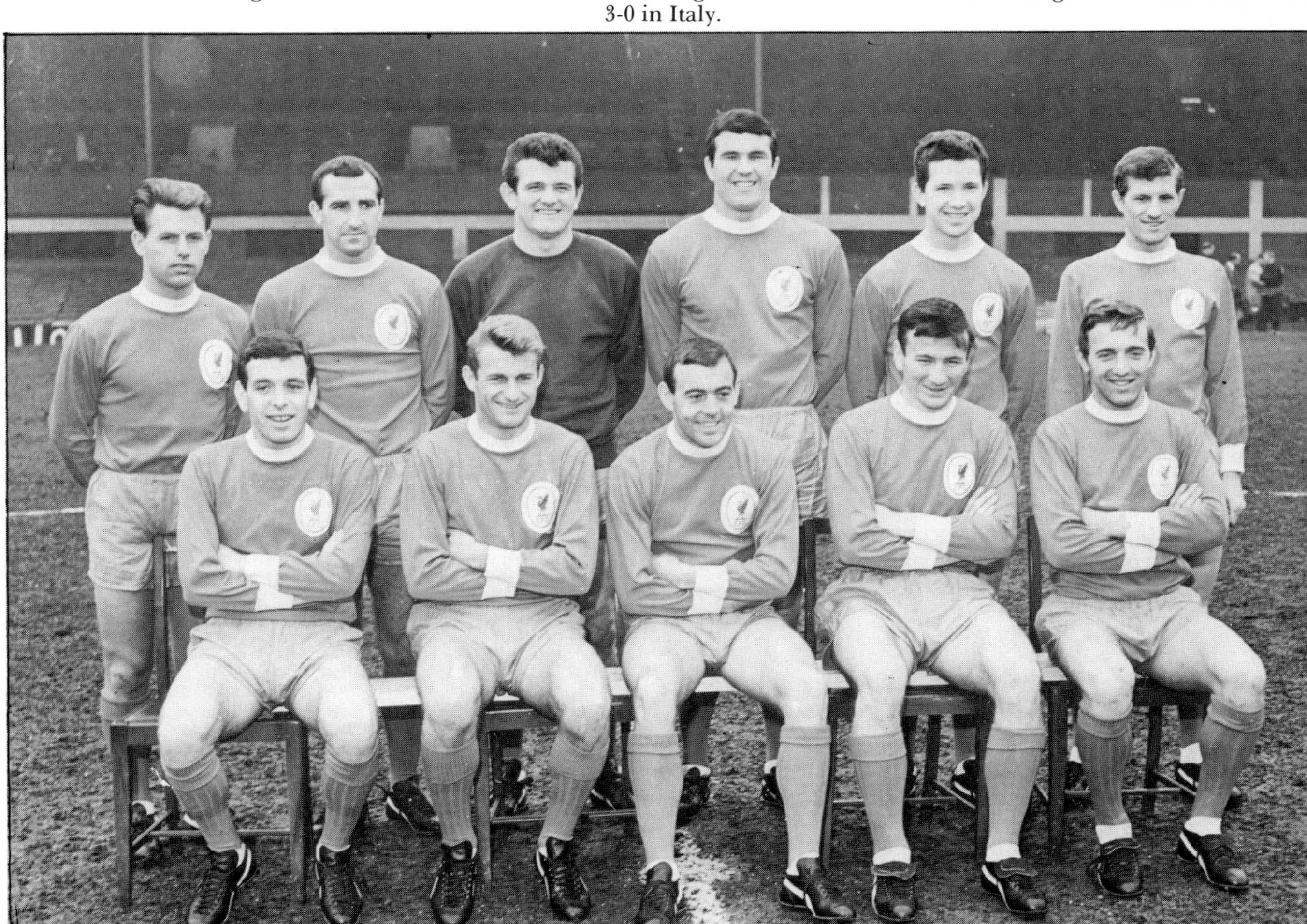

The Liverpool squad before the 1965 FA Cup Final against Leeds United. Back row (left to right): Gordon Milne, Gerry Byrne, Tommy Lawrence, Ron Yeats, Chris Lawler, Willie Stevenson. Front row: Ian Callaghan, Roger Hunt, Ian St John, Tommy Smith, Peter Thompson. Gordon Milne missed the Final through injury, Geoff Strong taking his place.

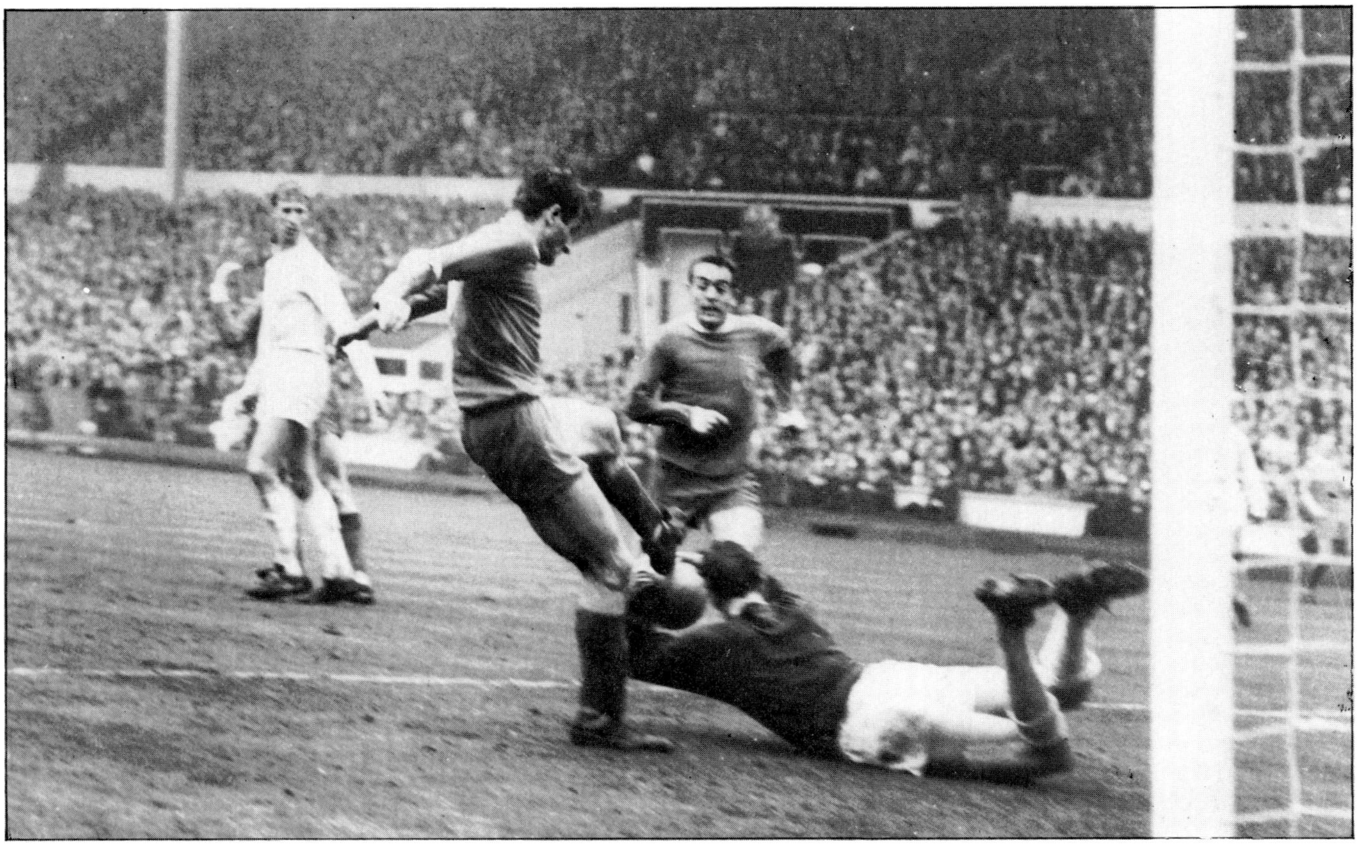

Leeds United's Gary Sprake dives at the feet of Liverpool's Roger Hunt during the 1965 FA Cup Final. Ian St John rushes in looking for the ball to fly clear, Jack Charlton looks back.

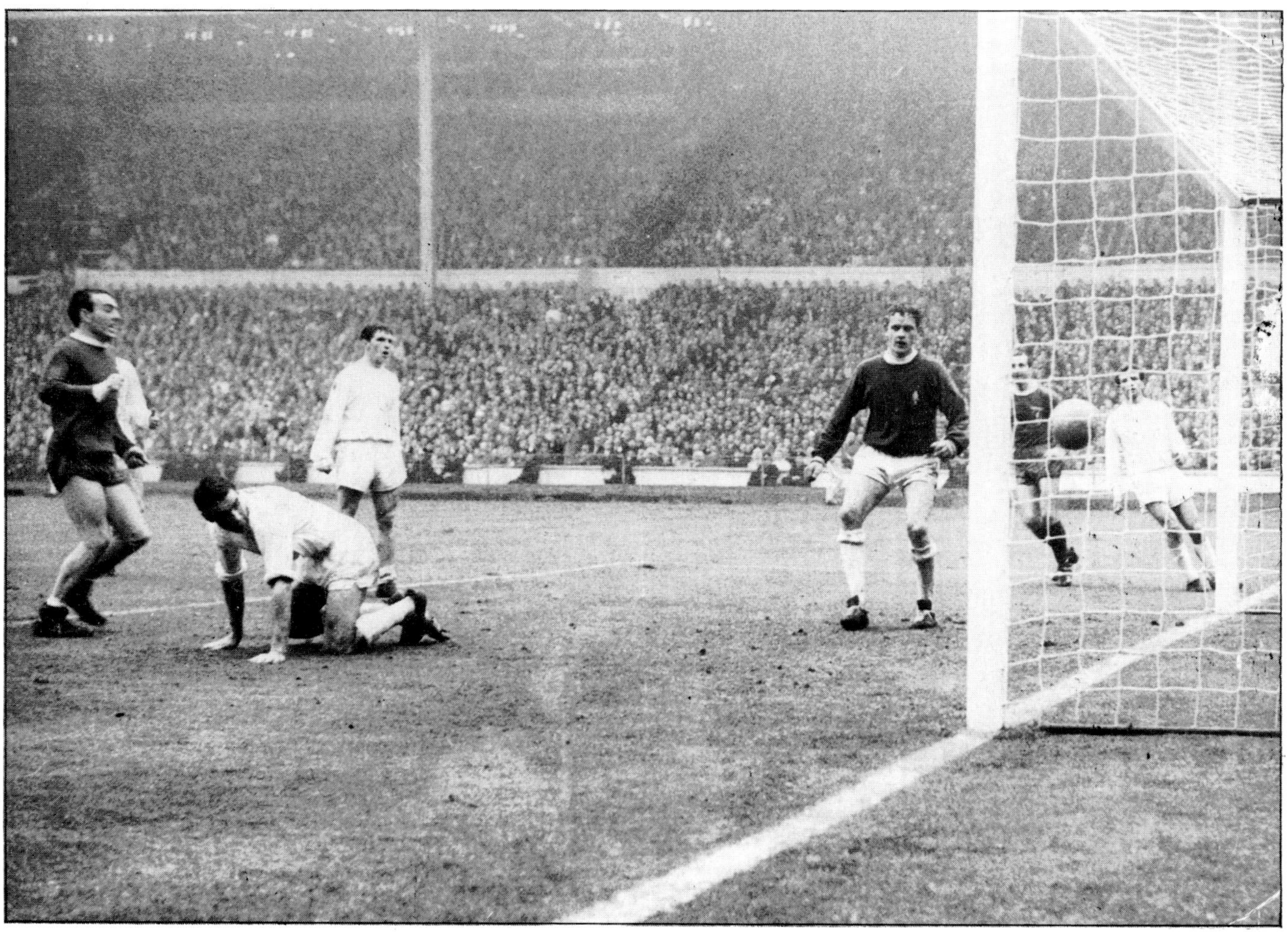

Gray Sprake watches helplessly as Roger Hunt (not in picture) scores Liverpool's first goal in extra-time of the 1965 Cup Final. The Reds eventually won 2-1 with full-back Gerry Byrne playing for most of the game with a broken collarbone. The other players in this picture (from left to right) are Ian St John, Willie Bell, Norman Hunter, Byrne and Paul Reaney.

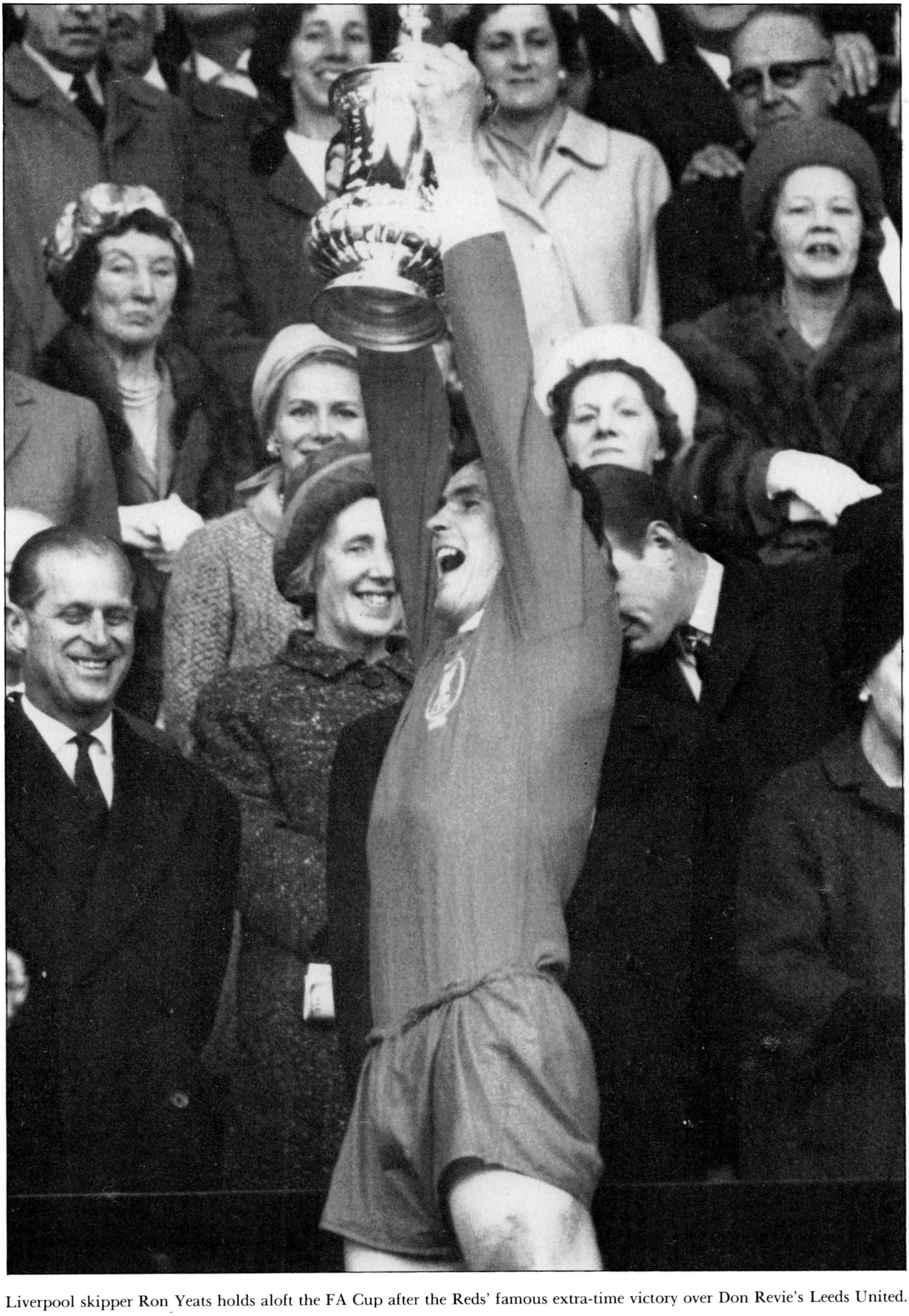

Liverpool skipper Ron Yeats holds aloft the FA Cup after the Reds' famous extra-time victory over Don Revie's Leeds United.

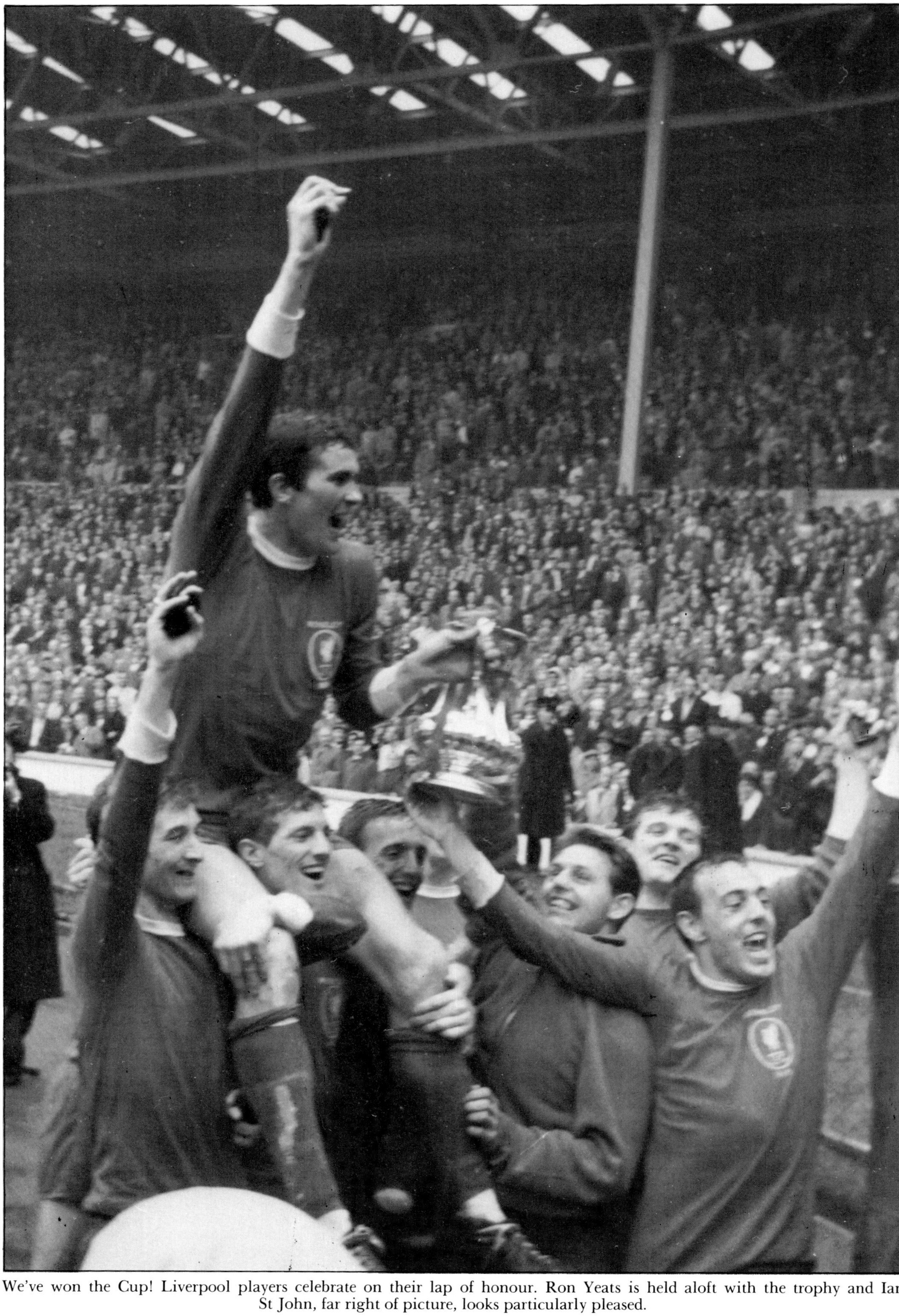

We've won the Cup! Liverpool players celebrate on their lap of honour. Ron Yeats is held aloft with the trophy and Ian St John, far right of picture, looks particularly pleased.

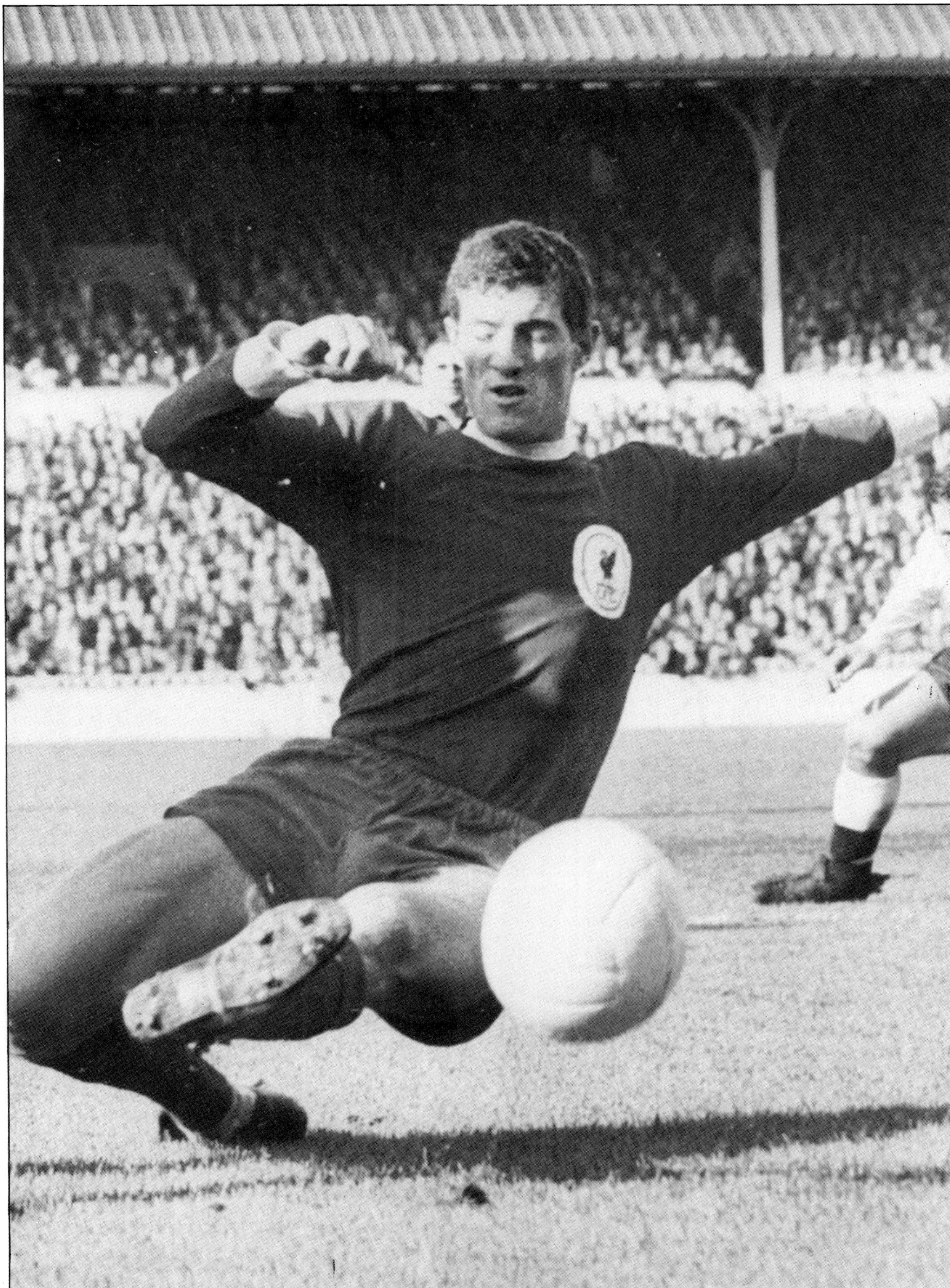

Former Rangers wing-half Willie Stevenson came back from Australian soccer to resume his League career with Liverpool in October 1962. It was a good move for Stevenson, who added two League Championship medals, an FA Cup winners' medal and a European Cup-winners' Cup runners-up medal to the honours he had already won in Scotland. He left Anfield for Stoke City in December 1967 for £48,000, having played in 238 senior games for the Reds.

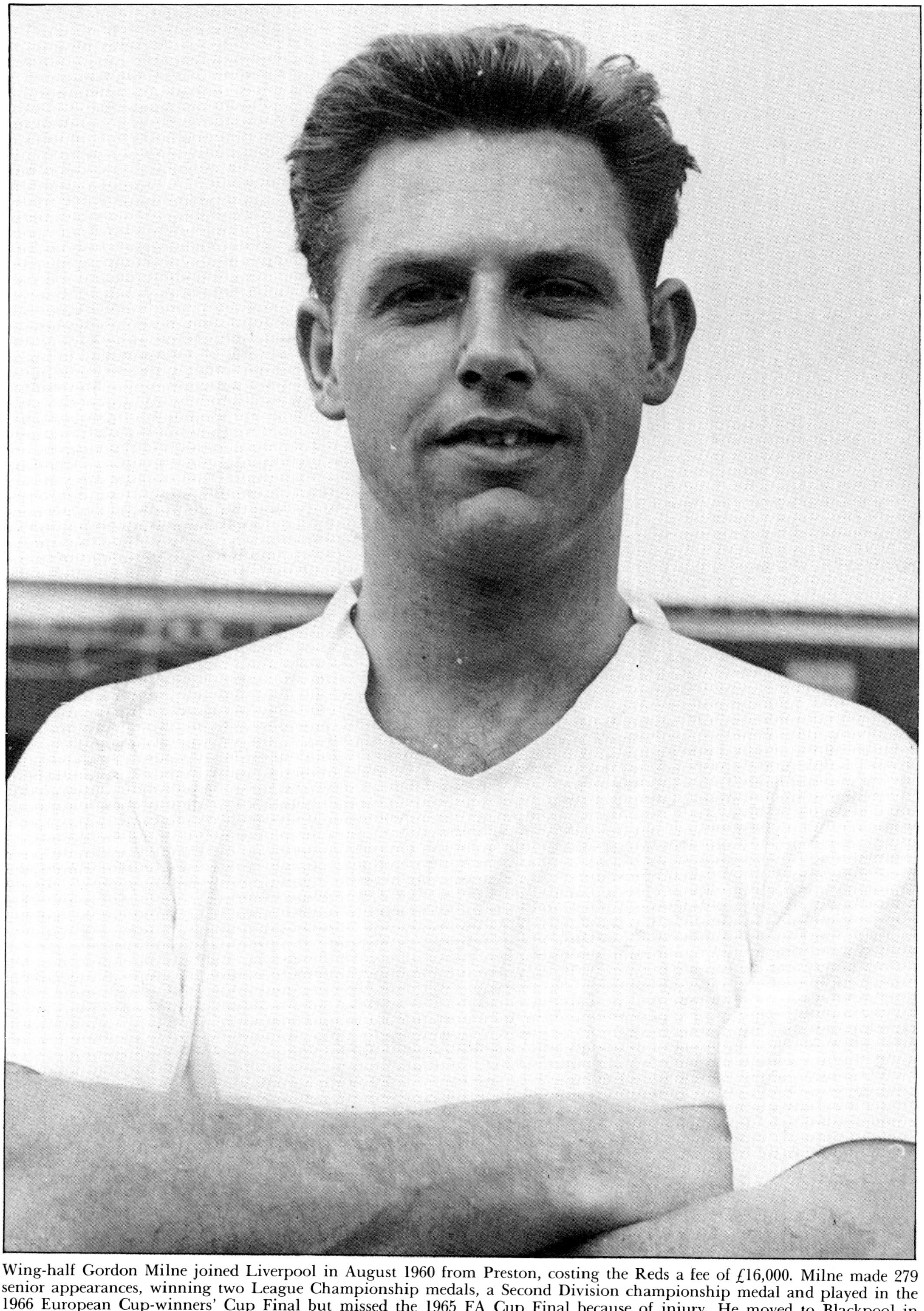

Wing-half Gordon Milne joined Liverpool in August 1960 from Preston, costing the Reds a fee of £16,000. Milne made 279 senior appearances, winning two League Championship medals, a Second Division championship medal and played in the 1966 European Cup-winners' Cup Final but missed the 1965 FA Cup Final because of injury. He moved to Blackpool in May 1967, for £30,000, and later had a long managerial career.

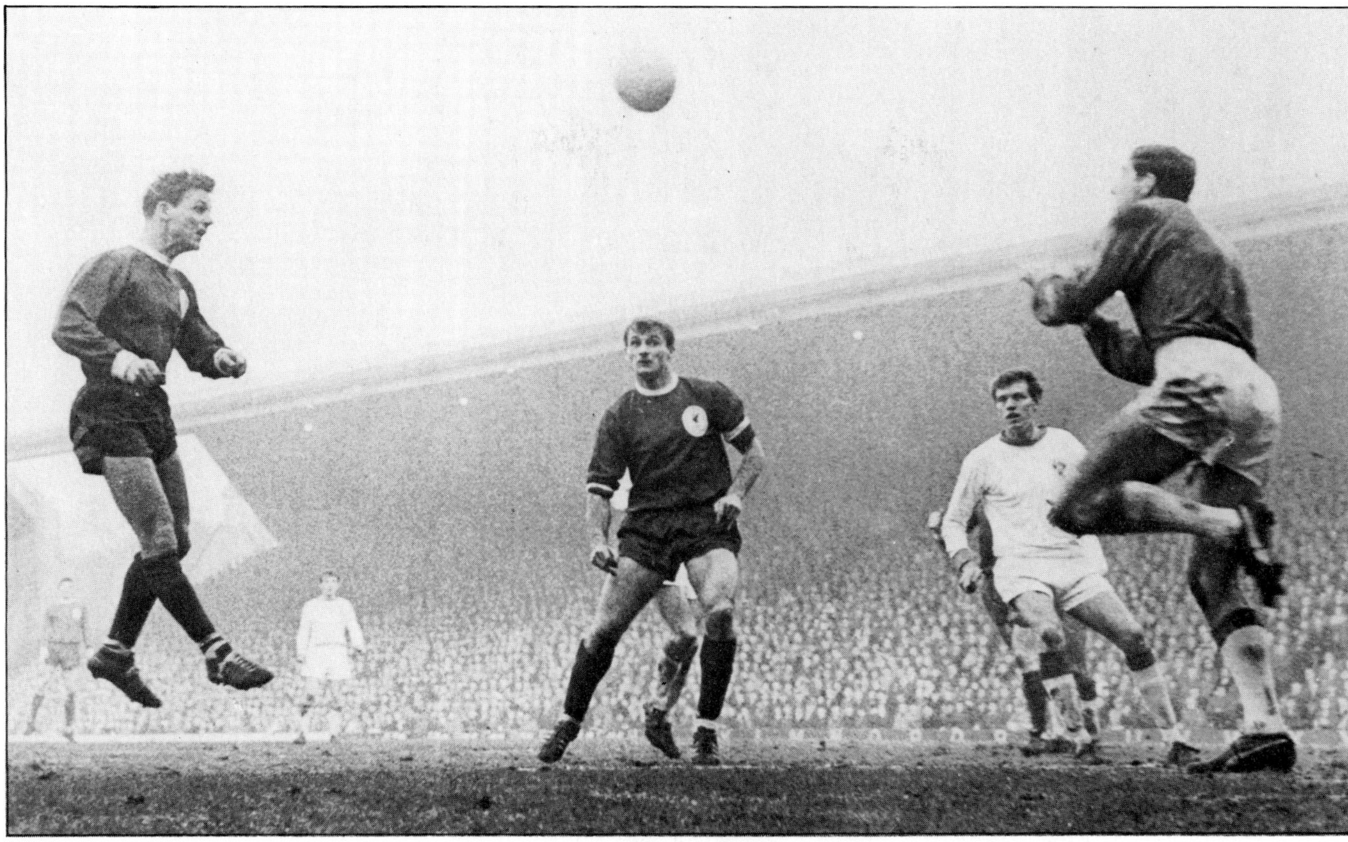

Gordon Milne heads Liverpool's third goal past Blackpool's Tony Waiters at Anfield in February 1966. The Reds won 4-1.

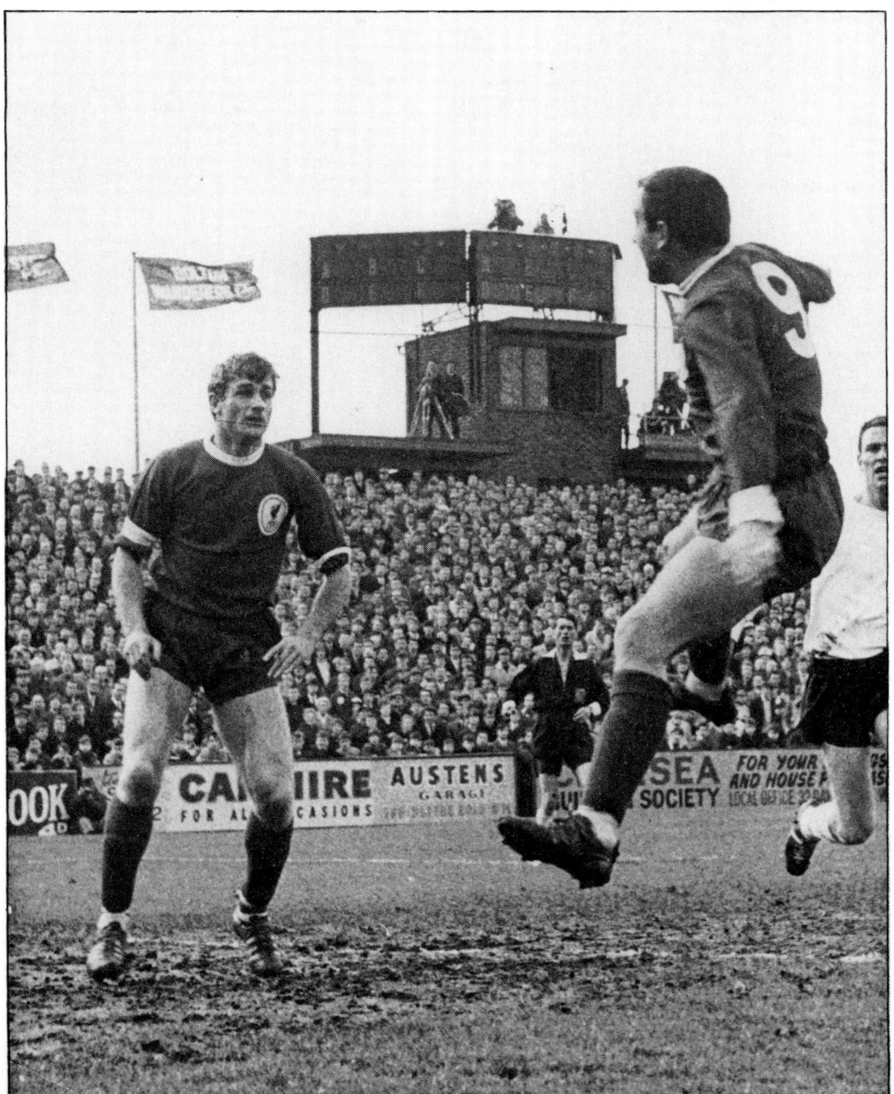

Liverpool regained the Football League Championship in 1965-6, but there was a shock along the way. This photograph shows Ian St John (left) and Roger Hunt in action at Craven Cottage in February 1966, when the Reds went down 2-0 to bottom-of-the-table Fulham. Two minutes from the end of the game, St John was sent off. He was only the third Liverpool player to be dismissed since the war and he was also one of the others, against Preston in March 1962.

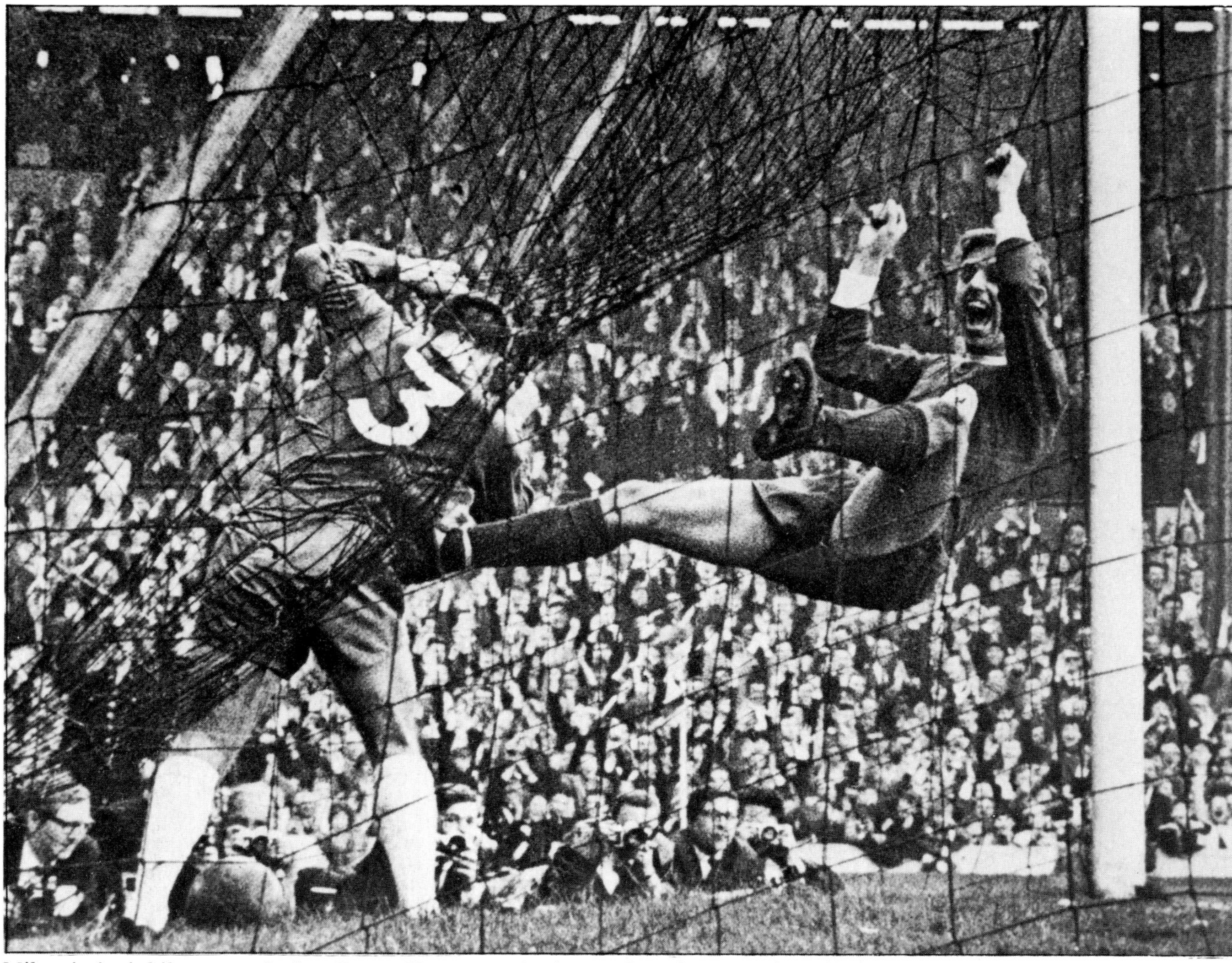

Milne is in jubilant mood after Roger Hunt scored Liverpool's winner against Chelsea at Anfield in early April 1966. It was a victory which clinched the Reds' seventh Football League Championship title.

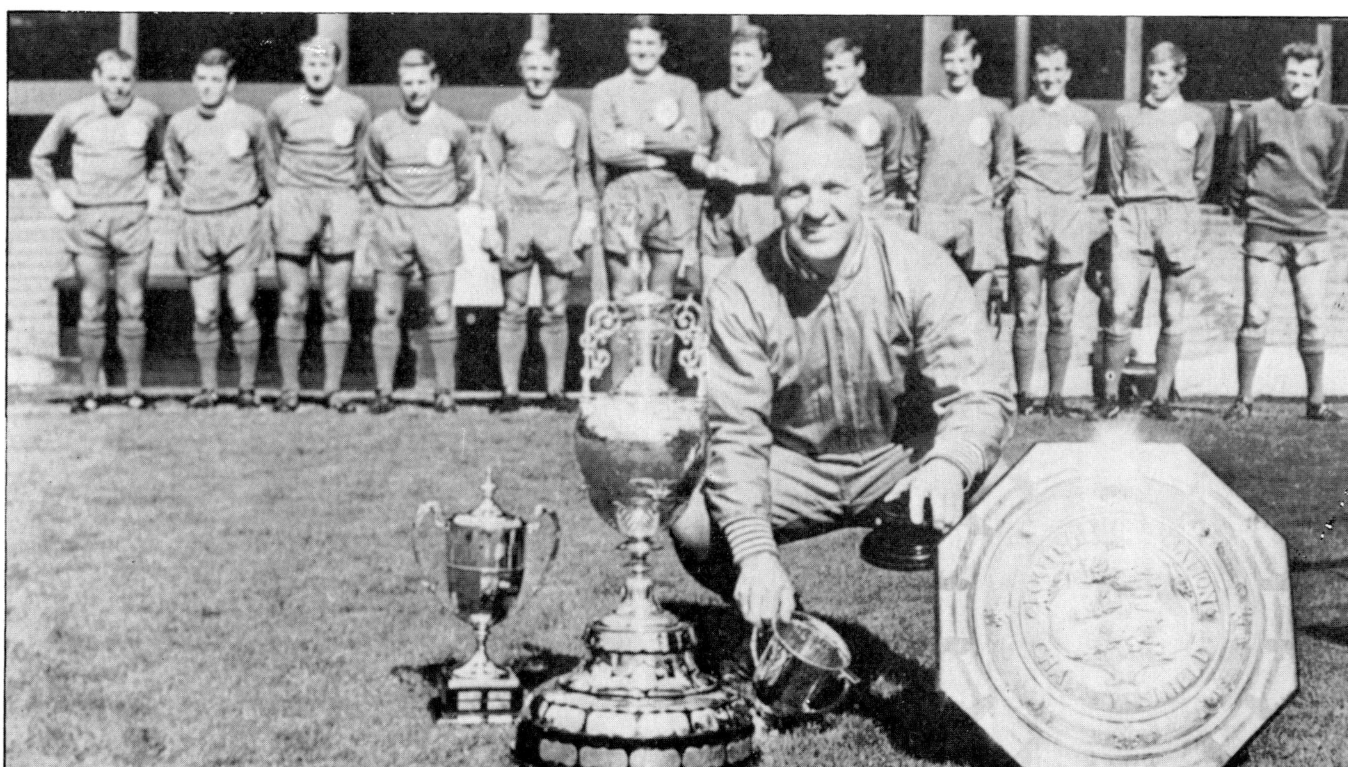

Liverpool manager Bill Shankly poses with souvenirs of success.

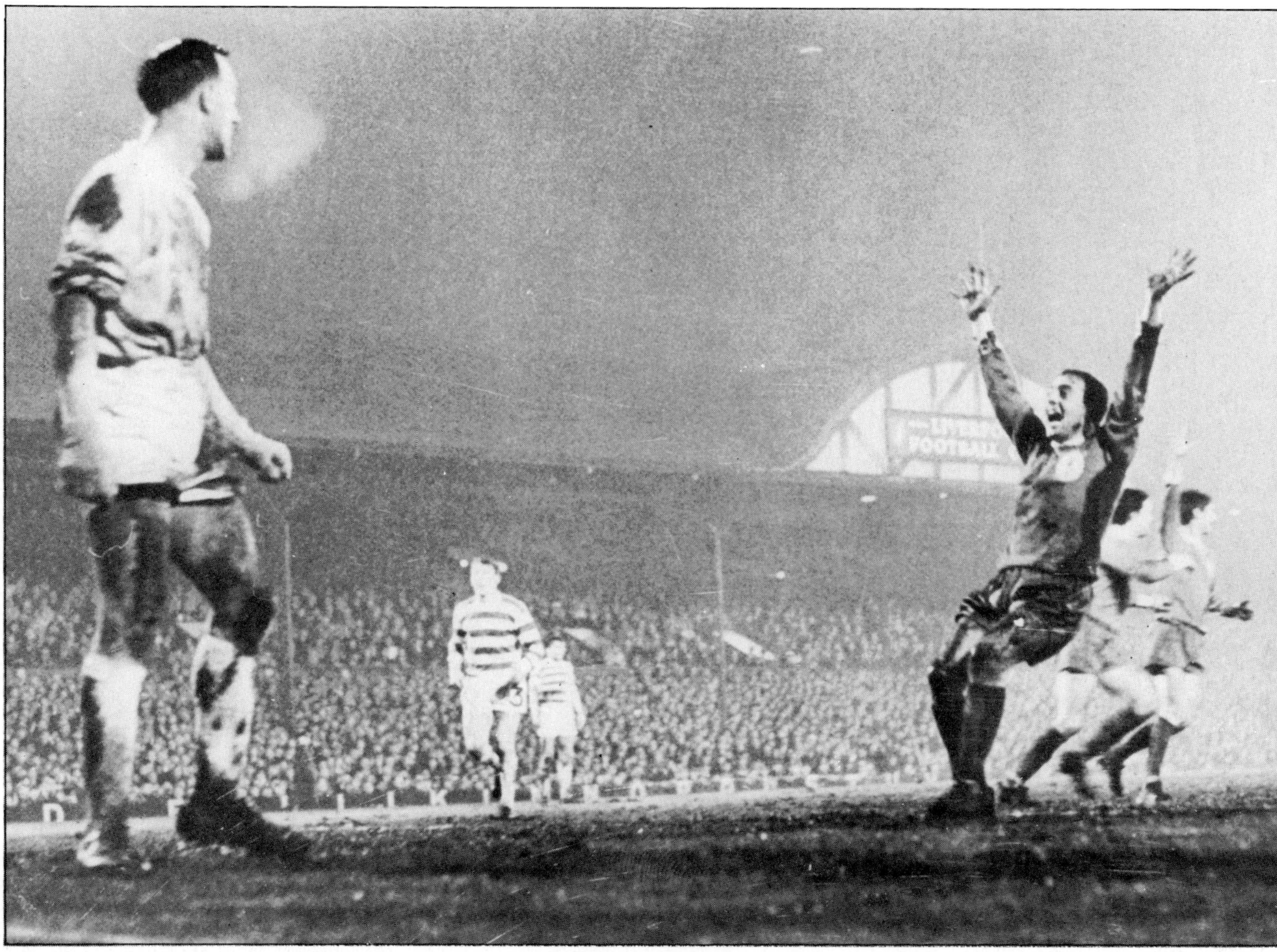

In 1966, the Reds also reached their first major European Final, in the Cup-winners' Cup. Here, Ian St John is celebrating a Liverpool goal in the second leg of the European semi-final against Celtic. The Reds lost 1-0 at Parkhead but won the return game 2-0 to go through on aggregate.

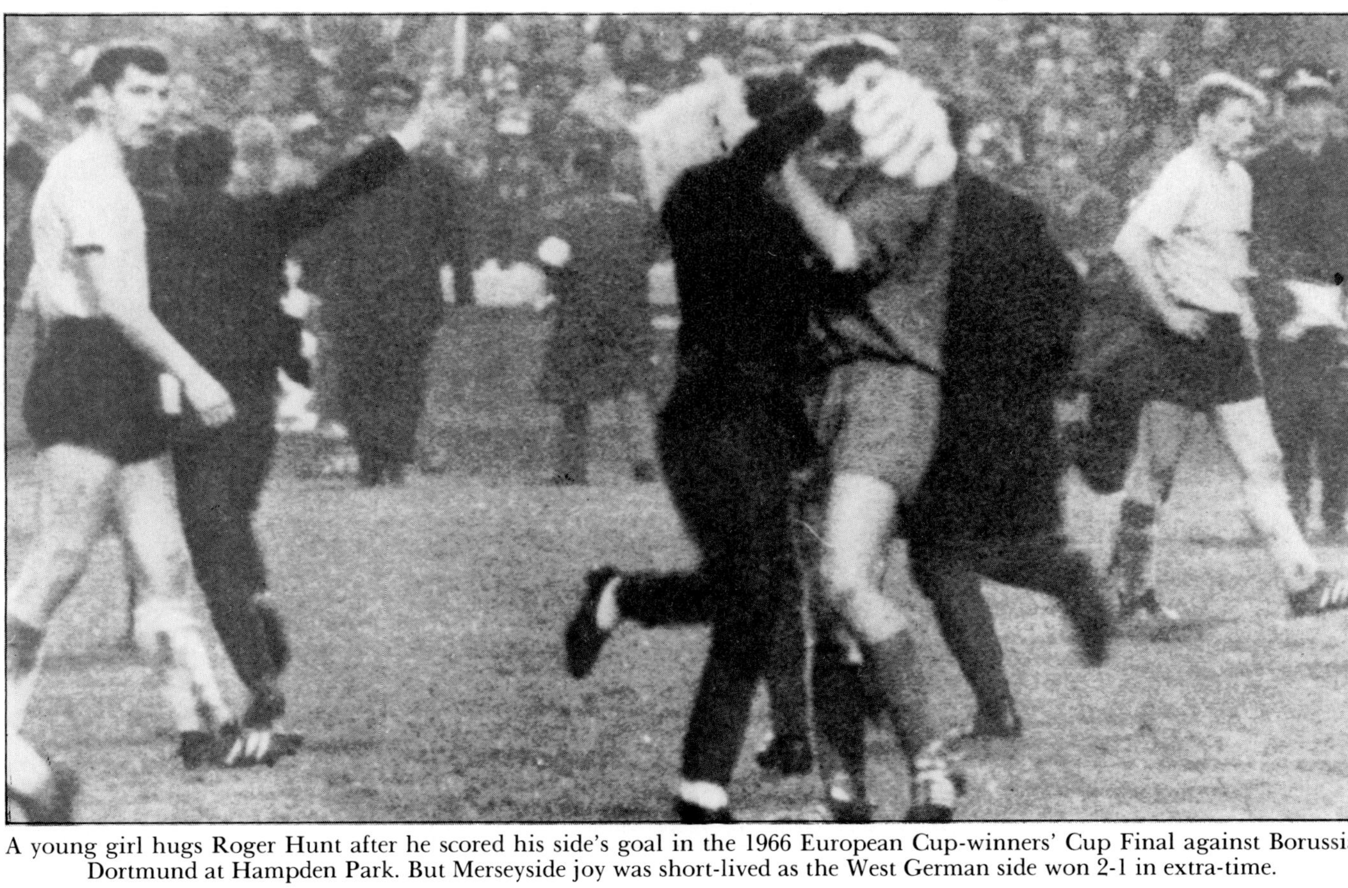

A young girl hugs Roger Hunt after he scored his side's goal in the 1966 European Cup-winners' Cup Final against Borussia Dortmund at Hampden Park. But Merseyside joy was short-lived as the West German side won 2-1 in extra-time.

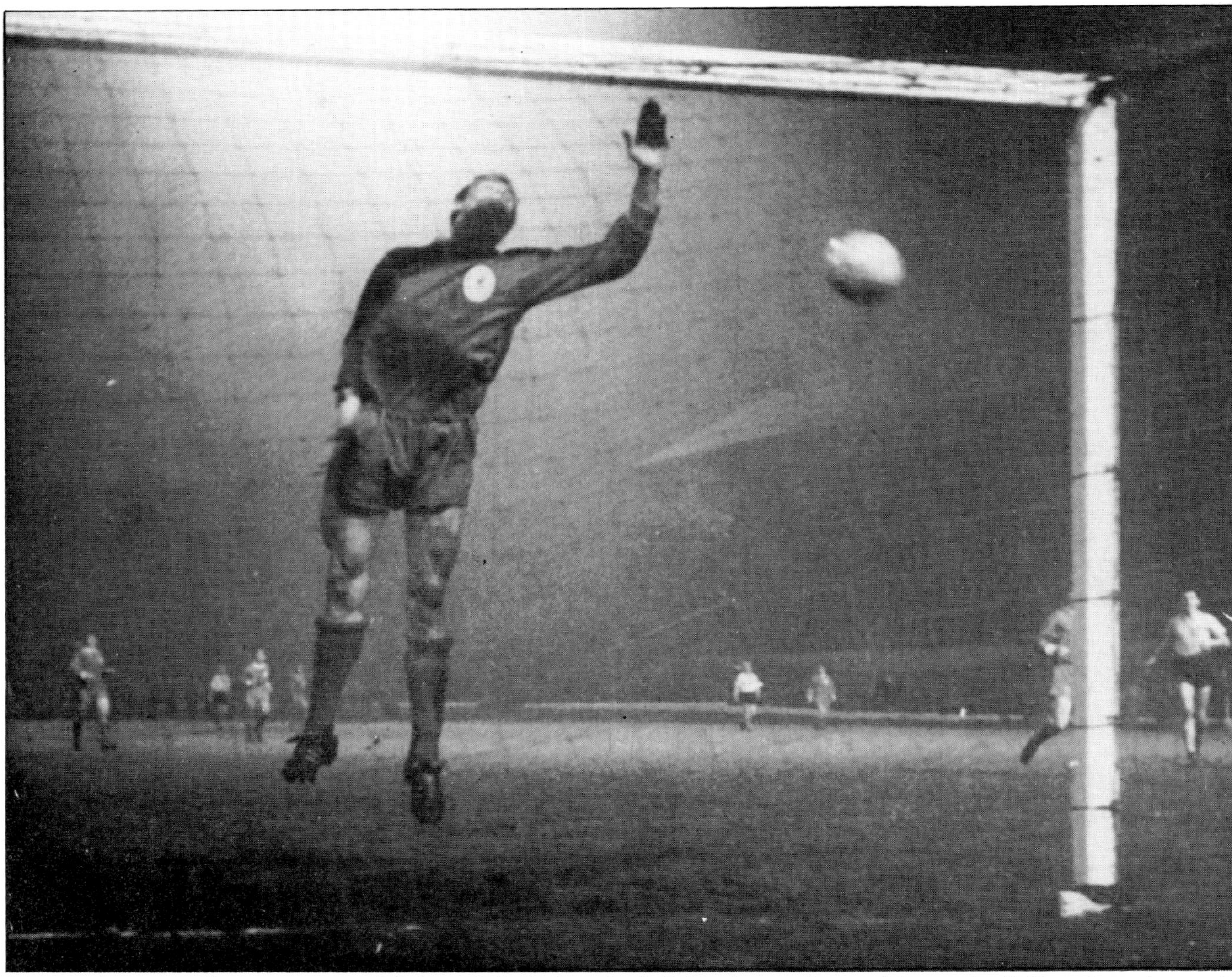

Liverpool centre-half tries to stop a lob from Libuda but the ball hit the crossbar and bounced off Yeats into the net for Borussia Dortmund's winning goal.

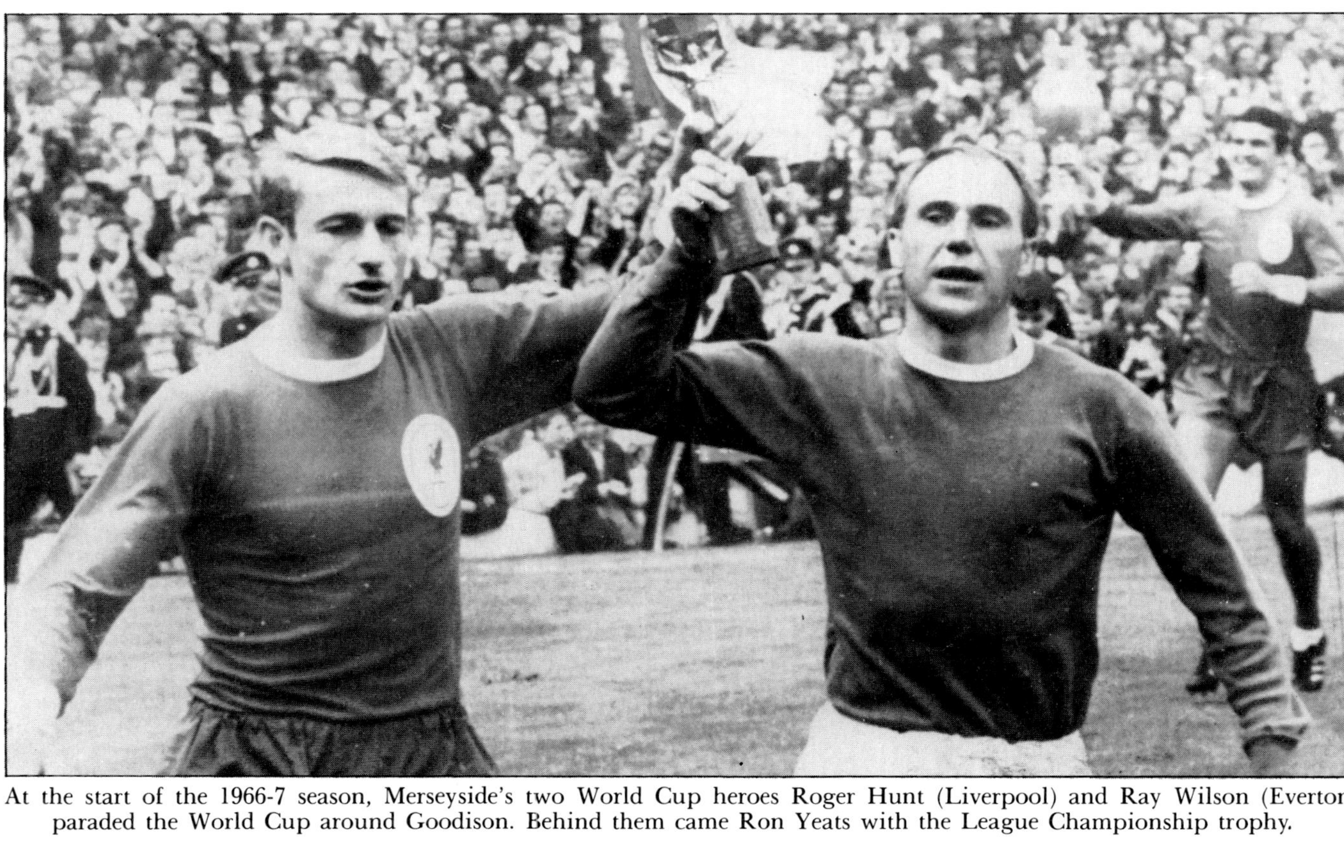

At the start of the 1966-7 season, Merseyside's two World Cup heroes Roger Hunt (Liverpool) and Ray Wilson (Everton) paraded the World Cup around Goodison. Behind them came Ron Yeats with the League Championship trophy.

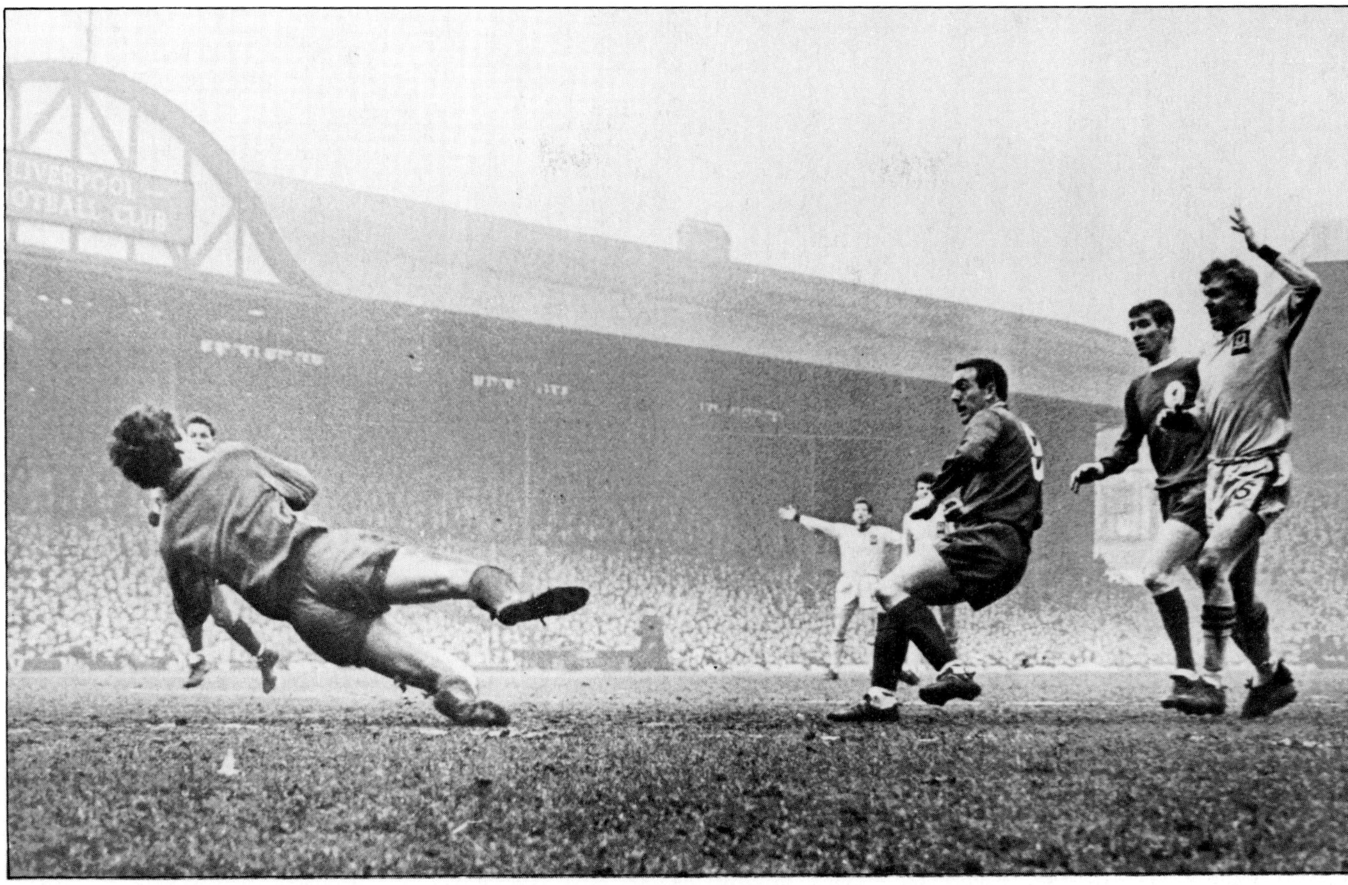

February 1967 and Ian St John's shot is blocked by Aston Villa's Colin Withers during the Reds' 1-0 FA Cup win at Anfield. The previous week, Liverpool had beaten Villa by the same score at home in a League game. Liverpool went out of the competition in the fifth round, losing to Everton, and finished fifth in Division One.

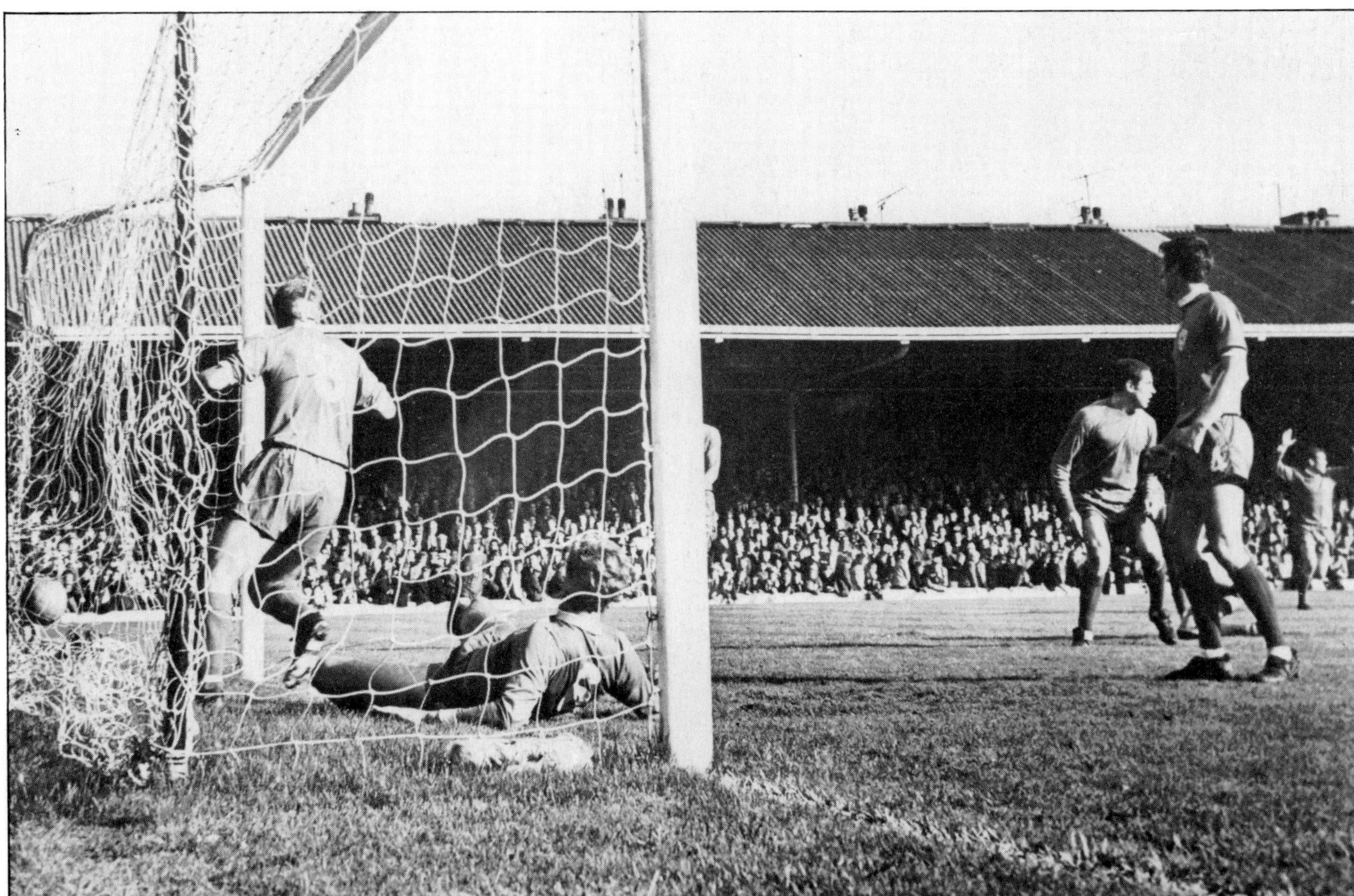

Roger Hunt (far left) follows his header into the Leicester City net at Filbert Street in October 1967 but his effort was disallowed for offside. The Reds went down 2-1.

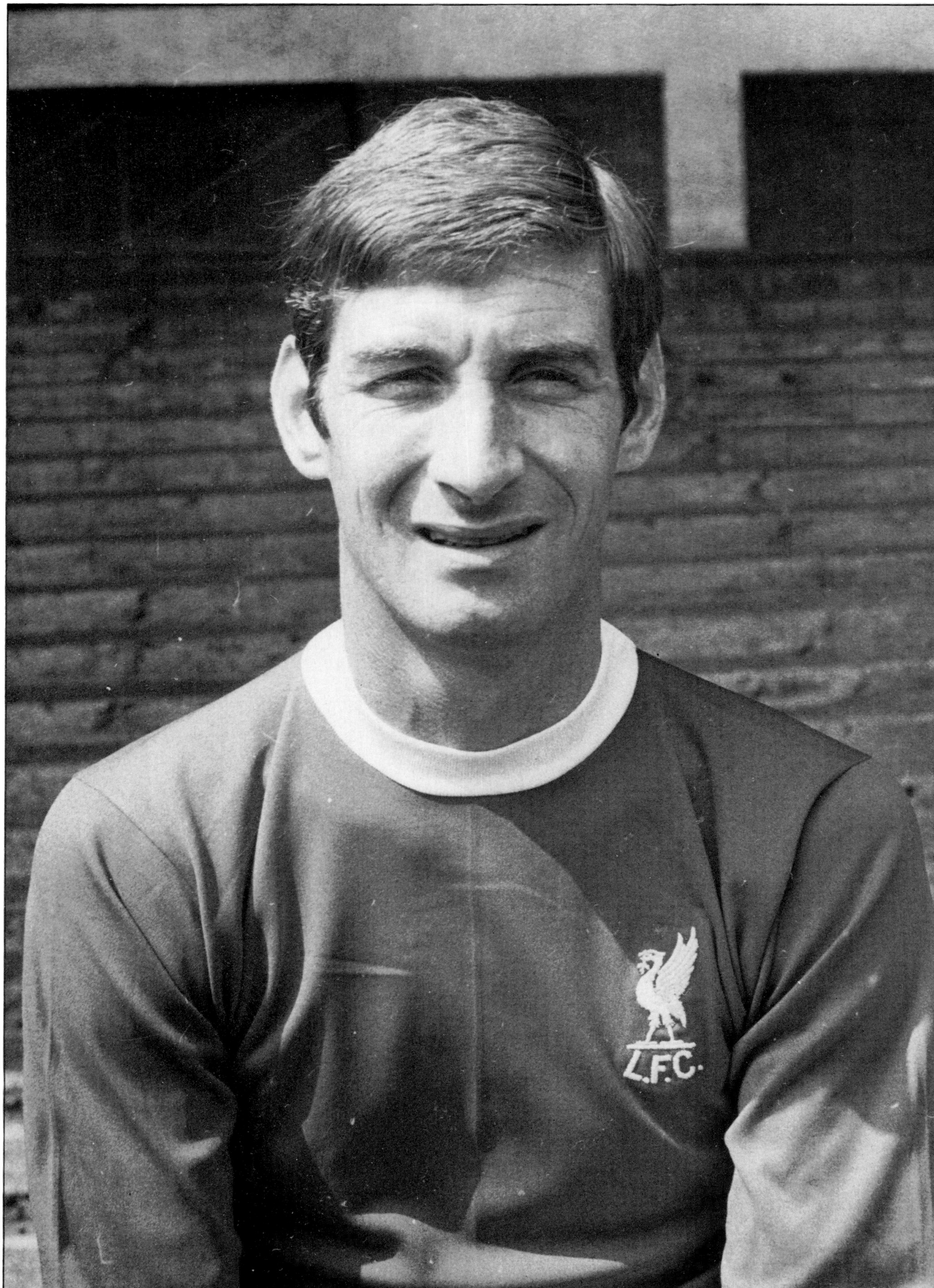

Utility player Geoff Strong was signed from Arsenal for £40,000 in November 1964 and went on to make 198 senior appearances for Liverpool, scoring 32 goals, before Coventry City paid £30,000 for him in August 1970. Whilst at Anfield, Strong gained an FA Cup winners' medal in 1965 and a League Championship medal 12 months later.

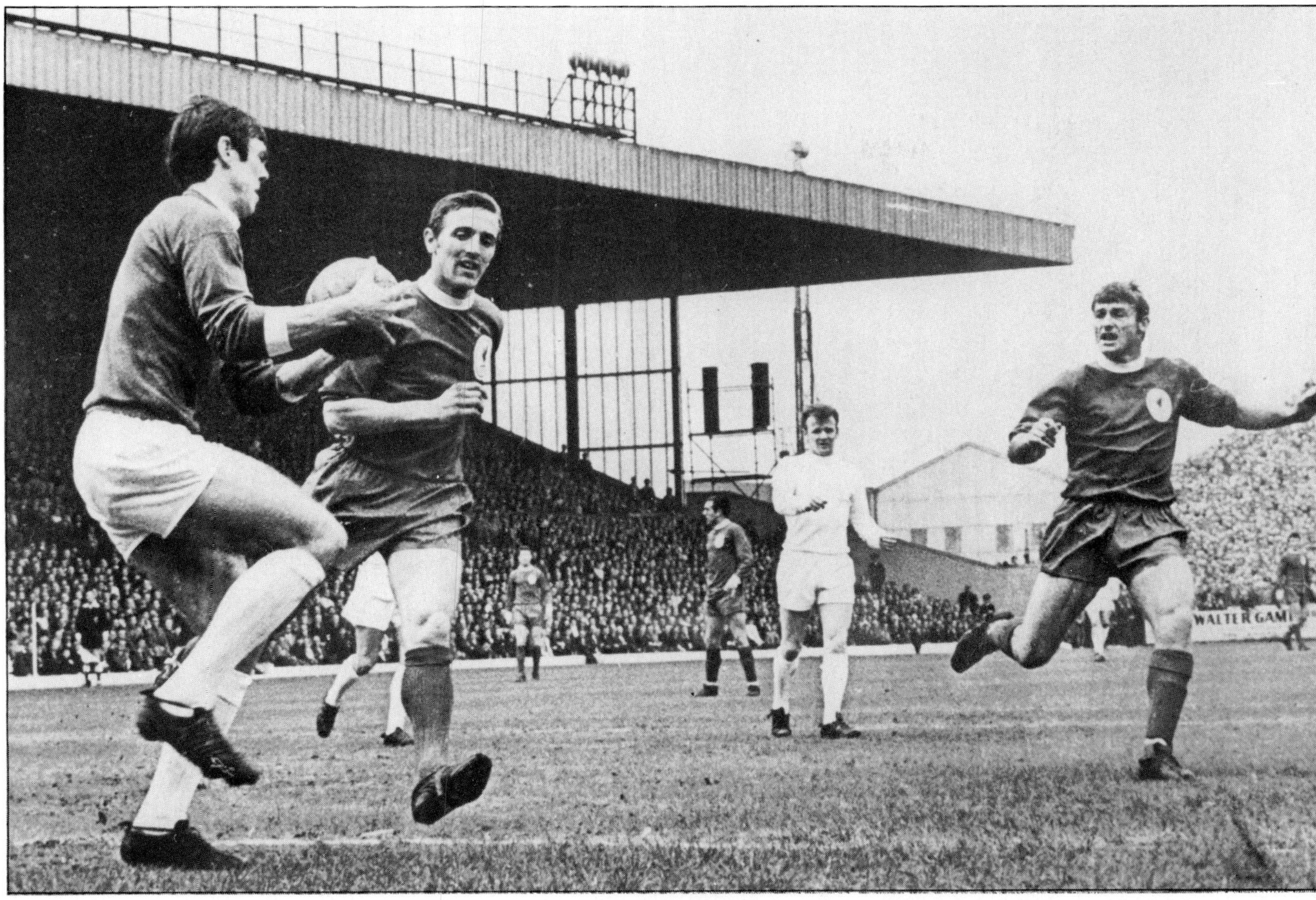

David Harvey grabs the ball from Peter Thompson as Roger Hunt looks on at Elland Road in May 1968. Liverpool won 2-1 but finished third in the table. In the FA Cup, Liverpool played nine games but reached only the sixth round, needing two games each to defeat Bournemouth, Walsall and Spurs before losing to West Brom in a second replay.

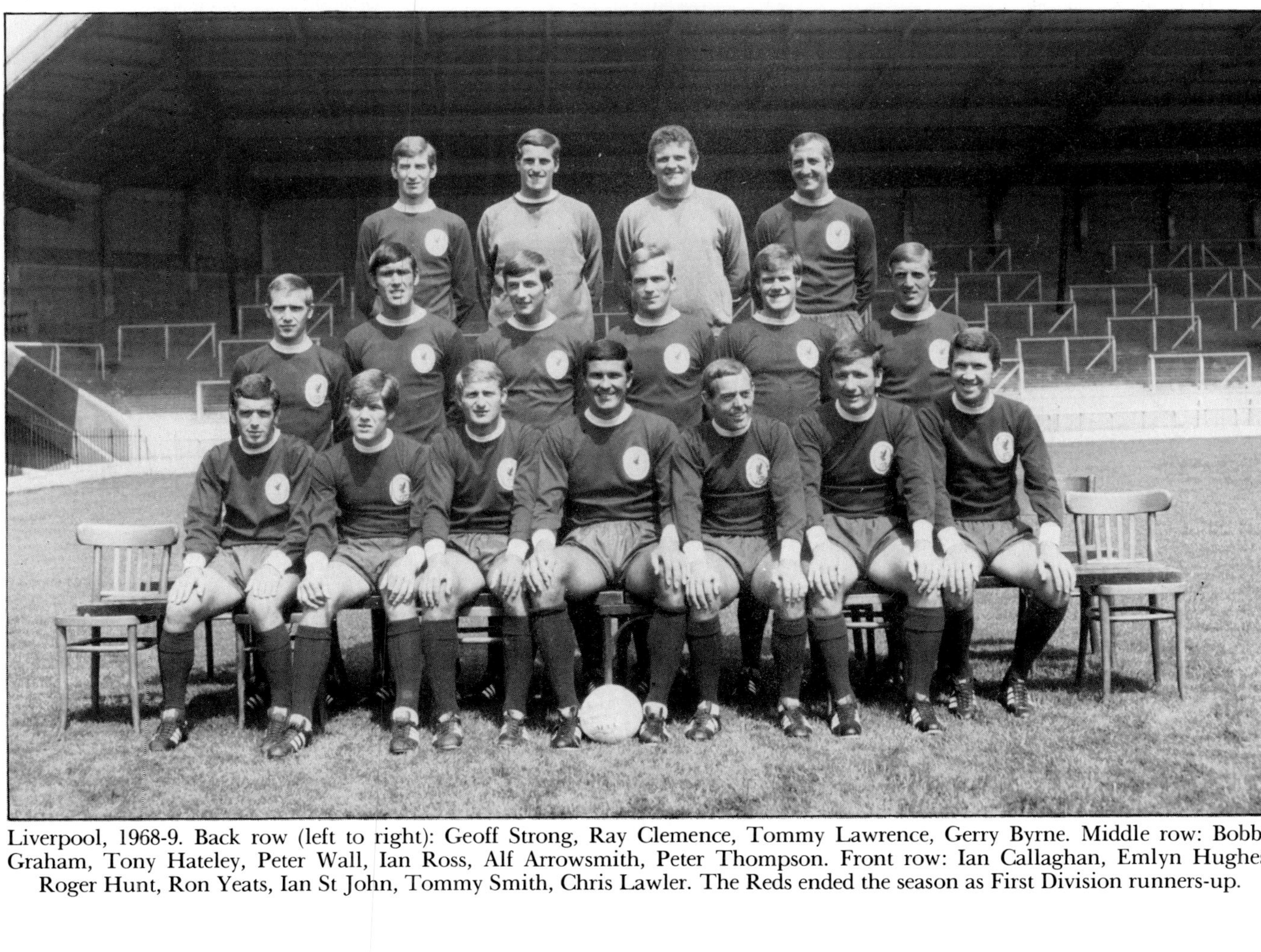

Liverpool, 1968-9. Back row (left to right): Geoff Strong, Ray Clemence, Tommy Lawrence, Gerry Byrne. Middle row: Bobby Graham, Tony Hateley, Peter Wall, Ian Ross, Alf Arrowsmith, Peter Thompson. Front row: Ian Callaghan, Emlyn Hughes, Roger Hunt, Ron Yeats, Ian St John, Tommy Smith, Chris Lawler. The Reds ended the season as First Division runners-up.

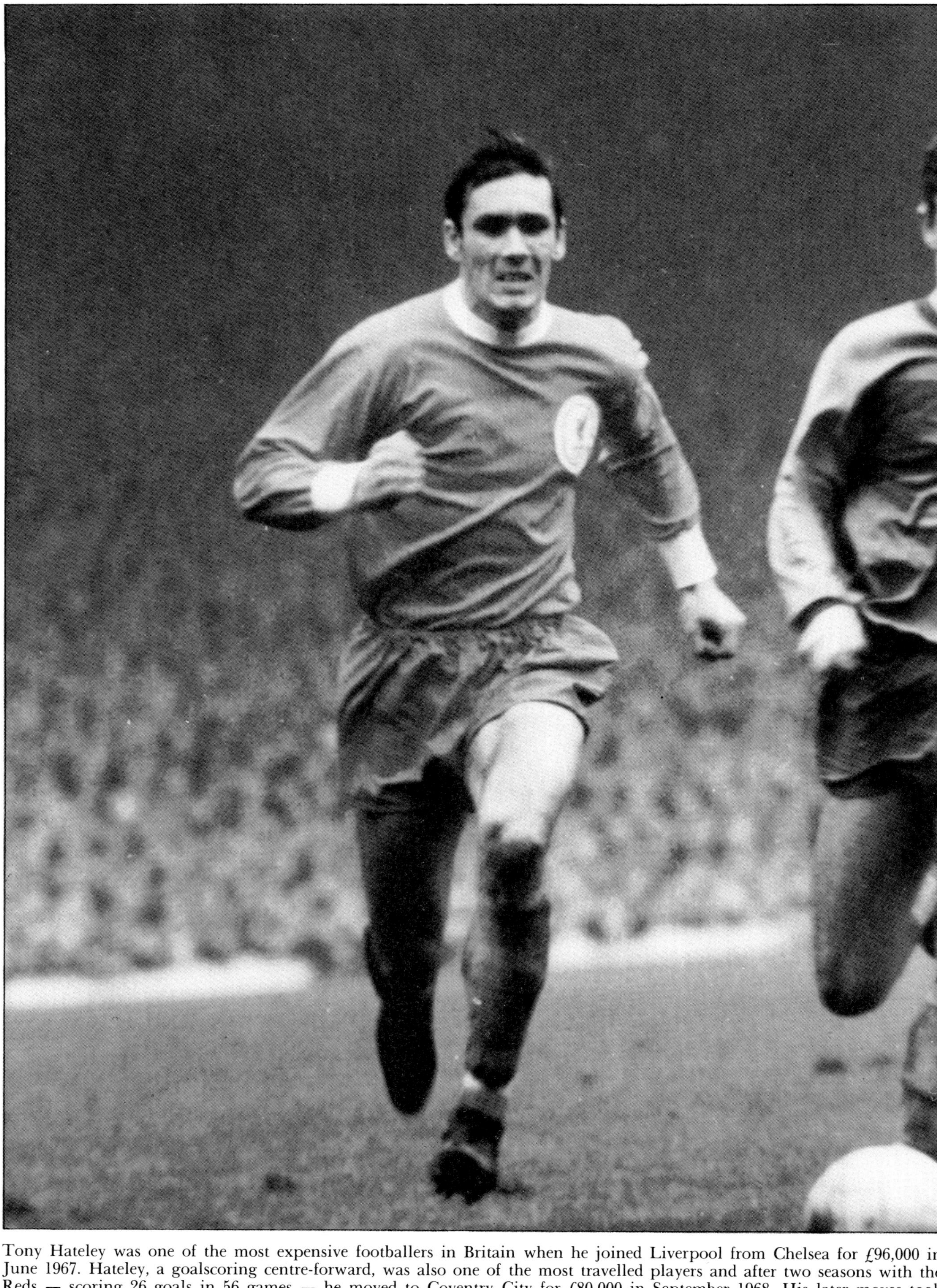

Tony Hateley was one of the most expensive footballers in Britain when he joined Liverpool from Chelsea for £96,000 in June 1967. Hateley, a goalscoring centre-forward, was also one of the most travelled players and after two seasons with the Reds — scoring 26 goals in 56 games — he moved to Coventry City for £80,000 in September 1968. His later moves took him to Birmingham City (for £60,000), Notts County (£20,000) and Oldham Athletic (£5,000). Hateley began his career with Notts County before joining Aston Villa in 1963 for £22,000 and then Chelsea, who paid £100,000 for him in October 1966. Despite his high value moves, he was never capped although his son, Mark, played for England. Altogether, Tony Hateley made 434 League appearances, scoring 211 goals.

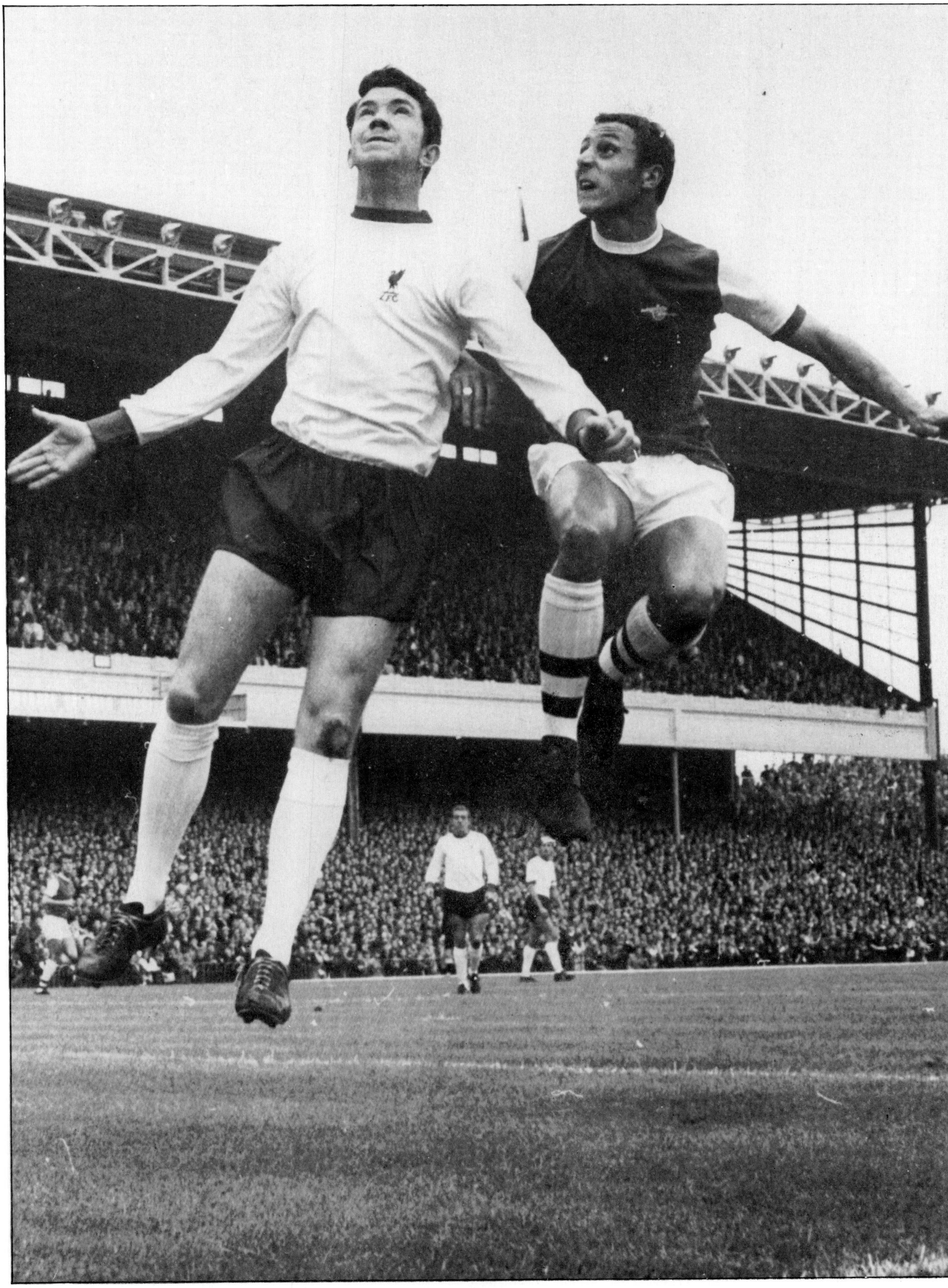

Chris Lawler and Arsenal's John Radford appear to be looking for the ball at Highbury in August 1968. Lawler, despite being a full-back, scored 61 goals in his 546 senior appearances for Liverpool after signing from local schools football in May 1959. Most of his goals came not from penalties or free-kicks but as a result of his great attacking flair. An England international, he was transferred to Portsmouth in October 1975 after gaining League Championship, FA Cup and UEFA Cup winners' medals.

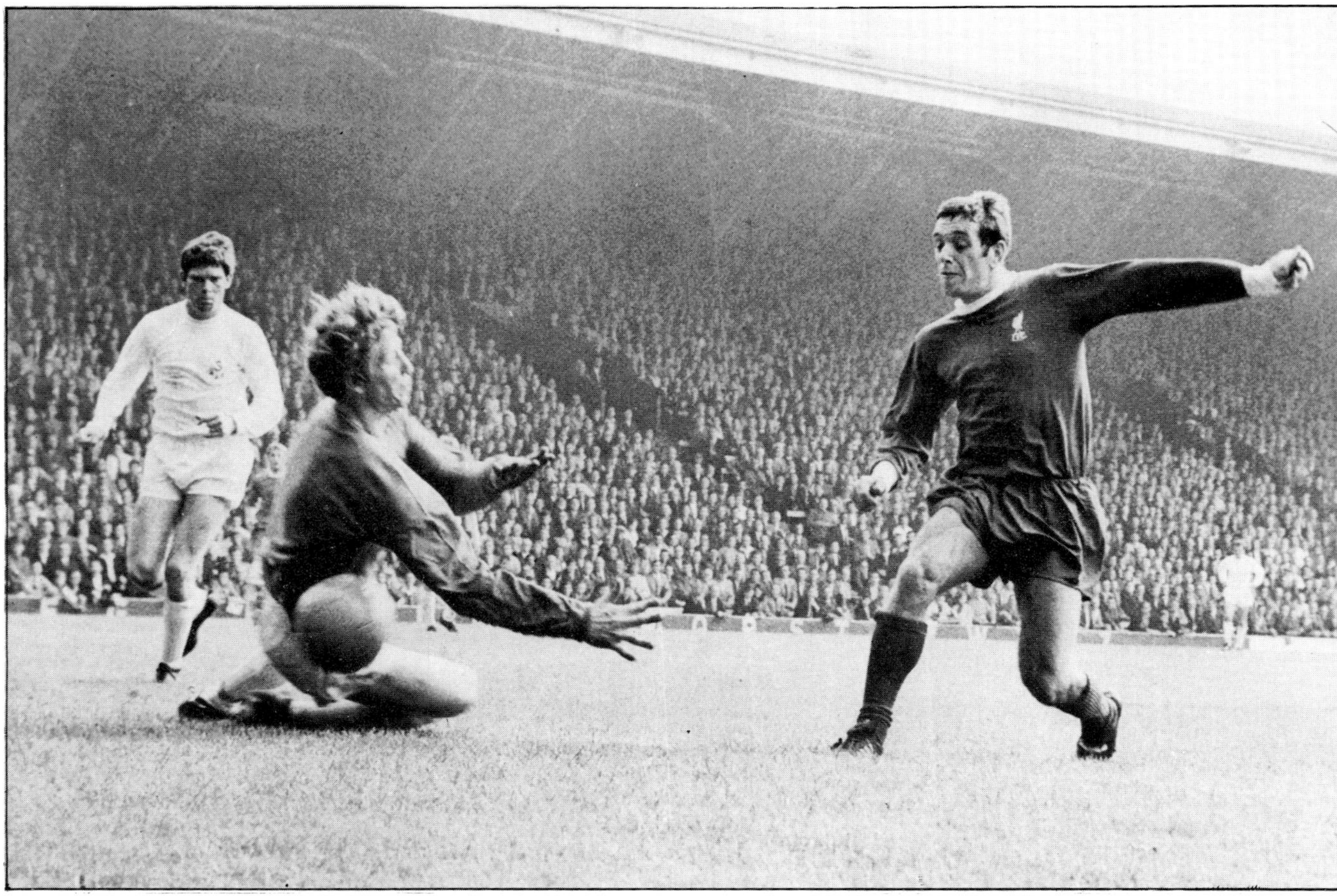

Ian Callaghan beats Sunderland's Jim Montgomery to score Liverpool's third goal a minute before half-time against the Wearsiders at Anfield in August 1968. Liverpool won 4-1.

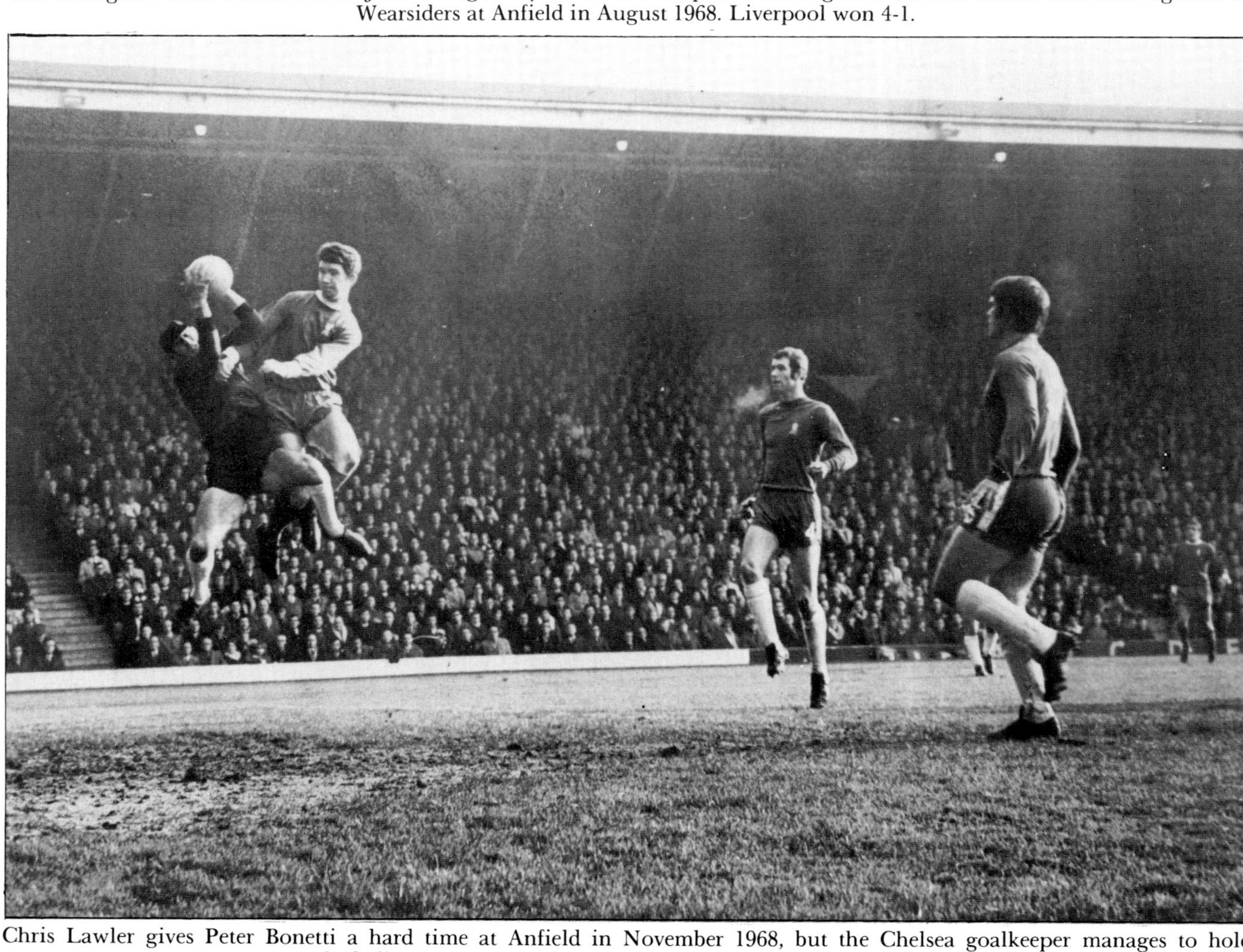

Chris Lawler gives Peter Bonetti a hard time at Anfield in November 1968, but the Chelsea goalkeeper manages to hold on to the ball. Peter Osgood and David Webb are the other Chelsea players.

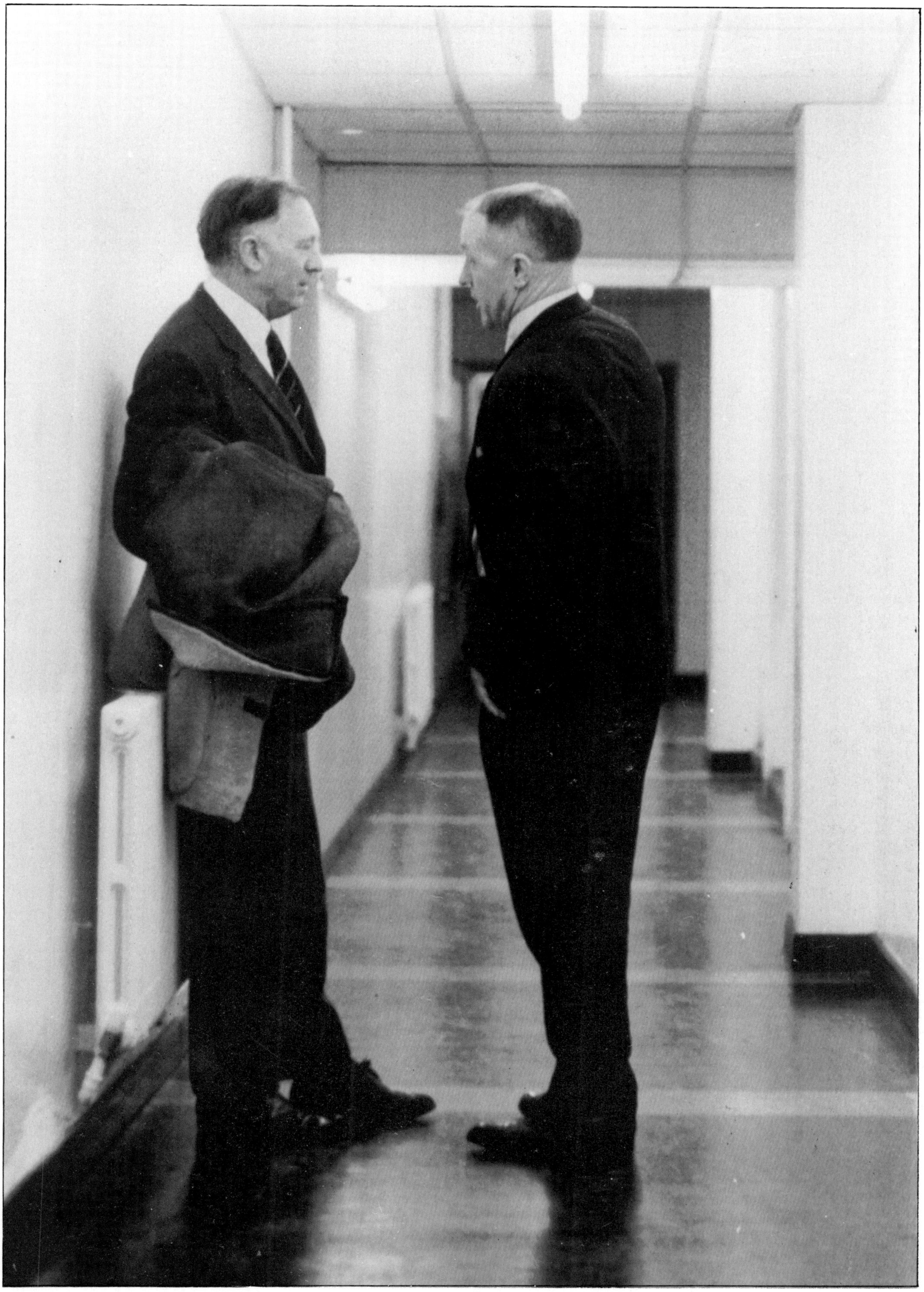

Two great football managers in the corridors of power. Liverpool's Bill Shankly and Manchester City's Joe Mercer share a quiet word.

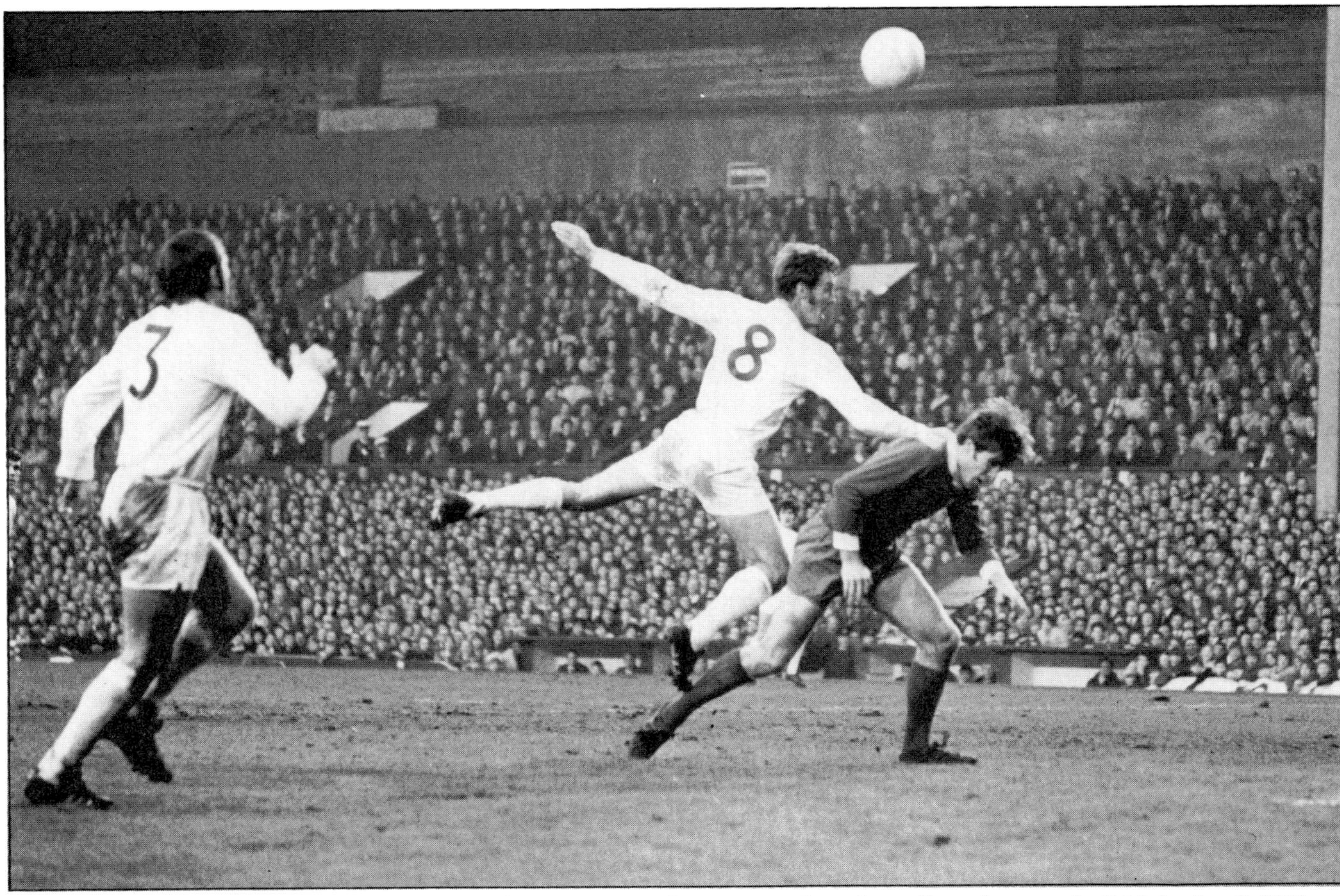

Emlyn Hughes is beaten by Leeds' Paul Madeley as Terry Cooper watches. A goalless draw at Anfield in April 1969 was enough to clinch the Championship for Leeds.

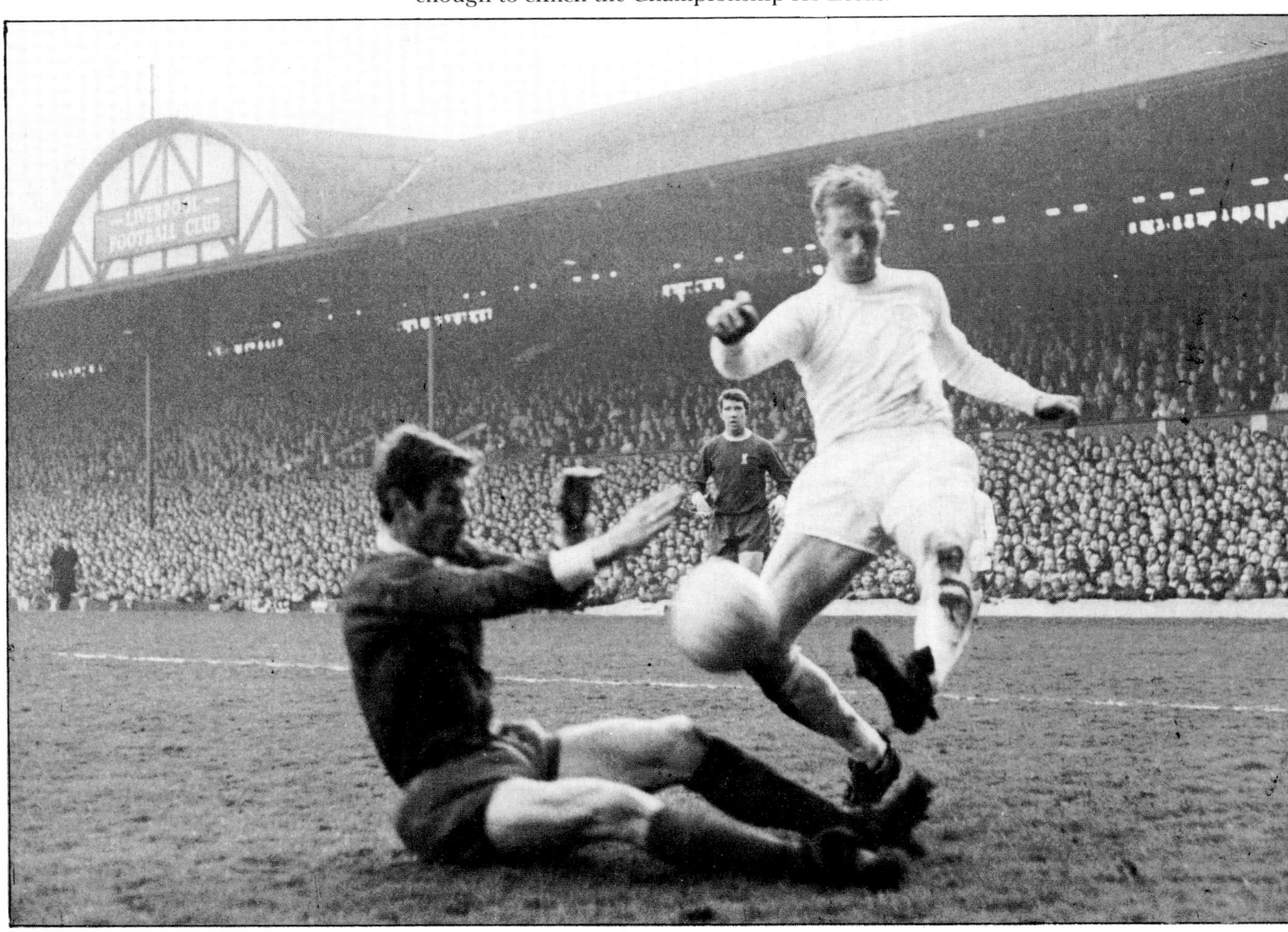

In the same match Leeds United's Jack Charlton finds his path blocked by Geoff Strong. Liverpool ended the season in runners-up spot behind Leeds.

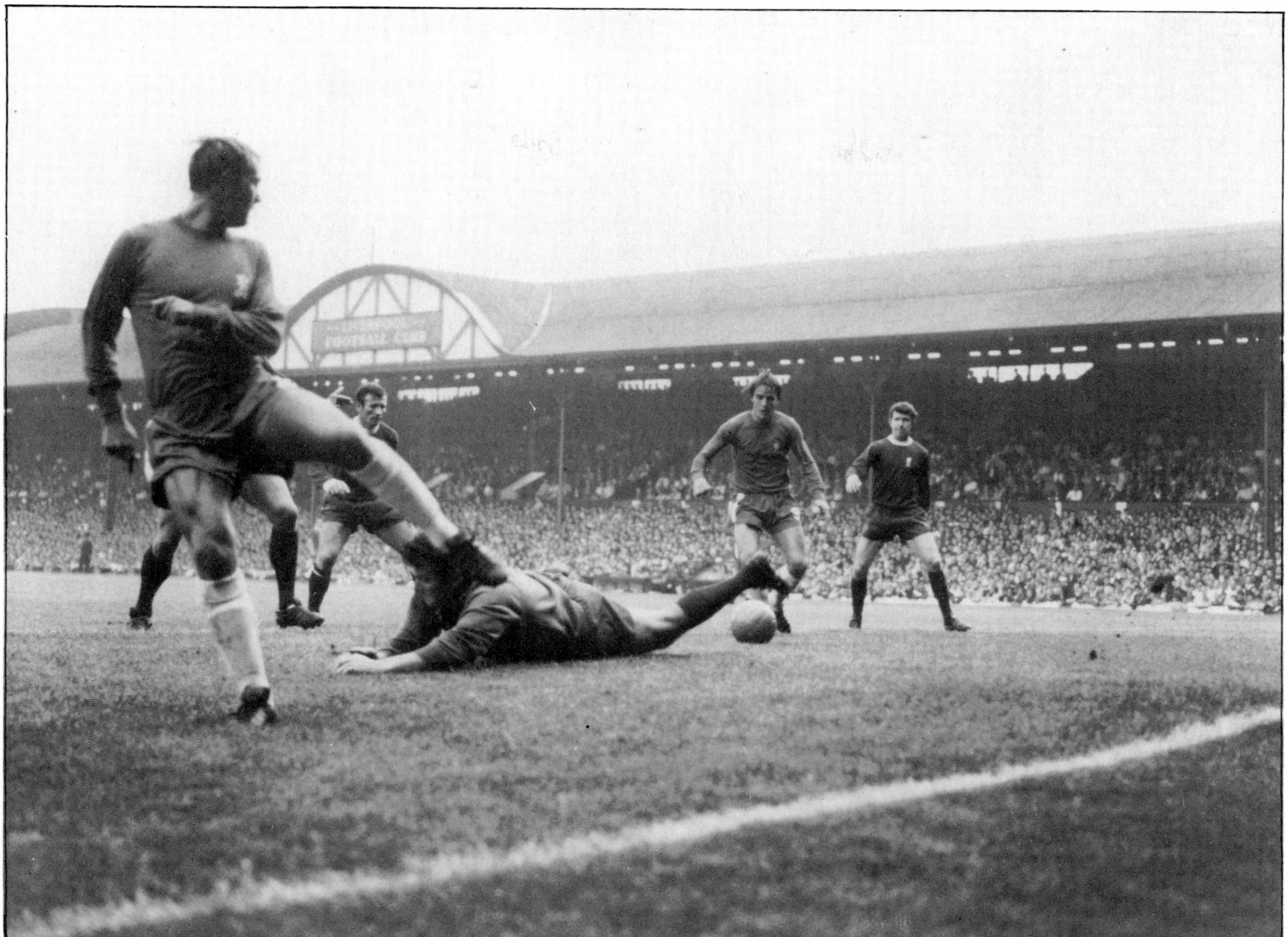

Tommy Lawrence dives at the feet of Chelsea's Tommy Baldwin at Anfield on the opening day of 1969-70. Ian Hutchinson (second right) scored Chelsea's only goal as the Reds stormed to a 4-1 win.

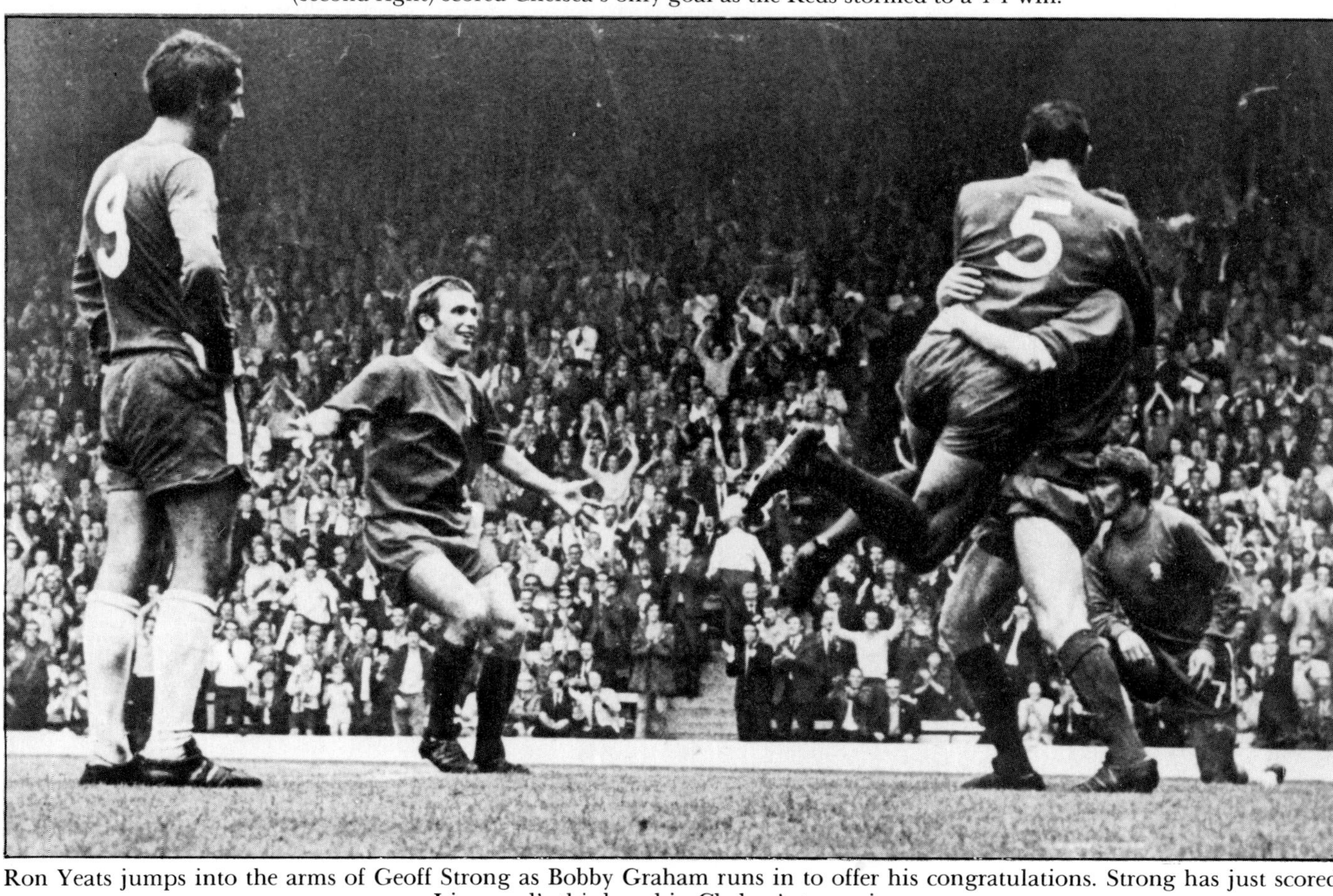

Ron Yeats jumps into the arms of Geoff Strong as Bobby Graham runs in to offer his congratulations. Strong has just scored Liverpool's third goal in Chelsea's trouncing.

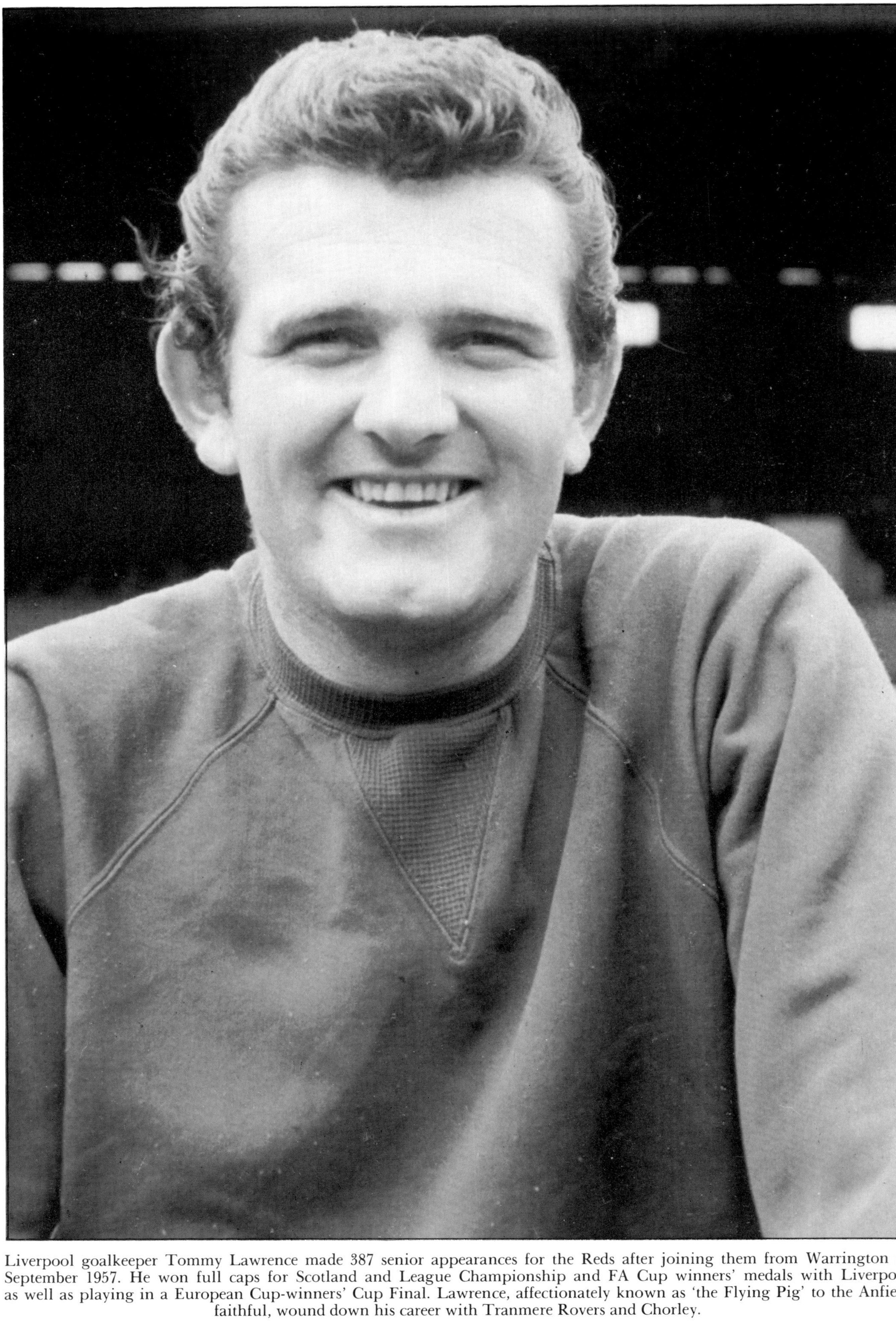

Liverpool goalkeeper Tommy Lawrence made 387 senior appearances for the Reds after joining them from Warrington in September 1957. He won full caps for Scotland and League Championship and FA Cup winners' medals with Liverpool as well as playing in a European Cup-winners' Cup Final. Lawrence, affectionately known as 'the Flying Pig' to the Anfield faithful, wound down his career with Tranmere Rovers and Chorley.

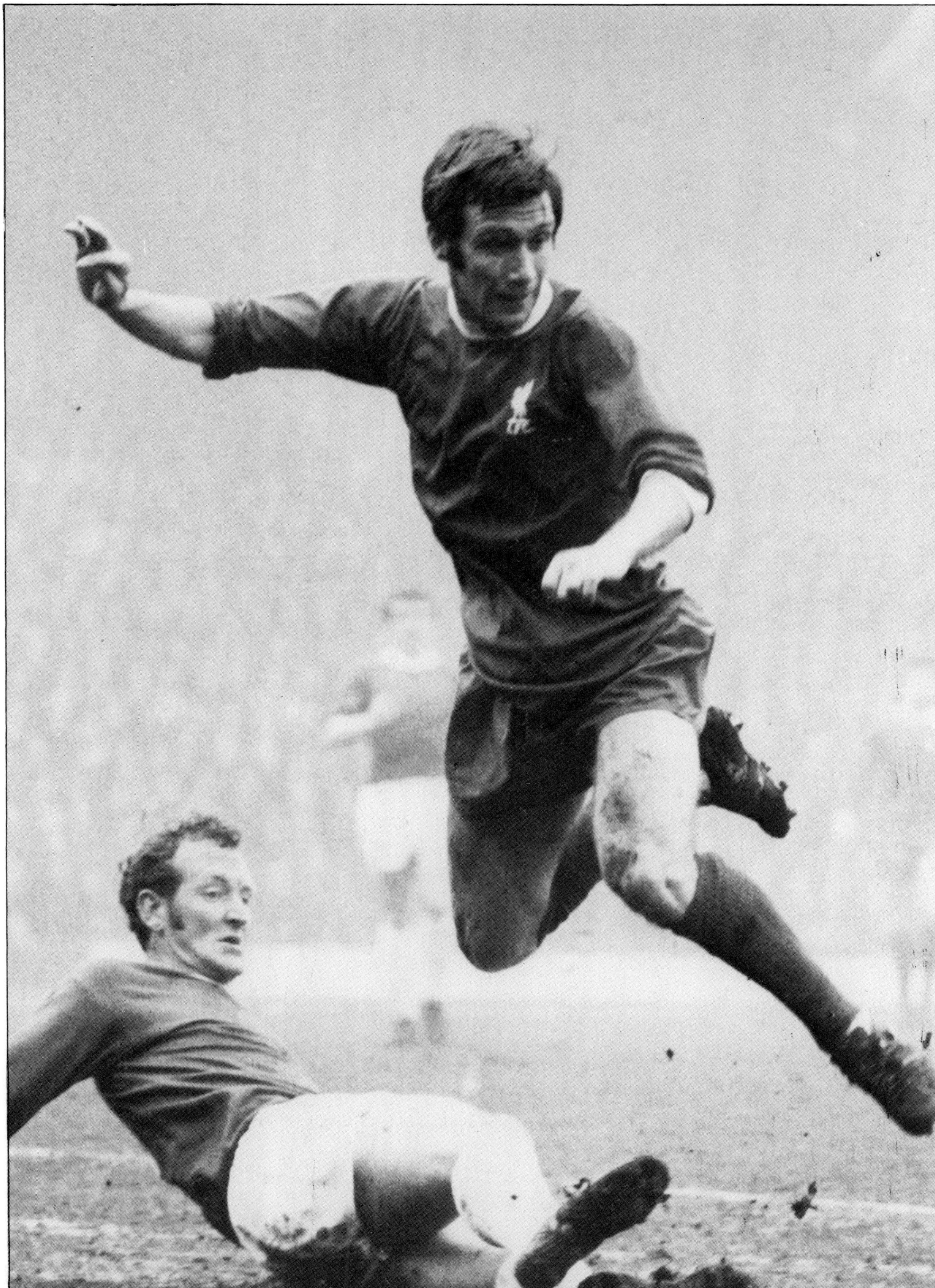

Bobby Graham of Liverpool rides a tackle from Everton's Sandy Brown. In 1969-70, the Reds won 3-0 at Goodison and lost 2-0 at Anfield to the eventual League Champions.

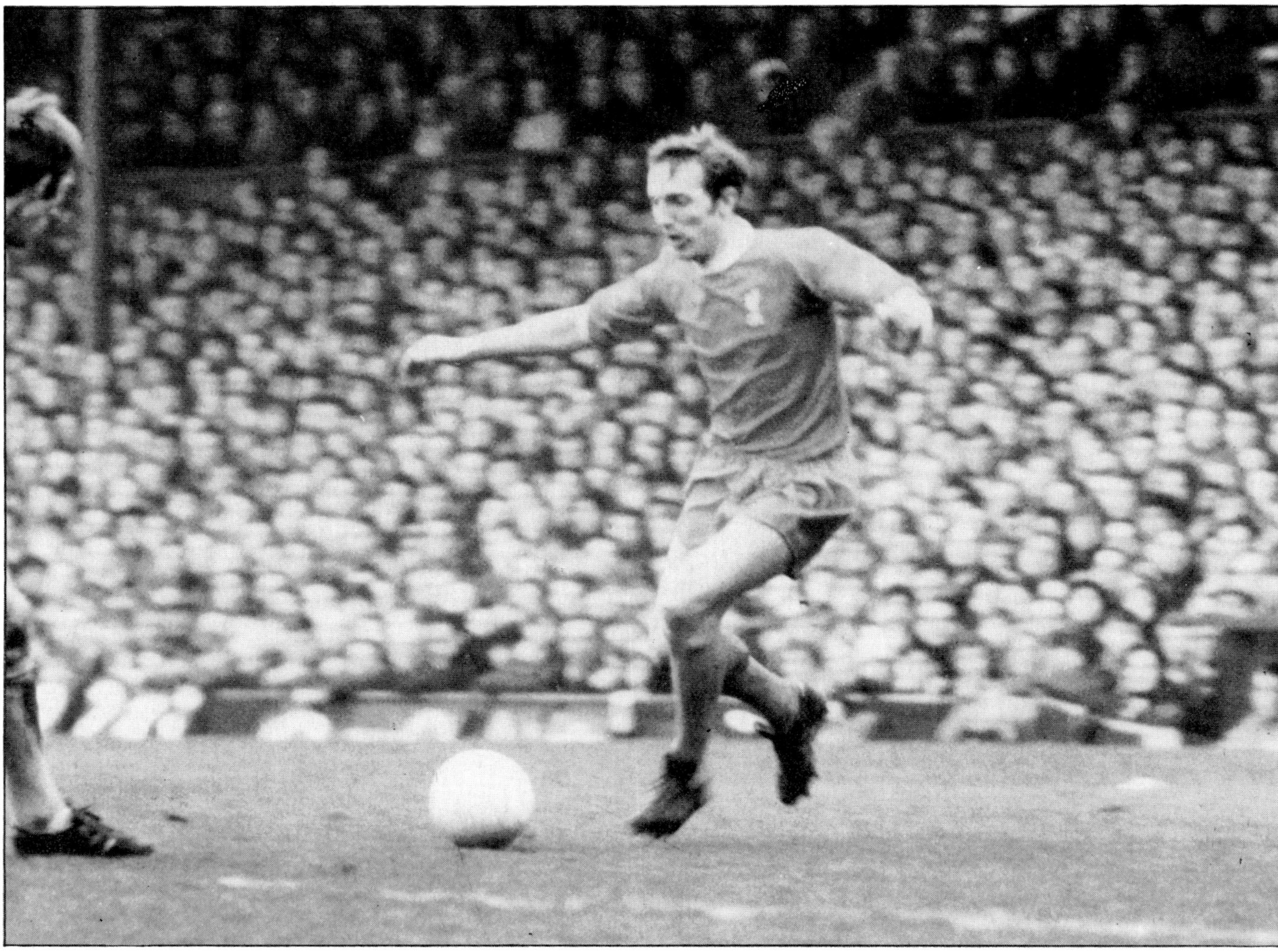

Peter Thompson was hailed as 'the new Tom Finney' when he emerged with Preston North End. Liverpool paid £37,000 for his signature in August 1963 and Thompson, a flying left winger, went on to make 412 senior appearances, scoring 54 goals, before being transferred to Bolton Wanderers for £18,000 in January 1974. He was capped for England and won League Championship and FA Cup winners' medals with Liverpool as well as playing in a European Cup-winners' Cup Final.

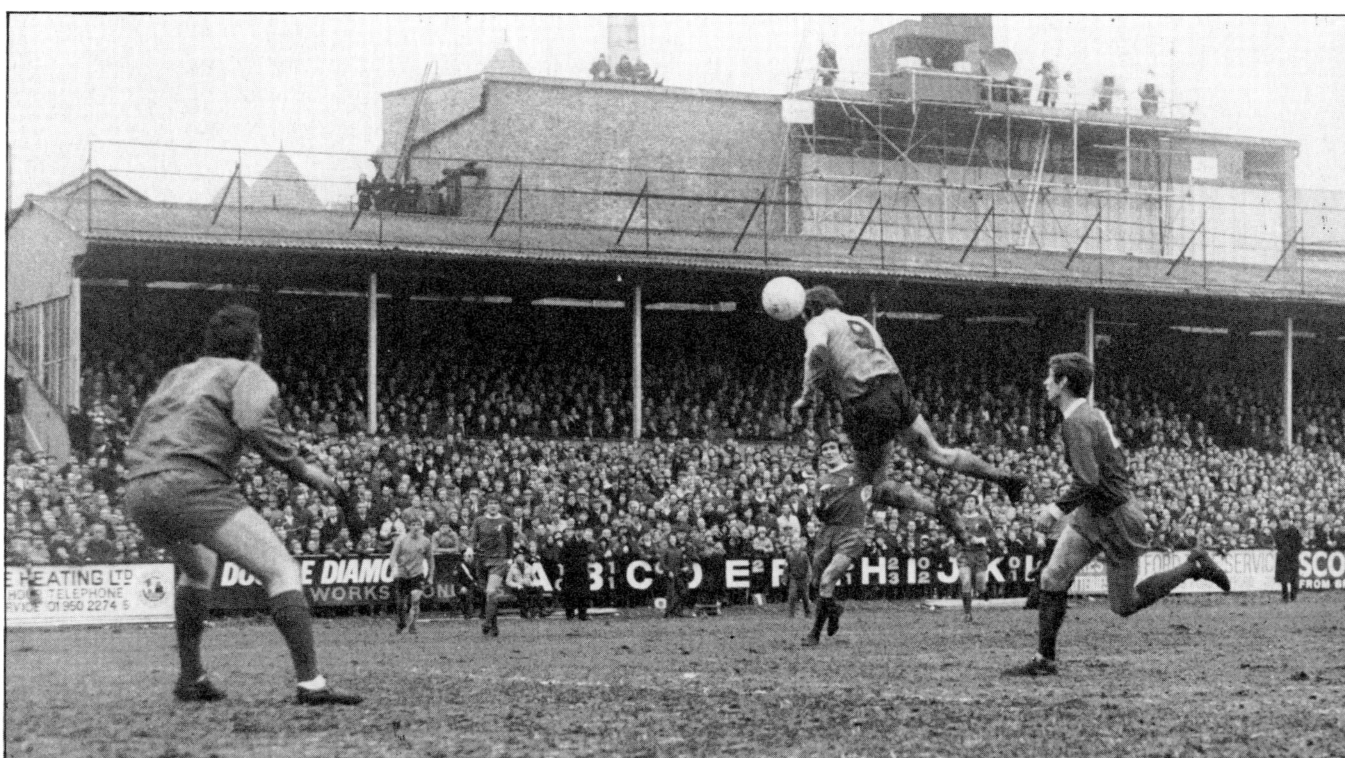

Liverpool ended the 1969-70 season in fifth place in Division One and were on the end of an FA Cup shock when they were beaten 1-0 in the quarter-final by Watford, from the lower reaches of the Second Division. This photograph shows Watford centre-forward Barry Endean scoring the only goal of the game at Vicarage Road with a header past Tommy Lawrence.

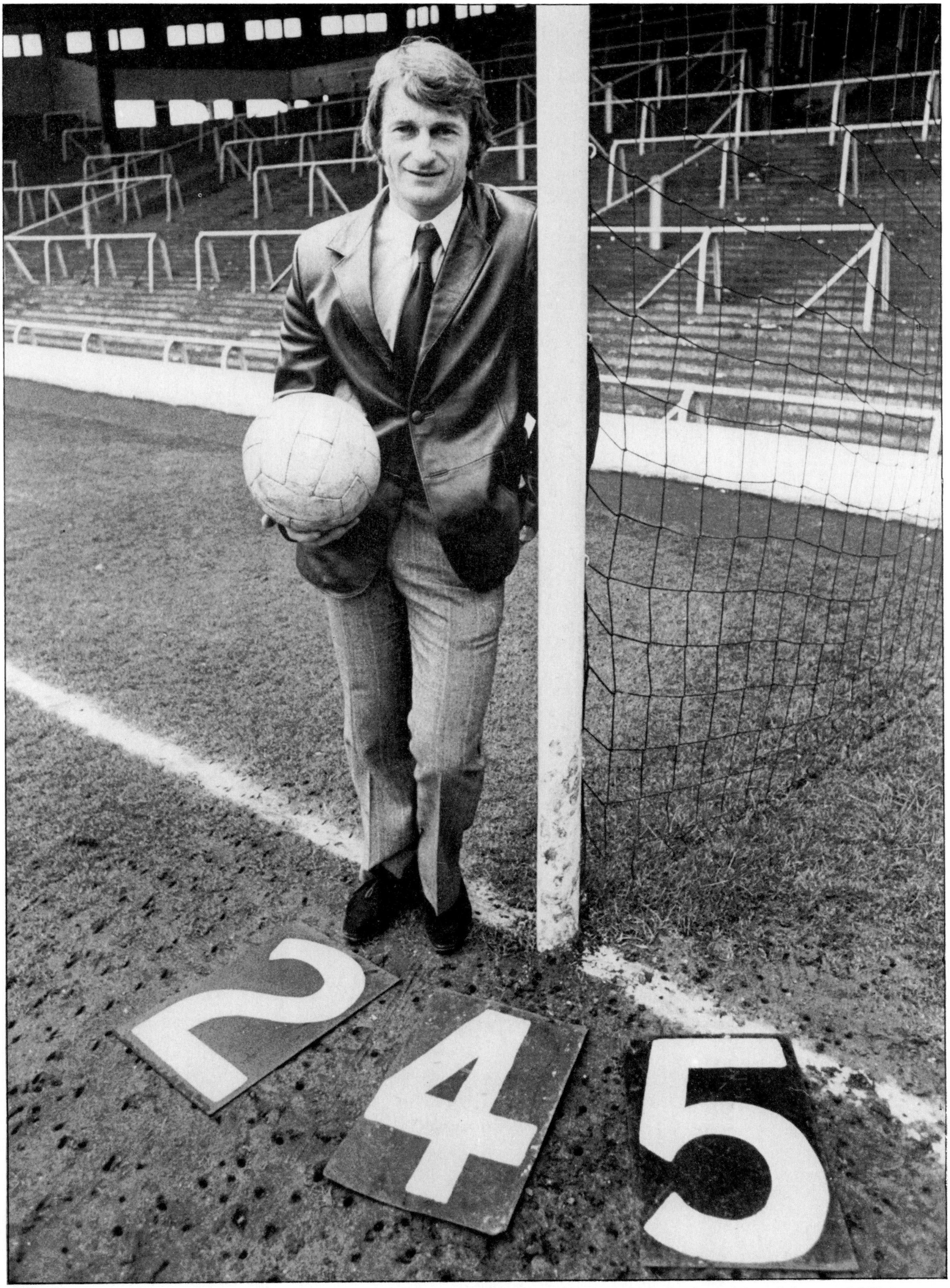

By the time he signed for Bolton Wanderers for £31,000 in December 1969, Roger Hunt had scored a club record 245 League goals for Liverpool. Hunt, who had joined Liverpool as an amateur in 1958, altogether scored 285 goals in 489 senior games for the Reds. He was a member of England's 1966 World Cup winning team. With the Reds he won First and Second Division championship and FA Cup winners' medals and played in a European Cup-winners' Cup Final.

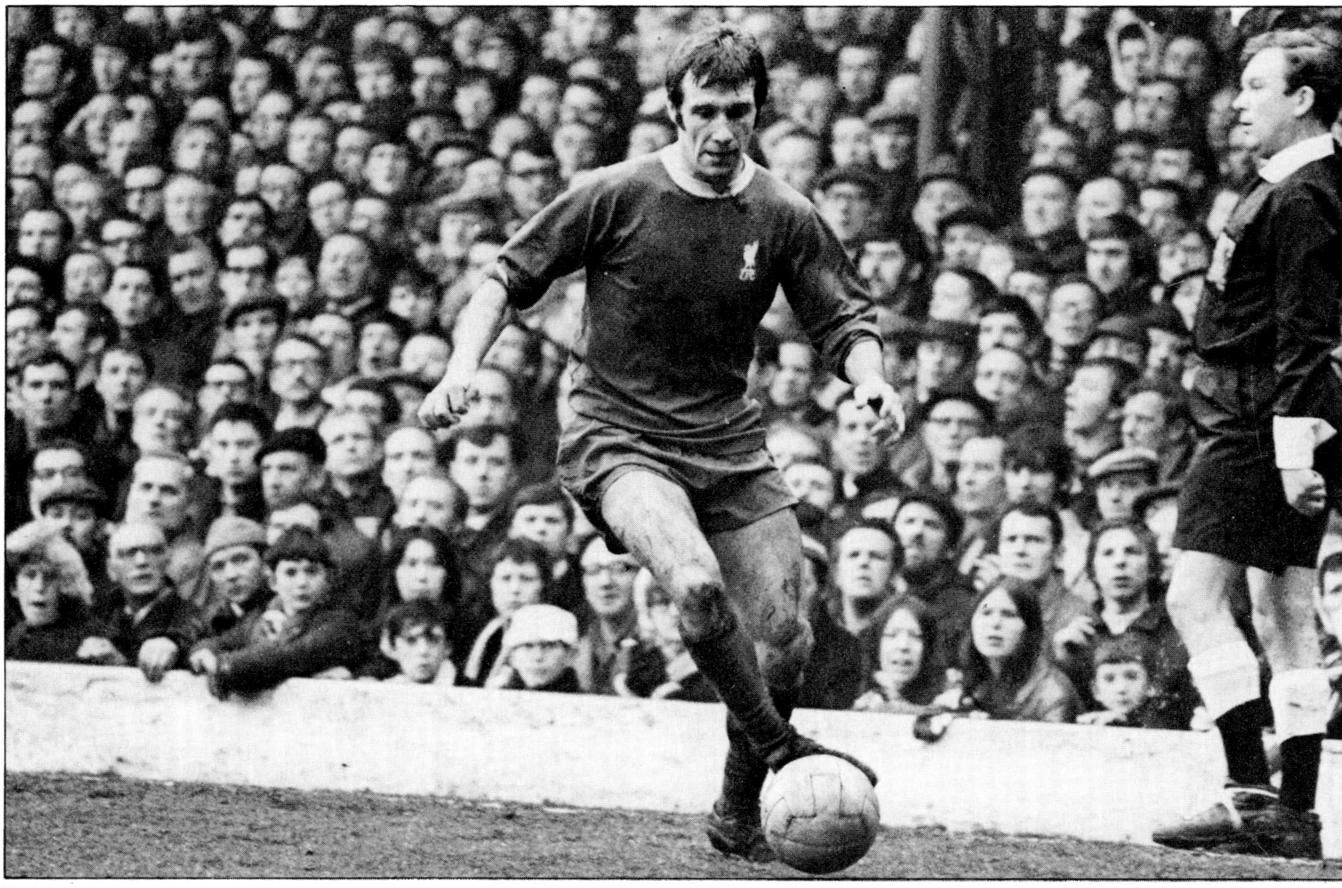

Bobby Graham, scorer of 42 goals in 131 senior appearances for Liverpool, joined the club from local schools football in 1960. A utility forward, who played mostly at centre-forward, had a chequered career at Anfield, over half his appearances coming in a 12-month spell from April 1969. He certainly had an impressive debut, though, scoring a hat-trick against Aston Villa in September 1964. Coventry City paid £70,000 for his services in March 1972.

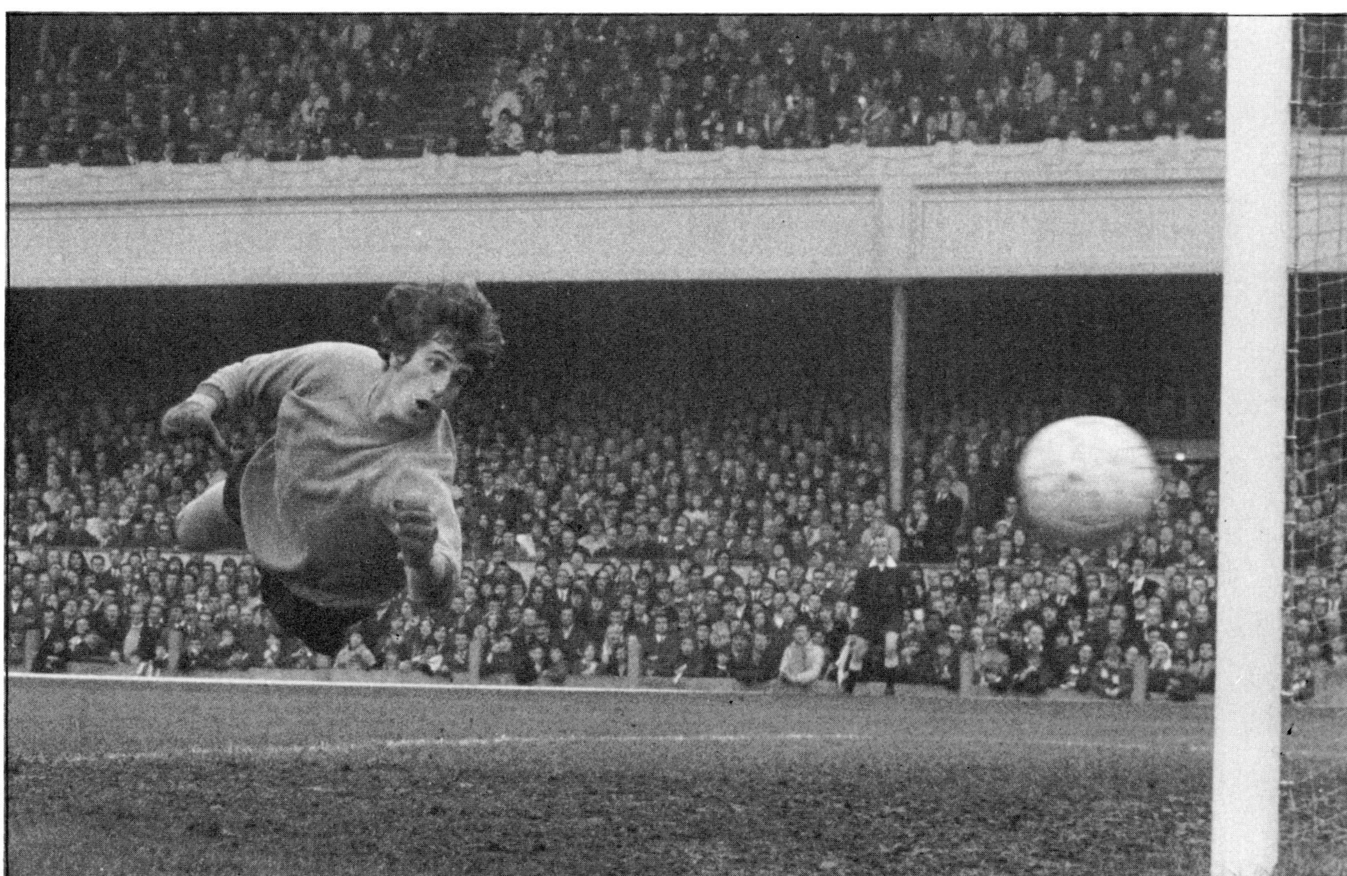

Ray Clemence is well beaten but the ball goes wide during an Arsenal attack at Highbury in November 1970. The Gunners won 2-0.

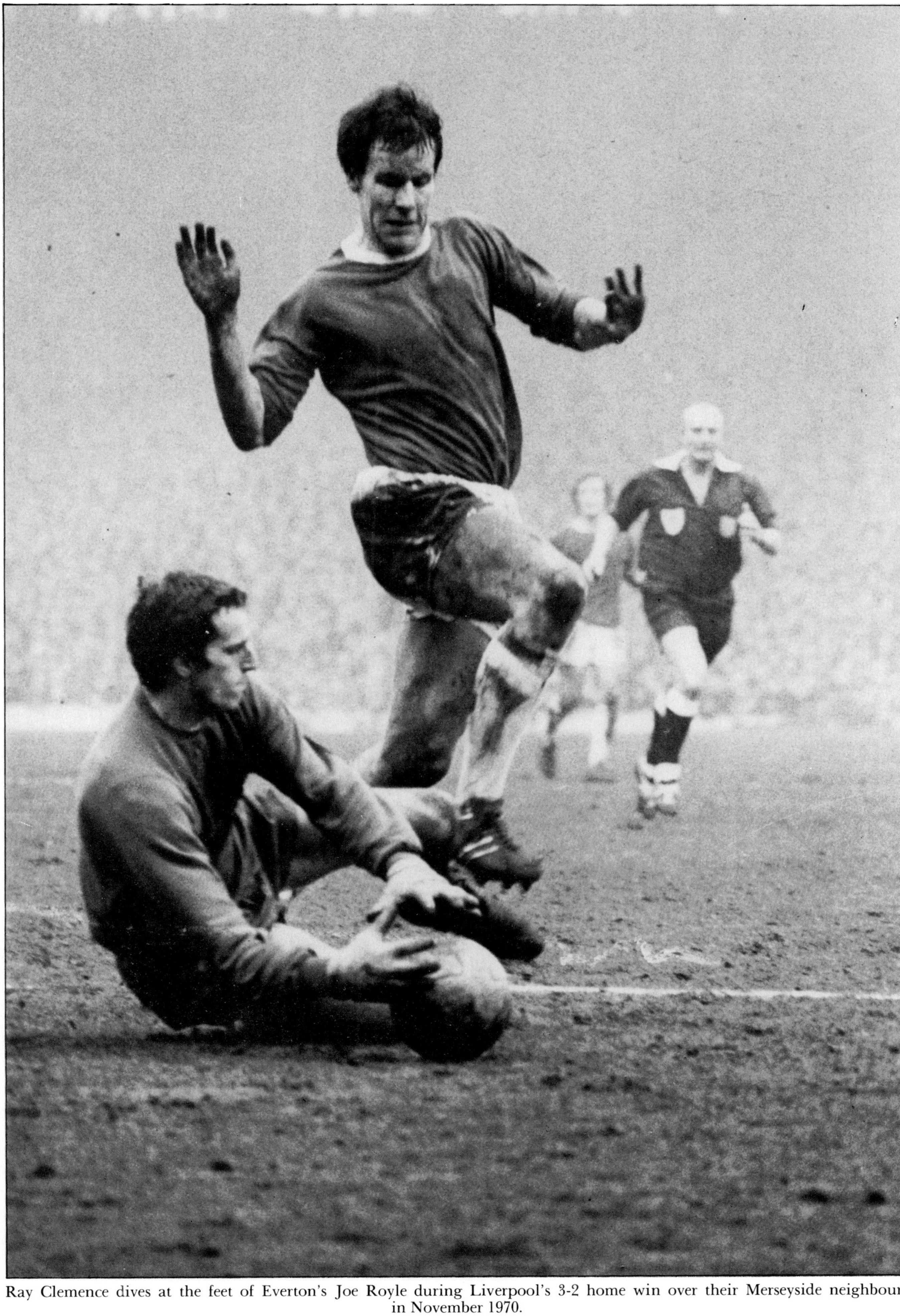

Ray Clemence dives at the feet of Everton's Joe Royle during Liverpool's 3-2 home win over their Merseyside neighbours in November 1970.

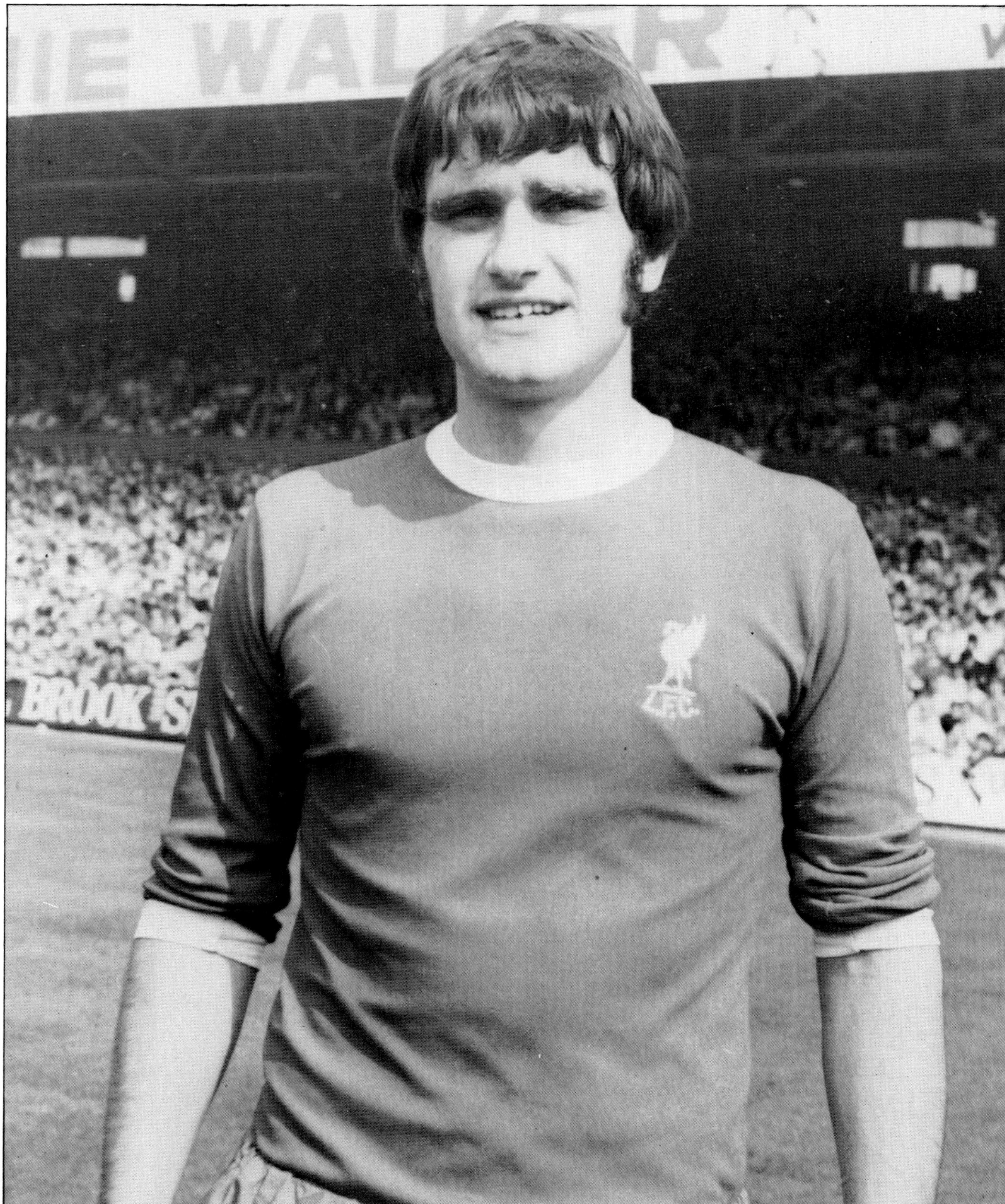

Centre-half Larry Lloyd joined the Reds from Bristol Rovers in April 1969 for £50,000. He was the sheet anchor of a miserly Liverpool defence and won England honours in his time at Anfield, as well as gaining a League Championship medal and a UEFA Cup winners' medal and playing in the 1966 European Cup-winners' Cup Final. He moved to Coventry City for £225,000 in August 1974 and later won European Cup, League Championship and FA Cup winners' medals under Brian Clough at Nottingham Forest. For Liverpool he made 217 senior appearances.

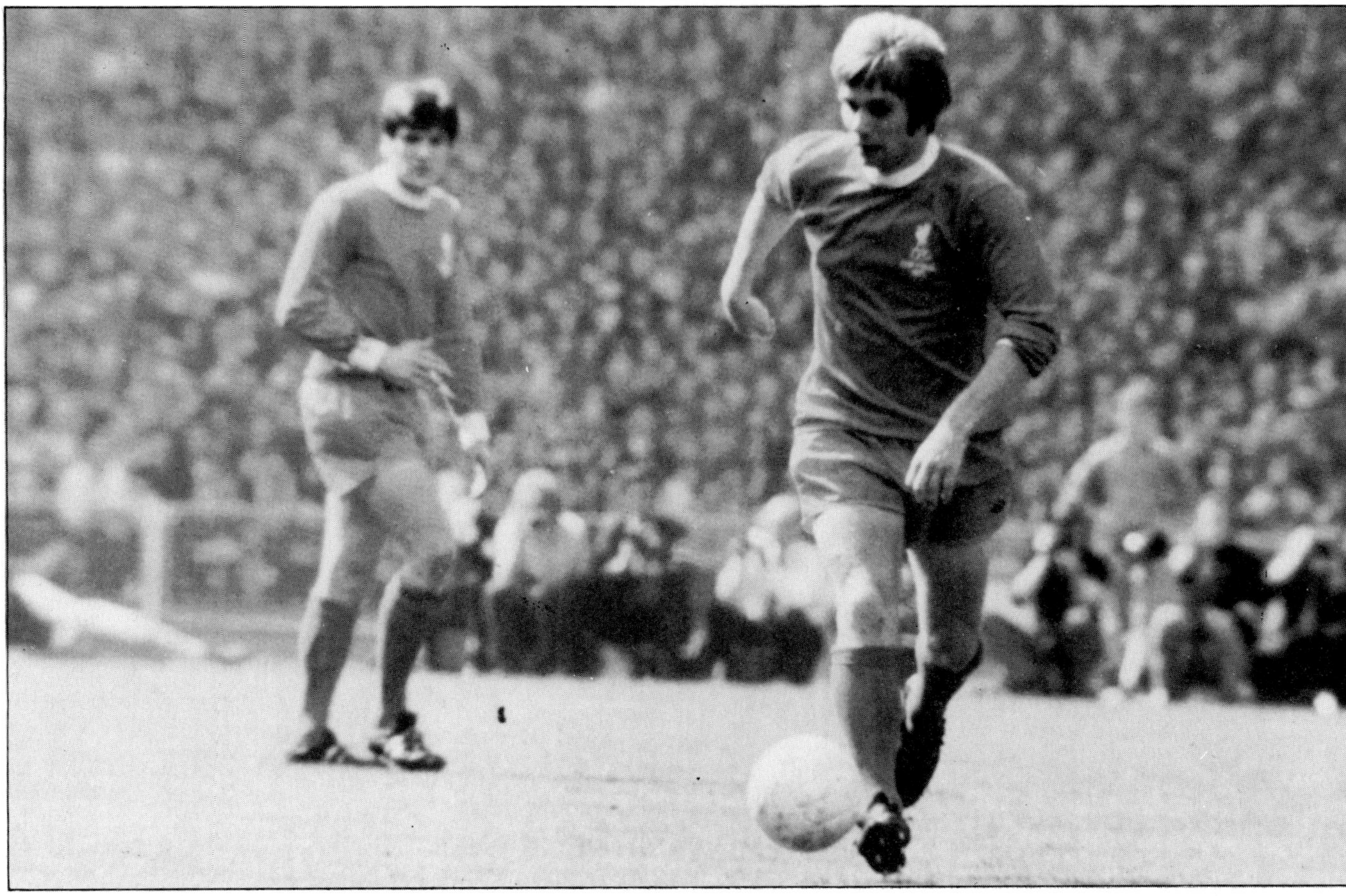

Alun Evans was the most expensive teenage footballer in Britain when Liverpool paid £100,000 to sign him from Wolves in September 1968. But his Anfield days were marred by a night-club incident, which left him facially scarred, and by a knee operation, and he moved to Aston Villa for £70,000 in June 1972. An England Under-23 international forward, his only honour with the Reds was an FA Cup runners-up medal in 1971. In all he made 110 senior appearances for Liverpool scoring 33 goals.

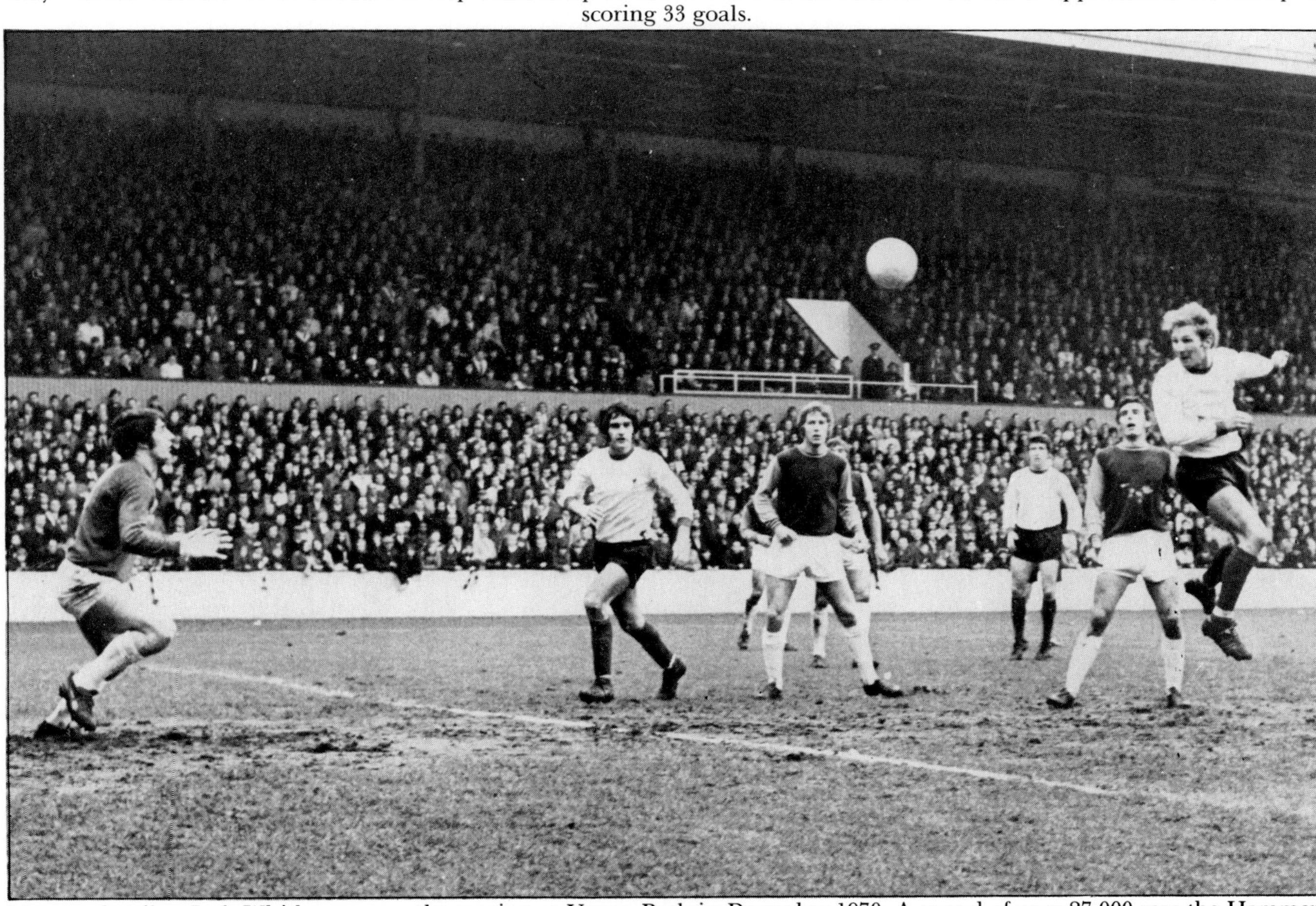

Liverpool striker Jack Whitham opens the scoring at Upton Park in December 1970. A crowd of over 27,000 saw the Hammers beaten 2-1.

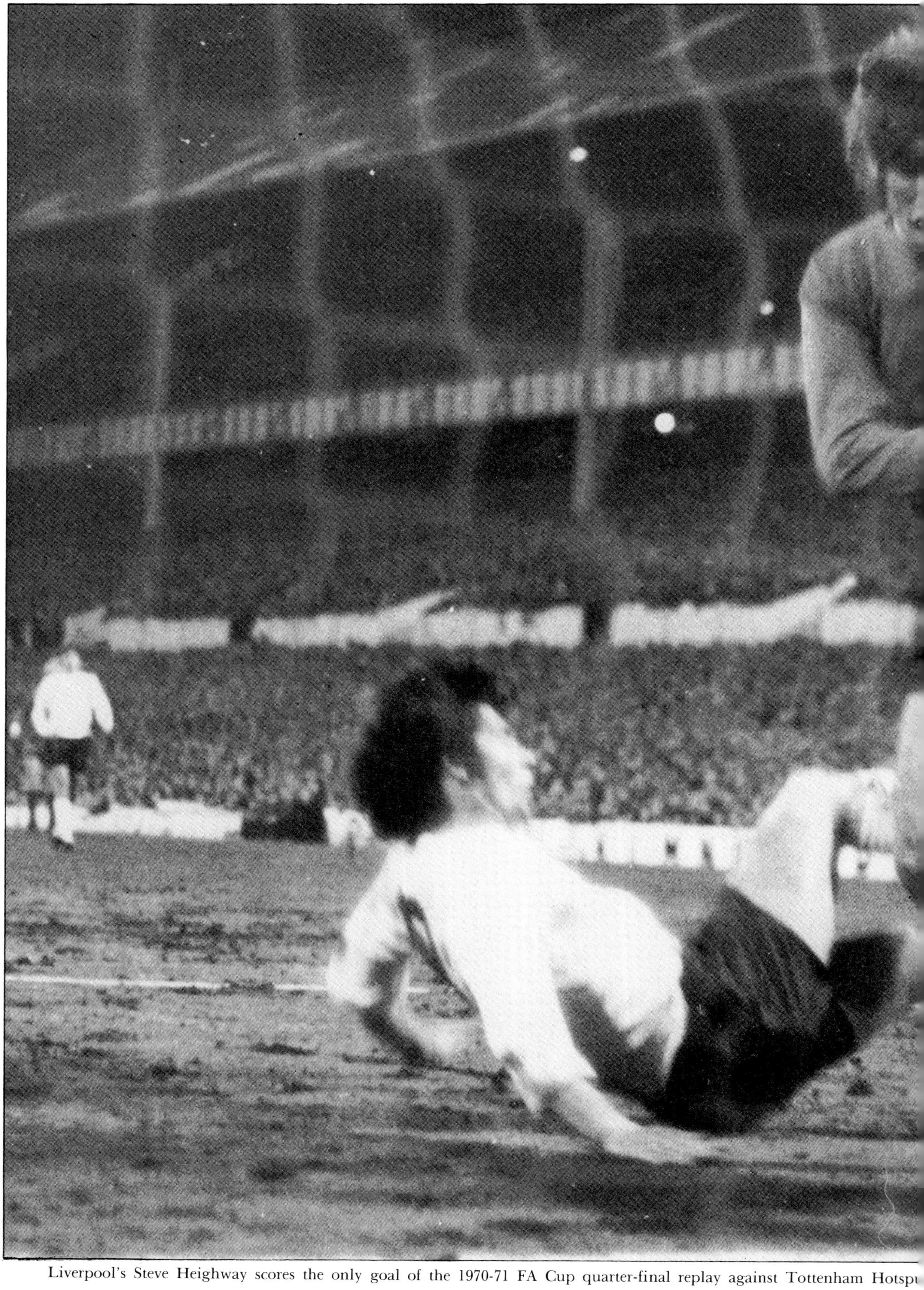

Liverpool's Steve Heighway scores the only goal of the 1970-71 FA Cup quarter-final replay against Tottenham Hotspu

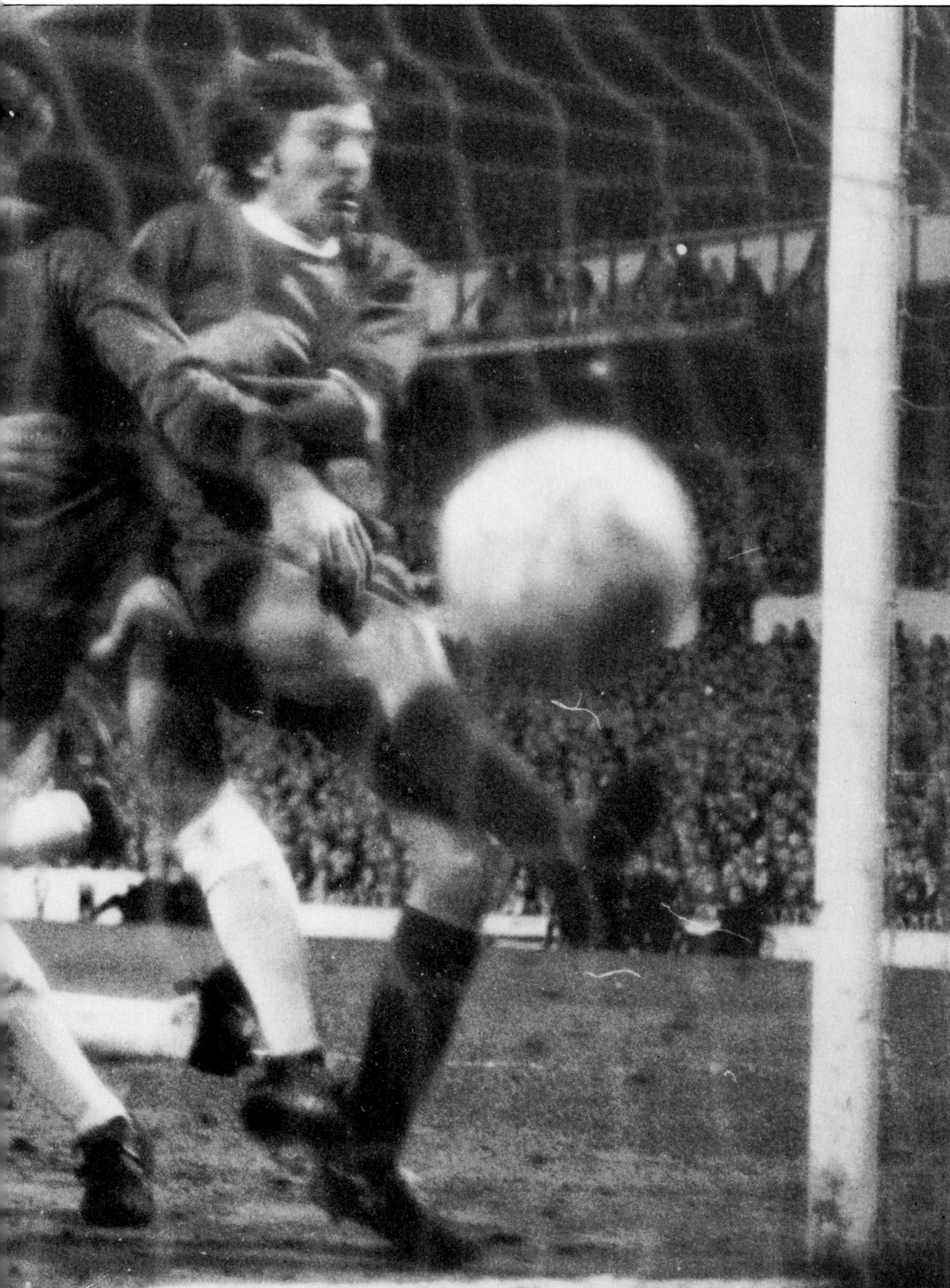

White Hart Lane. The Reds went through to meet Merseyside rivals Everton in the penultimate stage of the competition.

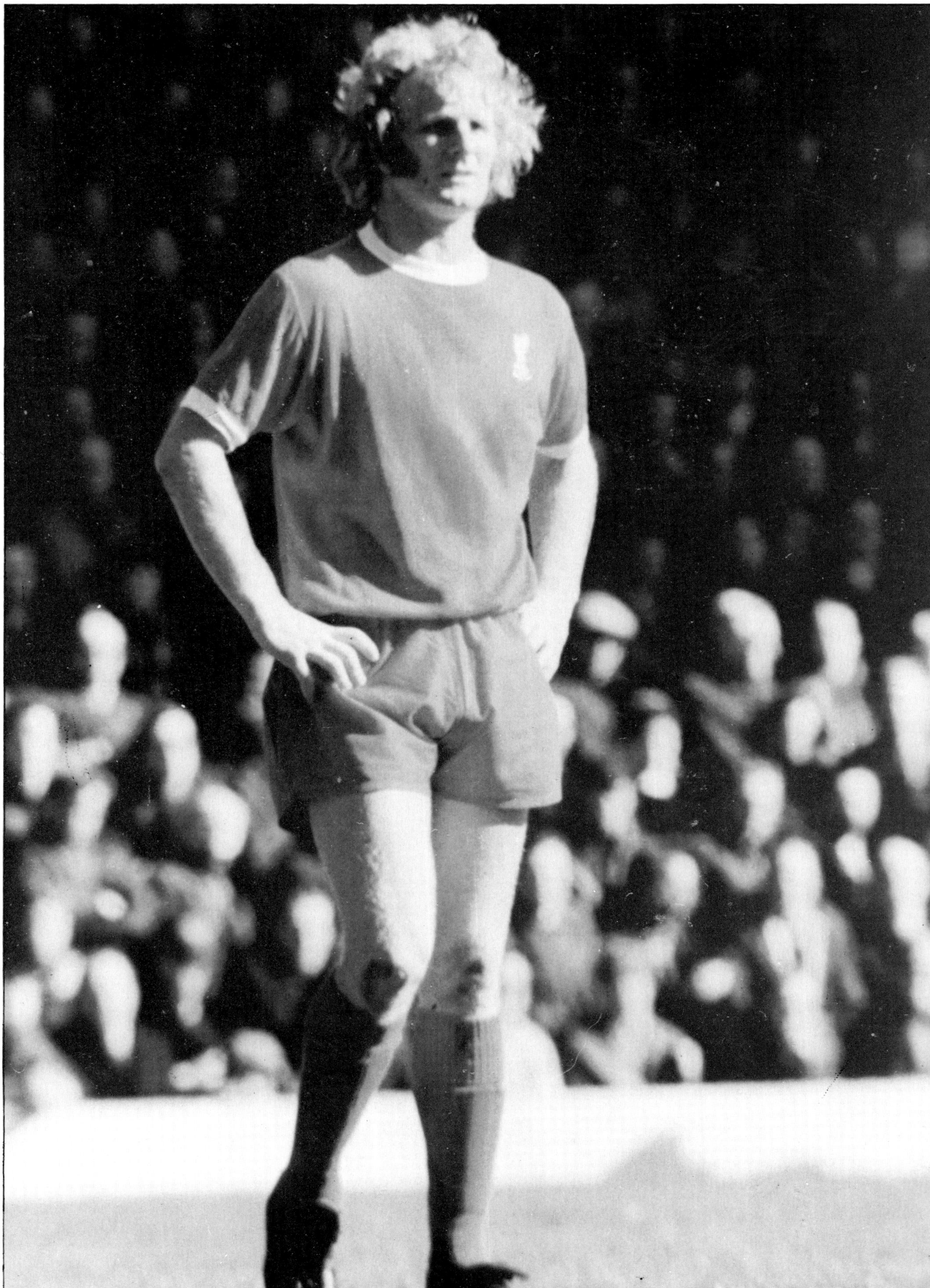

Left-back Alec Lindsay was signed from Bury for £67,000 in March 1969 and made 246 senior appearances before being transferred to Stoke City in 1977 for £20,000. He played for England and gained UEFA Cup, League Championship and FA Cup winners' medals at Anfield.

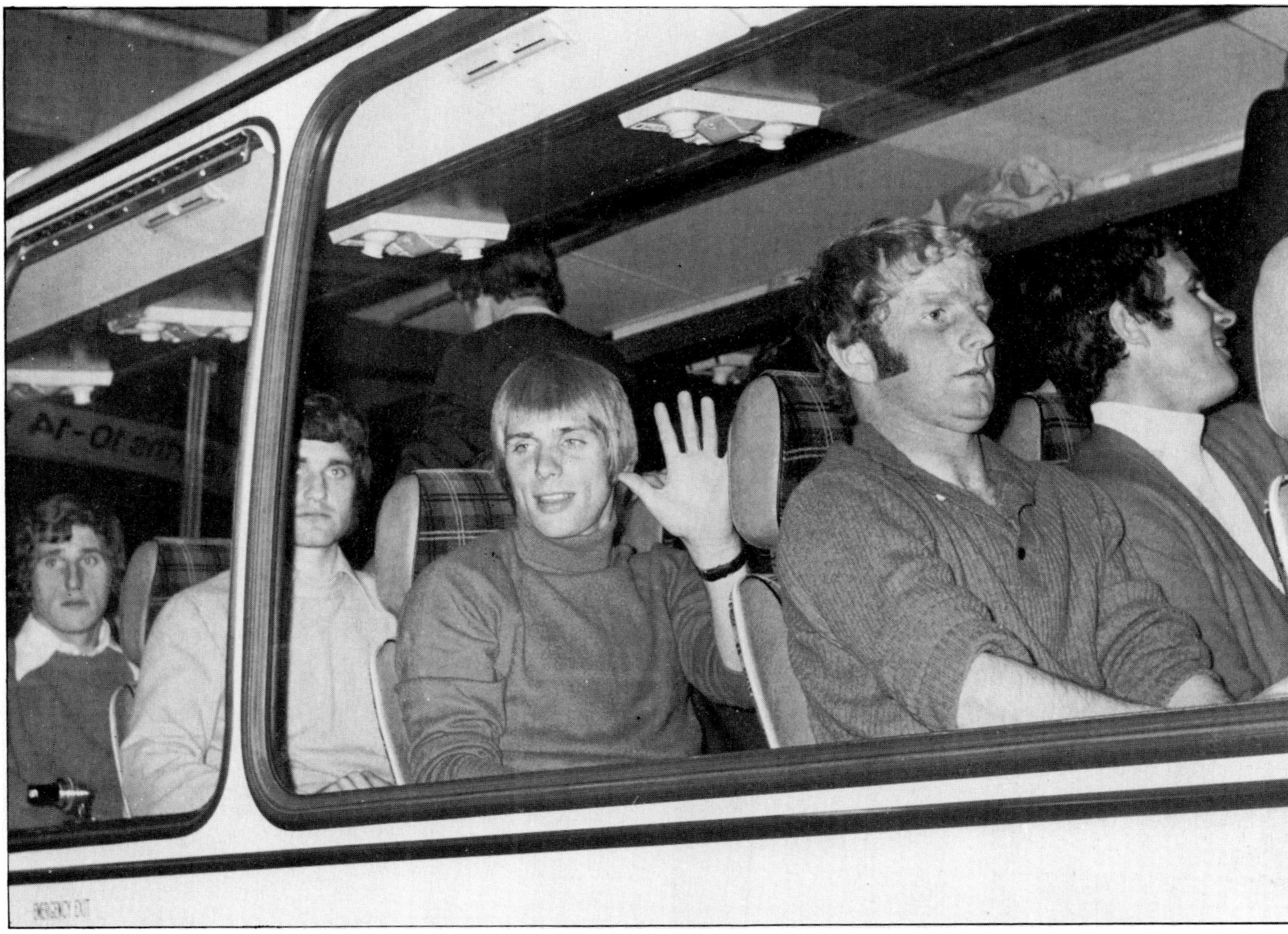

Liverpool players arrive in London for the 1971 FA Cup Final against Arsenal. Alun Evans gives the crowd a wave, but Alec Lindsay appears to be in pensive mood.

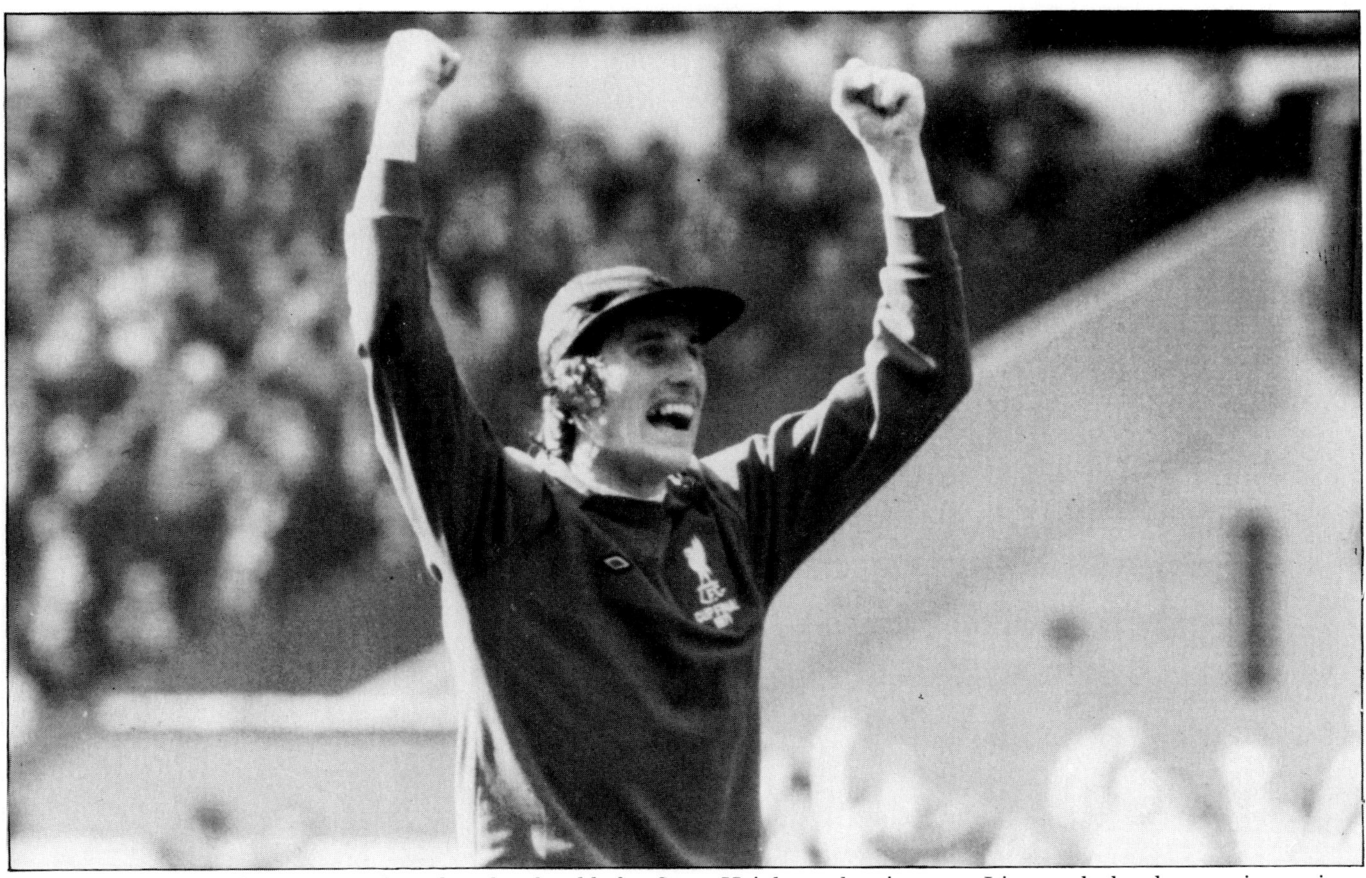

Ray Clemence looks happy enough and so he should, for Steve Heighway has just put Liverpool ahead two minutes into extra-time in the 1971 FA Cup Final. But the Merseysiders' day was to be spoiled.

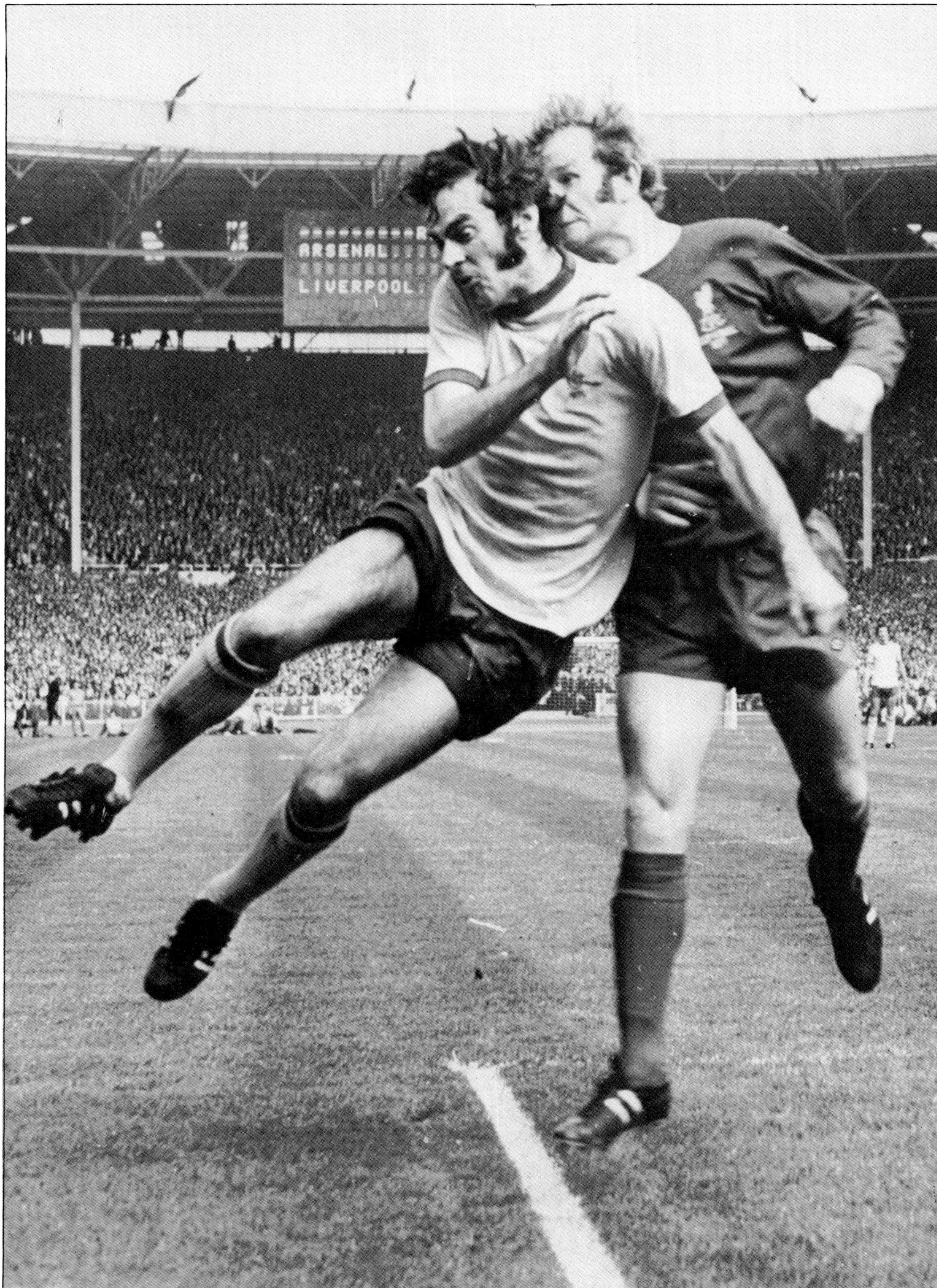

Alec Lindsay clashes with Arsenal's Peter Storey at Wembley in May 1971.

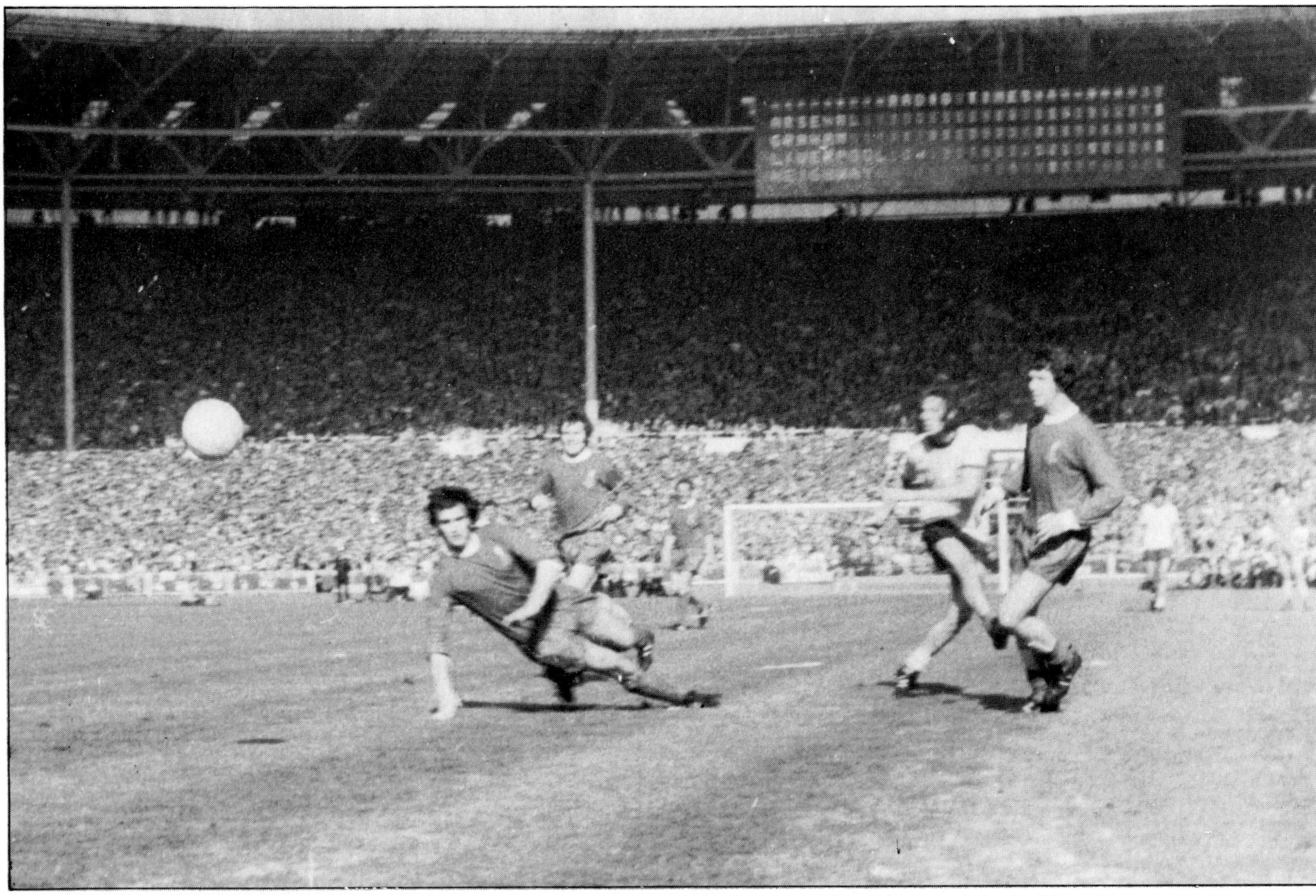

Charlie George scores the winning goal for Arsenal in extra-time in the 1971 FA Cup Final. The Gunners' victory over Liverpool gave them the League and Cup double, a feat not repeated until Liverpool themselves won the title and the premier knock-out trophy in 1986.

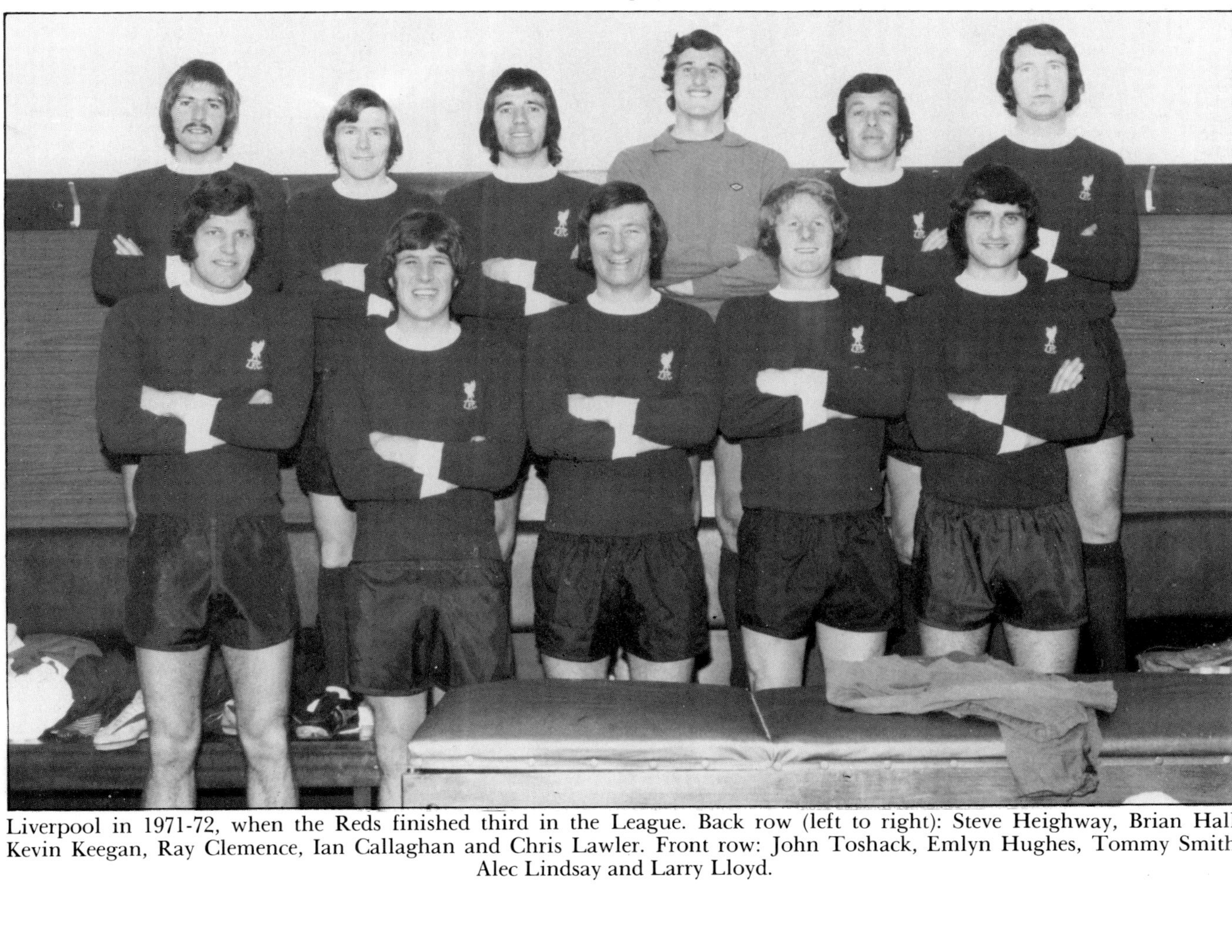

Liverpool in 1971-72, when the Reds finished third in the League. Back row (left to right): Steve Heighway, Brian Hall, Kevin Keegan, Ray Clemence, Ian Callaghan and Chris Lawler. Front row: John Toshack, Emlyn Hughes, Tommy Smith, Alec Lindsay and Larry Lloyd.

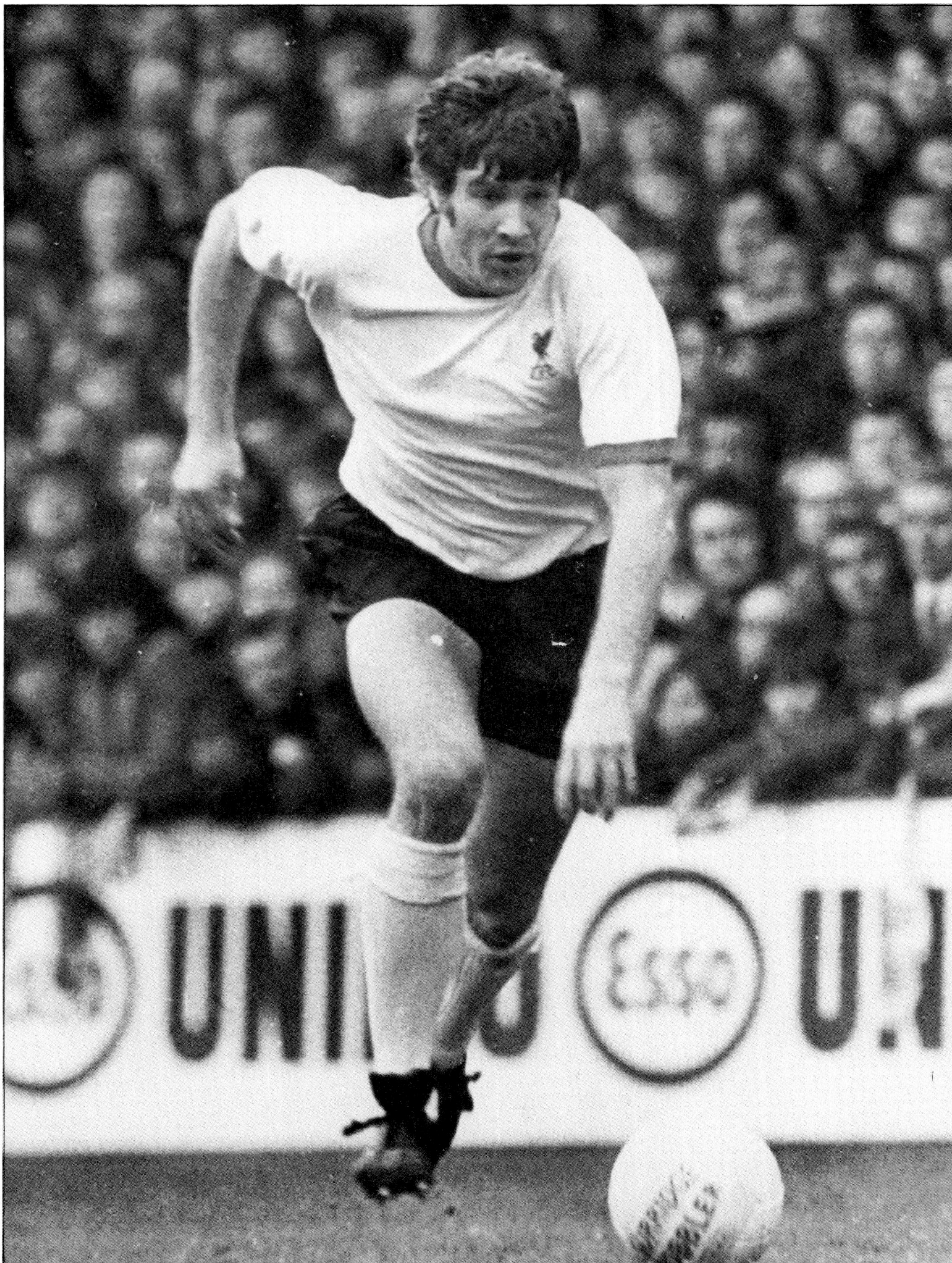

Emlyn Hughes — 'Crazy Horse' to the Liverpool fans — was one of the truly great names in the Reds' glory days of the 1970s. He signed from Blackpool in February 1967 for £65,000 and went on to skipper Liverpool as a powerful midfielder who also scored some spectacular goals. Hughes made 657 senior appearances, hitting 48 goals, before a £90,000 move to Wolves in August 1979. At Anfield he gained 62 full England caps and a host of winners' medals in the European Cup, UEFA Cup, League Championship and FA Cup. Hughes led Wolves to a League Cup victory in 1980 before becoming player-manager of Rotherham United. In recent times he has been a familar face as a television personality.

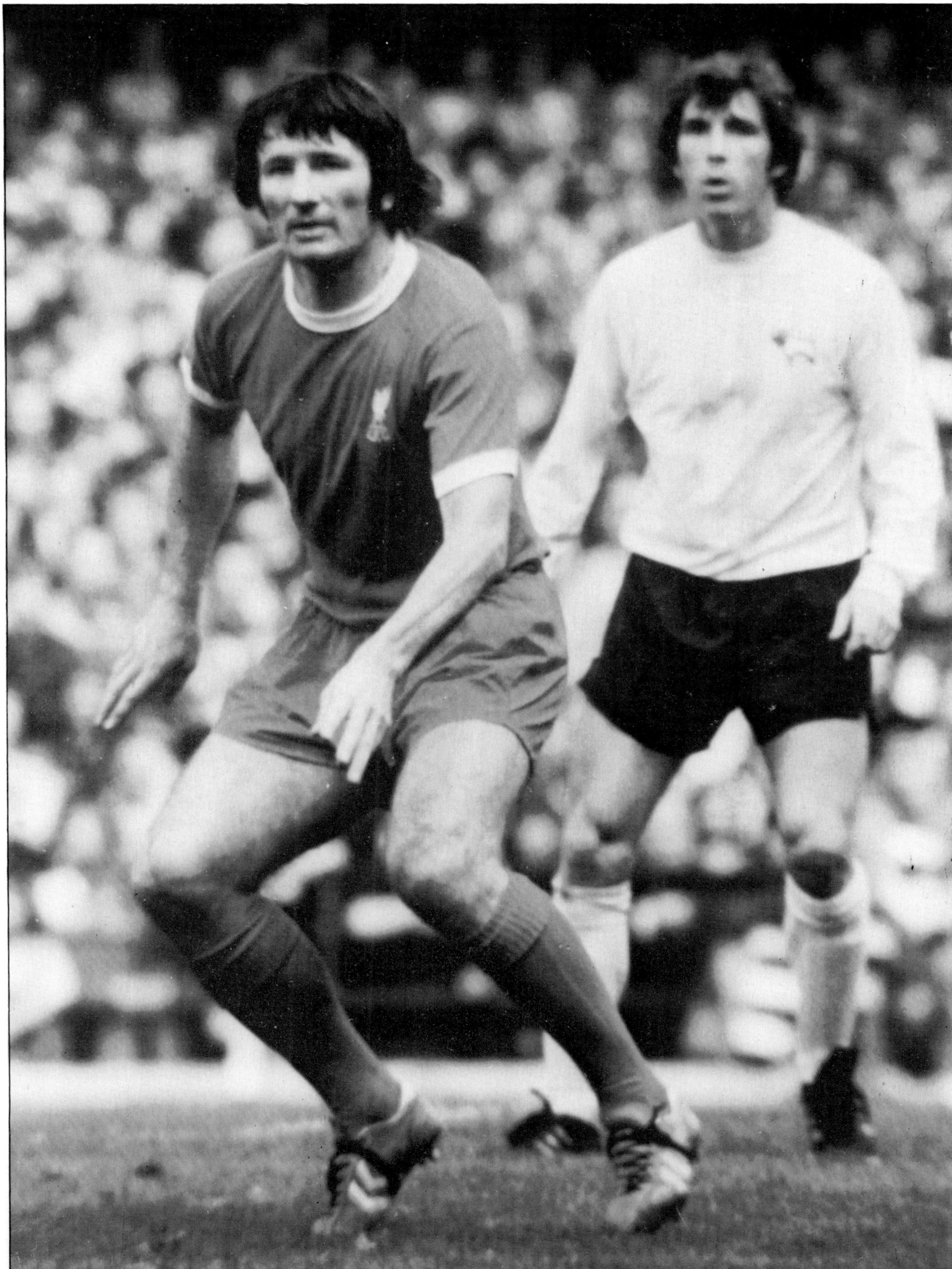

Tommy Smith was born in Liverpool and joined the Anfield groundstaff in May 1960 before signing full-time professional forms two years later. Smith is best remembered as a tough-tackling wing-half but he was also a fine footballer who began his career at inside-forward before moving to midfield and then defence. He won European, League and FA Cup honours with Liverpool as well as England caps. Smith appeared in 633 senior games for the Reds, scoring 48 goals. He moved to Swansea City in August 1978 before returning to Liverpool to coach the young players for a spell.

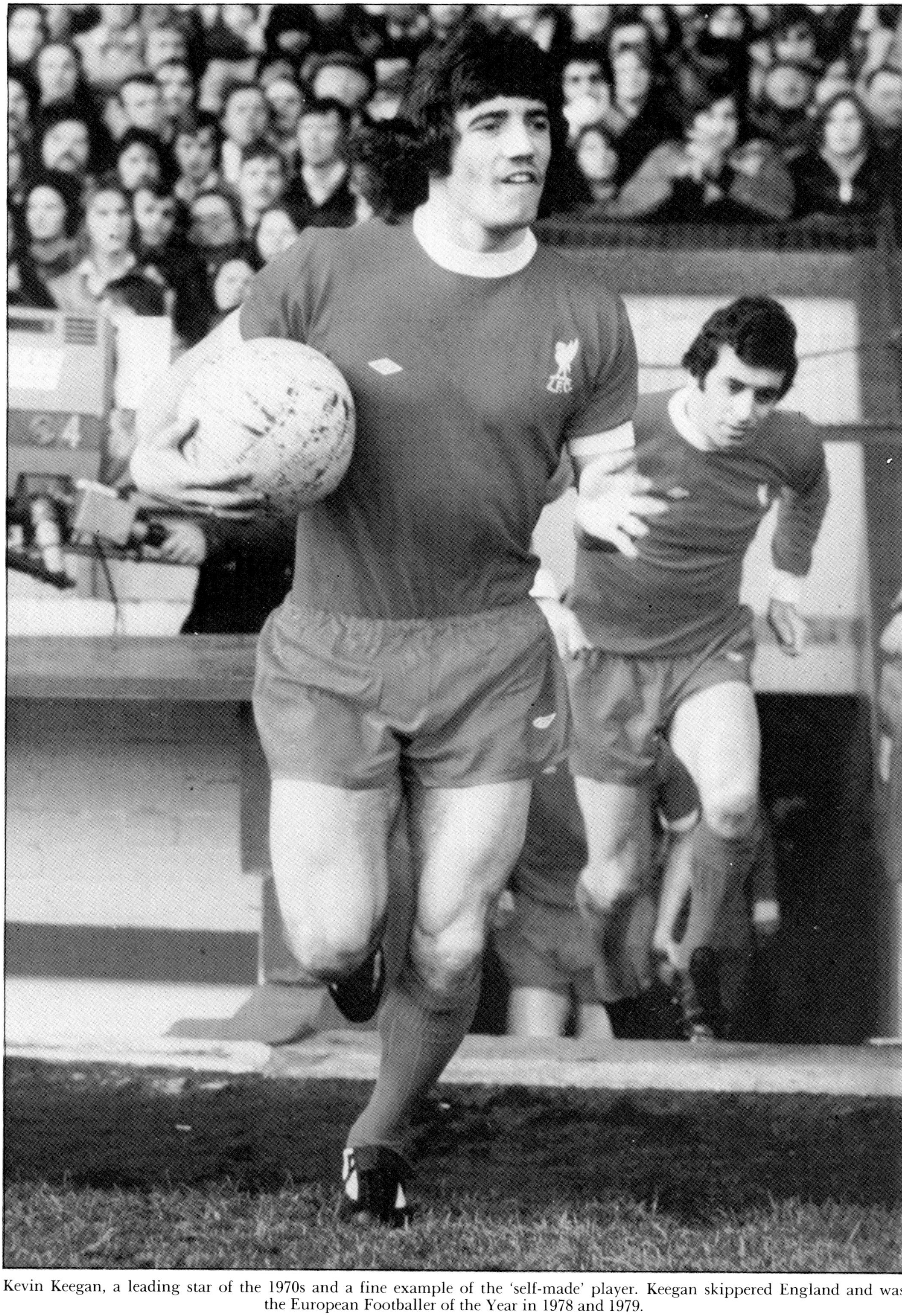

Kevin Keegan, a leading star of the 1970s and a fine example of the 'self-made' player. Keegan skippered England and was the European Footballer of the Year in 1978 and 1979.

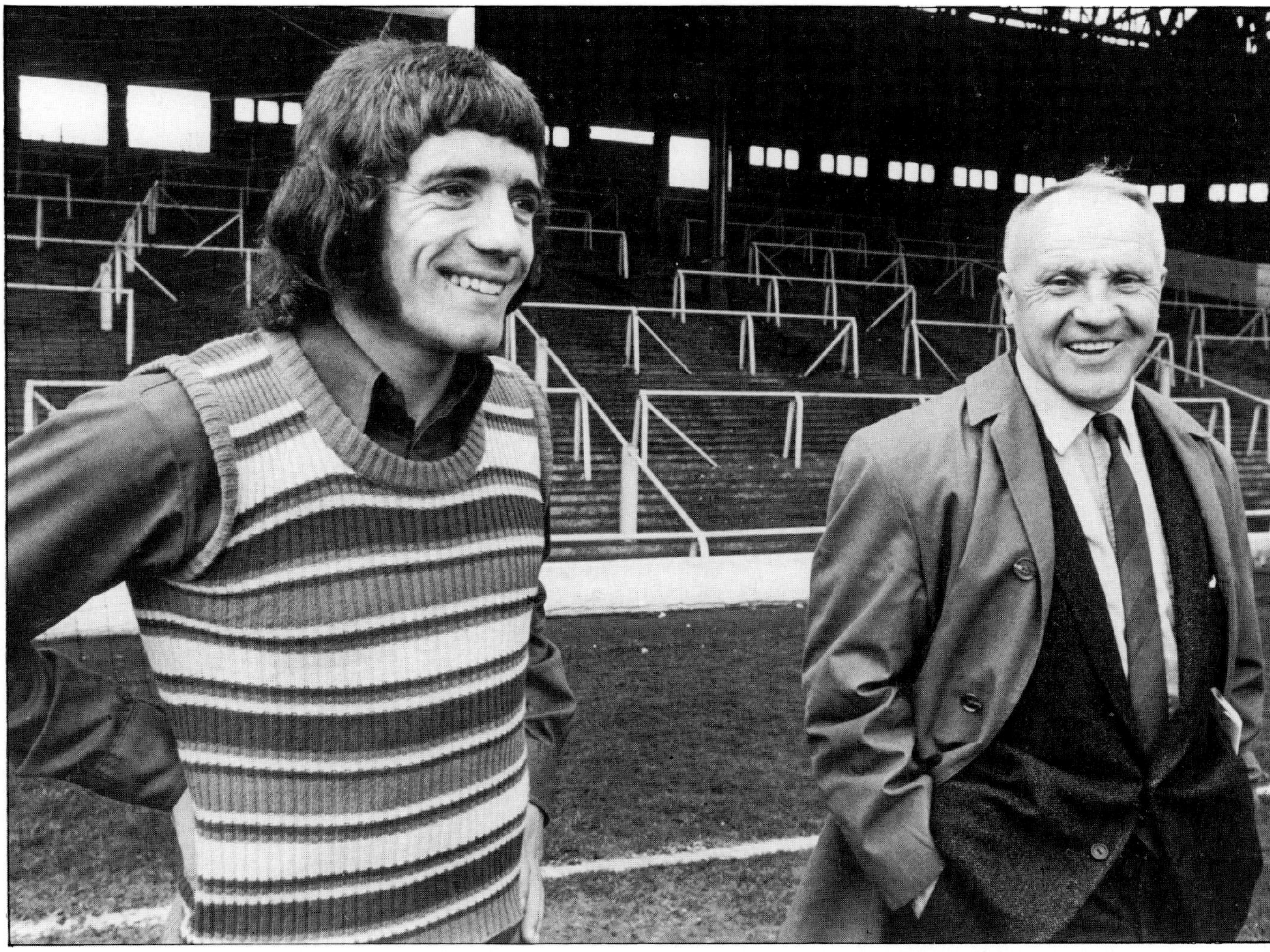

In May 1971, Bill Shankly made one of his shrewdest signings for Liverpool when he bought a young striker called Kevin Keegan from Scunthorpe United for £33,000. Keegan went on to become one of the greatest names in Liverpool's history, scoring 100 goals in 321 games as well as gaining England honours and sharing in the domestic and European glories under Shankly. Our picture shows Keegan and Shankly in the goalmouth at Anfield Road.

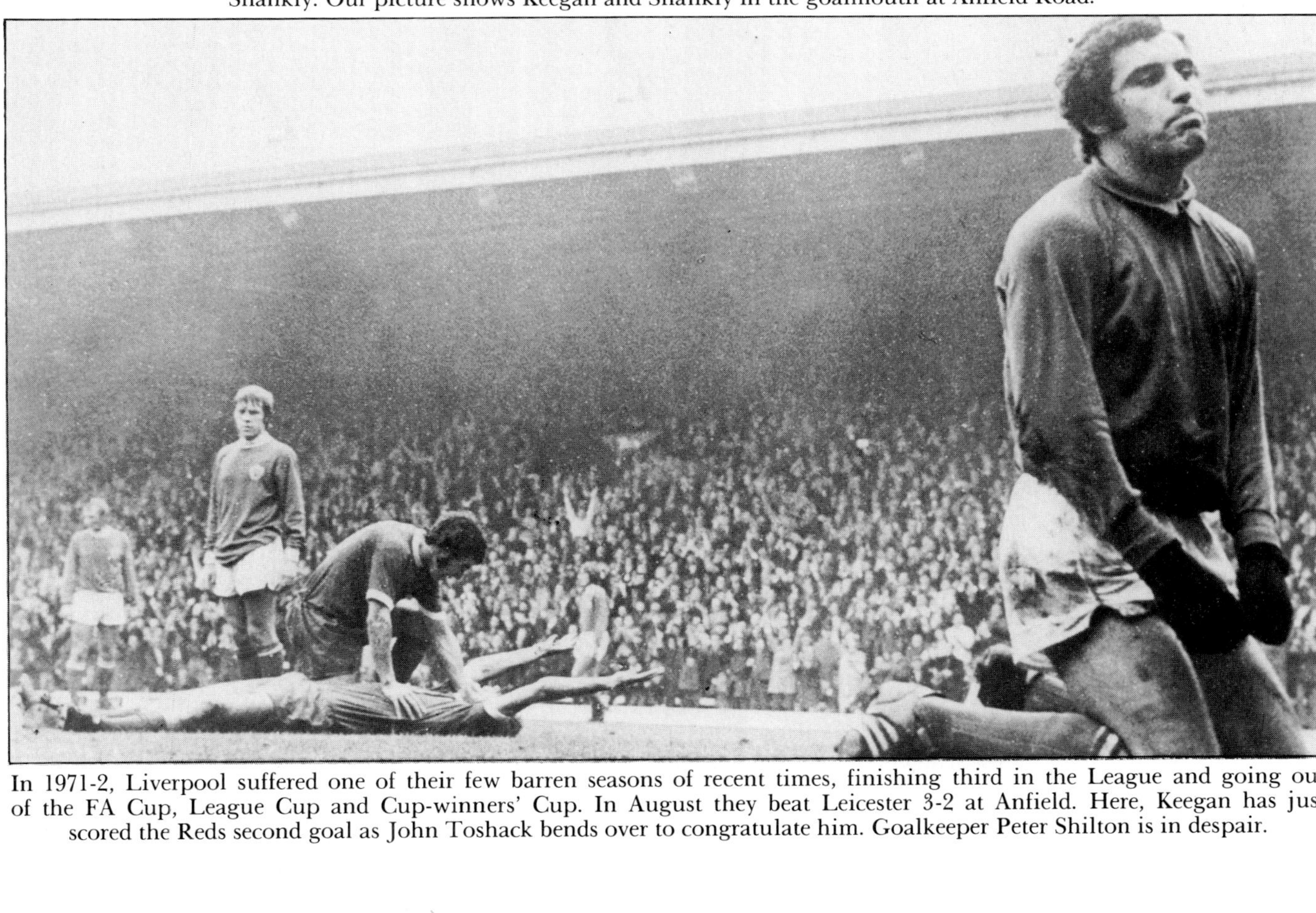

In 1971-2, Liverpool suffered one of their few barren seasons of recent times, finishing third in the League and going out of the FA Cup, League Cup and Cup-winners' Cup. In August they beat Leicester 3-2 at Anfield. Here, Keegan has just scored the Reds second goal as John Toshack bends over to congratulate him. Goalkeeper Peter Shilton is in despair.

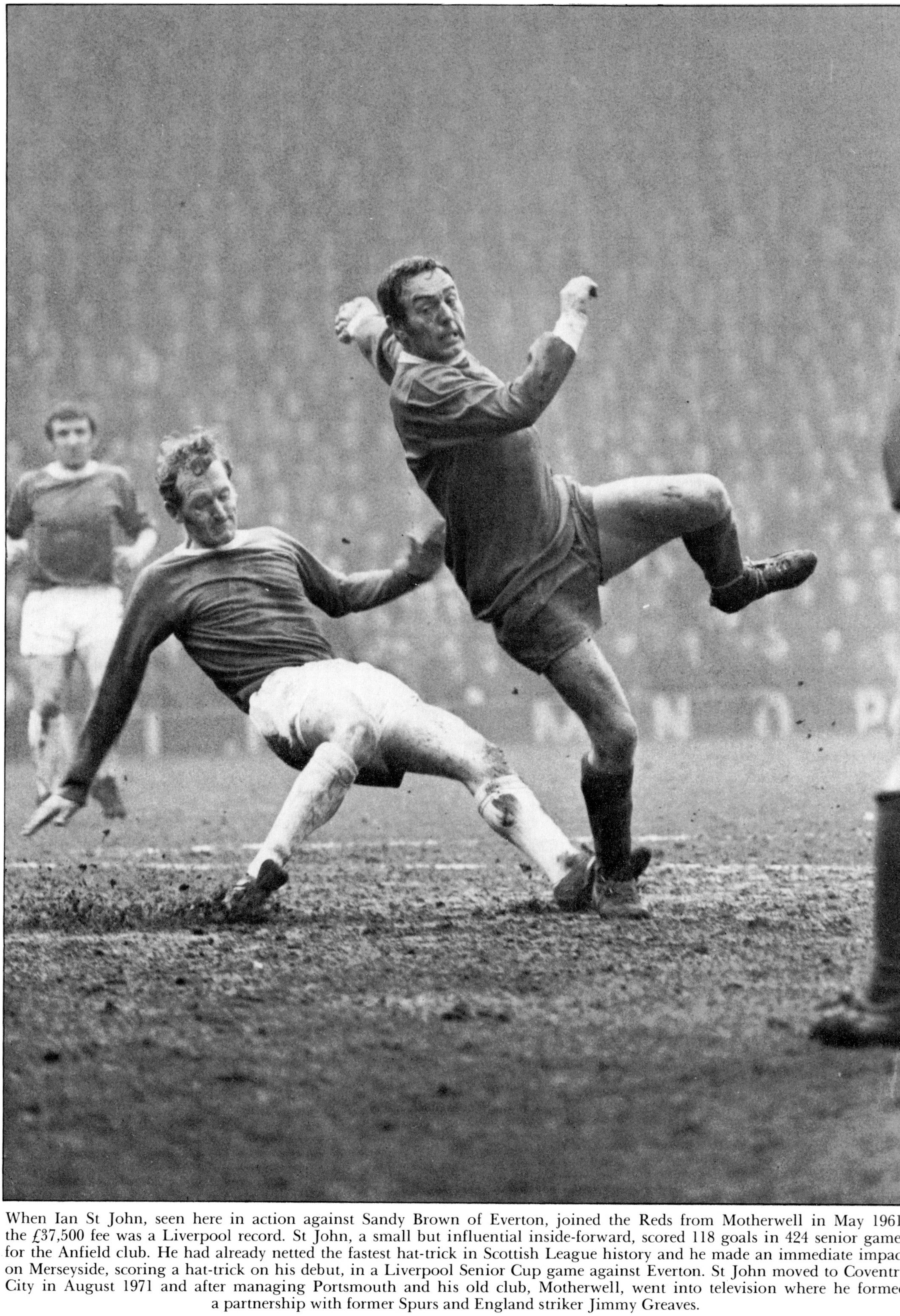

When Ian St John, seen here in action against Sandy Brown of Everton, joined the Reds from Motherwell in May 1961, the £37,500 fee was a Liverpool record. St John, a small but influential inside-forward, scored 118 goals in 424 senior games for the Anfield club. He had already netted the fastest hat-trick in Scottish League history and he made an immediate impact on Merseyside, scoring a hat-trick on his debut, in a Liverpool Senior Cup game against Everton. St John moved to Coventry City in August 1971 and after managing Portsmouth and his old club, Motherwell, went into television where he formed a partnership with former Spurs and England striker Jimmy Greaves.

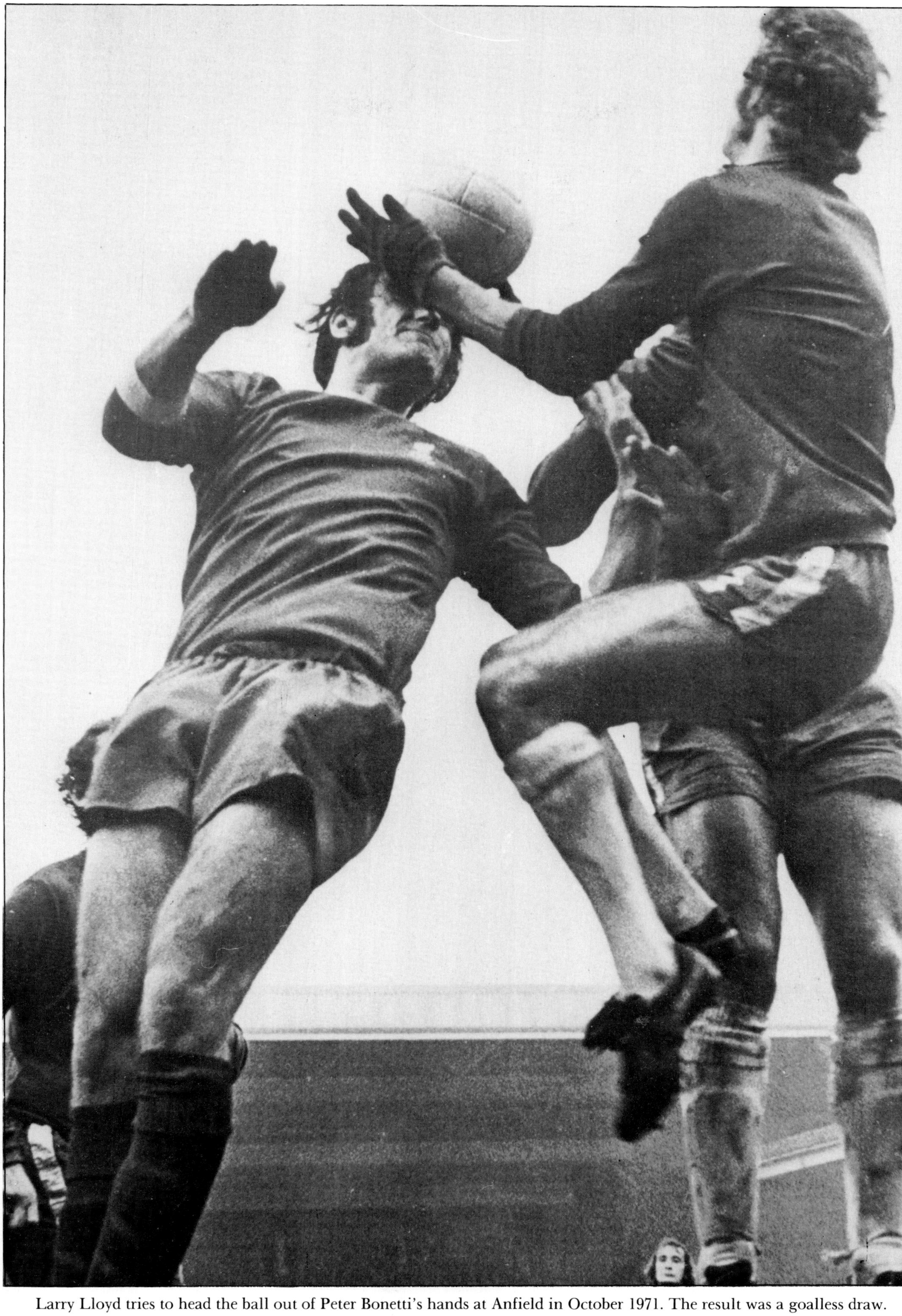

Larry Lloyd tries to head the ball out of Peter Bonetti's hands at Anfield in October 1971. The result was a goalless draw.

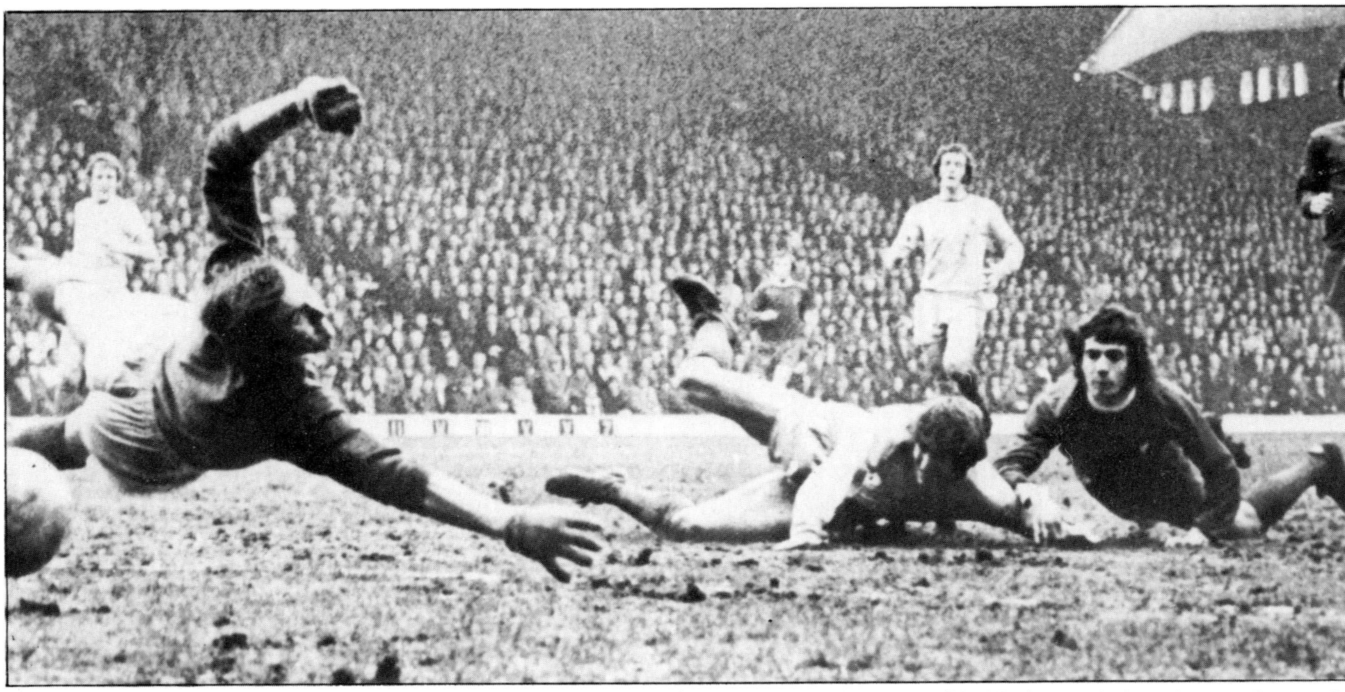

Kevin Keegan (right) looks to see his diving header beat the Coventry goalkeeper Bill Glazier to help Liverpool to a 3-1 win at Anfield in April 1972.

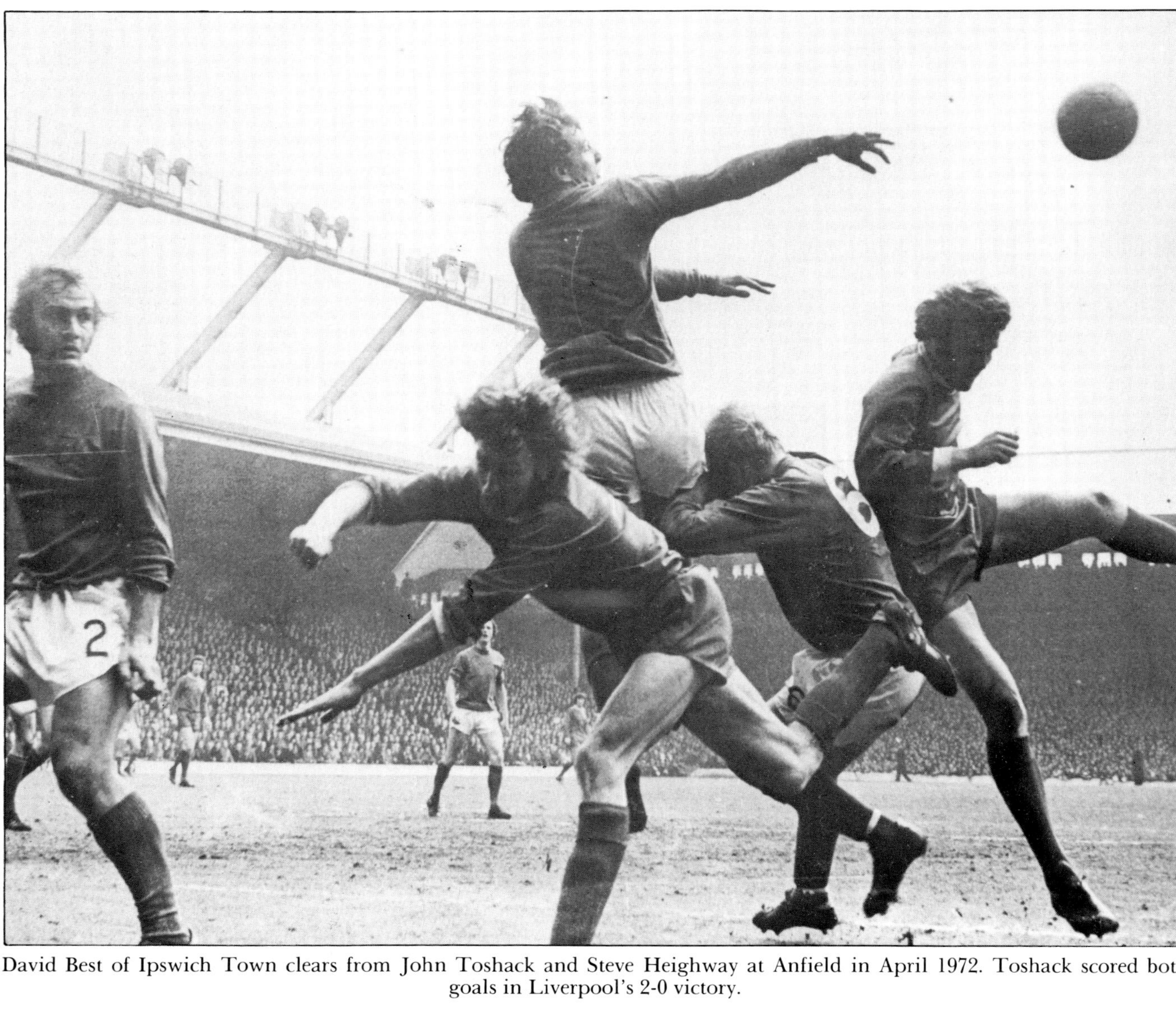

David Best of Ipswich Town clears from John Toshack and Steve Heighway at Anfield in April 1972. Toshack scored both goals in Liverpool's 2-0 victory.

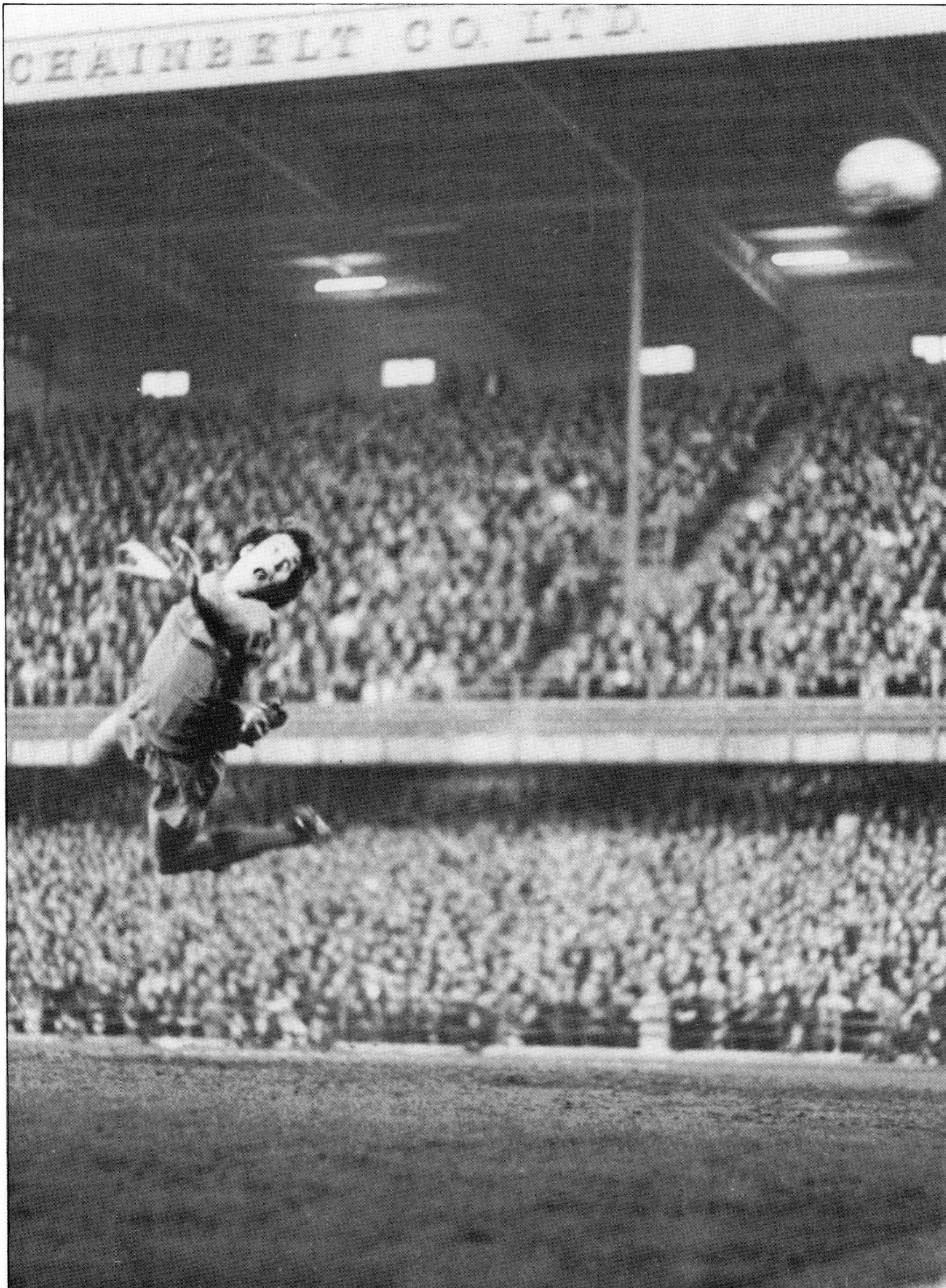

The goal that won a Championship. Derby County's John McGovern (out of picture) hammered home this shot for the only goal of the game at the Baseball Ground in May 1972. It was Derby's last game of the season and after the Reds drew 0-0 at Highbury a week later, and Leeds lost at Molineux, Derby took the title to leave Liverpool with a barren return for the season.

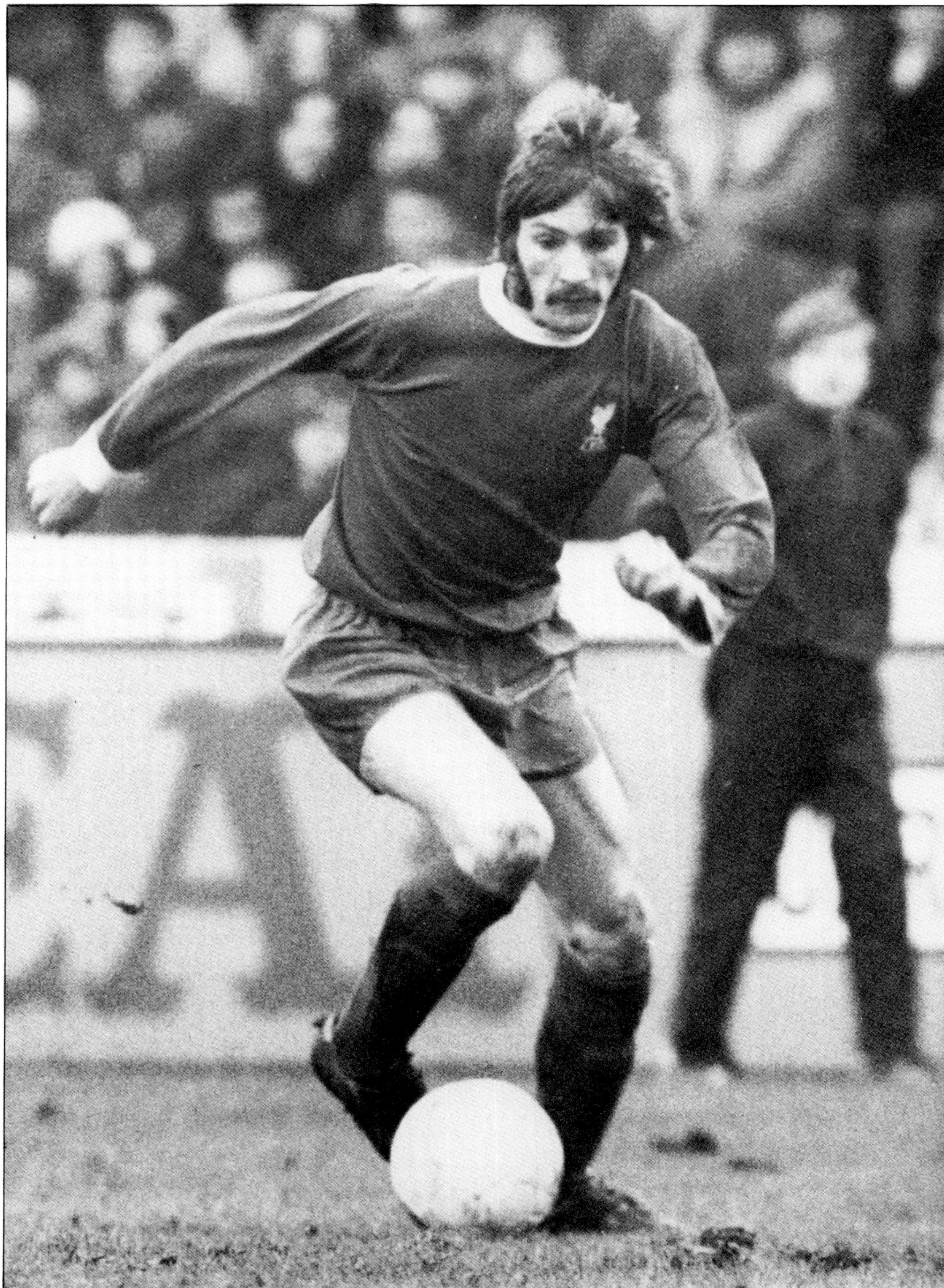

Steve Heighway was a major figure in Liverpool's triumphs of the 1970s. Born in Dublin, Heighway joined the Reds from amateur side Skelmersdale United. A Republic of Ireland international, he gained a BA (Econs) from Warwick University. Heighway was a fast, high-stepping attacker who scored 76 goals in 467 games for Liverpool before drifting out of the League and into the NASL with Minnesota Kicks in 1980.

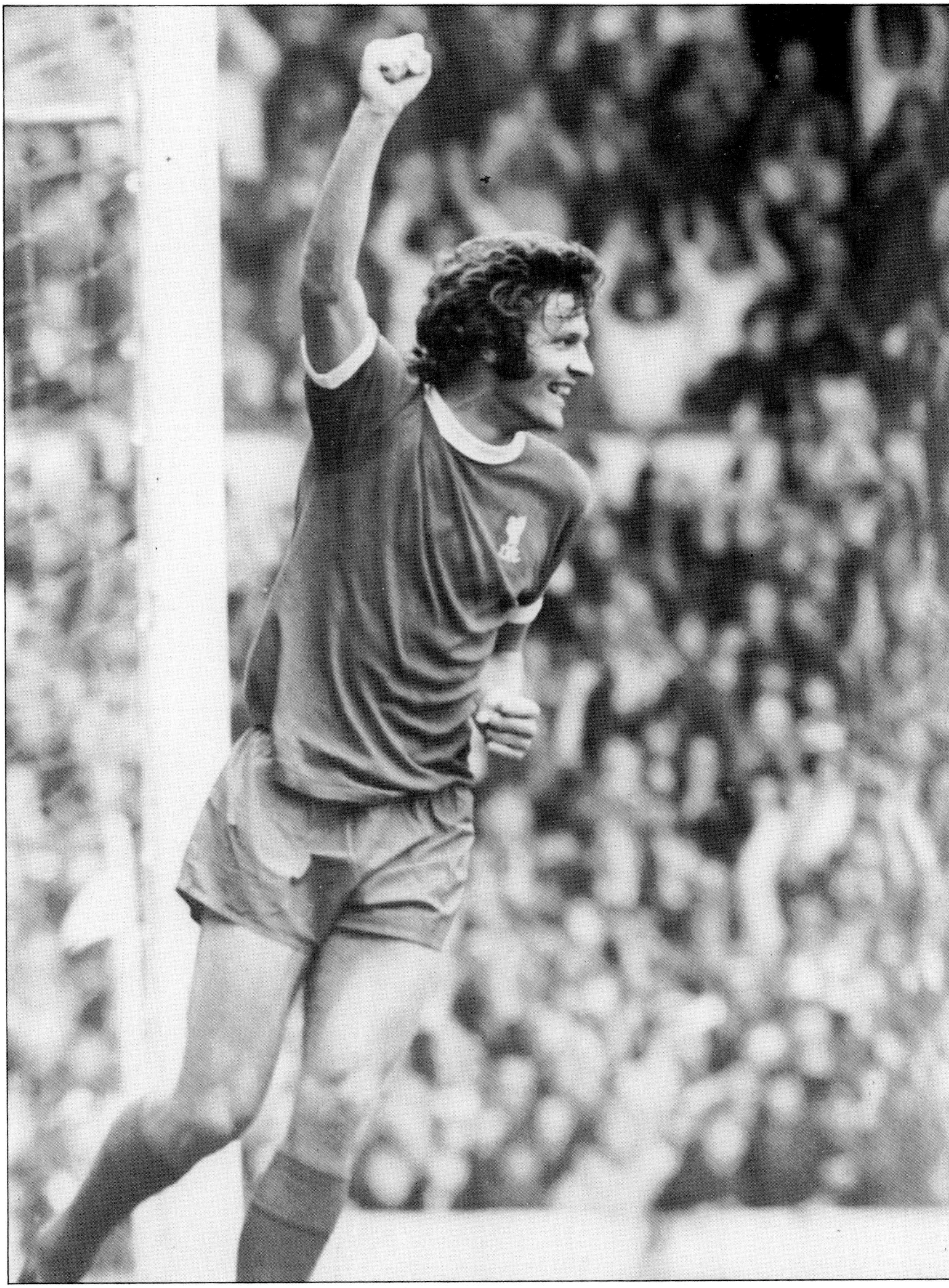

John Toshack celebrates after scoring the first goal in a 3-2 win over West Ham at Anfield in August 1972, as the Reds embarked on another Championship-winning season. Toshack joined Liverpool from Cardiff City for £110,000 in November 1970 and by the time he left to become player-manager of Swansea City in February 1978, he had gained League Championship, FA Cup and UEFA Cup winners' medals with the Anfield club. A big man, renowned for finding Kevin Keegan with flicked headers, Toshack scored 95 goals in 245 games for Liverpool.

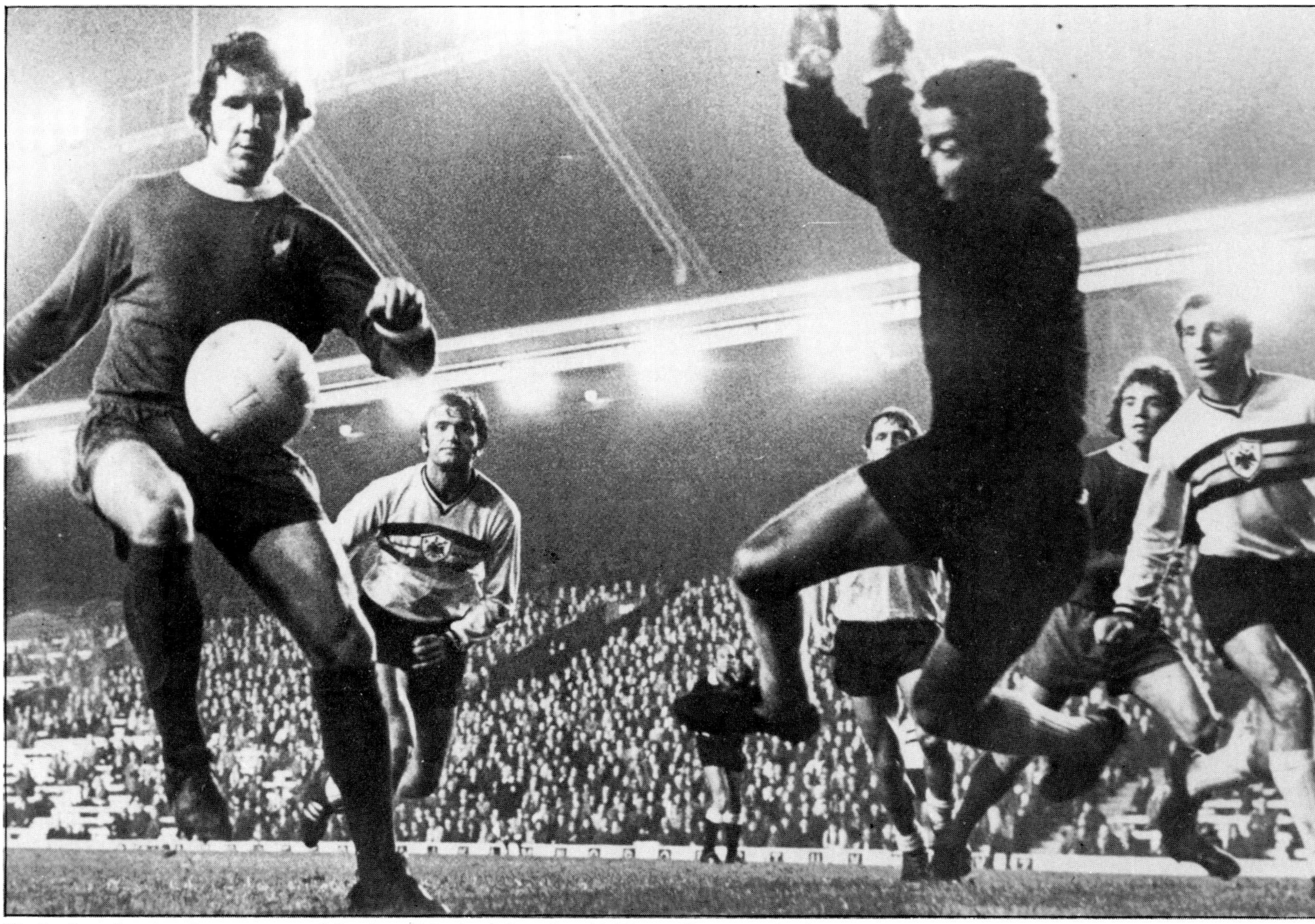

Chris Lawler is about to see his shot blocked by the AEK goalkeeper during the UEFA Cup second round first-leg game at Anfield in October 1972. Liverpool won the game 3-0 and eventually reached the Final, where they beat Borussia Mönchengladbach 3-2 on aggregate to lift the European trophy.

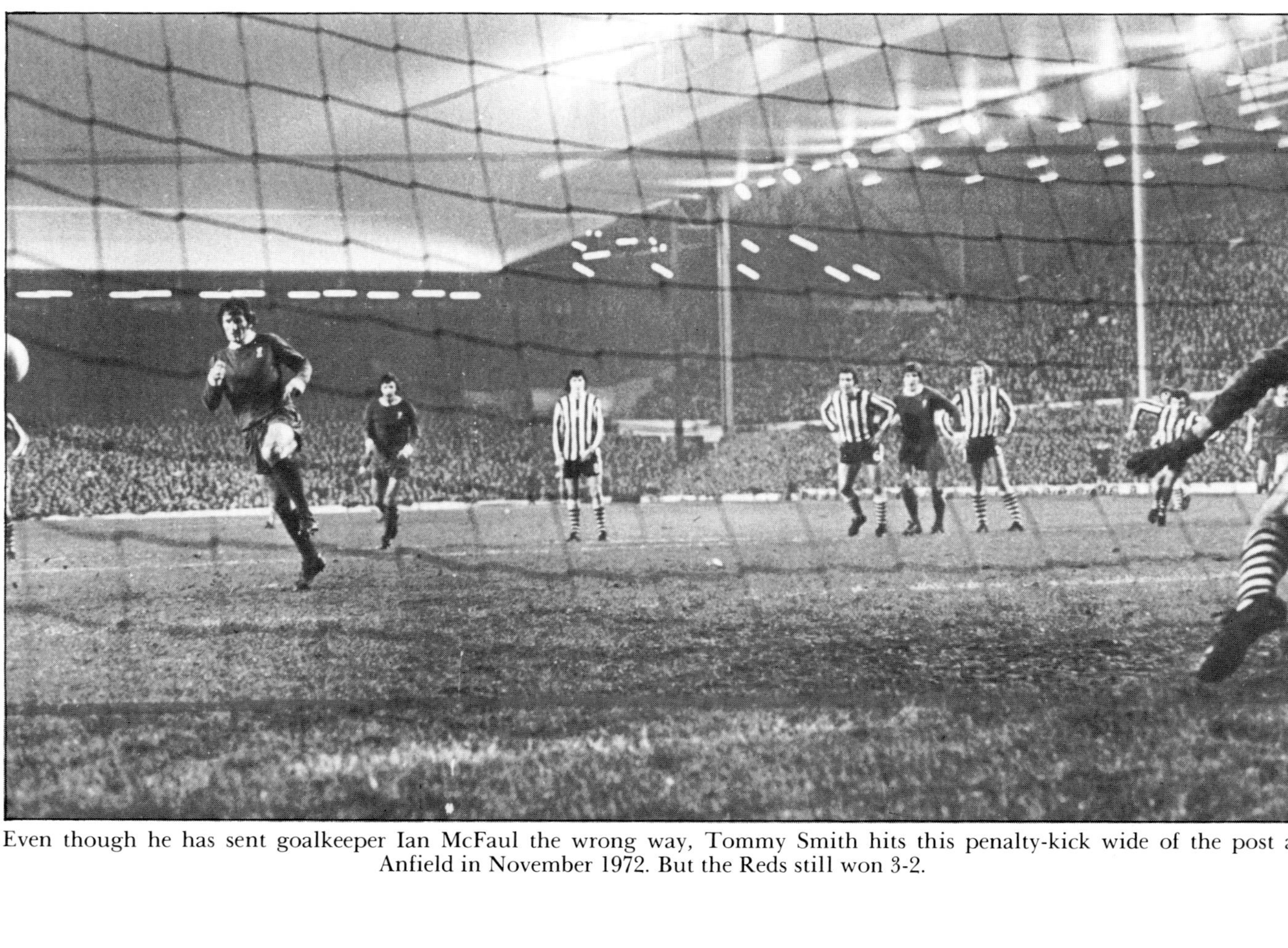

Even though he has sent goalkeeper Ian McFaul the wrong way, Tommy Smith hits this penalty-kick wide of the post at Anfield in November 1972. But the Reds still won 3-2.

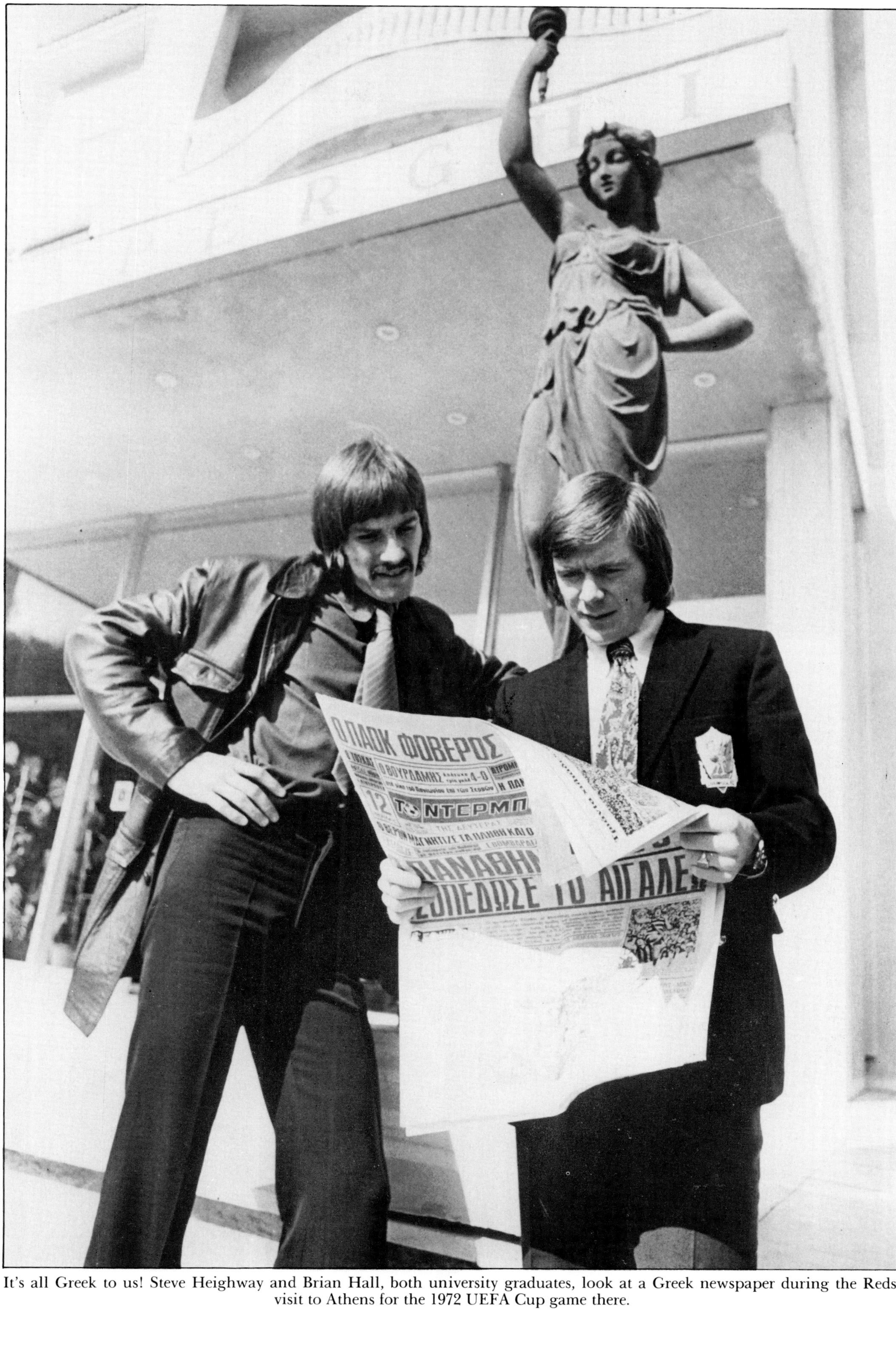

It's all Greek to us! Steve Heighway and Brian Hall, both university graduates, look at a Greek newspaper during the Reds' visit to Athens for the 1972 UEFA Cup game there.

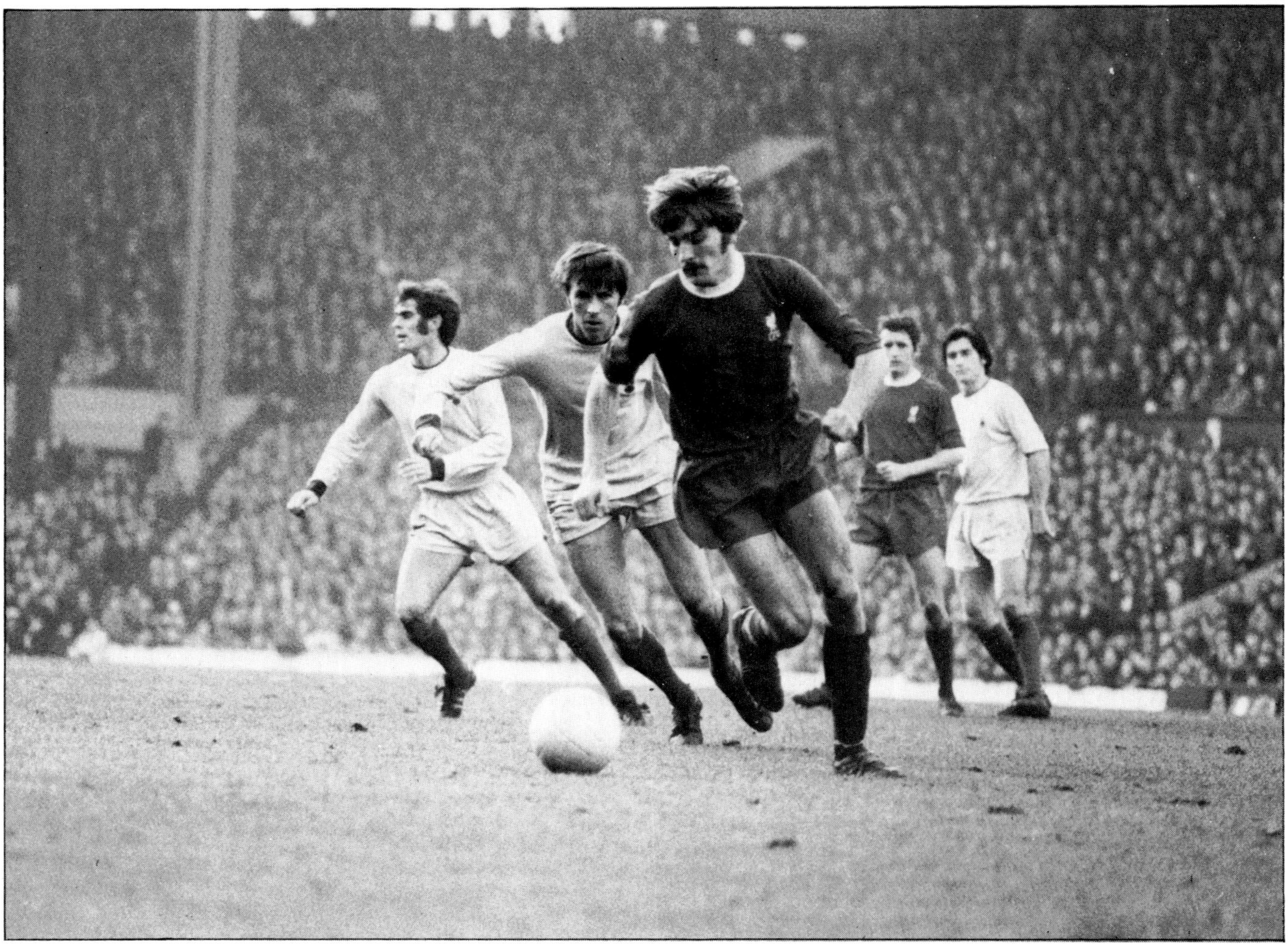

Steve Heighway bursts through the Coventry defence at Anfield in December 1972, a game which the Reds won 2-0 with goals from John Toshack.

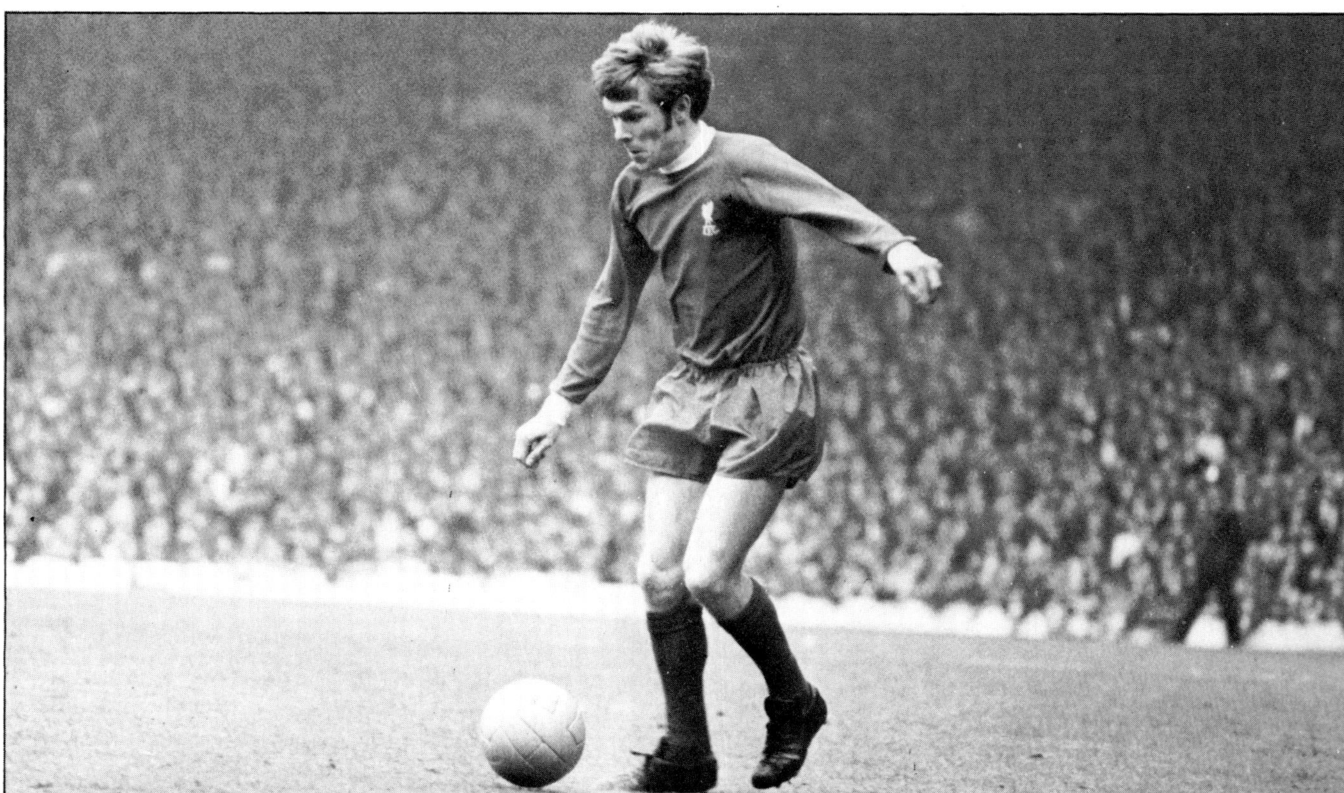

Brian Hall made 220 senior appearances for Liverpool. A BSc from Manchester University, Hall joined the Reds in July 1968 and was substitute in the first leg of the 1973 UEFA Cup Final. He played in the side which won the League Championship the same year and the FA Cup the following year. Hall, an energetic little midfielder, moved to Plymouth Argyle for £35,000 in 1976 and after a spell with Burnley became a schoolteacher.

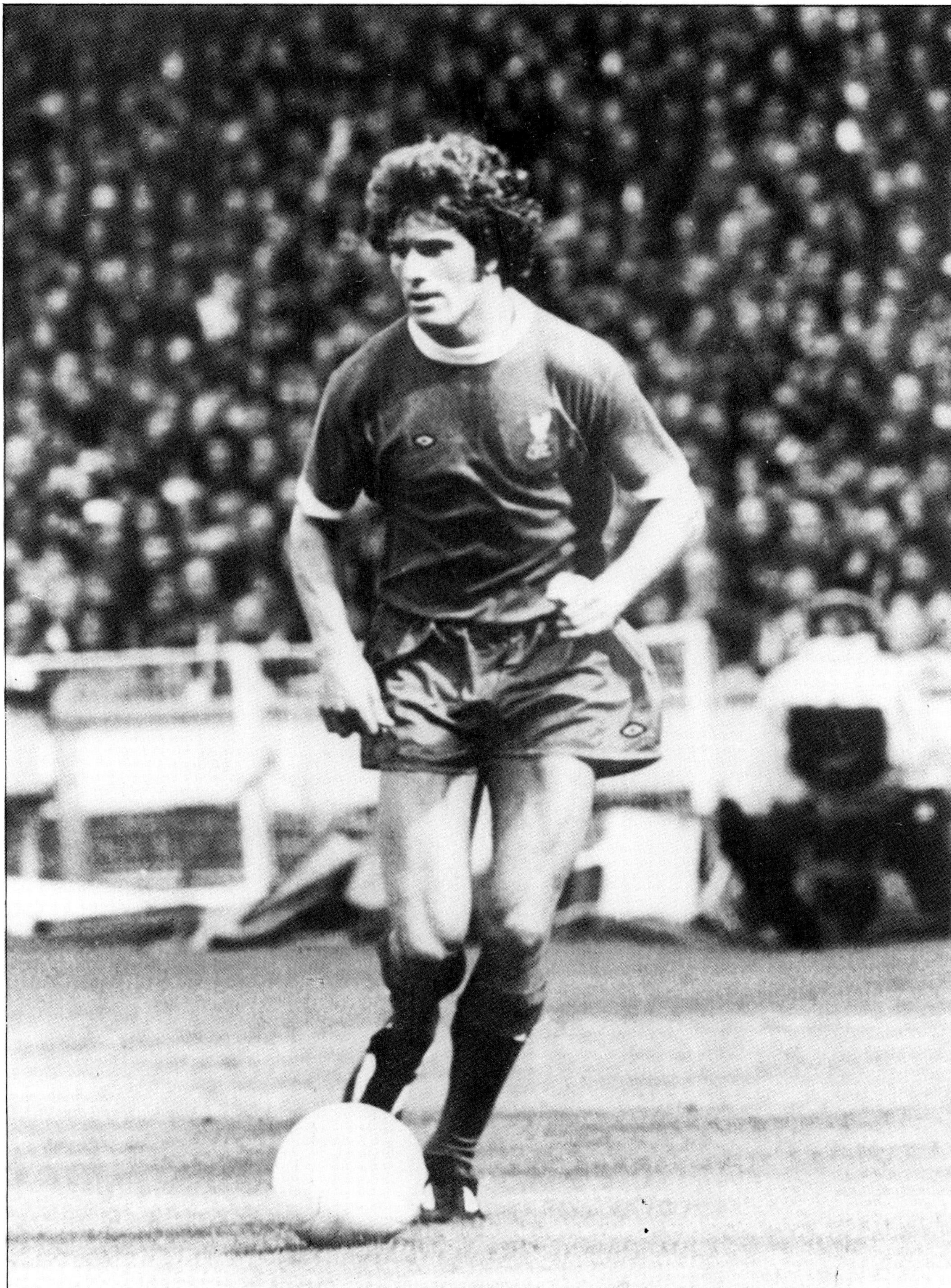

Phil Boersma scored 29 goals in 119 first-team appearances for Liverpool, the club he joined from junior football in 1965, becoming a full-time professional in September 1968. Boersma was a substitute in the second leg of the Reds' successful 1973 UEFA Cup Final and also played in the League Championship winning side that season. His chance had come when John Toshack was injured. Boersma moved to Middlesbrough for £72,000 in December 1975.

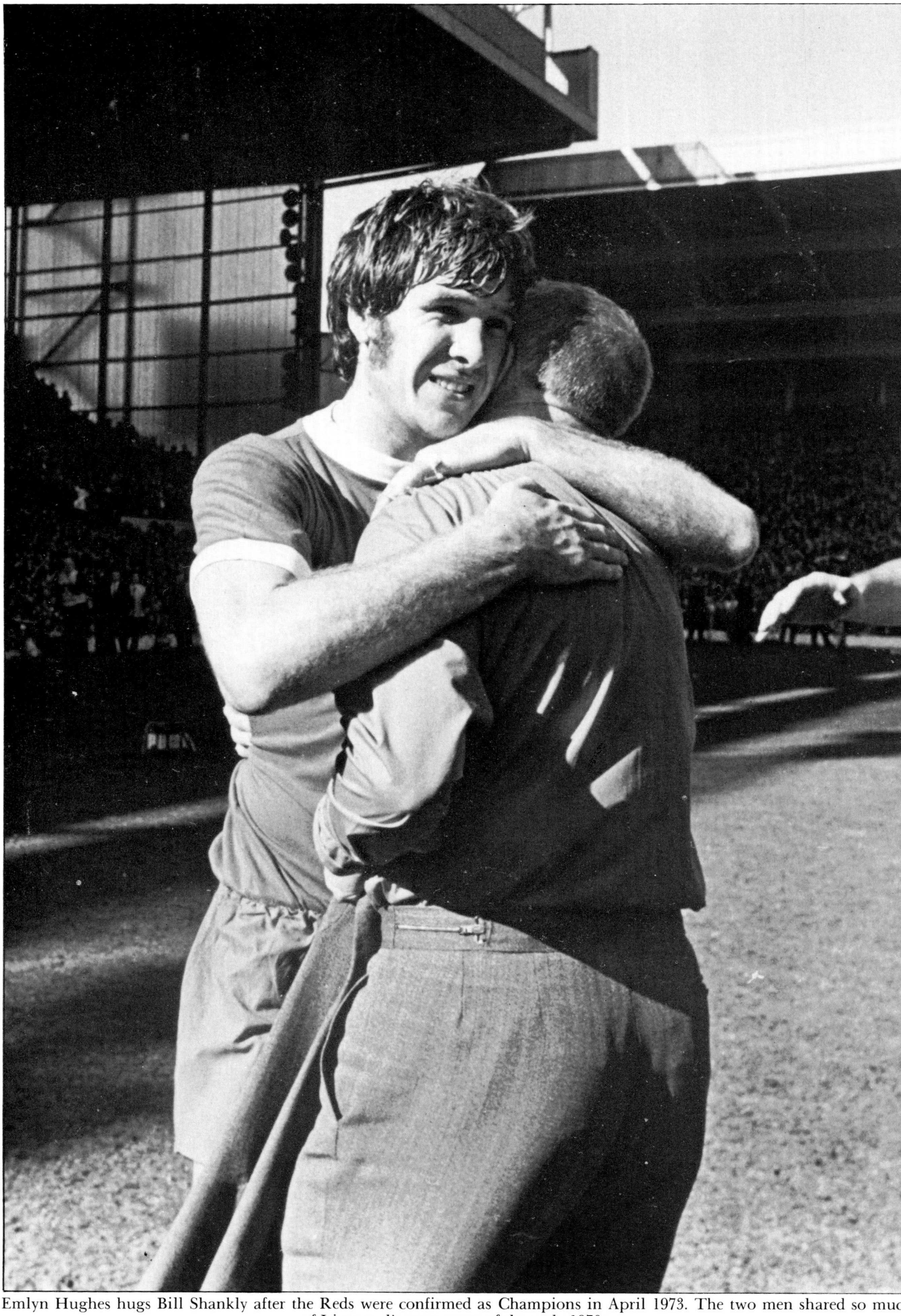

Emlyn Hughes hugs Bill Shankly after the Reds were confirmed as Champions in April 1973. The two men shared so much of Liverpool's great years of the early 1970s.

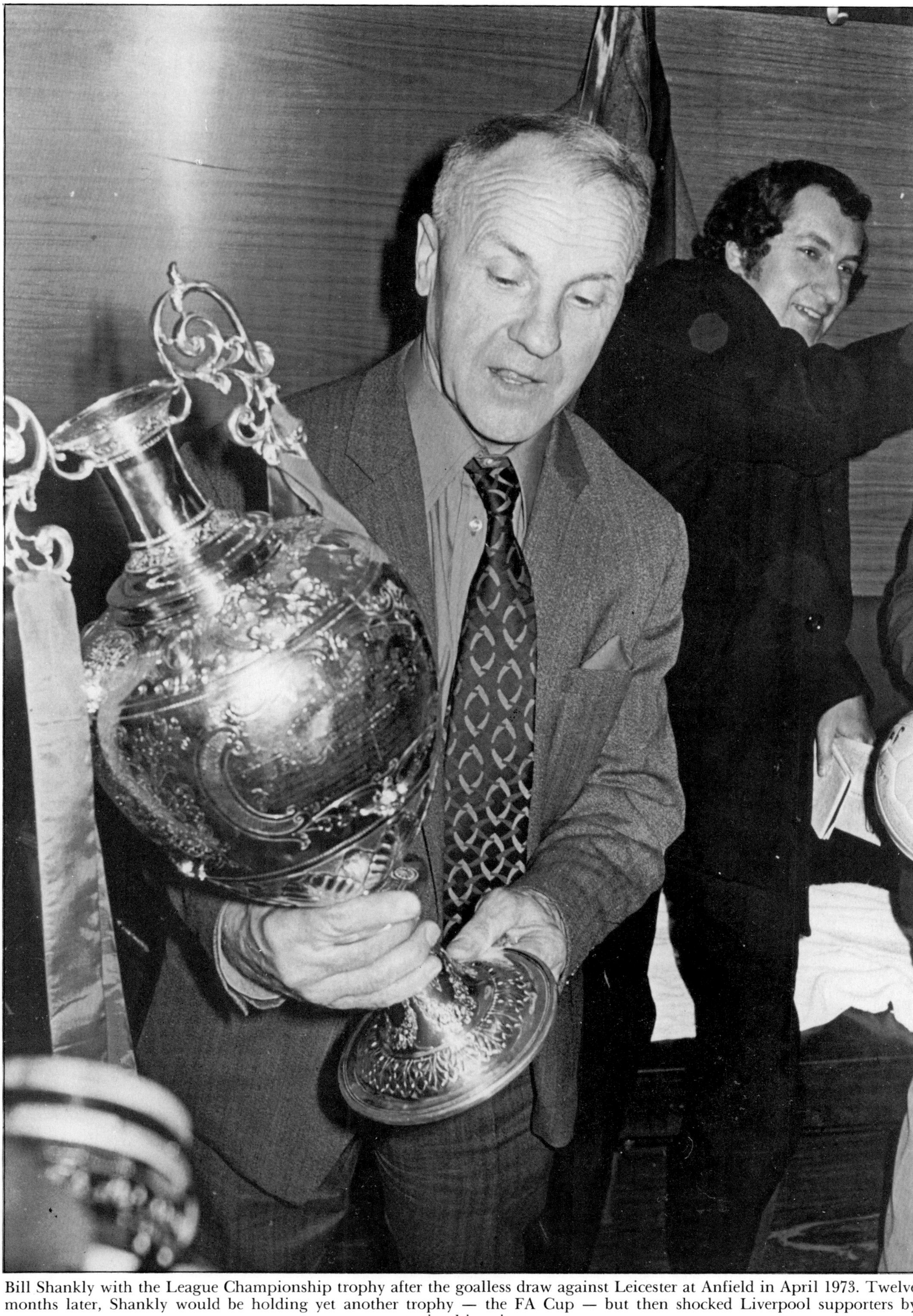

Bill Shankly with the League Championship trophy after the goalless draw against Leicester at Anfield in April 1973. Twelve months later, Shankly would be holding yet another trophy — the FA Cup — but then shocked Liverpool supporters by announcing his retirement.

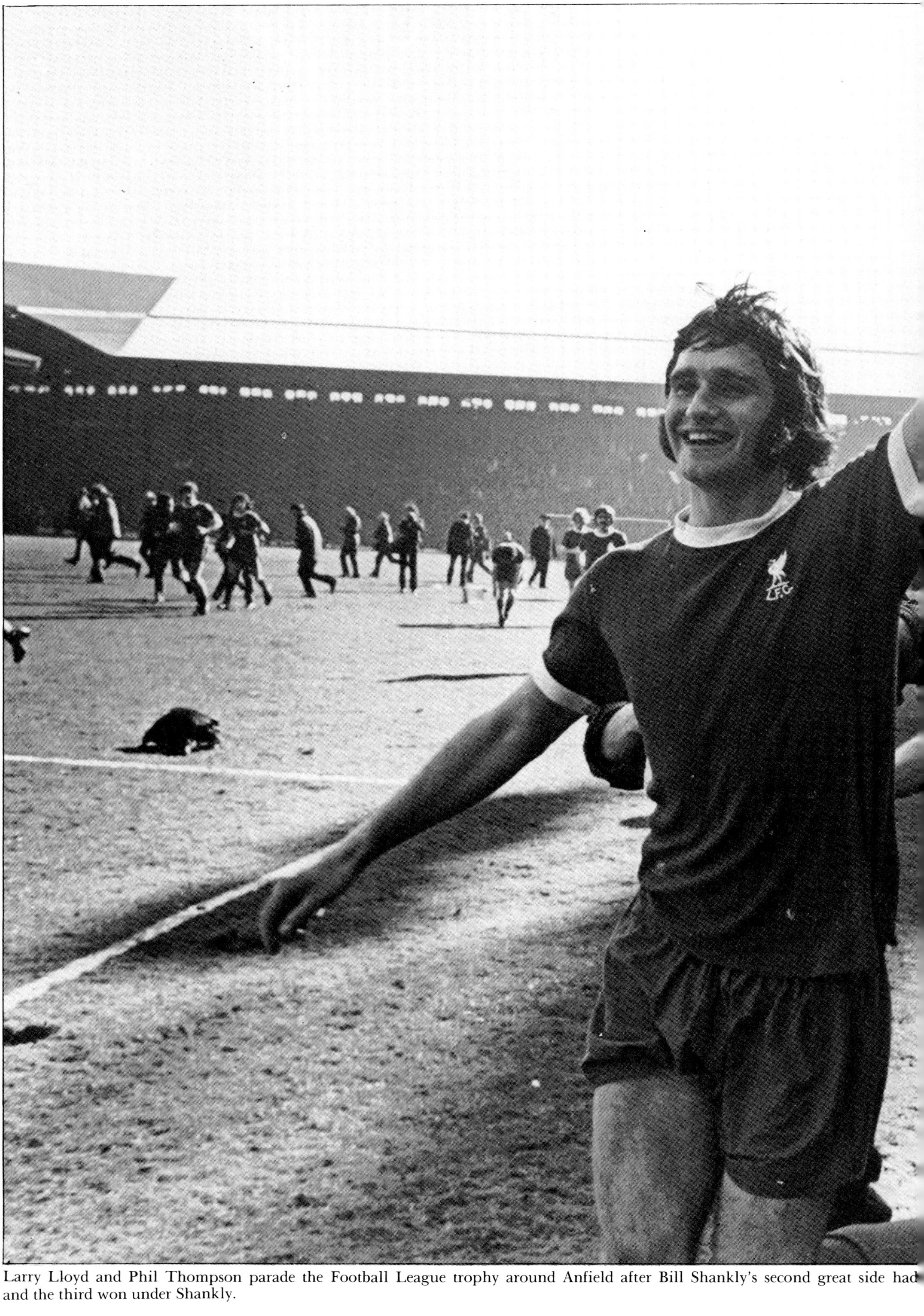

Larry Lloyd and Phil Thompson parade the Football League trophy around Anfield after Bill Shankly's second great side had and the third won under Shankly.

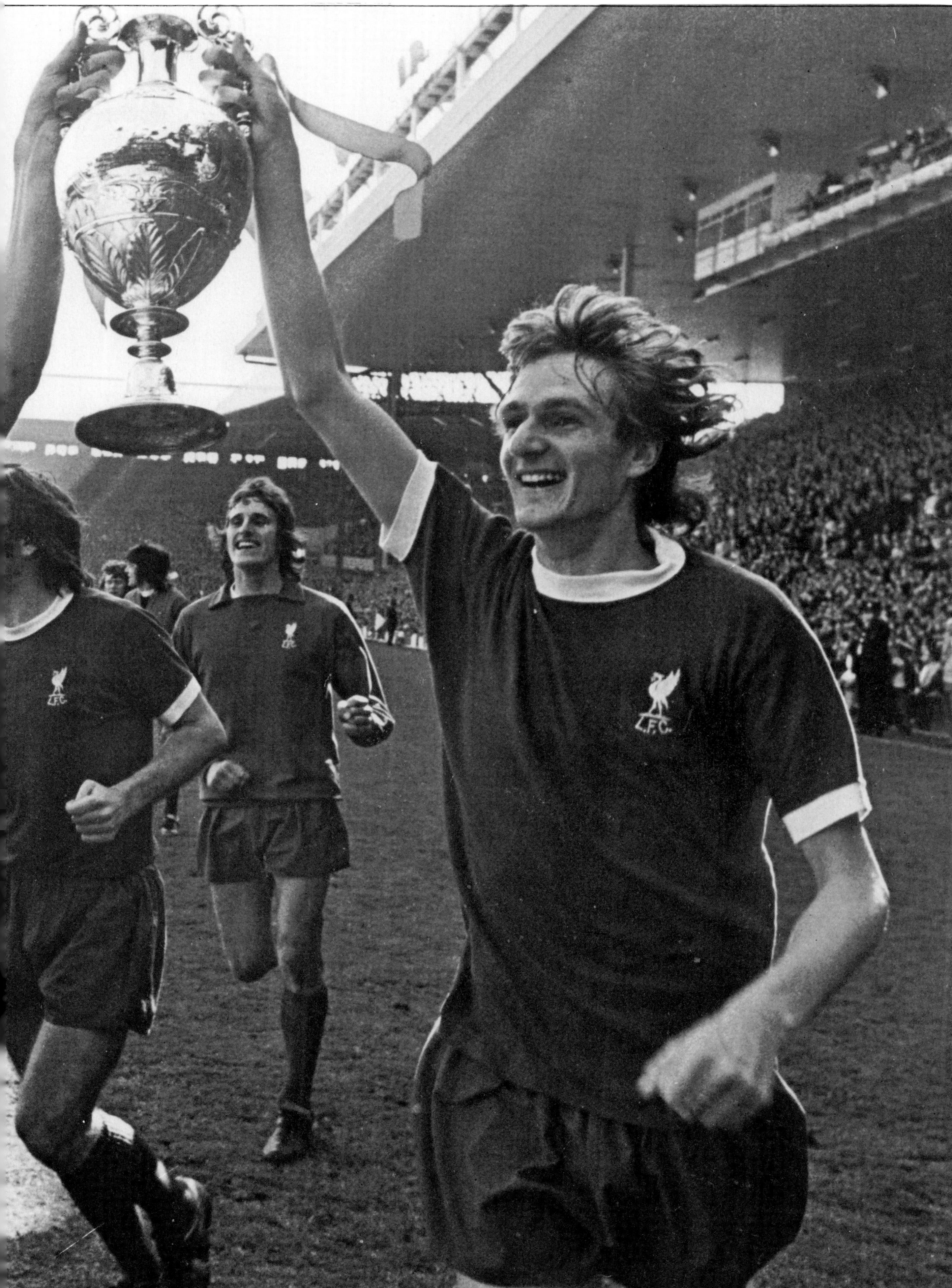

ched the title with a point against Leicester City in April 1973. It was the eighth League Championship in the club's history

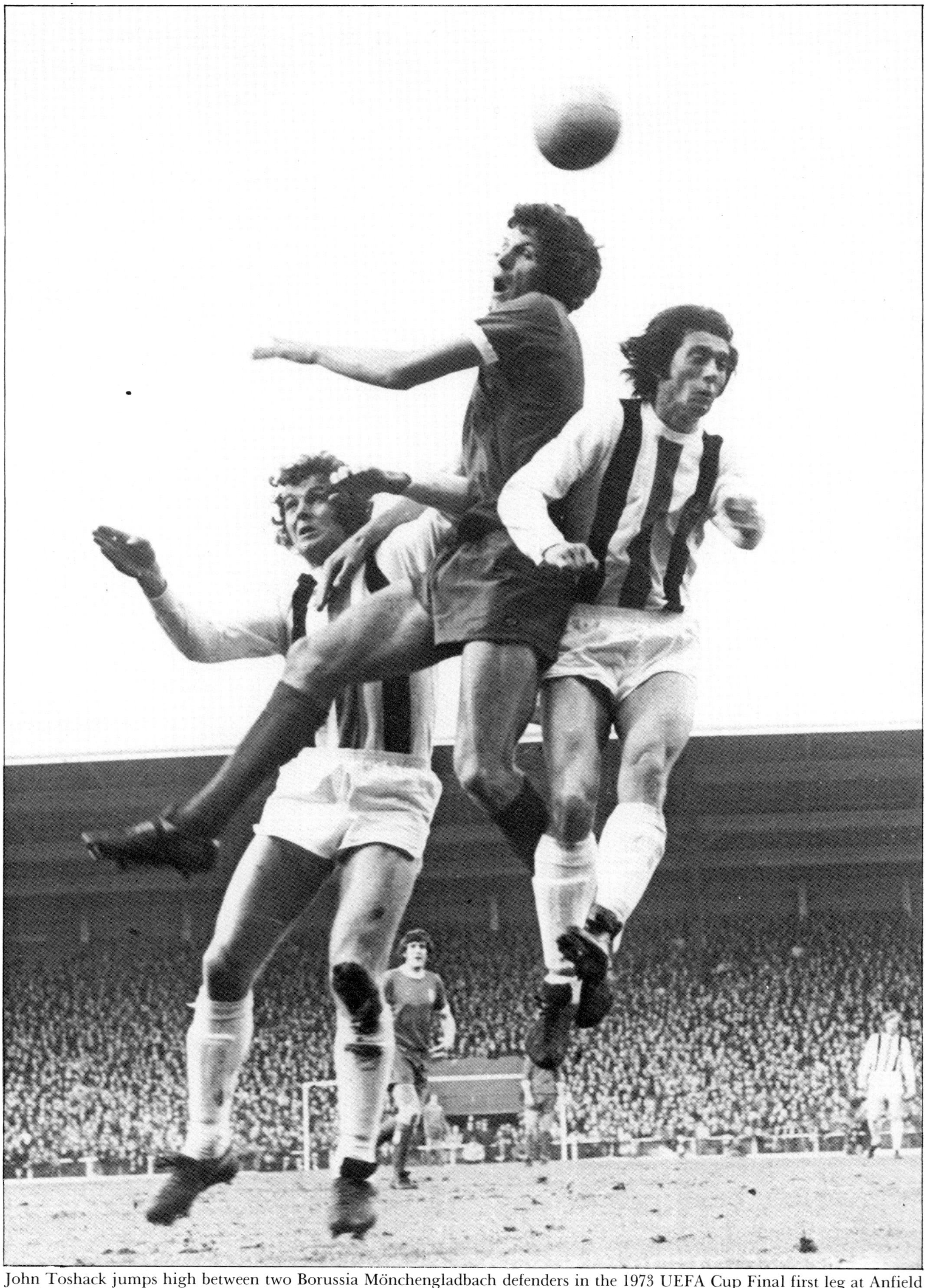

John Toshack jumps high between two Borussia Mönchengladbach defenders in the 1973 UEFA Cup Final first leg at Anfield in May 1973. Liverpool beat Eintracht Frankfurt, AEK Athens, Dynamo Berlin, Dynamo Dresden and Tottenham Hotspur on their way to the Final, where they won the first leg 3-0.

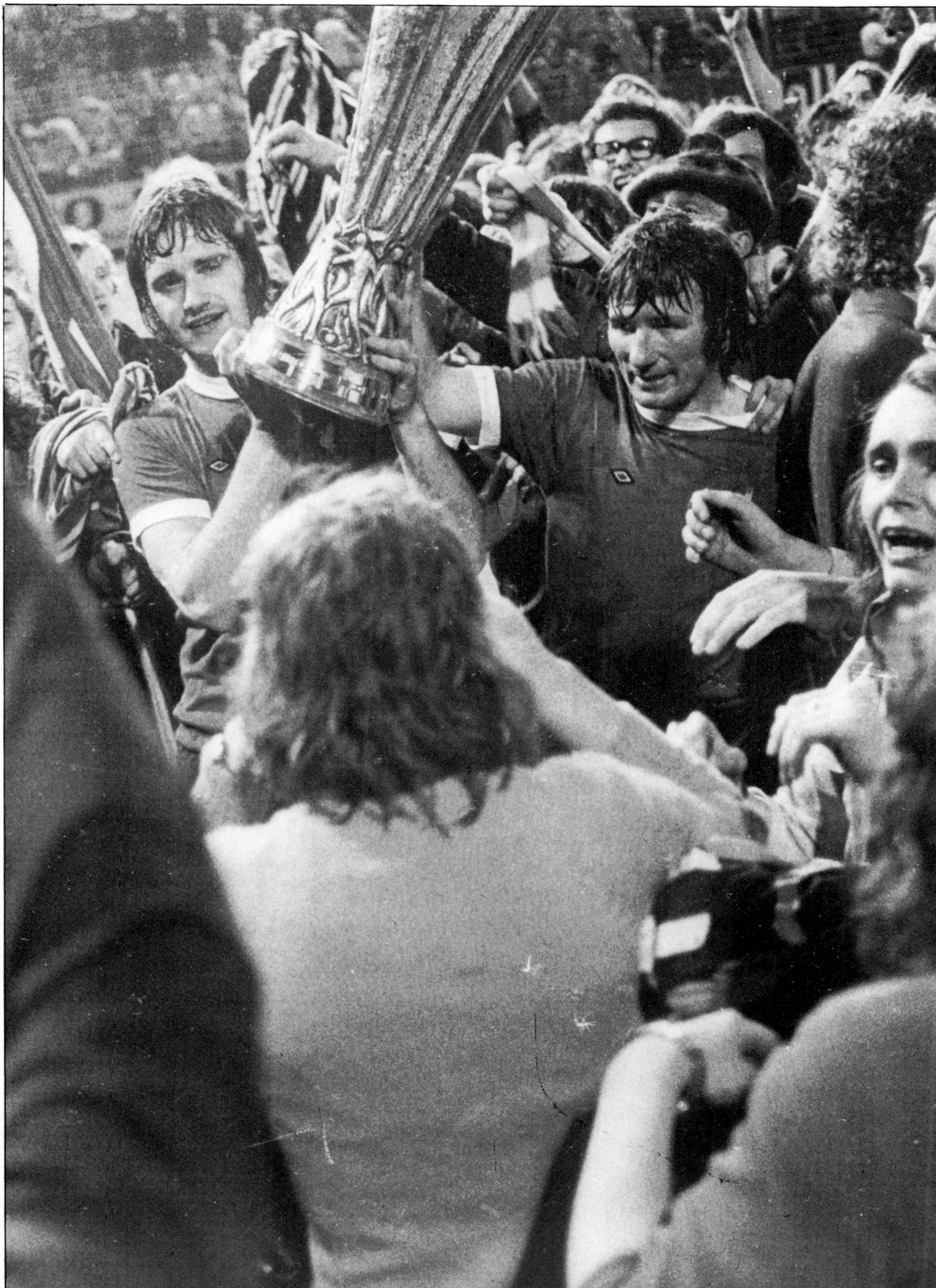

In West Germany, Liverpool went down 2-0 but had done enough to lift the UEFA Cup. Larry Lloyd and Tommy Smith carry the trophy as they force their way through a throng of delighted Merseyside fans.

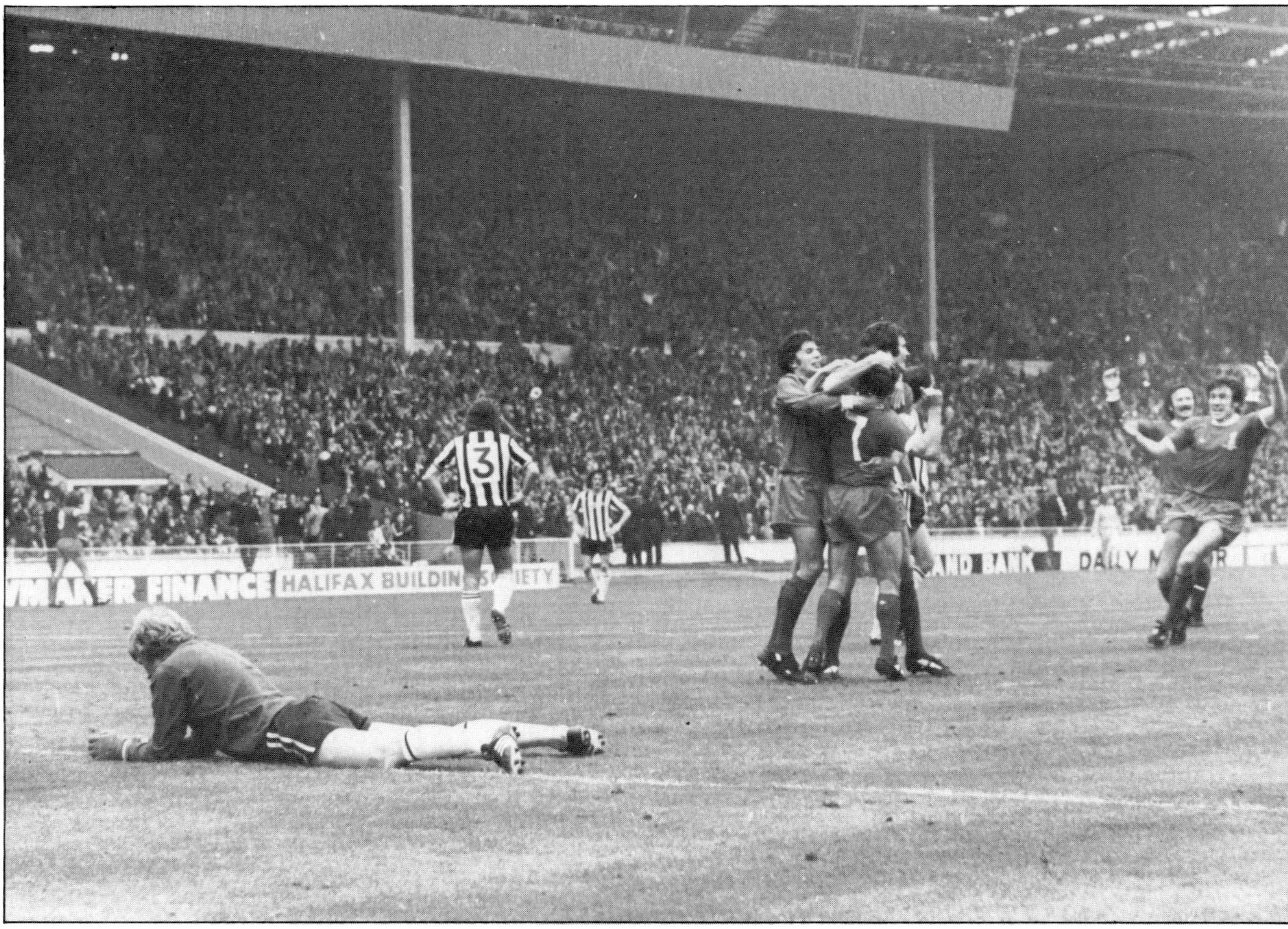

In 1973-4, Liverpool failed to retain their League title, finishing runners-up to Leeds United, but they gained compensation with an emphatic 3-0 victory over Newcastle United in the FA Cup Final. Kevin Keegan is mobbed by his teammates after opening the scoring in the 57th minute.

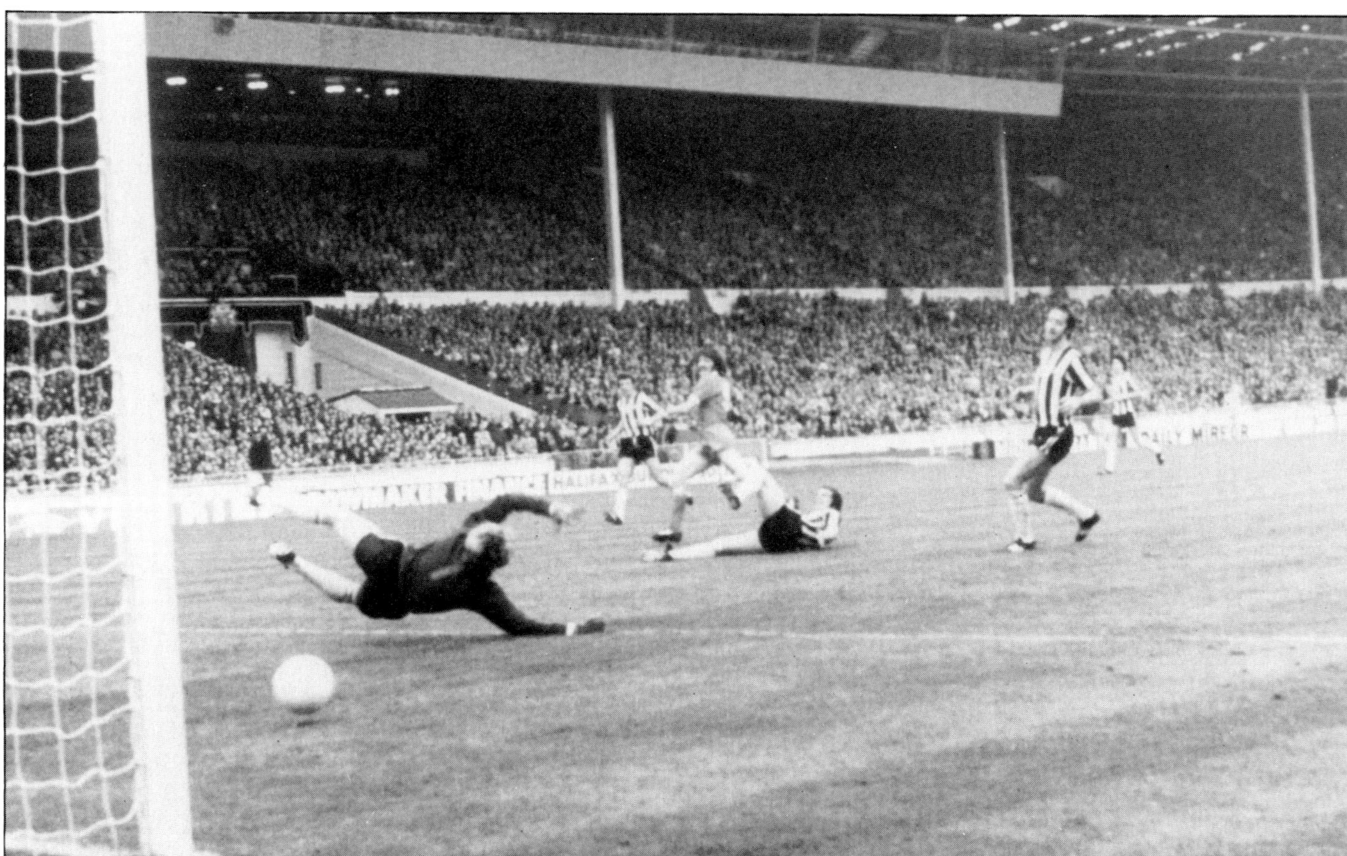

Steve Heighway (centre) beats Newcastle's Ian McFaul to make it 2-0 after 75 minutes.

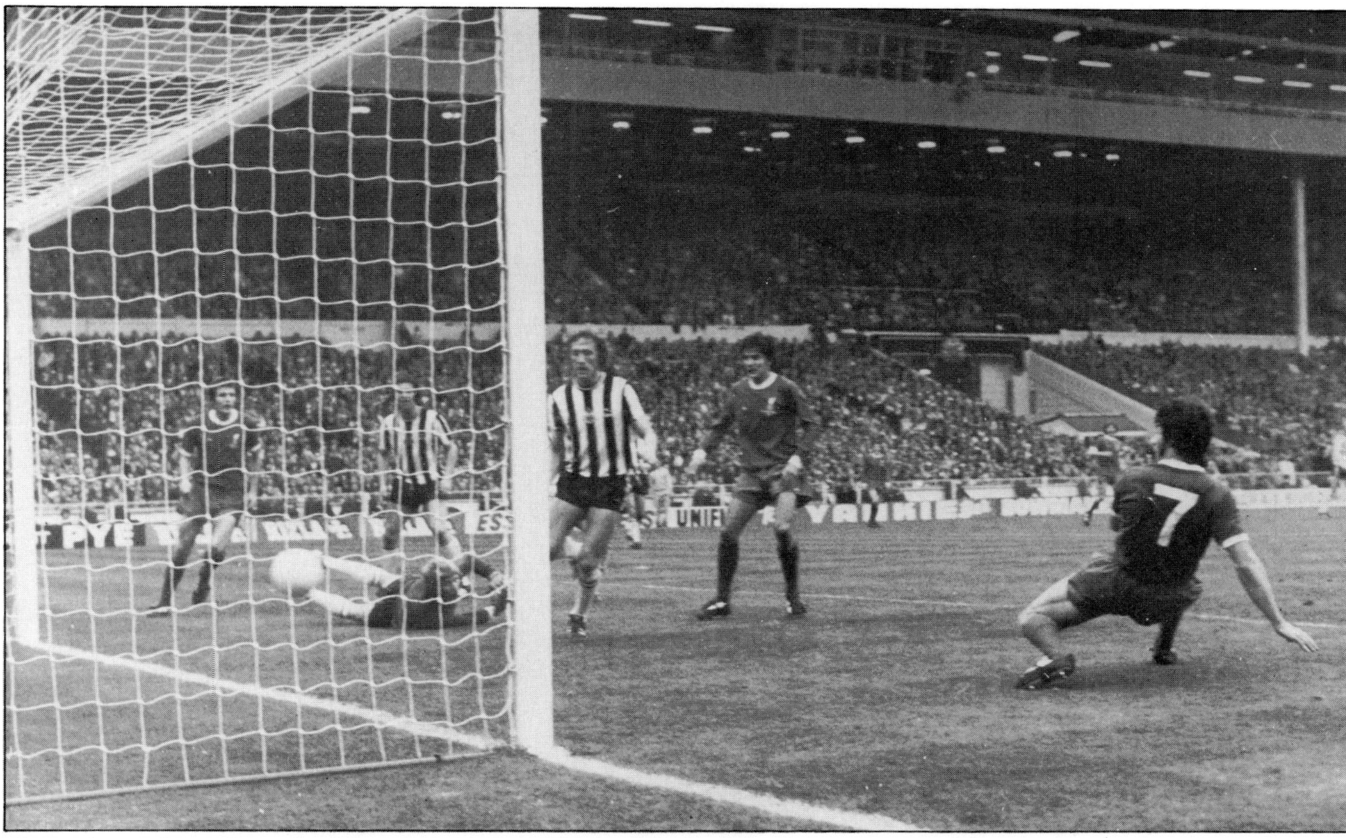

Two minutes from the end of the 1974 FA Cup Final, Kevin Keegan (7) completes the scoring. It was Keegan's sixth goal on the Wembley trail that year. Ironically, Keegan was later to become as big a cult figure on Tyneside as he had been on Merseyside.

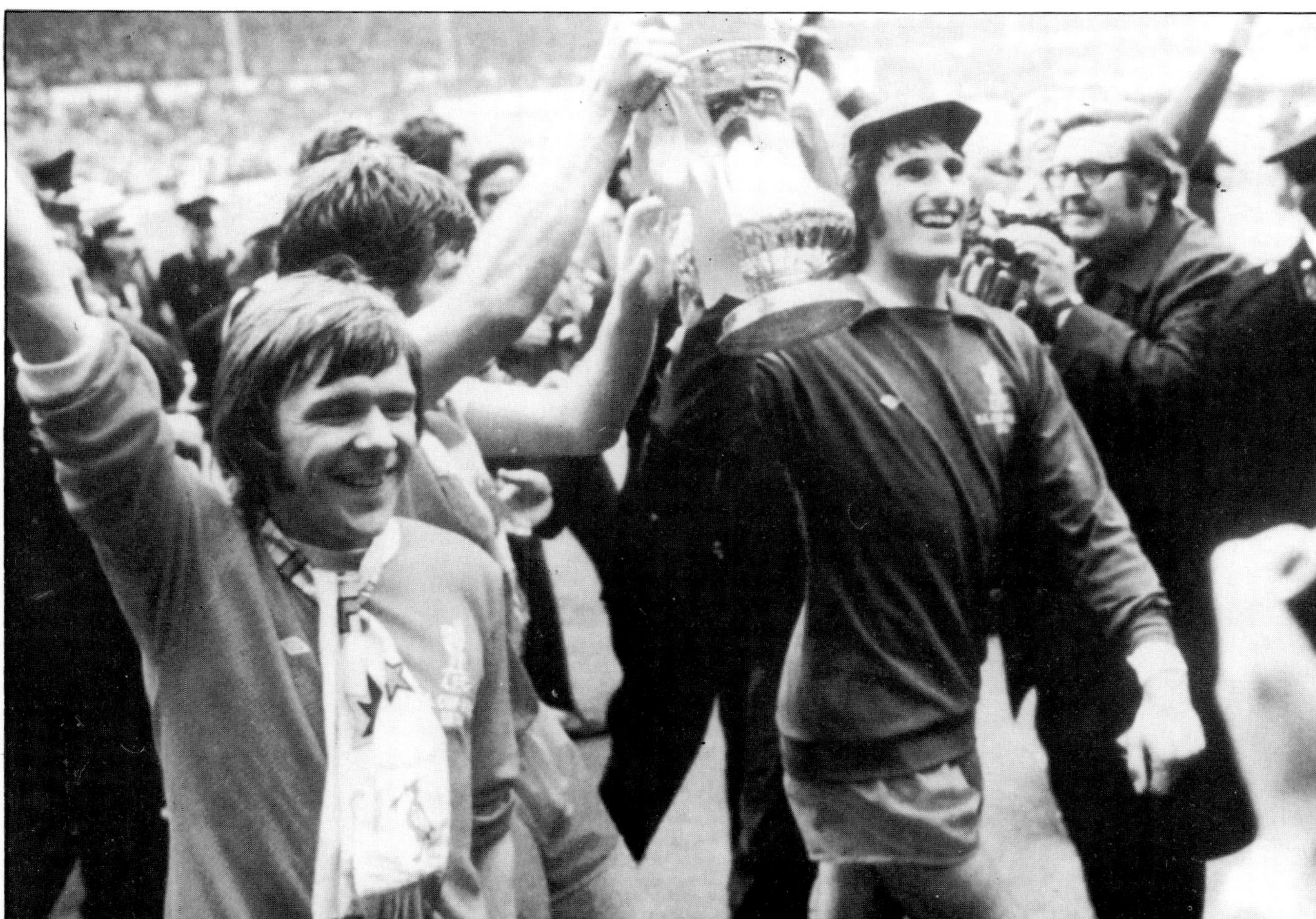

Brian Hall (left), Emlyn Hughes (partly hidden) and Ray Clemence parade the FA Cup around Wembley after the Reds had routed Newcastle.

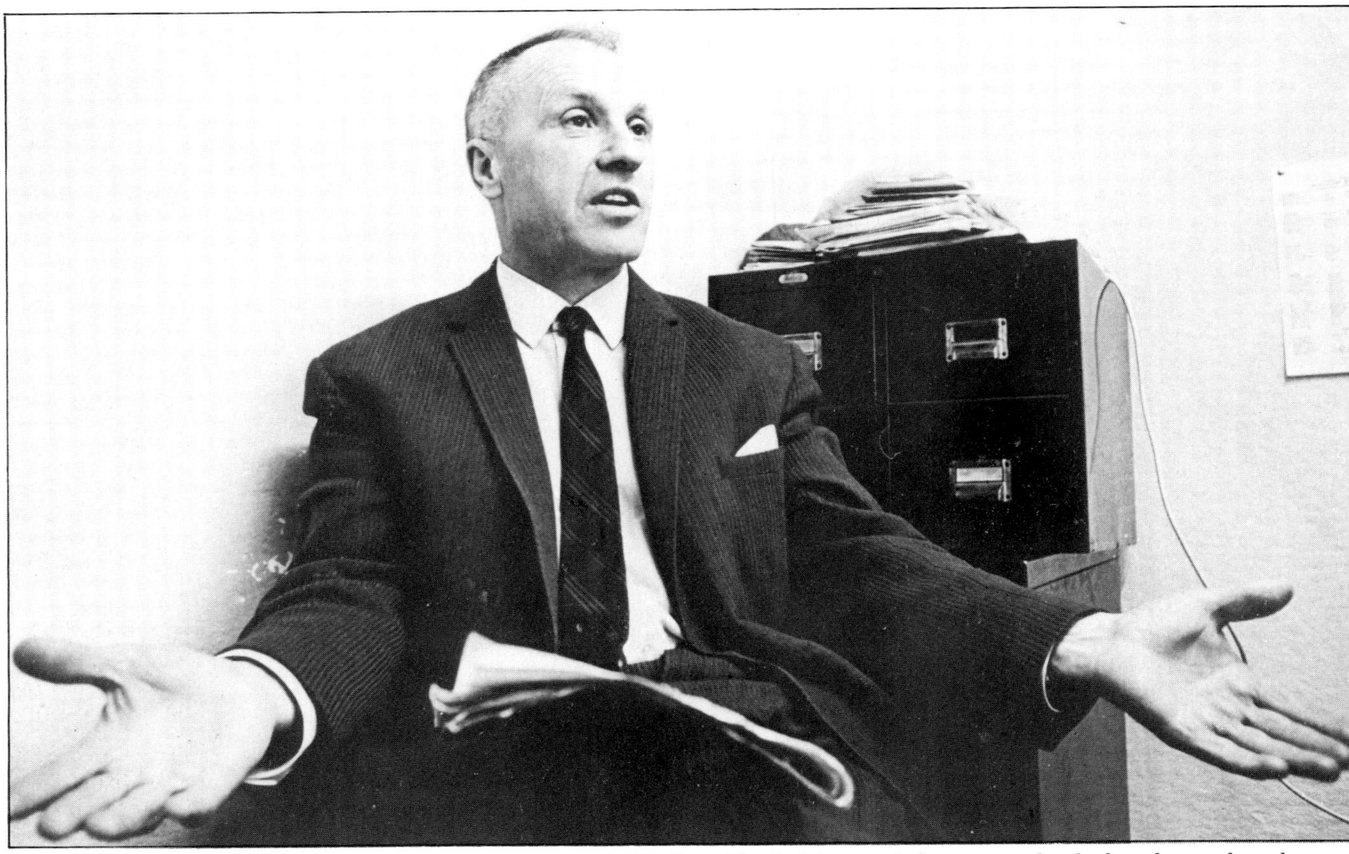

Bill Shankly holds court at Anfield. But after the 1974 FA Cup Final, Liverpool fans were shocked to learn that the man who had rebuilt their club to become the greatest in the land had decided to retire.

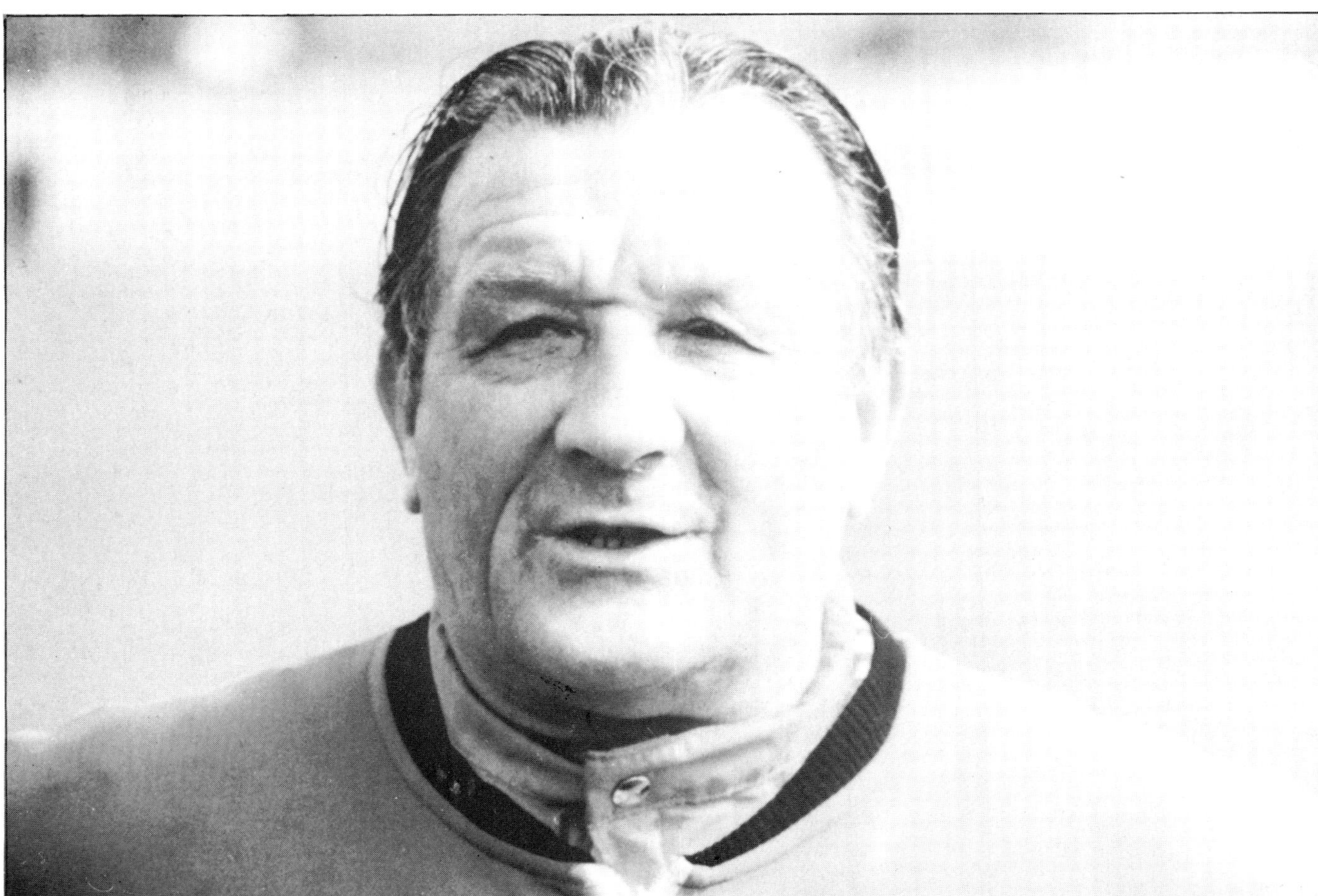

Former Liverpool wing-half Bob Paisley took over from Bill Shankly in 1974. Paisley, who had made 278 senior appearances for the Reds between 1945-6 and 1953-4, won a League Championship medal in 1946-7 but missed the 1950 FA Cup Final defeat by Arsenal, despite scoring in the semi-final against Everton. As manager he guided the Reds to new European and domestic triumphs, although the FA Cup, which had eluded him as a player, also escaped him as a manager.

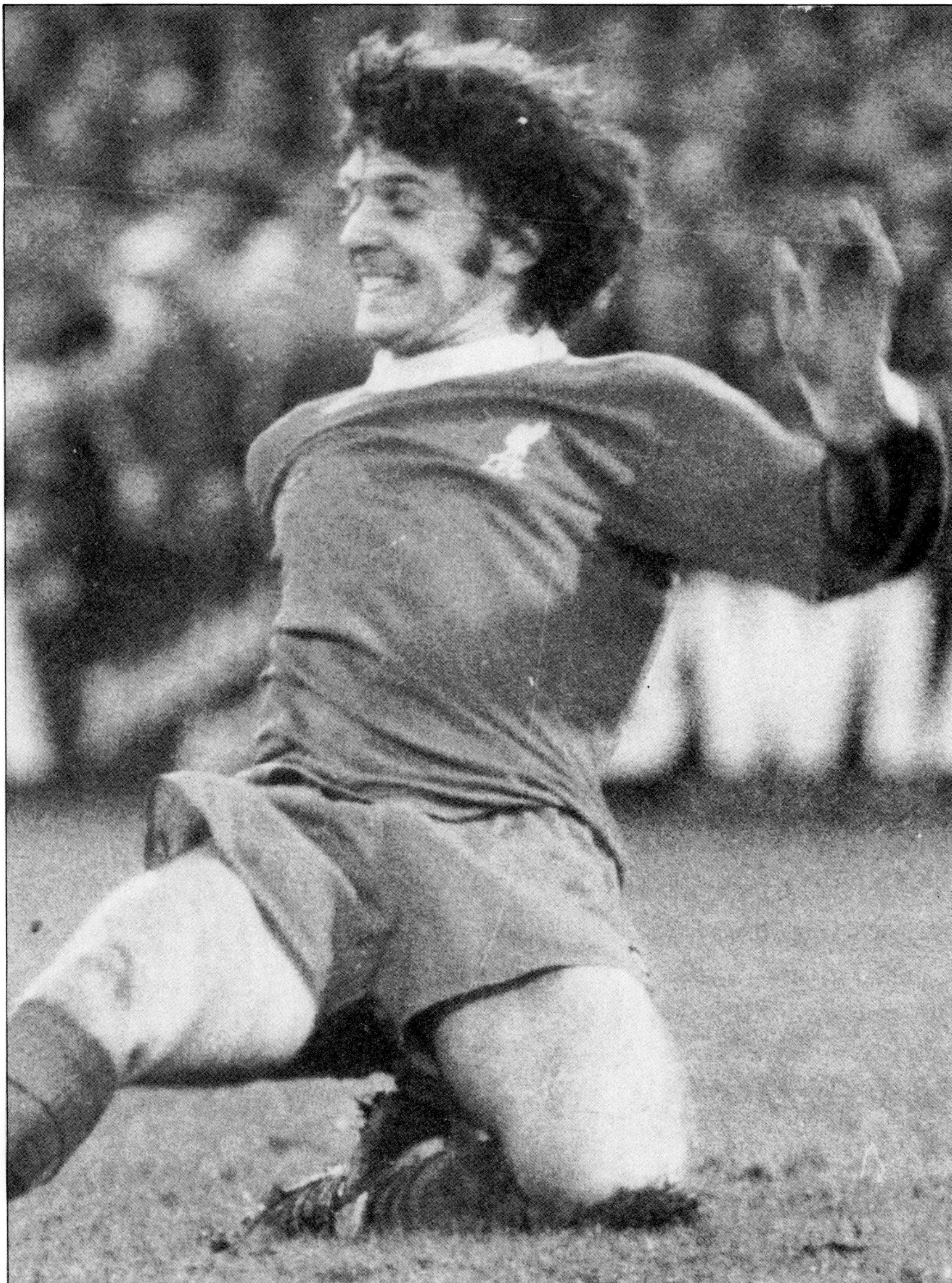

Former Hibernian midfielder Peter Cormack joined Liverpool from Nottingham Forest in July 1972 for a fee of £110,000. An old style inside-forward, Cormack developed into an attacking midfielder who made 125 League appearances for the Reds, helping them to two League Championships, an FA Cup Final victory and success in Europe too. He went to Bristol City for £50,000 in November 1976.

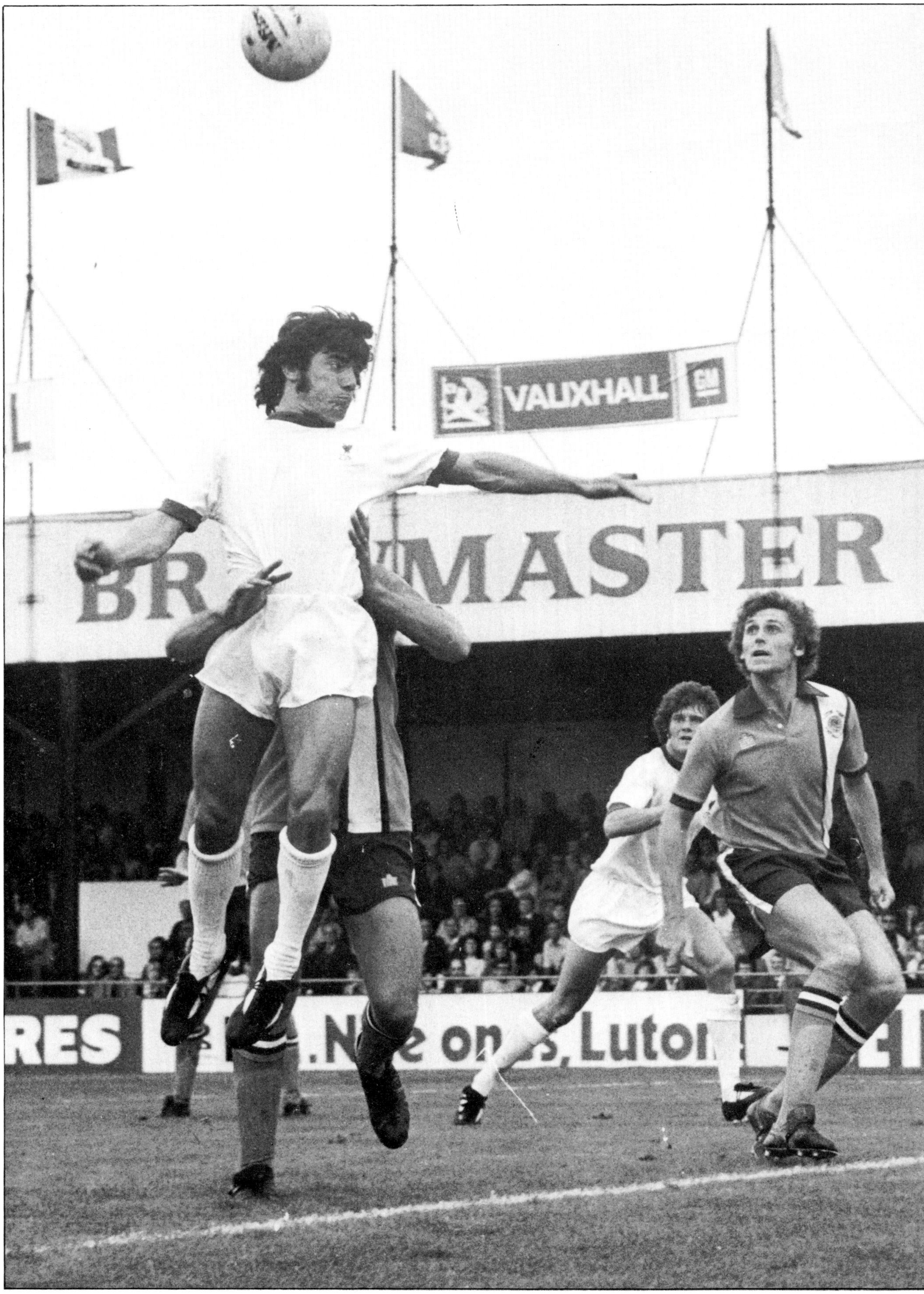

Apparently assisted by a Luton Town player, Kevin Keegan gets up to a high ball at Kenilworth Road in August 1974, when the FA Cup holders met the newly-promoted Hatters. The result was a 2-1 opening day win for the Reds. They ended the season in second place again, this time behind Derby County, and failed in the Cups.

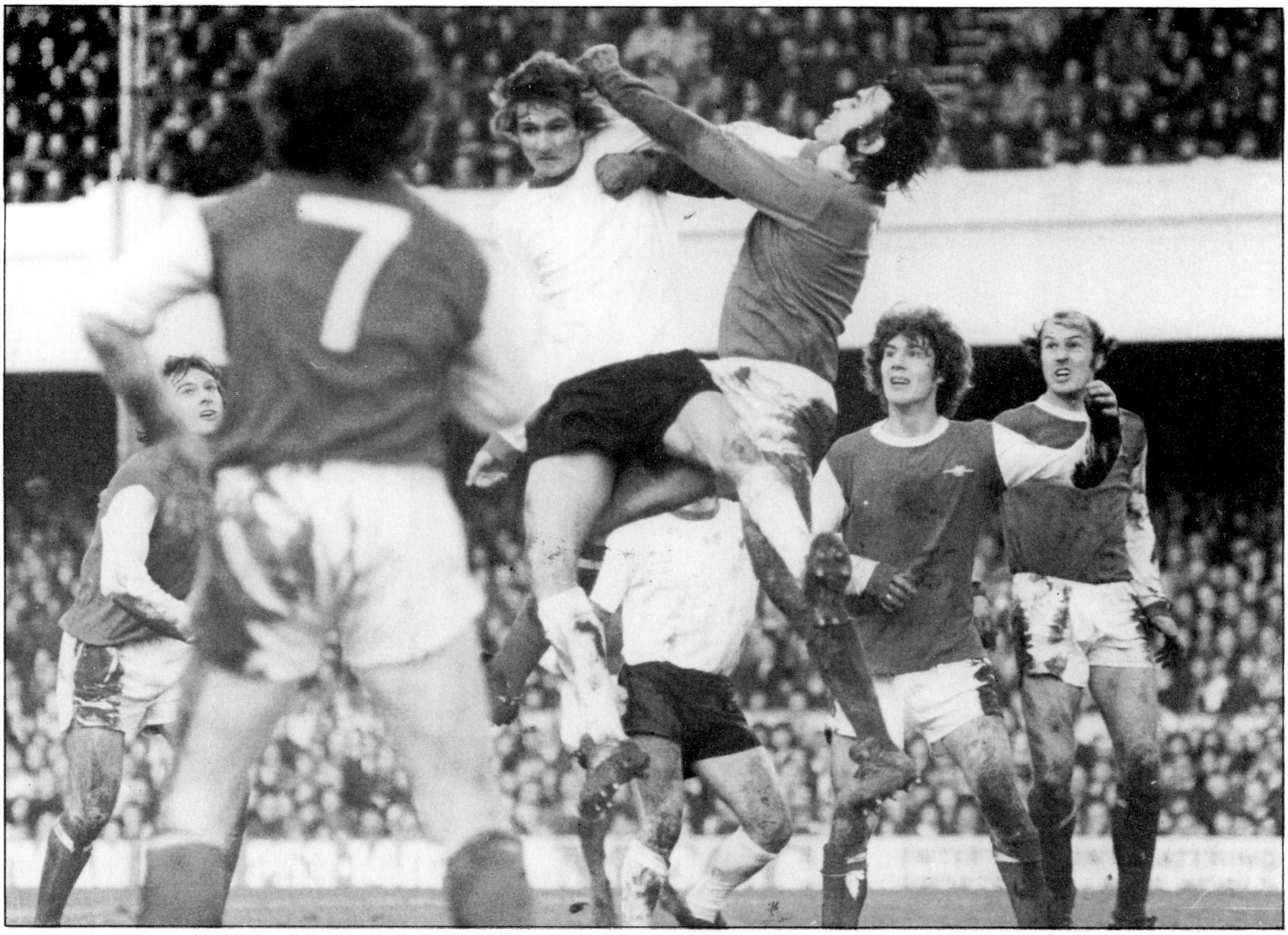

Anxious looks on the faces of Arsenal's Brian Kidd (second right) and Terry Mancini as the Gunners' goalkeeper Jimmy Rimmer and Liverpool's Phil Thompson battle it out in the air. The game at Highbury in February 1975 saw the Reds beaten 2-0.

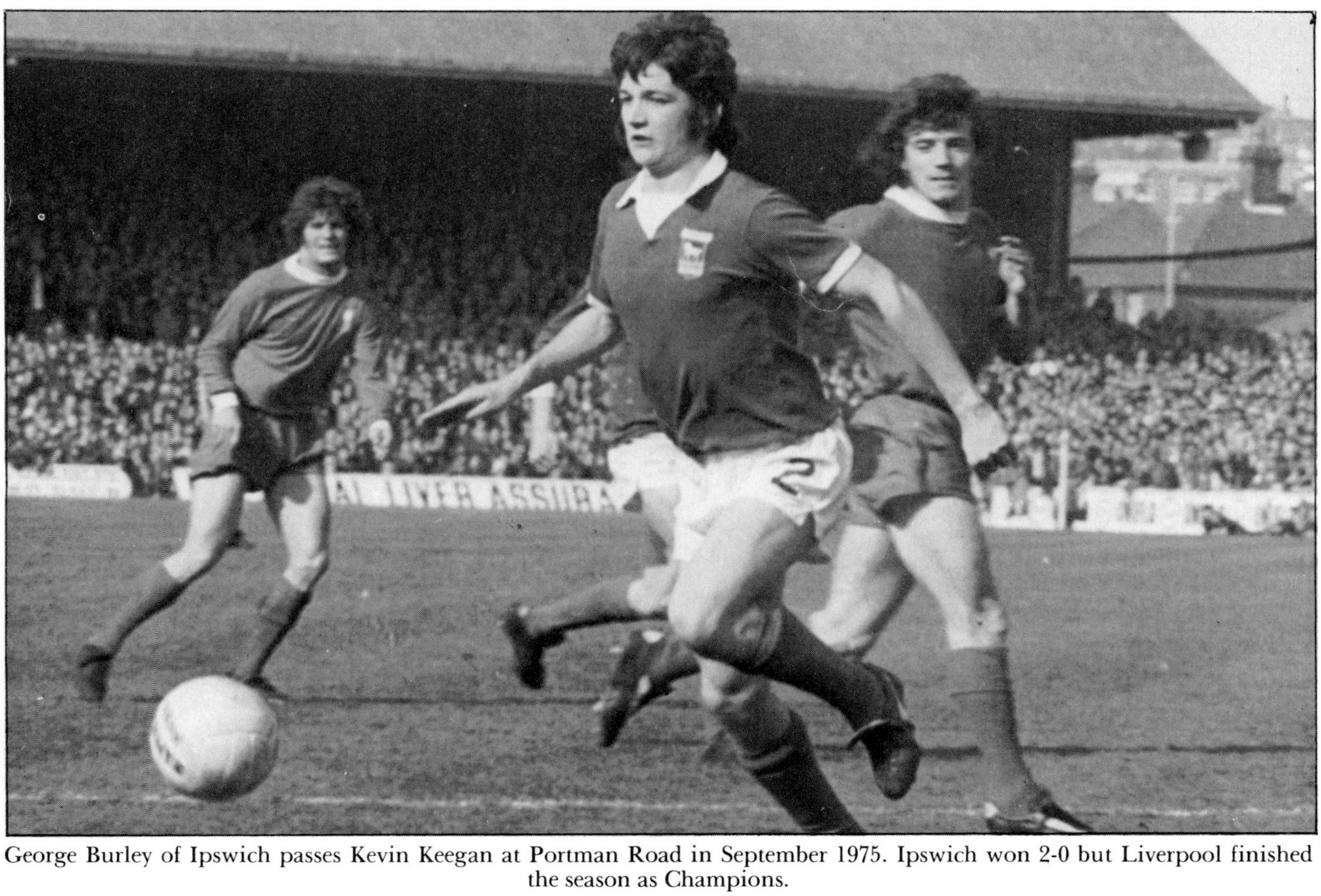

George Burley of Ipswich passes Kevin Keegan at Portman Road in September 1975. Ipswich won 2-0 but Liverpool finished the season as Champions.

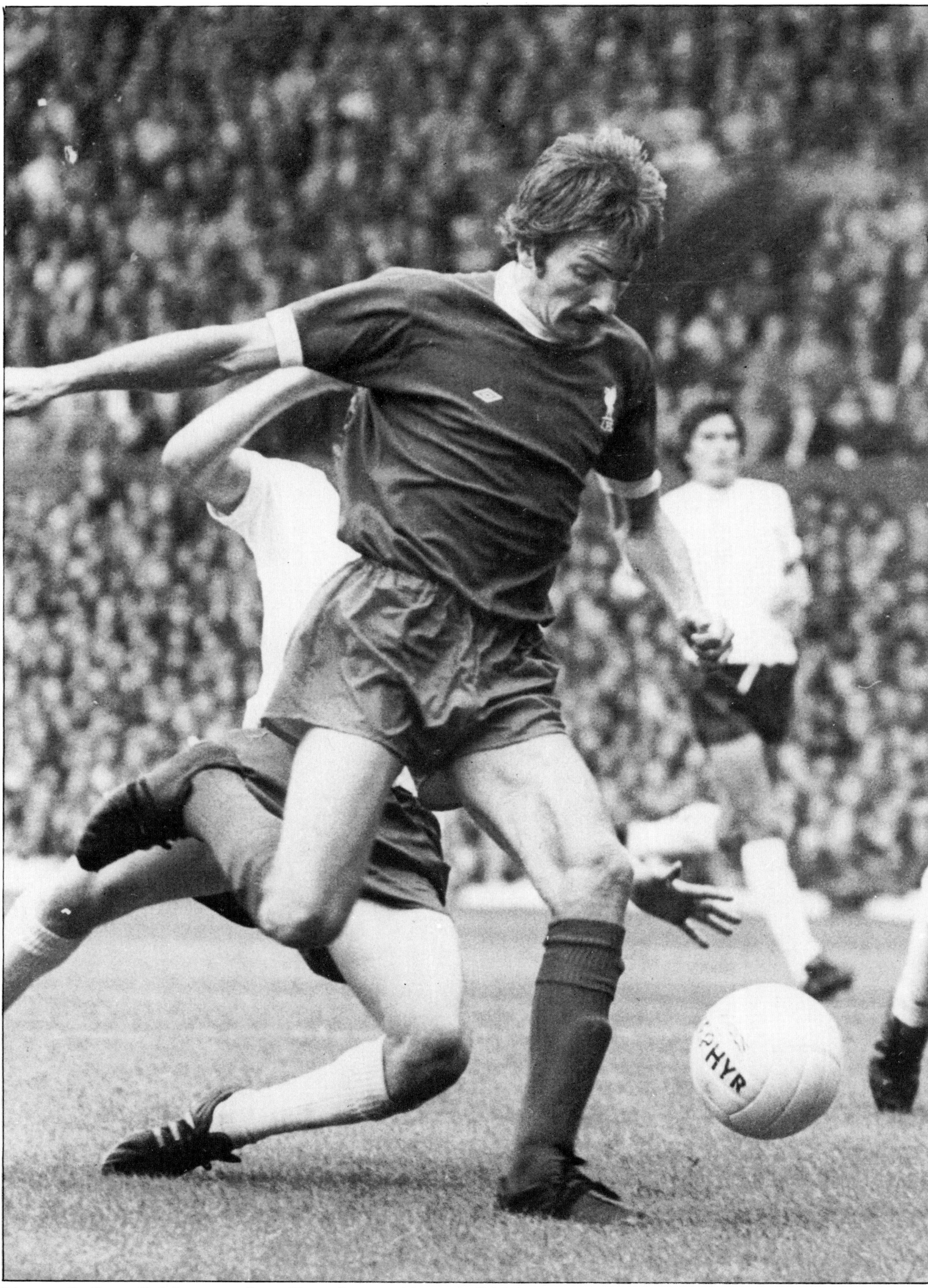

Liverpool's Steve Heighway evades a Tottenham tackle at Anfield in August 1975. The Reds had begun the season with a defeat and a draw. Spurs' visit looked to be prolonging their agony as the Londoners took a 2-0 half-time lead. But second-half goals from Keegan, Case and Heighway earned Liverpool their first win of a season which eventually saw them regain the title.

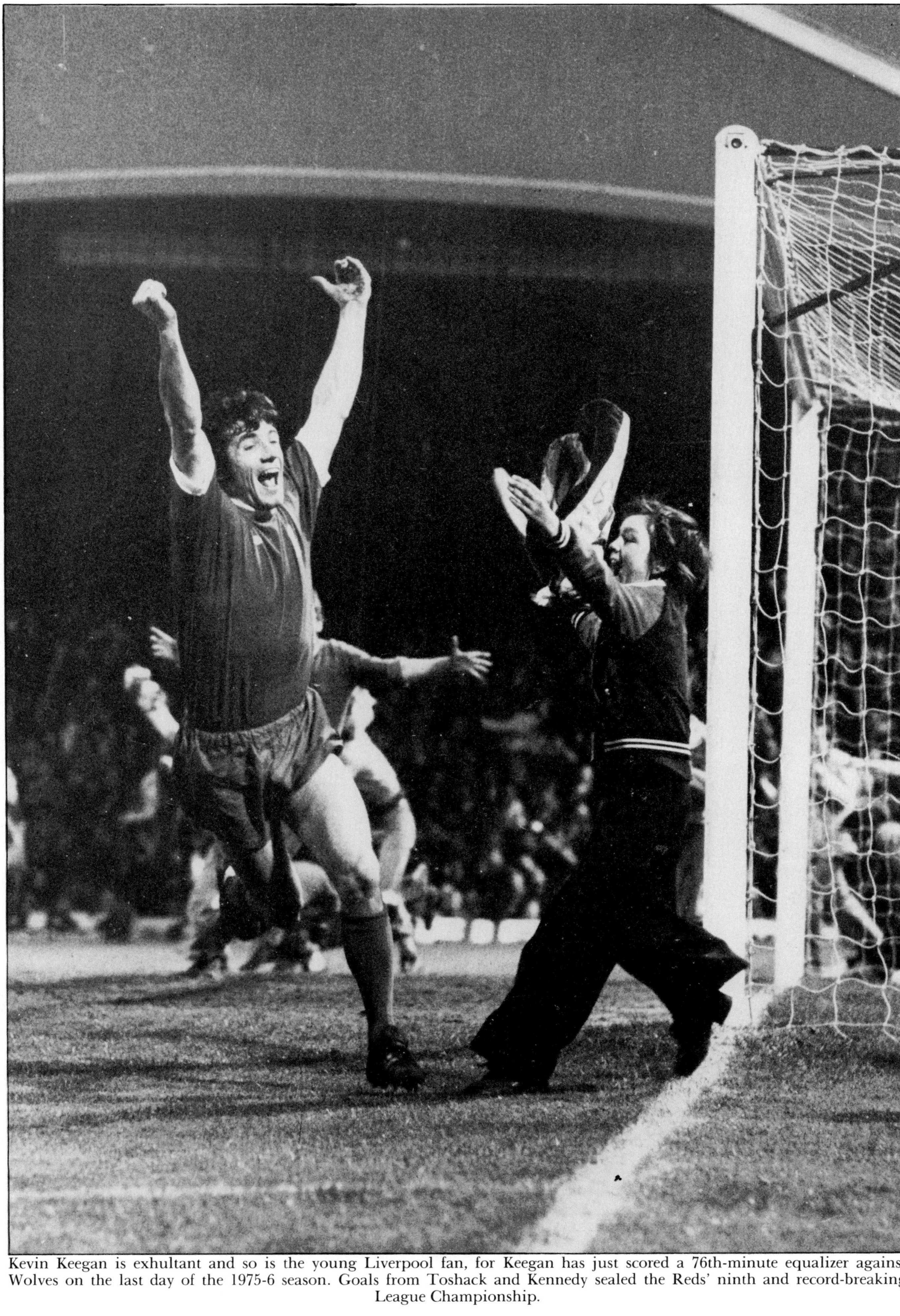

Kevin Keegan is exhultant and so is the young Liverpool fan, for Keegan has just scored a 76th-minute equalizer against Wolves on the last day of the 1975-6 season. Goals from Toshack and Kennedy sealed the Reds' ninth and record-breaking League Championship.

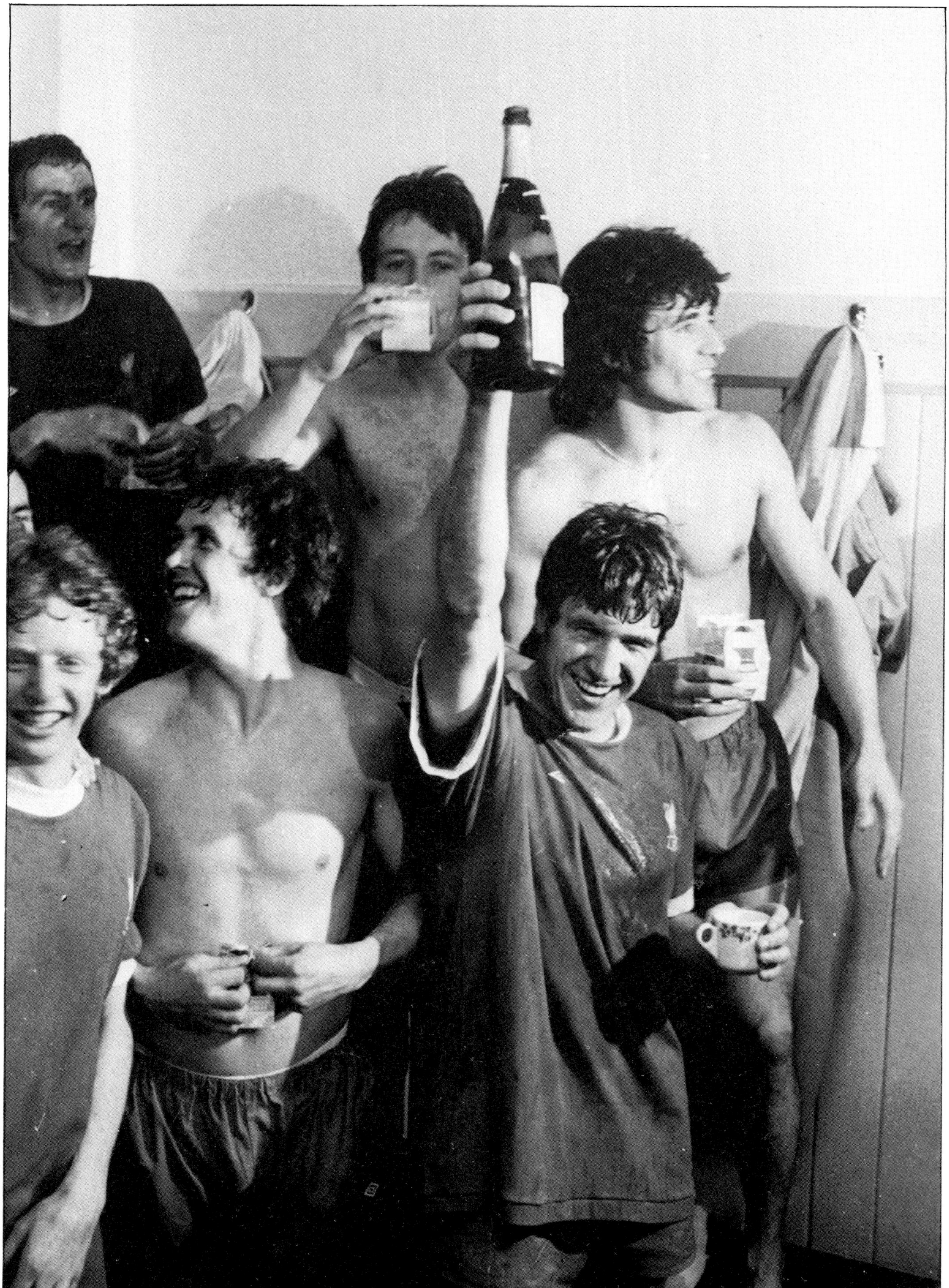

The champagne is uncorked and dressing-room celebrations can begin after another Championship victory. David Fairclough, Phil Neal and Emlyn Hughes are in the foreground, Phil Thompson, Jimmy Case and Kevin Keegan at the rear.

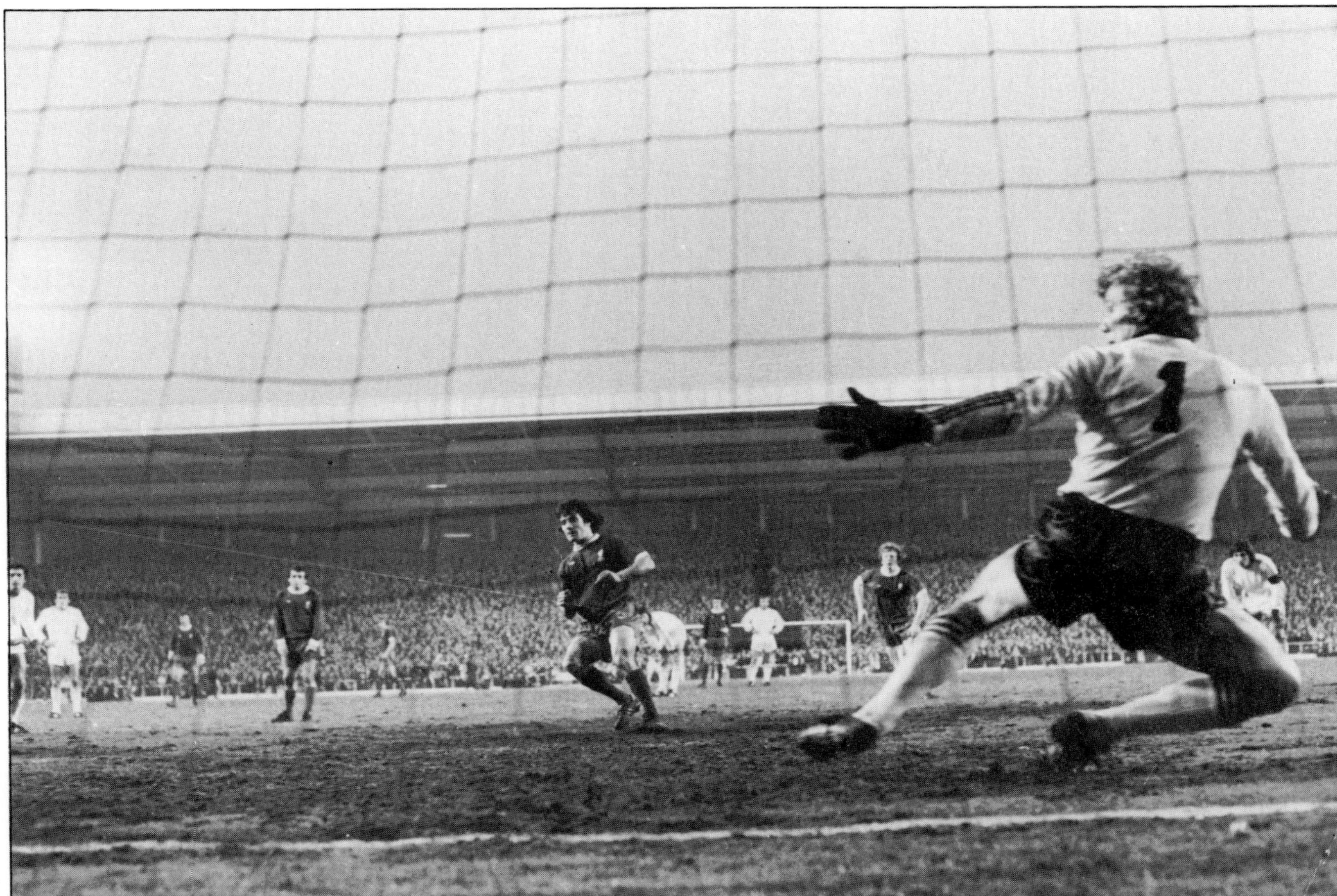

Kevin Keegan scores from the penalty-spot in the first leg of the 1976 UEFA Cup Final against FC Bruges. Keegan's goal completed a 3-2 win for Liverpool at Anfield after they had trailed 2-0 at half-time. A 1-1 draw in the second leg gave them the trophy for the second time.

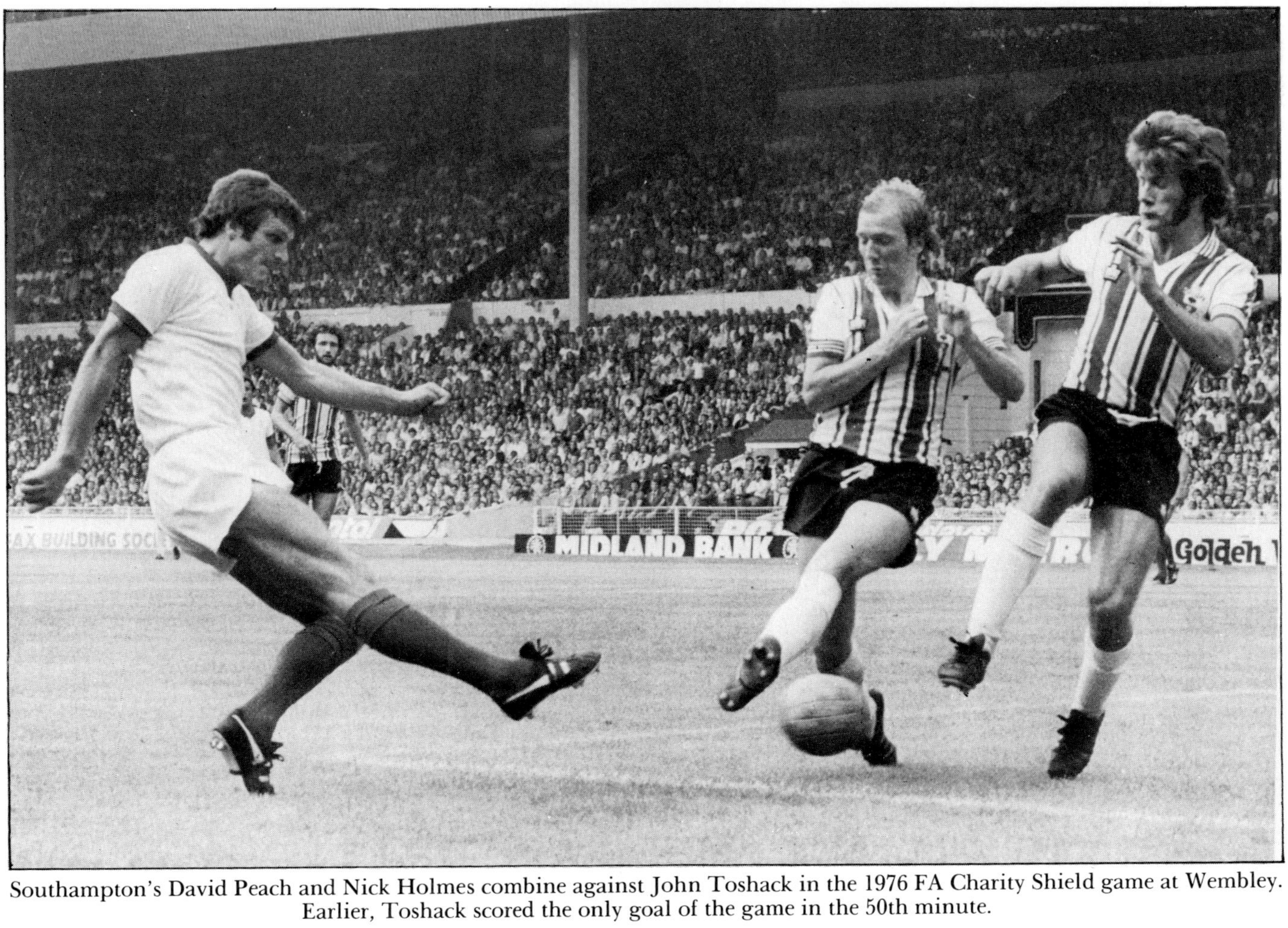

Southampton's David Peach and Nick Holmes combine against John Toshack in the 1976 FA Charity Shield game at Wembley. Earlier, Toshack scored the only goal of the game in the 50th minute.

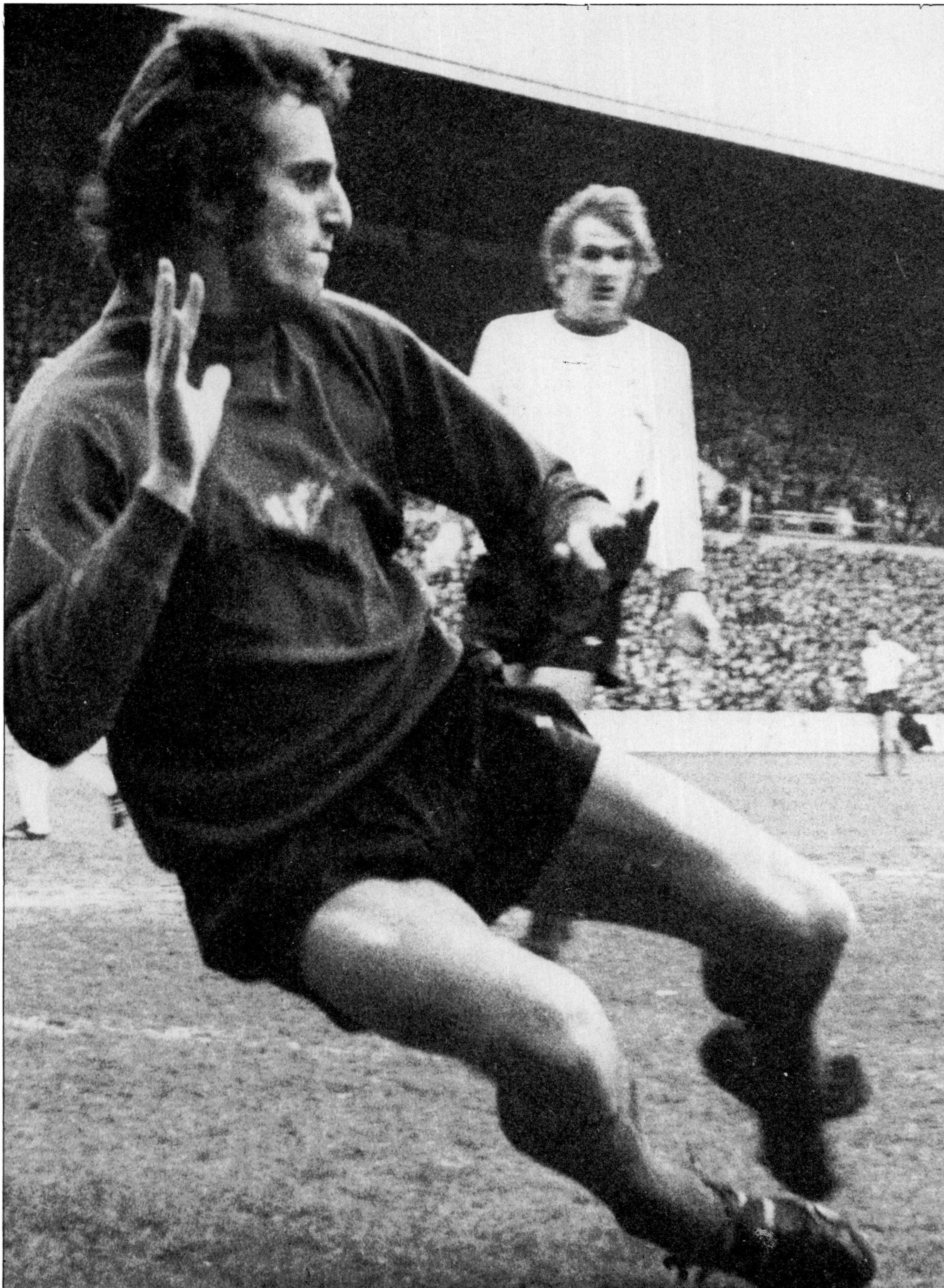

Like Kevin Keegan, Liverpool goalkeeper Ray Clemence joined the club from Scunthorpe United. Clemence came from the Old Show Ground for £18,000 in August 1965. By the time he moved to Tottenham Hotspur in August 1981 for £300,000, Clemence had made a staggering total of 656 first-team appearances for the Reds and would have won many more than his 61 England caps but for the presence of Peter Shilton.

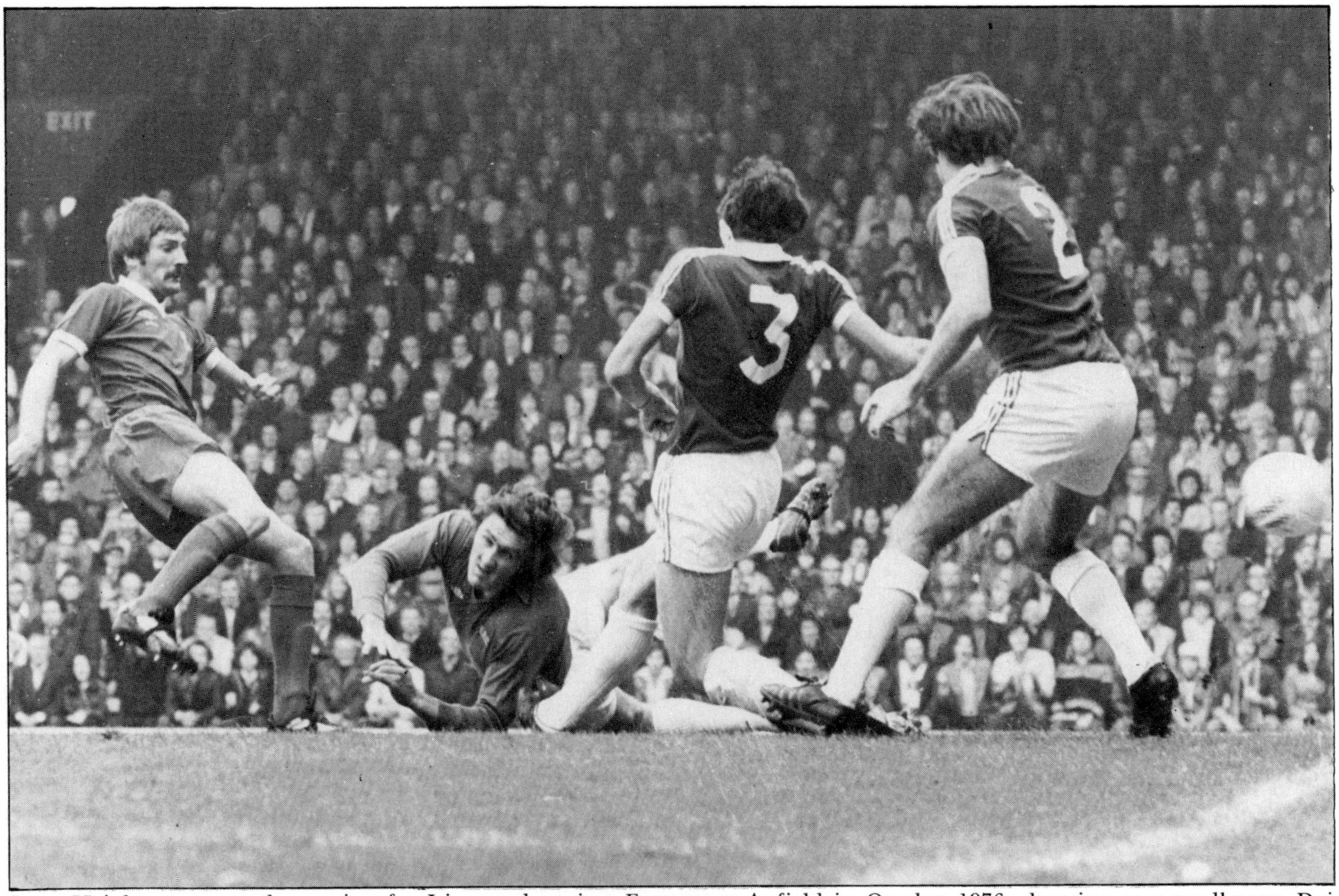

Steve Heighway opens the scoring for Liverpool against Everton at Anfield in October 1976, shooting past goalkeeper Dai Davies in the seventh minute. Five minutes later, Phil Neal scored from a penalty and John Toshack made it 3-0 before half-time. The Reds won 3-1 and went back to the top of Division One.

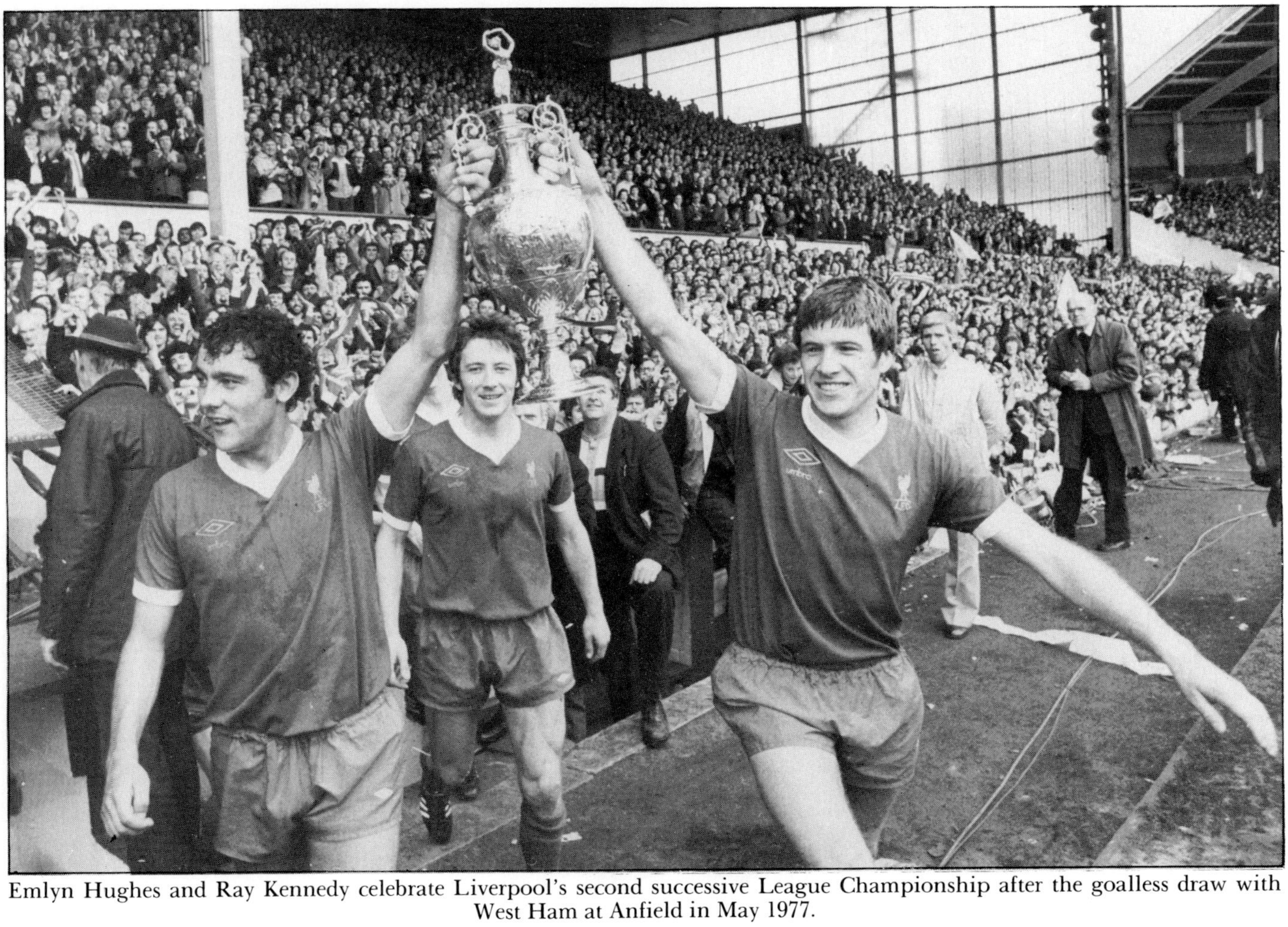

Emlyn Hughes and Ray Kennedy celebrate Liverpool's second successive League Championship after the goalless draw with West Ham at Anfield in May 1977.

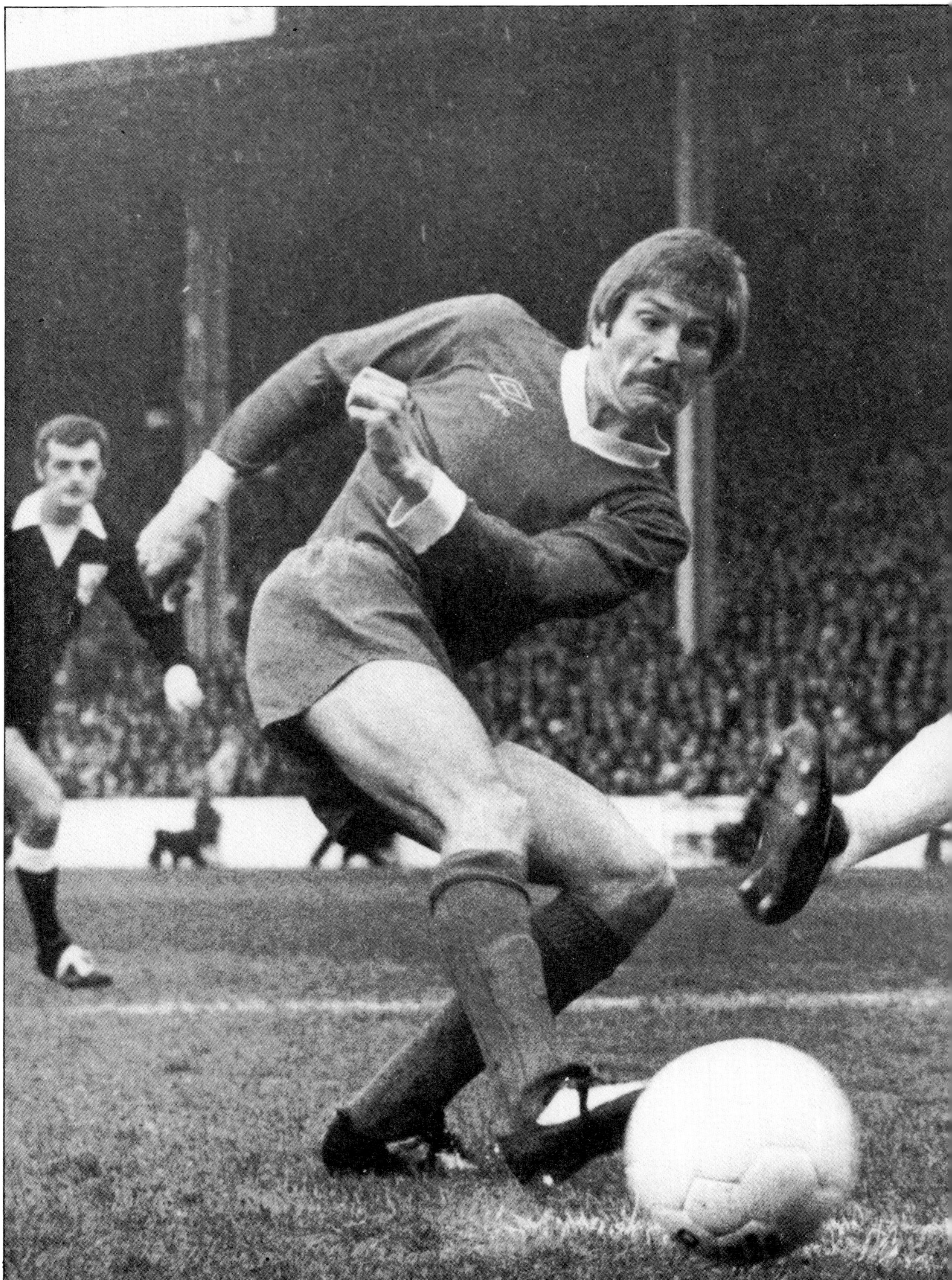

Steve Heighway tries a shot in the 1977 FA Cup semi-final as Everton's Terry Darracott lunges into t

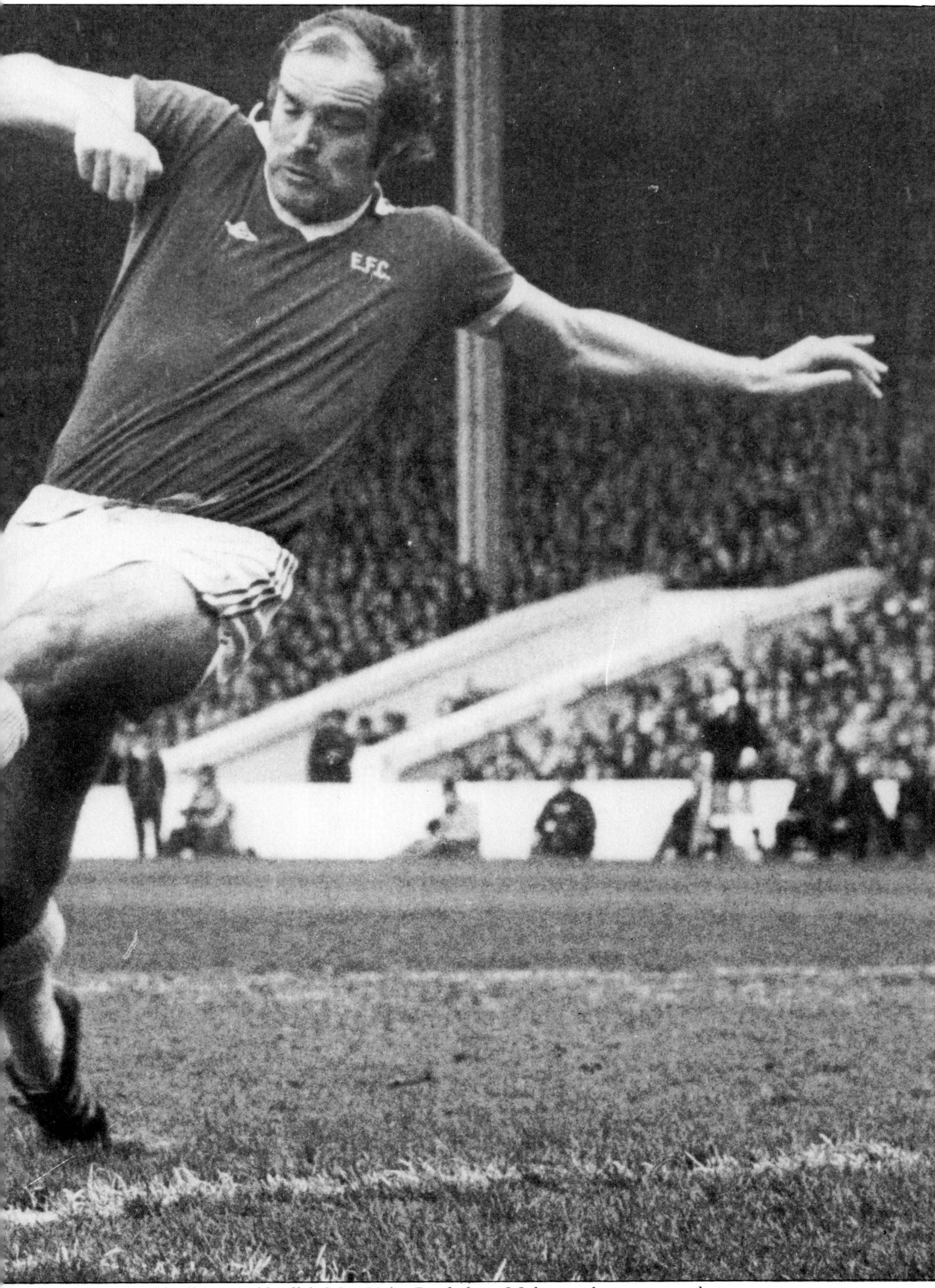

kle. The Reds won this all-Merseyside affair 3-0 at Maine Road after a 2-2 draw at the same ground.

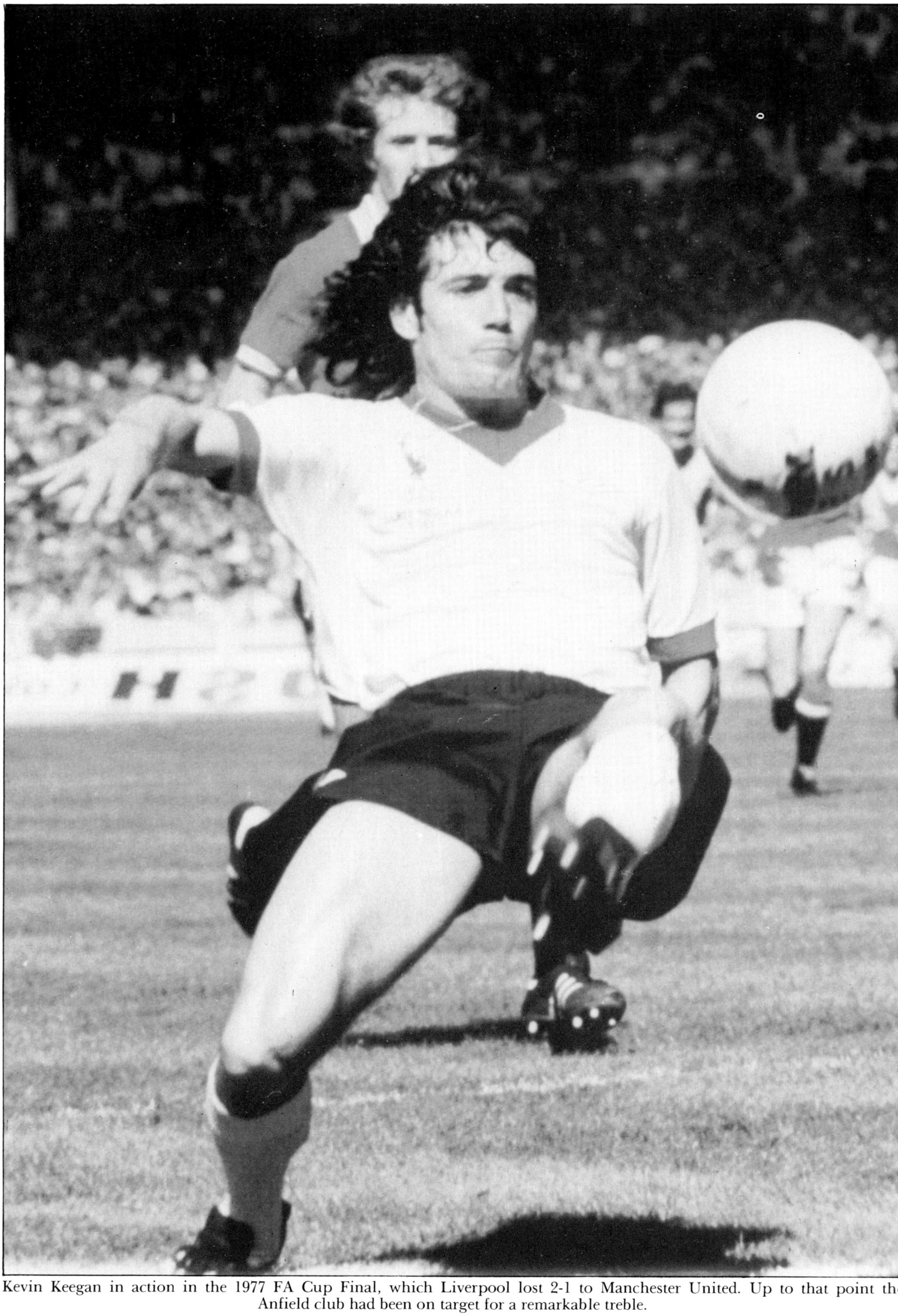

Kevin Keegan in action in the 1977 FA Cup Final, which Liverpool lost 2-1 to Manchester United. Up to that point the Anfield club had been on target for a remarkable treble.

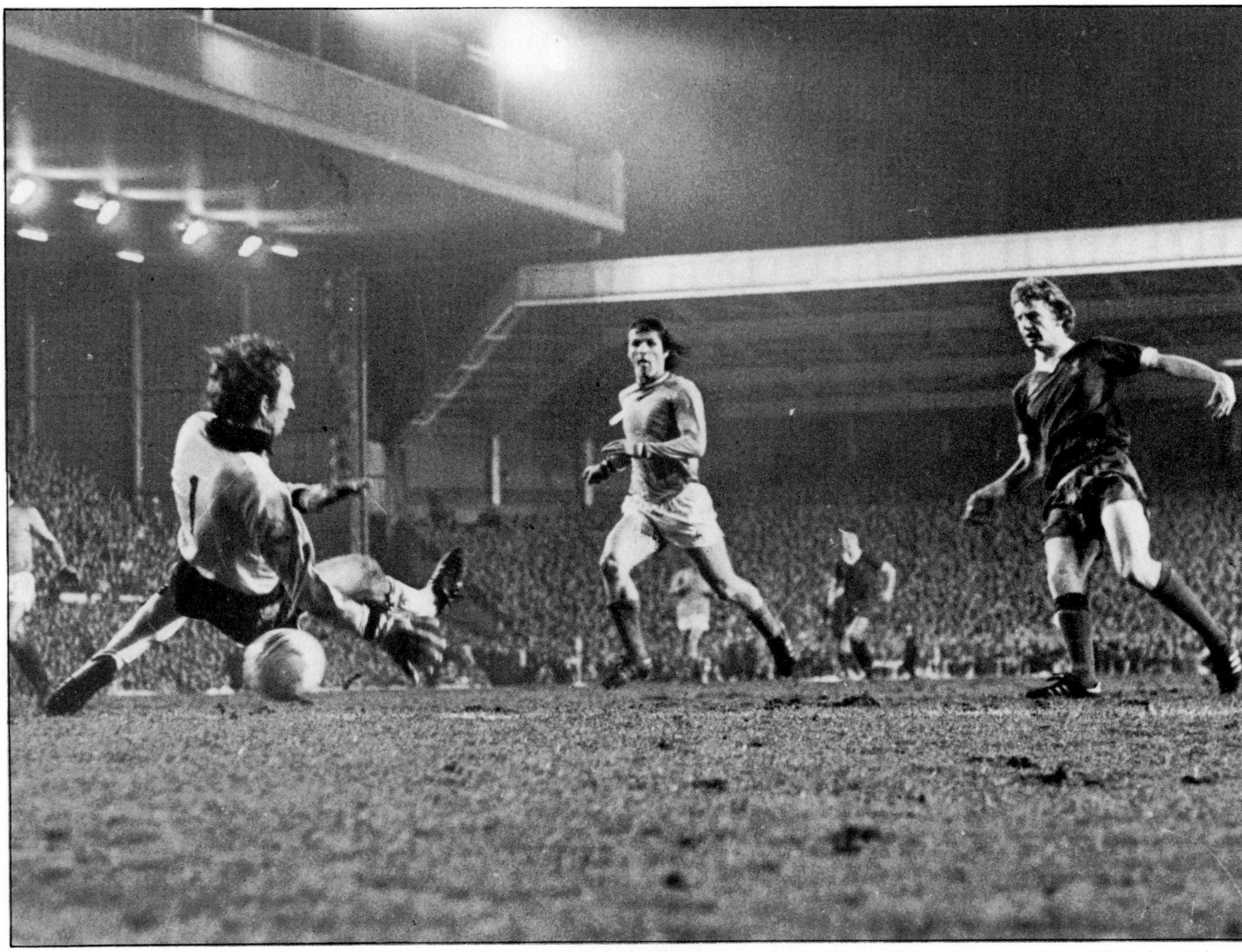

David Fairclough scores Liverpool's third goal in the European Cup quarter-final second-leg game against AS Saint-Etienne at Anfield in March 1977. In the semi-final, the Reds beat FC Zürich 6-1 on aggregate to meet Borussia Mönchengladbach in the Final in Rome.

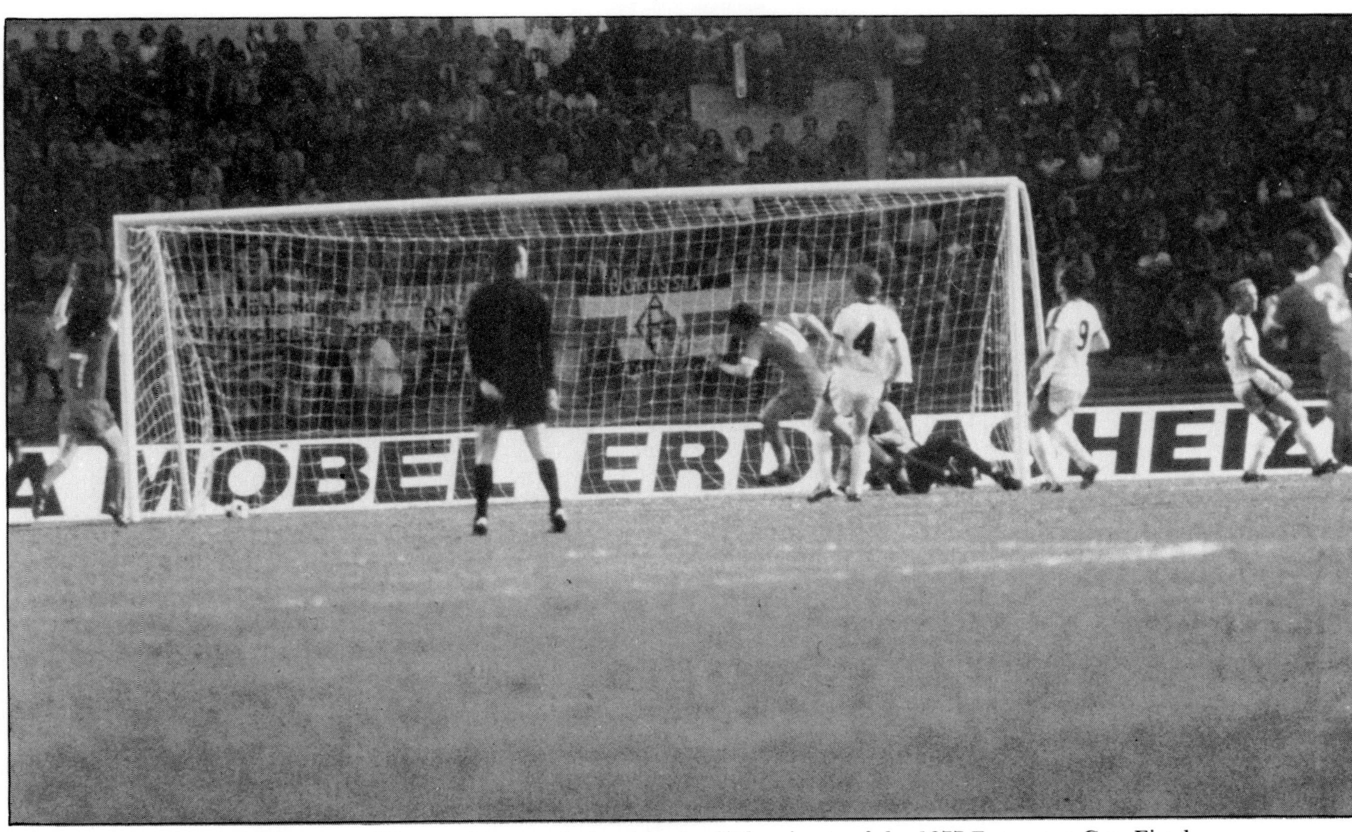

Terry McDermott (11) puts Liverpool ahead in the 27th minute of the 1977 European Cup Final.

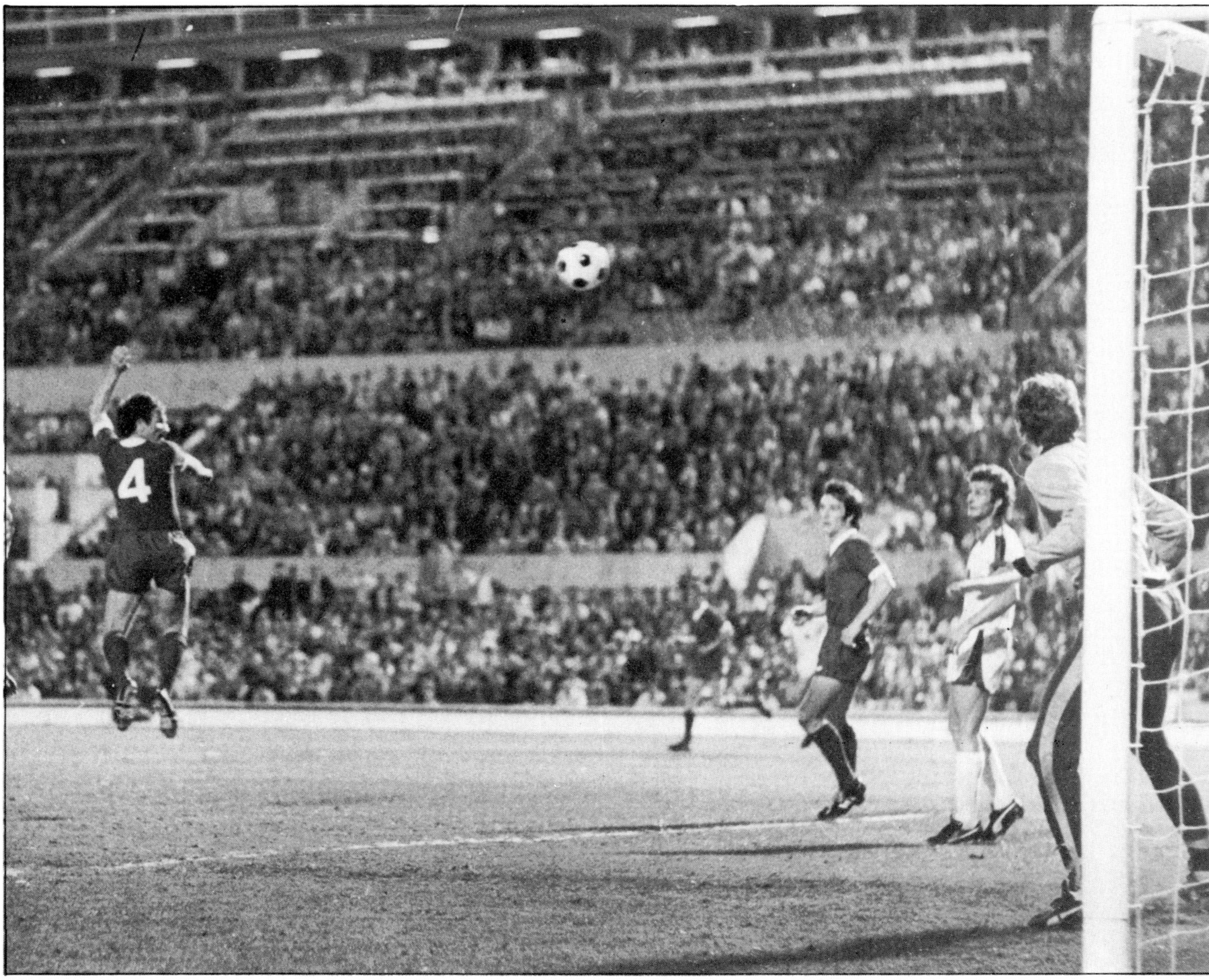

Tommy Smith nets the Reds' second with this header past the Germans' goalkeeper, Kneib.

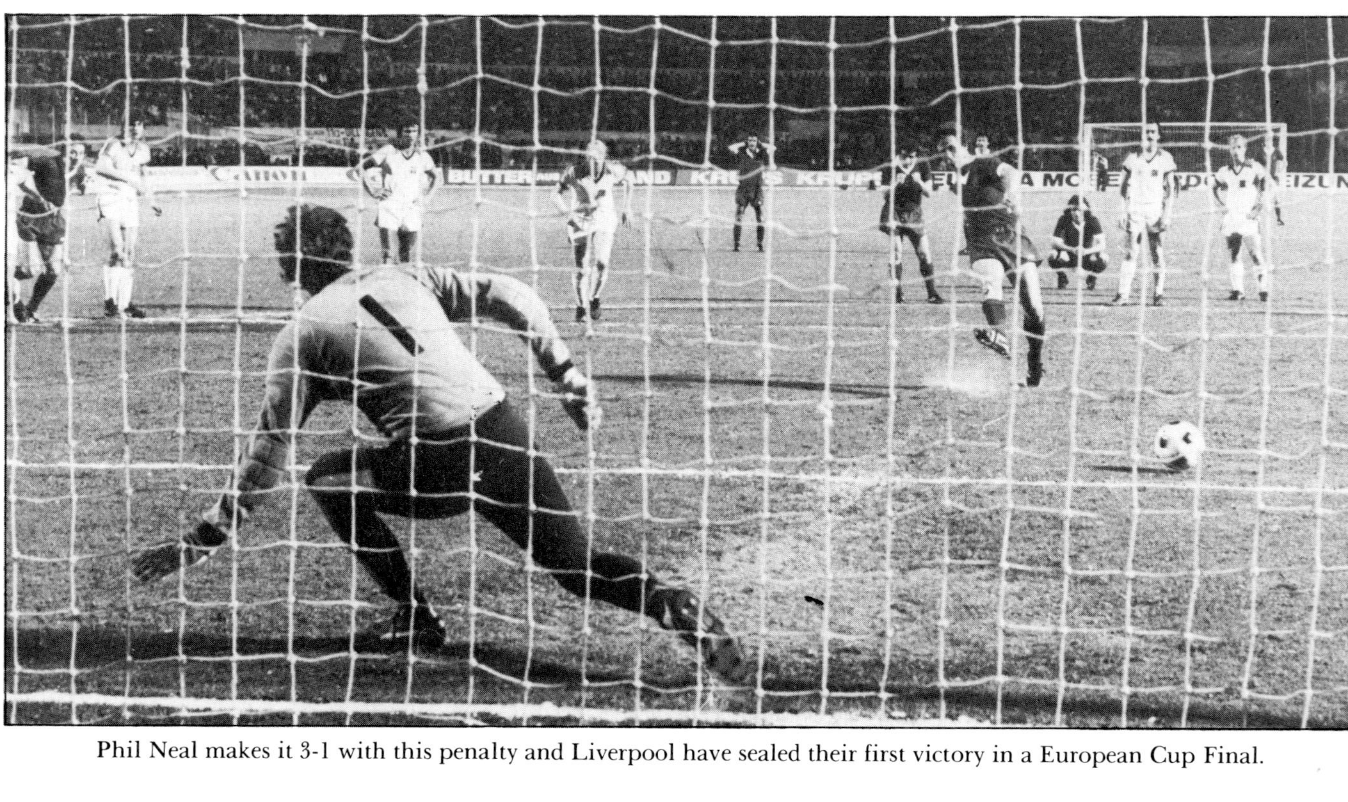

Phil Neal makes it 3-1 with this penalty and Liverpool have sealed their first victory in a European Cup Final.

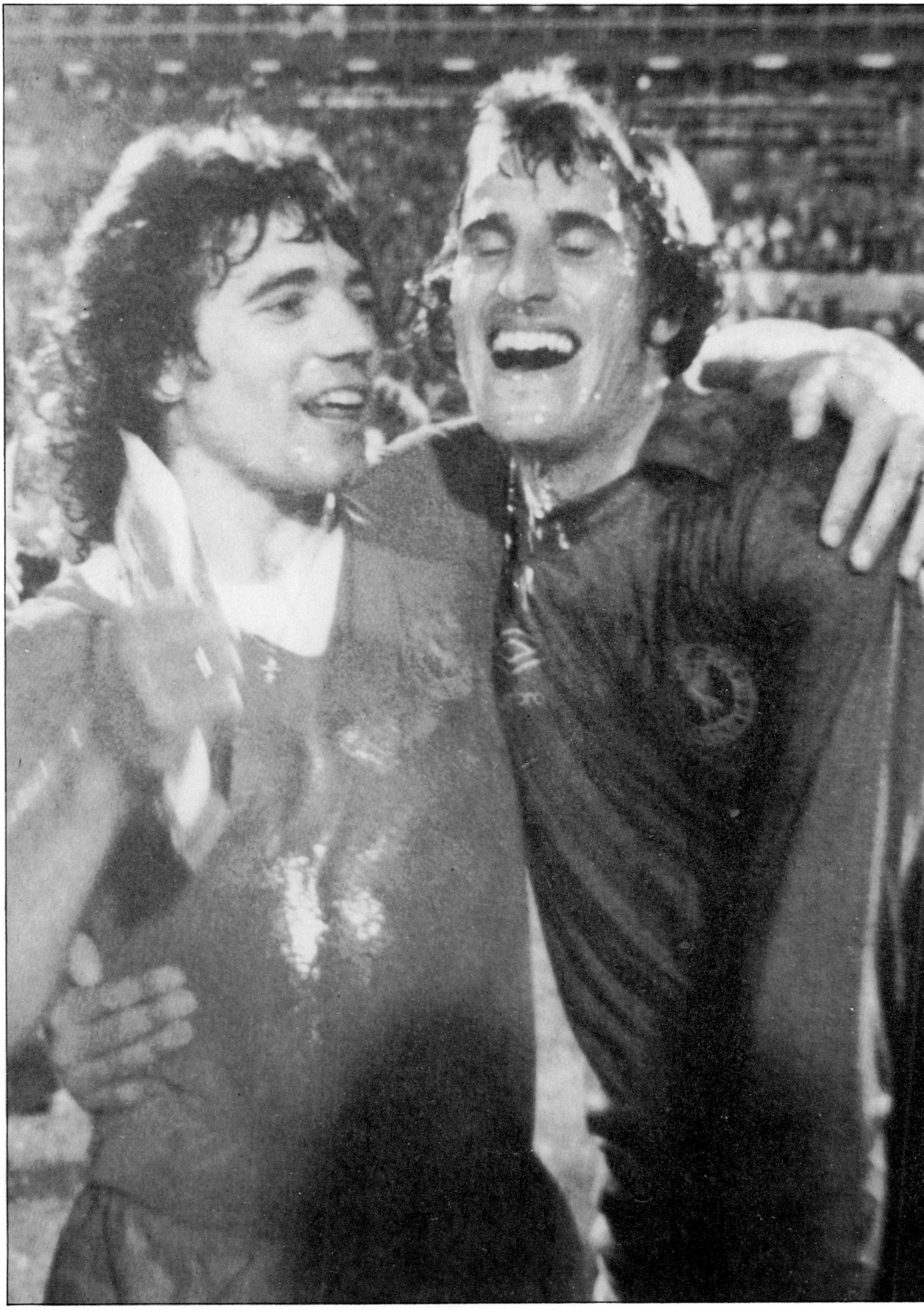

Kevin Keegan, man of the match in the 1977 European Cup Final, and Ray Clemence are in a deleriously happy mood after Liverpool's win over Borussia Mönchengladbach.

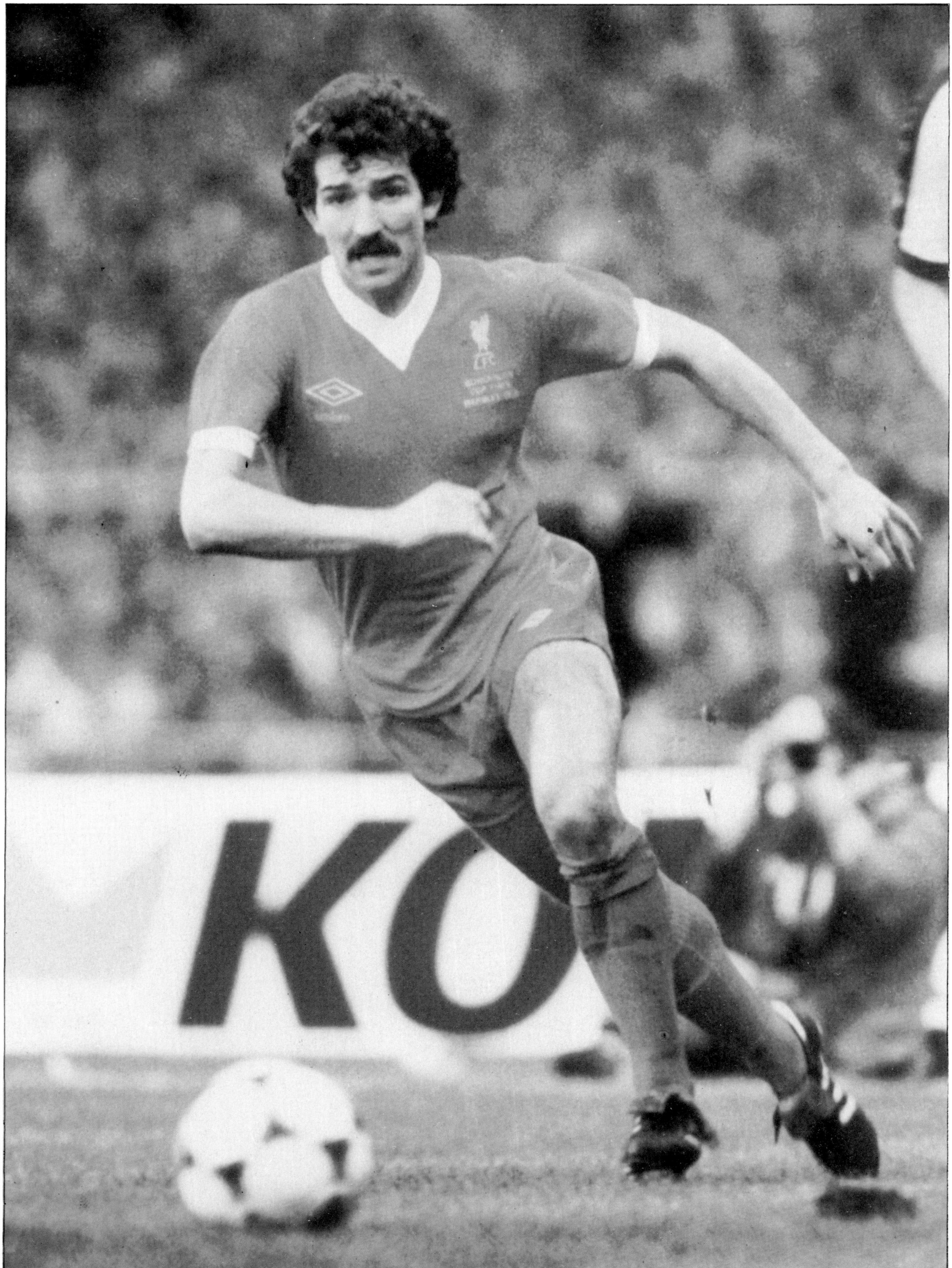

Graham Souness joined the Reds from Middlesbrough for £352,000 in January 1978 and in his first season won a European Cup winners' medal when he supplied the pass for Kenny Dalglish to score the only goal in the Final against Bruges. Souness went on to gain winners' medals in two more European Cup Finals as well as League Championship and League Cup winners' medals. A Scottish international, he scored 56 goals in 352 senior appearances for the Reds before moving to Sampdoria for £650,000 in June 1984 and then back to Anfield as manager via a spell as Rangers' boss.

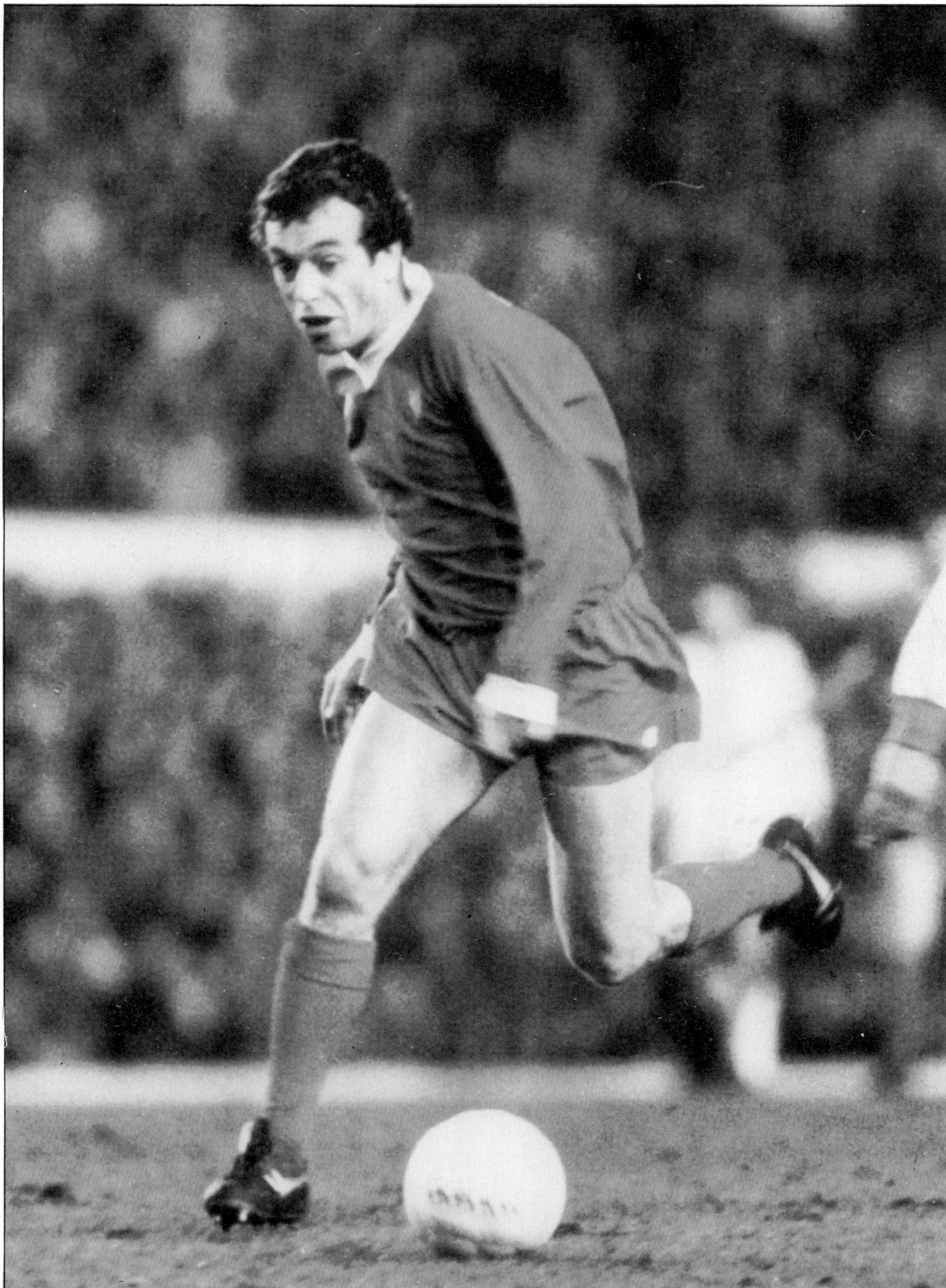

Ian Callaghan enjoyed a remarkably long career with Liverpool, the club he joined from school in 1957. Callaghan, a skilful midfielder, holds the Reds' League appearances record with 640 games and altogether played in 848 senior matches, scoring 60 goals, before moving to Swansea City in 1978. The Footballer of the Year in 1974, he won England honours and winners' medals in the European Cup, UEFA Cup and FA Cup as well as First and Second Division championship medals.

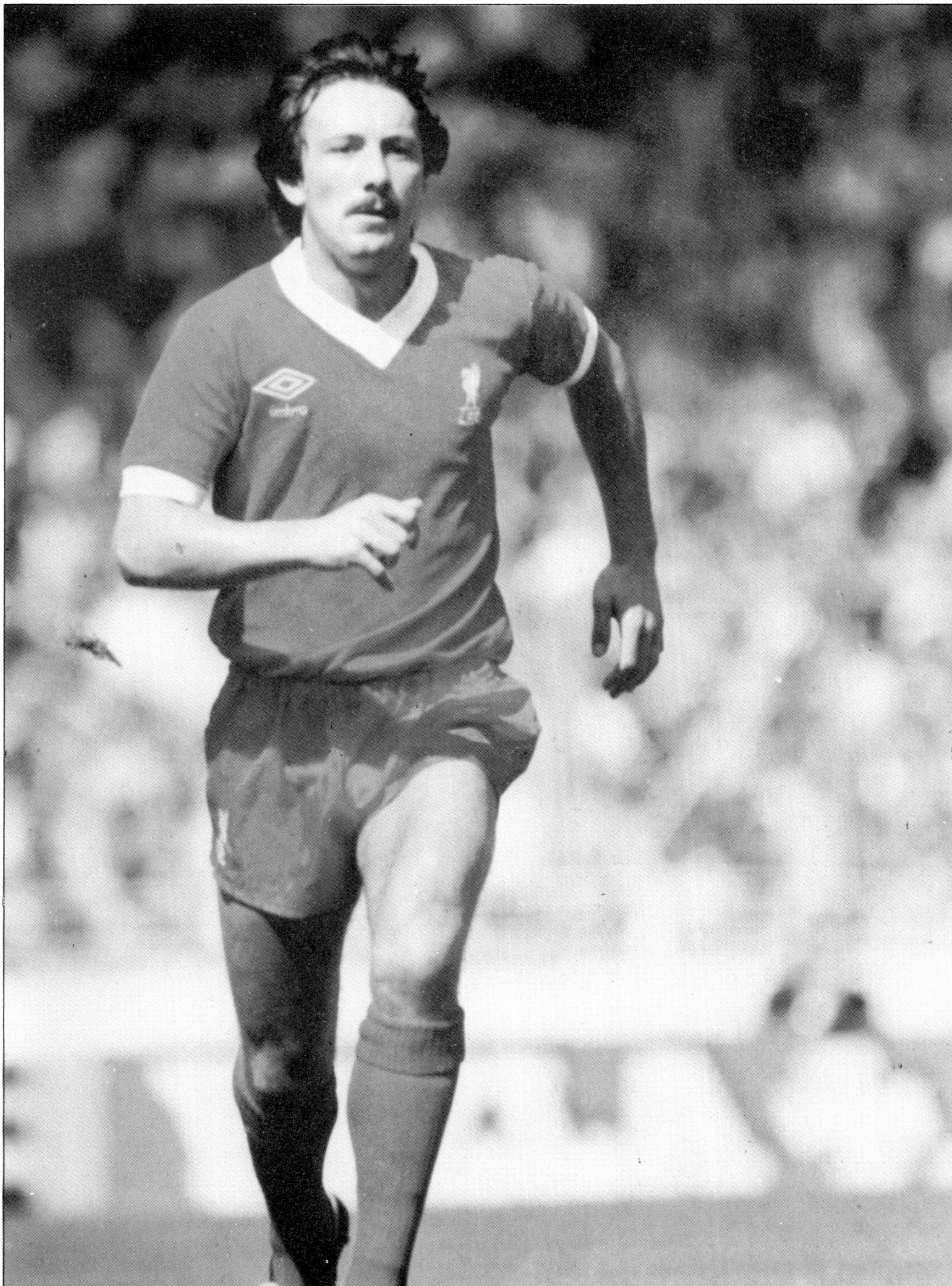

Jimmy Case, veteran of 261 senior games for Liverpool, was an amateur with the club before signing professional forms in May 1973, costing the Reds a £500 fee to South Liverpool. A hard-tackling ball-winner, Case won European Cup, UEFA Cup, League Championship, FA Cup and League Cup winners' medals with Liverpool before being transferred to Brighton for £350,000 in August 1981. He later extended his career with a move to Southampton and then Halifax Town.

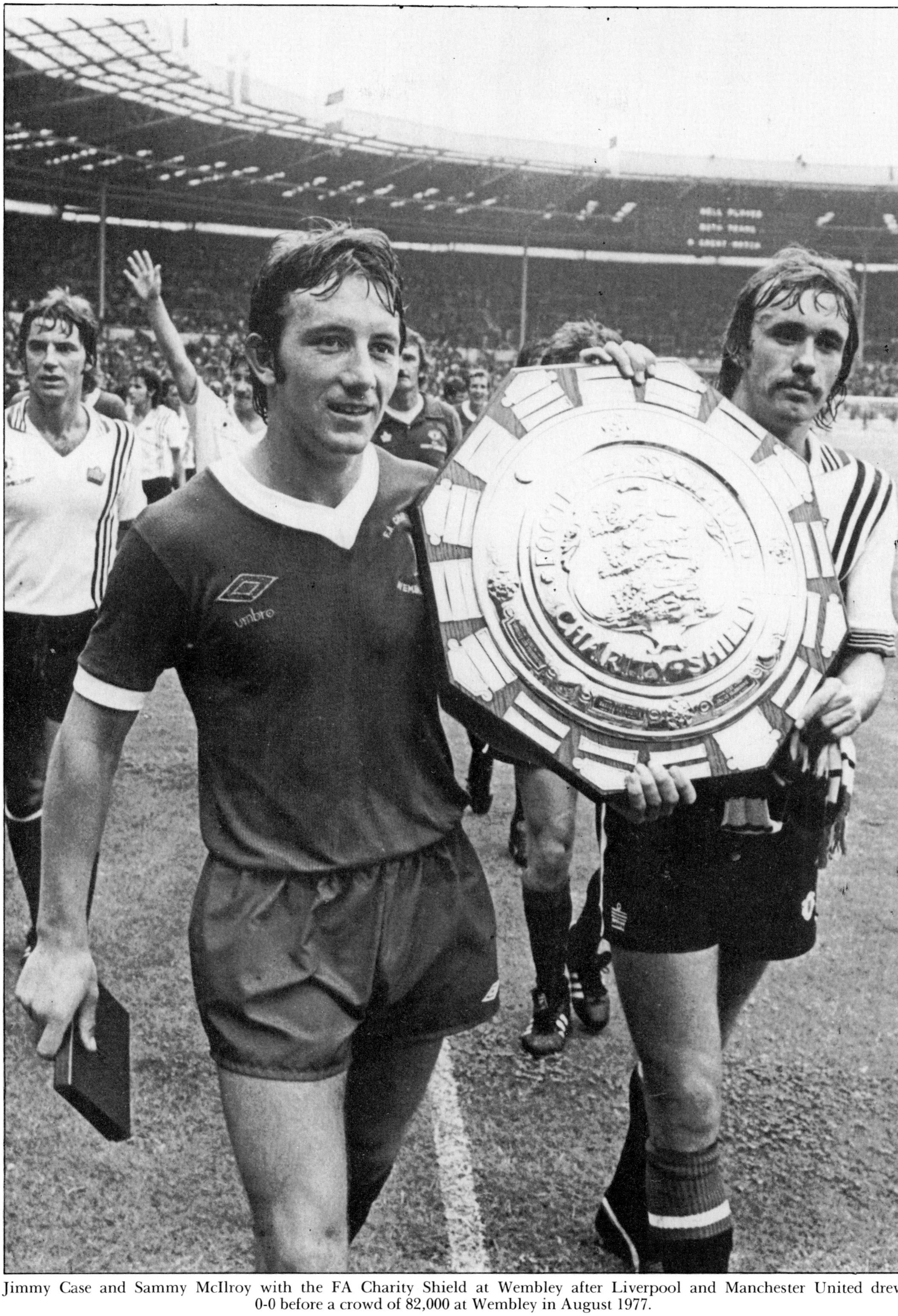

Jimmy Case and Sammy McIlroy with the FA Charity Shield at Wembley after Liverpool and Manchester United drew 0-0 before a crowd of 82,000 at Wembley in August 1977.

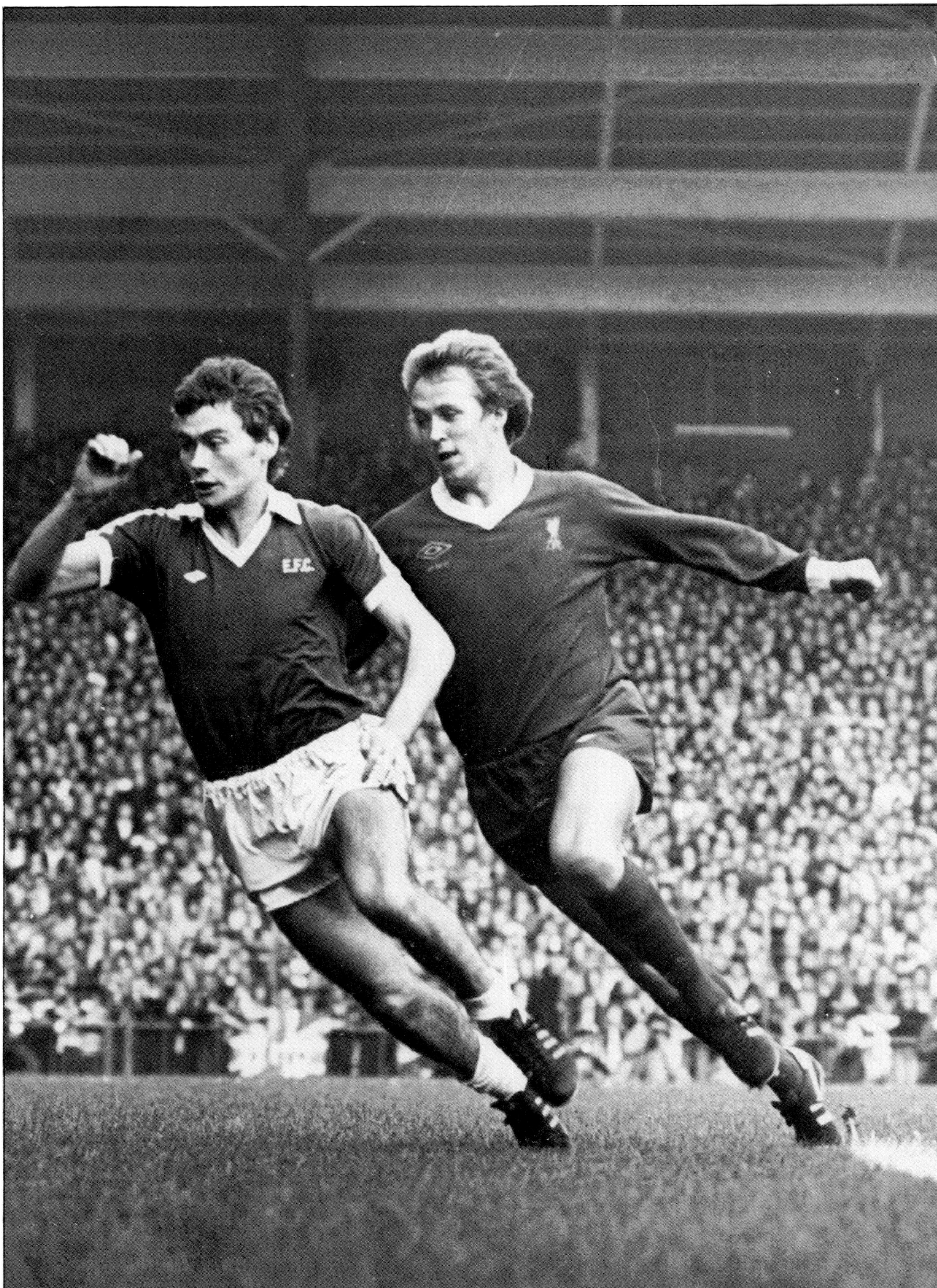

Phil Neal and Everton's Dave Thomas in action at Anfield in October 1977, in a Merseyside derby which ended in a goalless draw. Liverpool ended the 1977-8 season as runners-up to Nottingham Forest.

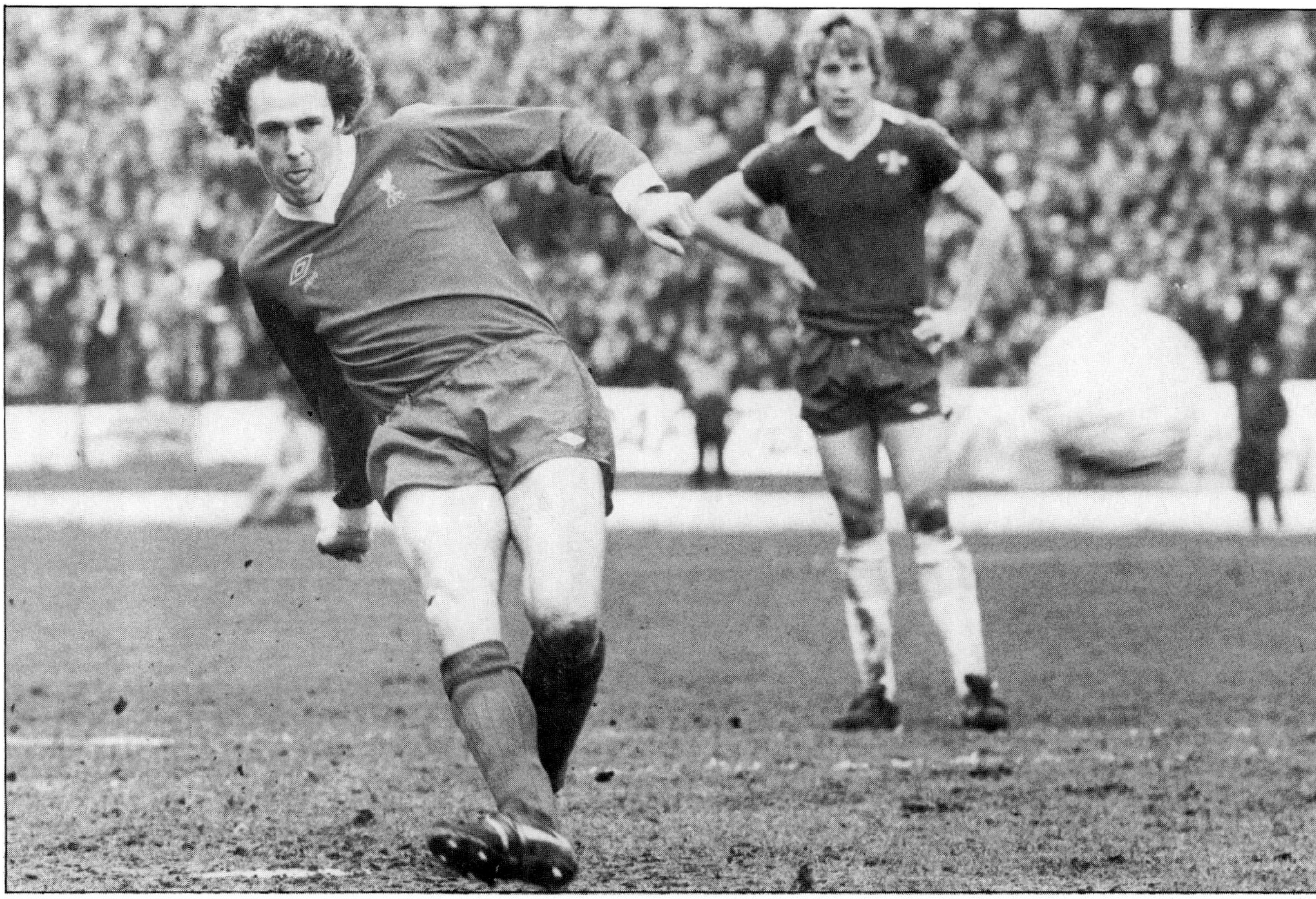

Phil Neal scores from the penalty-spot at Stamford Bridge in March 1978, but the Reds lost 3-1.

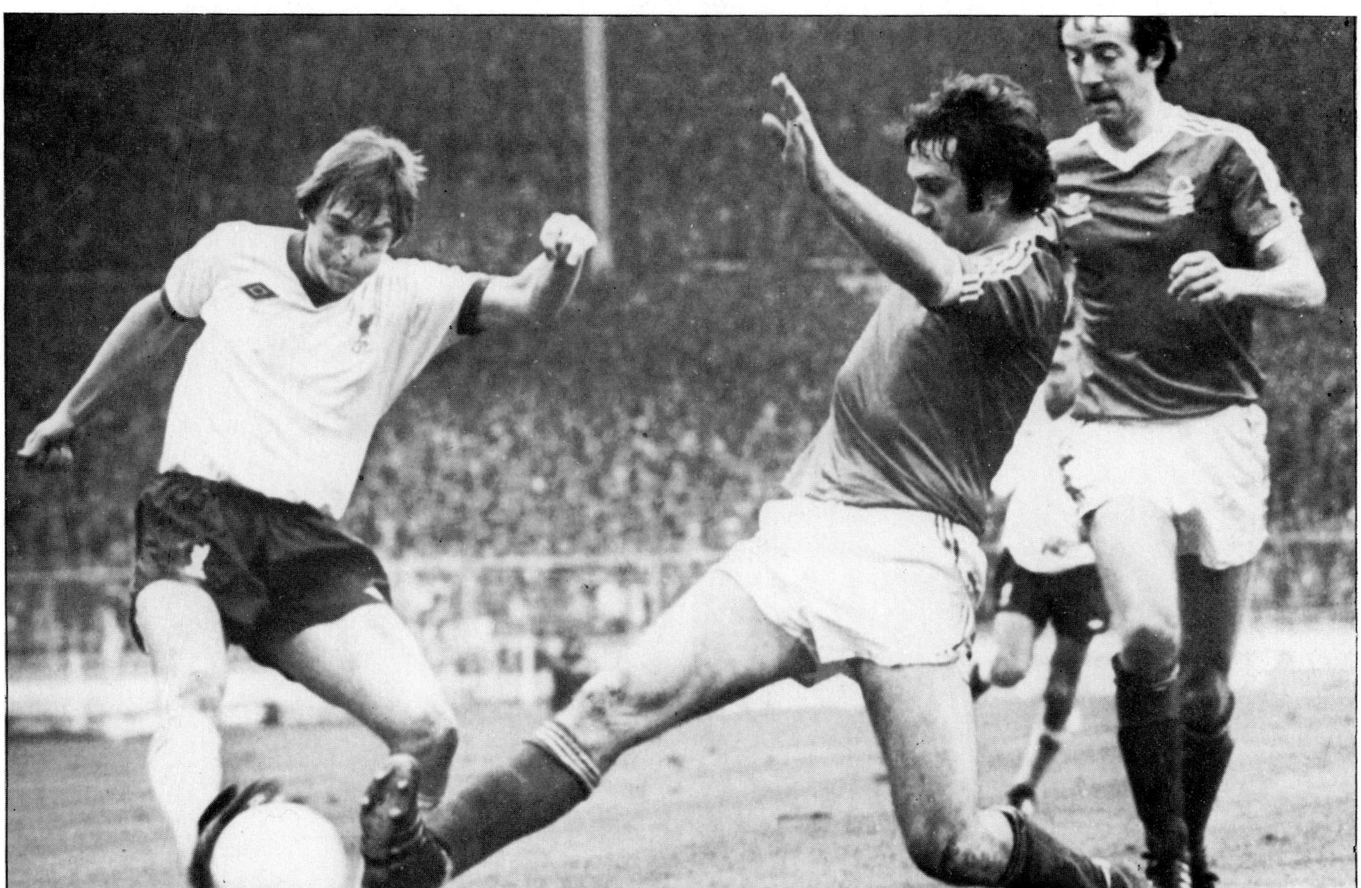

Kenny Dalglish (white shirt) gets in a shot as Nottingham Forest's Larry Lloyd, a former Liverpool player, and Frank Clark close in during the 1978 Football League Cup Final at Wembley. The game ended in a goalless draw before Brian Clough's team won the replay 1-0 at Old Trafford with a hotly disputed penalty-kick after Phil Thompson was adjudged to have brought down John O'Hare.

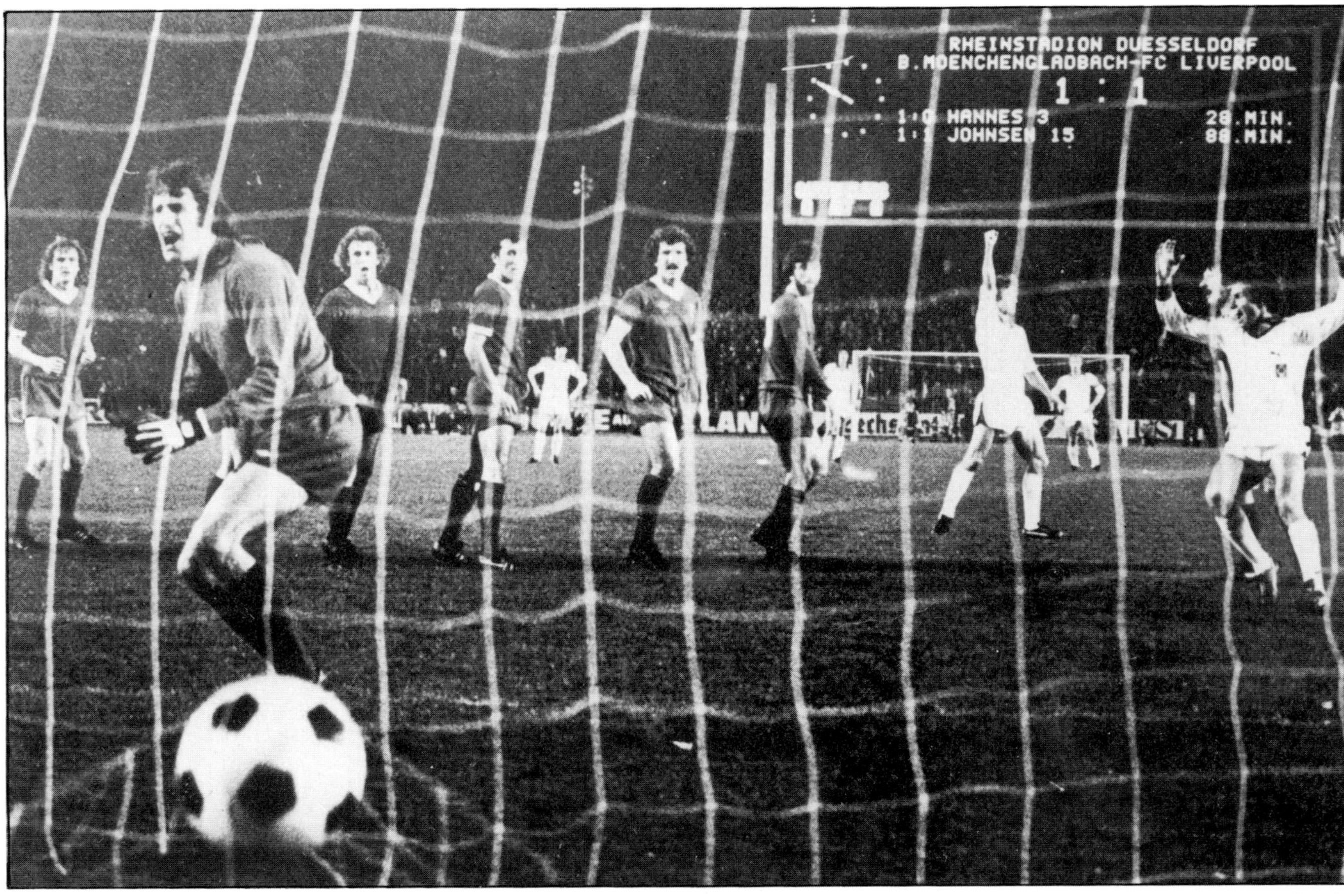

Horror is etched on the faces of the Liverpool defenders as Borussia Mönchengladbach snatch a last-minute victory in the first leg of the 1978 European Cup semi-final in Düsseldorf.

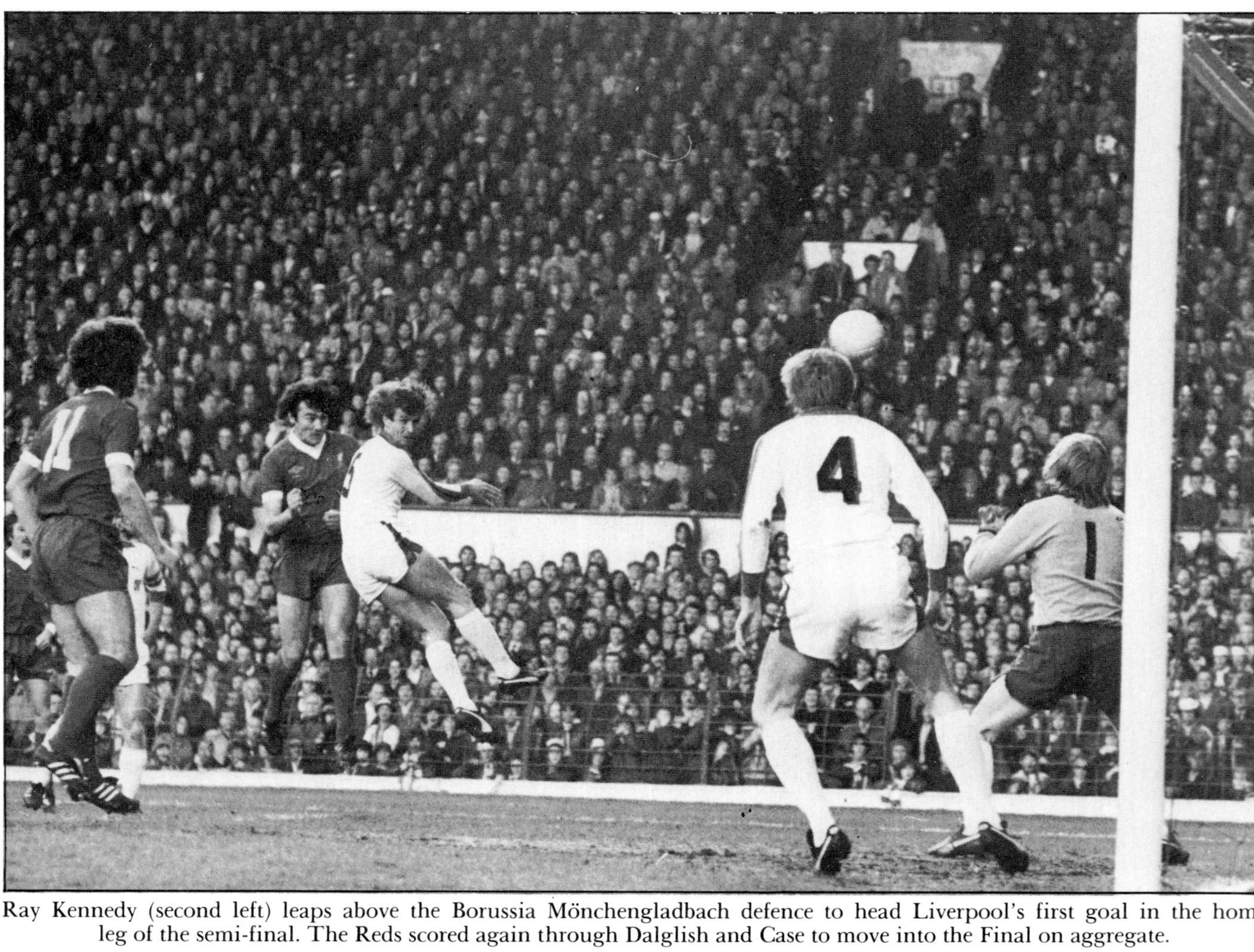

Ray Kennedy (second left) leaps above the Borussia Mönchengladbach defence to head Liverpool's first goal in the home leg of the semi-final. The Reds scored again through Dalglish and Case to move into the Final on aggregate.

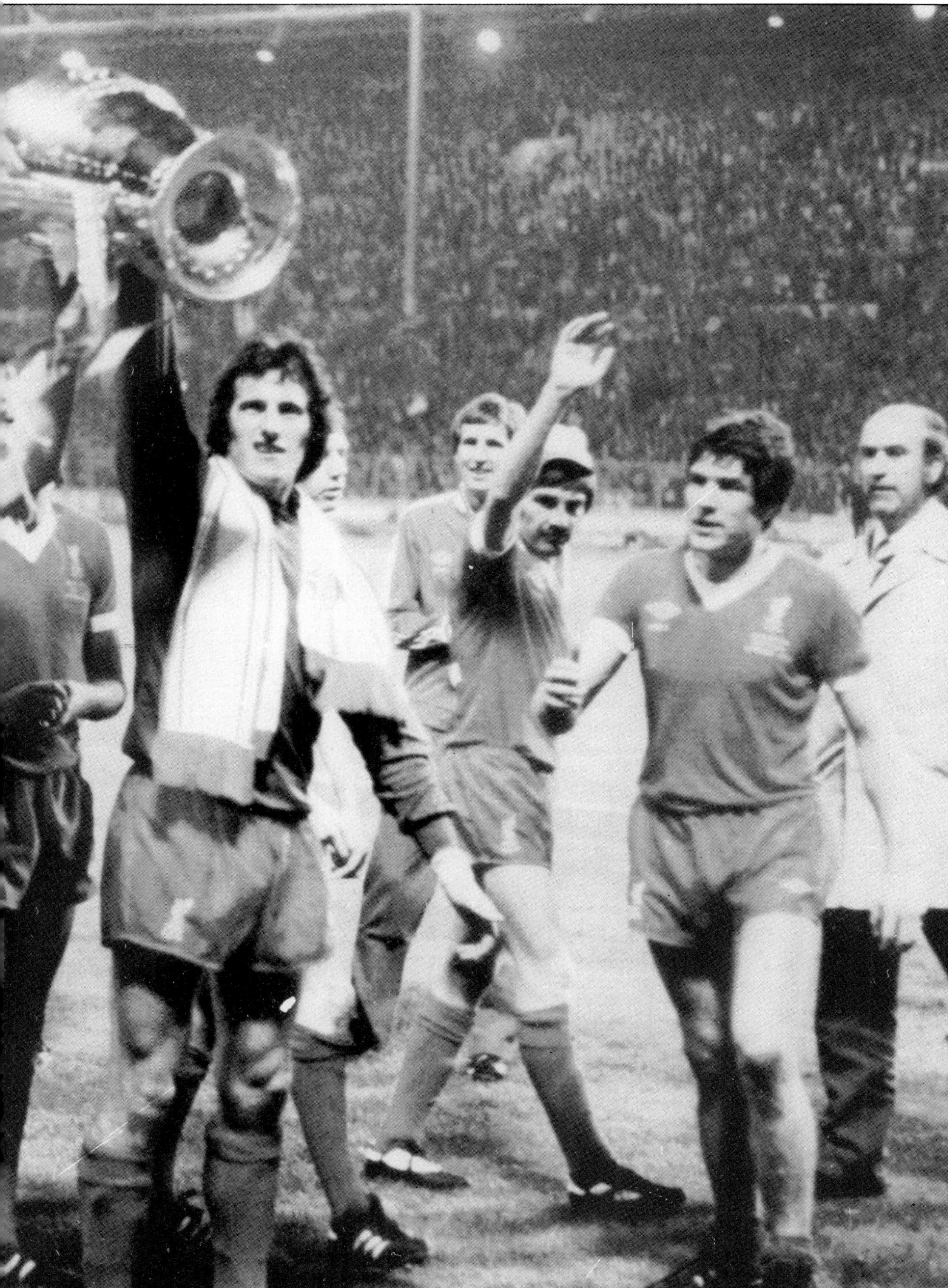

Reds retained the trophy with a 1-0 over Club Brugge KV.

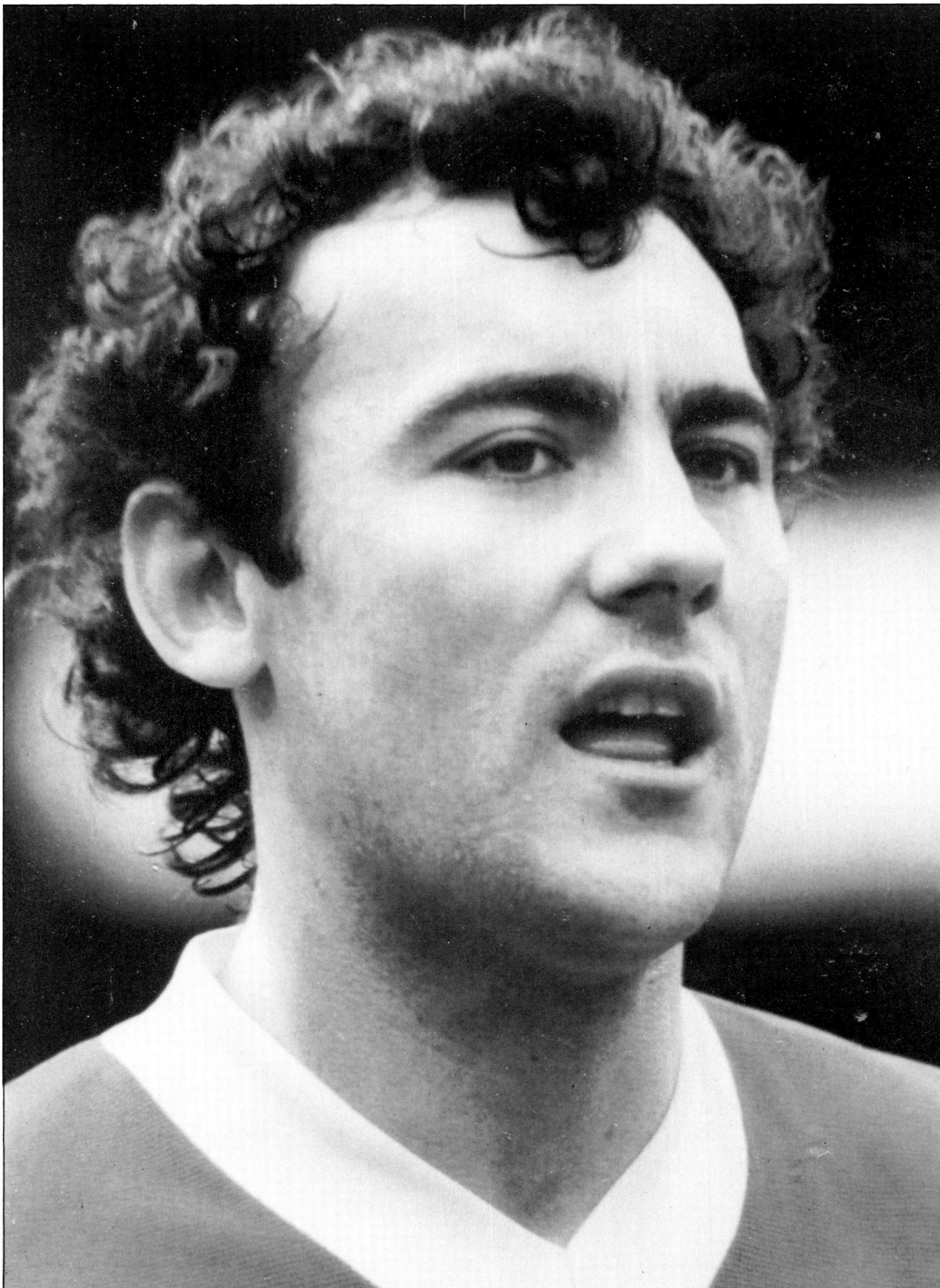

Midfielder Ray Kennedy was signed from Arsenal after playing in the Gunners' 1970-71 double-winning side which beat Liverpool in the FA Cup Final. He cost the Reds £180,000 in July 1974 and made 384 senior appearances, scoring 72 goals, and gaining winners' medals in the European Cup, UEFA Cup, League Championship and Football League Cup. He moved to Swansea City for £160,000 in January 1982.

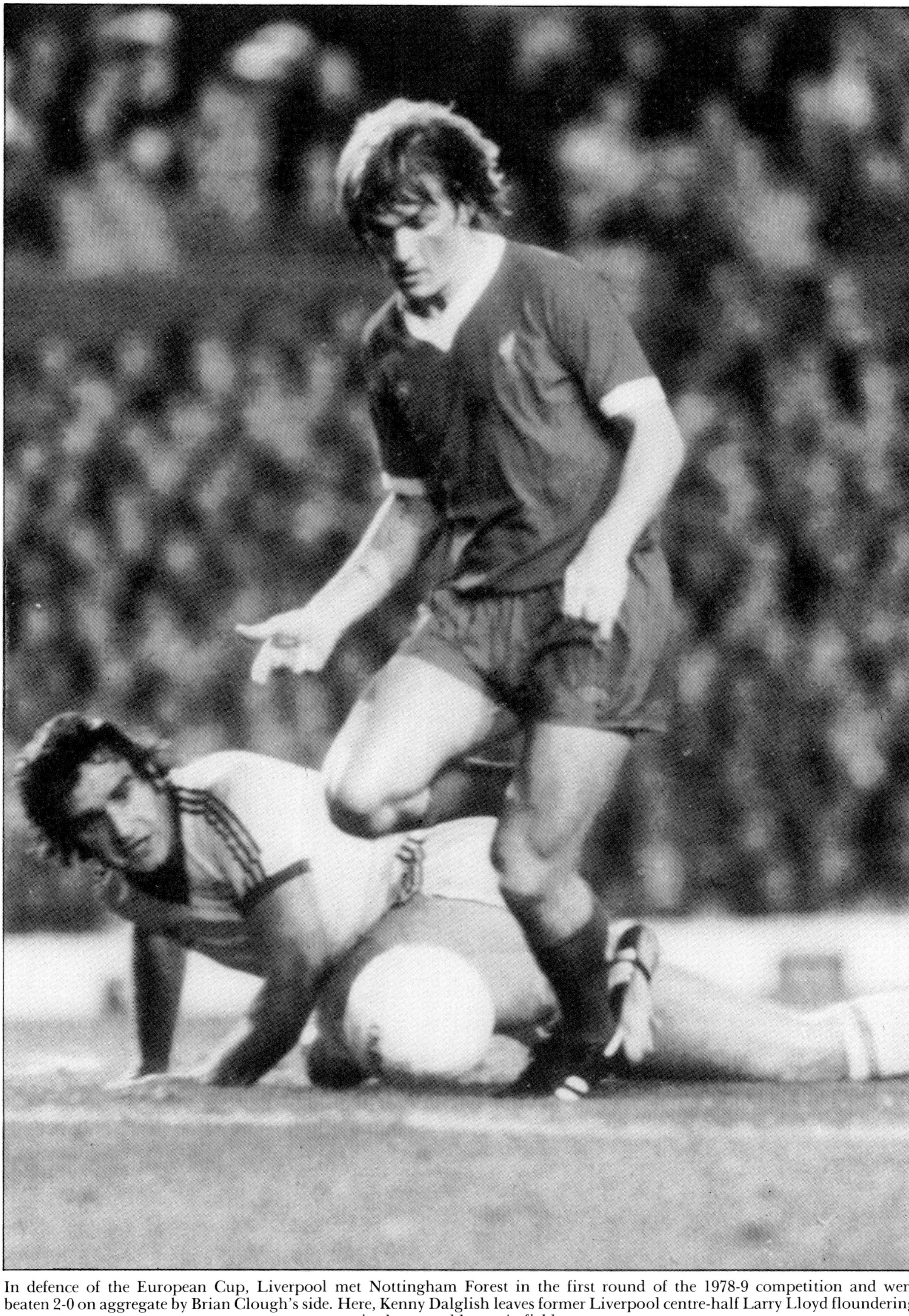

In defence of the European Cup, Liverpool met Nottingham Forest in the first round of the 1978-9 competition and were beaten 2-0 on aggregate by Brian Clough's side. Here, Kenny Dalglish leaves former Liverpool centre-half Larry Lloyd floundering in the second leg at Anfield.

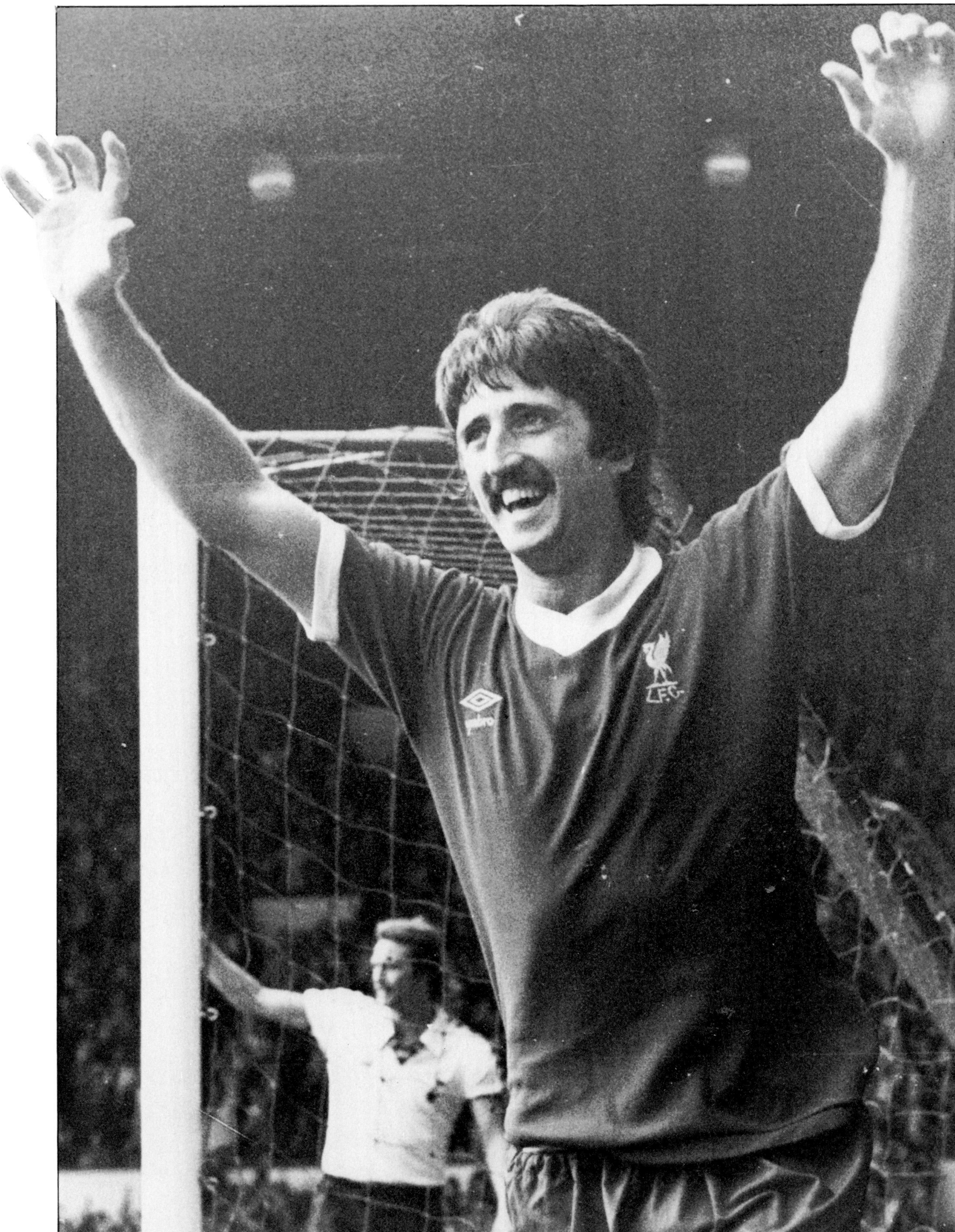

Liverpool's David Johnson celebrates after scoring one of his two goals in the 7-0 hammering of Tottenham Hotspur at Anfield in September 1978. The Reds went on to lift the Championship eight points ahead of Nottingham Forest. Johnson, a former Everton striker, joined Liverpool from Ipswich Town for £200,000 in 1973 but did not establish himself until 1978-9, when he scored 18 goals in the title-winning season.

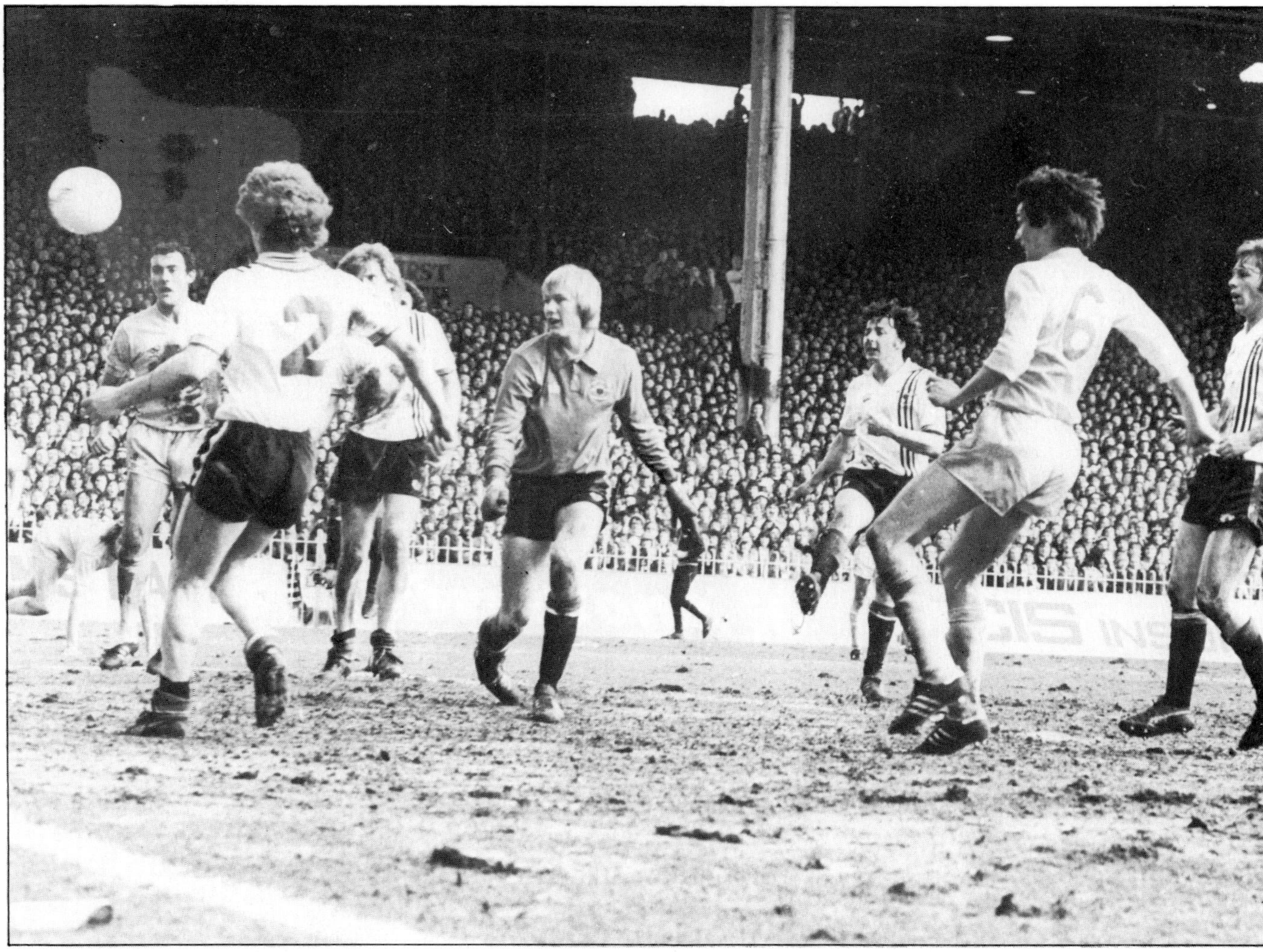

In the 1978-9 FA Cup, Liverpool reached the semi-final where they met Manchester United. They were beaten 1-0 at Goodison Park after a 2-2 draw at Maine Road. Here, Alan Hansen (6) hammers home Liverpool's equalizer in the first match as United goalkeeper Gary Bailey is caught stranded.

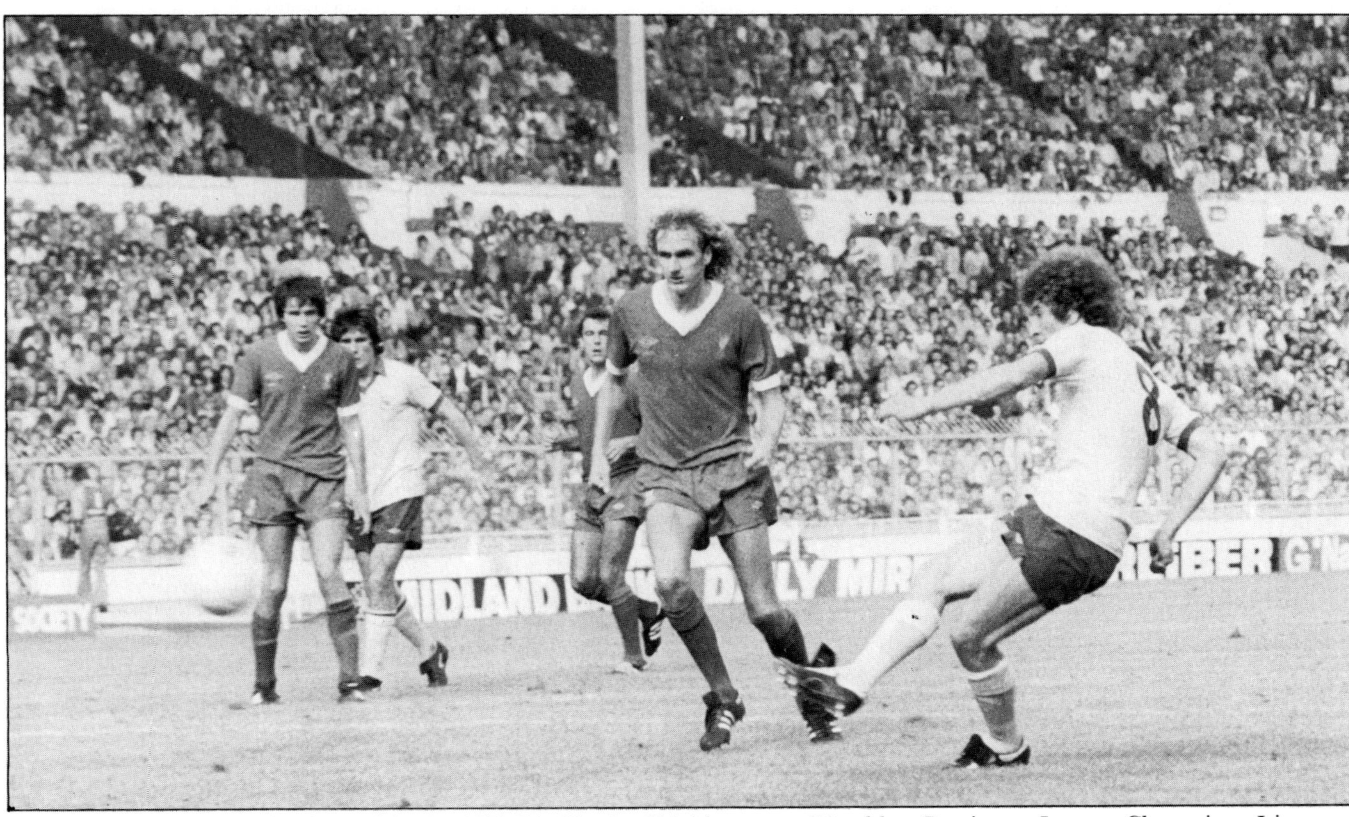

Alan Sunderland scores for Arsenal in the 1979 FA Charity Shield game at Wembley. But it was League Champions Liverpool who won the trophy, ending the game 3-1 winners over the FA Cup holders.

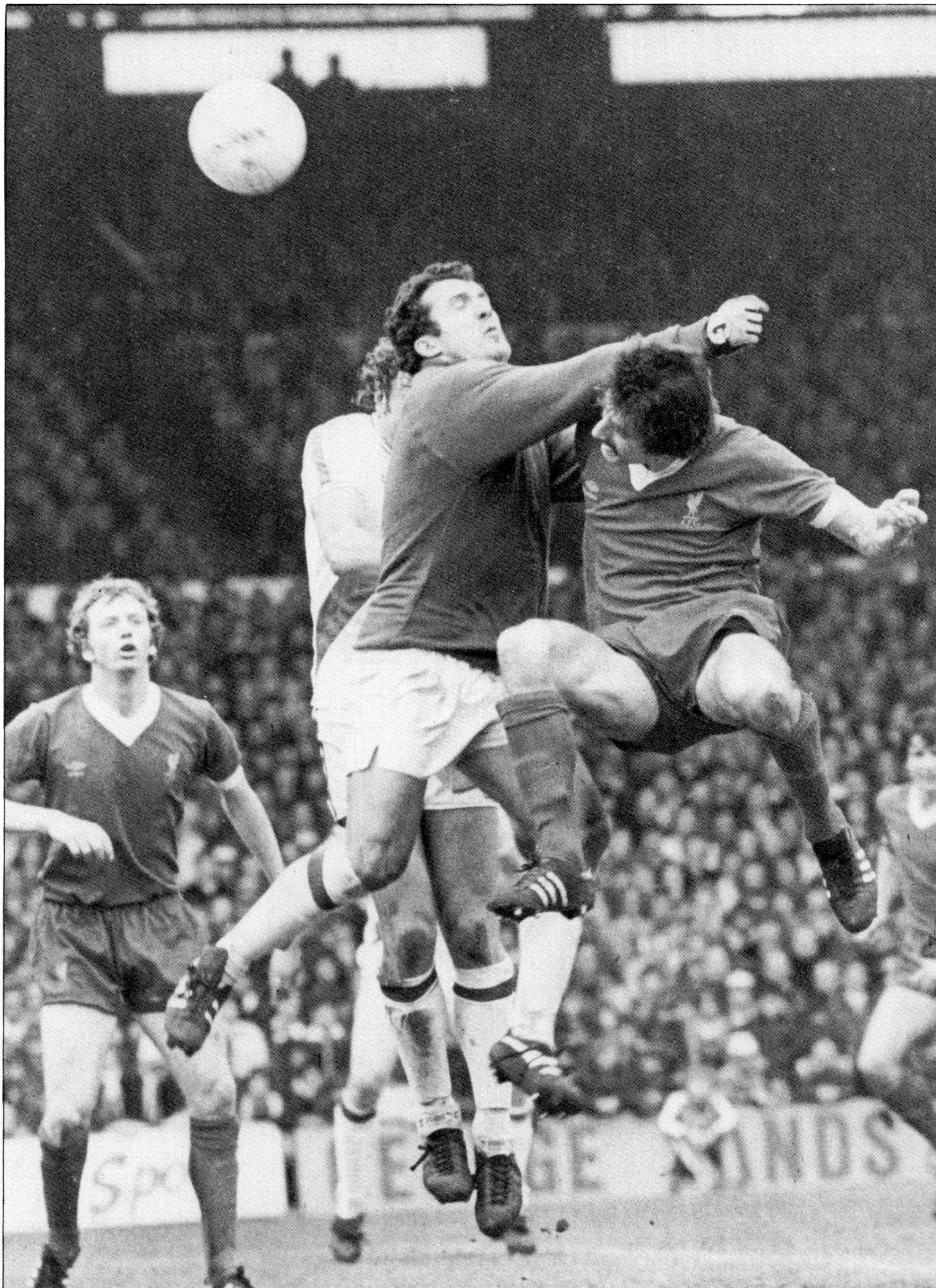

David Johnson and Crystal Palace's John Burridge in an aerial battle during the goalless draw at Selhurst Park in April 1980. Liverpool were now only one game away from the title.

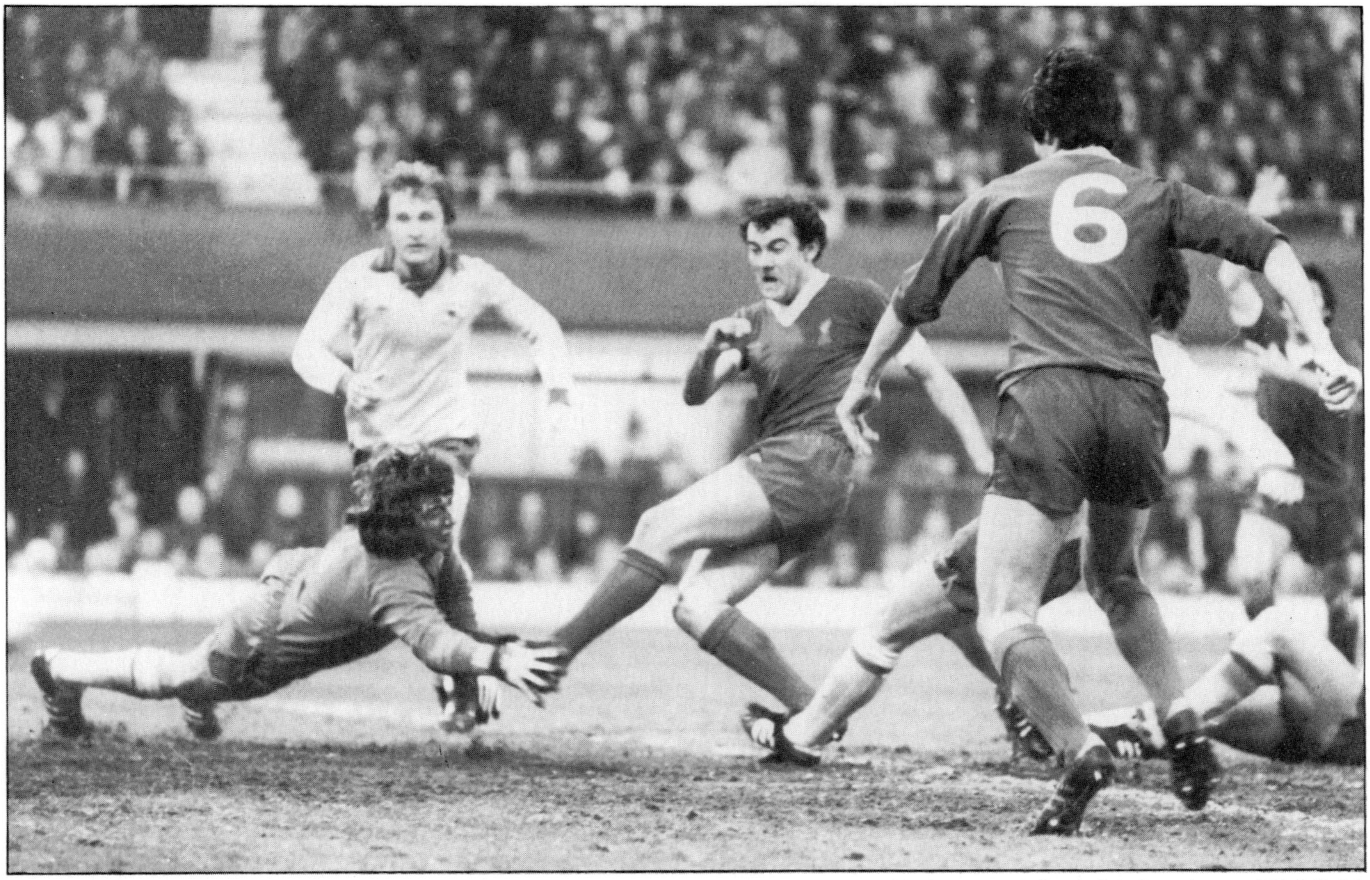

Arsenal's Pat Jennings dives bravely at the feet of Ray Kennedy during the 1980 FA Cup semi-final third replay at Highfield Road, Coventry. The Merseysiders went down 1-0.

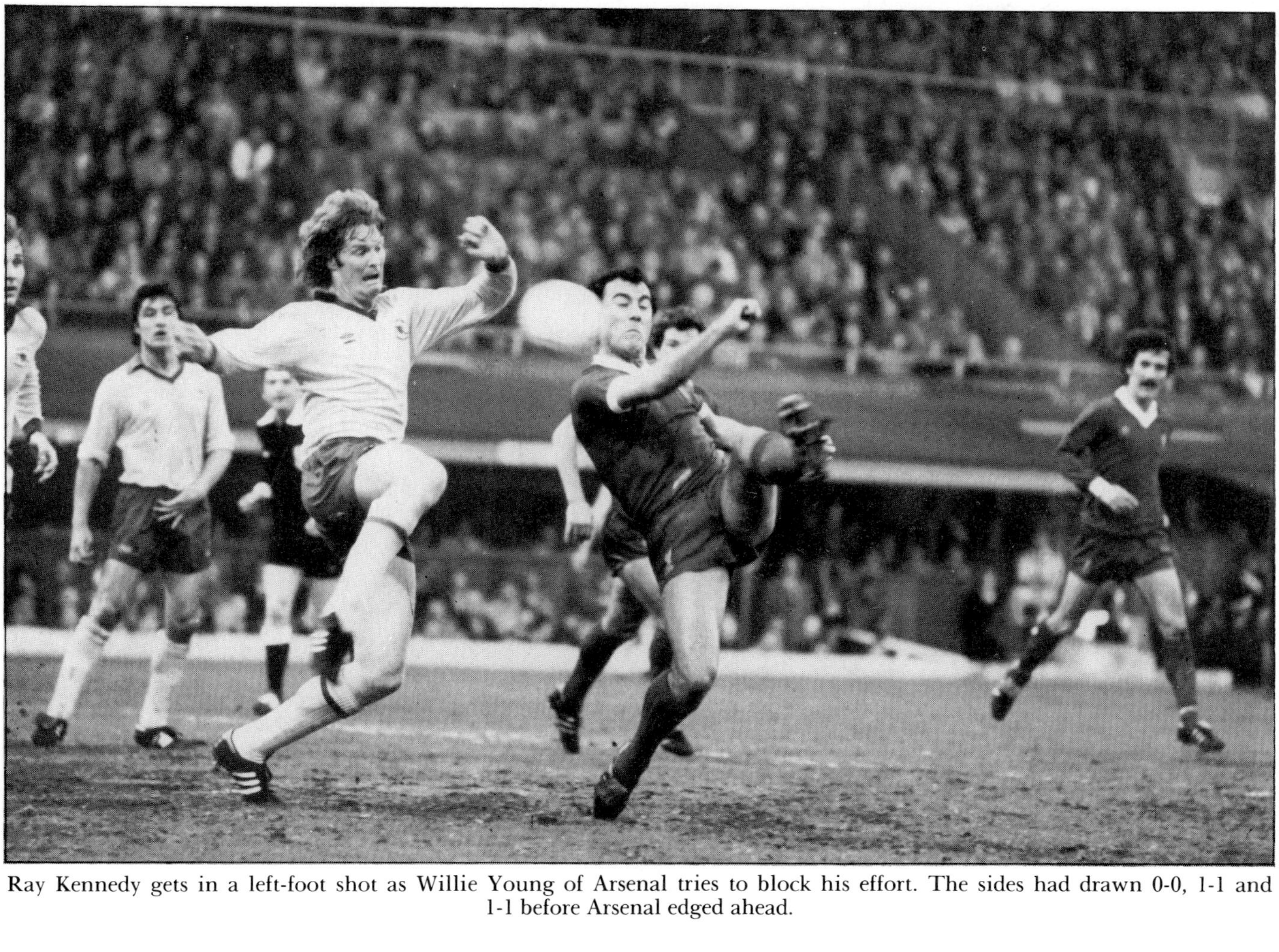

Ray Kennedy gets in a left-foot shot as Willie Young of Arsenal tries to block his effort. The sides had drawn 0-0, 1-1 and 1-1 before Arsenal edged ahead.

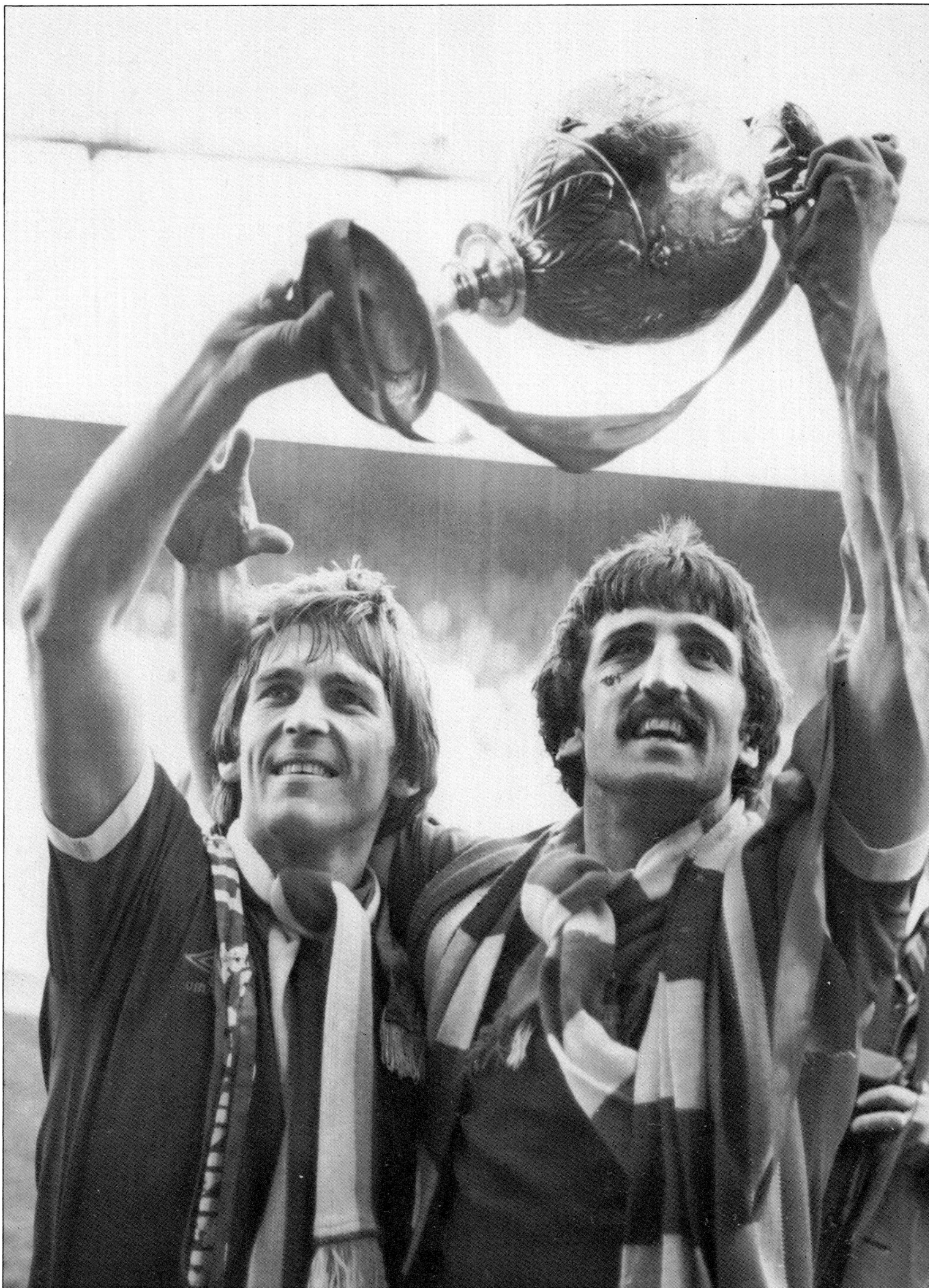

Kenny Dalglish and David Johnson with the League Championship trophy after the 4-1 win over Aston Villa at Anfield in May 1980. The Reds finished two points ahead of Manchester United, Johnson scoring 21 goals in 37 League games.

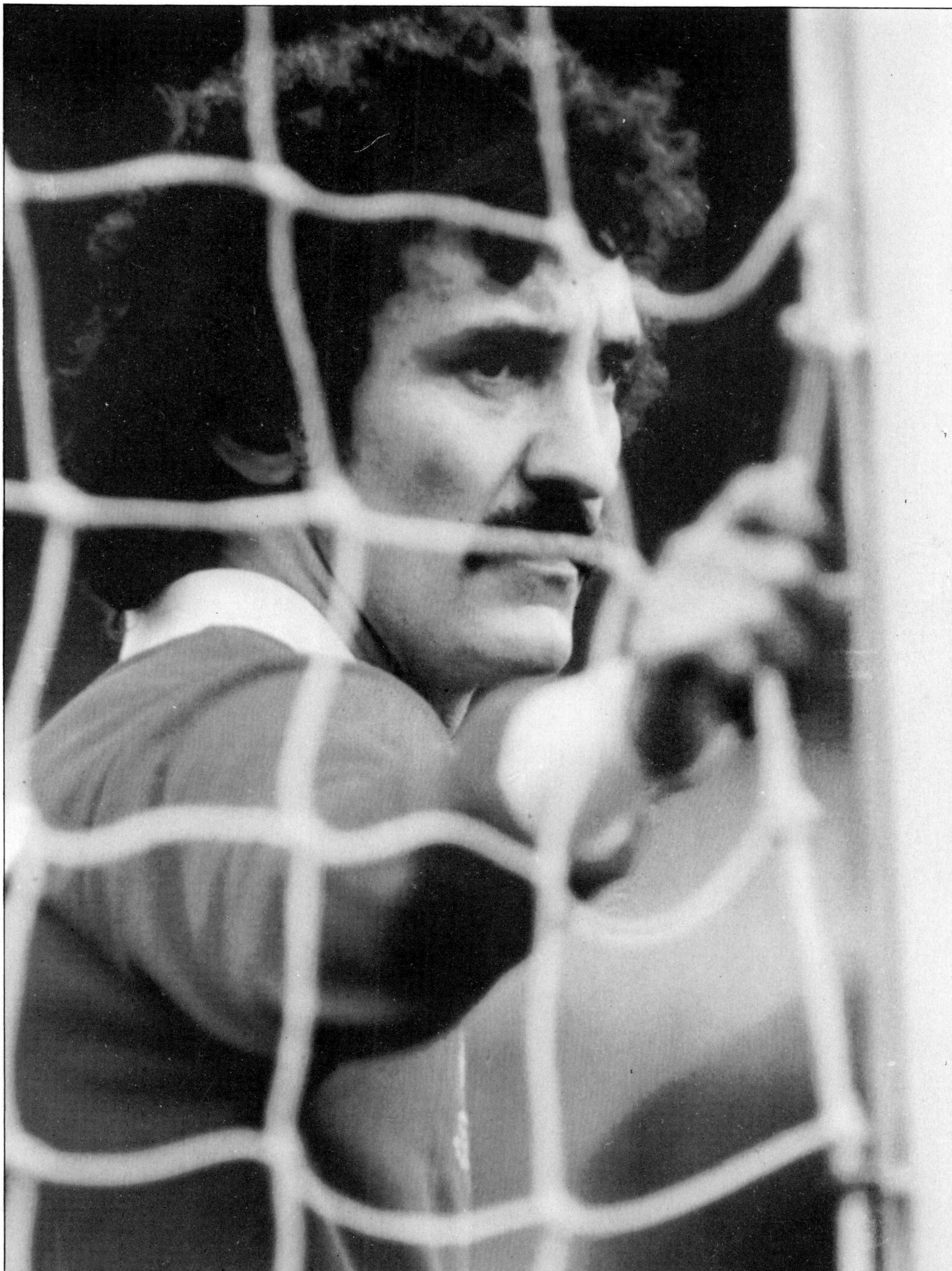

Terry McDermott, a £170,000 signing from Newcastle United in November 1974, was a hard-running midfielder and scorer of some spectacular goals. He made 322 senior appearances, scoring 75 times, and gaining three European Cup winners' medals, four League Championship medals and two Football League Cup winners' medals as well as playing in the 1977 FA Cup Final, adding that runners-up medal to the one he had gained with Newcastle against Liverpool in 1974. He also played for England. McDermott left Anfield to return to Newcastle for £100,000 in September 1982. He is currently Keegan's assistant at St James' Park.

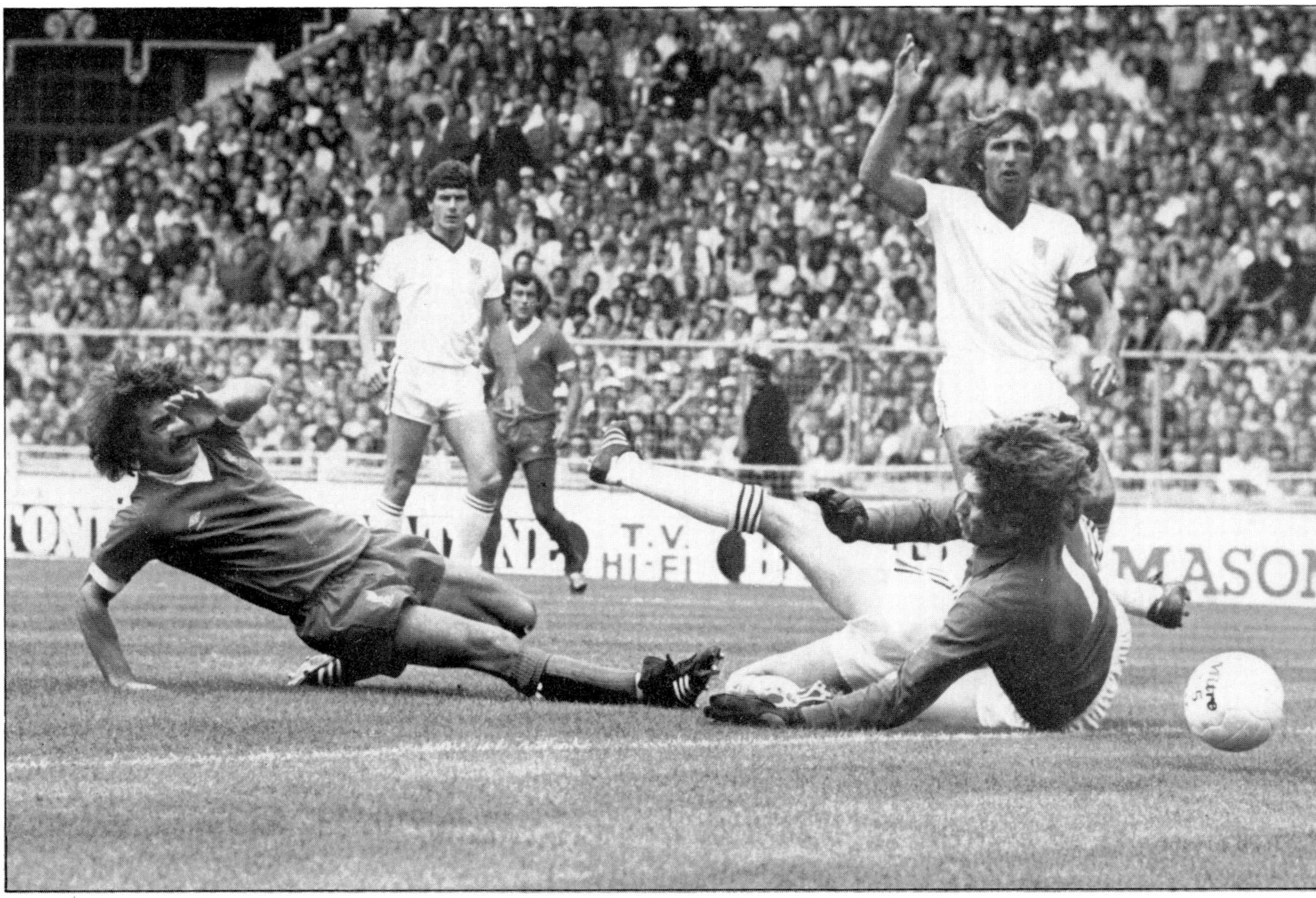

Terry McDermott scores the only goal of the FA Charity Shield game against West Ham United at Wembley in August 1980.

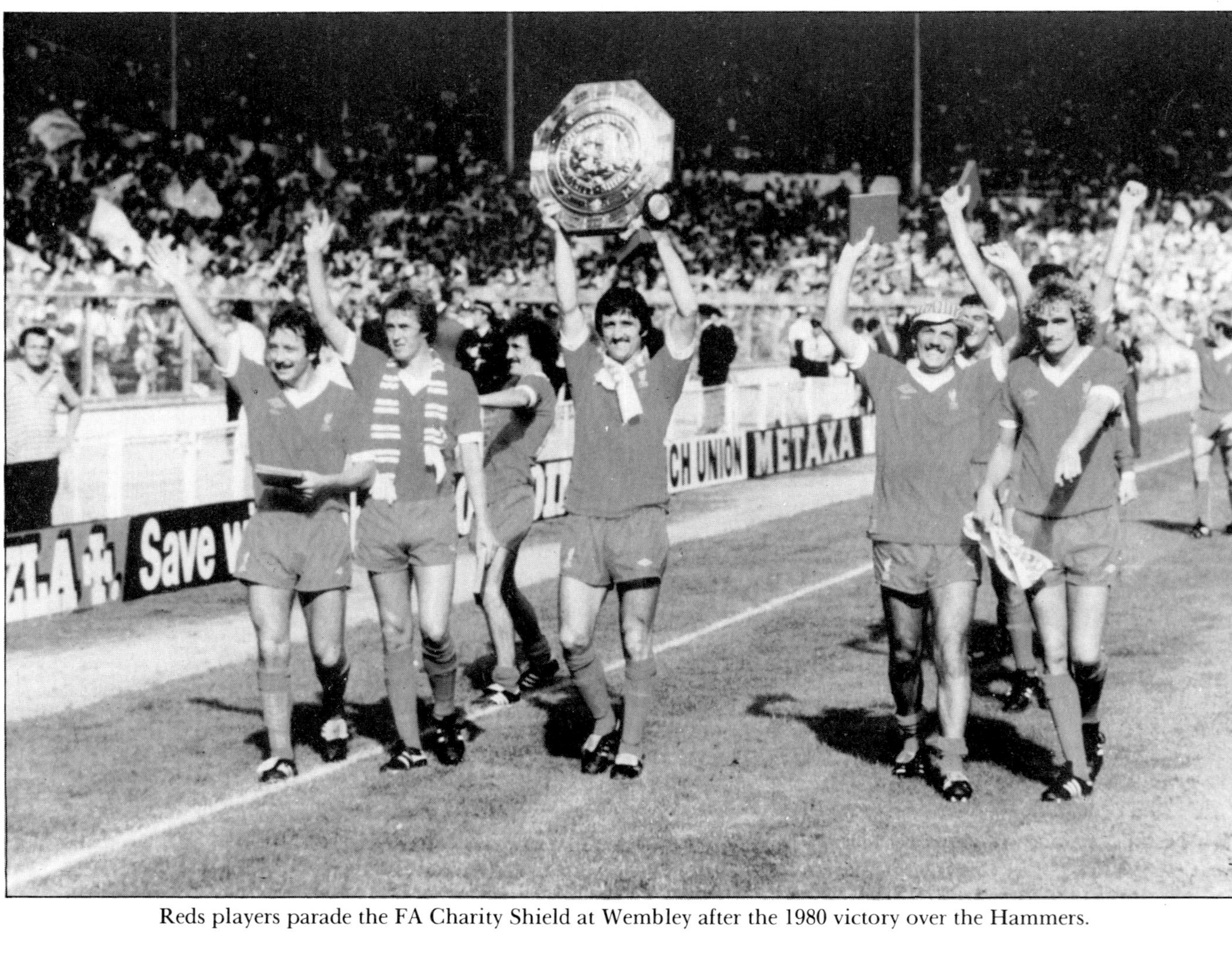

Reds players parade the FA Charity Shield at Wembley after the 1980 victory over the Hammers.

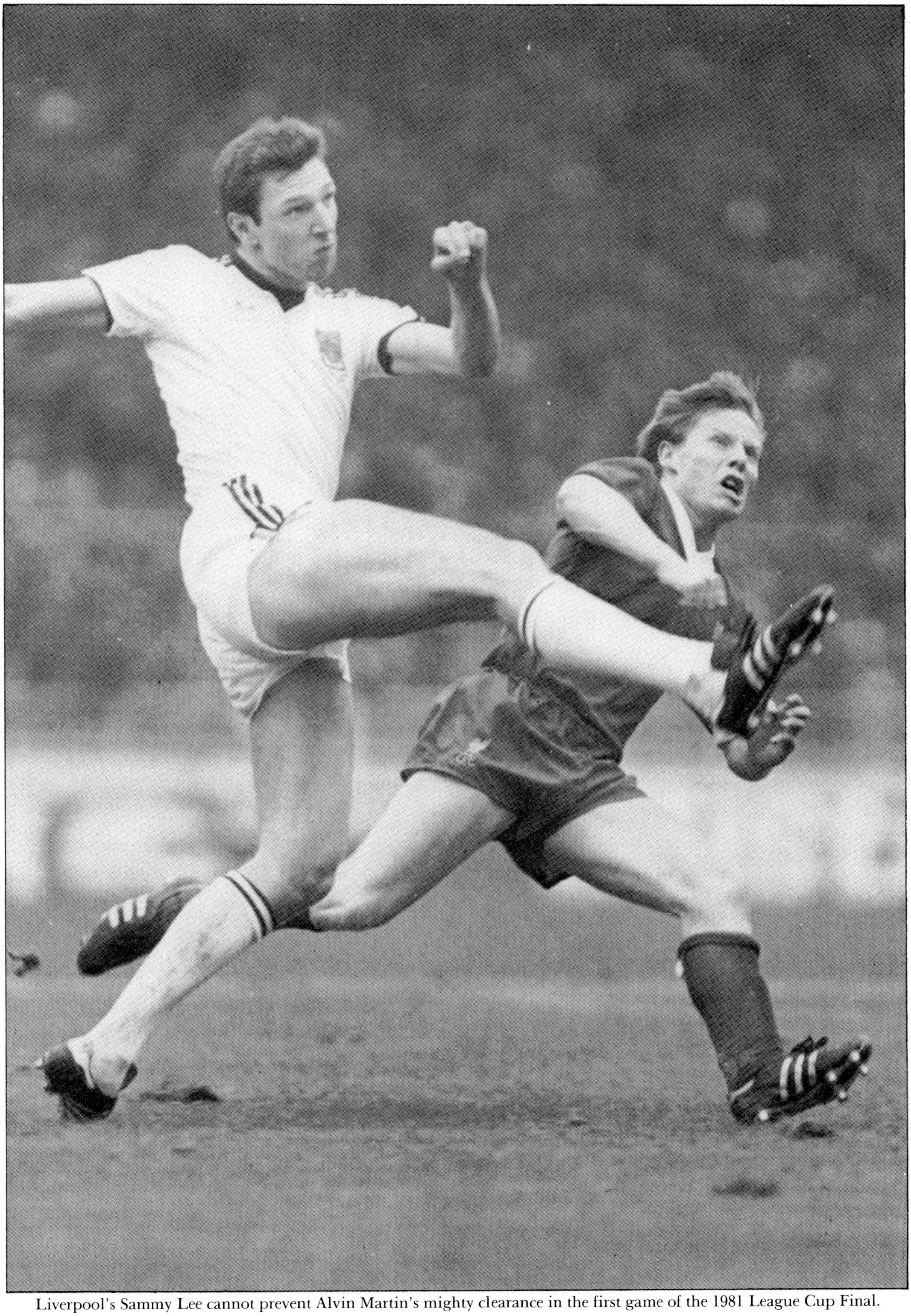

Liverpool's Sammy Lee cannot prevent Alvin Martin's mighty clearance in the first game of the 1981 League Cup Final.

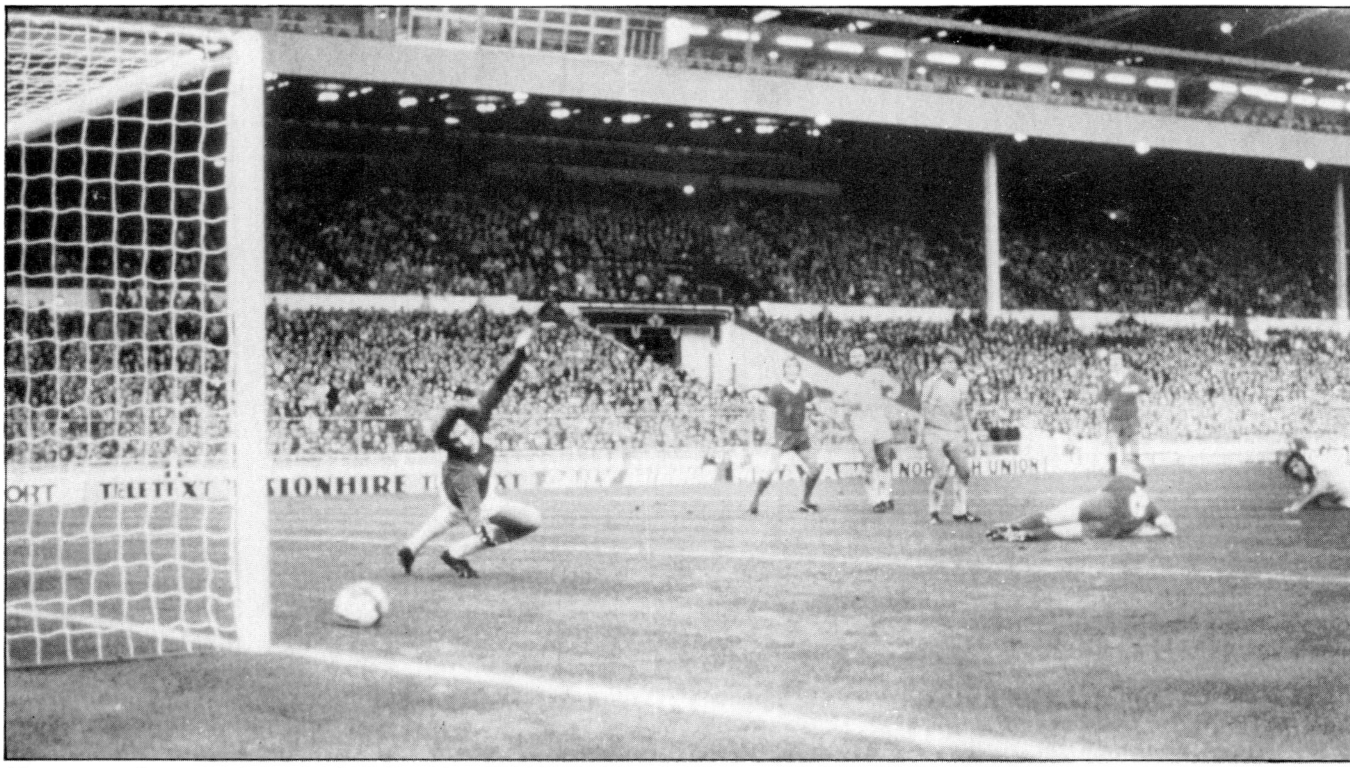

Alan Kennedy scores in extra-time for Liverpool in the 1981 League Cup Final against West Ham United at Wembley. The game ended in a 1-1 draw.

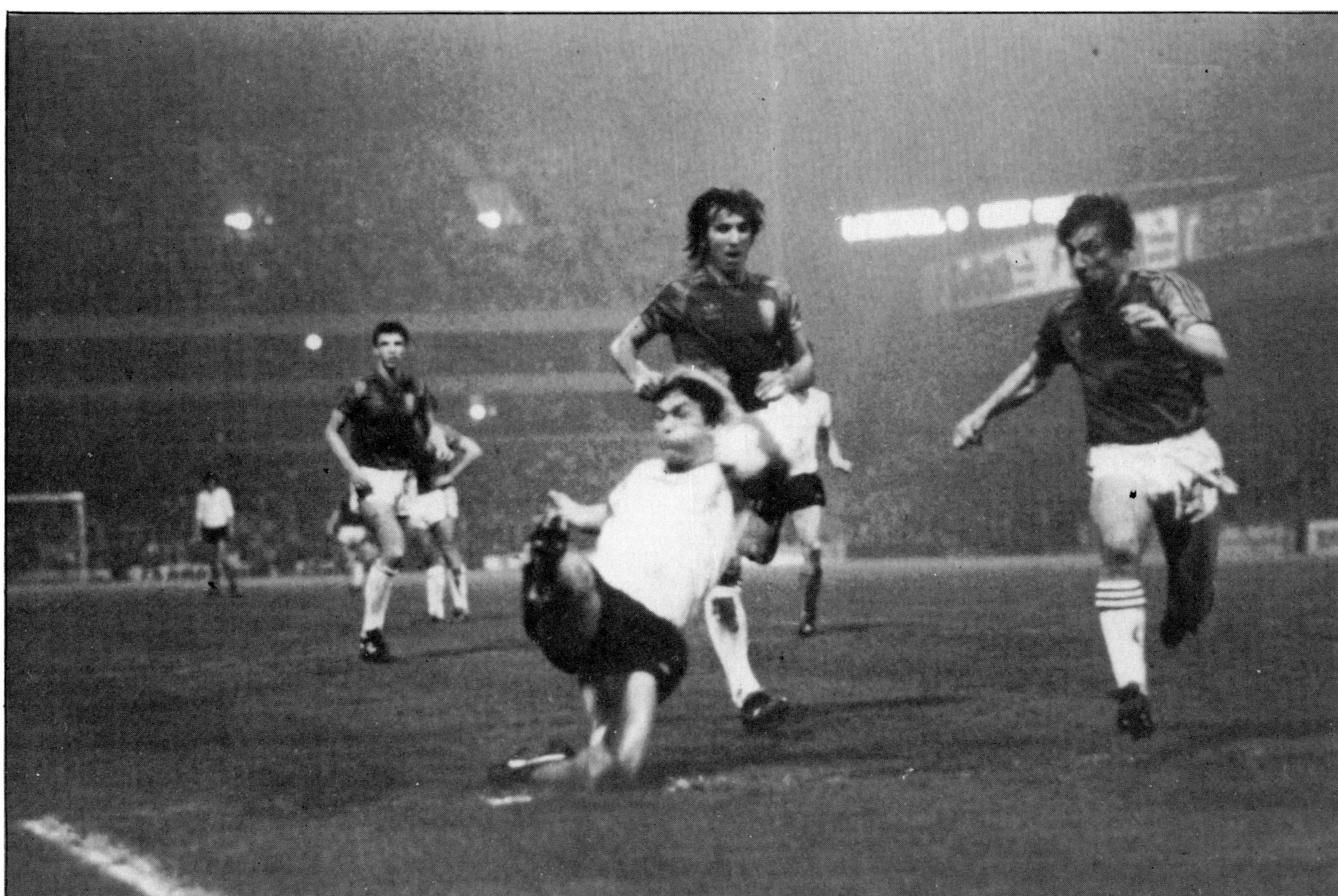

Kenny Dalglish scores Liverpool's first goal in the 1981 League Cup Final at Villa Park.

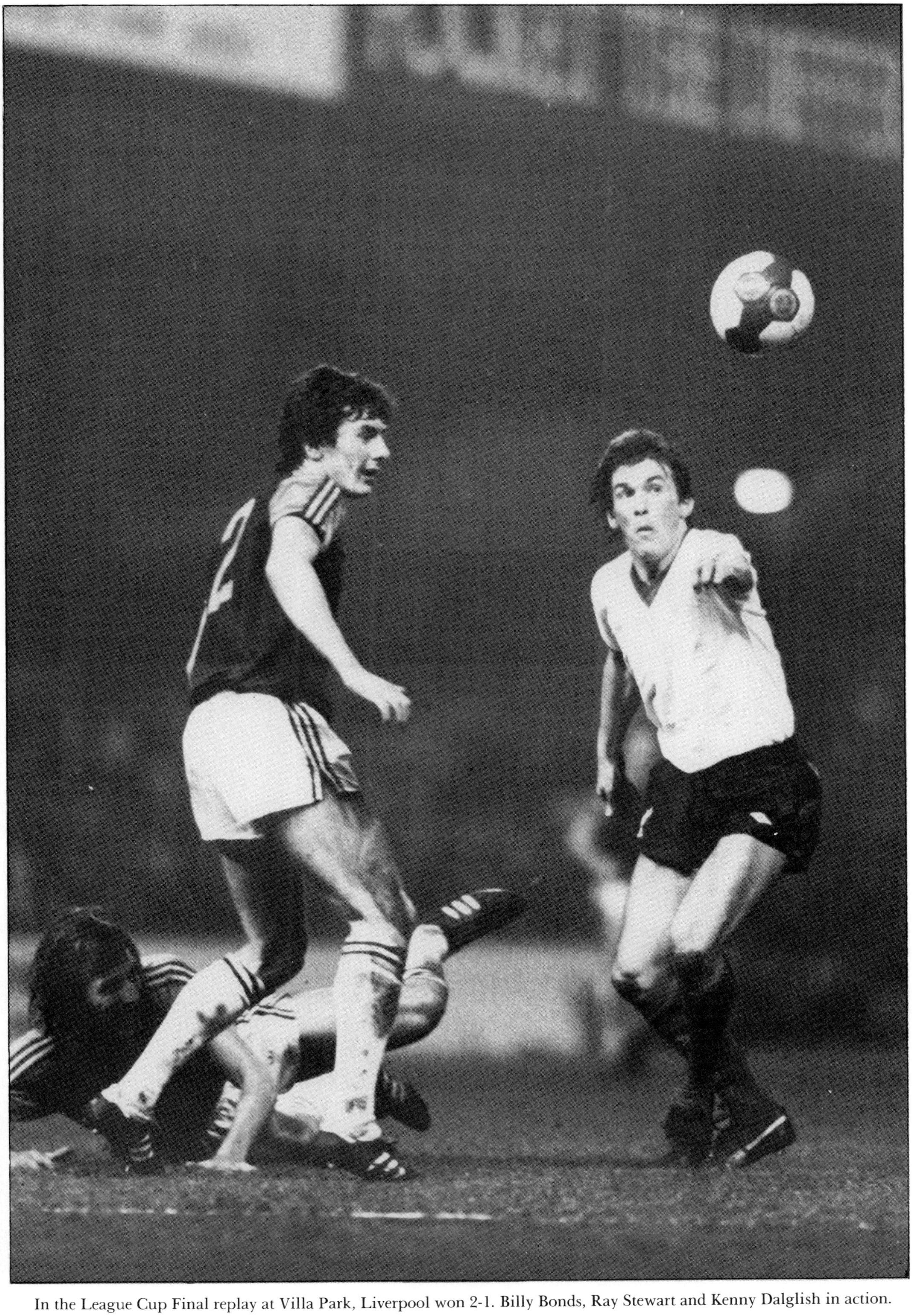

In the League Cup Final replay at Villa Park, Liverpool won 2-1. Billy Bonds, Ray Stewart and Kenny Dalglish in action.

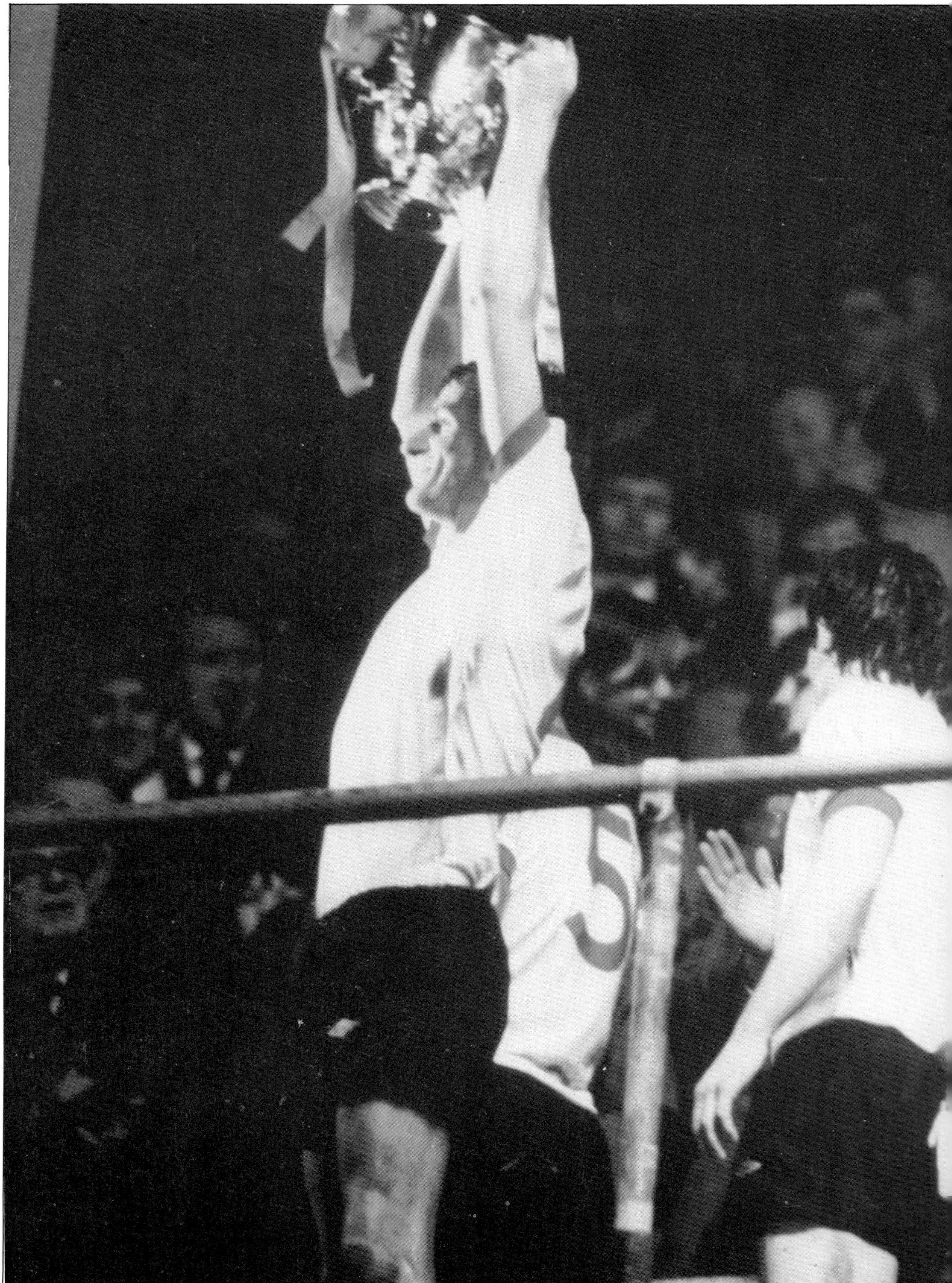

Phil Thompson collects the League Cup, t

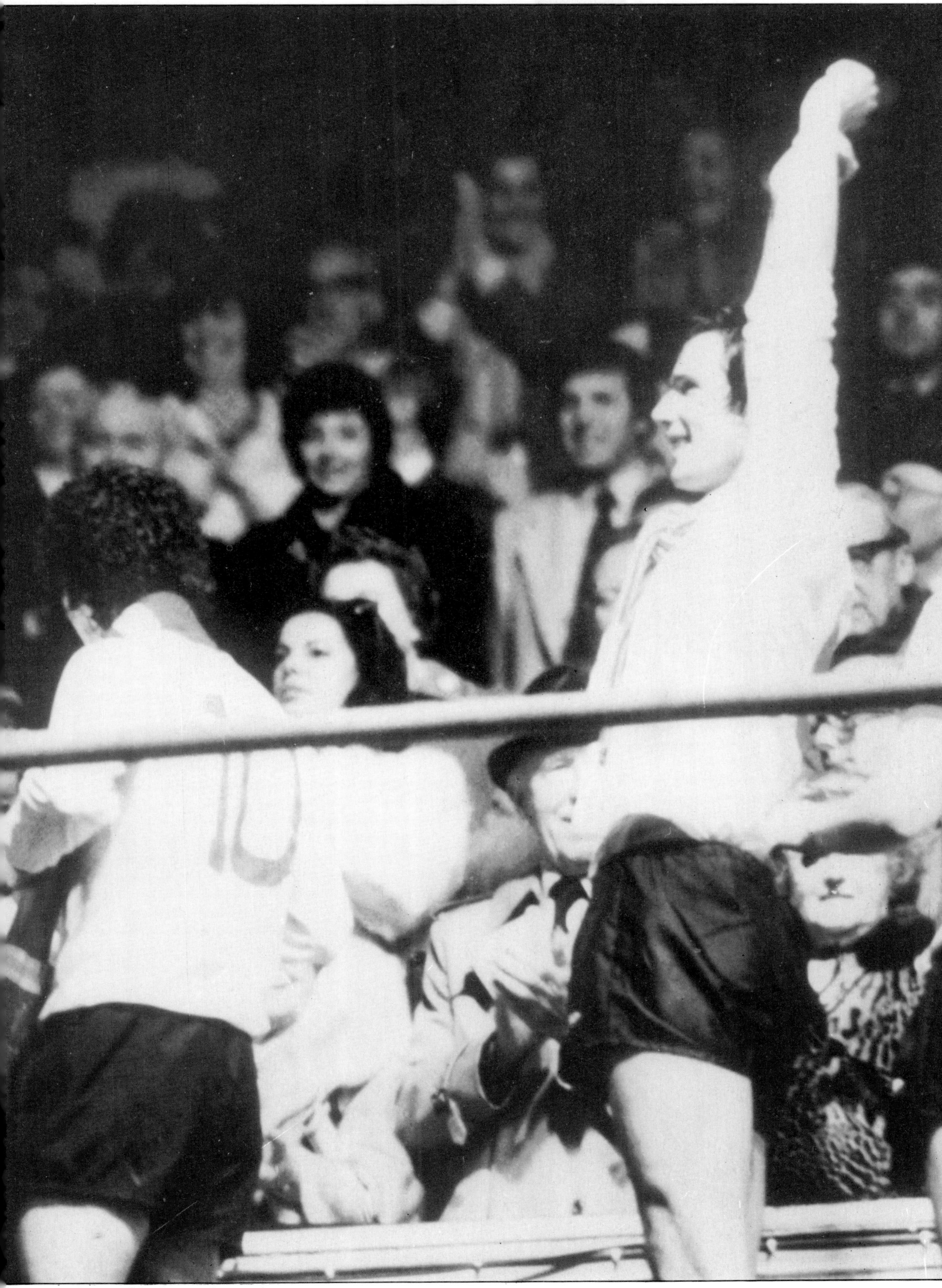

ırst time Liverpool had won the trophy.

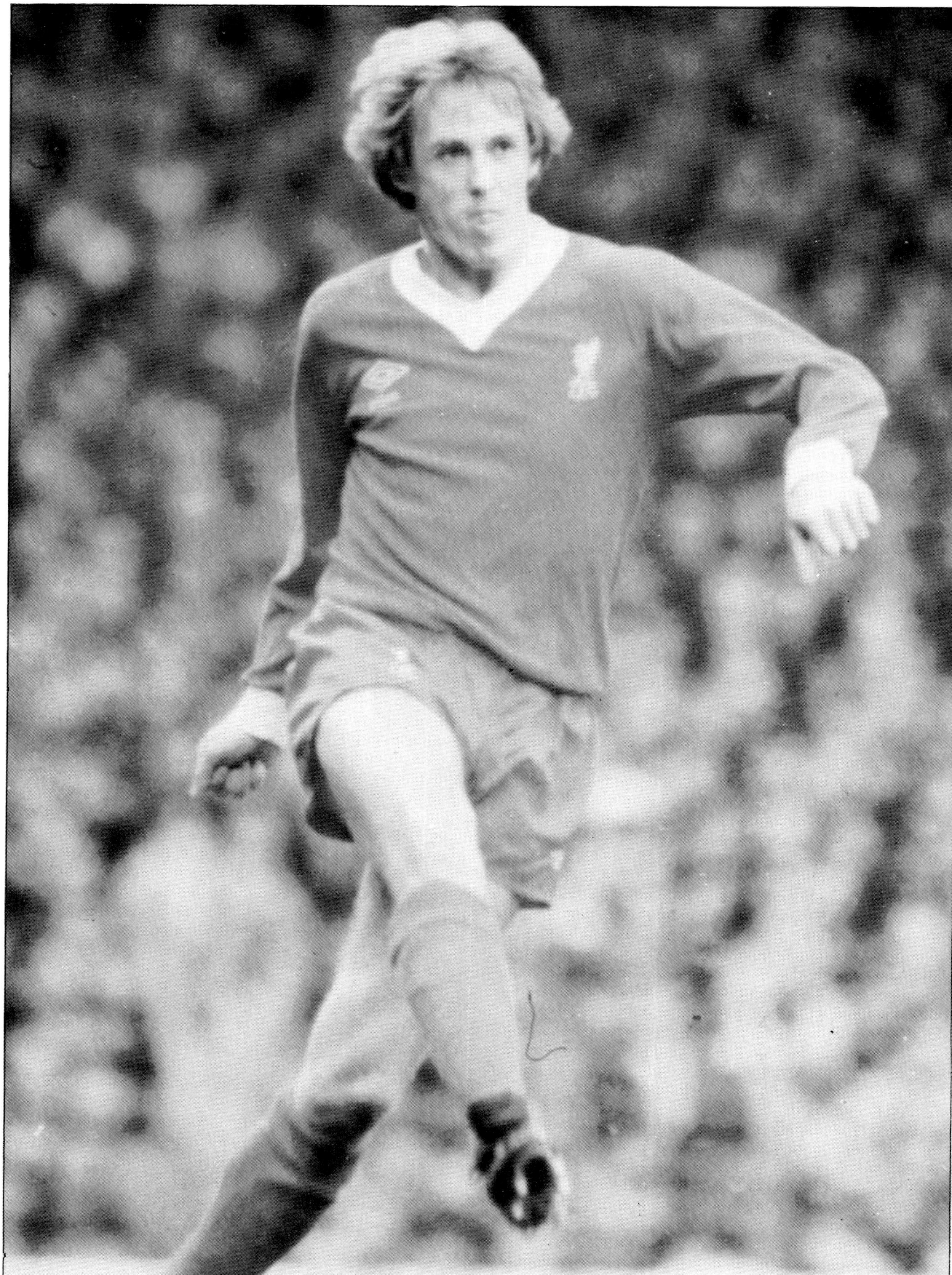

Phil Neal made 635 senior appearances for Liverpool, scoring 60 goals, after joining them from Northampton Town for £66,000 in October 1964. Neal, a right-back who proved to be an effective penalty-taker, won 50 England caps and a host of honours with Liverpool — winners' medals in the European Cup, UEFA Cup, League Championship, FA Cup and League Cup. In the ten seasons 1975-6 to 1984-5 he missed only one League game. Neal became player-manager of Bolton Wanderers in December 1985 and is currently assistant to Bobby Gould at Coventry City.

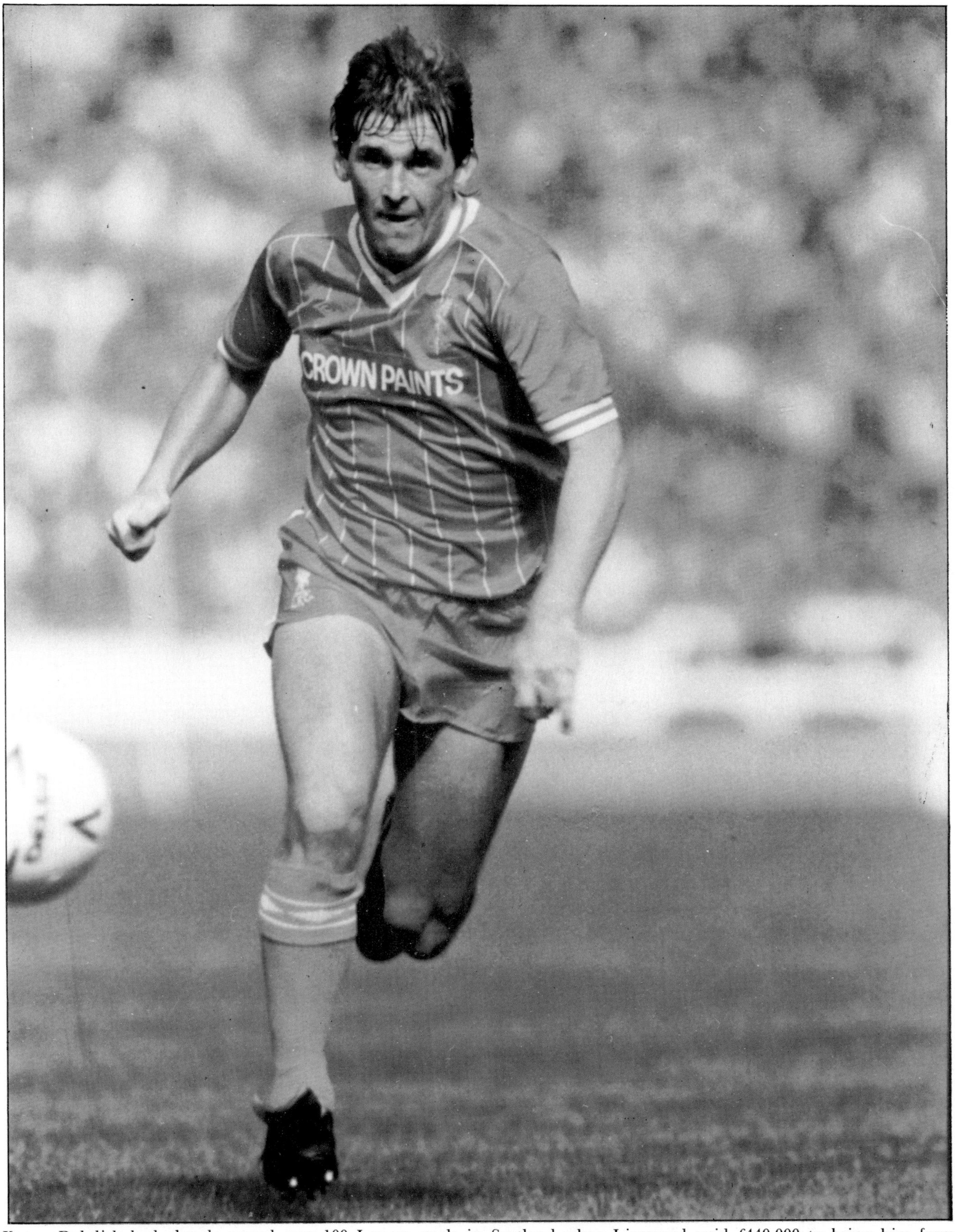

Kenny Dalglish had already scored over 100 League goals in Scotland when Liverpool paid £440,000 to bring him from Celtic in August 1977, then a record fee for a move between English and Scottish clubs. At Anfield, Dalglish repeated the feat to become the first man to score a century of League goals on both sides of the border. He also established the record for full Scottish caps — 102 — and with Liverpool won a huge number of honours to add to those he had gained with Celtic. With the Reds he lifted European Cup winners' medals as well as League Championship medals, League Cup winners' medals and an FA Cup winners' medal. Footballer of the Year in 1979, he became Liverpool's first player-manager in 1986 and took them to a League and FA Cup double in his first season, being voted Manager of the Year in 1986 and 1988. Dalglish shocked Liverpool by announcing his retirement from the game but returned to steer big-spending Blackburn Rovers into the Premier League in 1992.

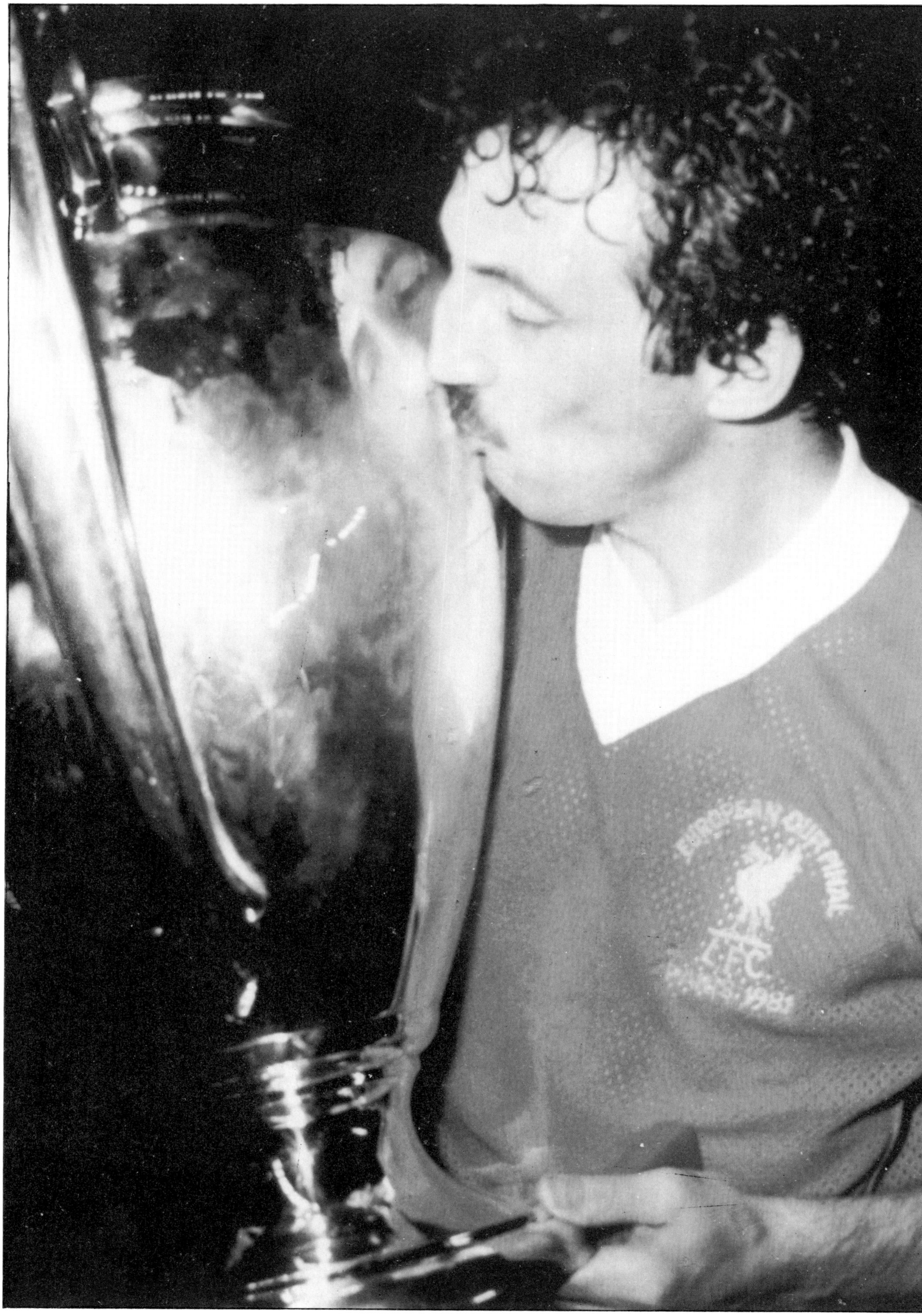

Scorer Alan Kennedy with the European Cup.

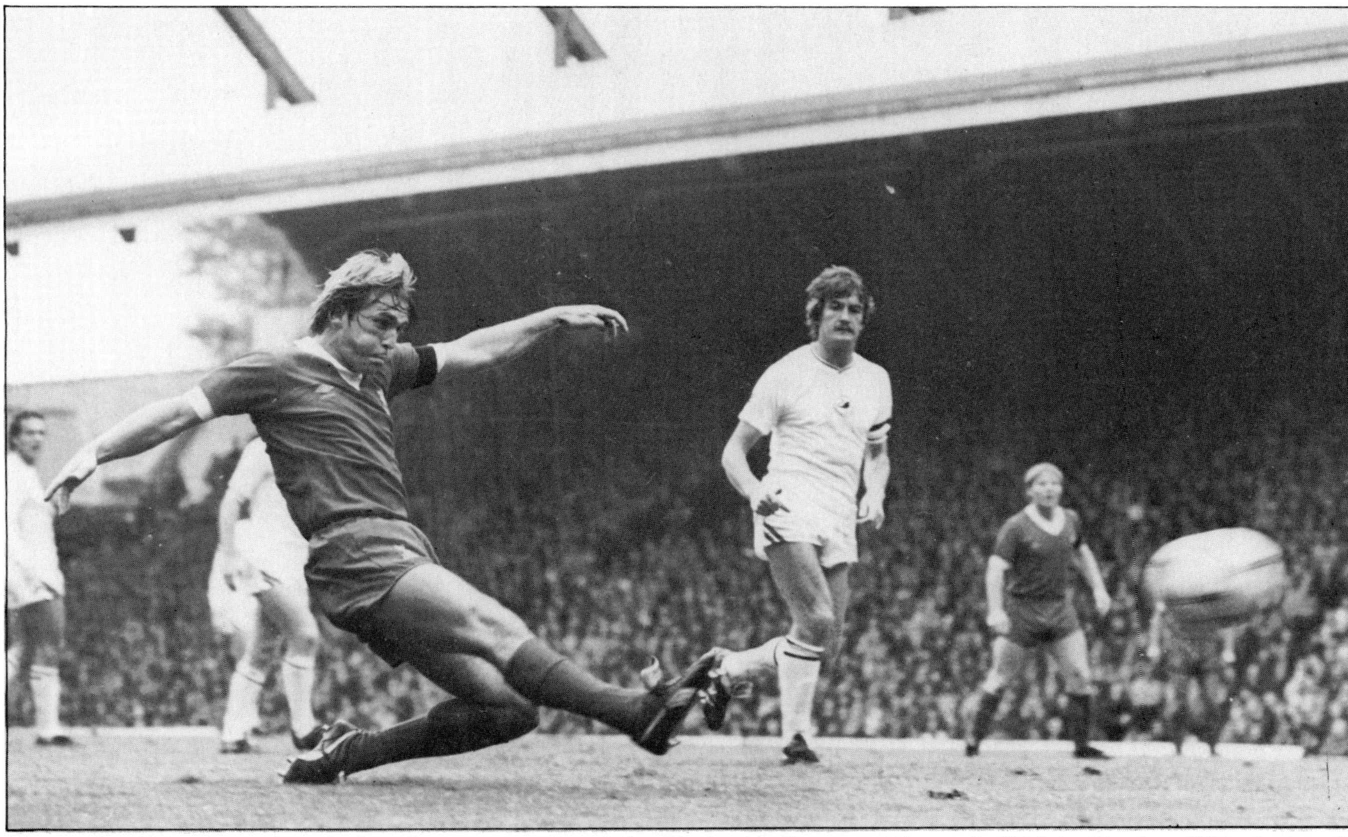

Kenny Dalglish tries a shot during the game against John Toshack's Swansea City at Anfield in October 1981, during the week in which the great Bill Shankly died. The Reds won 2-0, both goals coming from McDermott penalties.

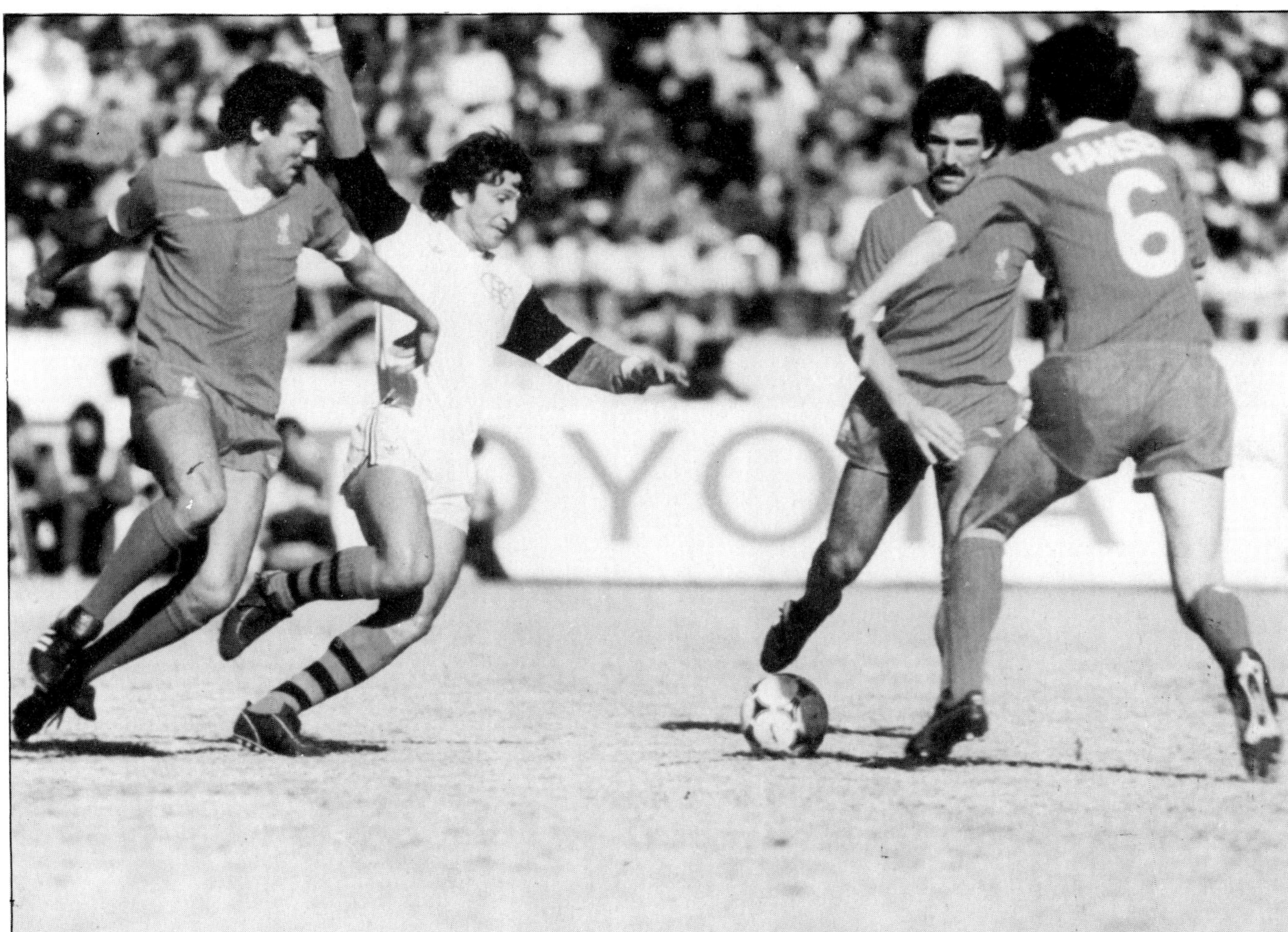

In December 1981, Liverpool met the South American champions, Flamenco, in the World Club Championship match in Tokyo, where they were beaten 3-0. Here, Zico, the Brazilian star, takes the ball through the Reds defence of Ray Kennedy, Graeme Souness and Alan Hansen.

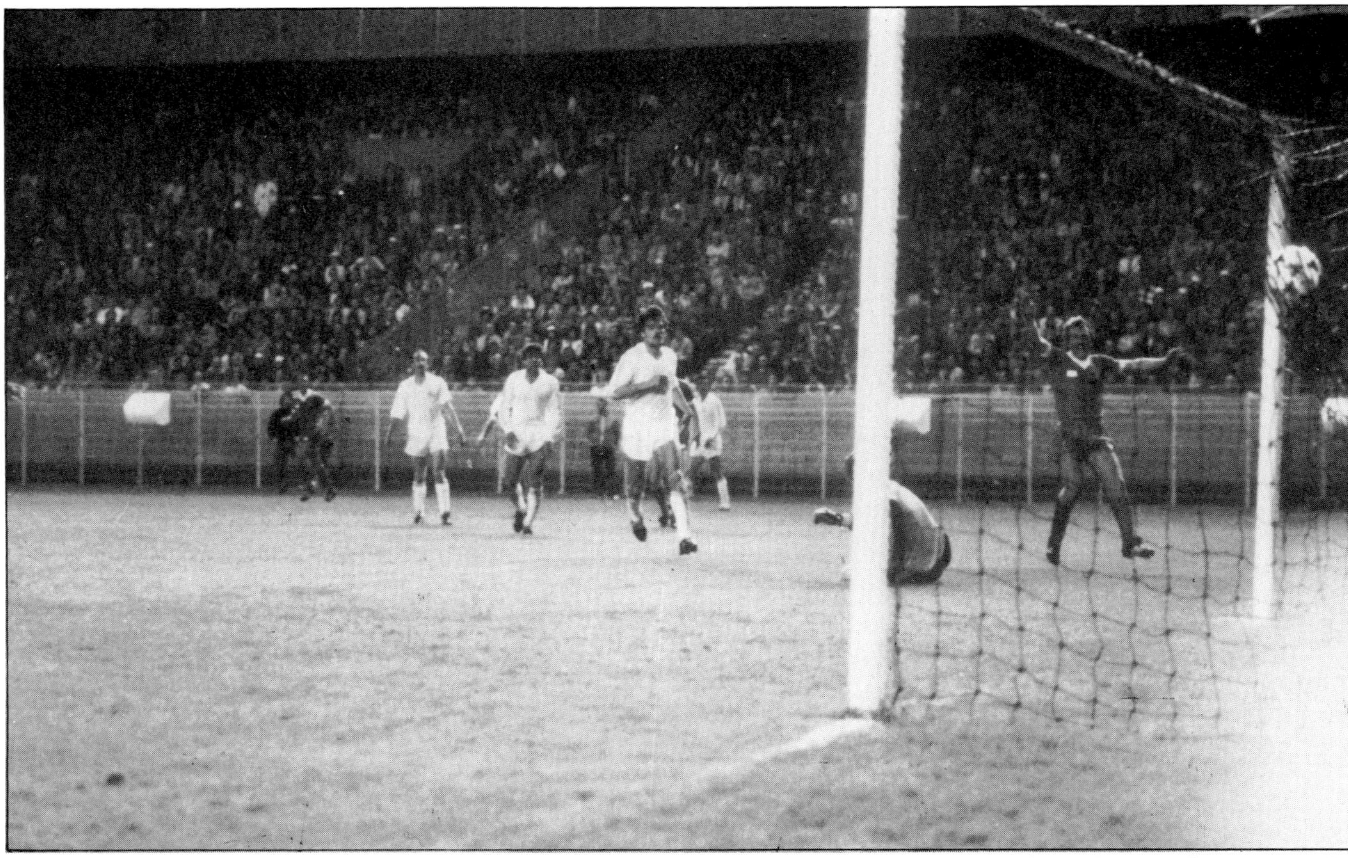

In the 1981 European Cup, the Reds beat OPS Oulu, Aberdeen, CFKA Sredets and Bayern Munich before meeting Real Madrid in the Final in Paris. Alan Kennedy (right) scores the only goal of the game nine minutes from the end of normal time.

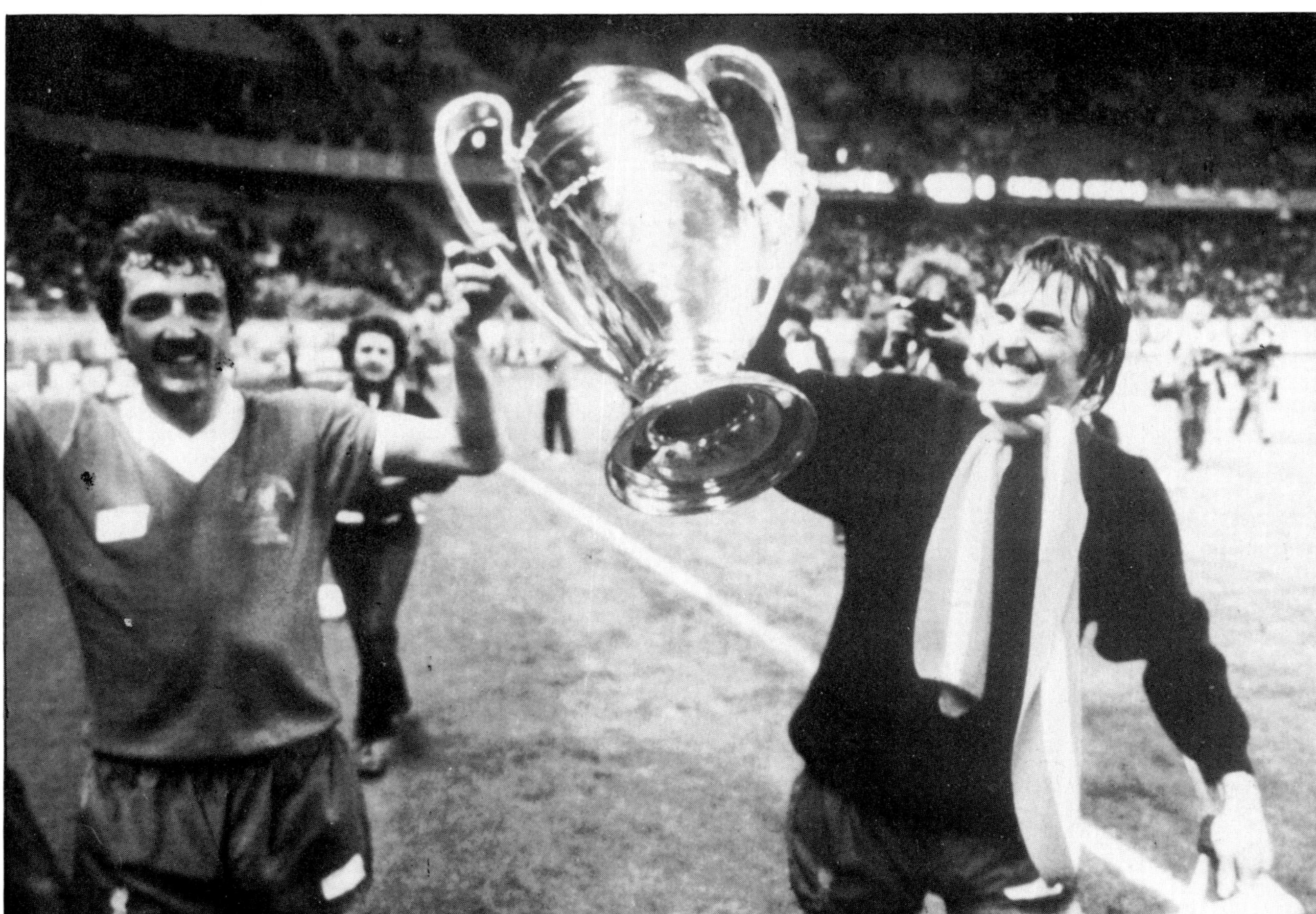

Alan Kennedy and Kenny Dalglish parade the European trophy around the Paris stadium.

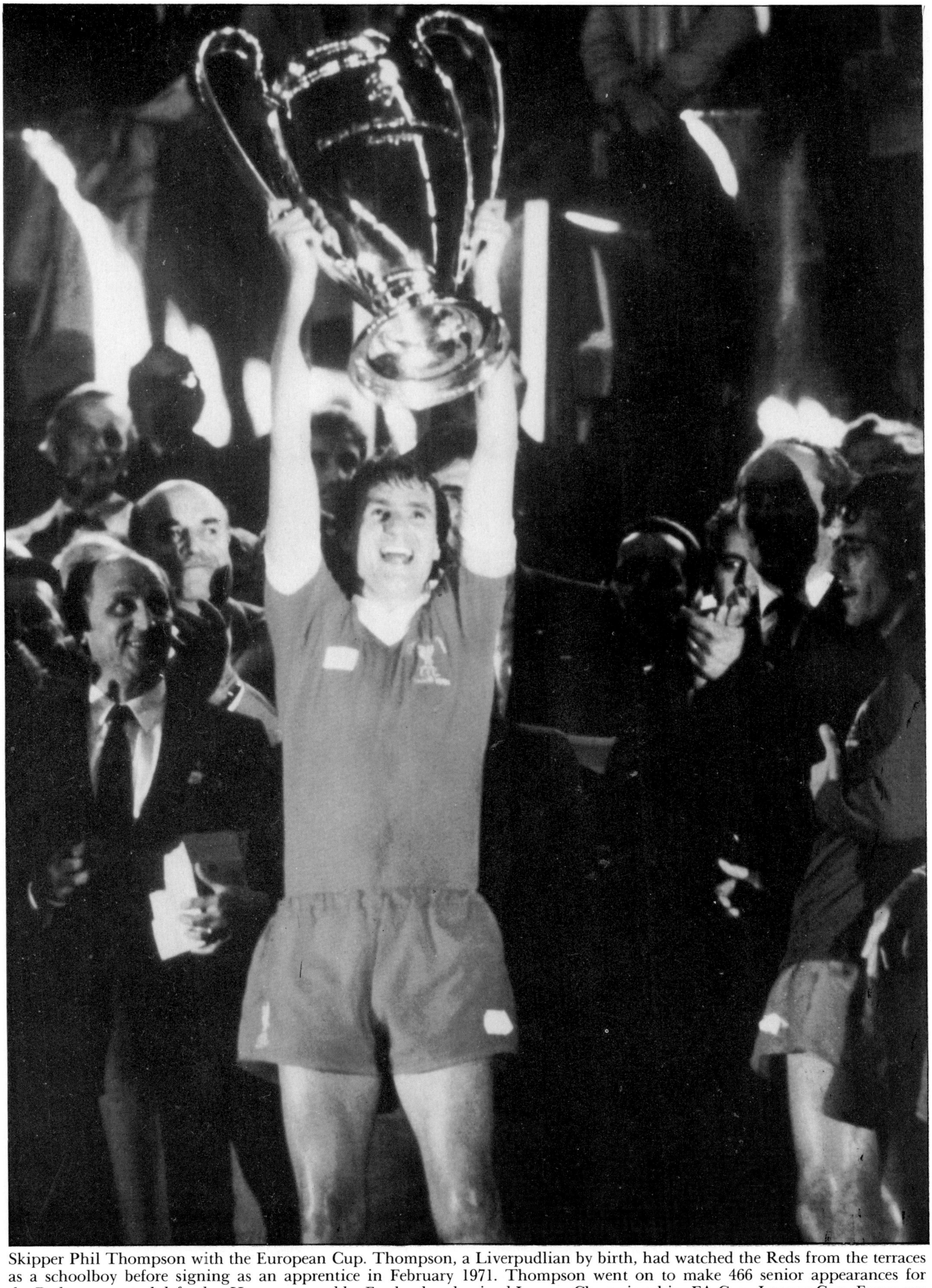

Skipper Phil Thompson with the European Cup. Thompson, a Liverpudlian by birth, had watched the Reds from the terraces as a schoolboy before signing as an apprentice in February 1971. Thompson went on to make 466 senior appearances for the Reds as a central defender. He was capped by England and gained League Championship, FA Cup, League Cup, European Cup and UEFA Cup winners' medals with the Reds before being transferred to Sheffield United in 1985. Thompson later returned to Anfield on the coaching staff, where he remained until 1992.

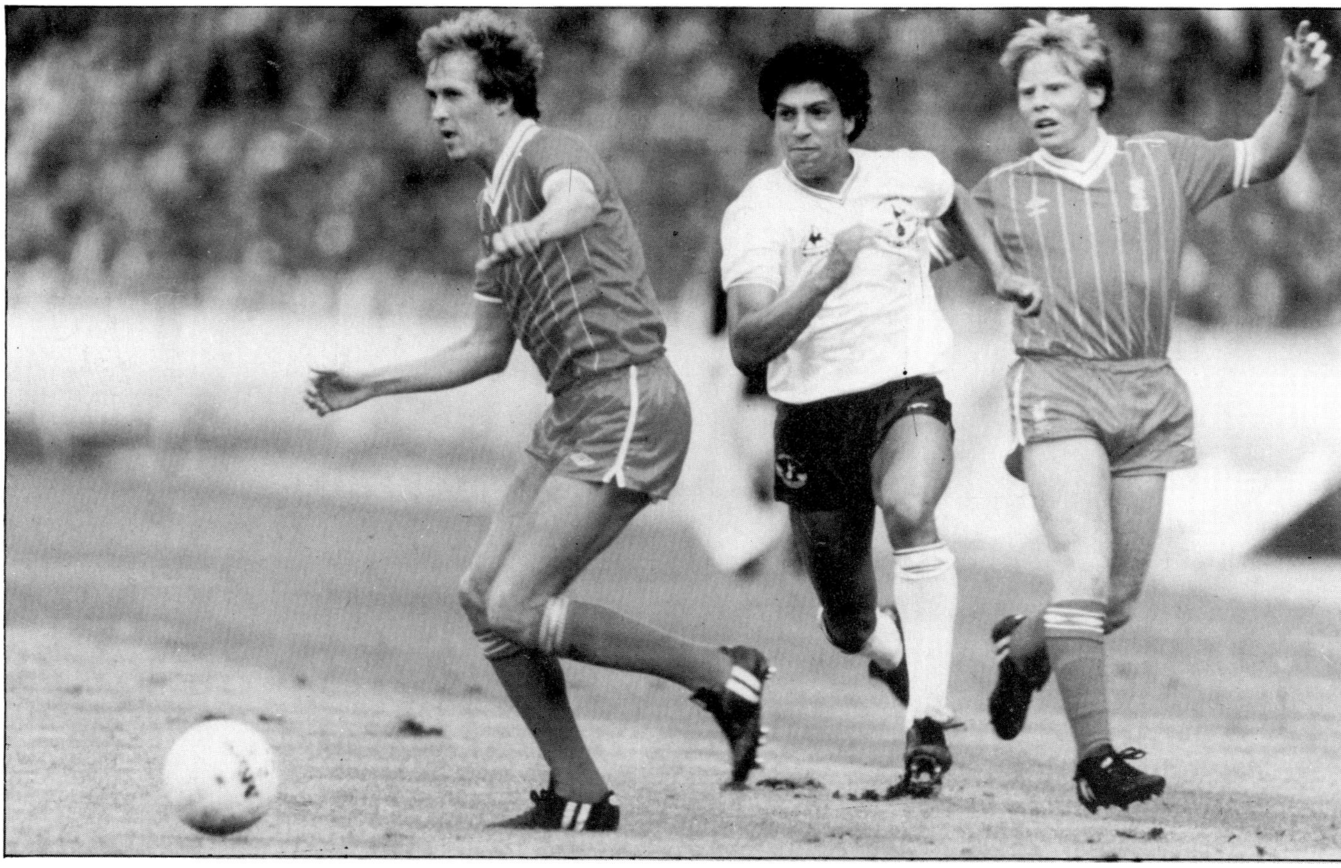

Phil Neal and Sammy Lee appear to have got the better of a determined Chris Hughton during the 1982 Milk Cup Final.

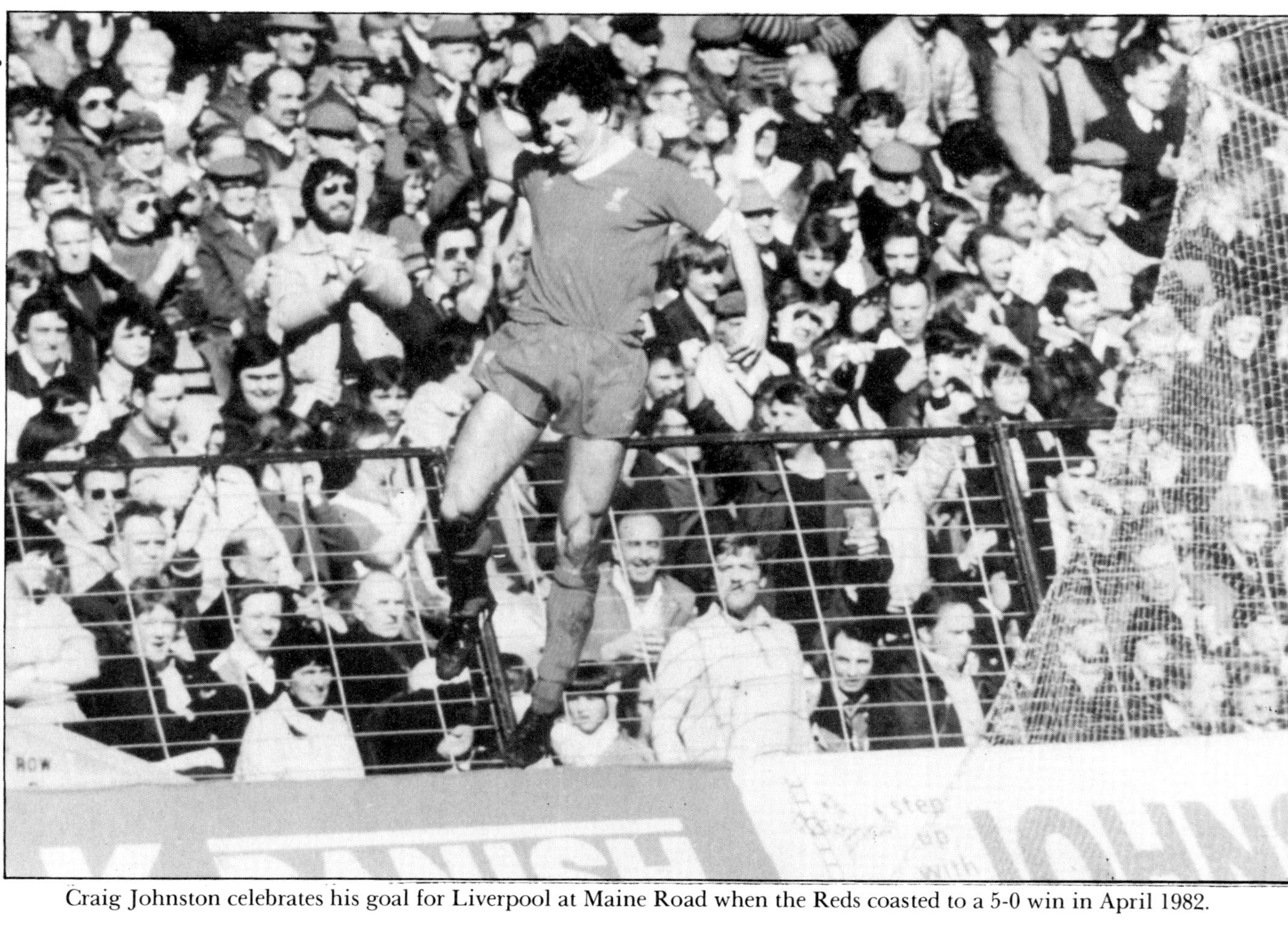

Craig Johnston celebrates his goal for Liverpool at Maine Road when the Reds coasted to a 5-0 win in April 1982.

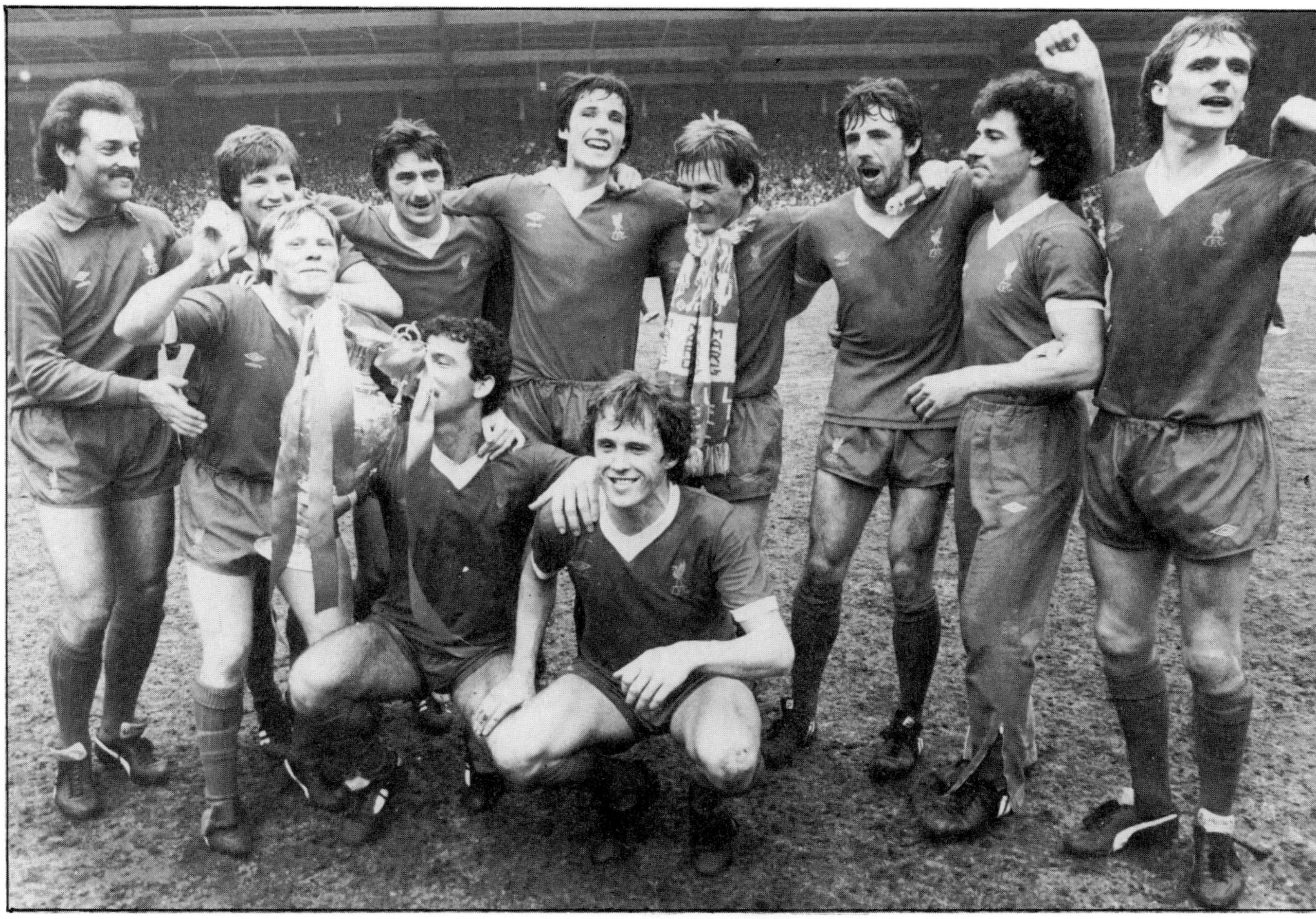

Liverpool players celebrate after beating Tottenham Hotspur in their final home game of the 1981-2 season to win the League Championship for a record 13th time. Players at the back (left to right) are Grobbelaar, Whelan, Rush, Hansen, Dalglish, Lawrenson, Johnston and Thompson. In front are Lee, Souness and Neal.

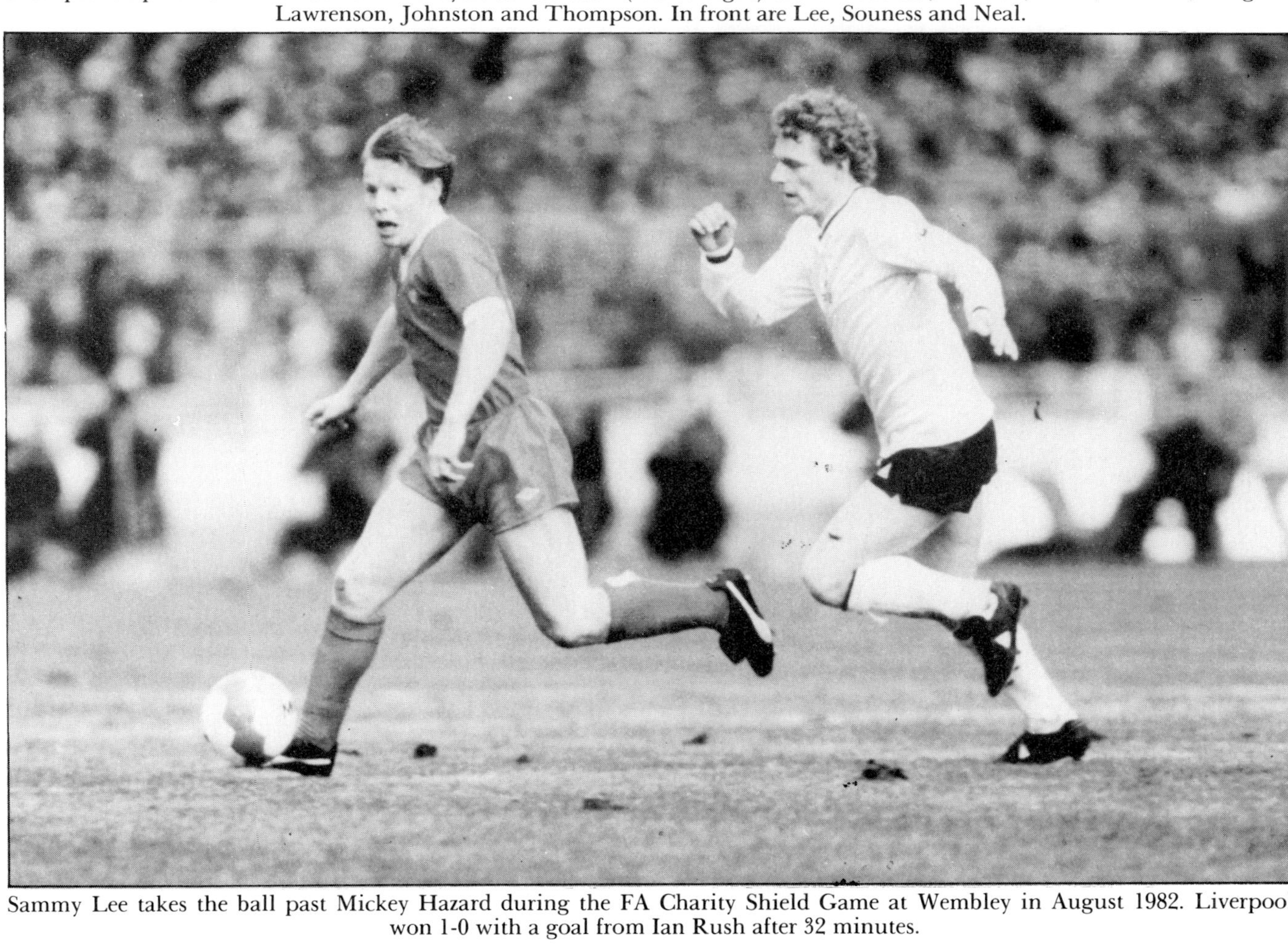

Sammy Lee takes the ball past Mickey Hazard during the FA Charity Shield Game at Wembley in August 1982. Liverpool won 1-0 with a goal from Ian Rush after 32 minutes.

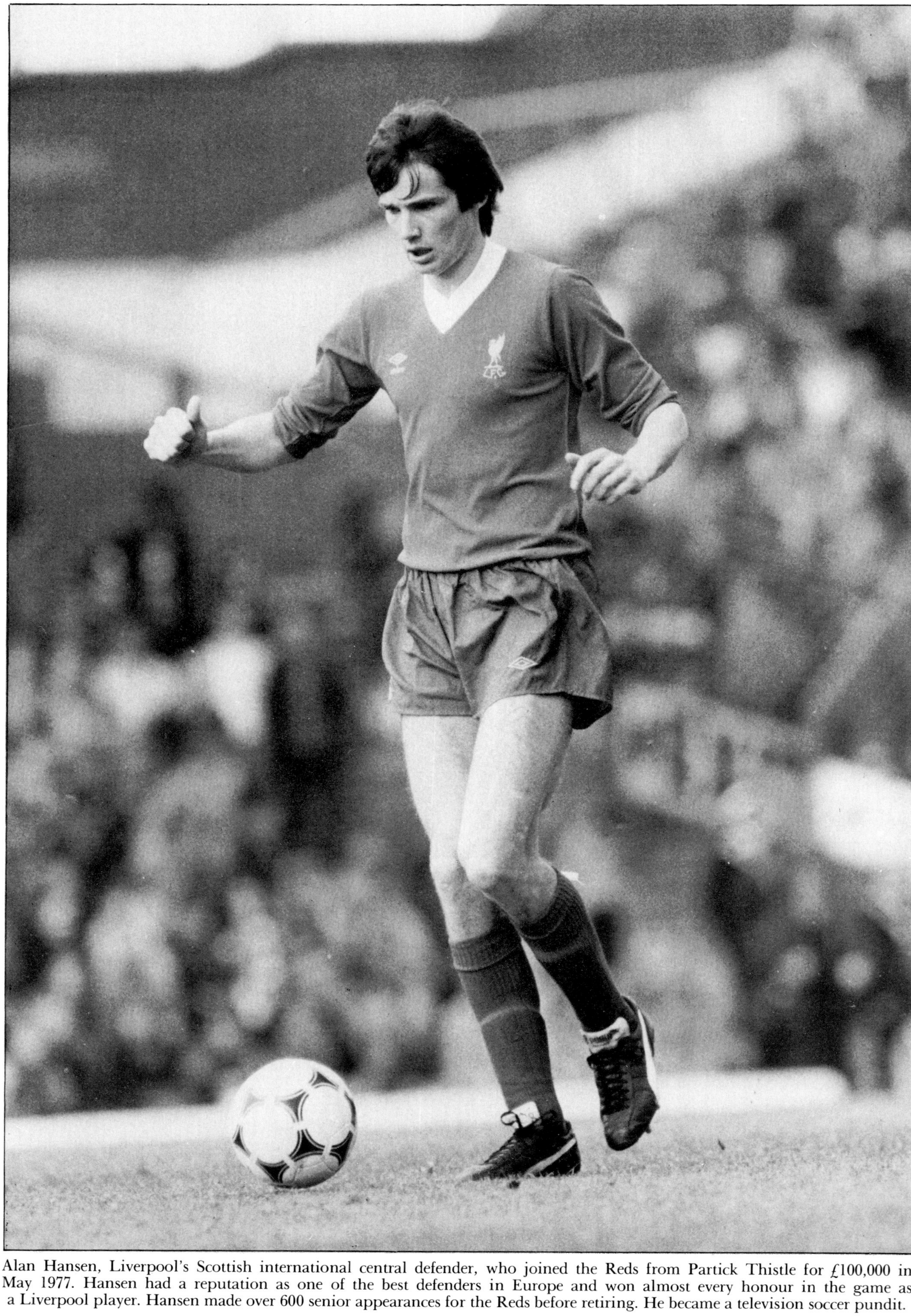
Alan Hansen, Liverpool's Scottish international central defender, who joined the Reds from Partick Thistle for £100,000 in May 1977. Hansen had a reputation as one of the best defenders in Europe and won almost every honour in the game as a Liverpool player. Hansen made over 600 senior appearances for the Reds before retiring. He became a television soccer pundit.

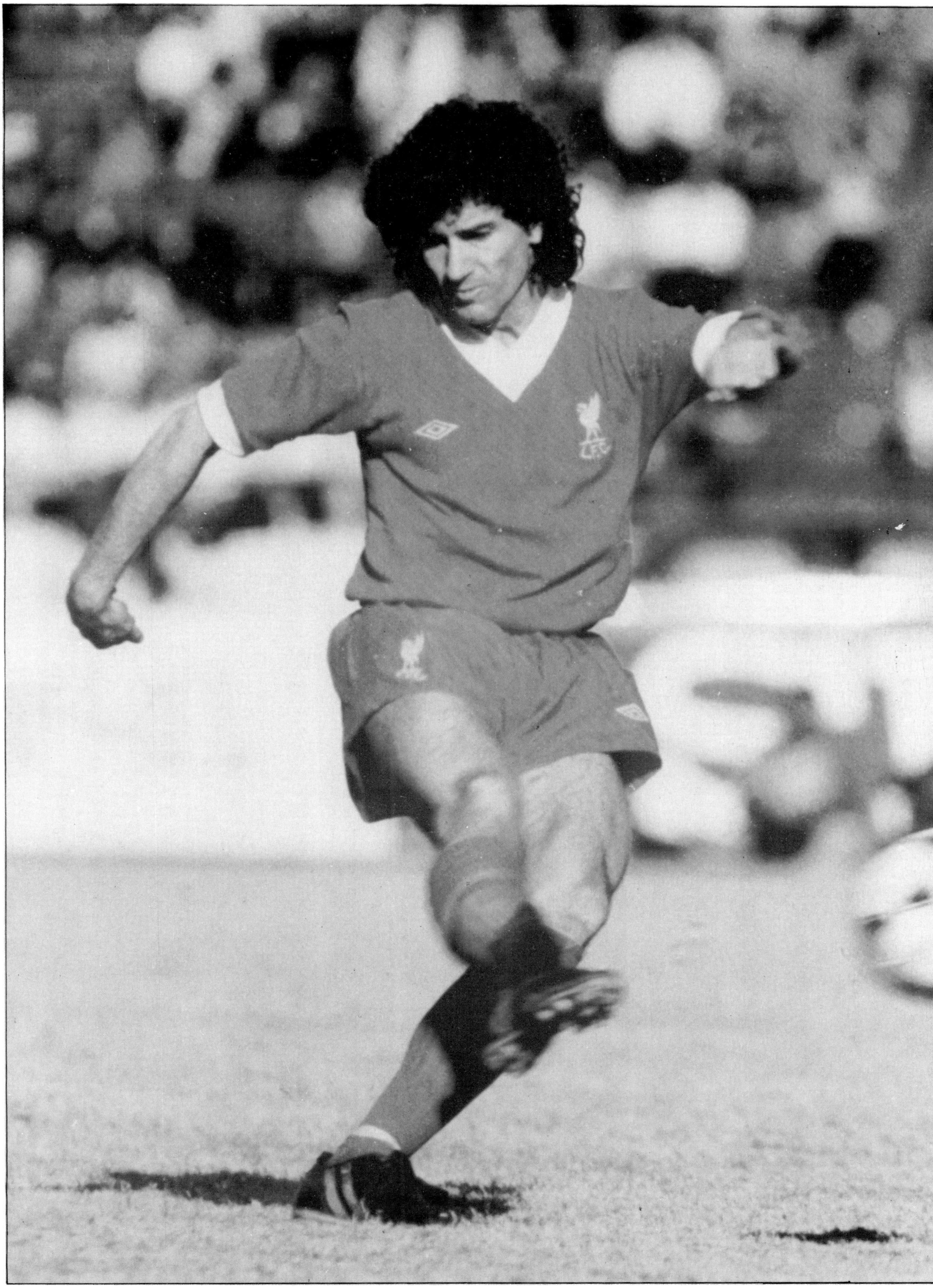

Although born in South Africa, Craig Johnston came into League football from Lake McQuarrie FC of Australia when he joined Middlesbrough in 1978. Liverpool paid £575,000 for the gifted midfielder in April 1981 and Johnston went on to win European Cup, League Championship, FA Cup and League Cup medals with the Reds. He made 259 senior appearances, scoring 39 goals, before returning to Australia in 1988.

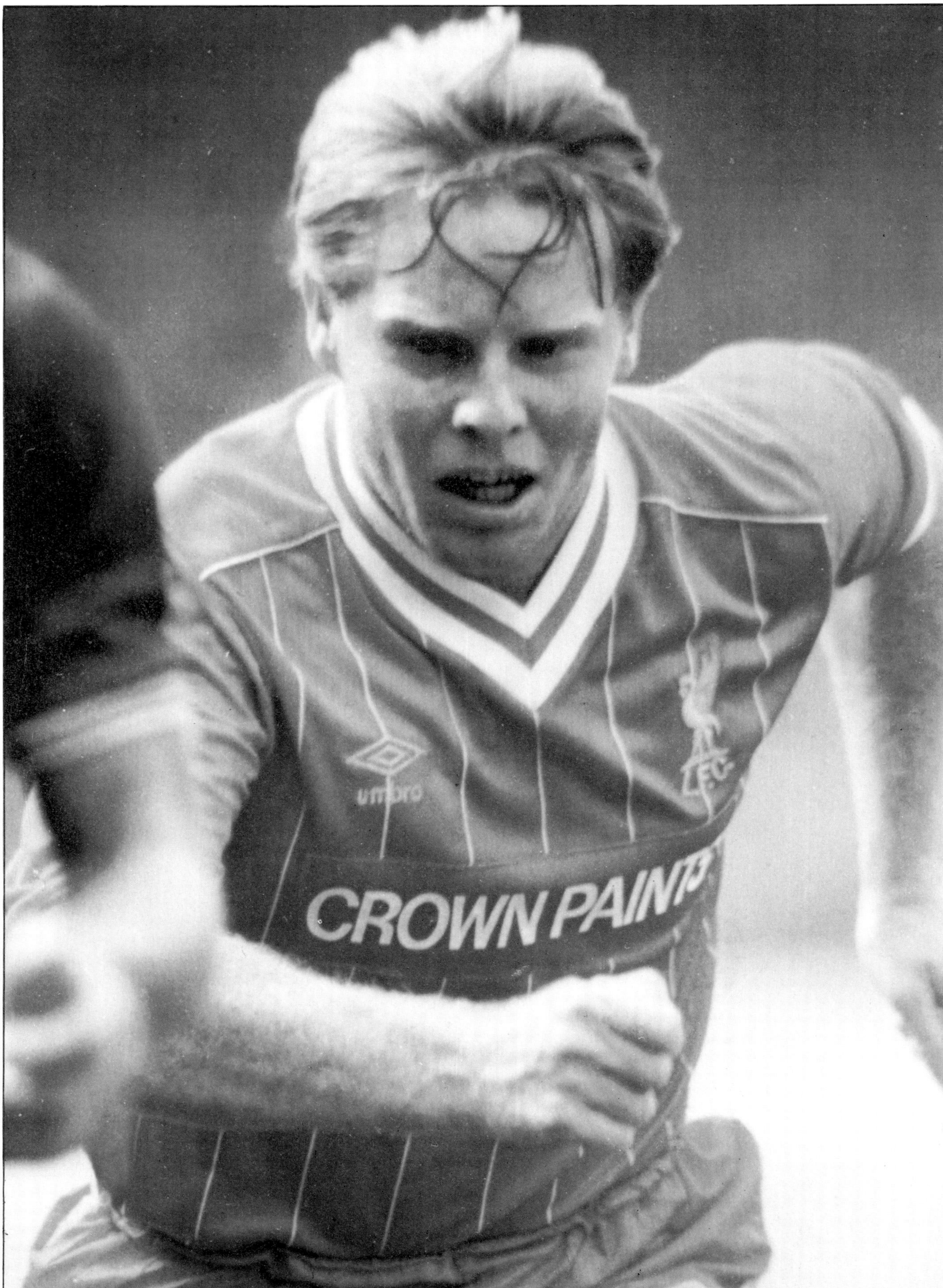

Sammy Lee made 286 appearances for Liverpool, the club he joined from Merseyside schools football in 1975. Lee, a constructive ball-winner who was capped by England, won his major honours — winners' medals in the European Cup, League Championship and League Cup — at Anfield between 1980 and 1984 but lost form during 1984-5 and after moving to QPR for £200,000 in August 1986 drifted into the Spanish League with Osasuna. He later played alongside Jimmy Case at Southampton and then returned to Anfield on the coaching staff.

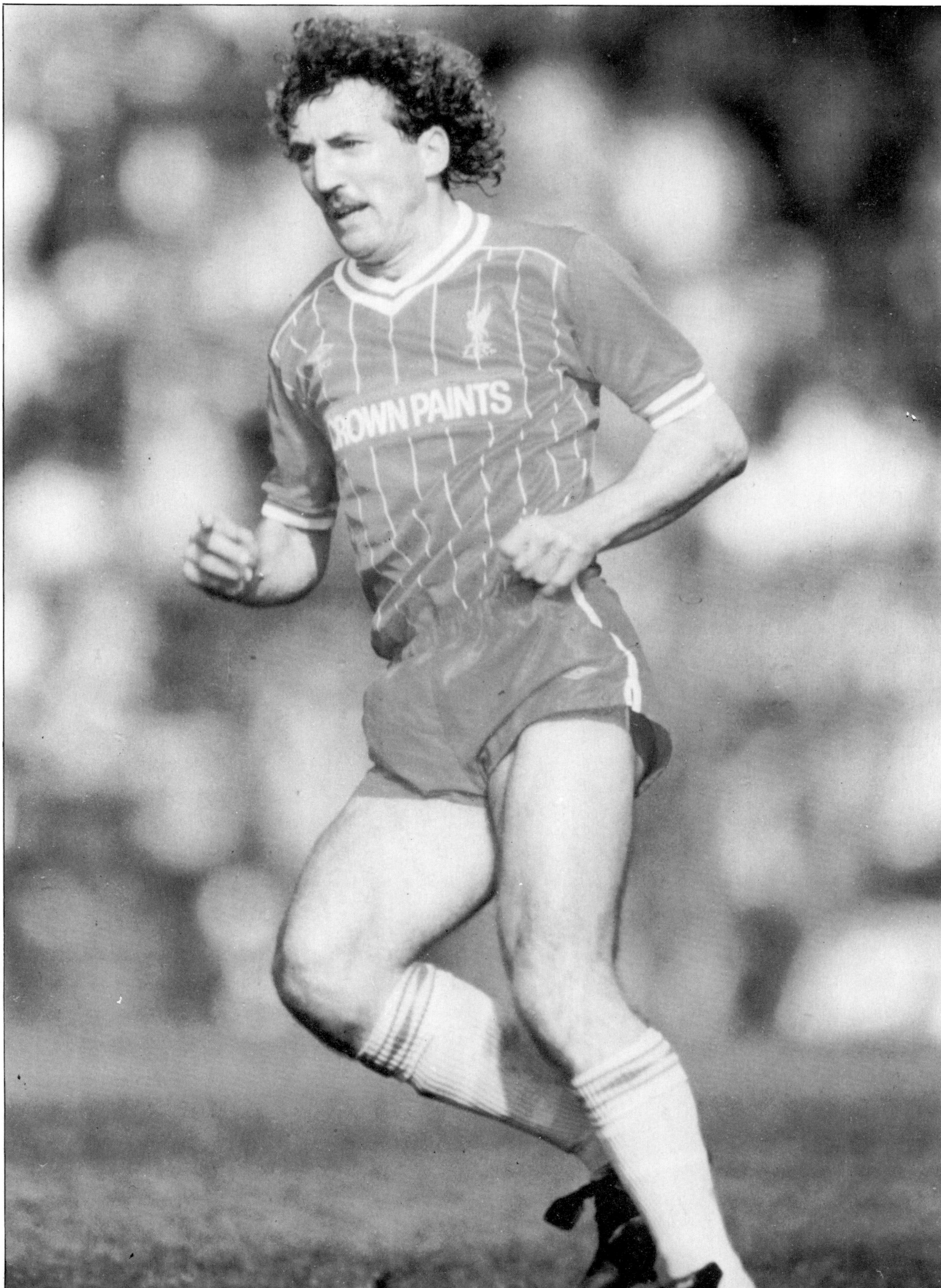

Alan Kennedy made 349 first-team appearances for Liverpool as a hard-tackling full-back. He joined the Reds in August 1978 from Newcastle United for £330,000 and left them for Sunderland in September 1985, for £100,000. With Liverpool he was capped by England and gained winners' medals in the European Cup, League Championship and Football League Cup. He played against the Reds in the 1974 FA Cup Final.

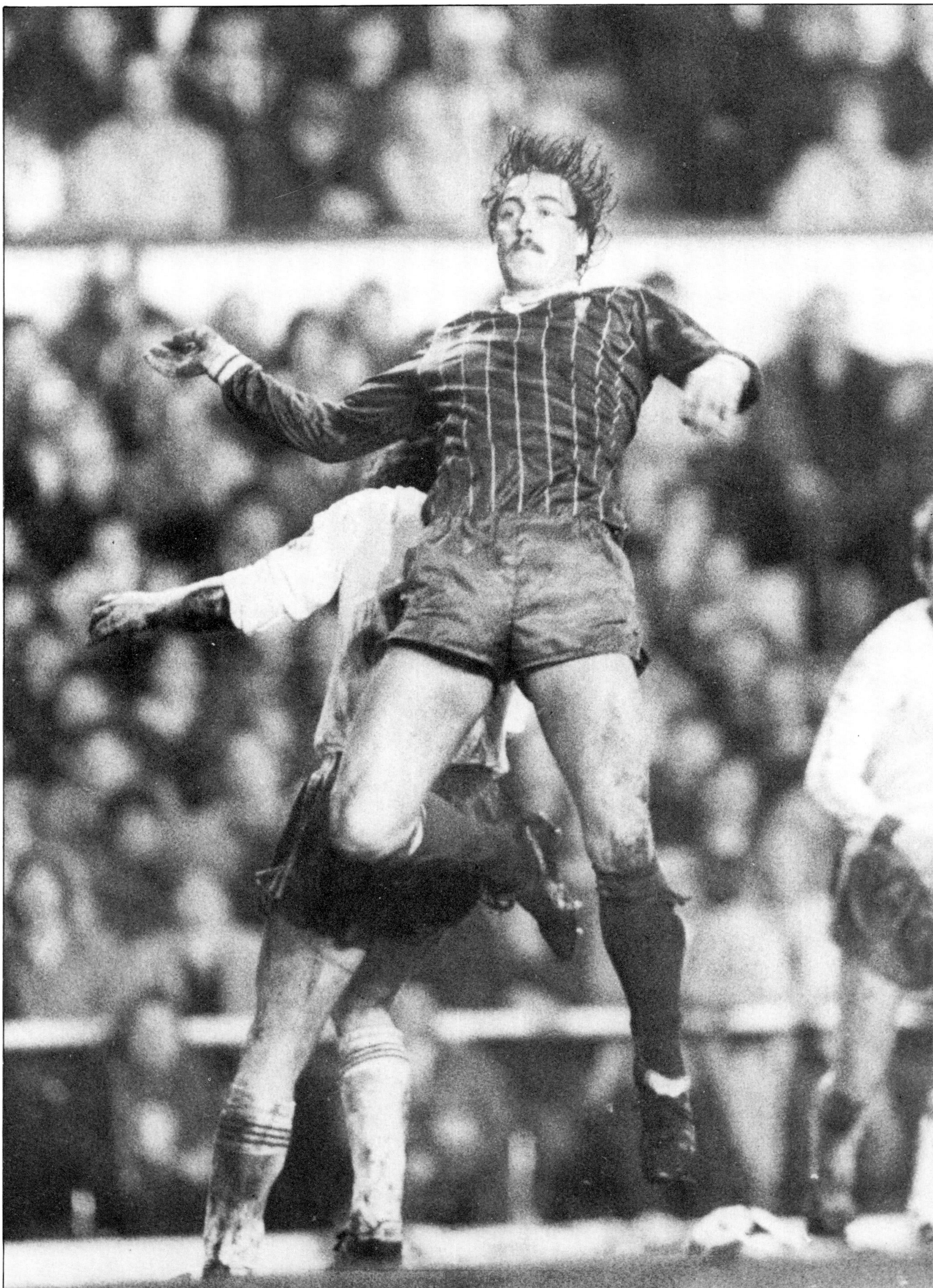

David Hodgson in action during the 1982-3 European Cup quarter-final home leg tie against Widzew Lódź. The Reds lost 2-0 in Poland and went down 3-2 at Anfield to go out on aggregate. Hodgson followed the trail taken by Souness and Johnston to Liverpool but made nothing like the same impact, making only 21 full League appearances.

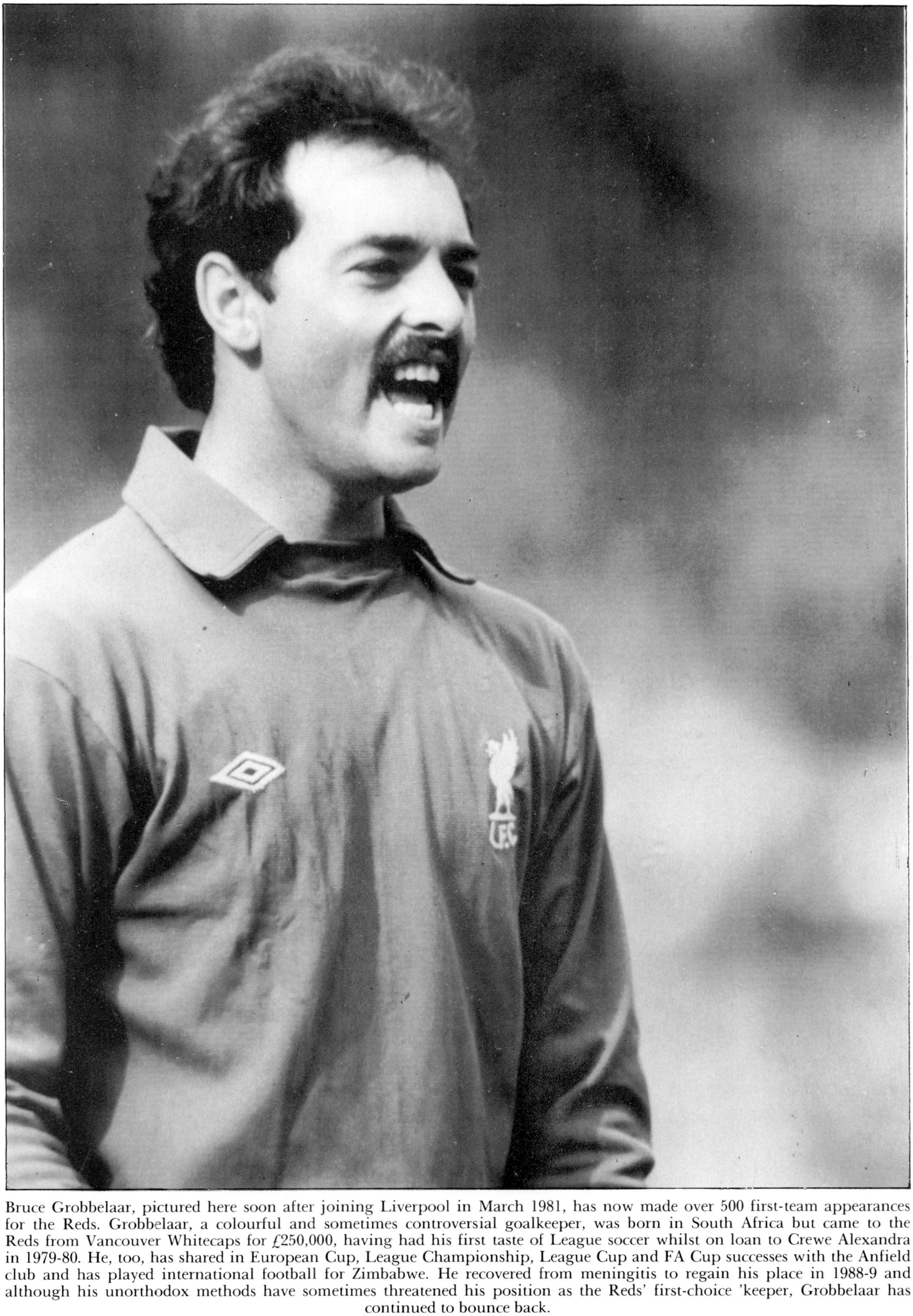

Bruce Grobbelaar, pictured here soon after joining Liverpool in March 1981, has now made over 500 first-team appearances for the Reds. Grobbelaar, a colourful and sometimes controversial goalkeeper, was born in South Africa but came to the Reds from Vancouver Whitecaps for £250,000, having had his first taste of League soccer whilst on loan to Crewe Alexandra in 1979-80. He, too, has shared in European Cup, League Championship, League Cup and FA Cup successes with the Anfield club and has played international football for Zimbabwe. He recovered from meningitis to regain his place in 1988-9 and although his unorthodox methods have sometimes threatened his position as the Reds' first-choice 'keeper, Grobbelaar has continued to bounce back.

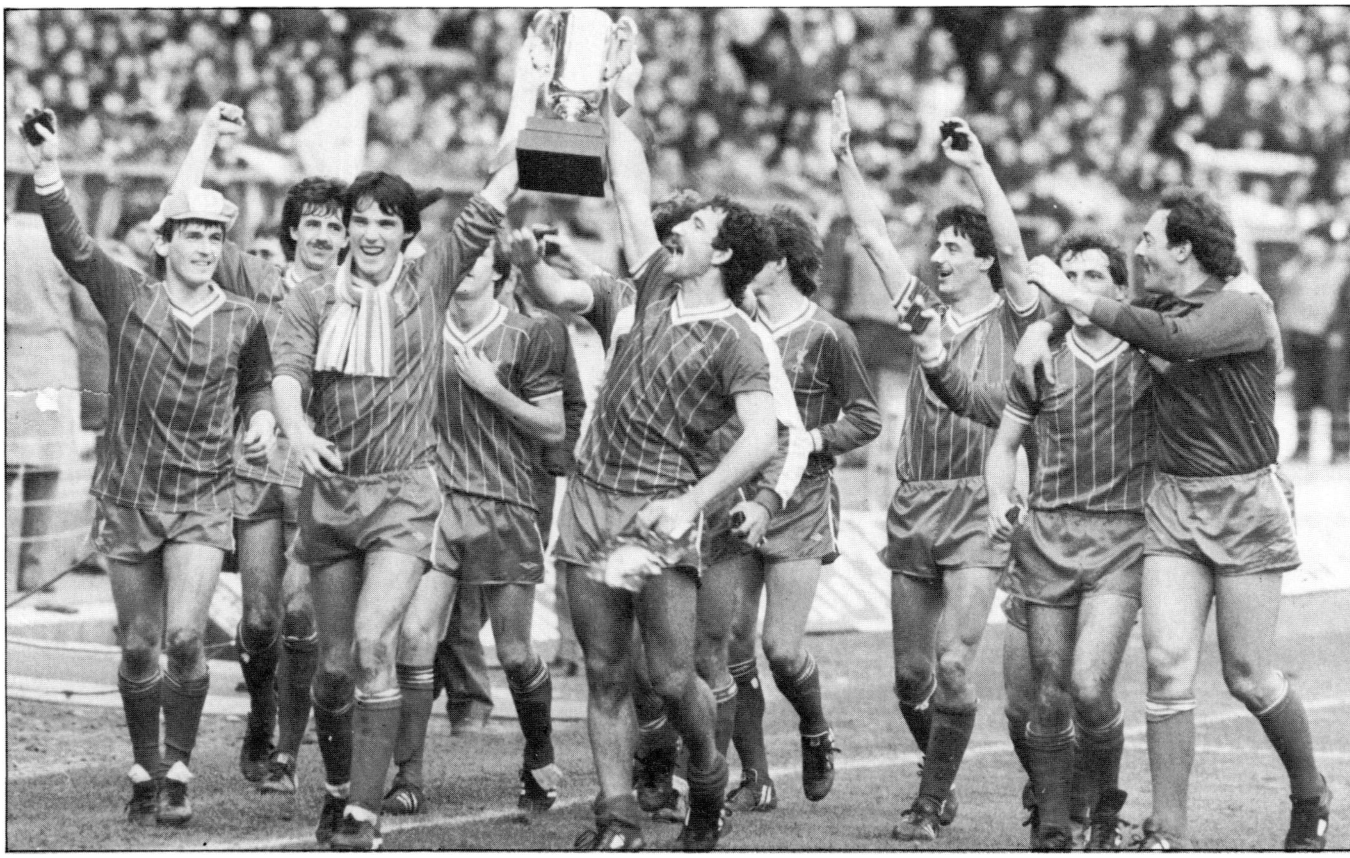

Liverpool players celebrate after retaining the Milk Cup by beating Manchester United 2-1 after extra-time in the 1983 Final.

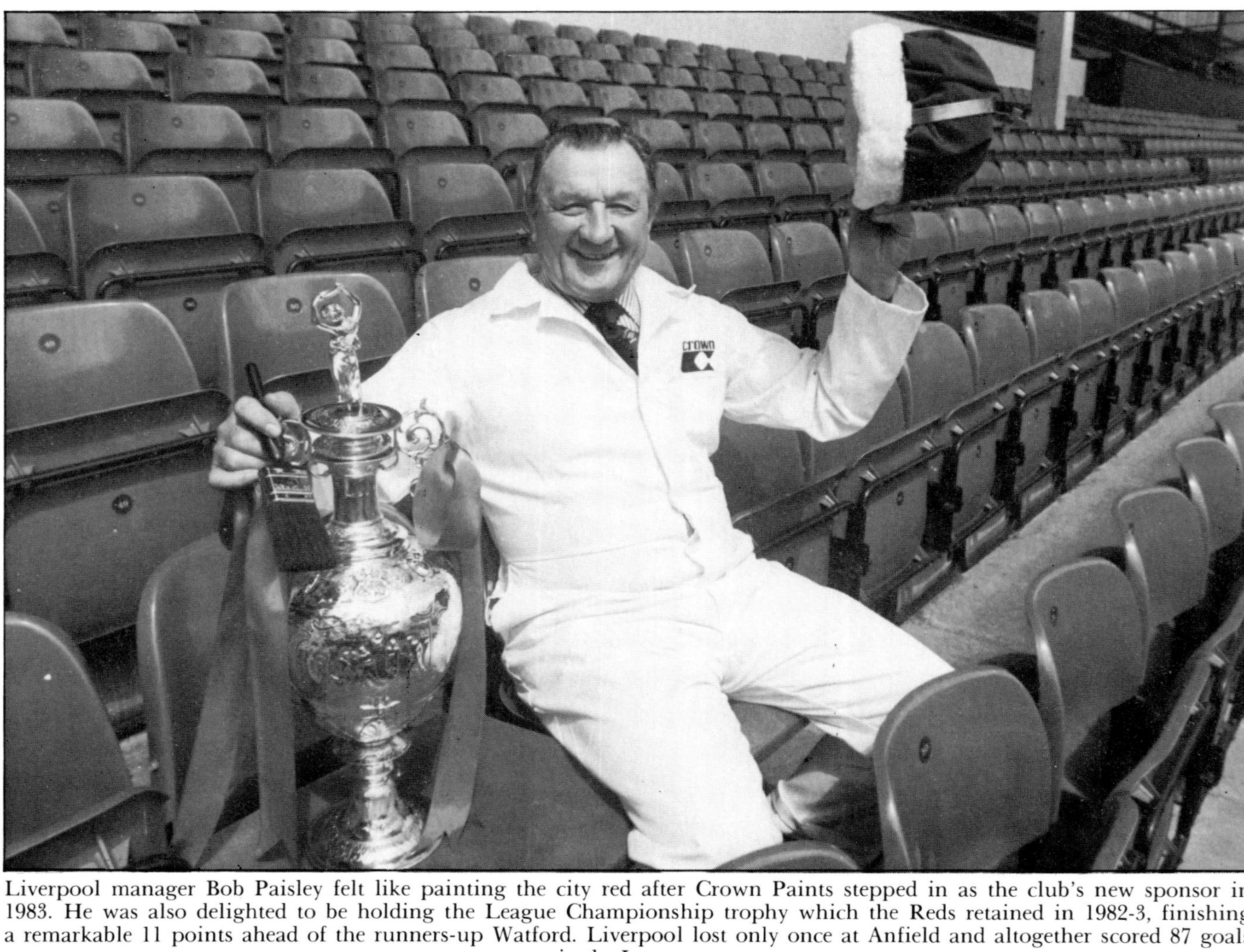

Liverpool manager Bob Paisley felt like painting the city red after Crown Paints stepped in as the club's new sponsor in 1983. He was also delighted to be holding the League Championship trophy which the Reds retained in 1982-3, finishing a remarkable 11 points ahead of the runners-up Watford. Liverpool lost only once at Anfield and altogether scored 87 goals in the League.

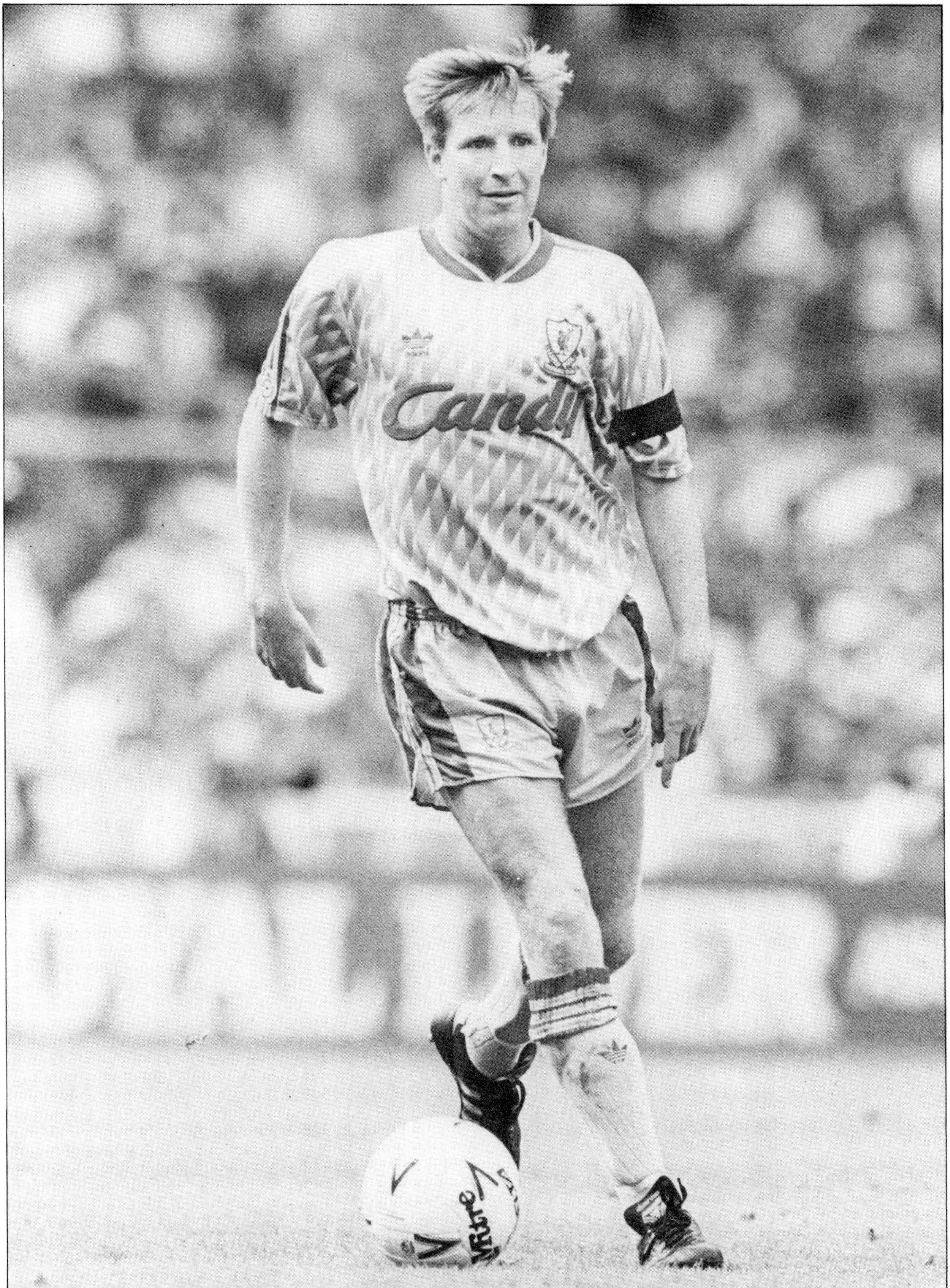

Ronnie Whelan has made nearly 500 senior appearances for Liverpool. A Republic of Ireland international midfielder, Whelan joined the Reds in October 1979 from the Dublin club Home Farm and has gained European Cup, League Championship, FA Cup and League Cup winners' medals with the Anfield club.

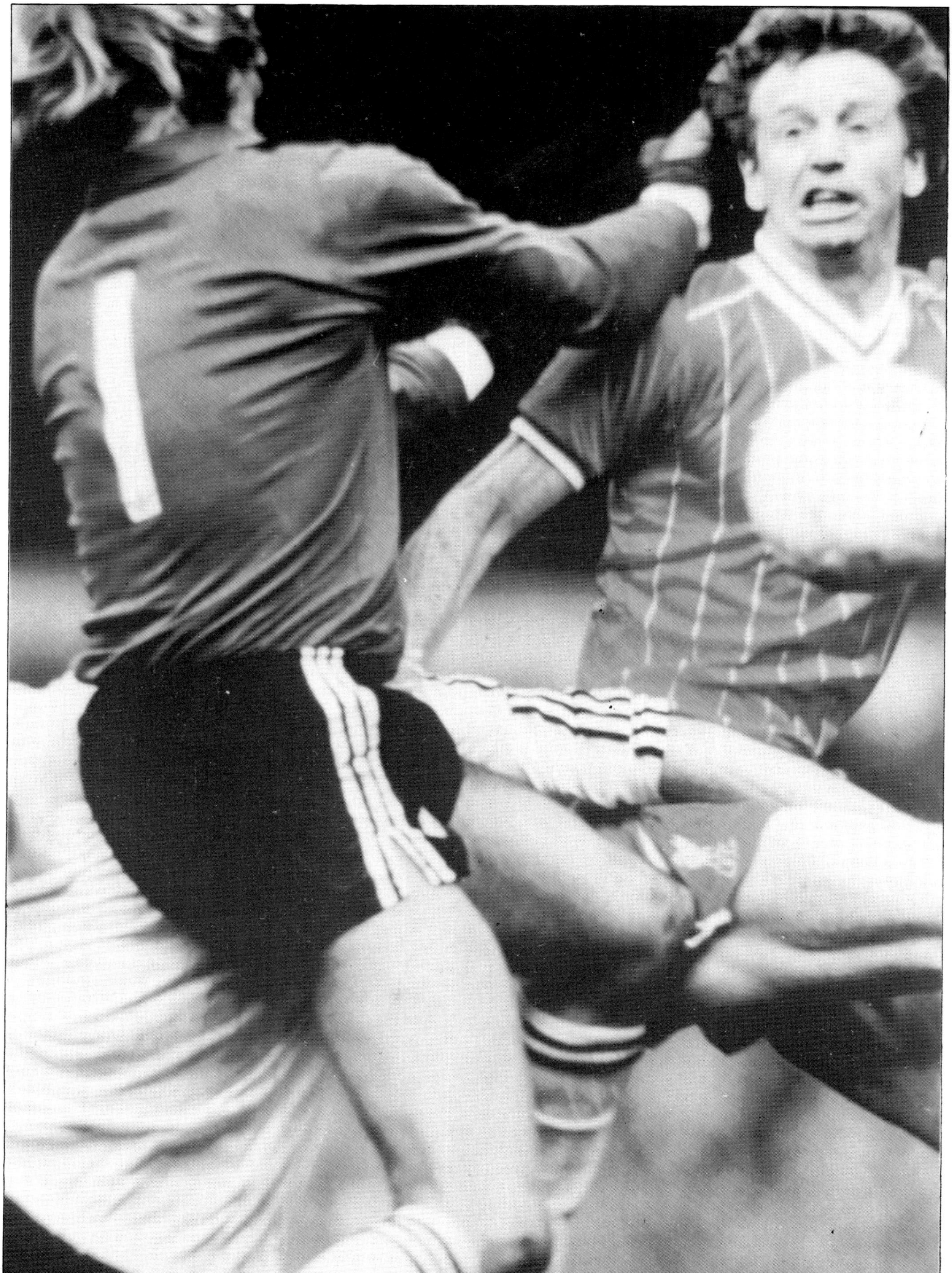

One player on his way out of Anfield after the 1982-3 Championship-winning season was David Fairclough, nicknamed 'Super Sub' because of his knack of coming on to score vital goals. Liverpool-born Fairclough joined the Reds from schools football in 1974. Although never a regular enough member of the side to qualify for a League Championship medal, Fairclough won European Cup and UEFA Cup winners' medals and a Milk Cup winners' medal.

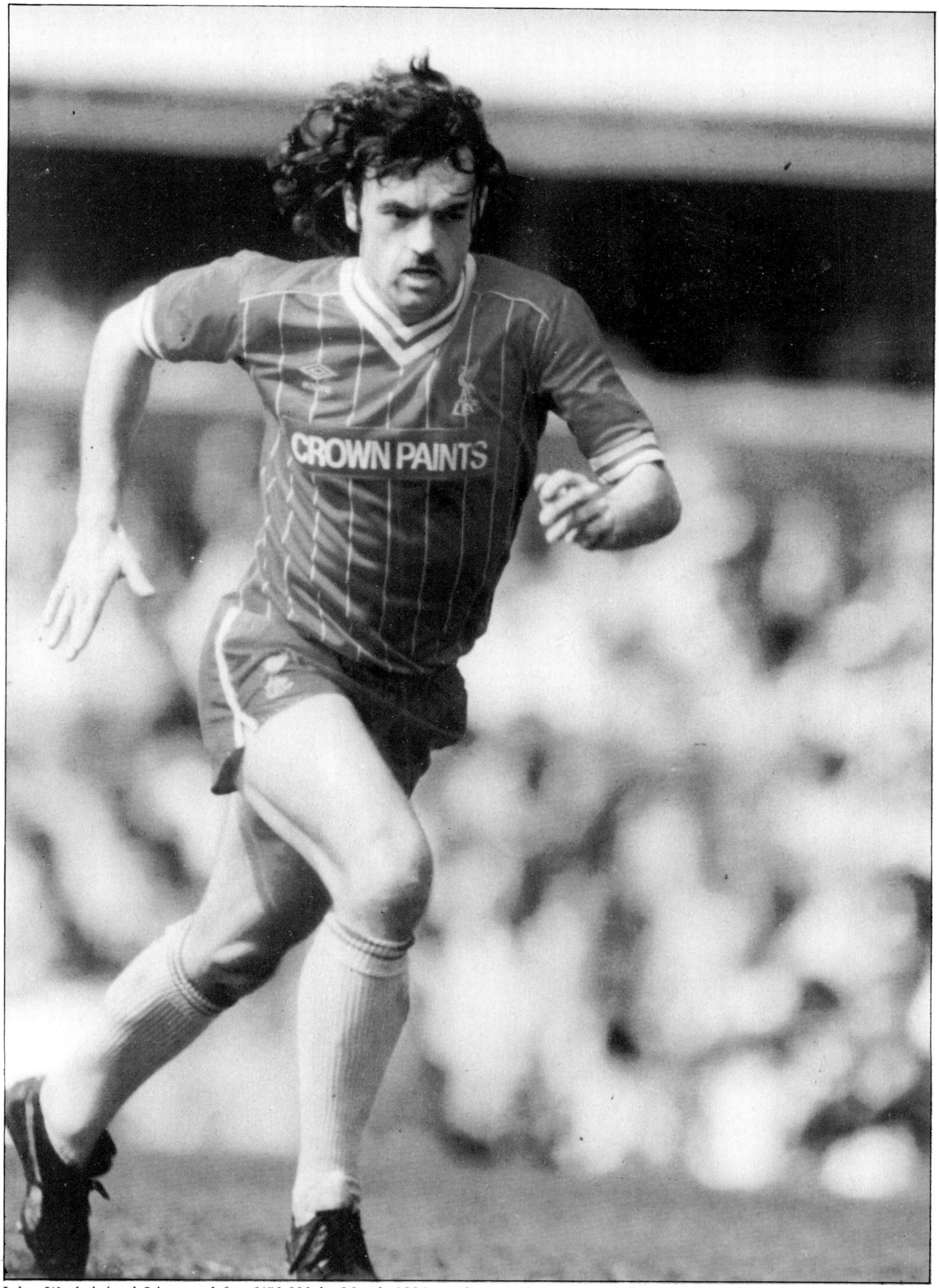

John Wark joined Liverpool for £450,000 in March 1984, as Graeme Souness was about to leave for Italy. Wark, a Scottish international midfielder, played for the Reds in a European Cup Final — he had winners' medals in the UEFA Cup and FA Cup whilst with Ipswich — before returning to Portman Road for £100,000 in January 1988. In 1992-3 he was still a leading member of the Ipswich team which had just been promoted to the Premier League.

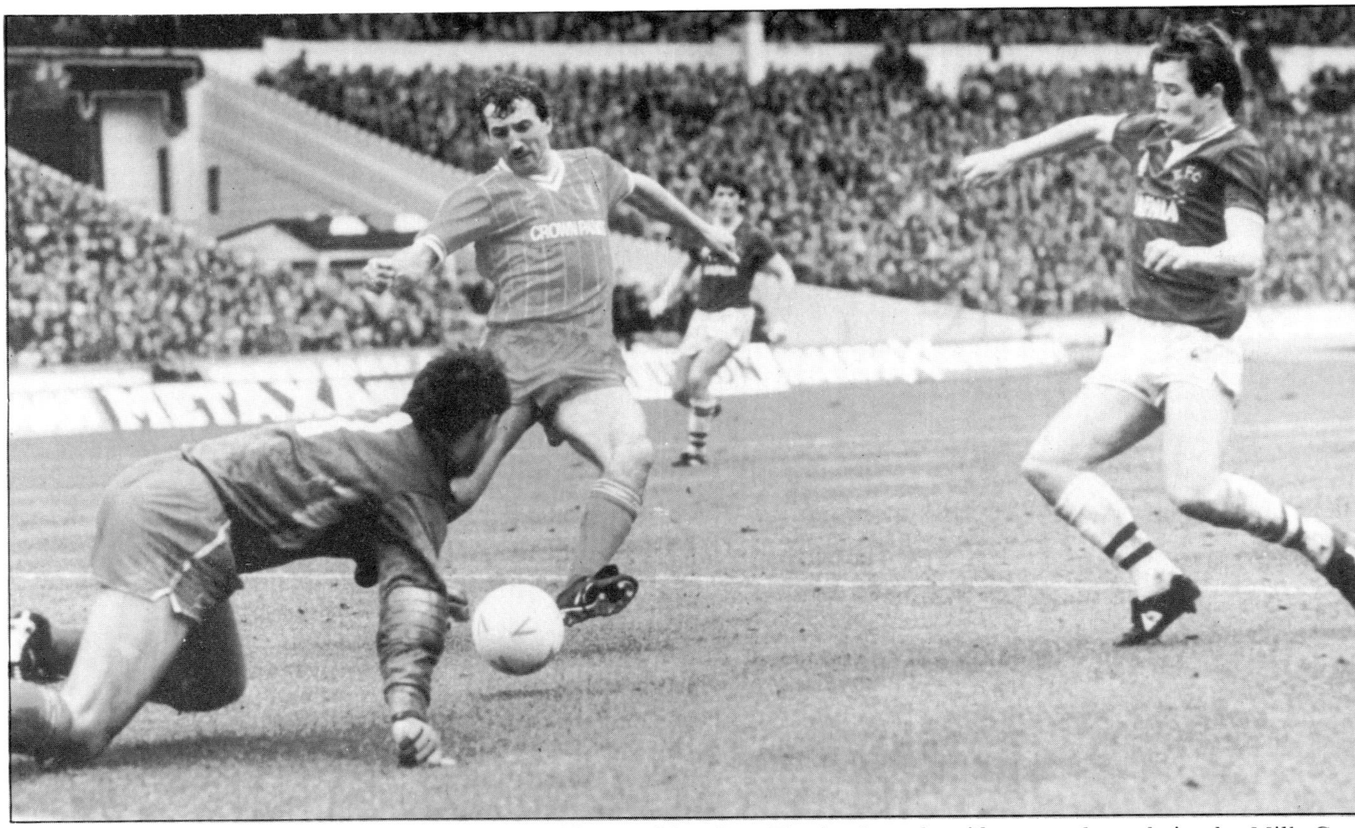

In 1984, Liverpool met Everton in an all-Merseyside Wembley Cup Final, when the sides won through in the Milk Cup. Here, Everton's Adrian Heath is beaten to the ball by Alan Kennedy as Bruce Grobbelaar scrambles after it. The sides drew 0-0 before Liverpool won the replay 1-0 at Maine Road.

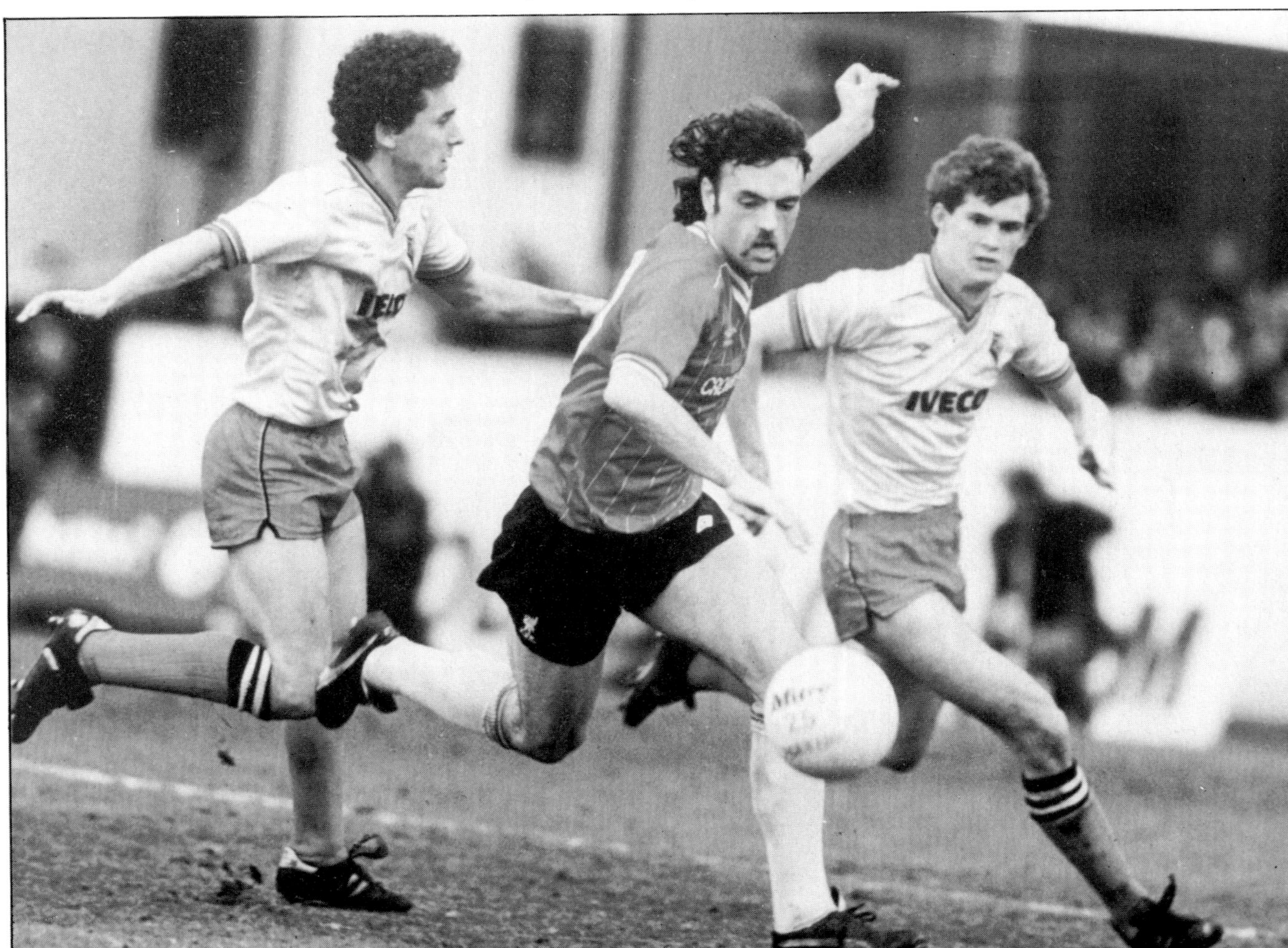

John Wark bursts through against Watford at Vicarage Road in March 1984. The Watford players are Wilf Rostron and Lee Sinnott. Wark and Rush hit the goals as Liverpool won 2-0.

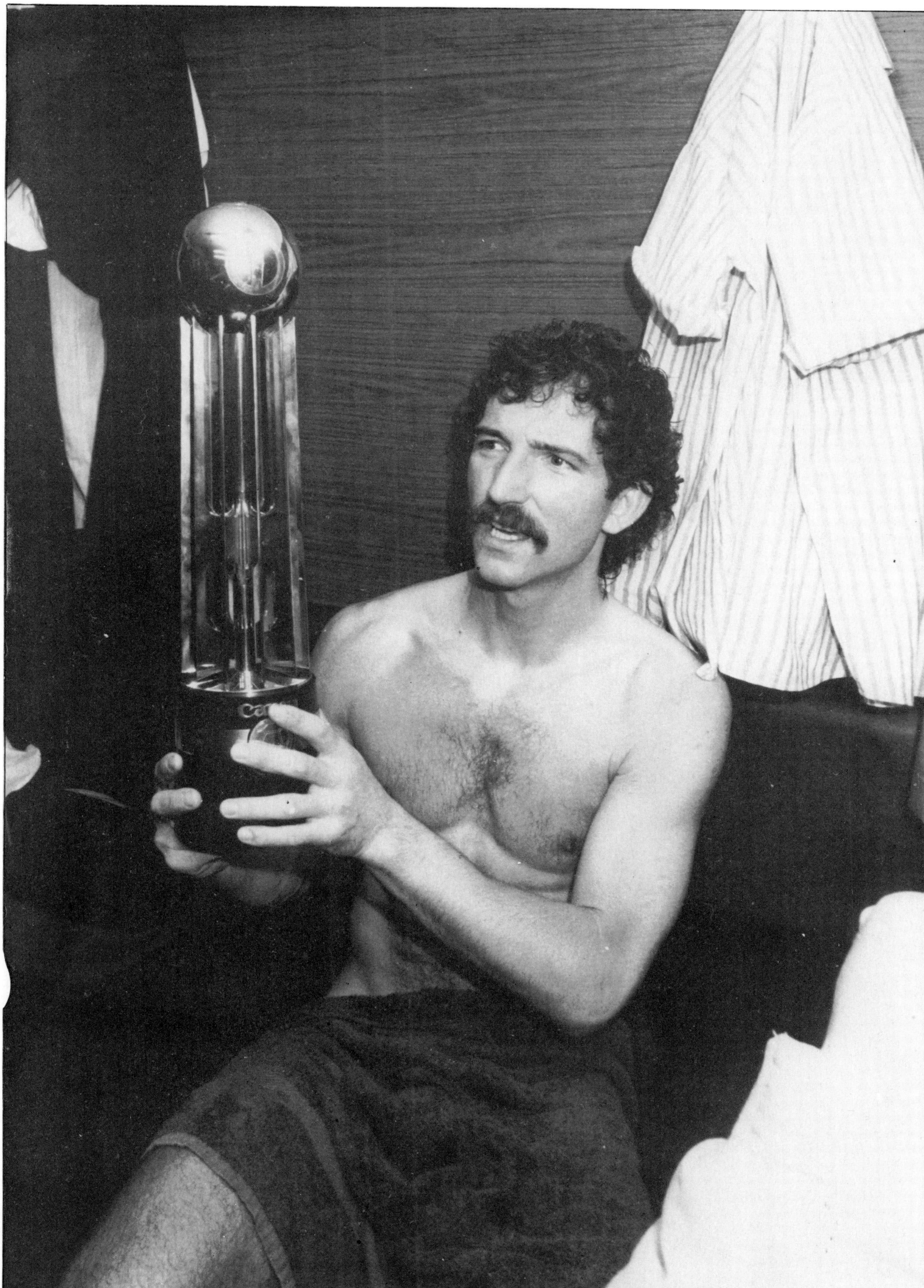

Liverpool skipper Graeme Souness pictured with the League Championship trophy after the Reds' 1-1 draw with Norwich City in the last game of 1983-4. Liverpool had thus completed a hat-trick of League titles, the first club to do so since Arsenal in the 1930s. The Reds finished three points ahead of Southampton.

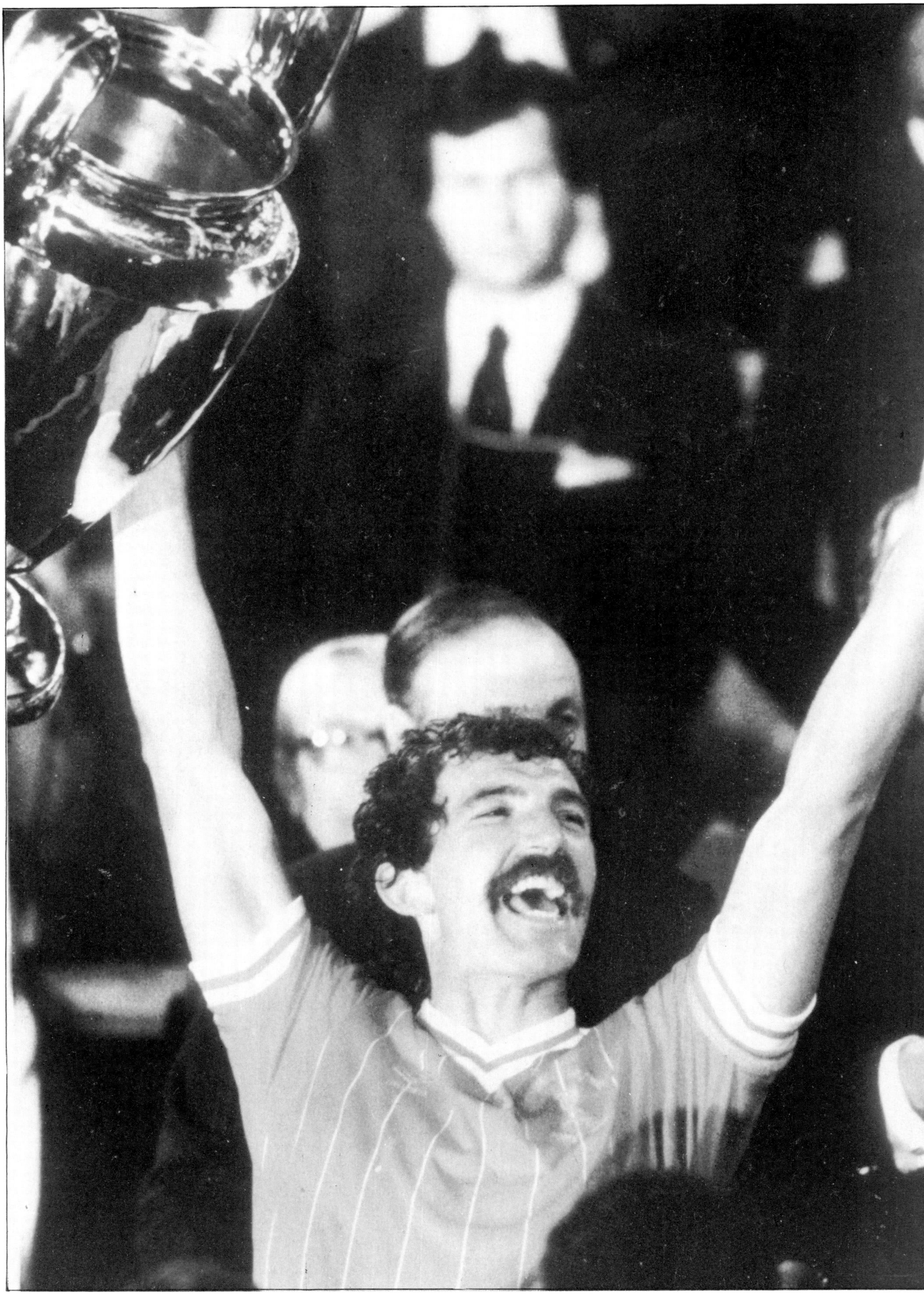

The 1983-4 season was one of the most memorable in Liverpool's glorious history, for besides completing a hat-trick of League Championships and winning the Milk Cup, the Reds also lifted the European Cup, beating AS Roma on penalties in Rome. Graeme Souness, soon to be playing in Italian football, lifts the European trophy.

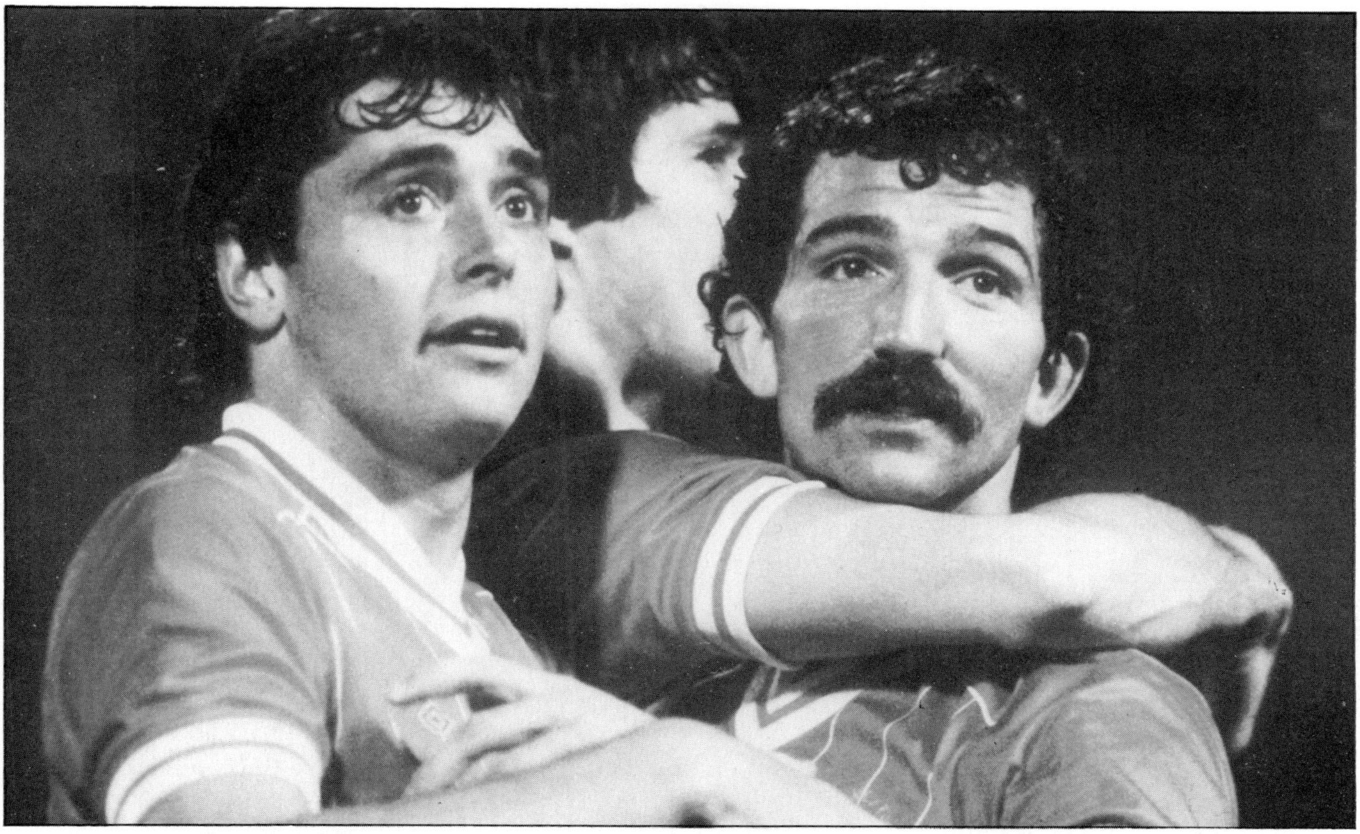

Michael Robinson and Graeme Souness look apprehensive. Robinson joined Liverpool from Brighton in August 1983 for £200,000. An aggresive, roving type of player he attracted a lot of money in his moves around the Football League which also took in Preston, Manchester City and QPR, the club he joined from Anfield for £100,000 in December 1984. Qualified through parentage, Robinson won 23 full caps for the Republic of Ireland. He played for Brighton in the 1983 FA Cup Final and in his short spell with Liverpool he won European Cup and League Championship medals. He was a member of QPR's 1986 League Cup Final team.

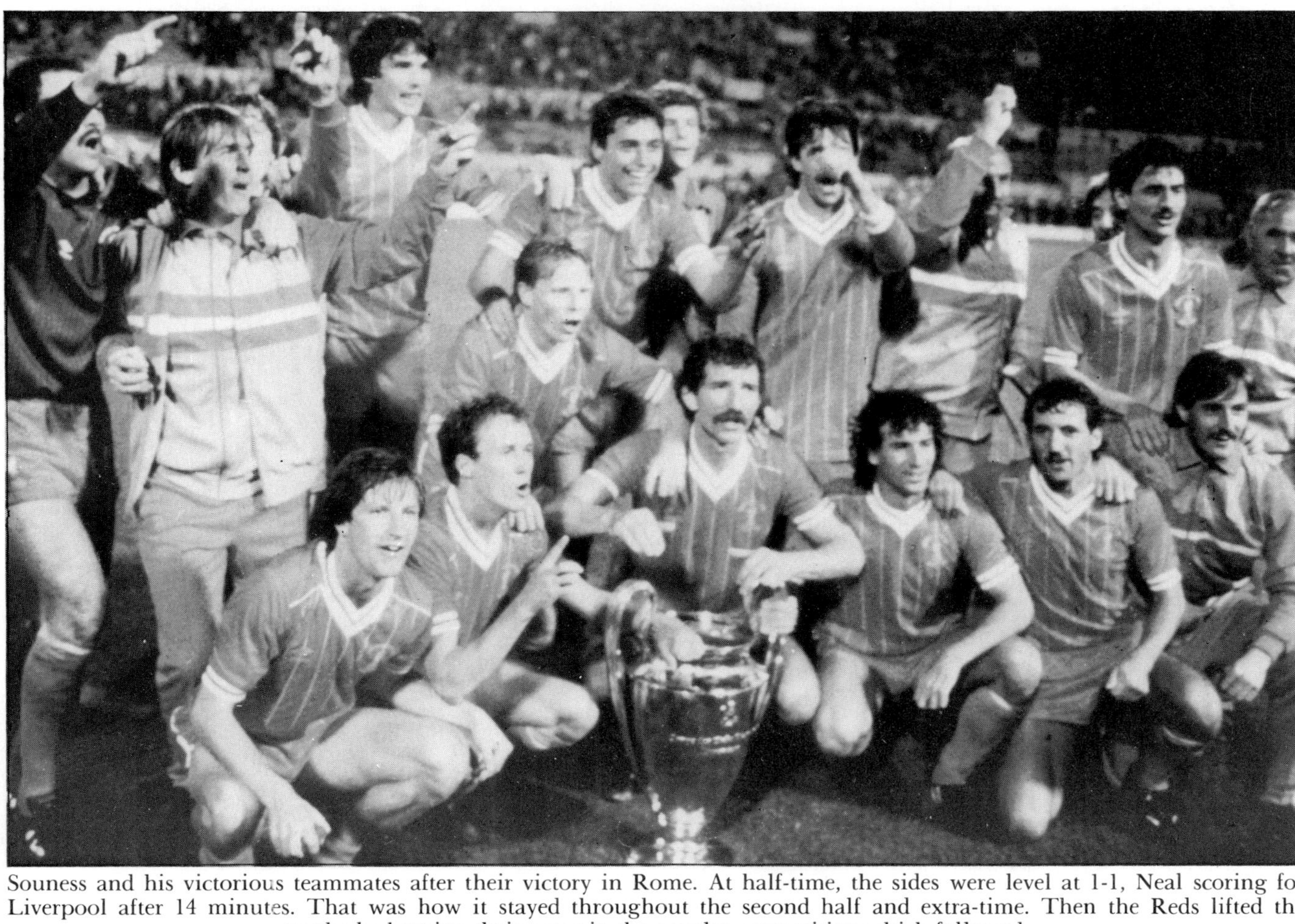

Souness and his victorious teammates after their victory in Rome. At half-time, the sides were level at 1-1, Neal scoring for Liverpool after 14 minutes. That was how it stayed throughout the second half and extra-time. Then the Reds lifted the trophy by keeping their nerve in the penalty competition which followed.

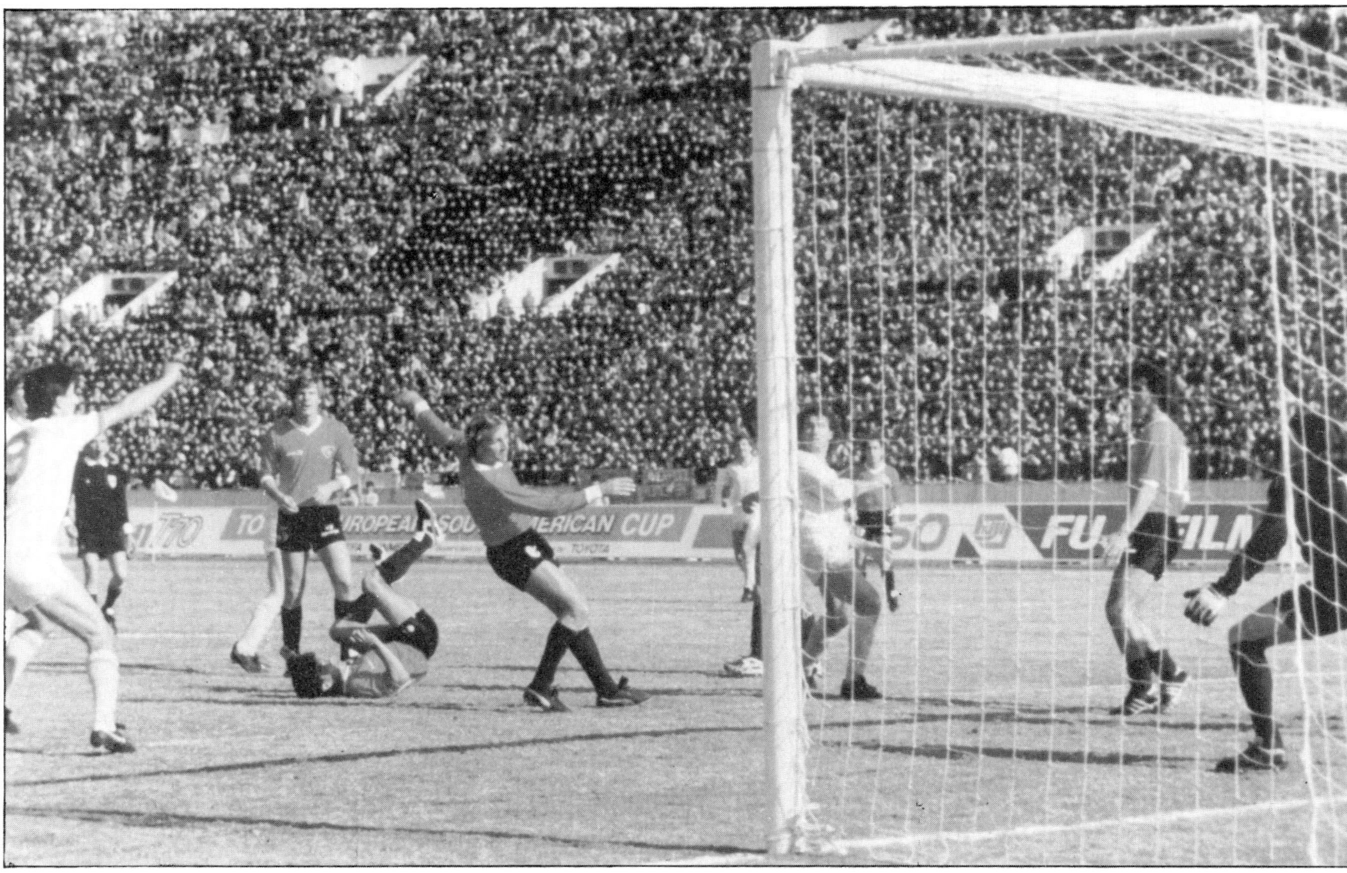

In December 1984, Liverpool met Independiente in the World Club Championship in Tokyo, where they lost 1-0. Here, the Reds appear to be appealing for something in the South Americans' goalmouth.

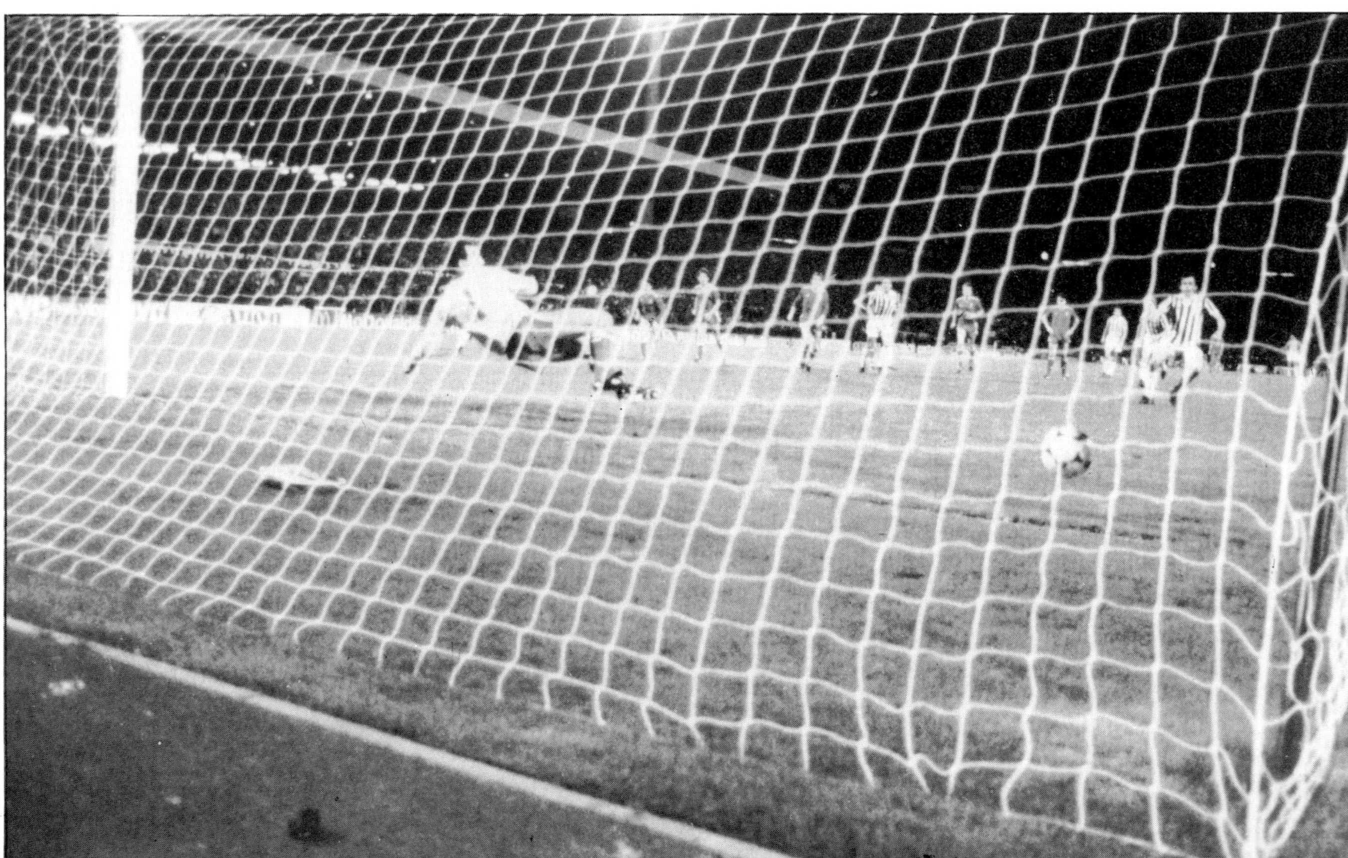

In 1984-5, Liverpool suffered a rare barren spell, ending the season without a trophy. They finished runners-up to neighbours Everton in the First Division and were knocked out of the FA Cup by Manchester United in the semi-final and by Tottenham in the third round of the Milk Cup. The season ended on a bitter note with the Heysel Stadium disaster at the European Cup Final in Brussels. The game eventually got under way but no one had any appetite for football. Here, Juventus' Michel Platini scores the only goal of the game from the penalty-spot.

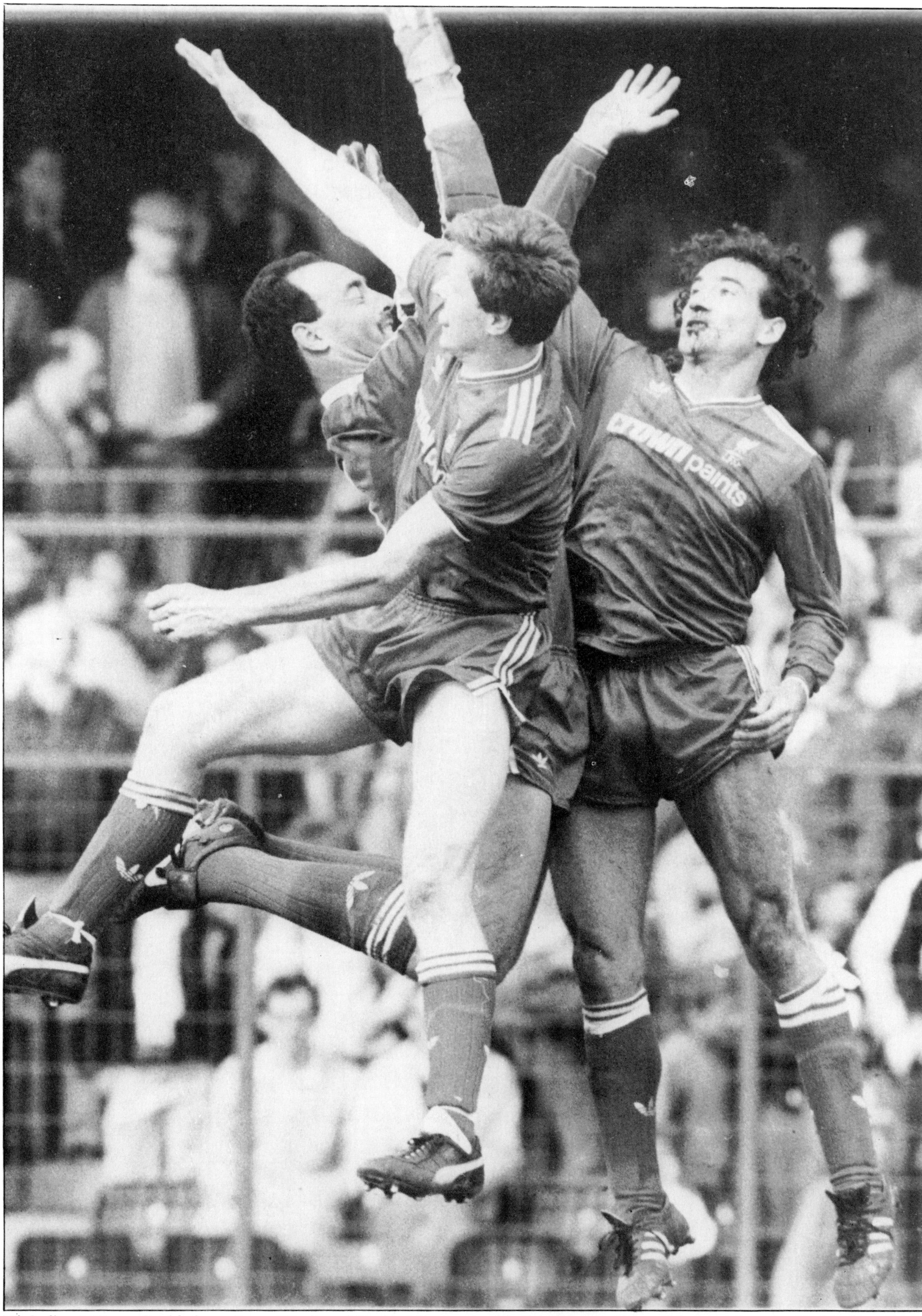

High fives! Bruce Grobbelaar, Steve Nicol and Craig Johnston celebrate another Championship after the Reds' victory over Chelsea at Stamford Bridge in May 1986 left them three points ahead of Everton.

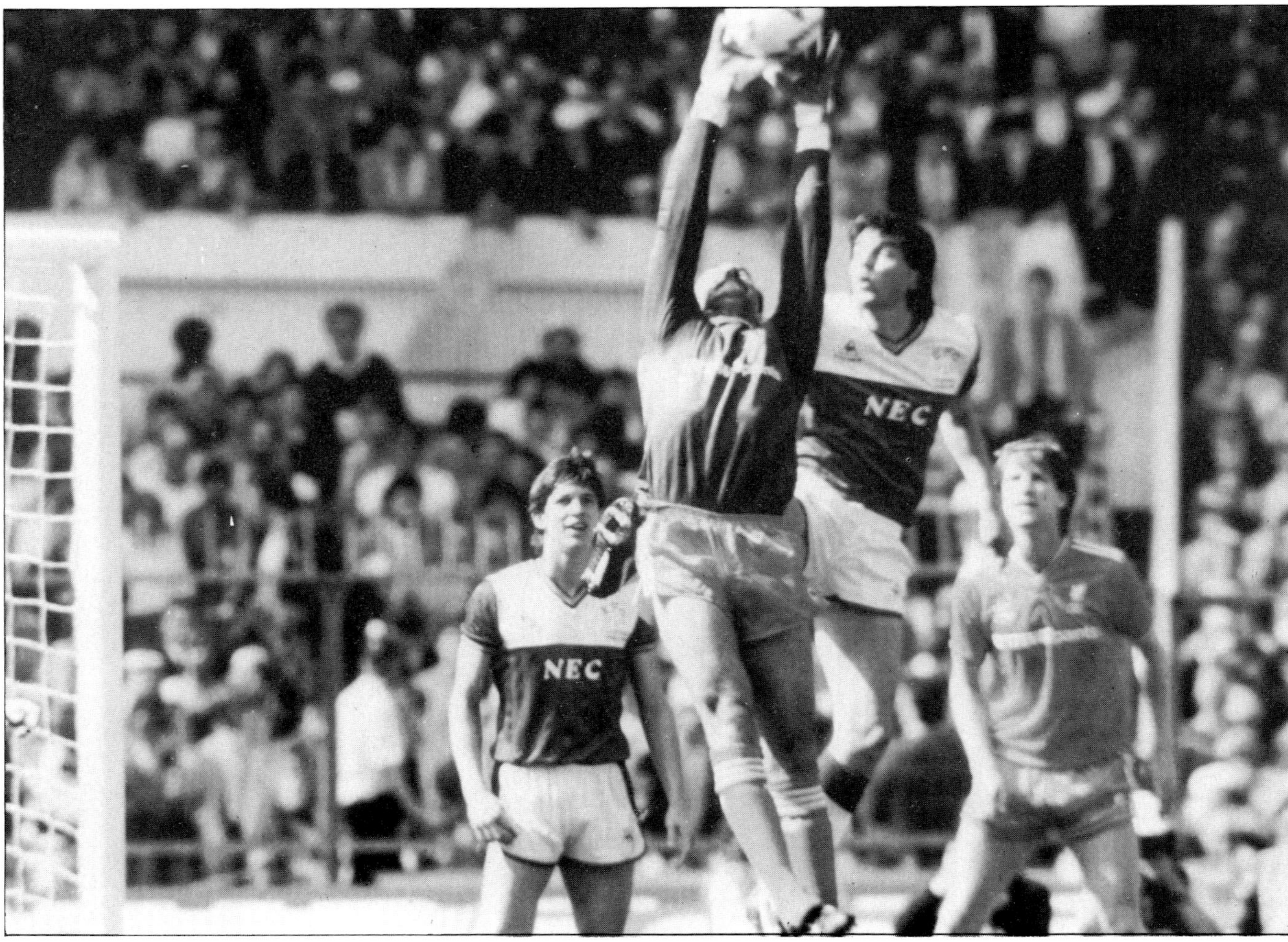

In 1986, Liverpool met Everton in another all-Merseyside Wembley Cup Final, this time in the FA Cup. The Reds lifted the trophy to seal a League and Cup double, winning 3-1 after extra-time. Bruce Grobbelaar outjumps Everton's Graeme Sharp.

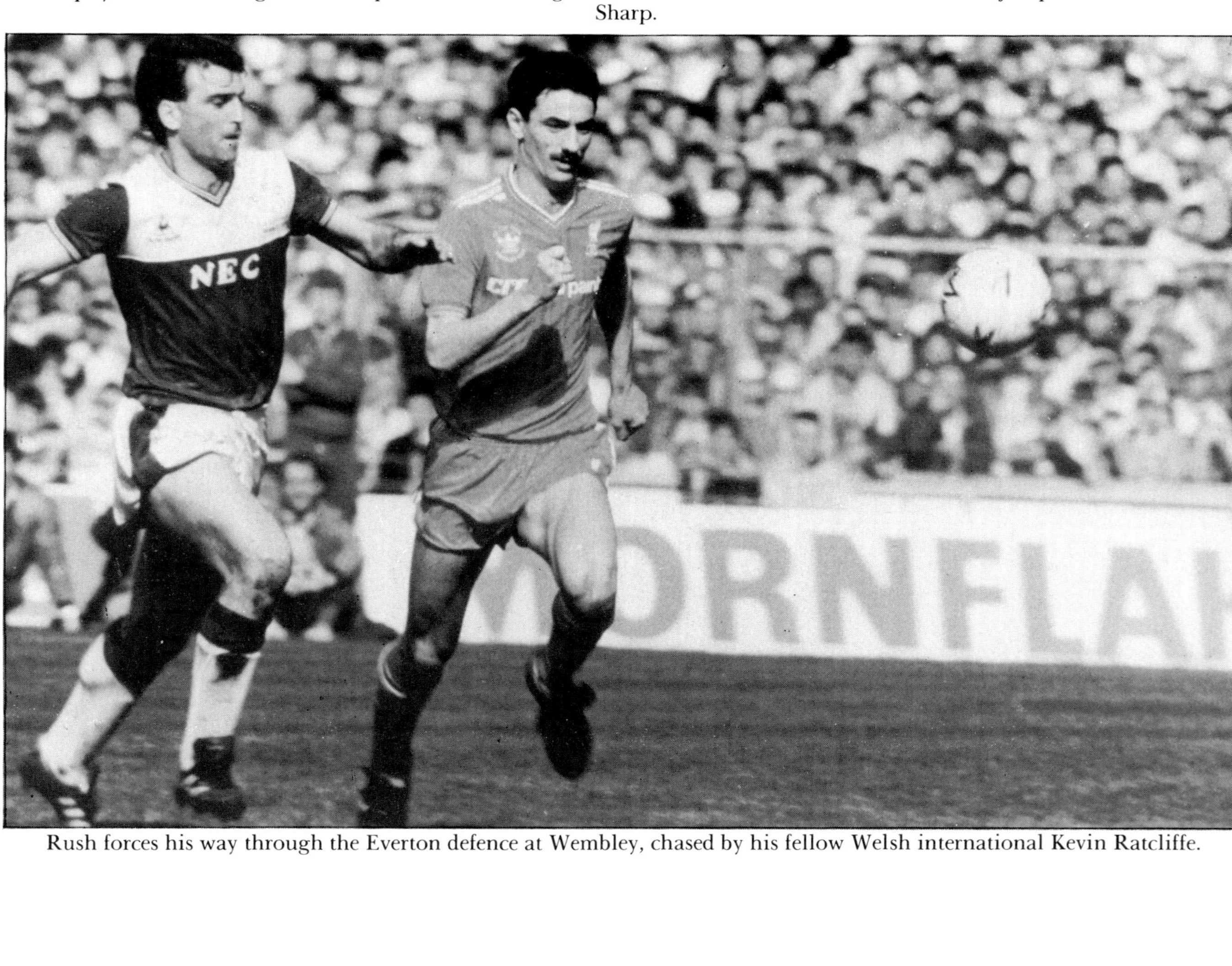

Rush forces his way through the Everton defence at Wembley, chased by his fellow Welsh international Kevin Ratcliffe.

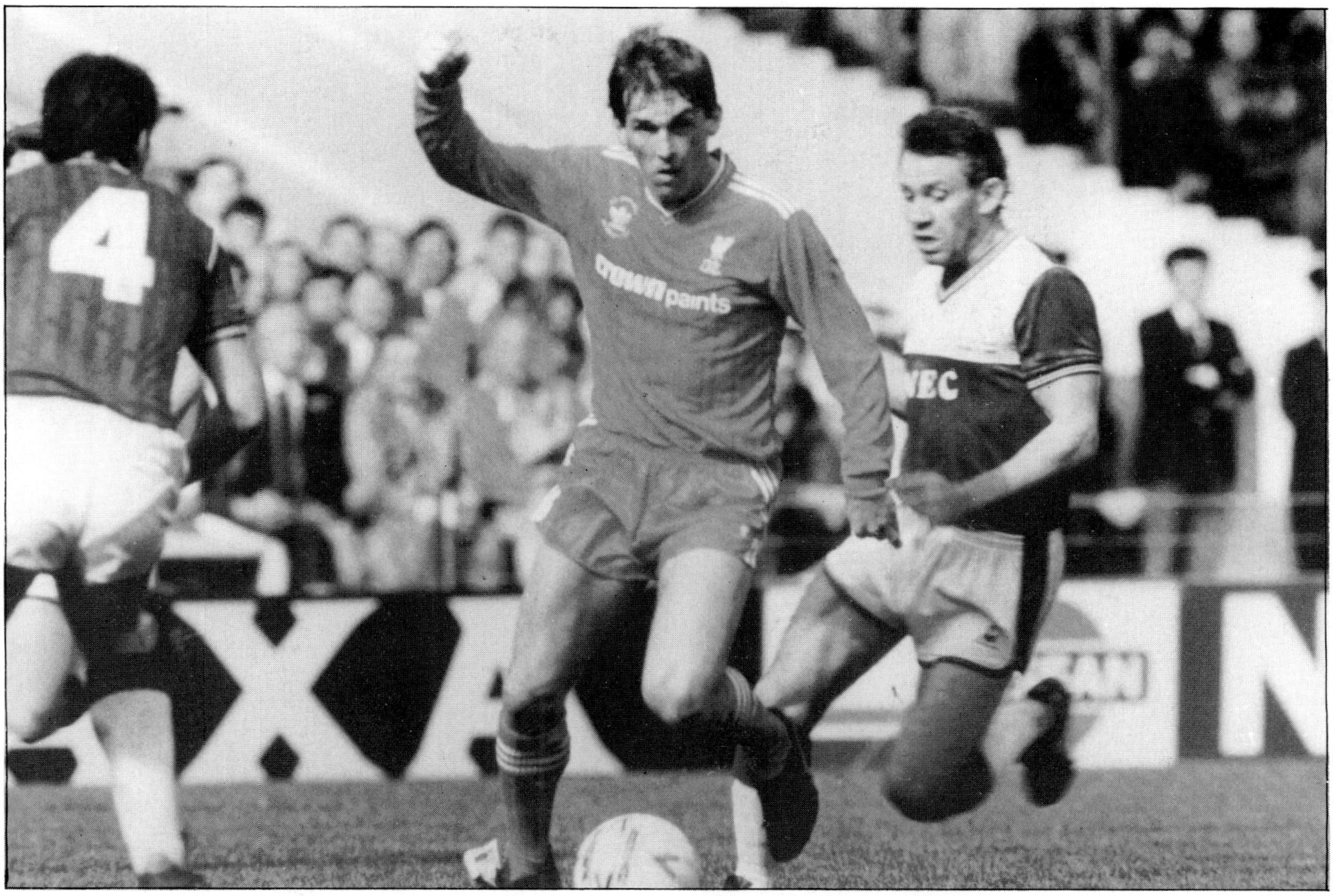

Kenny Dalglish sweeps the ball past Everton's Peter Reid at Wembley.

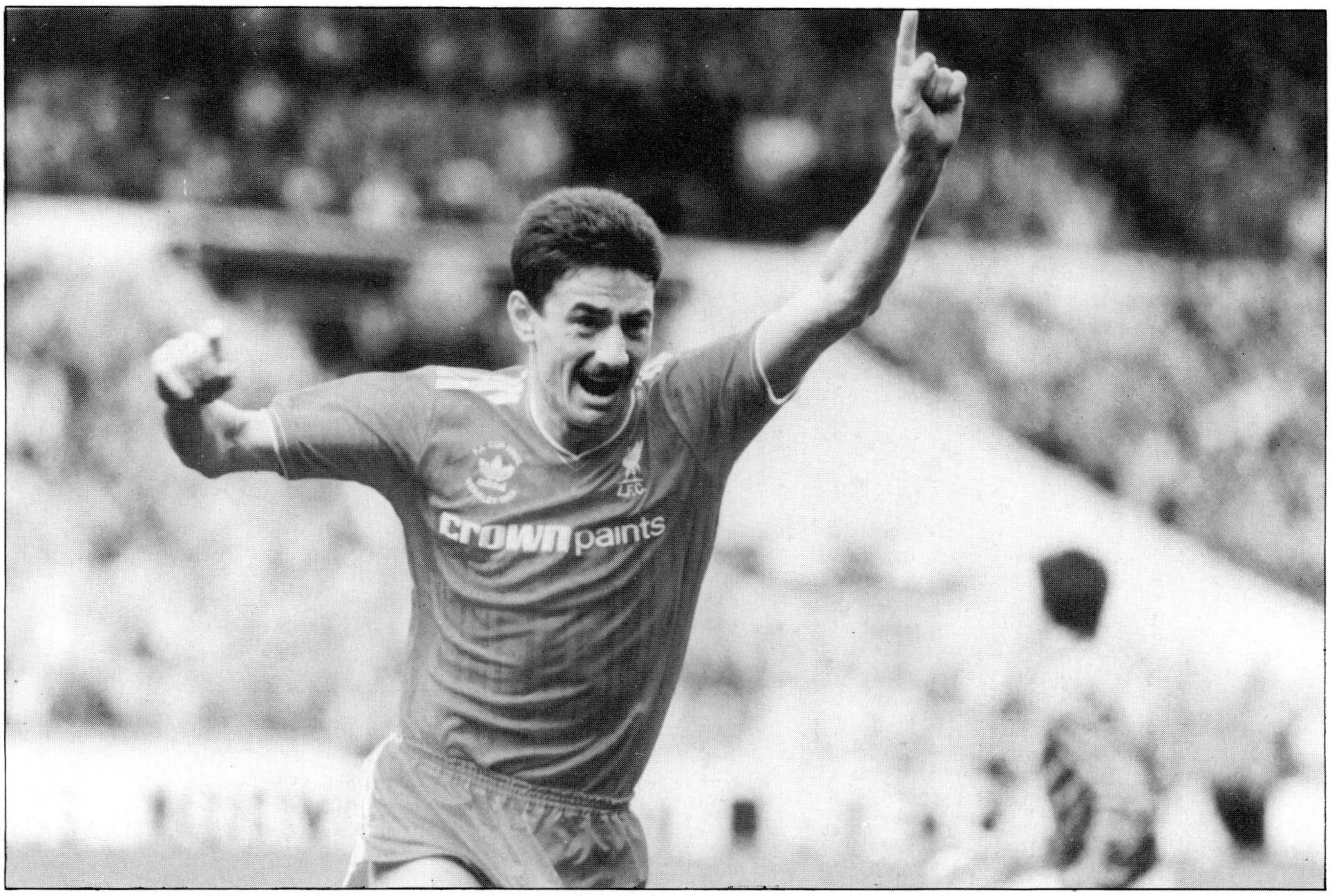

Everton took a first-half lead in the 1986 FA Cup Final but the Reds fought back with two goals from Ian Rush and one from Craig Johnston. Rush turns away in delight after scoring one of his goals.

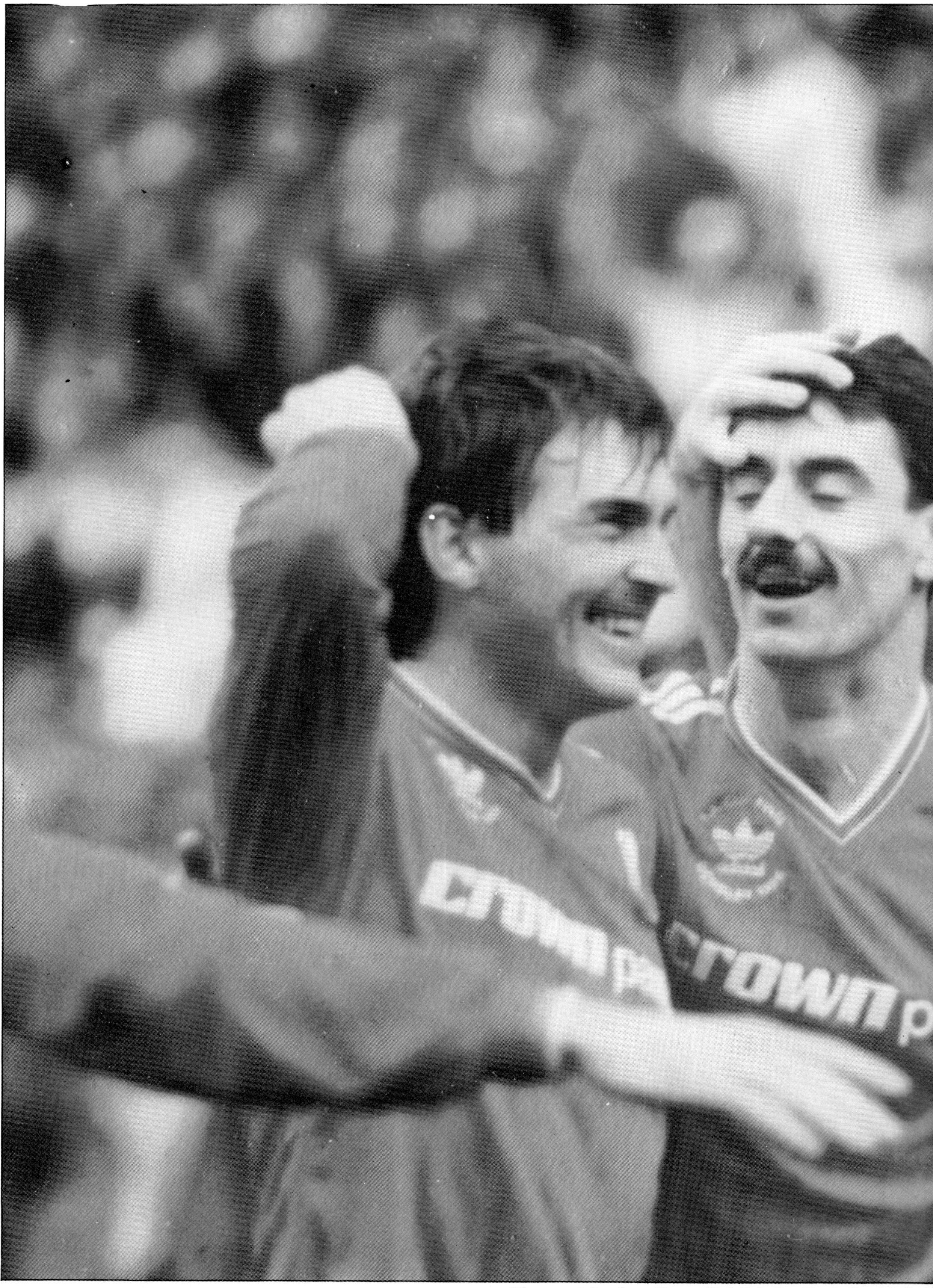

Victory celebrations. Kenny Dalglish, Ian Rush, Jan Molby

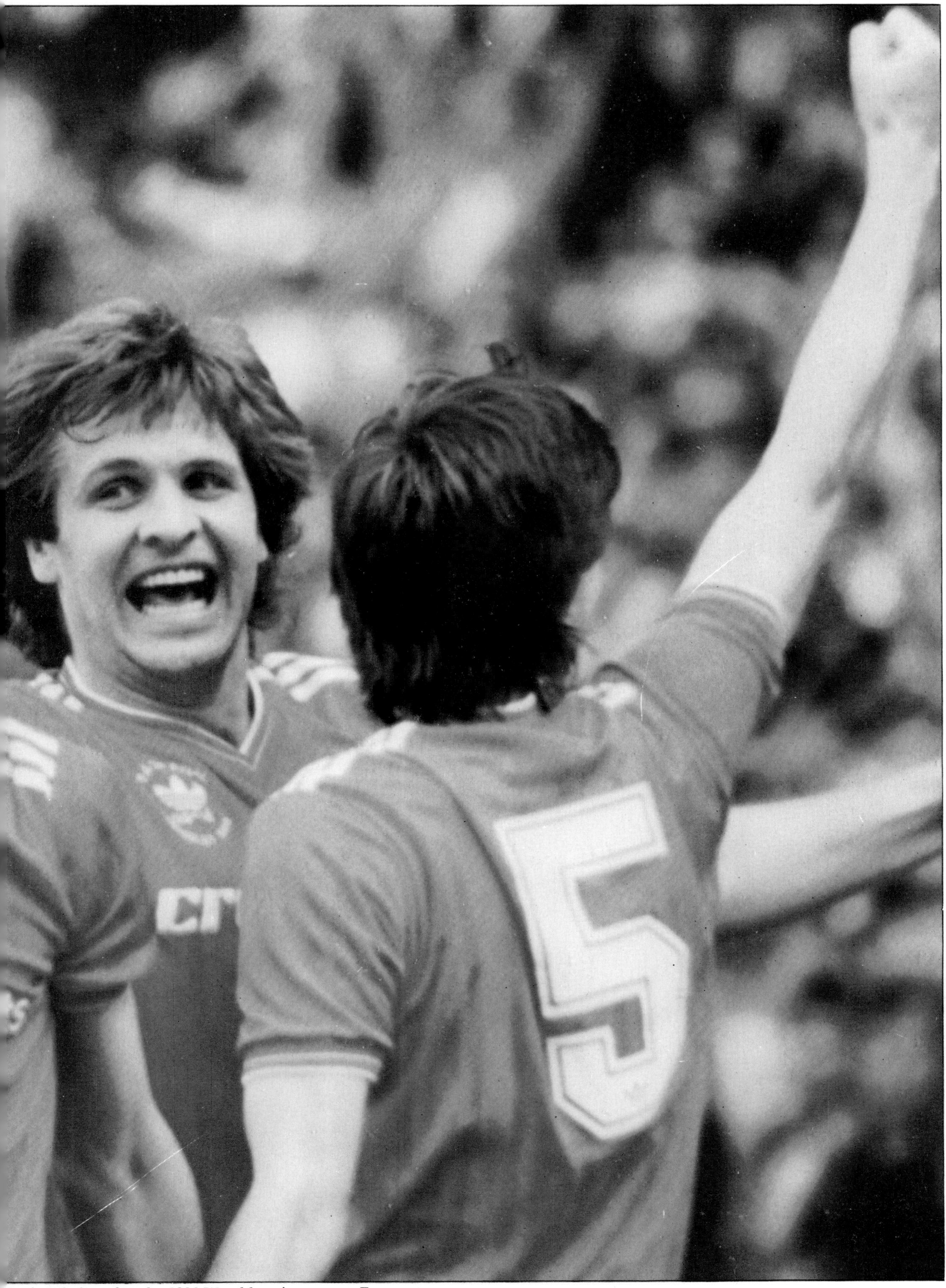

›nnie Whelan after the 1986 Wembley victory over Everton.

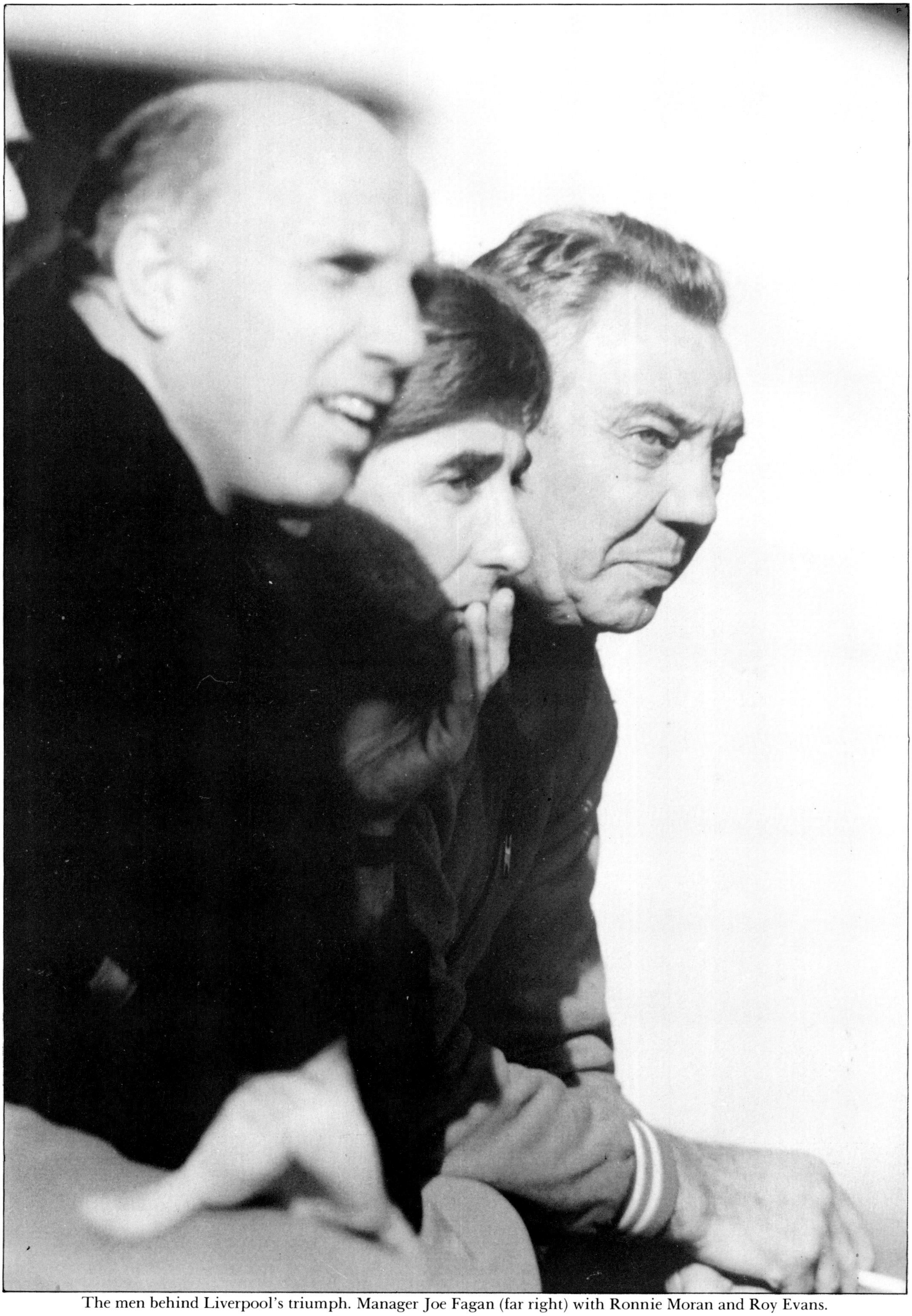

The men behind Liverpool's triumph. Manager Joe Fagan (far right) with Ronnie Moran and Roy Evans.

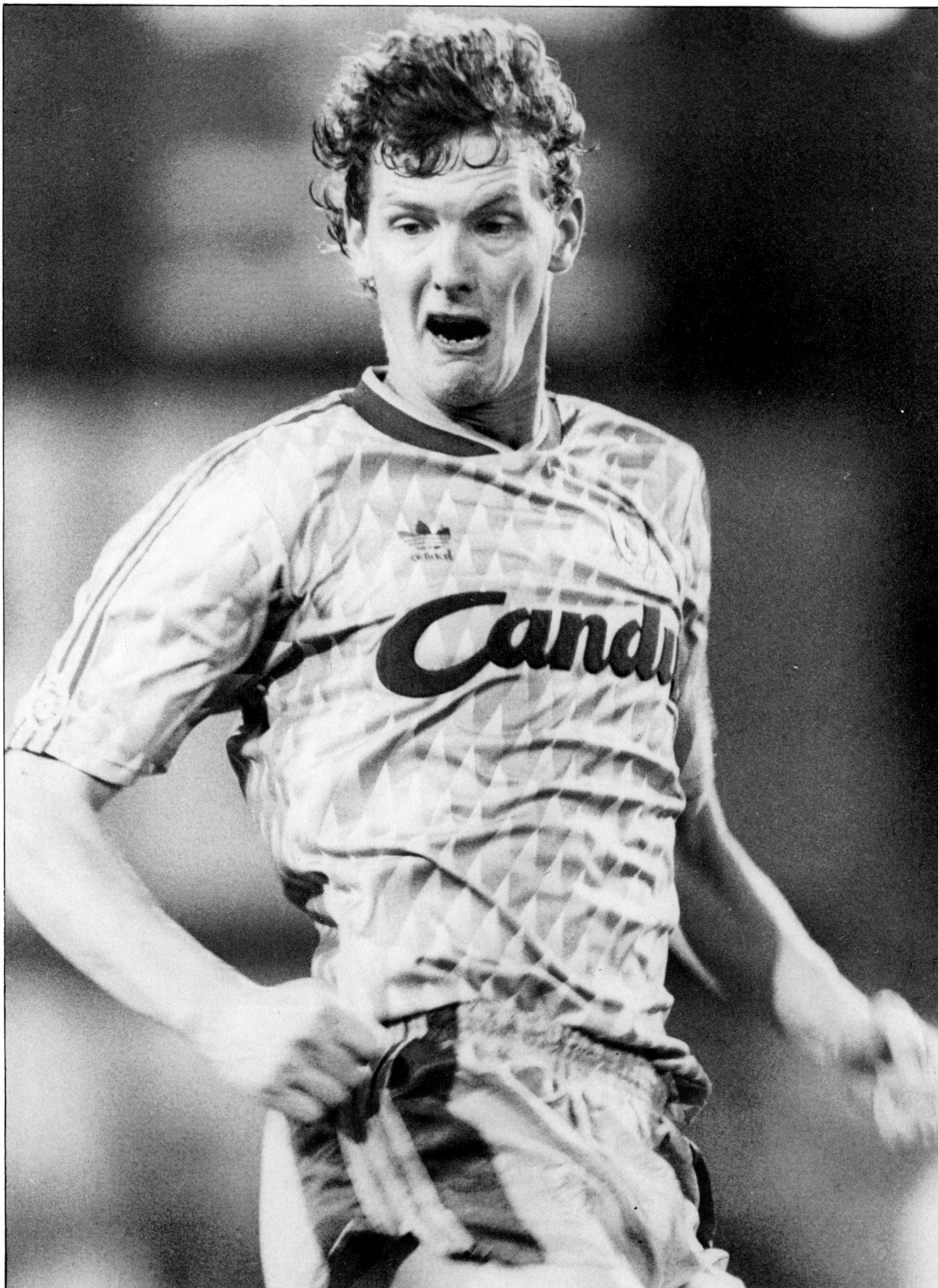

Scottish international defender Gary Gillespie joined the Reds from Falkirk in July 1983, for £325,000, and made around 200 senior appearances for Liverpool before moving to Celtic in August 1991 for £925,000. He gained three League Championship medals with the Merseysiders.

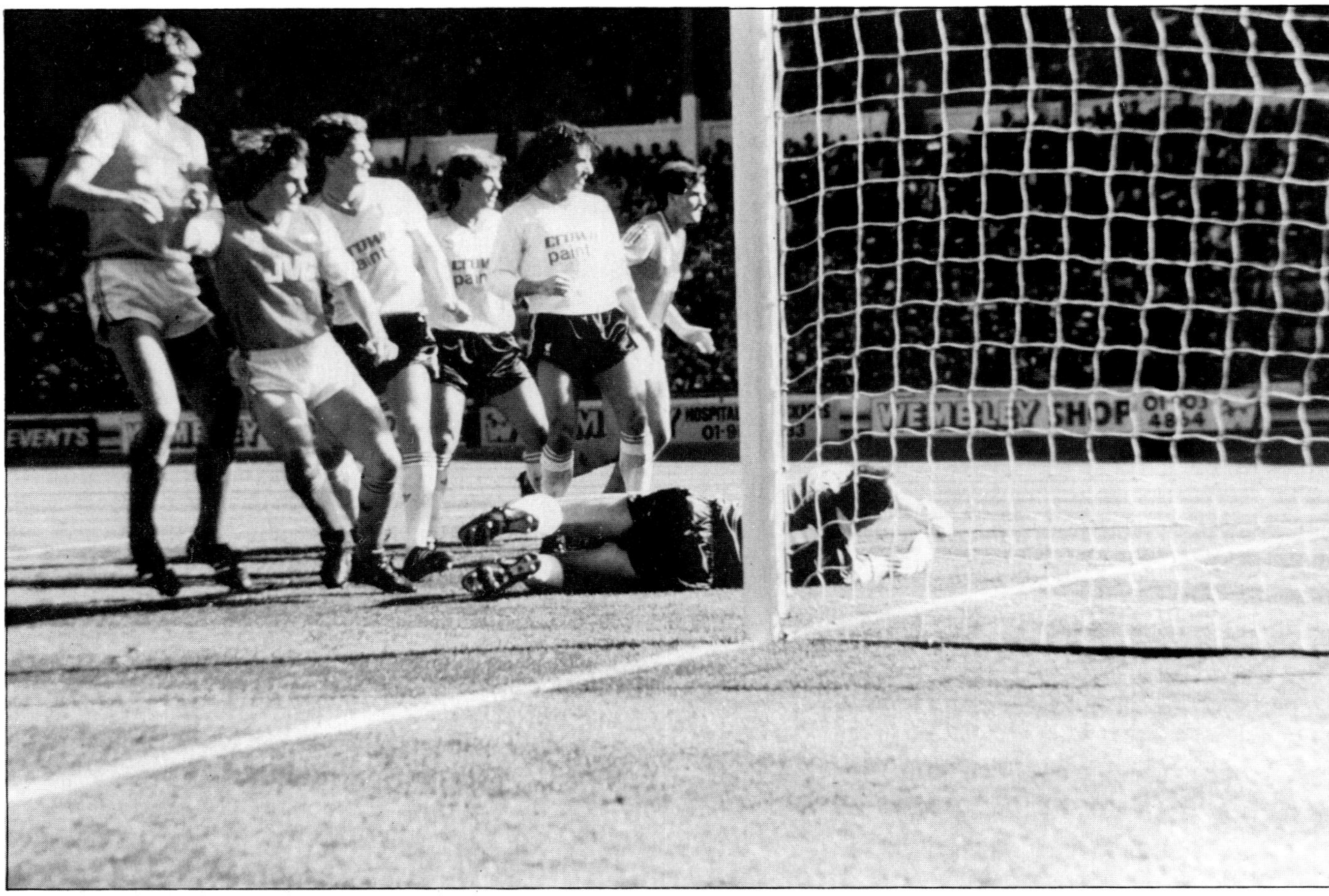

Charlie Nicholas (second left) scores the first of his two goals against Liverpool in the 1987 Littlewoods Cup Final at Wembley.

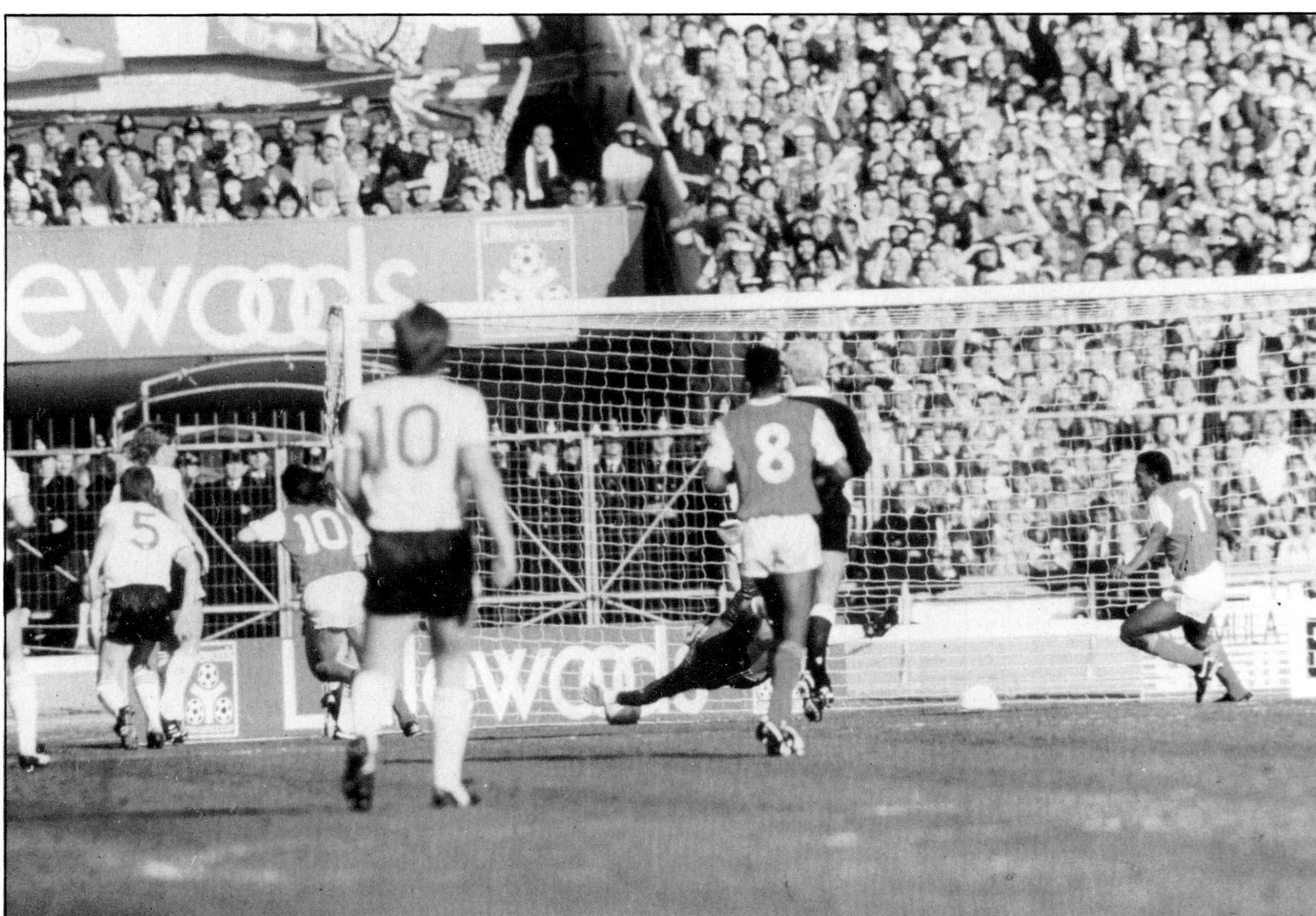

Nicholas (10) scores his second goal against the Reds, giving the Gunners a 2-1 win over Liverpool in the Littlewoods Final.

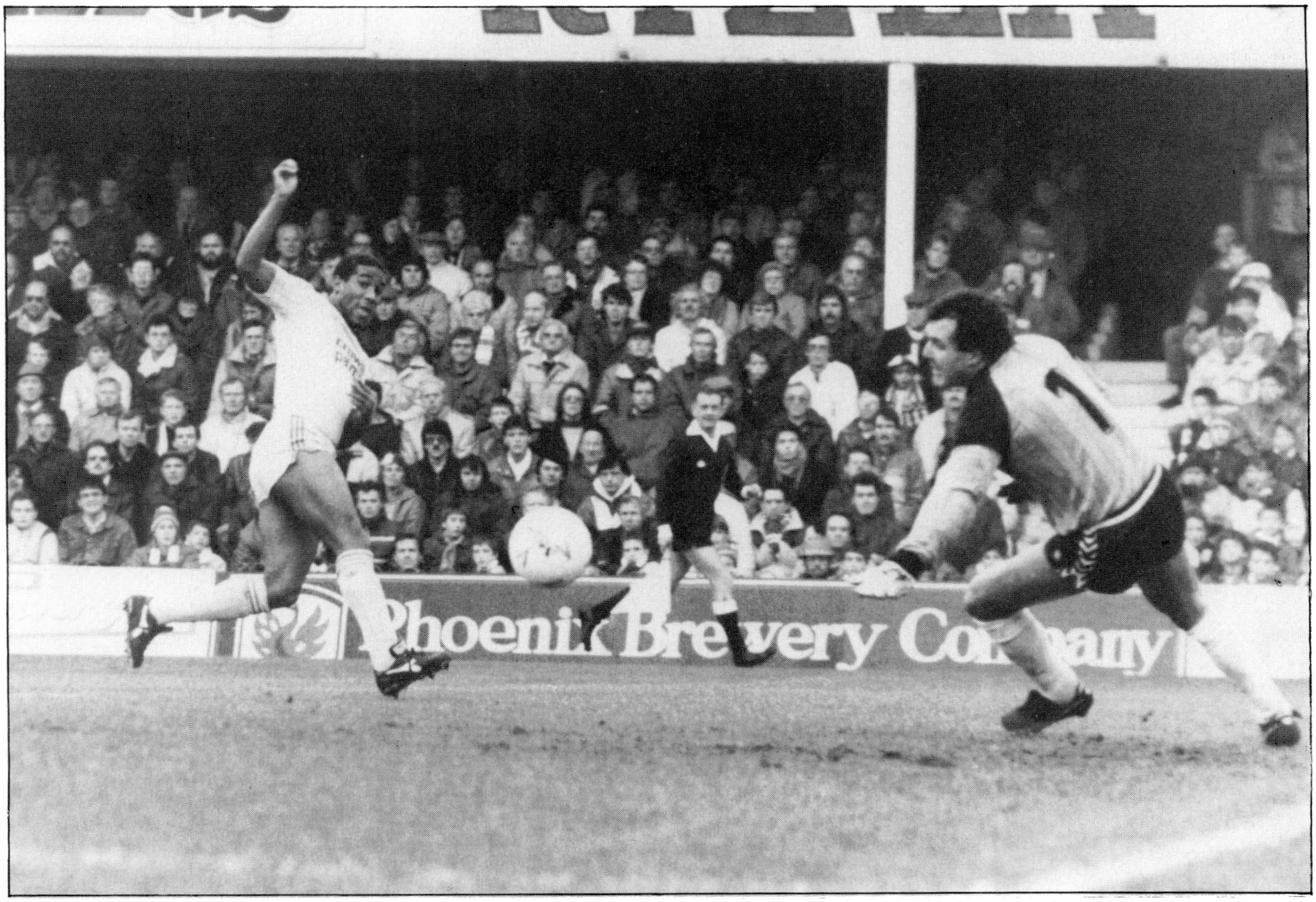

John Barnes scores the first of his two goals for Liverpool in their 2-2 draw at The Dell in December 1987. The Reds were 2-0 ahead after 40 minutes but allowed ther Saints to snatch a point.

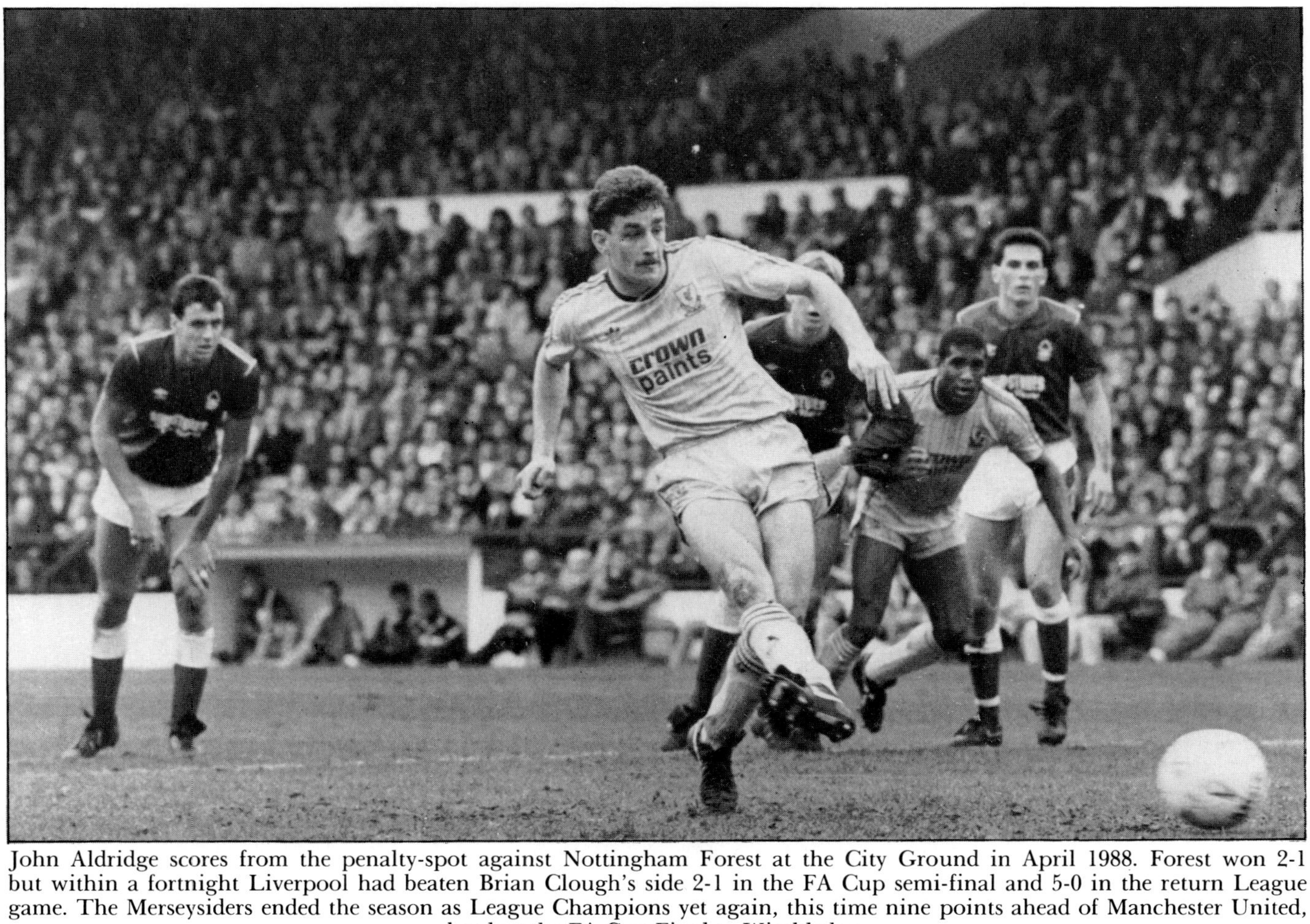

John Aldridge scores from the penalty-spot against Nottingham Forest at the City Ground in April 1988. Forest won 2-1 but within a fortnight Liverpool had beaten Brian Clough's side 2-1 in the FA Cup semi-final and 5-0 in the return League game. The Merseysiders ended the season as League Champions yet again, this time nine points ahead of Manchester United, but lost the FA Cup Final to Wimbledon.

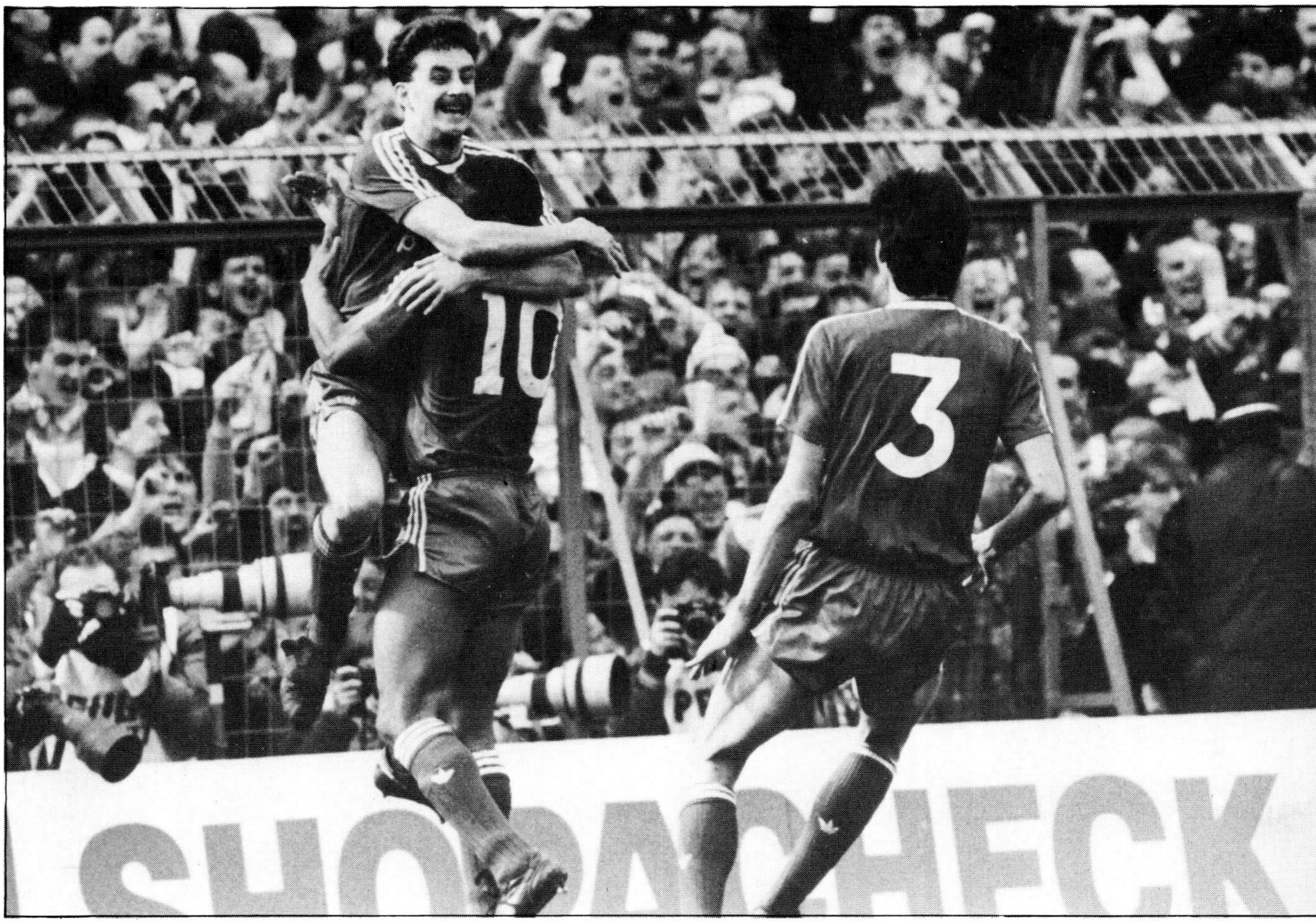

John Aldridge celebrates his first goal after three minutes of the 1988 FA Cup semi-final against Nottingham Forest at Hillsborough. The Reds won 2-1, Aldridge scoring again in the 51st minute.

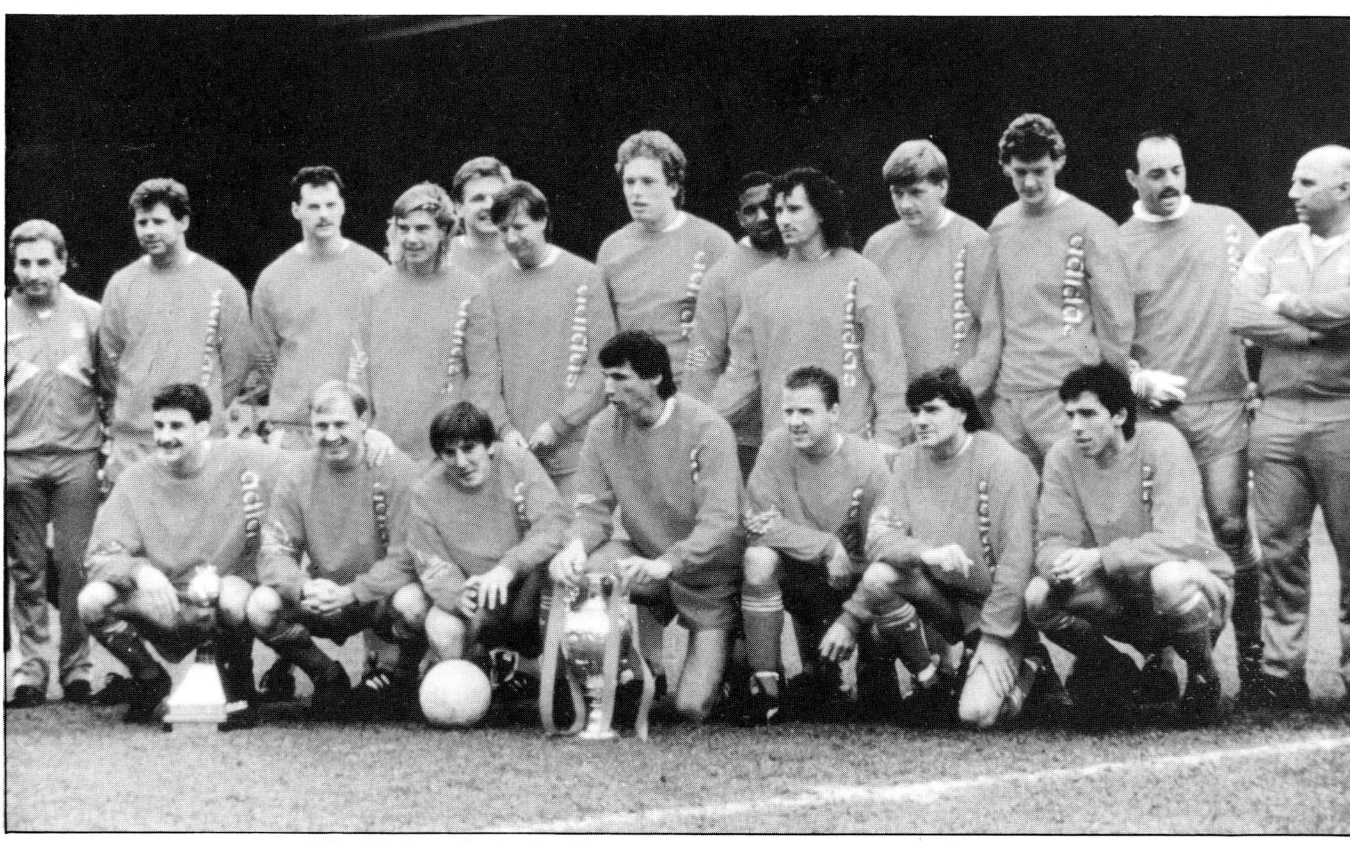

The Liverpool squad with the League Championship trophy in 1988.

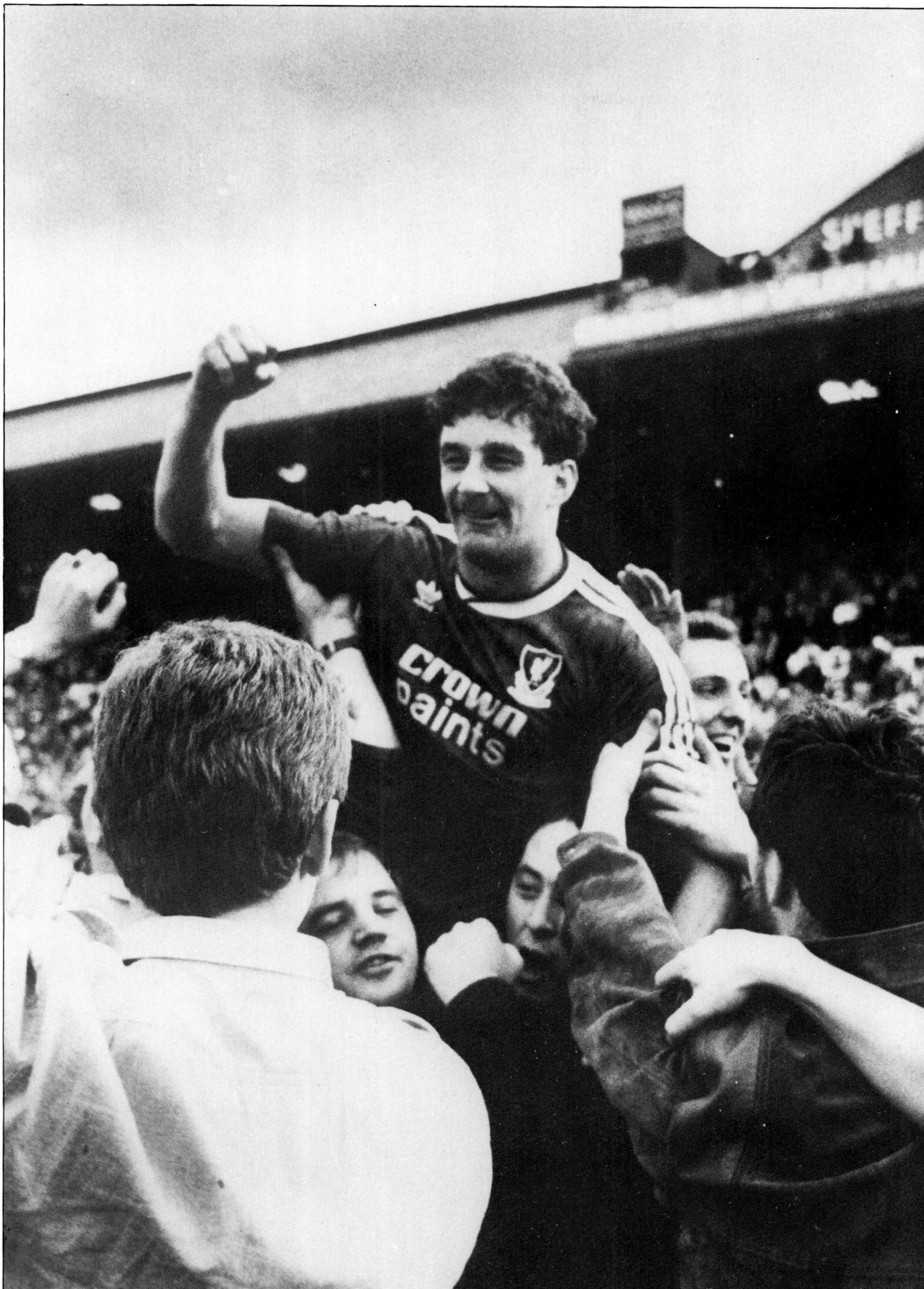

Another FA Cup Final in prospect. Liverpool's John Aldridge, two-goal hero of the 1988 semi-final, is carried off shoulder-high by Liverpool's adoring fans.

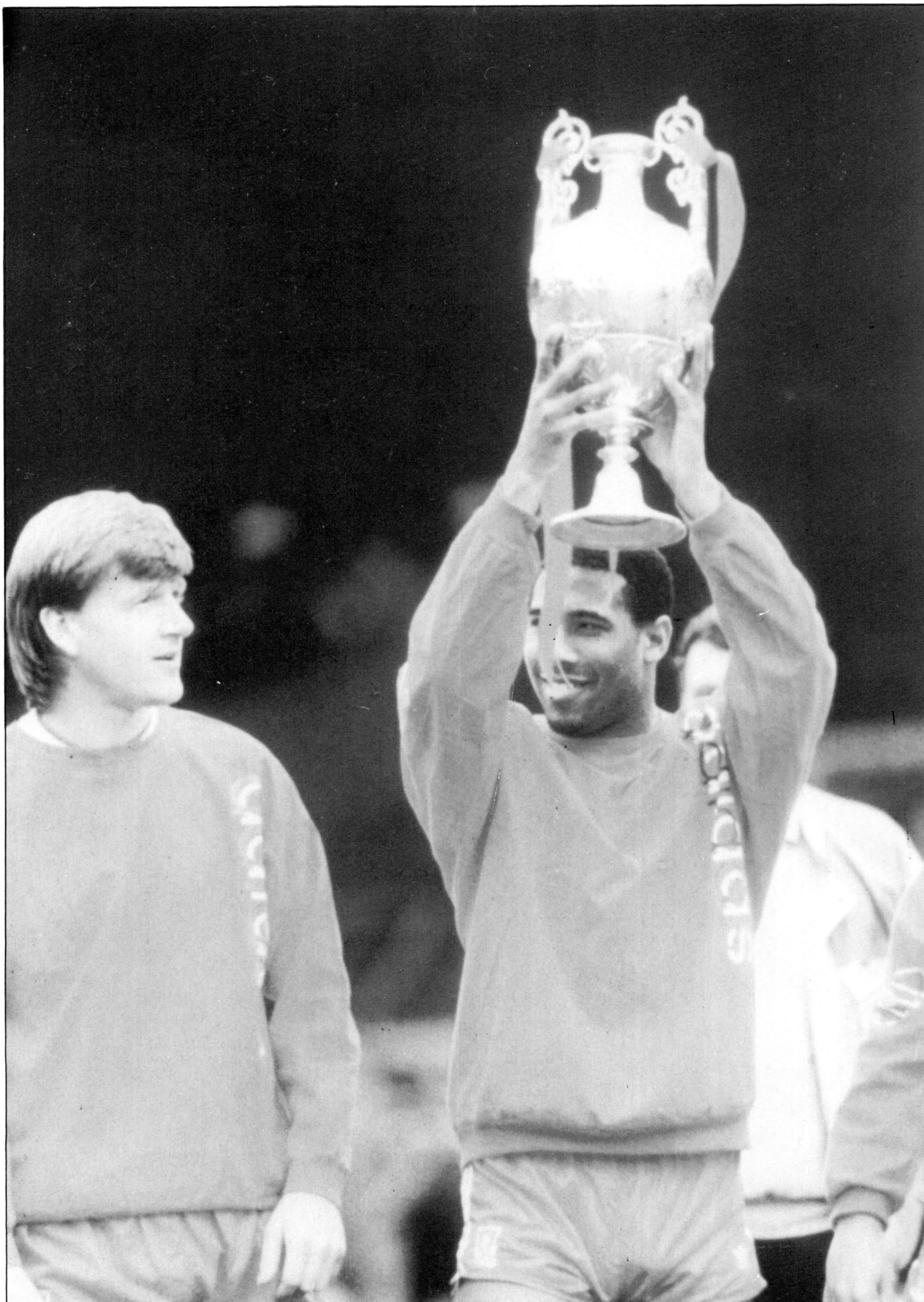

John Barnes with the Championship trophy in 1988.

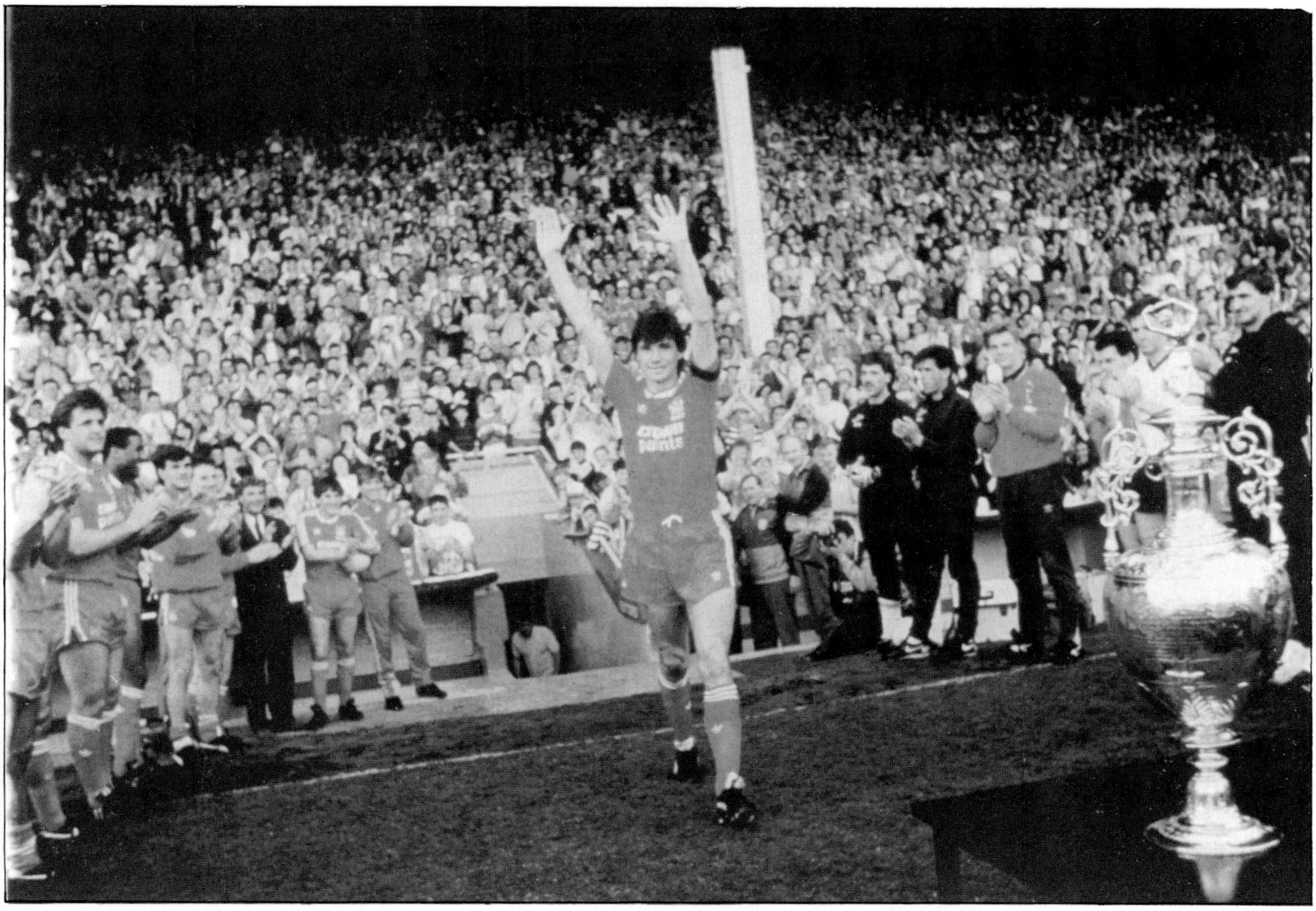

Alan Hansen steps up to receive the League Championship trophy at the end of the 1987-8 season, when the Reds finished nine points ahead of Manchester United.

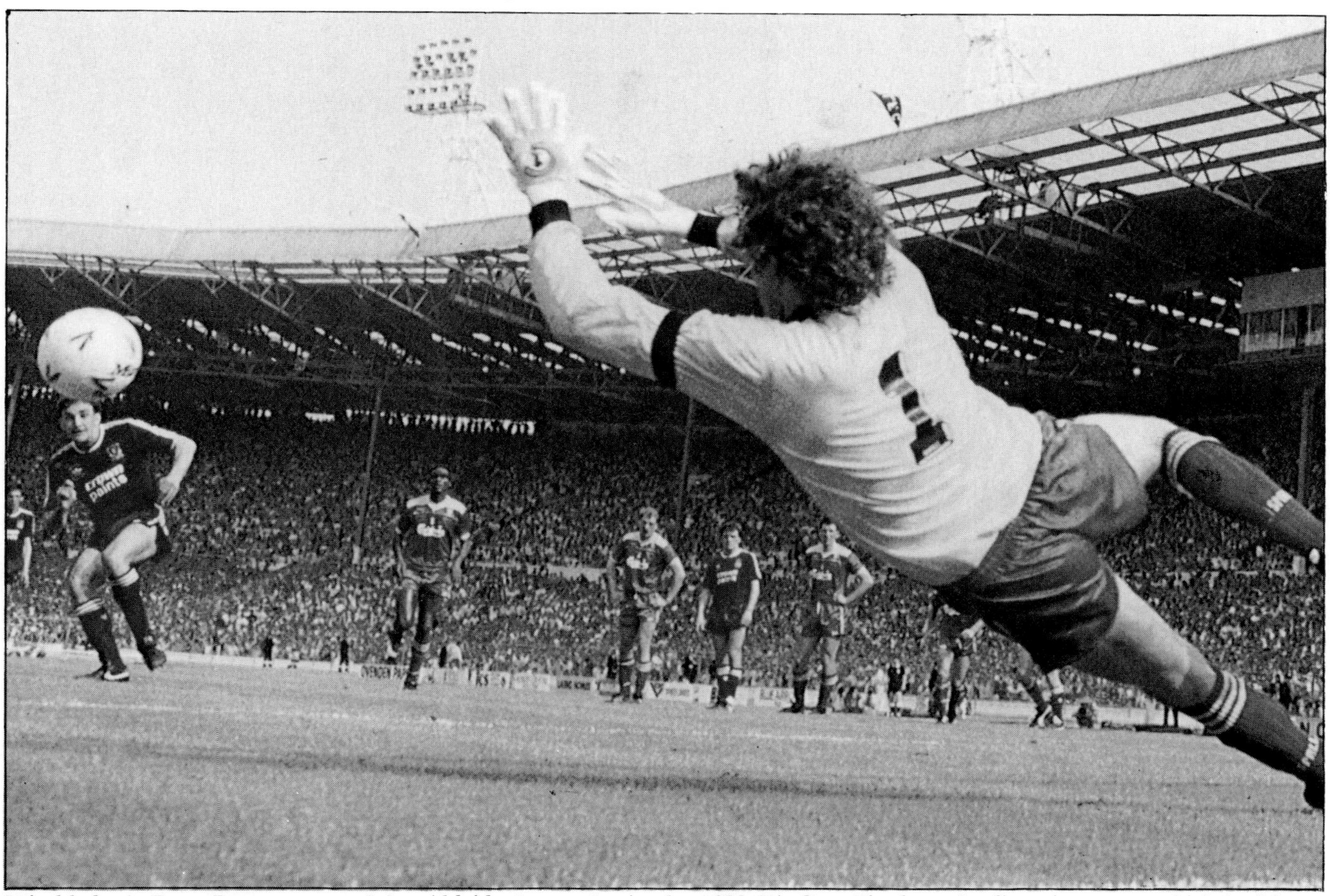

Wimbledon's Dave Beasant saves John Aldridge's penalty in the 1988 FA Cup Final — the first time a spot-kick had been missed in a Final — and the Reds went on to lose 1-0.

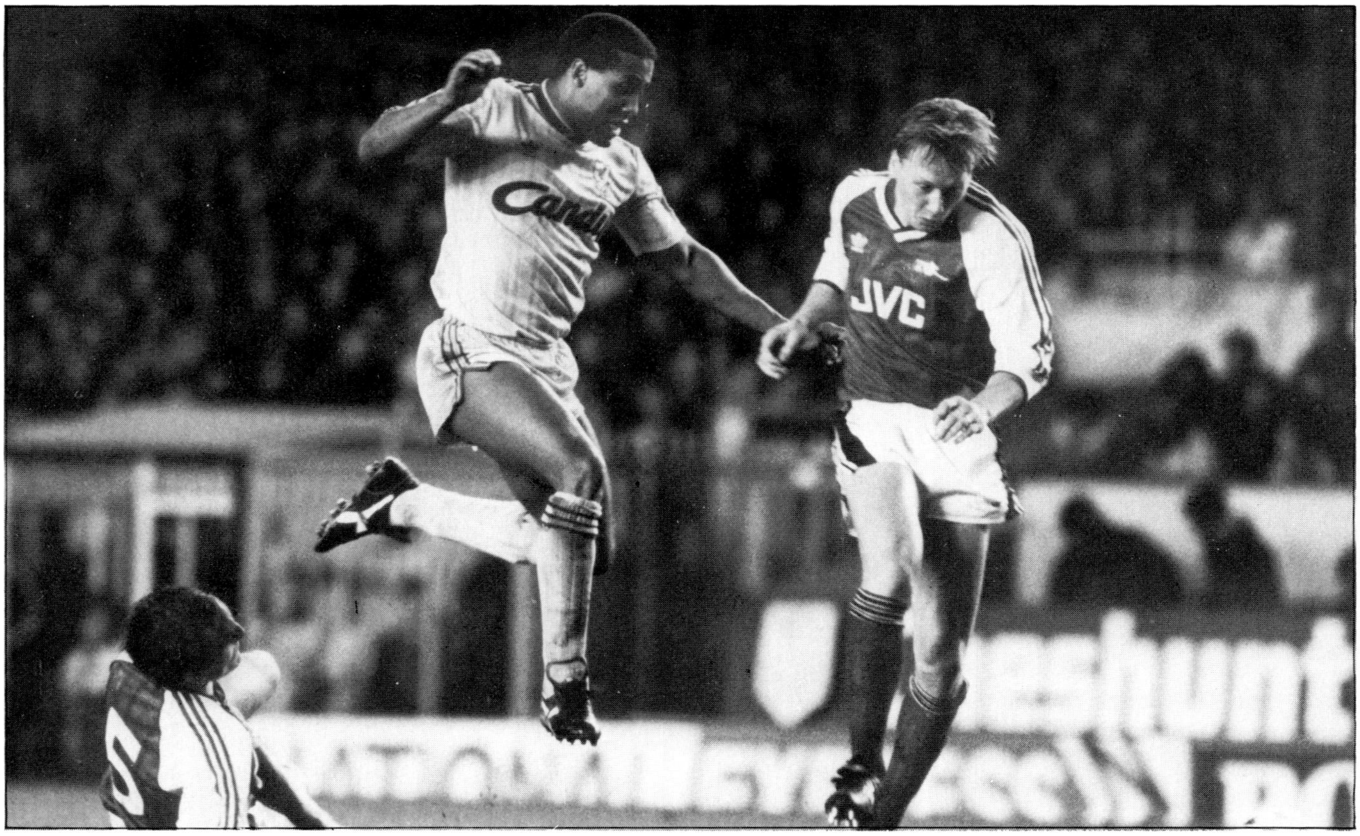

Liverpool reached the fourth round of the Littlewoods Cup in 1988-9 before losing to West Ham United. In the third round they overcame Arsenal 2-1 at Villa Park after two draws. John Barnes gets between Steve Bould and Lee Dixon in the goalless draw at Highbury.

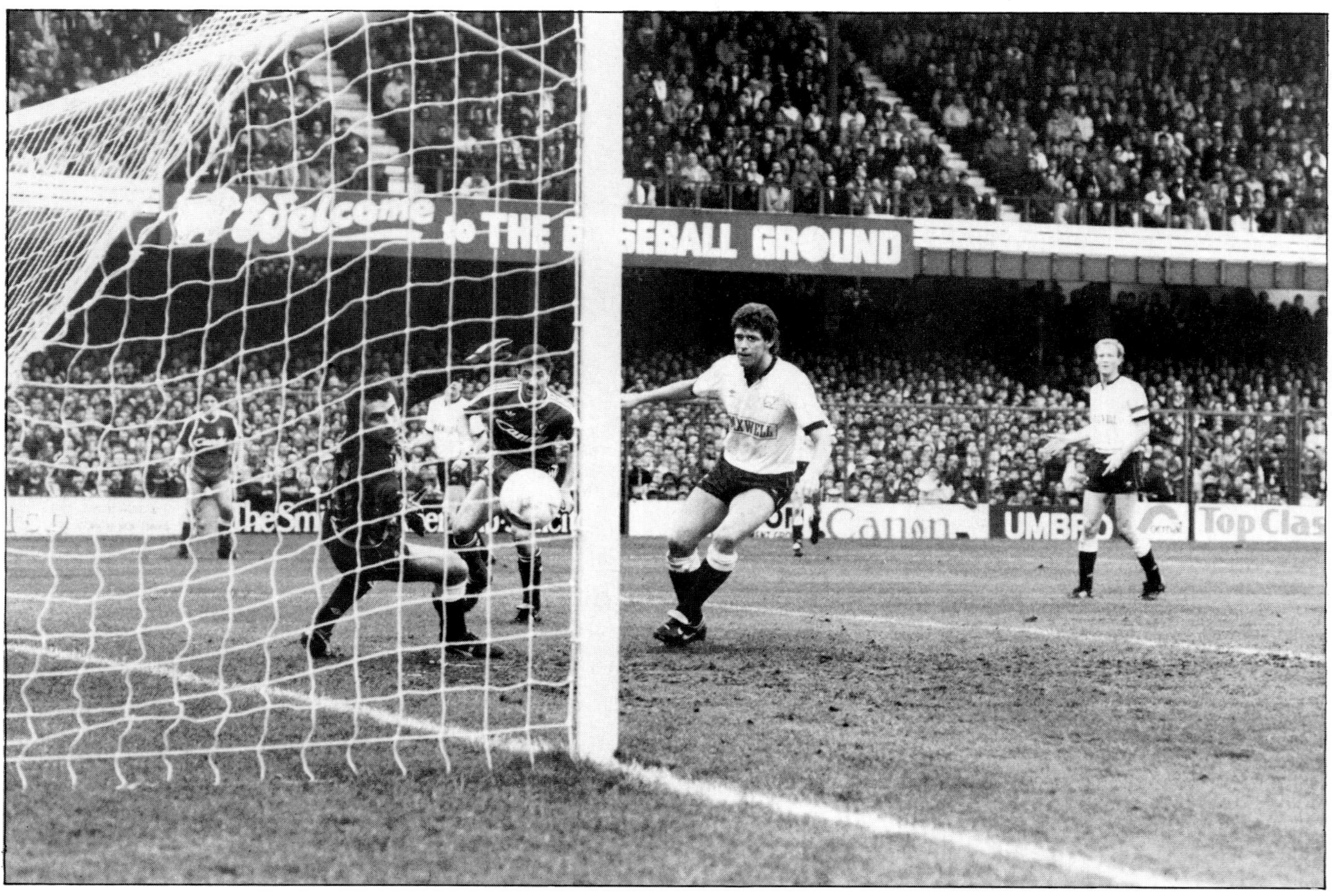

Ian Rush scores the only goal of the game against Derby County past Peter Shilton at the Baseball Ground on Boxing Day 1988. The Reds went on to finish runners-up.

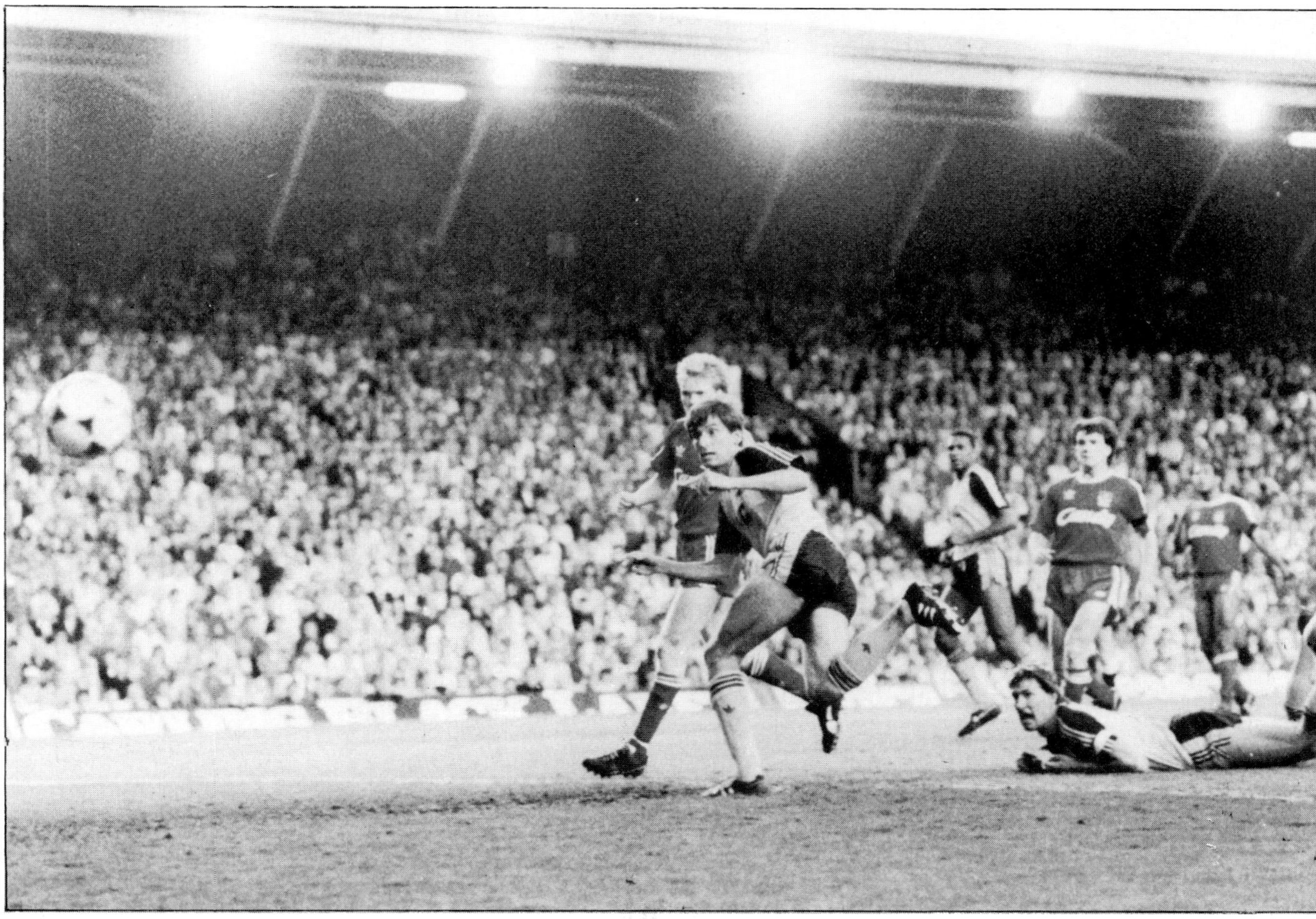

There can surely have never been a more dramatic finale to the Football League Championship than that of 1988-9 when Arsenal visited Highbury in the last game of the season needing to win by two clear goals to take the title. If they failed, then Liverpool would be Champions. After 52 minutes, Alan Smith put the Gunners ahead (above) but with only seconds remaining it still looked like Liverpool's title.

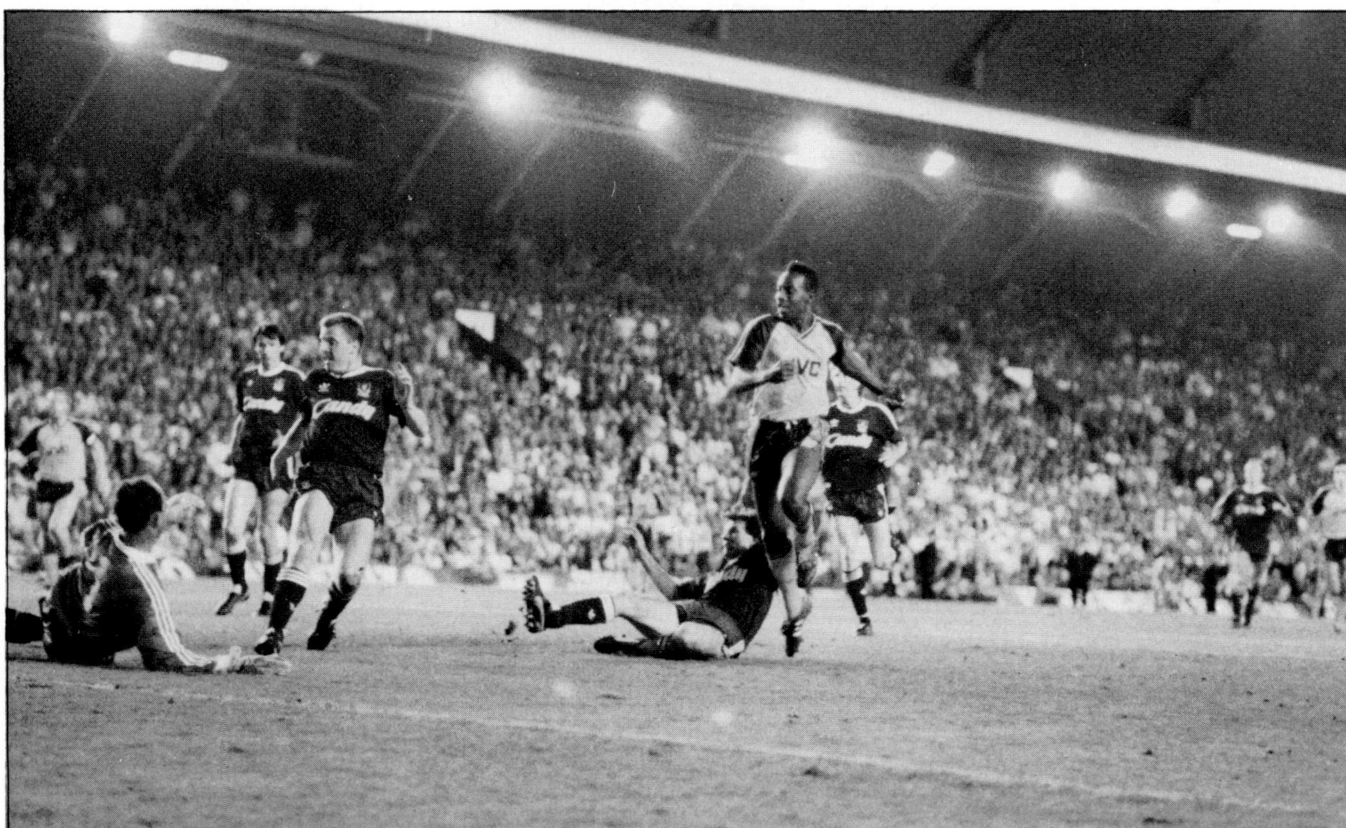

In the dying seconds, Michael Thomas stabbed the ball into the Liverpool net and Arsenal were Champions. In December 1991, Thomas joined the Anfield club.

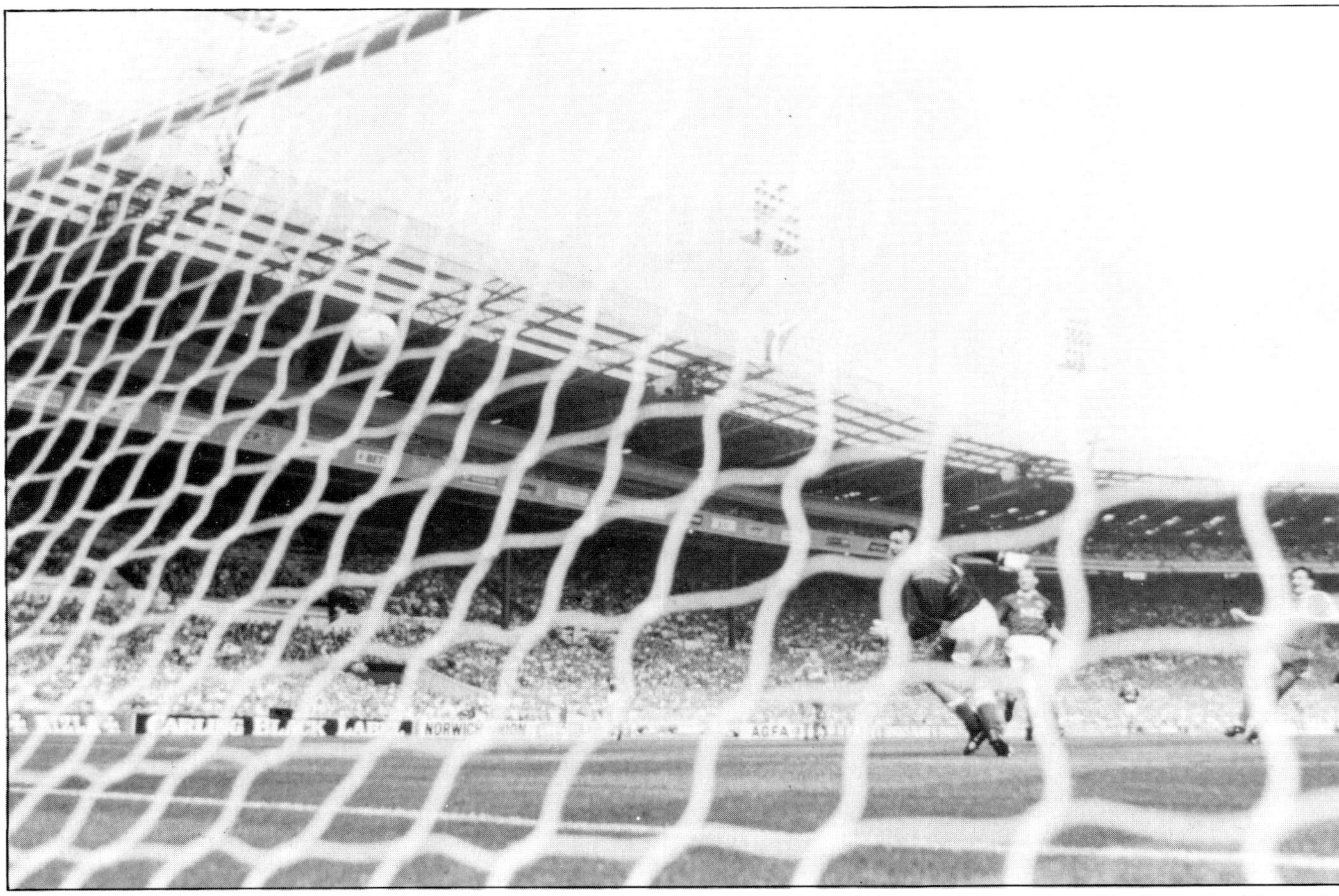

In 1989, Liverpool and Everton met yet again at Wembley, this occasion being another FA Cup Final as the Merseyside giants continued to dominate English football. John Aldridge puts Liverpool ahead in the fourth minute.

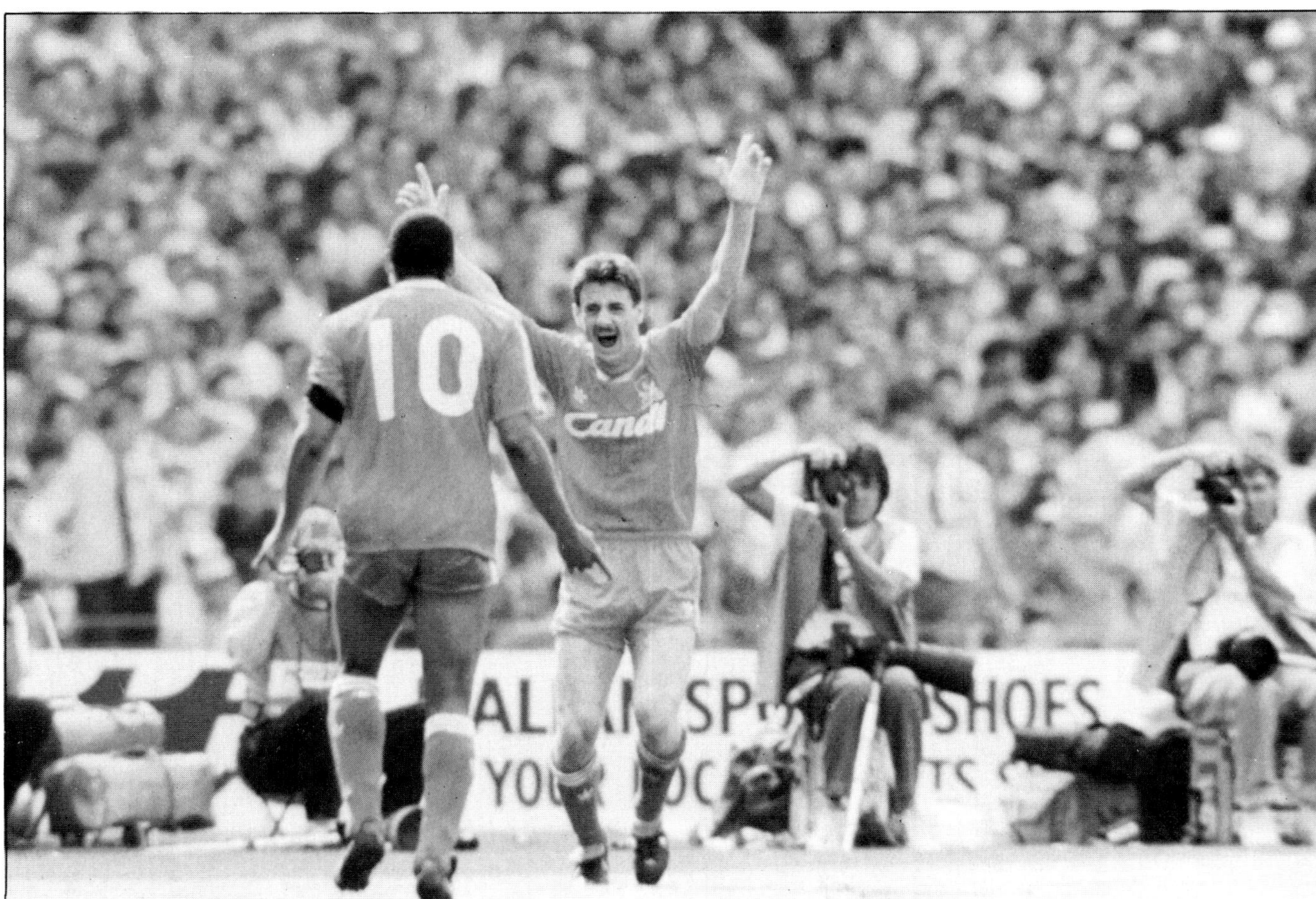

Ian Rush netted two extra-time goals and Liverpool were FA Cup holders for the fourth time in their history. John Barnes is about to congratulate Rush on his winner.

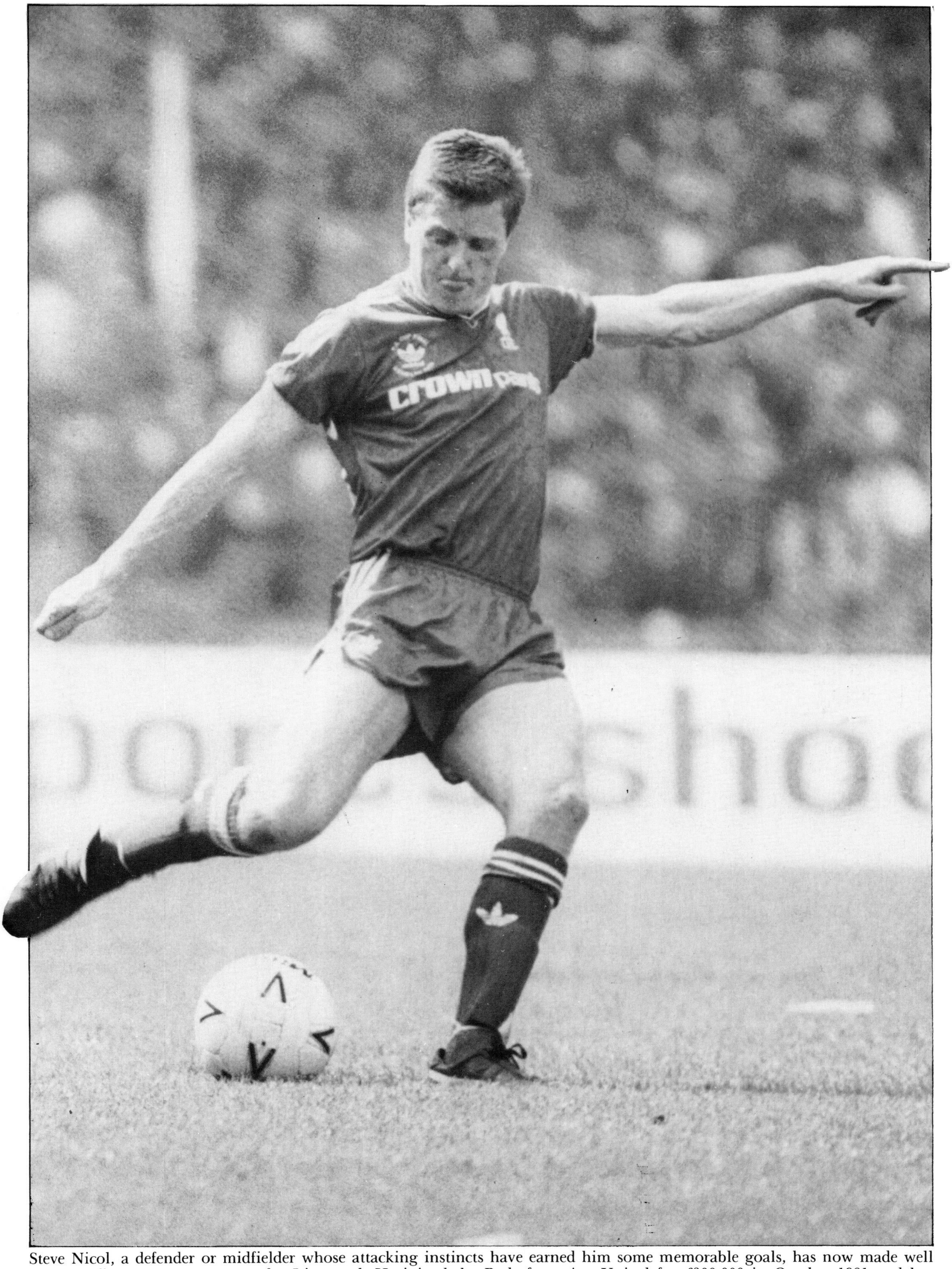

Steve Nicol, a defender or midfielder whose attacking instincts have earned him some memorable goals, has now made well over 300 first-team appearances for Liverpool. He joined the Reds from Ayr United for £300,000 in October 1981 and has won full Scotland honours as well as winners' medals in the European Cup, League Championship and FA Cup. His 14 appearances for Scotland Under-21s is still a record.

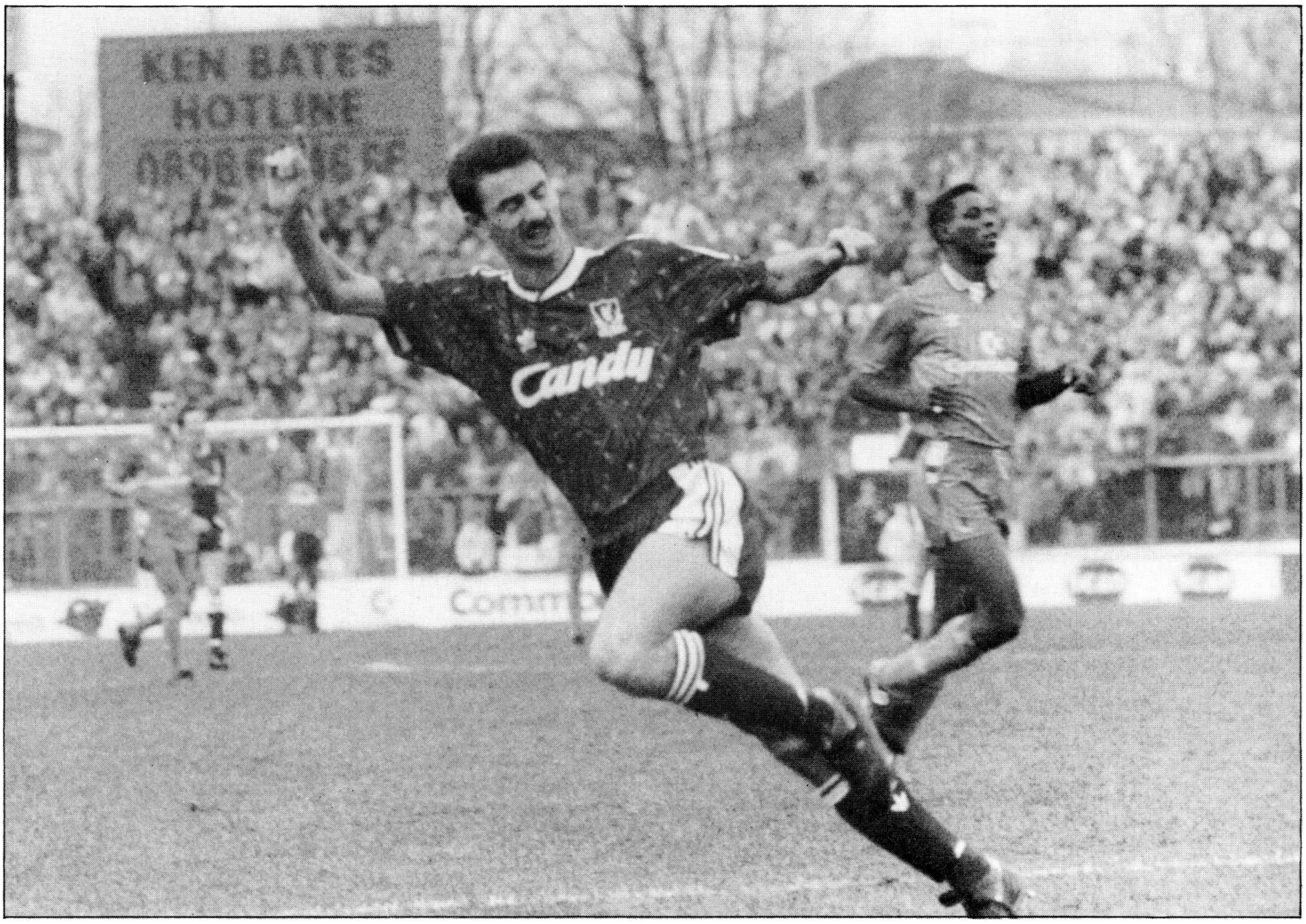

Ian Rush wheels away after scoring the first of his two goals in the 5-2 defeat of Chelsea at Stamford Bridge in December 1989. By the end of the season Liverpool were nine points ahead of their nearest rivals, Aston Villa, and so took the title for the 18th time.

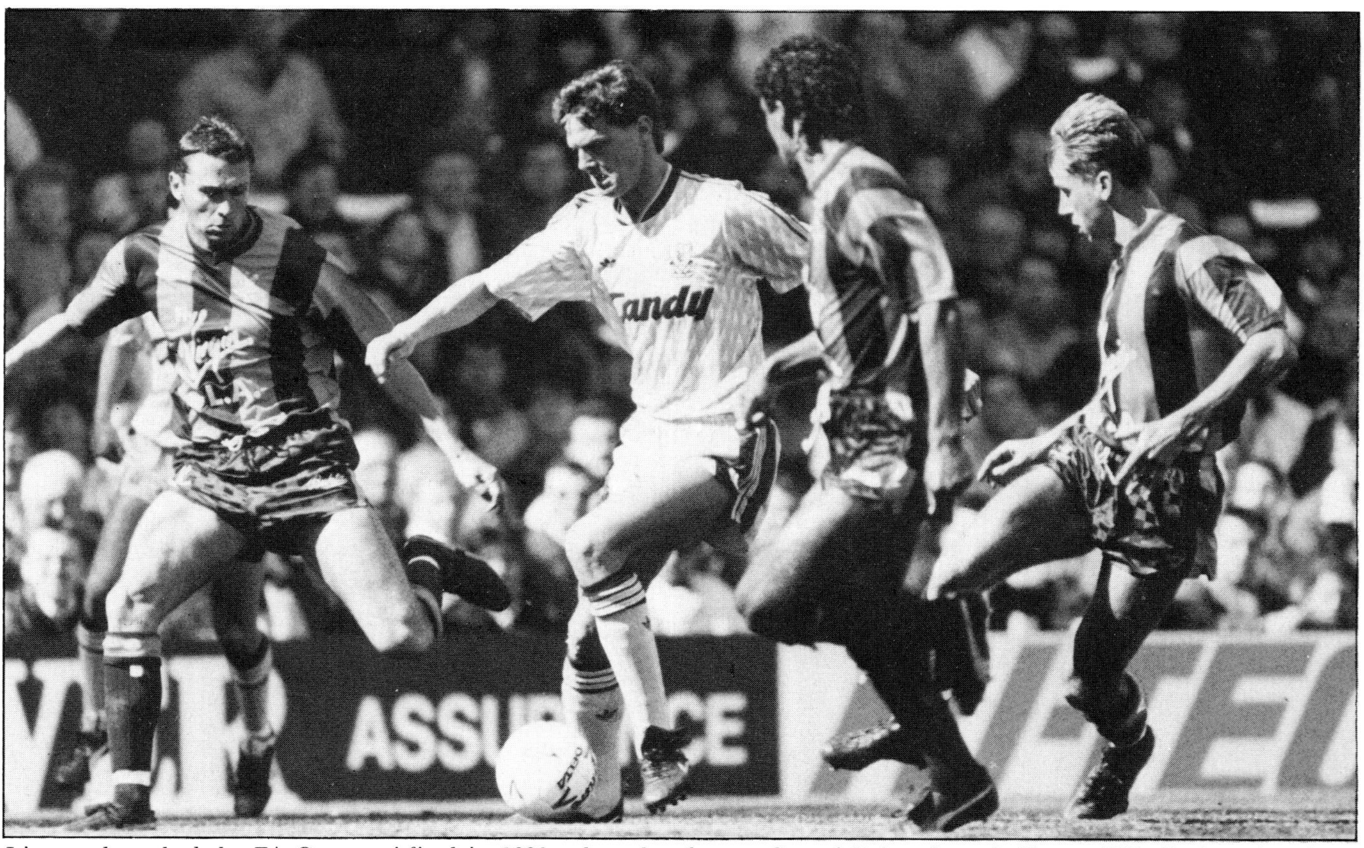

Liverpool reached the FA Cup semi-final in 1990, when they lost to Crystal Palace in a thriller at Villa Park, going down 4-3 after extra-time. Liverpool's Gary Gillespie is surrounded here by Palace defenders.

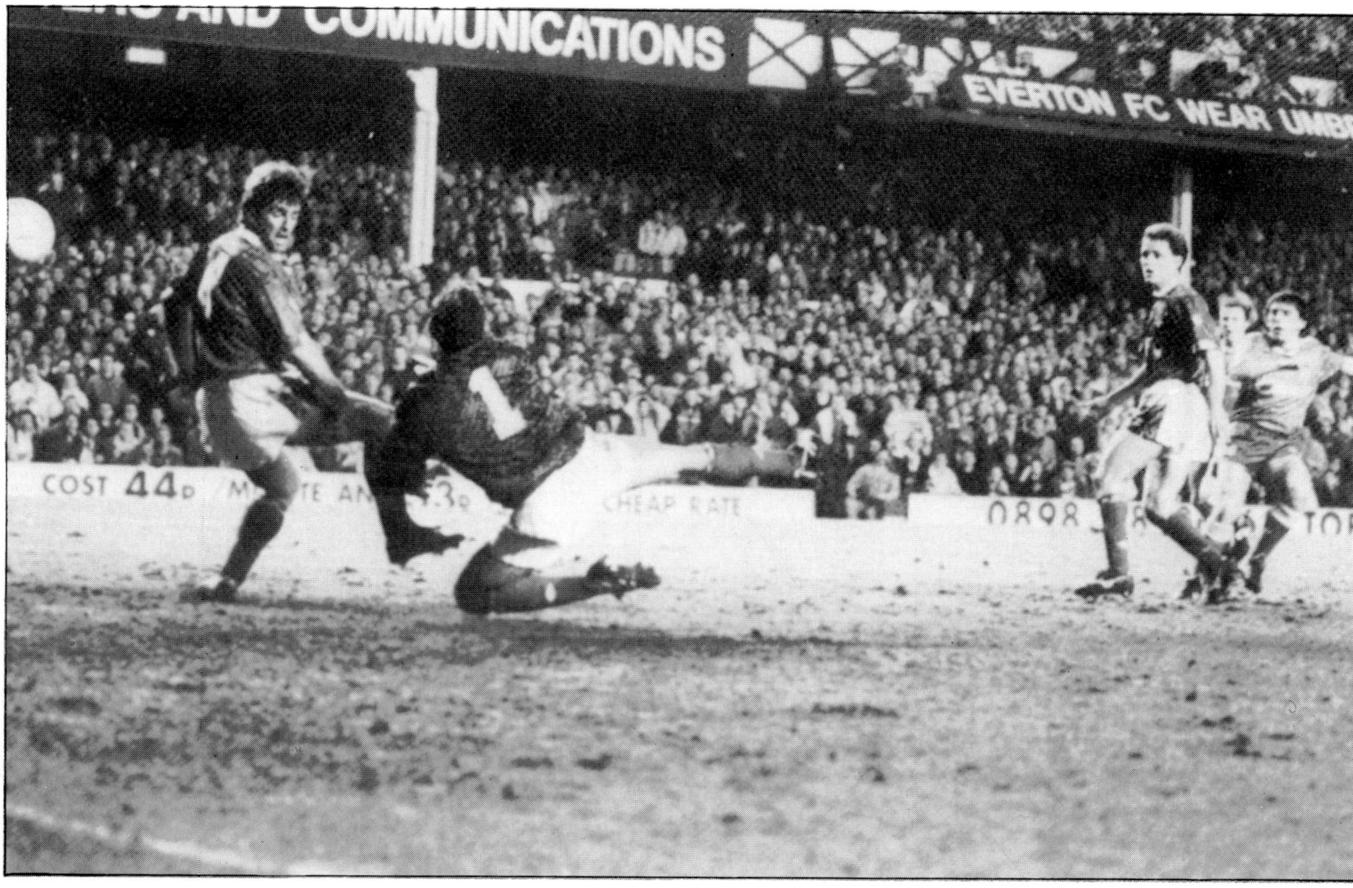

Peter Beardsley (far right) opens the scoring for Liverpool for the first of eight goals in a 4-4 thriller fifth-round FA Cup replay at Goodison Park in February 1991. The Blues eventually went through to the quarter-finals.

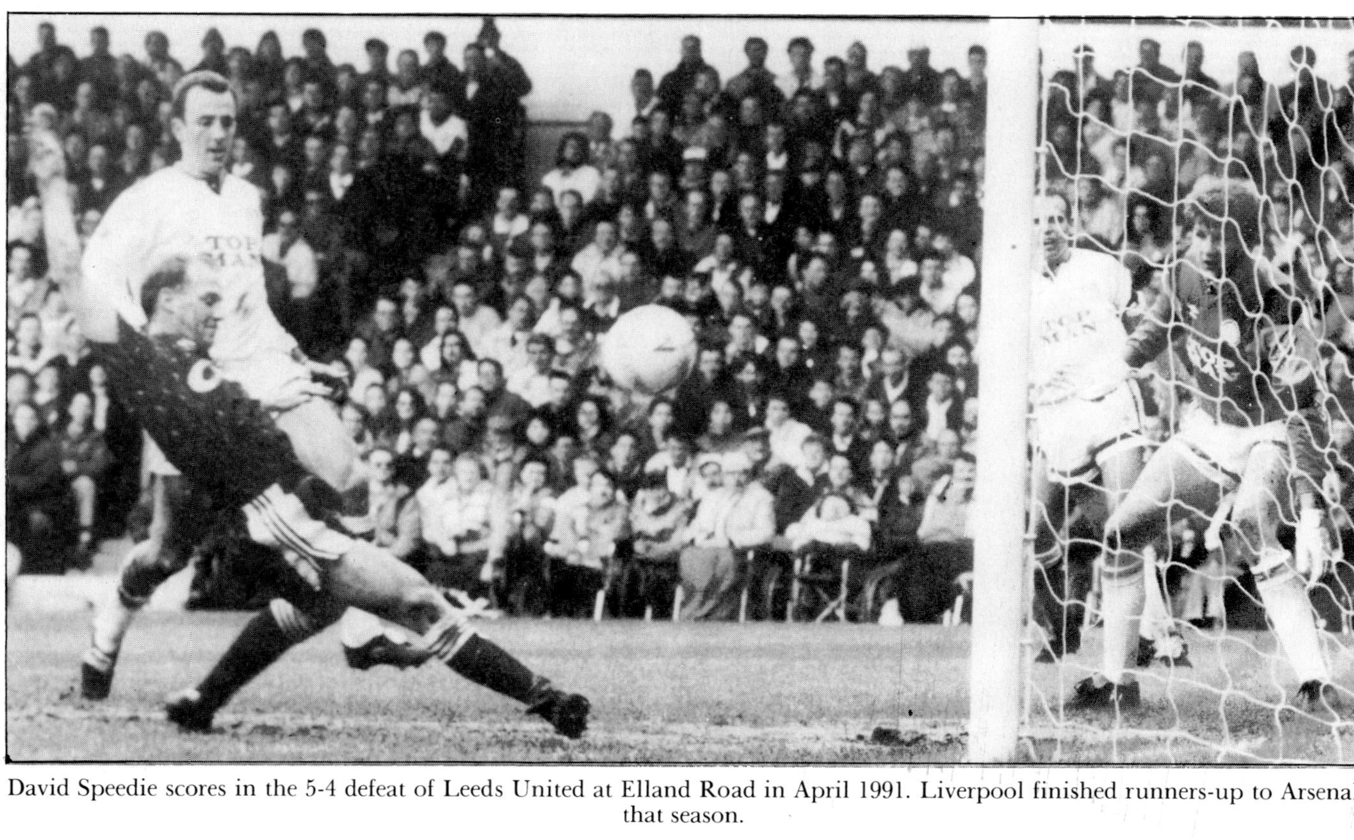

David Speedie scores in the 5-4 defeat of Leeds United at Elland Road in April 1991. Liverpool finished runners-up to Arsenal that season.

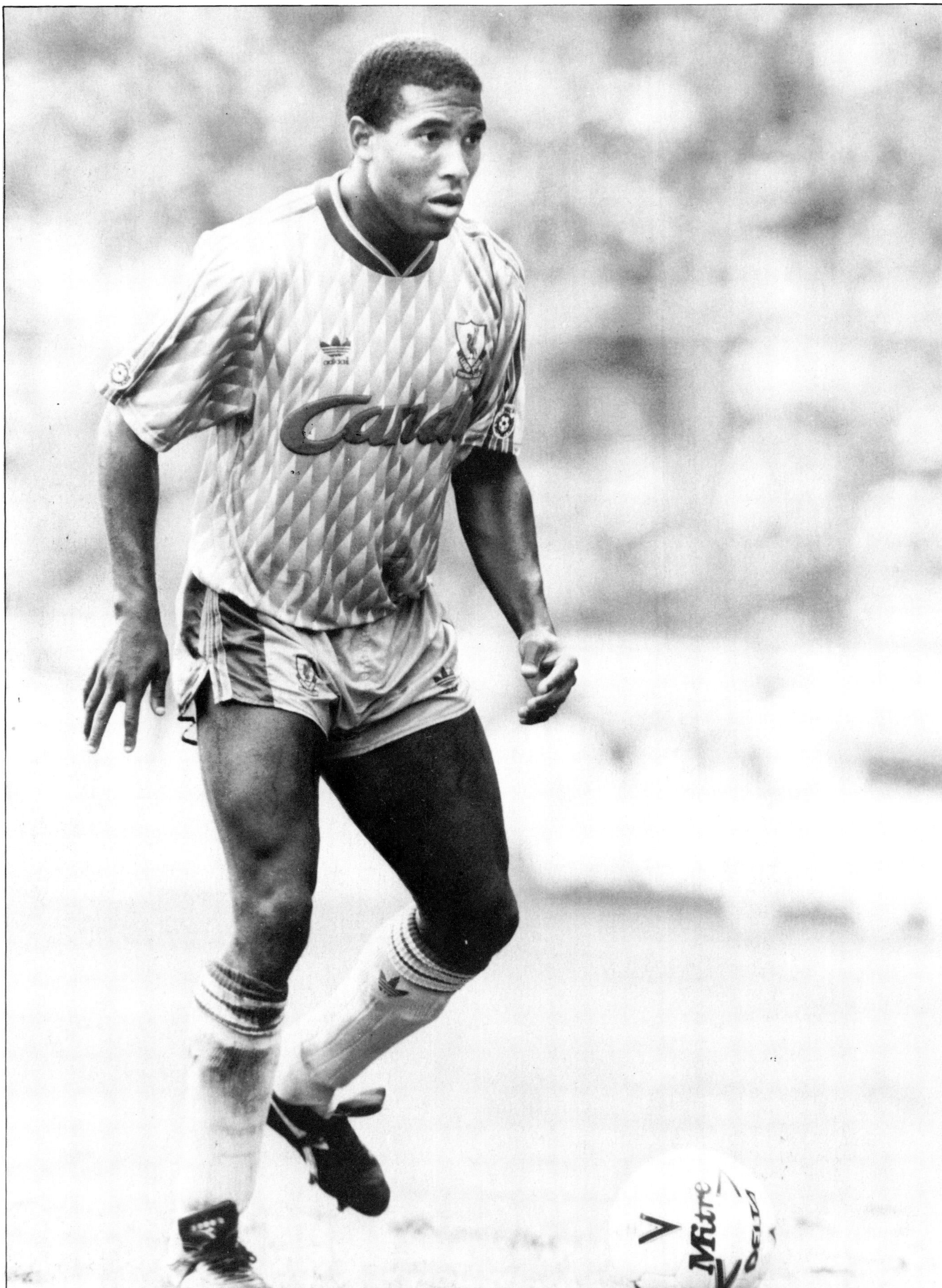

Winger John Barnes joined Liverpool from Watford in June 1987 for £900,000. Barnes, the 1988 Footballer of the Year, has won League Championship and FA Cup winners' medals with the Reds and won his 40th England cap in that year's European Championship. He was injured before the 1992 European Finals, in a friendly in Helsinki.

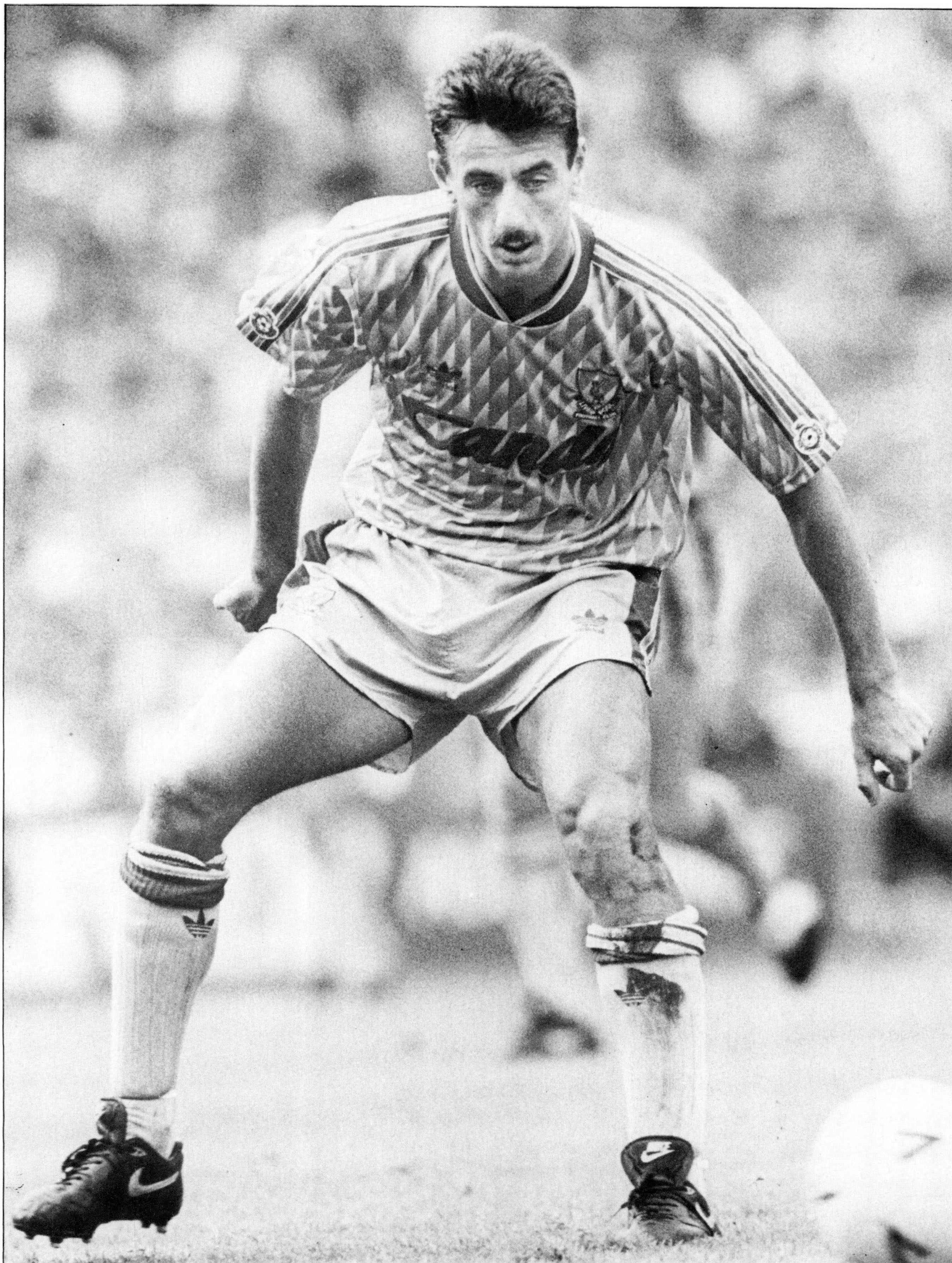

Ian Rush first joined Liverpool from Chester in April 1980 for £300,000, making him Britain's most expensive teenage footballer, a record once held by Alun Evans when he joined the Reds. Rush blossomed into a fine striker in a great team, scoring almost 200 goals for the club before a £3.2 million move to Juventus in June 1987. Just over a year later he returned to Anfield for £2.8 million. Welsh international Rush has gained a host of honours with Liverpool including winners' medals in the European Cup, League Championship, FA Cup and League Cup.

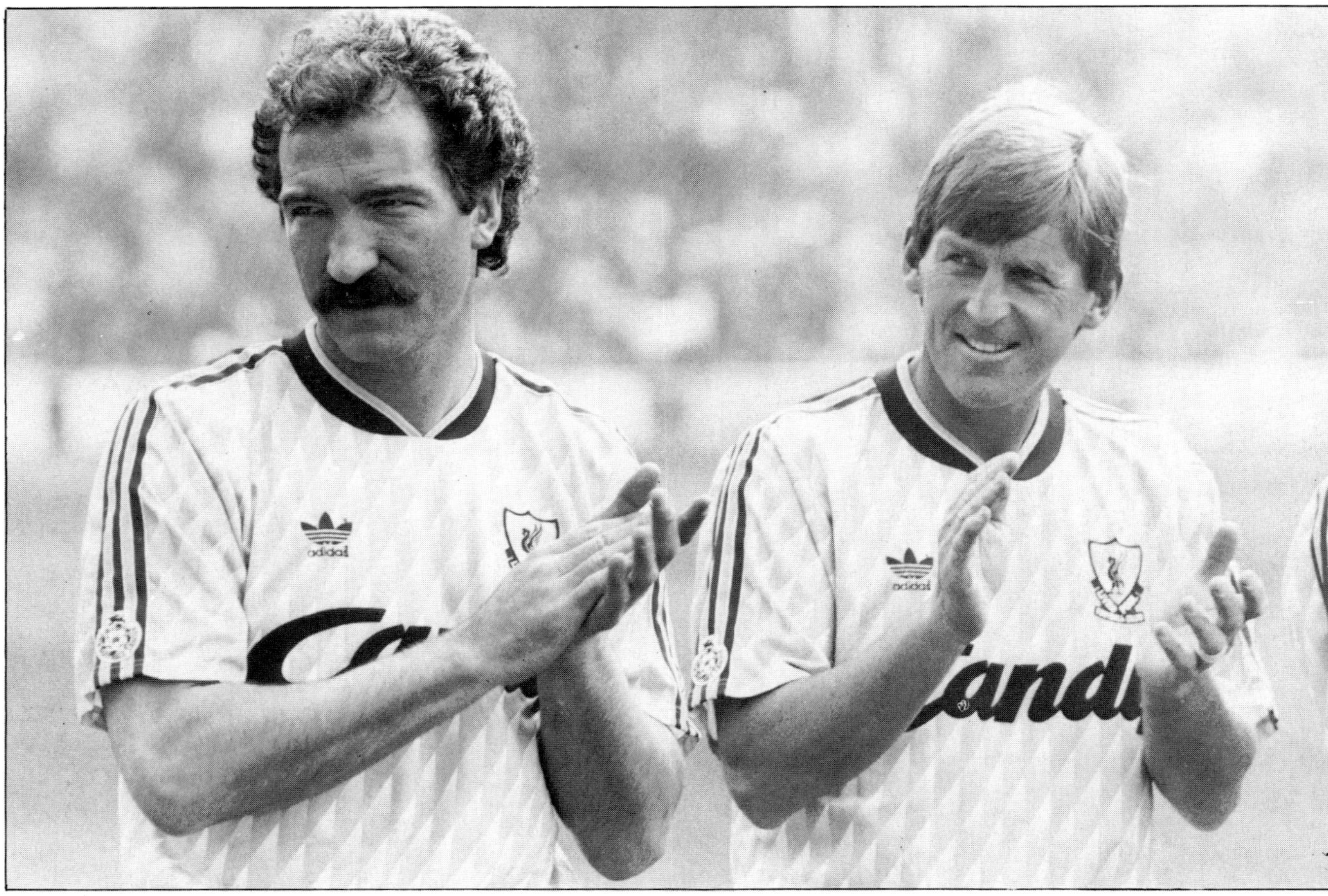

Liverpool boss Graeme Souness and his predecessor Kenny Dalglish in the Liverpool line-up for Ray Kennedy's testimonial game in April 1991.

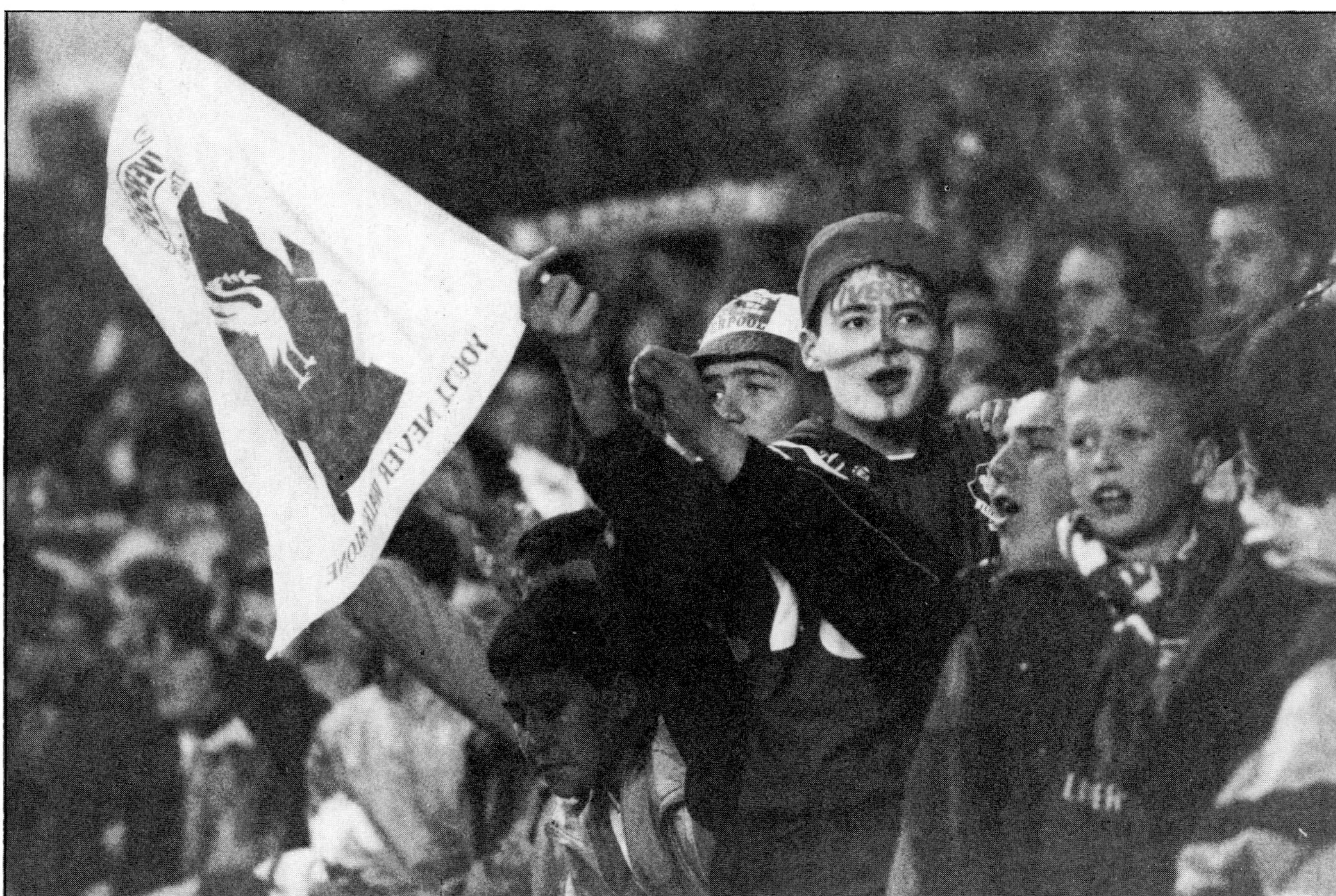

Liverpool fans pictured during the UEFA Cup second-round second-leg game against AJ Auxerre. The Reds lost 2-0 in France but won the second leg 3-0.

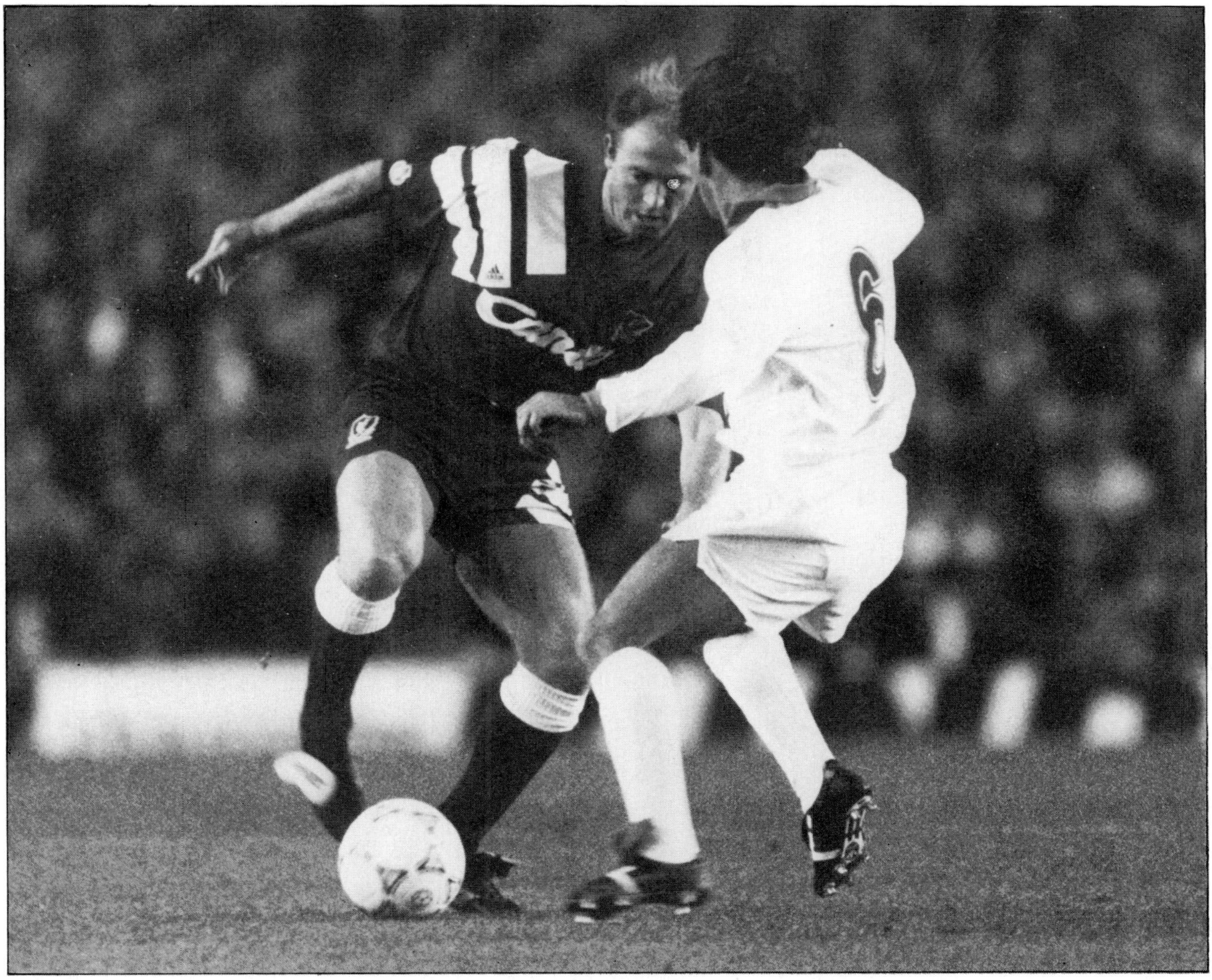

Steve McMahon and AJ Auxerre's Raphael Guerreiro scrapping for the ball. In the third round the Reds beat FC Swarovski Tirol before losing to Genoa in the quarter-final.

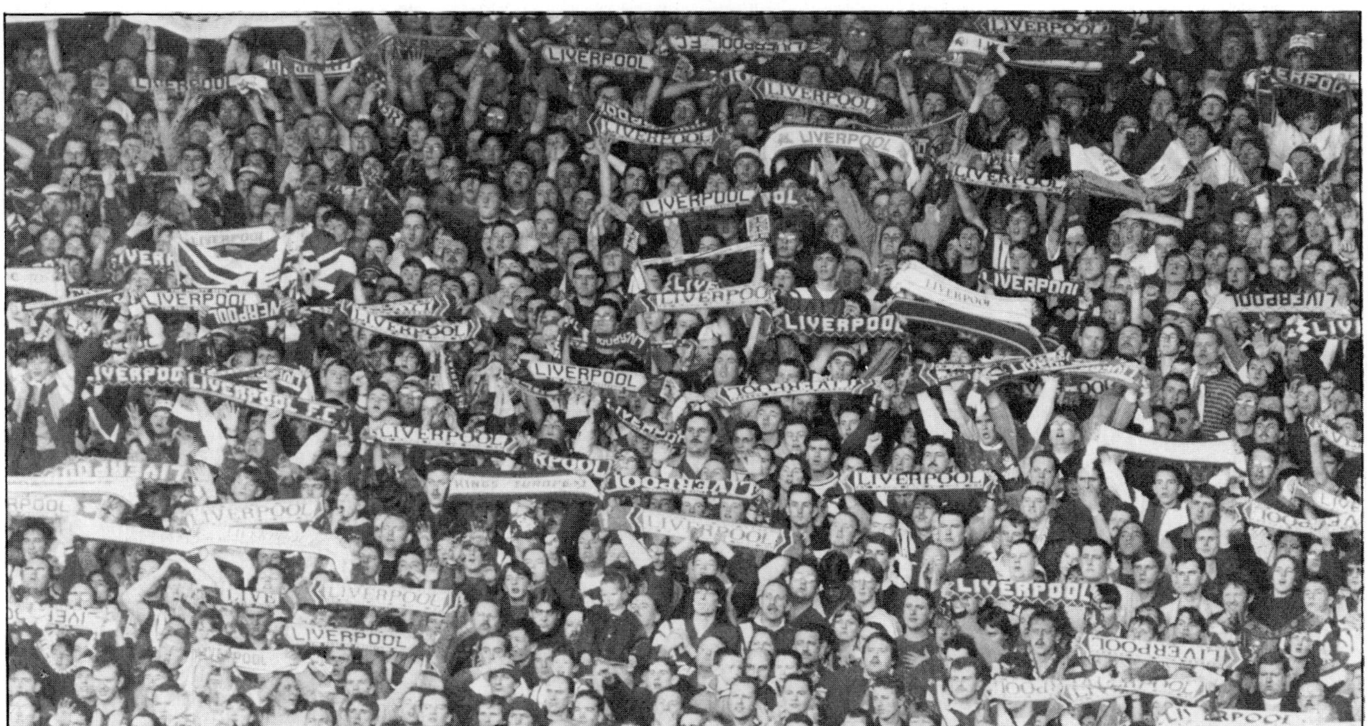

Liverpool's world-famous support at the Kop end of Anfield.

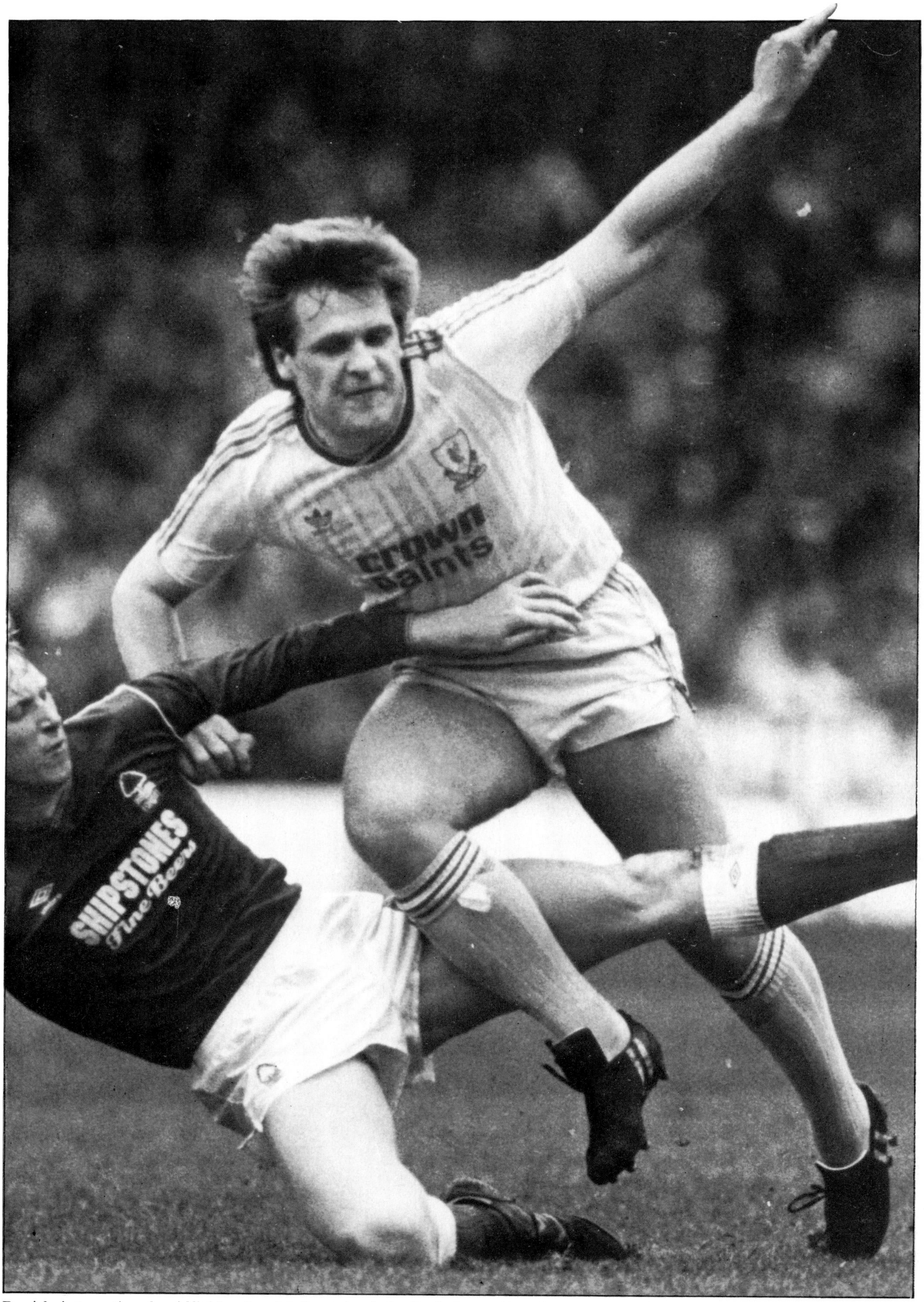

Danish international midfielder Jan Mølby joined the Reds from Ajax Amsterdam for £200,000 in August 1984. He was a key member of the 1986 double-winning side but was later side-lined through injury and received a three-month prison sentence for a motoring offence. He has made almost 300 senior appearances for the Reds.

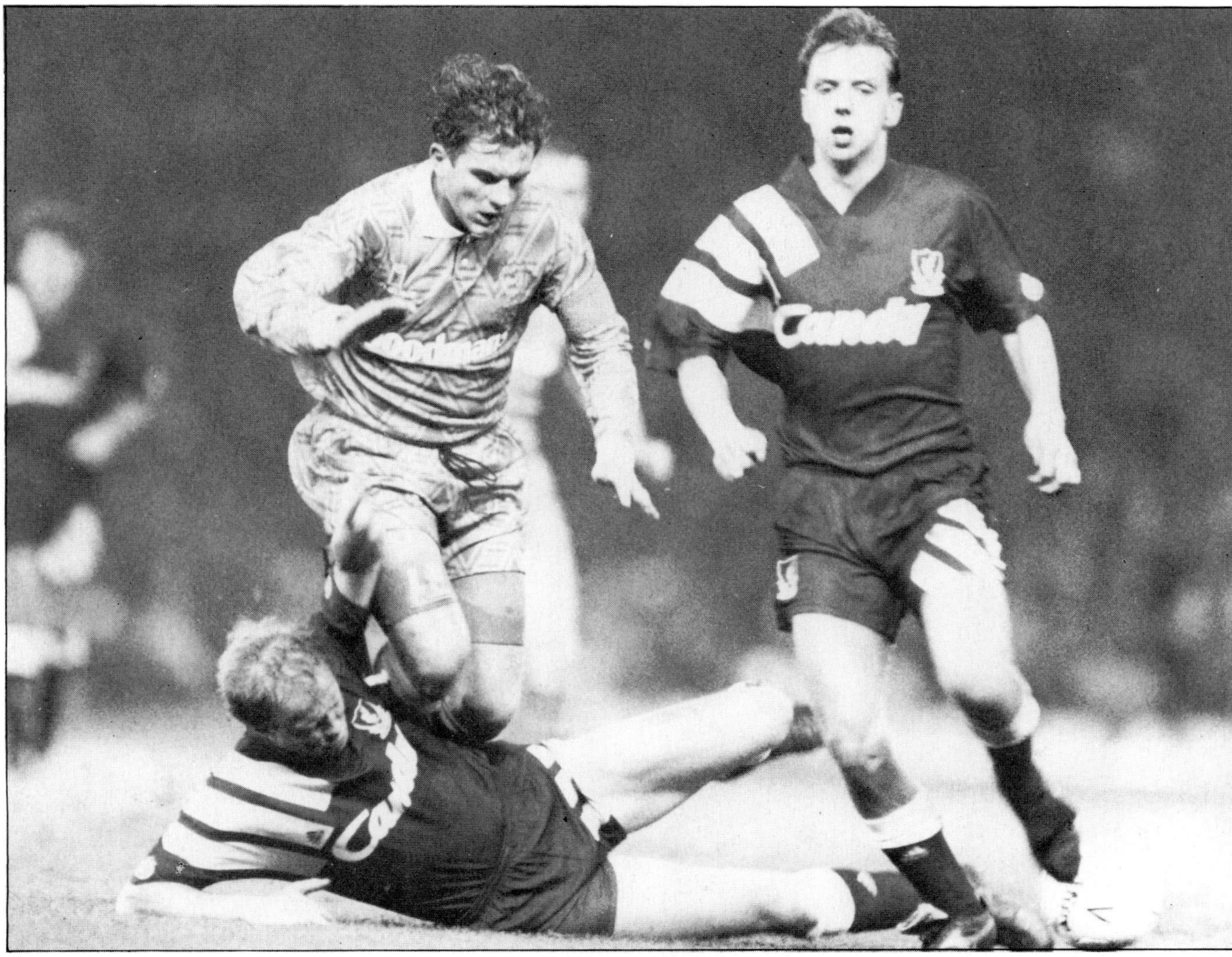

Portsmouth's Martin Kuhl finds his way blocked by Liverpool's England centre-half Mark Wright. The other player is the Reds' newest young star Rob Jones, also now an England player. Pompey threatened to bar Liverpool's path to the 1992 FA Cup Final but the Reds eventually went through on penalties.

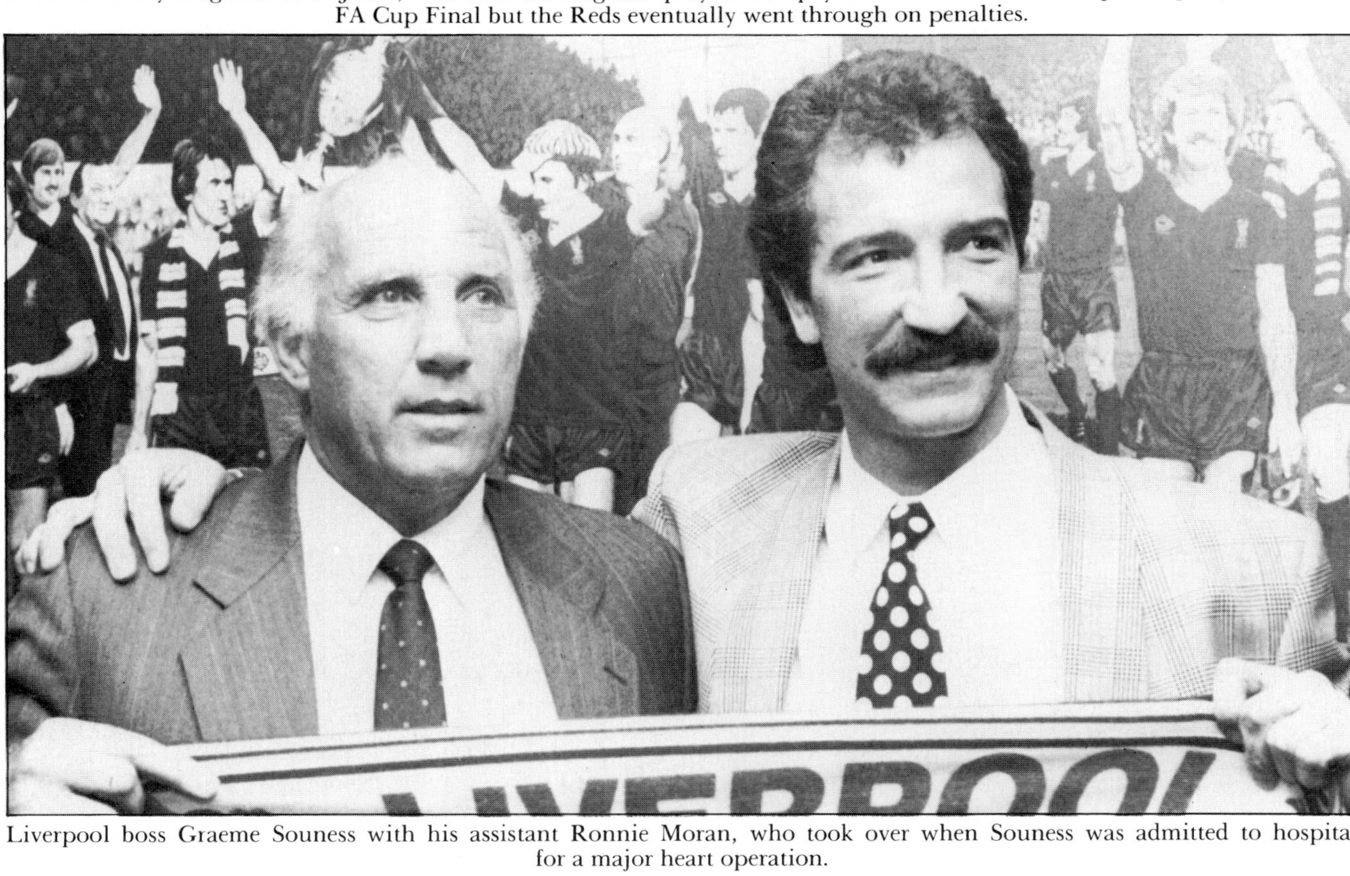

Liverpool boss Graeme Souness with his assistant Ronnie Moran, who took over when Souness was admitted to hospital for a major heart operation.

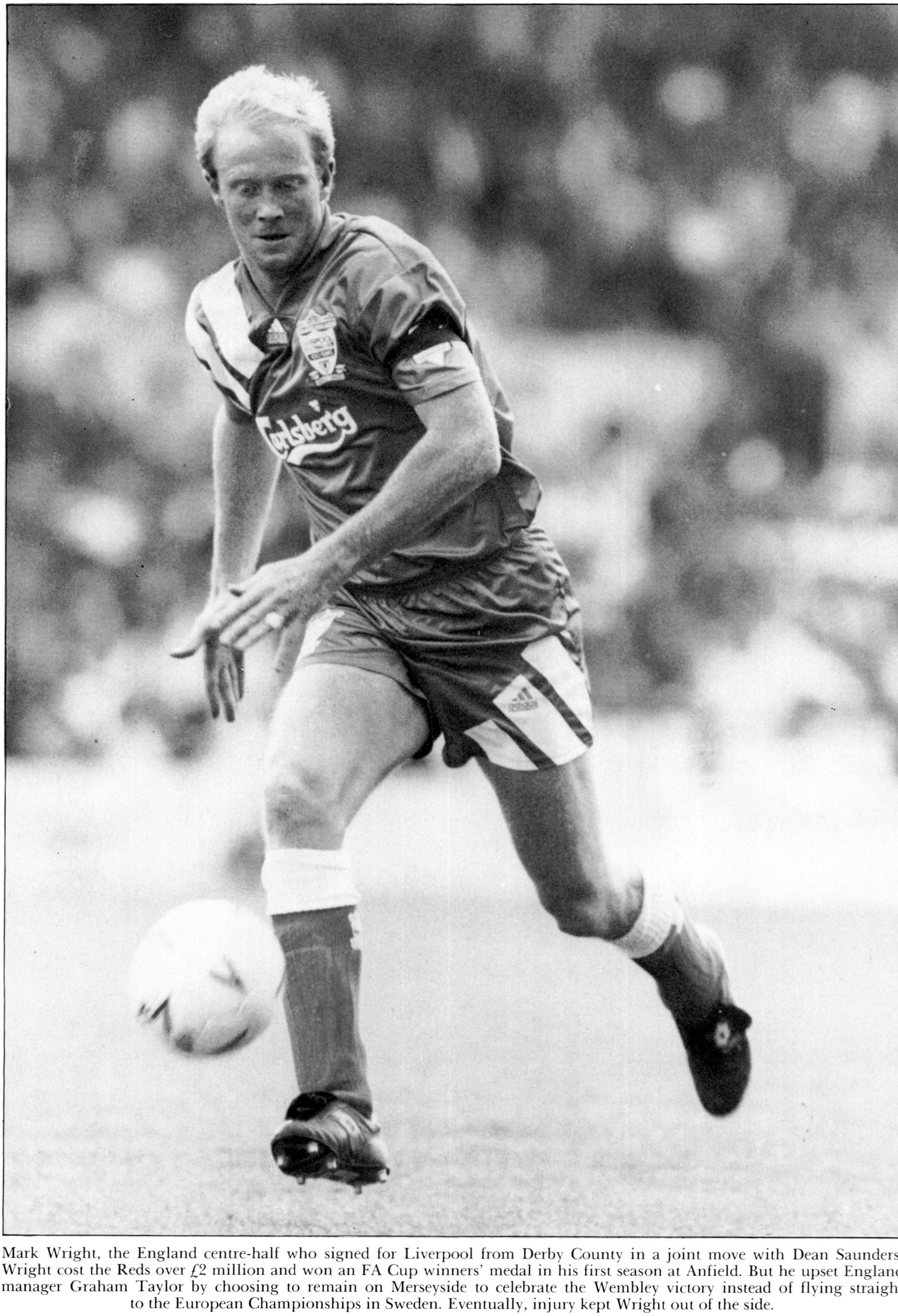

Mark Wright, the England centre-half who signed for Liverpool from Derby County in a joint move with Dean Saunders. Wright cost the Reds over £2 million and won an FA Cup winners' medal in his first season at Anfield. But he upset England manager Graham Taylor by choosing to remain on Merseyside to celebrate the Wembley victory instead of flying straight to the European Championships in Sweden. Eventually, injury kept Wright out of the side.

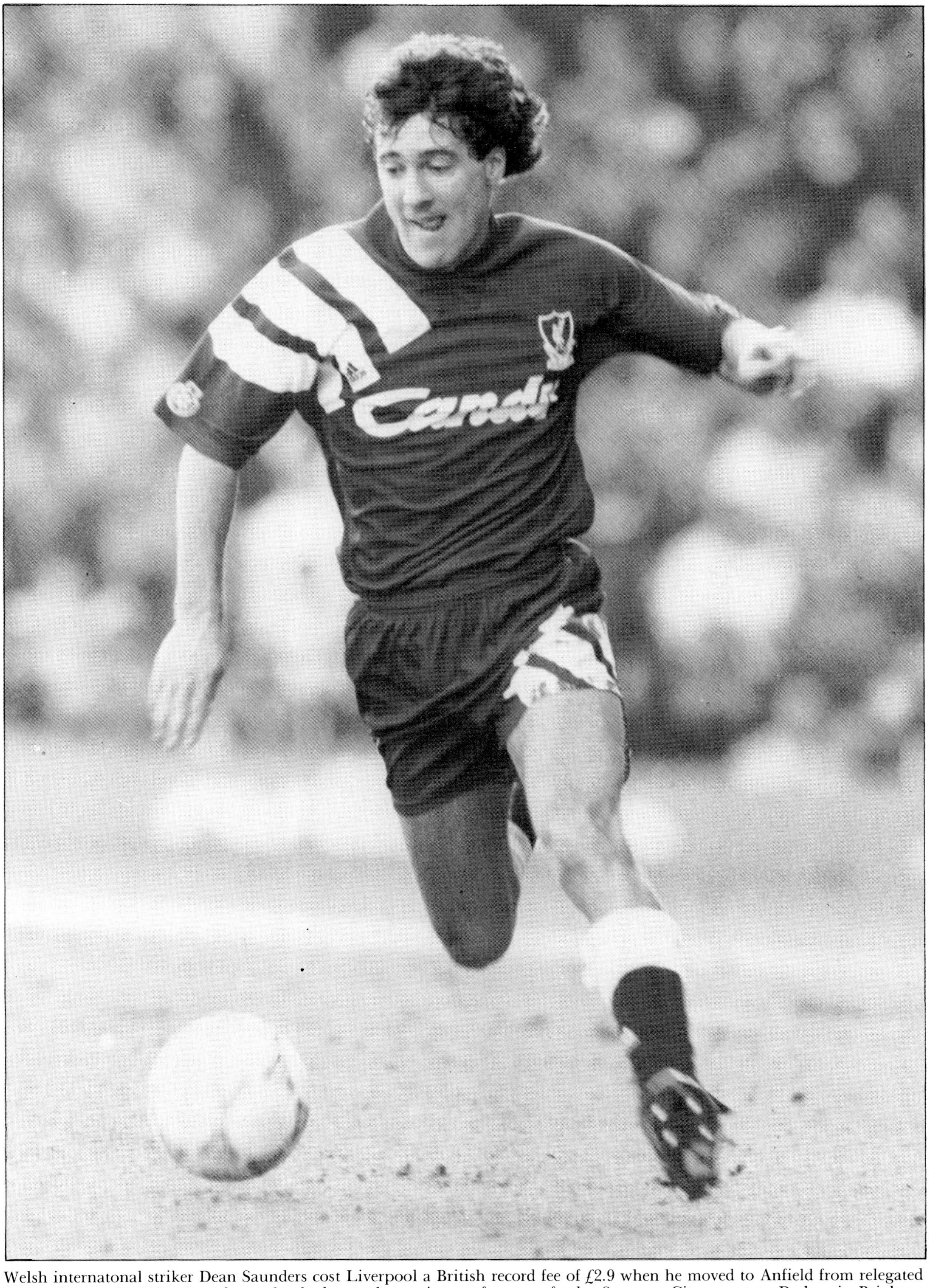

Welsh internatonal striker Dean Saunders cost Liverpool a British record fee of £2.9 when he moved to Anfield from relegated Derby County in 1991. Saunders, who had once been given a free transfer by Swansea City, went to Derby via Brighton and Oxford United. His move to Liverpool was not an unqualified success, however, and in September 1992 he moved to Aston Villa for £2.3 million.

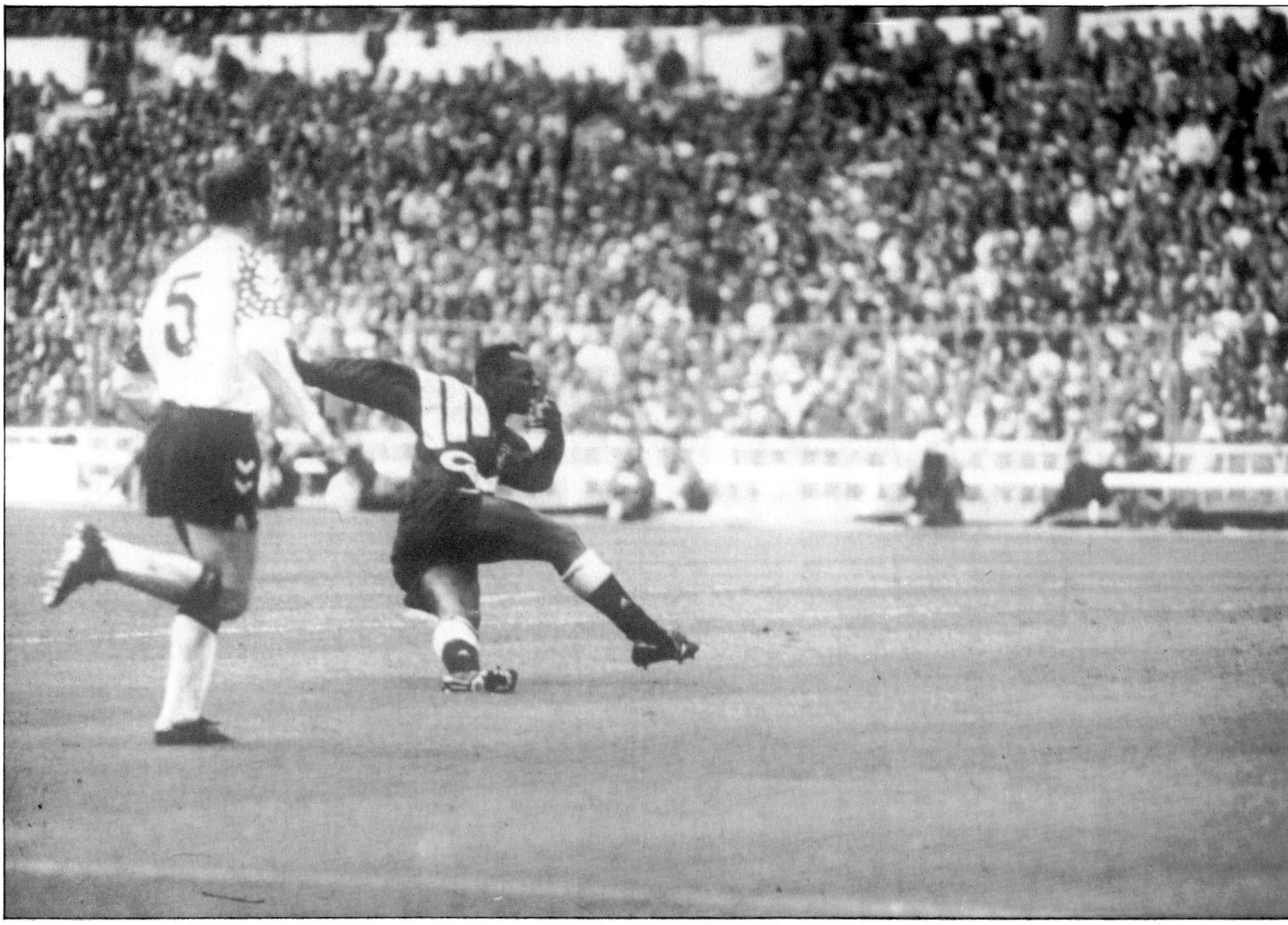

Michael Thomas scores Liverpool's first goal against Second Division Sunderland in the 1992 FA Cup Final.

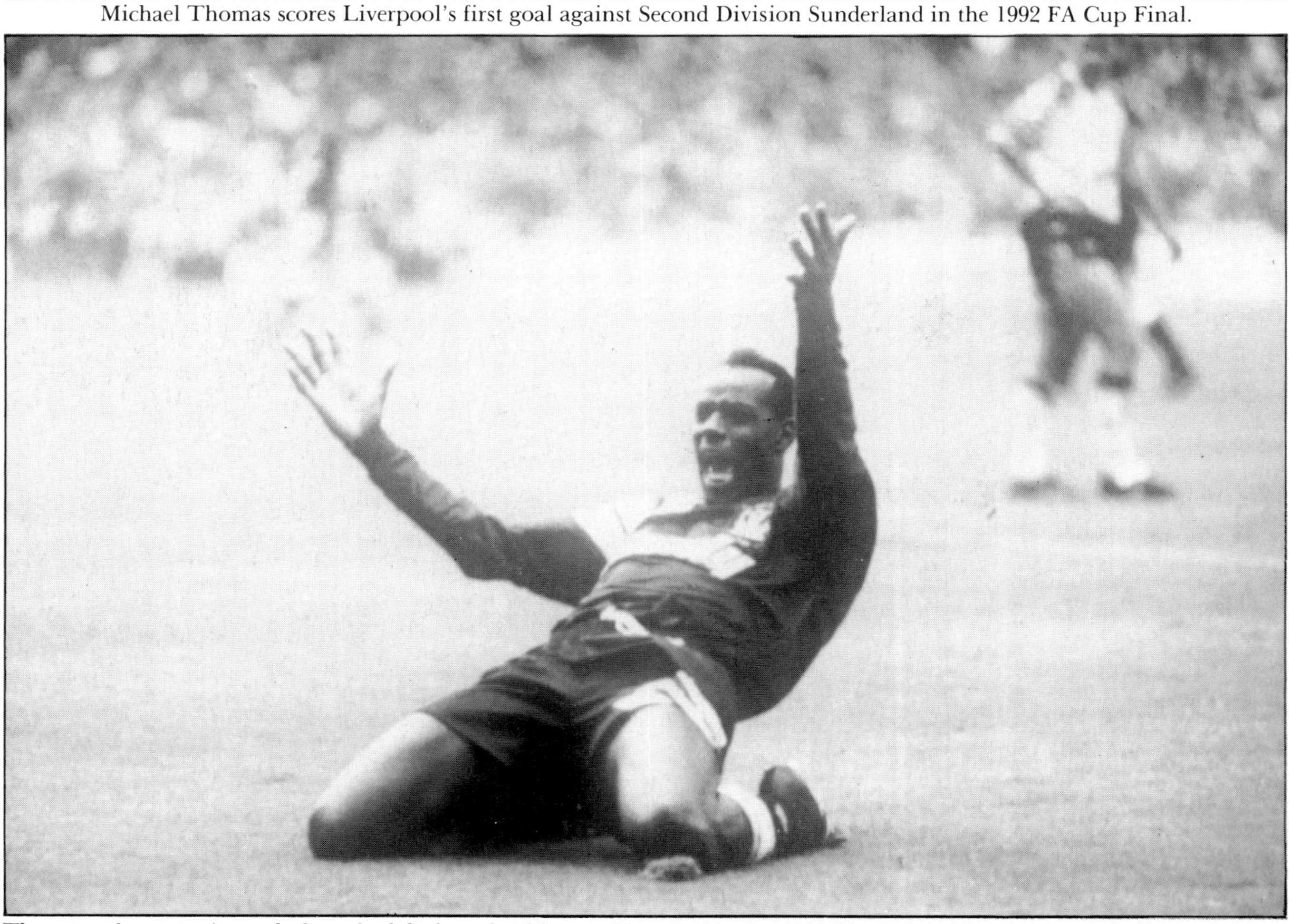

Thomas, who as an Arsenal player had dealt such a blow to Liverpool in the 1989 Championship-clincher at Anfield, celebrates putting the Merseysiders ahead at Wembley.

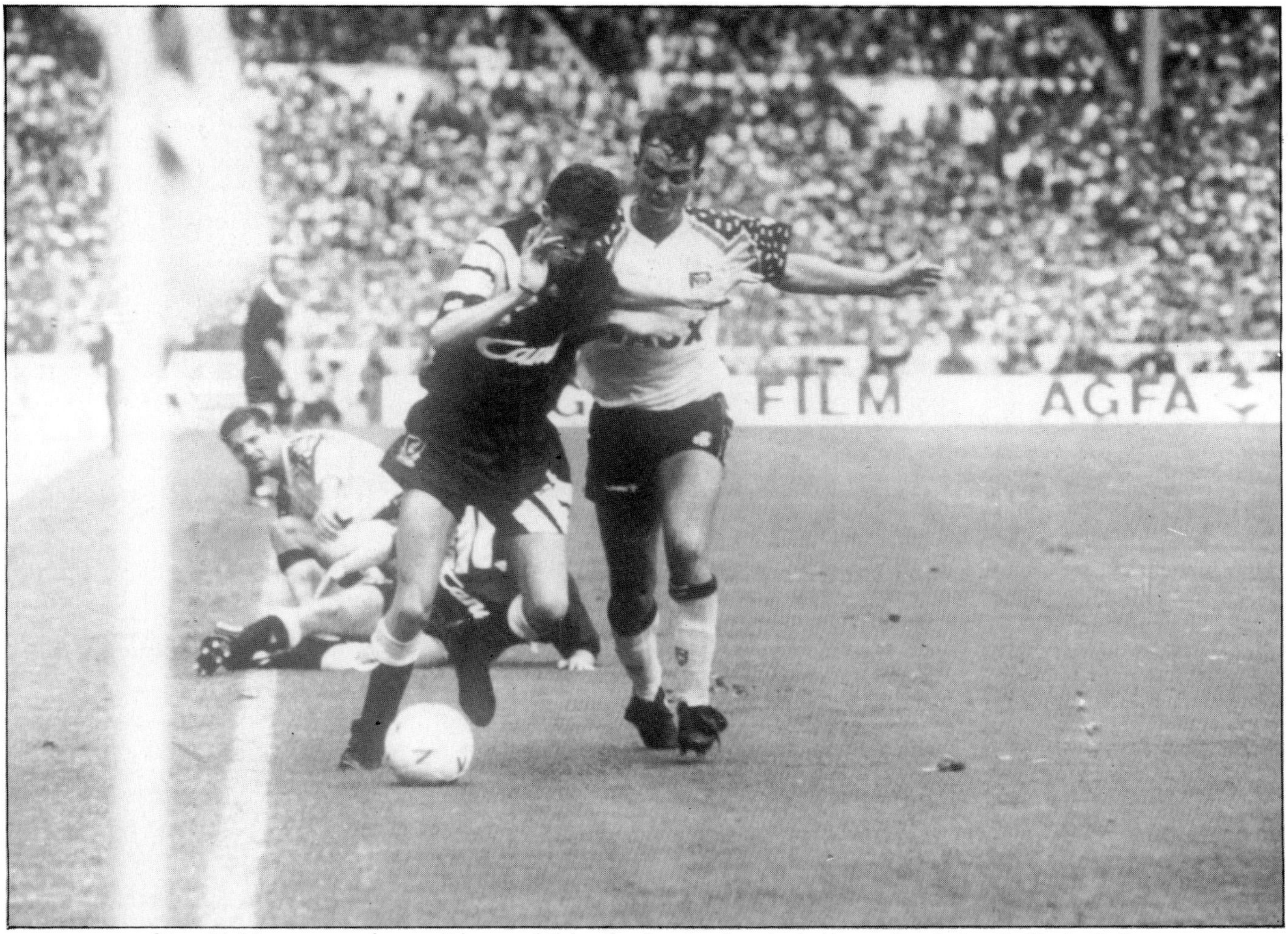

Steve McManaman, a former Liverpool Schools player, takes the ball past Sunderland's Kevin Ball.

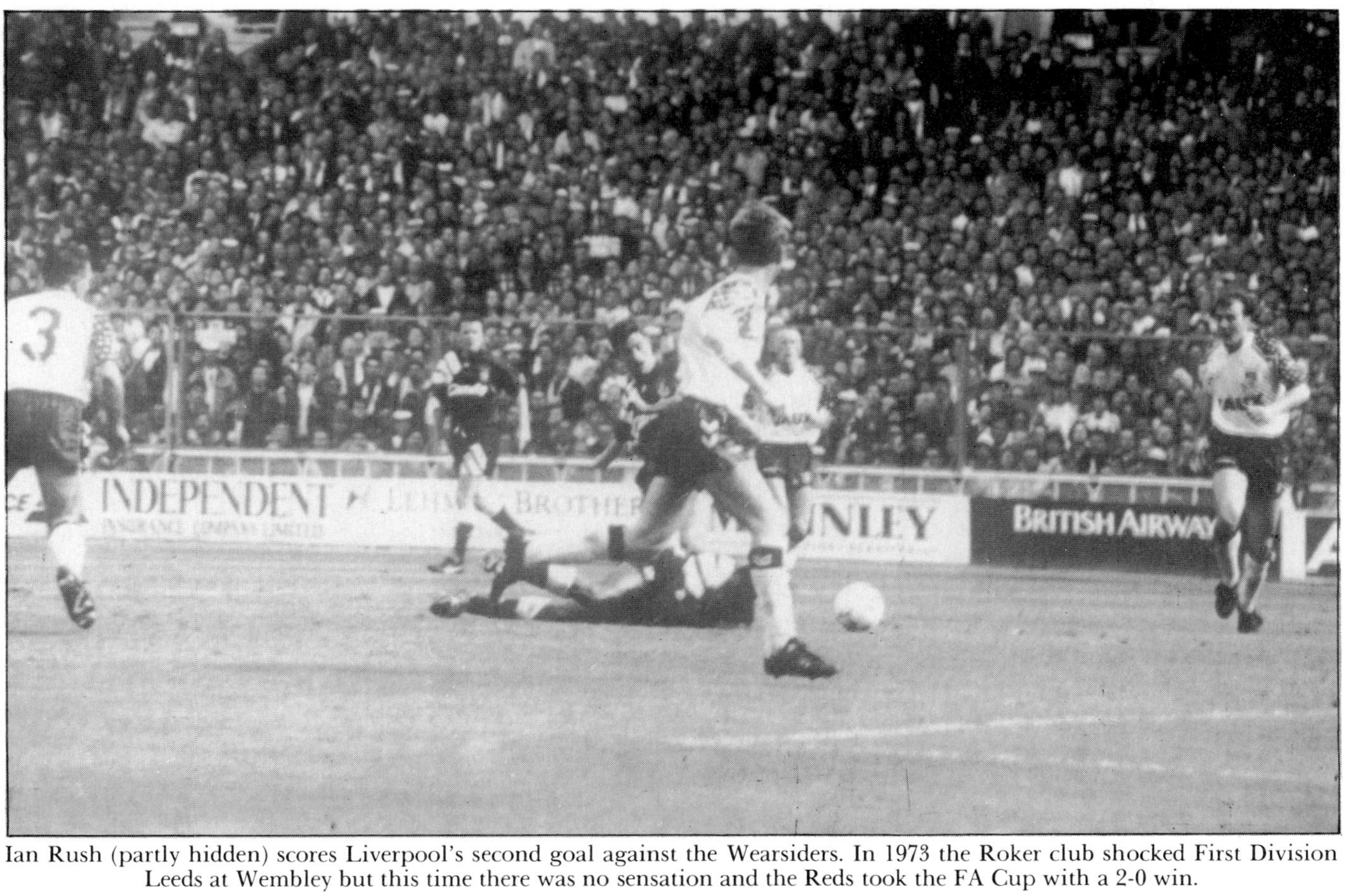

Ian Rush (partly hidden) scores Liverpool's second goal against the Wearsiders. In 1973 the Roker club shocked First Division Leeds at Wembley but this time there was no sensation and the Reds took the FA Cup with a 2-0 win.

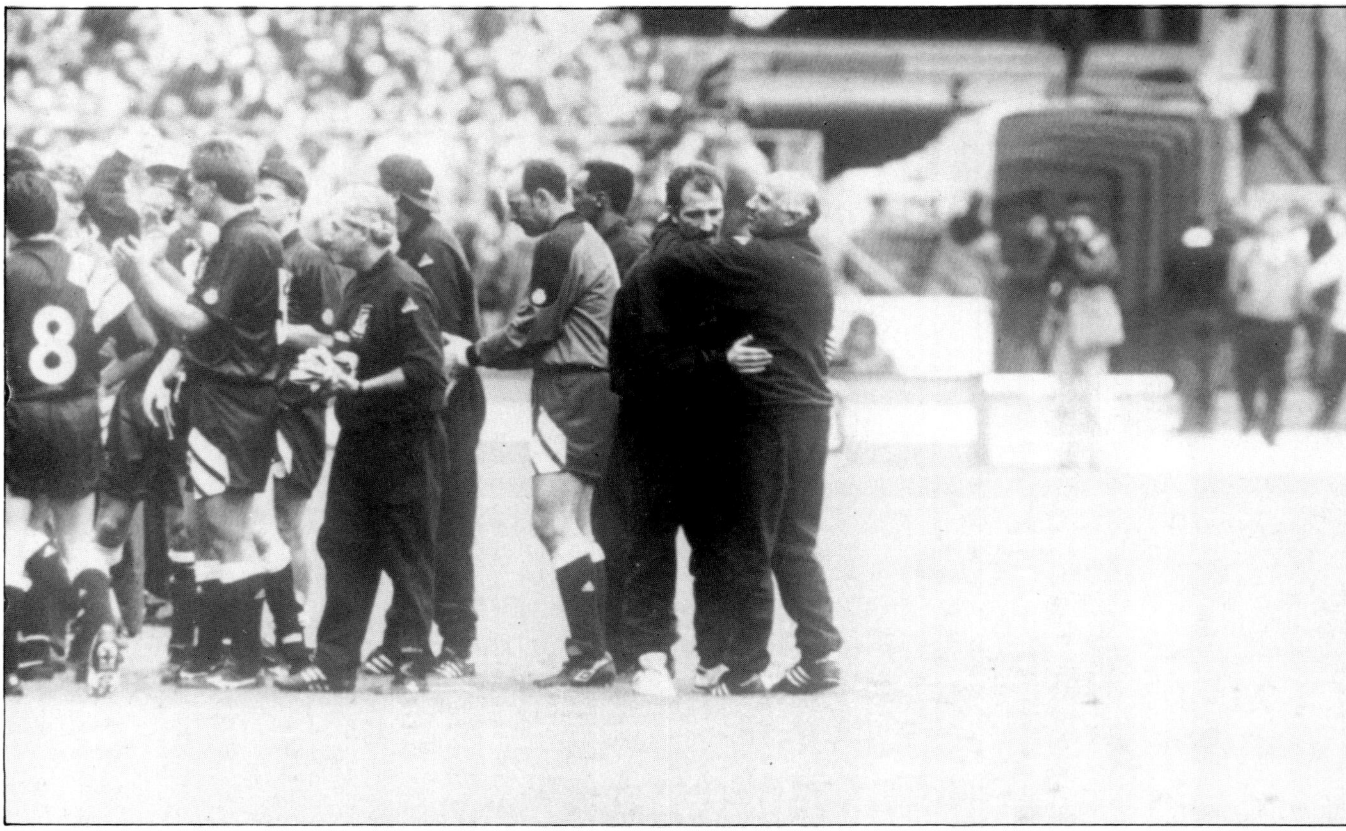

Graeme Souness, still recuperating from a major heart operation, gets a hug from caretaker boss Ronnie Moran after Liverpool's Wembley win.

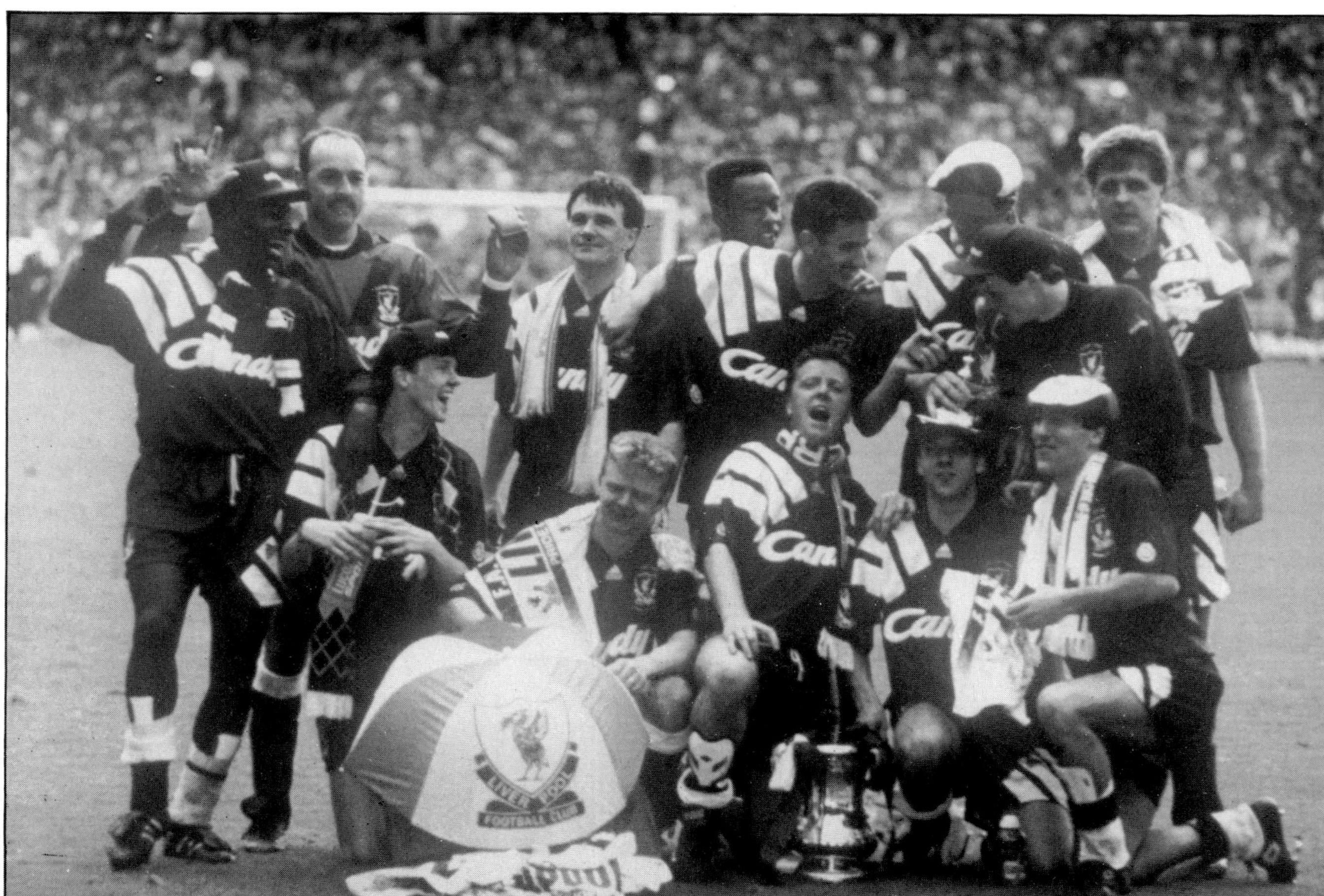

A so-familiar scene — Liverpool players celebrating after another Wembley victory. This time the FA Cup has been joined by a supporter's cap of outsize proportions.

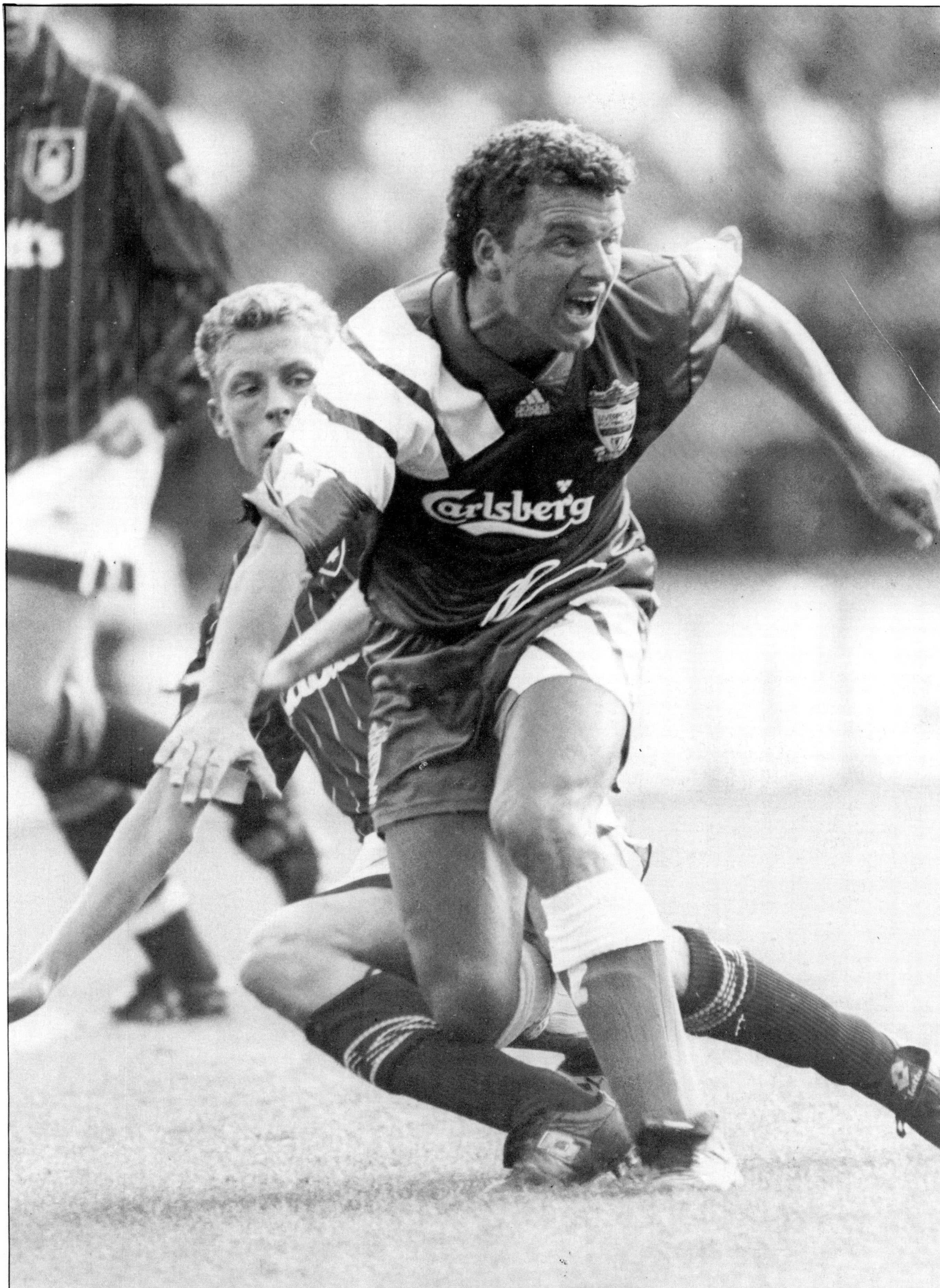

Paul Stewart joined Liverpool from Tottenham Hotspur in the close season of 1992. Stewart began his career with Blackpool, for whom he scored 56 goals in 201 League games, and then hit 26 goals in 51 League appearances for Manchester City. For Spurs he scored 28 goals in 131 League games.

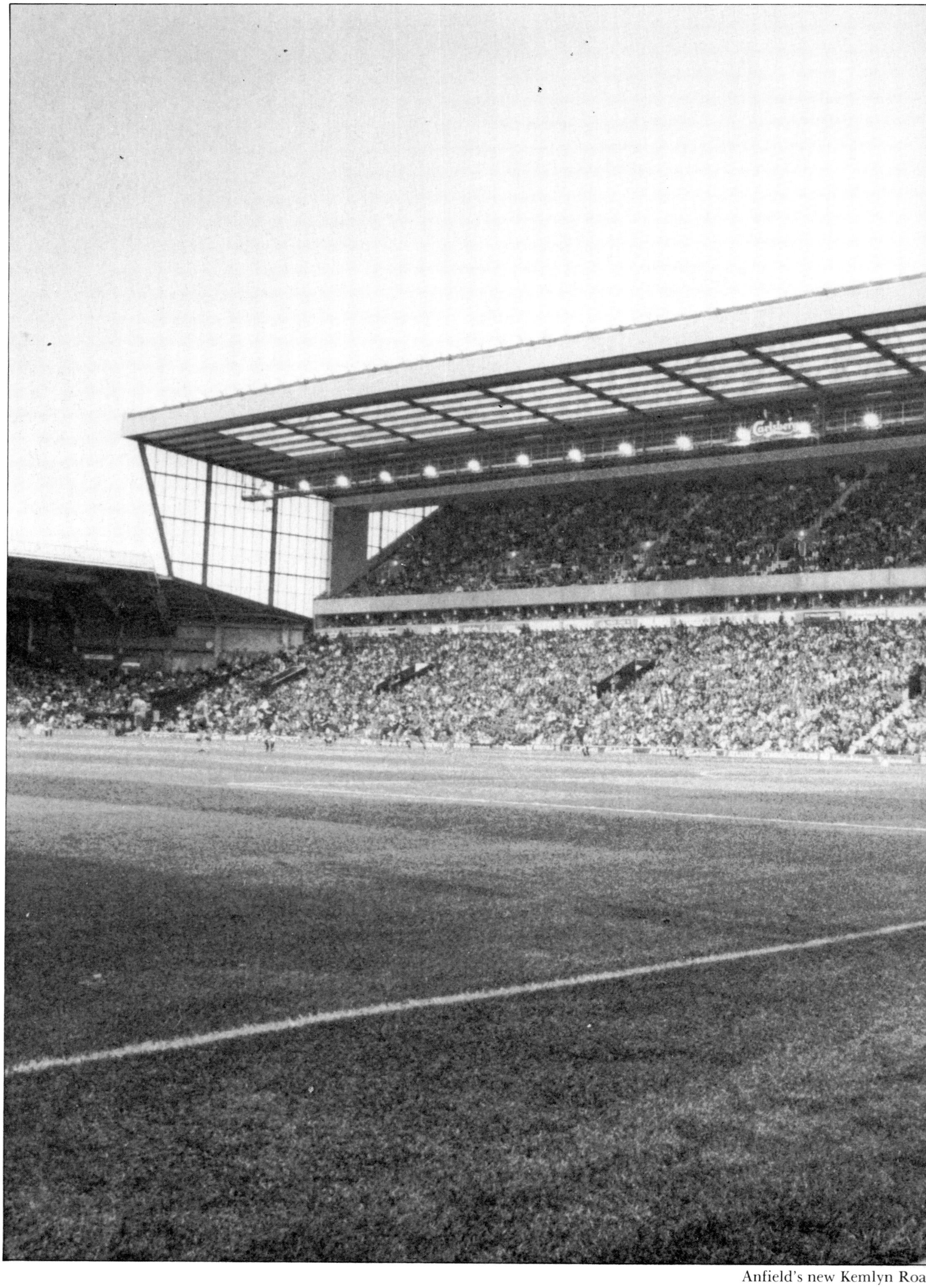

Anfield's new Kemlyn Roa

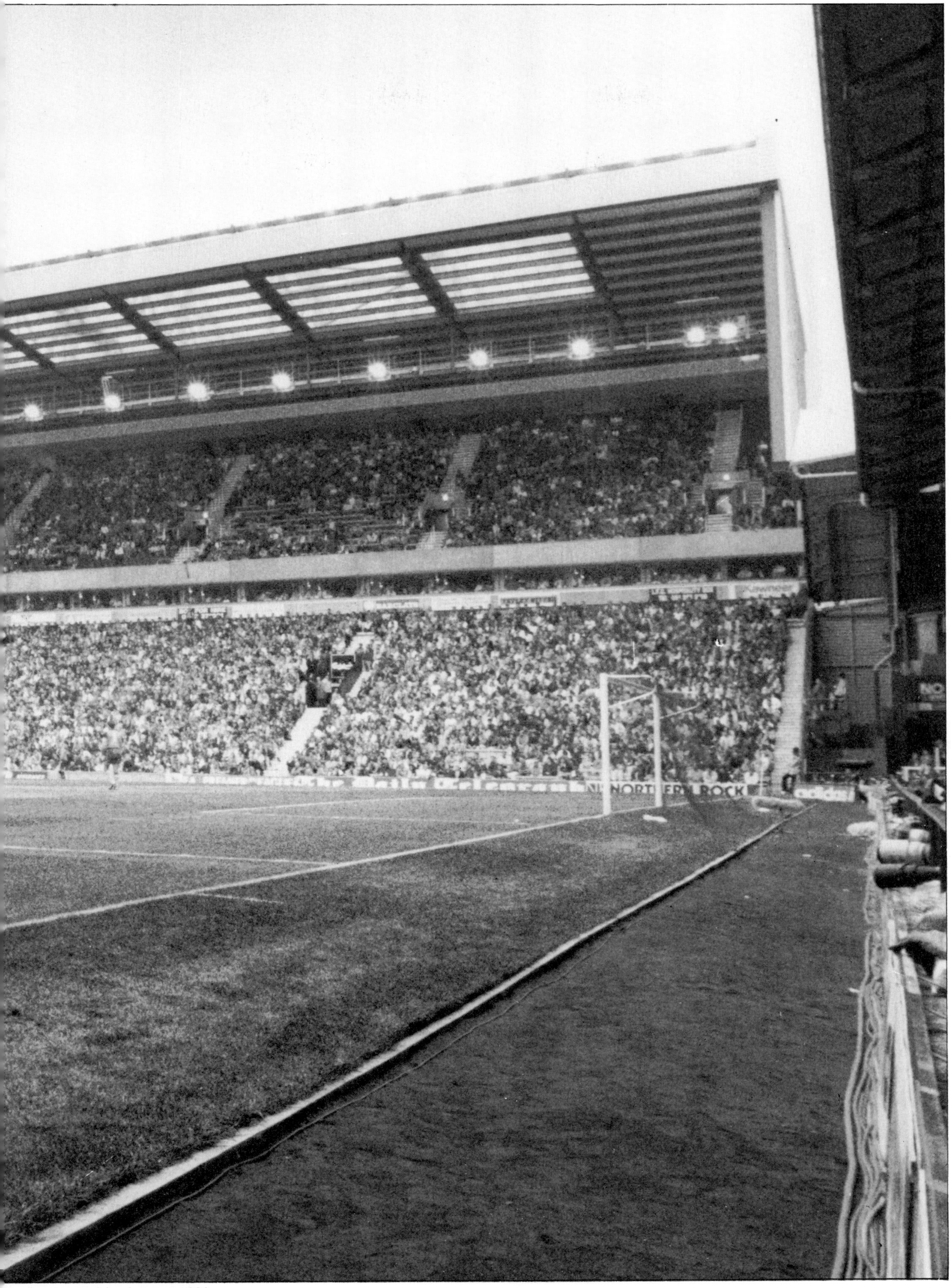

tand, pictured in August 1992.

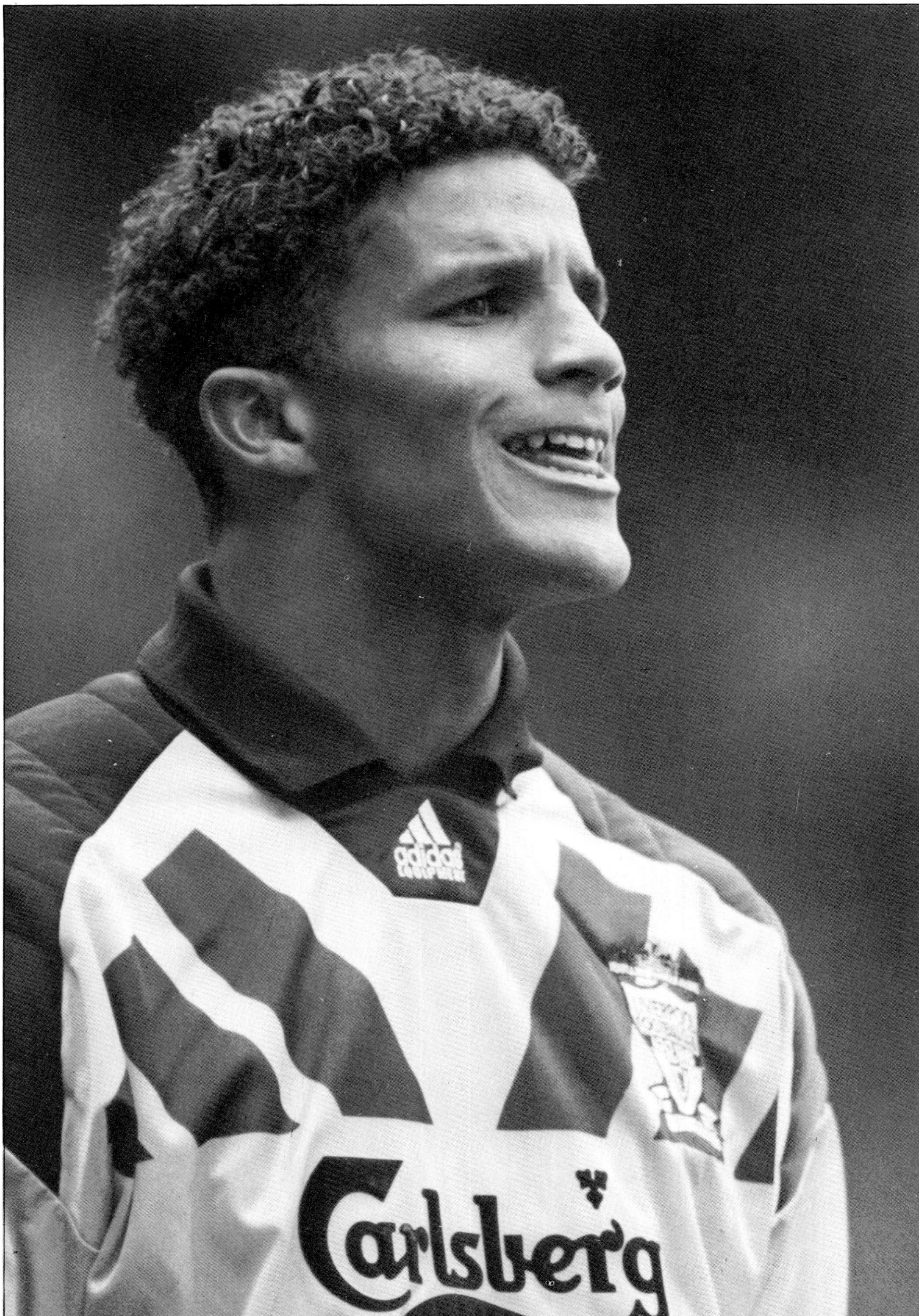

David James, Liverpool's England Under-21 goalkeeper who joined the Reds from Watford in the 1992 close season.

Liverpool in the Football League

DIVISION 2 1893-1894

	P	W	D	L	F	A	W	D	L	F	A	Pts
LIVERPOOL	**28**	**14**	**0**	**0**	**46**	**6**	**8**	**6**	**0**	**31**	**12**	**50**
Small Heath	28	12	0	2	68	19	9	0	5	35	25	42
Notts Co	28	12	1	1	55	14	6	2	6	15	17	39
Newcastle U	28	12	1	1	44	10	3	5	6	22	29	36
Grimsby T	28	11	1	2	47	16	4	1	9	24	42	32
Burton S	28	9	1	4	52	26	5	2	7	27	35	31
Burslem PV	28	10	2	2	43	20	3	2	9	23	44	30
Lincoln C	28	5	4	5	31	22	6	2	6	28	36	28
W Arsenal	28	9	1	4	33	19	3	3	8	19	36	28
Walsall TS	28	8	1	5	36	23	2	2	10	15	38	23
M'brough Iron	28	7	4	3	27	20	1	0	13	10	52	20
Crewe A	28	3	7	4	22	22	3	0	11	20	51	19
Ardwick	28	6	1	7	32	20	2	1	11	15	51	18
Rotherham T	28	5	1	8	28	42	1	2	11	16	49	15
Northwich V	28	3	3	8	17	34	0	0	14	13	64	9

Reds' leading League goalscorer: Stott 14

DIVISION 1 1894-1895

	P	W	D	L	F	A	W	D	L	F	A	Pts
Sunderland	30	13	2	0	51	14	8	3	4	29	23	47
Everton	30	12	2	1	47	18	6	4	5	35	32	42
Aston Villa	30	12	2	1	51	12	5	3	7	31	31	39
Preston NE	30	9	3	3	32	14	6	2	7	30	32	35
Blackburn R	30	9	5	1	40	15	2	5	8	19	34	32
Sheffield U	30	10	2	3	33	17	4	2	9	24	38	32
Nottingham F	30	10	1	4	33	22	3	4	8	17	34	31
Sheffield W	30	10	2	3	36	19	2	2	11	14	36	28
Burnley	30	8	2	5	28	24	3	3	10	16	32	26
Bolton W	30	8	3	4	45	23	1	4	10	16	39	25
Wolves	30	7	4	4	24	25	2	3	10	19	38	25
Small Heath	30	6	6	3	35	28	3	1	11	15	46	25
WBA	30	9	2	4	38	21	1	2	12	13	45	24
Stoke	30	7	3	5	35	25	2	3	10	15	42	24
Derby Co	30	4	5	6	23	23	3	4	8	22	45	23
LIVERPOOL	**30**	**6**	**4**	**5**	**38**	**28**	**1**	**4**	**10**	**13**	**42**	**22**

Reds' leading League goalscorer: Ross 12

DIVISION 2 1895-1896

	P	W	D	L	F	A	W	D	L	F	A	Pts
LIVERPOOL	**30**	**14**	**1**	**0**	**65**	**11**	**8**	**1**	**6**	**41**	**21**	**46**
Ardwick	30	12	3	0	37	9	9	1	5	26	29	46
Grimsby T	30	14	1	0	51	9	6	1	8	31	29	42
Burton W	30	12	1	2	43	15	7	3	5	26	25	42
Newcastle U	30	14	0	1	57	14	2	2	11	16	36	34
Newton Heath	30	12	2	1	48	15	3	1	11	18	42	33
W Arsenal	30	11	1	3	42	11	3	3	9	16	31	32
Leicester F	30	10	0	5	40	16	4	4	7	17	28	32
Darwen	30	9	4	2	55	22	3	2	10	17	45	30
Notts Co	30	8	1	6	41	22	4	1	10	16	32	26
Burton S	30	7	2	6	24	26	3	2	10	15	43	24
Loughboro' T	30	7	3	5	32	25	2	2	11	8	41	23
Lincoln C	30	7	1	7	36	24	2	3	10	17	51	22
Burslem PV	30	6	4	5	25	24	1	0	14	18	54	18
Rotherham T	30	7	2	6	27	26	0	1	14	7	71	17
Crewe A	30	5	2	8	22	28	0	1	14	8	67	13

Reds' leading League goalscorer: Allan 25

DIVISION 1 1896-1897

	P	W	D	L	F	A	W	D	L	F	A	Pts
Aston Villa	30	10	3	2	36	16	11	2	2	37	22	47
Sheffield U	30	6	4	5	22	16	7	6	2	20	13	36
Derby Co	30	10	2	3	45	22	6	2	7	25	28	36
Preston NE	30	8	4	3	35	21	3	8	4	20	19	34
LIVERPOOL	**30**	**7**	**6**	**2**	**25**	**10**	**5**	**3**	**7**	**21**	**28**	**33**
Sheffield W	30	9	4	2	29	11	1	7	7	13	26	31
Everton	30	8	1	6	42	29	6	2	7	20	28	31
Bolton W	30	7	3	5	22	18	5	3	7	18	25	30
Bury	30	7	5	3	25	15	3	5	7	14	29	30
Wolves	30	6	4	5	26	14	5	2	8	19	27	28
Nottingham F	30	8	3	4	30	16	1	5	9	14	33	26
WBA	30	7	2	6	18	16	3	4	8	15	40	26
Stoke	30	8	3	4	30	18	3	0	12	18	41	25
Blackburn R	30	8	1	6	27	25	3	2	10	8	37	25
Sunderland	30	4	6	5	21	21	3	3	9	13	26	23
Burnley	30	4	5	6	25	25	2	2	11	18	36	19

Reds' leading League goalscorer: Allan 17

DIVISION 1 1897-1898

	P	W	D	L	F	A	W	D	L	F	A	Pts
Sheffield U	30	9	4	2	27	14	8	4	3	29	17	42
Sunderland	30	12	2	1	27	8	4	3	8	16	22	37
Wolves	30	10	4	1	36	14	4	3	8	21	27	35
Everton	30	11	3	1	33	12	2	6	7	15	27	35
Sheffield W	30	12	0	3	39	15	3	3	9	12	27	33
Aston Villa	30	12	1	2	47	21	2	4	9	14	30	33
WBA	30	8	5	2	25	16	3	5	7	19	29	32
Nottingham F	30	7	5	3	30	19	4	4	7	17	30	31
LIVERPOOL	**30**	**7**	**4**	**4**	**27**	**16**	**4**	**2**	**9**	**21**	**29**	**28**
Derby Co	30	10	3	2	40	19	1	3	11	17	42	28
Bolton W	30	9	2	4	18	13	2	2	11	10	28	26
Preston NE	30	7	5	3	26	15	1	3	11	9	28	24
Notts Co	30	4	6	5	23	23	4	2	9	13	23	24
Bury	30	8	3	4	25	19	0	5	10	14	32	24
Blackburn R	30	4	7	4	20	22	3	3	9	19	32	24
Stoke	30	8	3	4	21	14	0	5	10	14	41	24

Reds' leading League goalscorer: Becton 11

DIVISION 1 1898-1899

	P	W	D	L	F	A	W	D	L	F	A	Pts
Aston Villa	34	15	2	0	58	13	4	5	8	18	27	45
LIVERPOOL	**34**	**12**	**3**	**2**	**29**	**10**	**7**	**2**	**8**	**20**	**23**	**43**
Burnley	34	11	5	1	32	15	4	4	9	13	32	39
Everton	34	10	2	5	25	13	5	6	6	23	28	38
Notts Co	34	9	6	2	33	20	3	7	7	14	31	37
Blackburn R	34	9	5	3	41	23	5	3	9	19	29	36
Sunderland	34	11	3	3	26	10	4	3	10	15	31	36
Wolves	34	9	5	3	30	13	5	2	10	24	35	35
Derby Co	34	11	5	1	46	19	1	6	10	16	38	35
Bury	34	9	5	3	31	18	5	2	10	17	31	35
Nottingham F	34	6	6	5	22	18	5	5	7	20	24	33
Stoke	34	10	4	3	29	17	3	3	11	18	35	33
Newcastle U	34	9	3	5	33	18	2	5	10	16	30	30
WBA	34	11	1	5	28	9	1	5	11	14	48	30
Preston NE	34	10	4	3	29	14	0	5	12	15	33	29
Sheffield U	34	7	8	2	31	20	2	3	12	14	31	29
Bolton W	34	6	5	6	24	21	3	2	12	13	30	25
Sheffield W	34	8	2	7	26	24	0	6	11	6	37	24

Reds' leading League goalscorers: Morgan & Robertson 10

DIVISION 1 1899-1900

	P	W	D	L	F	A	W	D	L	F	A	Pts
Aston Villa	34	12	4	1	45	18	10	2	5	32	17	50
Sheffield U	34	11	5	1	40	11	7	7	3	23	22	48
Sunderland	34	12	2	3	27	9	7	1	9	23	26	41
Wolves	34	8	4	5	28	16	7	5	5	20	21	39
Newcastle U	34	10	5	2	34	15	3	5	9	19	28	36
Derby Co	34	11	2	4	32	15	3	6	8	13	28	36
Manchester C	34	10	3	4	33	15	3	5	9	17	29	34
Nottingham F	34	12	3	2	42	16	1	5	11	14	39	34
Stoke	34	9	5	3	24	15	4	3	10	13	30	34
LIVERPOOL	**34**	**9**	**4**	**4**	**31**	**19**	**5**	**1**	**11**	**18**	**26**	**33**
Everton	34	11	1	5	30	15	2	6	9	17	34	33
Bury	34	12	2	3	29	14	1	4	12	11	30	32
WBA	34	8	6	3	27	11	3	2	12	16	40	30
Blackburn R	34	12	2	3	38	22	1	2	14	11	39	30
Notts Co	34	5	7	5	29	22	4	4	9	17	38	29
Preston NE	34	9	3	5	28	20	3	1	13	10	28	28
Burnley	34	10	2	5	28	17	1	3	13	6	37	27
Glossop NE	34	4	6	7	19	22	0	4	13	12	52	18

Reds' leading League goalscorer: Walker 10

DIVISION 1 1900-1901

	P	W	D	L	F	A	W	D	L	F	A	Pts
LIVERPOOL	**34**	**12**	**2**	**3**	**36**	**13**	**7**	**5**	**5**	**23**	**22**	**45**
Sunderland	34	12	3	2	43	11	3	10	4	14	15	43
Notts Co	34	13	2	2	39	18	5	2	10	15	28	40
Nottingham F	34	10	4	3	32	14	6	3	8	21	22	39
Bury	34	11	3	3	31	10	5	4	8	22	27	39
Newcastle U	34	10	5	2	27	13	4	5	8	15	24	38
Everton	34	10	4	3	37	17	6	1	10	18	25	37
Sheffield W	34	13	2	2	38	16	0	8	9	14	26	36
Blackburn R	34	9	4	4	24	18	3	5	9	15	29	33
Bolton W	34	10	5	2	21	12	3	2	12	18	43	33
Manchester C	34	12	3	2	32	16	1	3	13	16	42	32
Derby Co	34	10	4	3	43	18	2	3	12	12	24	31
Wolves	34	6	10	1	21	15	3	3	11	18	40	31
Sheffield U	34	8	4	5	22	23	4	3	10	13	29	31
Aston Villa	34	8	5	4	32	18	2	5	10	13	33	30
Stoke	34	8	3	6	23	15	3	2	12	23	42	27
Preston NE	34	6	4	7	29	30	3	3	11	20	45	25
WBA	34	4	4	9	21	27	3	4	10	14	35	22

Reds' leading League goalscorer: Raybould 16

DIVISION 1 1901-1902

	P	W	D	L	F	A	W	D	L	F	A	Pts
Sunderland	34	12	3	2	32	14	7	3	7	18	21	44
Everton	34	11	2	4	31	11	6	5	6	22	24	41
Newcastle U	34	11	3	3	41	14	3	6	8	7	20	37
Blackburn R	34	12	2	3	36	16	3	4	10	16	32	36
Nottingham F	34	11	4	2	32	13	2	5	10	11	30	35
Derby Co	34	11	5	1	26	10	2	4	11	13	31	35
Bury	34	11	5	1	31	9	2	3	12	13	29	34
Aston Villa	34	9	5	3	27	13	4	3	10	15	27	34
Sheffield W	34	9	5	3	30	14	4	3	10	18	38	34
Sheffield U	34	10	5	2	38	13	3	2	12	15	35	33
LIVERPOOL	**34**	**8**	**3**	**6**	**28**	**16**	**2**	**9**	**6**	**14**	**22**	**32**
Bolton W	34	10	6	1	38	17	2	2	13	13	39	32
Notts Co	34	12	2	3	44	19	2	2	13	7	38	32
Wolves	34	12	3	2	32	13	1	3	13	14	44	32
Grimsby T	34	11	3	3	33	16	2	3	12	11	44	32
Stoke	34	10	4	3	31	12	1	5	11	14	43	31
Small Heath	34	8	5	4	31	14	3	3	11	16	31	30
Manchester C	34	10	3	4	28	17	1	3	13	14	41	28

Reds' leading League goalscorer: Raybould 16

DIVISION 1 1902-1903

	P	W	D	L	F	A	W	D	L	F	A	Pts
Sheffield W	34	12	3	2	31	7	7	1	9	23	29	42
Aston Villa	34	11	3	3	43	18	8	0	9	18	22	41
Sunderland	34	10	5	2	27	11	6	4	7	24	25	41
Sheffield U	34	11	0	6	36	22	6	5	6	22	22	39
LIVERPOOL	**34**	**11**	**3**	**3**	**48**	**21**	**6**	**1**	**10**	**20**	**28**	**38**
Stoke	34	11	2	4	29	11	4	5	8	17	27	37
WBA	34	10	2	5	37	27	6	2	9	17	26	36
Bury	34	14	1	2	41	14	2	2	13	13	29	35
Derby Co	34	13	2	2	34	11	3	1	13	16	36	35
Nottingham F	34	10	3	4	33	22	4	4	9	16	25	35
Wolves	34	12	2	3	34	17	2	3	12	14	40	33
Everton	34	10	2	5	28	18	3	4	10	17	29	32
Middlesbrough	34	10	3	4	27	16	4	1	12	14	34	32
Newcastle U	34	12	1	4	31	11	2	3	12	10	40	32
Notts Co	34	8	5	4	25	16	4	2	11	16	33	31
Blackburn R	34	9	2	6	27	24	3	3	11	17	39	29
Grimsby T	34	6	5	6	28	22	2	4	11	15	40	25
Bolton W	34	6	2	9	18	20	2	1	14	19	53	19

Reds' leading League goalscorer: Raybould 31

DIVISION 1 1905-1906

	P	W	D	L	F	A	W	D	L	F	A	Pts
LIVERPOOL	**38**	**14**	**3**	**2**	**49**	**15**	**9**	**2**	**8**	**30**	**31**	**51**
Preston NE	38	12	5	2	36	15	5	8	6	18	24	47
Sheffield W	38	12	5	2	40	20	6	3	10	23	32	44
Newcastle U	38	12	4	3	49	23	6	3	10	25	25	43
Manchester C	38	11	2	6	46	23	8	3	8	27	31	43
Bolton W	38	13	1	5	51	22	4	6	9	30	45	41
Birmingham	38	14	2	3	49	20	3	5	11	16	39	41
Aston Villa	38	13	2	4	51	19	4	4	11	21	37	40
Blackburn R	38	10	5	4	34	18	6	3	10	20	34	40
Stoke	38	12	5	2	41	15	4	2	13	13	40	39
Everton	38	12	1	6	44	30	3	6	10	26	36	37
W Arsenal	38	12	4	3	43	21	3	3	13	19	43	37
Sheffield U	38	10	4	5	33	23	5	2	12	24	39	36
Sunderland	38	13	2	4	40	21	2	3	14	21	49	35
Derby Co	38	10	5	4	27	16	4	2	13	12	42	35
Notts Co	38	8	9	2	34	21	3	3	13	21	50	34
Bury	38	8	5	6	30	26	3	5	11	27	48	32
Middlesbrough	38	10	4	5	41	23	0	7	12	15	48	31
Nottingham F	38	11	2	6	40	27	2	3	14	18	52	31
Wolves	38	7	5	7	38	28	1	2	16	20	71	23

Reds' leading League goalscorer: Hewitt 23

DIVISION 1 1908-1909

	P	W	D	L	F	A	W	D	L	F	A	Pts
Newcastle U	38	14	1	4	32	20	10	4	5	33	21	53
Everton	38	11	3	5	51	28	7	7	5	31	29	46
Sunderland	38	14	0	5	41	23	7	2	10	37	40	44
Blackburn R	38	6	6	7	29	26	8	7	4	32	24	41
Sheffield W	38	15	0	4	48	24	2	6	11	19	37	40
W Arsenal	38	9	3	7	24	18	5	7	7	28	31	38
Aston Villa	38	8	7	4	31	22	6	3	10	27	34	38
Bristol C	38	7	7	5	24	25	6	5	8	21	33	38
Middlesbrough	38	11	2	6	38	21	3	7	9	21	32	37
Preston NE	38	8	7	4	29	17	5	4	10	19	27	37
Chelsea	38	8	7	4	33	22	6	2	11	23	39	37
Sheffield U	38	9	5	5	31	25	5	4	10	20	34	37
Manchester U	38	10	3	6	37	33	5	4	10	21	35	37
Nottingham F	38	9	2	8	39	24	5	6	8	27	33	36
Notts Co	38	9	4	6	31	23	5	4	10	20	25	36
LIVERPOOL	**38**	**9**	**5**	**5**	**36**	**25**	**6**	**1**	**12**	**21**	**40**	**36**
Bury	38	9	6	4	35	27	5	2	12	28	50	36
Bradford C	38	7	6	6	27	20	5	4	10	20	27	34
Manchester C	38	12	3	4	50	23	3	1	15	17	46	34
Leicester F	38	6	6	7	32	41	2	3	14	22	61	25

Reds' leading League goalscorer: Orr 20

DIVISION 1 1903-1904

	P	W	D	L	F	A	W	D	L	F	A	Pts
Sheffield W	34	14	3	0	34	10	6	4	7	14	18	47
Manchester C	34	10	4	3	35	19	9	2	6	36	26	44
Everton	34	13	0	4	36	12	6	5	6	23	20	43
Newcastle U	34	12	3	2	31	13	6	3	8	27	32	42
Aston Villa	34	13	1	3	41	16	4	6	7	29	32	41
Sunderland	34	12	3	2	41	15	5	2	10	22	34	39
Sheffield U	34	9	6	2	40	21	6	2	9	22	36	38
Wolves	34	10	6	1	29	23	4	2	11	15	43	36
Nottingham F	34	7	3	7	29	26	4	6	7	28	31	31
Middlesbrough	34	9	3	5	30	17	0	9	8	16	30	30
Small Heath	34	8	5	4	25	19	3	3	11	14	33	30
Bury	34	6	8	3	25	20	1	7	9	15	33	29
Notts Co	34	9	3	5	27	26	3	2	12	10	35	29
Derby Co	34	7	3	7	41	33	2	7	8	17	27	28
Blackburn R	34	7	5	5	29	23	4	1	12	19	37	28
Stoke	34	9	2	6	45	26	1	5	11	9	31	27
LIVERPOOL	**34**	**7**	**5**	**5**	**24**	**20**	**2**	**3**	**12**	**25**	**42**	**26**
WBA	34	4	8	5	19	19	3	2	12	17	41	24

Reds' leading League goalscorer: Cox 10

DIVISION 1 1906-1907

	P	W	D	L	F	A	W	D	L	F	A	Pts
Newcastle U	38	18	1	0	51	12	4	6	9	23	34	51
Bristol C	38	12	3	4	37	18	8	5	6	29	29	48
Everton	38	16	2	1	50	10	4	3	12	20	36	45
Sheffield U	38	13	4	2	36	17	4	7	8	21	38	45
Aston Villa	38	13	4	2	51	19	6	2	11	27	33	44
Bolton W	38	10	4	5	35	18	8	4	7	24	29	44
W Arsenal	38	15	1	3	38	15	5	3	11	28	44	44
Manchester U	38	10	6	3	33	15	7	2	10	20	41	42
Birmingham	38	13	5	1	41	17	2	3	14	11	35	38
Sunderland	38	10	4	5	42	31	4	5	10	23	35	37
Middlesbrough	38	11	2	6	33	21	4	4	11	23	42	36
Blackburn R	38	10	3	6	40	25	4	4	11	16	34	35
Sheffield W	38	8	5	6	33	26	4	6	9	16	34	35
Preston NE	38	13	4	2	35	19	1	3	15	9	38	35
LIVERPOOL	**38**	**9**	**2**	**8**	**45**	**32**	**4**	**5**	**10**	**19**	**33**	**33**
Bury	38	9	4	6	30	23	4	2	13	28	45	32
Manchester C	38	7	7	5	29	25	3	5	11	24	52	32
Notts Co	38	6	9	4	31	18	2	6	11	15	32	31
Derby Co	38	8	6	5	29	19	1	3	15	12	40	27
Stoke	38	7	6	6	27	22	1	4	14	14	42	26

Reds' leading League goalscorer: Raybould 15

DIVISION 1 1909-1910

	P	W	D	L	F	A	W	D	L	F	A	Pts
Aston Villa	38	17	2	0	62	19	6	5	8	22	23	53
LIVERPOOL	**38**	**13**	**3**	**3**	**47**	**23**	**8**	**3**	**8**	**31**	**34**	**48**
Blackburn R	38	13	6	0	47	17	5	3	11	26	38	45
Newcastle U	38	11	3	5	33	22	8	4	7	37	34	45
Manchester U	38	14	2	3	41	20	5	5	9	28	41	45
Sheffield U	38	10	5	4	42	19	6	5	8	20	22	42
Bradford C	38	12	3	4	38	17	5	5	9	26	30	42
Sunderland	38	12	3	4	40	18	6	2	11	26	33	41
Notts Co	38	10	5	4	41	26	5	5	9	26	33	40
Everton	38	8	6	5	30	28	8	2	9	21	28	40
Sheffield W	38	11	4	4	38	28	4	5	10	22	35	39
Preston NE	38	14	2	3	36	13	1	3	15	16	45	35
Bury	38	8	3	8	35	30	4	6	9	27	36	33
Nottingham F	38	4	7	8	19	34	7	4	8	35	38	33
Tottenham H	38	10	6	3	35	23	1	4	14	18	46	32
Bristol C	38	9	5	5	28	18	3	3	13	17	42	32
Middlesbrough	38	8	4	7	34	36	3	5	11	22	37	31
W Arsenal	38	6	5	8	17	19	5	4	10	20	48	31
Chelsea	38	10	4	5	32	24	1	3	15	15	46	29
Bolton W	38	7	2	10	31	34	2	4	13	13	37	24

Reds' leading League goalscorer: Orr 20

DIVISION 2 1904-1905

	P	W	D	L	F	A	W	D	L	F	A	Pts
LIVERPOOL	**34**	**14**	**3**	**0**	**60**	**12**	**13**	**1**	**3**	**33**	**13**	**58**
Bolton W	34	15	0	2	53	16	12	2	3	34	16	56
Manchester U	34	16	0	1	60	10	8	5	4	21	20	53
Bristol C	34	12	3	2	40	12	7	1	9	26	33	42
Chesterfield	34	9	6	2	26	11	5	5	7	18	24	39
Gainsboro' T	34	11	4	2	32	15	3	4	10	29	43	36
Barnsley	34	11	4	2	29	13	3	1	13	9	43	33
Bradford C	34	8	5	4	31	20	4	3	10	14	29	32
Lincoln C	34	9	4	4	31	16	3	3	11	11	24	31
WBA	34	8	2	7	28	20	5	2	10	28	28	30
Burnley	34	10	1	6	31	21	2	5	10	12	31	30
Glossop	34	7	5	5	23	14	3	5	9	14	32	30
Grimsby T	34	9	3	5	22	14	2	5	10	11	32	30
Leicester F	34	8	3	6	30	25	3	4	10	10	30	29
Blackpool	34	8	5	4	26	15	1	5	11	10	33	28
Burslem PV	34	7	4	6	28	25	3	3	11	19	47	27
Burton U	34	7	2	8	20	29	1	2	14	10	55	20
Doncaster R	34	3	2	12	12	32	0	0	17	11	49	8

Reds' leading League goalscorer: Robinson 23

DIVISION 1 1907-1908

	P	W	D	L	F	A	W	D	L	F	A	Pts
Manchester U	38	15	1	3	43	19	8	5	6	38	29	52
Aston Villa	38	9	6	4	47	24	8	3	8	30	35	43
Manchester C	38	12	5	2	36	19	4	6	9	26	35	43
Newcastle U	38	11	4	4	41	24	4	8	7	24	30	42
Sheffield W	38	14	0	5	50	25	5	4	10	23	39	42
Middlesbrough	38	12	2	5	32	16	5	5	9	22	29	41
Bury	38	8	7	4	29	22	6	4	9	29	39	39
LIVERPOOL	**38**	**11**	**2**	**6**	**43**	**24**	**5**	**4**	**10**	**25**	**37**	**38**
Nottingham F	38	11	6	2	42	21	2	5	12	17	41	37
Bristol C	38	8	7	4	29	21	4	5	10	29	40	36
Everton	38	11	4	4	34	24	4	2	13	24	40	36
Preston NE	38	9	7	3	33	18	3	5	11	14	35	36
Chelsea	38	8	3	8	30	35	6	5	8	23	27	36
W Arsenal	38	9	8	2	32	18	3	4	12	19	45	*36
Blackburn R	38	10	7	2	35	23	2	5	12	16	40	*36
Sunderland	38	11	2	6	53	31	5	1	3	25	44	35
Sheffield U	38	8	6	5	27	22	4	5	10	25	36	35
Notts Co	38	9	3	7	24	19	4	5	10	15	32	34
Bolton W	38	10	3	6	35	26	4	2	13	17	32	33
Birmingham	38	6	6	7	22	28	3	6	10	18	32	30

**Woolwich Arsenal & Blackburn Rovers finished in equal 14th place*

Reds' leading League goalscorer: J.Hewitt 21

DIVISION 1 1910-1911

	P	W	D	L	F	A	W	D	L	F	A	Pts
Manchester U	38	14	4	1	47	18	8	4	7	25	22	52
Aston Villa	38	15	3	1	50	18	7	4	8	19	23	51
Sunderland	38	10	6	3	44	22	5	9	5	23	26	45
Everton	38	12	3	4	34	17	7	4	8	16	19	45
Bradford C	38	13	1	5	33	16	7	4	8	18	26	45
Sheffield W	38	10	5	4	24	15	7	3	9	23	33	42
Oldham A	38	13	4	2	30	12	3	5	11	14	29	41
Newcastle U	38	8	7	4	37	18	7	3	9	24	25	40
Sheffield U	38	8	3	8	27	21	7	5	7	22	22	38
W Arsenal	38	9	6	4	24	14	4	6	9	17	35	38
Notts Co	38	9	6	4	21	16	5	4	10	16	29	38
Blackburn R	38	12	2	5	40	14	1	9	9	22	40	37
LIVERPOOL	**38**	**11**	**3**	**5**	**38**	**19**	**4**	**4**	**11**	**15**	**34**	**37**
Preston NE	38	8	5	6	25	19	4	6	9	15	30	35
Tottenham H	38	10	5	4	40	23	3	1	15	12	40	32
Middlesbrough	38	9	5	5	31	21	2	5	12	18	42	32
Manchester C	38	7	5	7	26	26	2	8	9	17	32	31
Bury	38	8	9	2	27	18	1	2	16	16	53	29
Bristol C	38	8	4	7	23	21	3	1	15	20	45	27
Nottingham F	38	5	4	10	28	31	4	3	12	27	44	25

Reds' leading League goalscorer: Parkinson 19

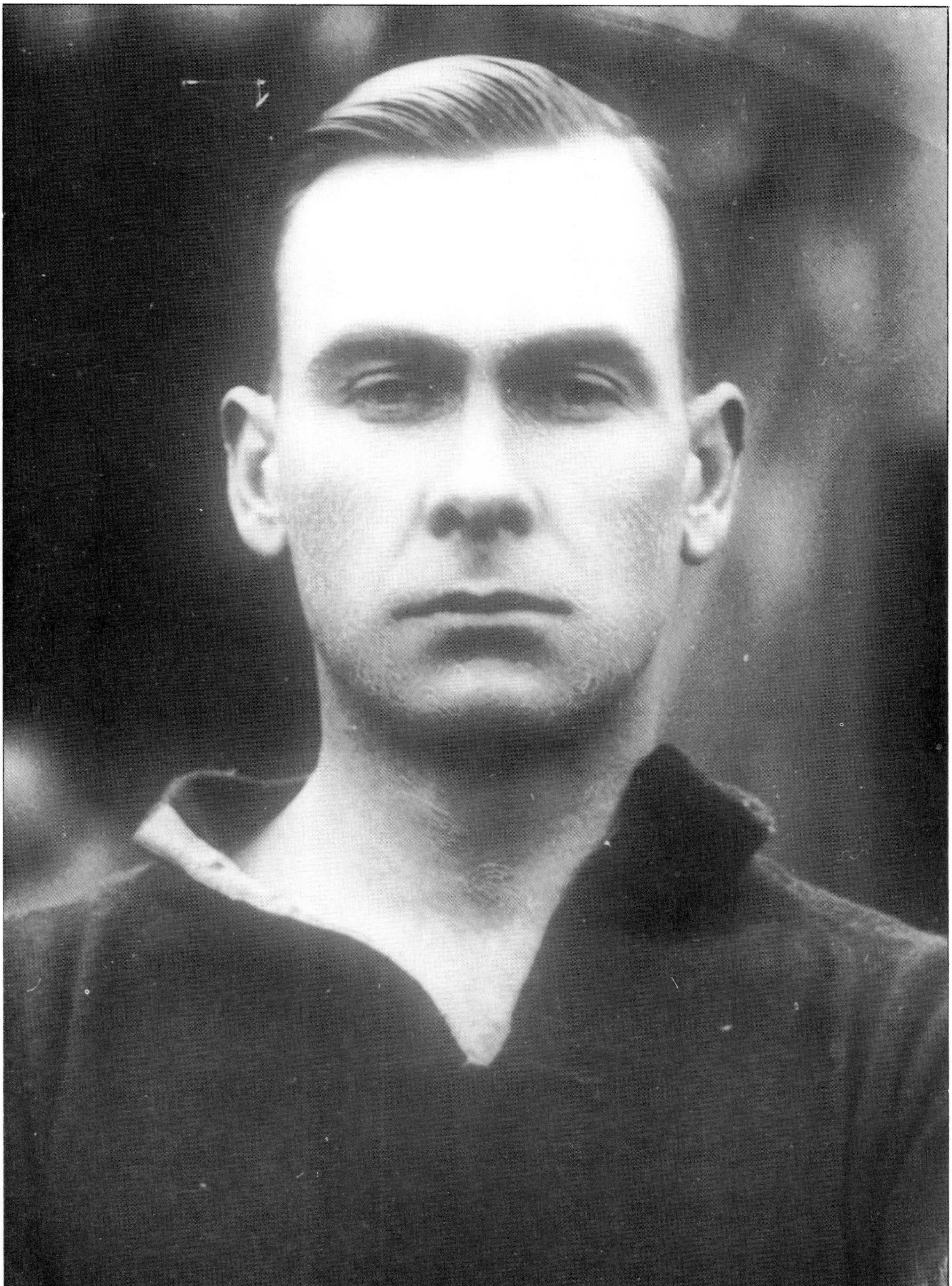

Gordon Hodgson scored 240 goals in 378 League and FA Cup appearances for Liverpool after joining the Anfield club from South African football during the 1925-6 season. Hodgson set a club record with 36 League goals in 1930-31. He was capped for England three times and his overall tally of 232 League goals was a club record until Roger Hunt surpassed it. Hodgson was transferred to Leeds United in December 1935.

DIVISION 1 1911-1912

	P	W	D	L	F	A	W	D	L	F	A	Pts
Blackburn R	38	13	6	0	35	10	7	3	9	25	33	49
Everton	38	13	5	1	29	12	7	1	11	17	30	46
Newcastle U	38	10	4	5	37	25	8	4	7	27	25	44
Bolton W	38	14	2	3	35	15	6	1	12	19	28	43
Sheffield W	38	11	3	5	44	17	5	6	8	25	32	41
Aston Villa	38	12	2	5	48	22	5	5	9	28	41	41
Middlesbrough	38	11	6	2	35	17	5	2	12	21	28	40
Sunderland	38	10	6	3	37	14	4	5	10	21	37	39
WBA	38	10	6	3	23	15	5	3	11	20	32	39
W Arsenal	38	12	3	4	38	19	3	5	11	17	40	38
Bradford C	38	12	3	4	31	15	3	5	11	15	35	38
Tottenham H	38	10	4	5	35	20	4	5	10	18	33	37
Manchester U	38	9	5	5	29	19	4	6	9	16	41	37
Sheffield U	38	10	4	5	47	29	3	6	10	16	27	36
Manchester C	38	10	5	4	39	20	3	4	12	17	38	35
Notts Co	38	9	4	6	26	20	5	3	11	20	43	35
LIVERPOOL	**38**	**8**	**4**	**7**	**27**	**23**	**4**	**6**	**9**	**22**	**32**	**34**
Oldham A	38	10	3	6	32	19	2	7	10	14	35	34
Preston NE	38	8	4	7	26	25	5	3	11	14	32	33
Bury	38	6	5	8	23	25	0	4	15	9	34	21

Reds' leading League goalscorer: Parkinson 12

DIVISION 1 1912-1913

	P	W	D	L	F	A	W	D	L	F	A	Pts
Sunderland	38	14	2	3	47	17	11	2	6	39	26	54
Aston Villa	38	13	4	2	57	21	6	8	5	29	31	50
Sheffield W	38	12	4	3	44	23	9	3	7	31	32	49
Manchester U	38	13	3	3	41	14	6	5	8	28	29	46
Blackburn R	38	10	5	4	54	21	6	8	5	25	22	45
Manchester C	38	12	3	4	34	15	6	5	8	19	22	44
Derby Co	38	10	2	7	40	29	7	6	6	29	37	42
Bolton W	38	10	6	3	36	20	6	4	9	26	43	42
Oldham A	38	11	7	1	33	12	3	7	9	17	43	42
WBA	38	8	7	4	30	20	5	5	9	27	30	38
Everton	38	8	2	9	28	31	7	5	7	20	23	37
LIVERPOOL	**38**	**12**	**2**	**5**	**40**	**24**	**4**	**3**	**12**	**21**	**47**	**37**
Bradford C	38	10	5	4	33	22	2	6	11	17	38	35
Newcastle U	38	8	5	6	30	23	5	3	11	17	24	34
Sheffield U	38	10	5	4	36	24	4	1	14	20	46	34
Middlesbrough	38	6	9	4	29	22	5	1	13	26	47	32
Tottenham H	38	9	3	7	28	25	3	3	13	17	47	30
Chelsea	38	7	2	10	29	40	4	4	11	22	33	28
Notts Co	38	6	4	9	19	20	1	5	13	9	36	23
W Arsenal	38	1	8	10	11	31	2	4	13	15	43	18

Reds' leading League goalscorer: Metcalfe 15

DIVISION 1 1913-1914

	P	W	D	L	F	A	W	D	L	F	A	Pts
Blackburn R	38	14	4	1	51	15	6	7	6	27	27	51
Aston Villa	38	11	3	5	36	21	8	3	8	29	29	44
Middlesbrough	38	14	2	3	55	20	5	3	11	22	40	43
Oldham A	38	11	5	3	34	16	6	4	9	21	29	43
WBA	38	11	7	1	30	16	4	6	9	16	26	43
Bolton W	38	13	4	2	41	14	3	6	10	24	38	42
Sunderland	38	11	3	5	32	17	6	3	10	31	35	40
Chelsea	38	12	3	4	28	18	4	4	11	18	37	39
Bradford C	38	8	6	5	23	17	4	8	7	17	23	38
Sheffield U	38	11	4	4	36	19	5	1	13	27	41	37
Newcastle U	38	9	6	4	27	18	4	5	10	12	30	37
Burnley	38	10	4	5	43	20	2	8	9	18	33	36
Manchester C	38	9	3	7	28	23	5	5	9	23	30	36
Manchester U	38	8	4	7	27	23	7	2	10	25	39	36
Everton	38	8	7	4	32	18	4	4	11	14	37	35
LIVERPOOL	**38**	**8**	**4**	**7**	**27**	**25**	**6**	**3**	**10**	**19**	**37**	**35**
Tottenham H	38	9	6	4	30	19	3	4	12	20	43	34
Sheffield W	38	8	4	7	34	34	5	4	10	19	36	34
Preston NE	38	9	4	6	39	31	3	2	14	13	38	30
Derby Co	38	6	5	8	34	32	2	6	11	21	39	27

Reds' leading League goalscorer: Miller 16

DIVISION 1 1914-1915

	P	W	D	L	F	A	W	D	L	F	A	Pts
Everton	38	8	5	6	44	29	11	3	5	32	18	46
Oldham A	38	11	5	3	46	25	6	6	7	24	31	45
Blackburn R	38	11	4	4	51	27	7	3	9	32	34	43
Burnley	38	12	1	6	38	18	6	6	7	23	29	43
Manchester C	38	9	7	3	29	15	6	6	7	20	24	43
Sheffield U	38	11	5	3	28	13	4	8	7	21	28	43
Sheffield W	38	10	7	2	43	23	5	6	8	18	31	43
Sunderland	38	11	3	5	46	30	7	2	10	35	42	41
Bradford	38	11	4	4	40	20	6	3	10	29	45	41
WBA	38	11	5	3	31	9	4	5	10	18	34	40
Bradford C	38	11	7	1	40	18	2	7	10	15	31	40
Middlesbrough	38	10	6	3	42	24	3	6	10	20	50	38
LIVERPOOL	**38**	**11**	**5**	**3**	**45**	**34**	**3**	**4**	**12**	**20**	**41**	**37**
Aston Villa	38	10	5	4	39	32	3	6	10	23	40	37
Newcastle U	38	8	4	7	29	23	3	6	10	17	25	32
Notts Co	38	8	7	4	28	18	1	6	12	13	39	31
Bolton W	38	8	5	6	35	27	3	3	13	33	57	30
Manchester U	38	8	6	5	27	19	1	6	12	19	43	30
Chelsea	38	8	6	5	32	25	0	7	12	19	40	29
Tottenham H	38	7	7	5	30	29	1	5	13	27	61	28

Reds' leading League goalscorer: Pagnam 24

DIVISION 1 1919-1920

	P	W	D	L	F	A	W	D	L	F	A	Pts
WBA	42	17	1	3	65	21	11	3	7	39	26	60
Burnley	42	13	5	3	43	27	8	4	9	22	32	51
Chelsea	42	15	3	3	33	10	7	2	12	23	41	49
LIVERPOOL	**42**	**12**	**5**	**4**	**35**	**18**	**7**	**5**	**9**	**24**	**26**	**48**
Sunderland	42	17	2	2	45	16	5	2	14	27	43	48
Bolton W	42	11	3	7	35	29	8	6	7	37	36	47
Manchester C	42	14	5	2	52	27	4	4	13	19	35	45
Newcastle U	42	11	5	5	31	13	6	4	11	13	26	43
Aston Villa	42	11	3	7	49	36	7	3	11	26	37	42
Arsenal	42	11	5	5	32	21	4	7	10	24	37	42
Bradford	42	8	6	7	31	26	7	6	8	29	37	42
Manchester U	42	6	8	7	20	17	7	6	8	34	33	40
Middlesbrough	42	10	5	6	35	23	5	5	11	26	42	40
Sheffield U	42	14	5	2	43	20	2	3	16	16	49	40
Bradford C	42	10	6	5	36	25	4	5	12	18	38	39
Everton	42	8	6	7	42	29	4	8	9	27	39	38
Oldham A	42	12	4	5	33	19	3	4	14	16	33	38
Derby Co	42	12	5	4	36	18	1	7	13	11	39	38
Preston NE	42	9	6	6	35	27	5	4	12	22	46	38
Blackburn R	42	11	4	6	48	30	2	7	12	16	47	37
Notts Co	42	9	8	4	39	25	3	4	14	17	49	36
Sheffield W	42	6	4	11	14	23	1	5	15	14	41	23

Reds' leading League goalscorer: Chambers 15

DIVISION 1 1920-1921

	P	W	D	L	F	A	W	D	L	F	A	Pts
Burnley	42	17	3	1	56	16	6	10	5	23	20	59
Manchester C	42	19	2	0	50	13	5	4	12	20	37	54
Bolton W	42	15	6	0	53	17	4	8	9	24	36	52
LIVERPOOL	**42**	**11**	**7**	**3**	**41**	**17**	**7**	**8**	**6**	**22**	**18**	**51**
Newcastle U	42	14	3	4	43	18	6	7	8	23	27	50
Tottenham H	42	15	2	4	46	16	4	7	10	24	32	47
Everton	42	9	8	4	40	26	8	5	8	26	29	47
Middlesbrough	42	10	6	5	29	21	7	6	8	24	32	46
Arsenal	42	9	8	4	31	25	6	6	9	28	38	44
Aston Villa	42	11	4	6	39	21	7	3	11	24	49	43
Blackburn R	42	7	9	5	36	27	6	6	9	21	32	41
Sunderland	42	11	4	6	34	19	3	9	9	23	41	41
Manchester U	42	9	4	8	34	26	6	6	9	30	42	40
WBA	42	8	7	6	31	23	5	7	9	23	35	40
Bradford C	42	7	9	5	38	28	5	6	10	23	35	39
Preston NE	42	10	4	7	38	25	5	5	11	23	40	39
Huddersfield T	42	11	4	6	26	16	4	5	12	16	33	39
Chelsea	42	9	7	5	35	24	4	6	11	13	34	39
Oldham A	42	6	9	6	23	26	3	6	12	26	60	33
Sheffield U	42	5	11	5	22	19	1	7	13	20	49	30
Derby Co	42	3	12	6	21	23	2	4	15	11	35	26
Bradford	42	6	5	10	29	35	2	3	16	14	41	24

Reds' leading League goalscorer: Chambers 22

DIVISION 1 1921-1922

	P	W	D	L	F	A	W	D	L	F	A	Pts
LIVERPOOL	**42**	**15**	**4**	**2**	**43**	**15**	**7**	**9**	**5**	**20**	**21**	**57**
Tottenham H	42	15	3	3	43	17	6	6	9	22	22	51
Burnley	42	16	3	2	49	18	6	2	13	23	36	49
Cardiff C	42	13	2	6	40	26	6	8	7	21	27	48
Aston Villa	42	16	3	2	50	19	6	0	15	24	36	47
Bolton W	42	12	4	5	40	24	8	3	10	28	35	47
Newcastle U	42	11	5	5	36	19	7	5	9	23	26	46
Middlesbrough	42	12	6	3	46	19	4	8	9	33	50	46
Chelsea	42	9	6	6	17	16	8	6	7	23	27	46
Manchester C	42	13	7	1	44	21	5	2	14	21	49	45
Sheffield U	42	11	3	7	32	17	4	7	10	27	37	40
Sunderland	42	13	4	4	46	23	3	4	14	14	39	40
WBA	42	8	6	7	26	23	7	4	10	25	40	40
Huddersfield T	42	12	3	6	33	14	3	6	12	20	40	39
Blackburn R	42	7	6	8	35	31	6	6	9	19	26	38
Preston NE	42	12	7	2	33	20	1	5	15	9	45	38
Arsenal	42	10	6	5	27	19	5	1	15	20	37	37
Birmingham	42	9	2	10	25	29	6	5	10	23	31	37
Oldham A	42	8	7	6	21	15	5	4	12	17	35	37
Everton	42	10	7	4	42	22	2	5	14	15	33	36
Bradford C	42	8	5	8	28	30	3	5	13	20	42	32
Manchester U	42	7	7	7	25	26	1	5	15	16	47	28

Reds' leading League goalscorer: Chambers 19

DIVISION 1 1922-1923

	P	W	D	L	F	A	W	D	L	F	A	Pts
LIVERPOOL	**42**	**17**	**3**	**1**	**50**	**13**	**9**	**5**	**7**	**20**	**18**	**60**
Sunderland	42	15	5	1	50	25	7	5	9	22	29	54
Huddersfield T	42	14	2	5	35	15	7	9	5	25	17	53
Newcastle U	42	13	6	2	31	11	5	6	10	14	26	48
Everton	42	14	4	3	41	20	6	3	12	22	39	47
Aston Villa	42	15	3	3	42	11	3	7	11	22	40	46
WBA	42	12	7	2	38	10	5	4	12	20	39	45
Manchester C	42	14	6	1	38	16	3	5	13	12	33	45
Cardiff C	42	15	2	4	51	18	3	5	13	22	41	43
Sheffield U	42	11	7	3	41	20	5	3	13	27	44	42
Arsenal	42	13	4	4	38	16	3	6	12	23	46	42
Tottenham H	42	11	3	7	34	22	6	4	11	16	28	41
Bolton W	42	11	8	2	36	17	3	4	14	14	41	40
Blackburn R	42	12	7	2	32	19	2	5	14	15	43	40
Burnley	42	12	3	6	39	24	4	3	14	19	35	38
Preston NE	42	12	3	6	41	26	1	8	12	19	38	37
Birmingham	42	10	4	7	25	19	3	7	11	16	38	37
Middlesbrough	42	11	4	6	41	25	2	6	13	16	38	36
Chelsea	42	5	13	3	29	20	4	5	12	16	33	36
Nottingham F	42	12	2	7	25	23	1	6	14	16	47	34
Stoke	42	7	9	5	28	19	3	1	17	19	48	30
Oldham A	42	9	6	6	21	20	1	4	16	14	45	30

Reds' leading League goalscorer: Chambers 22

DIVISION 1 1923-1924

	P	W	D	L	F	A	W	D	L	F	A	Pts
Huddersfield T	42	15	5	1	35	9	8	6	7	25	24	57
Cardiff C	42	14	5	2	35	13	8	8	5	26	21	57
Sunderland	42	12	7	2	38	20	10	2	9	33	34	53
Bolton W	42	13	6	2	45	13	5	8	8	23	21	50
Sheffield U	42	12	5	4	39	16	7	7	7	30	33	50
Aston Villa	42	10	10	1	33	11	8	3	10	19	26	49
Everton	42	13	7	1	43	18	5	6	10	19	35	49
Blackburn R	42	14	5	2	40	13	3	6	12	14	37	45
Newcastle U	42	13	5	3	40	21	4	5	12	20	33	44
Notts Co	42	9	7	5	21	15	5	7	9	23	34	42
Manchester C	42	11	7	3	34	24	4	5	12	20	47	42
LIVERPOOL	**42**	**11**	**5**	**5**	**35**	**20**	**4**	**6**	**11**	**14**	**28**	**41**
West Ham U	42	10	6	5	26	17	3	9	9	14	26	41
Birmingham	42	10	4	7	25	19	3	9	9	16	30	39
Tottenham H	42	9	6	6	30	22	3	8	10	20	34	38
WBA	42	10	6	5	43	30	2	8	11	8	32	38
Burnley	42	10	5	6	39	27	2	7	12	16	33	36
Preston NE	42	8	4	9	34	27	4	6	11	18	40	34
Arsenal	42	8	5	8	25	24	4	4	13	15	39	33
Nottingham F	42	7	9	5	19	15	3	3	15	23	49	32
Chelsea	42	7	9	5	23	21	2	5	14	8	32	32
Middlesbrough	42	6	4	11	23	23	1	4	16	14	37	22

Reds' leading League goalscorer: Walsh 16

DIVISION 1 1924-1925

	P	W	D	L	F	A	W	D	L	F	A	Pts
Huddersfield T	42	10	8	3	31	10	11	8	2	38	18	58
WBA	42	13	6	2	40	17	10	4	7	18	17	56
Bolton W	42	18	2	1	61	13	4	9	8	15	21	55
LIVERPOOL	**42**	**13**	**5**	**3**	**43**	**20**	**7**	**5**	**9**	**20**	**35**	**50**
Bury	42	13	4	4	35	20	4	11	6	19	31	49
Newcastle U	42	11	6	4	43	18	5	10	6	18	24	48
Sunderland	42	13	6	2	39	14	6	4	11	25	37	48
Birmingham	42	10	8	3	27	17	7	4	10	22	36	46
Notts Co	42	11	6	4	29	12	5	7	9	13	19	45
Manchester C	42	11	7	3	44	29	6	2	13	32	39	43
Cardiff C	42	11	5	5	35	19	5	6	10	21	32	43
Tottenham H	42	9	8	4	32	16	6	4	11	20	27	42
West Ham U	42	12	7	2	37	12	3	5	13	25	48	42
Sheffield U	42	10	5	6	34	25	3	8	10	21	38	39
Aston Villa	42	10	7	4	34	25	3	6	12	24	46	39
Blackburn R	42	7	6	8	31	26	4	7	10	22	40	35
Everton	42	11	4	6	25	20	1	7	13	15	40	35
Leeds U	42	9	8	4	29	17	2	4	15	17	42	34
Burnley	42	7	8	6	28	31	4	4	13	18	44	34
Arsenal	42	12	3	6	33	17	2	2	17	13	41	33
Preston NE	42	8	2	11	29	35	2	4	15	8	39	26
Nottingham F	42	5	6	10	17	23	1	6	14	12	42	24

Reds' leading League goalscorer: Forshaw 19

DIVISION 1 1925-1926

	P	W	D	L	F	A	W	D	L	F	A	Pts
Huddersfield T	42	14	6	1	50	17	9	5	7	42	43	57
Arsenal	42	16	2	3	57	19	6	6	9	30	44	52
Sunderland	42	17	2	2	67	30	4	4	13	29	50	48
Bury	42	12	4	5	55	34	8	3	10	30	43	47
Sheffield U	42	15	3	3	72	29	4	5	12	30	53	46
Aston Villa	42	12	7	2	56	25	4	5	12	30	51	44
LIVERPOOL	**42**	**9**	**8**	**4**	**43**	**27**	**5**	**8**	**8**	**27**	**36**	**44**
Bolton W	42	11	6	4	46	31	6	4	11	29	45	44
Manchester U	42	12	4	5	40	26	7	2	12	26	47	44
Newcastle U	42	13	3	5	59	33	3	7	11	25	42	42
Everton	42	9	9	3	42	26	3	9	9	30	44	42
Blackburn R	42	11	6	4	59	33	4	5	12	32	47	41
WBA	42	13	5	3	59	29	3	3	15	20	49	40
Birmingham	42	14	2	5	35	25	2	6	13	31	56	40
Tottenham H	42	11	4	6	45	36	4	5	12	21	43	39
Cardiff C	42	8	5	8	30	25	8	2	11	31	51	39
Leicester C	42	11	3	7	42	32	3	7	11	28	48	38
West Ham U	42	14	2	5	45	27	1	5	15	18	49	37
Leeds U	42	11	5	5	38	28	3	3	15	26	48	36
Burnley	42	7	7	7	43	35	6	3	12	42	73	36
Manchester C	42	8	7	6	48	42	4	4	13	41	58	35
Notts Co	42	11	4	6	37	26	2	3	16	17	48	33

Reds' leading League goalscorer: Forshaw 27

DIVISION 1 1926-1927

	P	W	D	L	F	A	W	D	L	F	A	Pts
Newcastle U	42	19	1	1	64	20	6	5	10	32	38	56
Huddersfield T	42	13	6	2	41	19	4	11	6	35	41	51
Sunderland	42	15	3	3	70	28	6	4	11	28	42	49
Bolton W	42	15	5	1	54	19	4	5	12	30	43	48
Burnley	42	15	4	2	55	30	4	5	12	36	50	47
West Ham U	42	9	6	6	50	36	10	2	9	36	34	46
Leicester C	42	13	4	4	58	33	4	8	9	27	37	46
Sheffield U	42	12	6	3	46	33	5	4	12	28	53	44
LIVERPOOL	**42**	**13**	**4**	**4**	**47**	**27**	**5**	**3**	**13**	**22**	**34**	**43**
Aston Villa	42	11	4	6	51	34	7	3	11	30	49	43
Arsenal	42	12	5	4	47	30	5	4	12	30	56	43
Derby Co	42	14	4	3	60	28	3	3	15	26	45	41
Tottenham H	42	11	4	6	48	33	5	5	11	28	45	41
Cardiff C	42	12	3	6	31	17	4	6	11	24	48	41
Manchester U	42	9	8	4	29	19	4	6	11	23	45	40
Sheffield W	42	15	3	3	49	29	0	6	15	26	63	39
Birmingham	42	13	3	5	36	17	4	1	16	28	56	38
Blackburn R	42	9	5	7	40	40	6	3	12	37	56	38
Bury	42	8	5	8	43	38	4	7	10	25	39	36
Everton	42	10	6	5	35	30	2	4	15	29	60	34
Leeds U	42	9	7	5	43	31	2	1	18	26	57	30
WBA	42	10	4	7	47	33	1	4	16	18	53	30

Reds' leading League goalscorer: Chambers 17

DIVISION 1 1927-1928

	P	W	D	L	F	A	W	D	L	F	A	Pts
Everton	42	11	8	2	60	28	9	5	7	42	38	53
Huddersfield T	42	15	1	5	57	31	7	6	8	34	37	51
Leicester C	42	14	5	2	66	25	4	7	10	30	47	48
Derby Co	42	12	4	5	59	30	5	6	10	37	53	44
Bury	42	13	1	7	53	35	7	3	11	27	45	44
Cardiff C	42	12	7	2	44	27	5	3	13	26	53	44
Bolton W	42	12	5	4	47	26	4	6	11	34	40	43
Aston Villa	42	13	3	5	52	30	4	6	11	26	43	43
Newcastle U	42	9	7	5	49	41	6	6	9	30	40	43
Arsenal	42	10	6	5	49	33	3	9	9	33	53	41
Birmingham	42	10	7	4	36	25	3	8	10	34	50	41
Blackburn R	42	13	5	3	41	22	3	4	14	25	56	41
Sheffield U	42	12	4	5	56	42	3	6	12	23	44	40
Sheffield W	42	9	6	6	45	29	4	7	10	36	49	39
Sunderland	42	9	5	7	37	29	6	4	11	37	47	39
LIVERPOOL	**42**	**10**	**6**	**5**	**54**	**36**	**3**	**7**	**11**	**30**	**51**	**39**
West Ham U	42	9	7	5	48	34	5	4	12	33	54	39
Manchester U	42	12	6	3	51	27	4	1	16	21	53	39
Burnley	42	12	5	4	55	31	4	2	15	27	67	39
Portsmouth	42	13	4	4	40	23	3	3	15	26	67	39
Tottenham H	42	12	3	6	47	34	3	5	13	27	52	38
Middlesbrough	42	7	9	5	46	35	4	6	11	35	53	37

Reds' leading League goalscorer: Hodgson 23

DIVISION 1 1928-1929

	P	W	D	L	F	A	W	D	L	F	A	Pts
Sheffield W	42	18	3	0	55	16	3	7	11	31	46	52
Leicester C	42	16	5	0	67	22	5	4	12	29	45	51
Aston Villa	42	16	2	3	62	30	7	2	12	36	51	50
Sunderland	42	16	2	3	67	30	4	5	12	26	45	47
LIVERPOOL	**42**	**11**	**4**	**6**	**53**	**28**	**6**	**8**	**7**	**37**	**36**	**46**
Derby Co	42	12	5	4	56	24	6	5	10	30	47	46
Blackburn R	42	11	6	4	42	26	6	5	10	30	37	45
Manchester C	42	12	3	6	63	40	6	6	9	32	46	45
Arsenal	42	11	6	4	43	25	5	7	9	34	47	45
Newcastle U	42	15	2	4	48	29	4	4	13	22	43	44
Sheffield U	42	12	5	4	57	30	3	6	12	29	55	41
Manchester U	42	8	8	5	32	23	6	5	10	34	53	41
Leeds U	42	11	5	5	42	28	5	4	12	29	56	41
Bolton W	42	10	6	5	44	25	4	6	11	29	55	40
Birmingham	42	8	7	6	37	32	7	3	11	31	45	40
Huddersfield T	42	9	6	6	45	23	5	5	11	25	38	39
West Ham U	42	11	6	4	55	31	4	3	14	31	65	39
Everton	42	11	2	8	38	31	6	2	13	25	44	38
Burnley	42	12	5	4	55	32	3	3	15	26	71	38
Portsmouth	42	13	2	6	43	26	2	4	15	13	54	36
Bury	42	9	5	7	38	35	3	2	16	24	64	31
Cardiff C	42	7	7	7	34	26	1	6	14	9	33	29

Reds' leading League goalscorer: Hodgson 30

DIVISION 1 1929-1930

	P	W	D	L	F	A	W	D	L	F	A	Pts
Sheffield W	42	15	4	2	56	20	11	4	6	49	37	60
Derby Co	42	16	4	1	61	32	5	4	12	29	50	50
Manchester C	42	12	5	4	51	33	7	4	10	40	48	47
Aston Villa	42	13	1	7	54	33	8	4	9	38	50	47
Leeds U	42	15	2	4	52	22	5	4	12	27	41	46
Blackburn R	42	15	2	4	65	36	4	5	12	34	57	45
West Ham U	42	14	2	5	51	26	5	3	13	35	53	43
Leicester C	42	12	5	4	57	42	5	4	12	29	48	43
Sunderland	42	13	3	5	50	35	5	4	12	26	45	43
Huddersfield T	42	9	7	5	32	21	8	2	11	31	48	43
Birmingham	42	13	3	5	40	21	3	6	12	27	41	41
LIVERPOOL	**42**	**11**	**5**	**5**	**33**	**29**	**5**	**4**	**12**	**30**	**50**	**41**
Portsmouth	42	10	6	5	43	25	5	4	12	23	37	40
Arsenal	42	10	2	9	49	26	4	9	8	29	40	39
Bolton W	42	11	5	5	46	24	4	4	13	28	50	39
Middlesbrough	42	11	3	7	48	31	5	3	13	34	53	38
Manchester U	42	11	4	6	39	34	4	4	13	28	54	38
Grimsby T	42	8	6	7	39	39	7	1	13	34	50	37
Newcastle U	42	13	4	4	52	32	2	3	16	19	60	37
Sheffield U	42	12	2	7	59	39	3	4	14	32	57	36
Burnley	42	11	5	5	53	34	3	3	15	26	63	36
Everton	42	6	7	8	48	46	6	4	11	32	46	35

Reds' leading League goalscorer: Smith 23

DIVISION 1 1930-1931

	P	W	D	L	F	A	W	D	L	F	A	Pts
Arsenal	42	14	5	2	67	27	14	5	2	60	32	66
Aston Villa	42	17	3	1	86	34	8	6	7	42	44	59
Sheffield W	42	14	3	4	65	32	8	5	8	37	43	52
Portsmouth	42	11	7	3	46	26	7	6	8	38	41	49
Huddersfield T	42	10	8	3	45	27	8	4	9	36	38	48
Derby Co	42	12	6	3	56	31	6	4	11	38	48	46
Middlesbrough	42	13	5	3	57	28	6	3	12	41	62	46
Manchester C	42	13	2	6	41	29	5	8	8	34	41	46
LIVERPOOL	**42**	**11**	**6**	**4**	**48**	**28**	**4**	**6**	**11**	**38**	**57**	**42**
Blackburn R	42	14	3	4	54	28	3	5	13	29	56	42
Sunderland	42	12	4	5	61	38	4	5	12	28	47	41
Chelsea	42	13	4	4	42	19	2	6	13	22	48	40
Grimsby T	42	13	2	6	55	31	4	3	14	27	56	39
Bolton W	42	12	6	3	45	26	3	3	15	23	55	39
Sheffield U	42	10	7	4	49	31	4	3	14	29	53	38
Leicester C	42	12	4	5	50	38	4	2	15	30	57	38
Newcastle U	42	9	2	10	41	45	6	4	11	37	42	36
West Ham U	42	11	3	7	56	44	3	5	13	23	50	36
Birmingham	42	11	3	7	37	28	2	7	12	18	42	36
Blackpool	42	8	7	6	41	44	3	3	15	30	81	32
Leeds U	42	10	3	8	49	31	2	4	15	19	50	31
Manchester U	42	6	6	9	30	37	1	2	18	23	78	22

Reds' leading League goalscorer: Hodgson 36

DIVISION 1 1931-1932

	P	W	D	L	F	A	W	D	L	F	A	Pts
Everton	42	18	0	3	84	30	8	4	9	32	34	56
Arsenal	42	14	5	2	52	16	8	5	8	38	32	54
Sheffield W	42	14	4	3	60	28	8	2	11	36	54	50
Huddersfield T	42	11	8	2	47	21	8	2	11	33	42	48
Aston Villa	42	15	1	5	64	28	4	7	10	40	44	46
WBA	42	12	4	5	46	21	8	2	11	31	34	46
Sheffield U	42	13	3	5	47	32	7	3	11	33	43	46
Portsmouth	42	14	2	5	37	21	5	5	11	25	41	45
Birmingham	42	13	5	3	48	22	5	3	13	30	45	44
LIVERPOOL	**42**	**13**	**4**	**4**	**56**	**38**	**6**	**2**	**13**	**25**	**55**	**44**
Newcastle U	42	13	5	3	52	31	5	1	15	28	56	42
Chelsea	42	12	4	5	43	27	4	4	13	26	46	40
Sunderland	42	11	4	6	42	29	4	6	11	25	44	40
Manchester C	42	10	5	6	49	30	3	7	11	34	43	38
Derby Co	42	13	5	3	51	25	1	5	15	20	50	38
Blackburn R	42	12	3	6	57	41	4	3	14	32	54	38
Bolton W	42	15	1	5	51	25	2	3	16	21	55	38
Middlesbrough	42	12	3	6	41	29	3	5	13	23	60	38
Leicester C	42	11	3	7	46	39	4	4	13	28	55	37
Blackpool	42	9	4	8	42	40	3	5	13	23	62	33
Grimsby T	42	11	4	6	39	28	2	2	17	28	70	32
West Ham U	42	9	5	7	35	37	3	2	16	27	70	31

Reds' leading League goalscorer: Hodgson 26

DIVISION 1 1932-1933

	P	W	D	L	F	A	W	D	L	F	A	Pts
Arsenal	42	14	3	4	70	27	11	5	5	48	34	58
Aston Villa	42	16	2	3	60	29	7	6	8	32	38	54
Sheffield W	42	15	5	1	46	20	6	4	11	34	48	51
WBA	42	16	1	4	50	23	4	8	9	33	47	49
Newcastle U	42	15	2	4	44	24	7	3	11	27	39	49
Huddersfield T	42	11	6	4	32	17	7	5	9	34	36	47
Derby Co	42	11	8	2	49	25	4	6	11	27	44	44
Leeds U	42	10	6	5	39	24	5	8	8	20	38	44
Portsmouth	42	14	3	4	39	22	4	4	13	35	54	43
Sheffield U	42	14	3	4	50	30	3	6	12	24	50	43
Everton	42	13	6	2	54	24	3	3	15	27	50	41
Sunderland	42	8	7	6	33	31	7	3	11	30	49	40
Birmingham	42	13	3	5	40	23	1	8	12	17	34	39
LIVERPOOL	**42**	**10**	**6**	**5**	**53**	**33**	**4**	**5**	**12**	**26**	**51**	**39**
Blackburn R	42	11	6	4	48	41	3	4	14	28	61	38
Manchester C	42	12	3	6	47	30	4	2	15	21	41	37
Middlesbrough	42	8	5	8	35	33	6	4	11	28	40	37
Chelsea	42	9	4	8	38	29	5	3	13	25	44	35
Leicester C	42	9	9	3	43	25	2	4	15	32	64	35
Wolves	42	10	4	7	56	48	3	5	13	24	48	35
Bolton W	42	10	7	4	49	33	2	2	17	29	59	33
Blackpool	42	11	2	8	44	35	3	3	15	25	50	33

Reds' leading League goalscorer: Hodgson 24

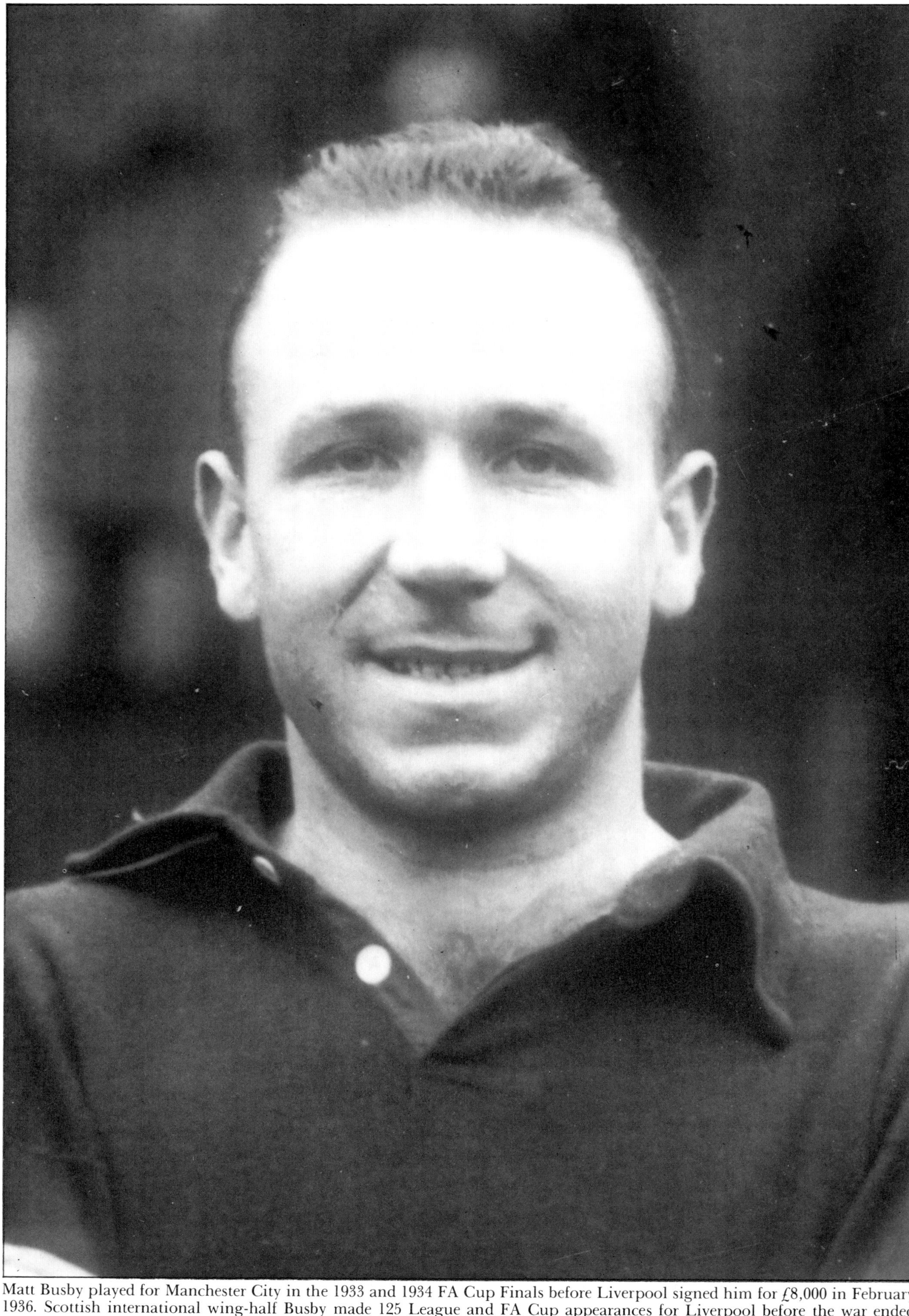

Matt Busby played for Manchester City in the 1933 and 1934 FA Cup Finals before Liverpool signed him for £8,000 in February 1936. Scottish international wing-half Busby made 125 League and FA Cup appearances for Liverpool before the war ended his career. In 1945 he began a remarkable career as manager of Manchester United.

DIVISION 1 1933-1934

	P	W	D	L	F	A	W	D	L	F	A	Pts
Arsenal	42	15	4	2	45	19	10	5	6	30	28	59
Huddersfield T	42	16	3	2	53	19	7	7	7	37	42	56
Tottenham H	42	14	3	4	51	24	7	4	10	28	32	49
Derby Co	42	11	8	2	45	22	6	3	12	23	32	45
Manchester C	42	14	4	3	50	29	3	7	11	15	43	45
Sunderland	42	14	6	1	57	17	2	6	13	24	39	44
WBA	42	12	4	5	49	28	5	6	10	29	42	44
Blackburn R	42	16	5	0	57	21	2	2	17	17	60	43
Leeds U	42	13	5	3	52	21	4	3	14	23	45	42
Portsmouth	42	11	5	5	31	21	4	7	10	21	34	42
Sheffield W	42	9	5	7	33	24	7	4	10	29	43	41
Stoke C	42	11	5	5	33	19	4	6	11	25	52	41
Aston Villa	42	10	5	6	45	34	4	7	10	33	41	40
Everton	42	9	7	5	38	27	3	9	9	24	36	40
Wolves	42	13	4	4	50	28	1	8	12	24	58	40
Middlesbrough	42	13	3	5	51	27	3	4	14	17	53	39
Leicester C	42	10	6	5	36	26	4	5	12	23	48	39
LIVERPOOL	**42**	**10**	**6**	**5**	**52**	**37**	**4**	**4**	**13**	**27**	**50**	**38**
Chelsea	42	12	3	6	44	24	2	5	14	23	45	36
Birmingham	42	8	6	7	29	20	4	6	11	25	36	36
Newcastle U	42	6	11	4	42	29	4	3	14	26	48	34
Sheffield U	42	11	5	5	40	25	1	2	18	18	76	31

Reds' leading League goalscorer: Hodgson 23

DIVISION 1 1934-1935

	P	W	D	L	F	A	W	D	L	F	A	Pts
Arsenal	42	15	4	2	74	17	8	8	5	41	29	58
Sunderland	42	13	4	4	57	24	6	12	3	33	27	54
Sheffield W	42	14	7	0	42	17	4	6	11	28	47	49
Manchester C	42	13	5	3	53	25	7	3	11	29	42	48
Grimsby T	42	13	6	2	49	25	4	5	12	29	35	45
Derby Co	42	10	4	7	44	28	8	5	8	37	38	45
LIVERPOOL	**42**	**13**	**4**	**4**	**53**	**29**	**6**	**3**	**12**	**32**	**59**	**45**
Everton	42	14	5	2	64	32	2	7	12	25	56	44
WBA	42	10	8	3	55	33	7	2	12	28	50	44
Stoke C	42	12	5	4	46	20	6	1	14	25	50	42
Preston NE	42	11	5	5	33	22	4	7	10	29	45	42
Chelsea	42	11	5	5	49	32	5	4	12	24	50	41
Aston Villa	42	11	6	4	50	36	3	7	11	24	52	41
Portsmouth	42	10	5	6	41	24	5	5	11	30	48	40
Blackburn R	42	12	5	4	42	23	2	6	13	24	55	39
Huddersfield T	42	11	5	5	52	27	3	5	13	24	44	38
Wolves	42	13	3	5	65	38	2	5	14	23	56	38
Leeds U	42	10	6	5	48	35	3	6	12	27	57	38
Birmingham	42	10	3	8	36	36	3	7	11	27	45	36
Middlesbrough	42	8	9	4	38	29	2	5	14	32	61	34
Leicester C	42	9	4	8	39	30	3	5	13	22	56	33
Tottenham H	42	8	8	5	34	31	2	2	17	20	62	30

Reds' leading League goalscorer: Hodgson 27

DIVISION 1 1935-1936

	P	W	D	L	F	A	W	D	L	F	A	Pts
Sunderland	42	17	2	2	71	33	8	4	9	38	41	56
Derby Co	42	13	5	3	43	23	5	7	9	18	29	48
Huddersfield T	42	12	7	2	32	15	6	5	10	27	41	48
Stoke C	42	13	3	5	35	24	7	4	10	22	33	47
Brentford	42	11	5	5	48	25	6	7	8	33	35	46
Arsenal	42	9	9	3	44	22	6	6	9	34	26	45
Preston NE	42	15	3	3	44	18	3	5	13	23	46	44
Chelsea	42	11	7	3	39	27	4	6	11	26	45	43
Manchester C	42	13	2	6	44	17	4	6	11	24	43	42
Portsmouth	42	14	4	3	39	22	3	4	14	15	45	42
Leeds U	42	11	5	5	41	23	4	6	11	25	41	41
Birmingham	42	10	6	5	38	31	5	5	11	23	32	41
Bolton W	42	11	4	6	41	27	3	9	9	26	49	41
Middlesbrough	42	12	6	3	56	23	3	4	14	28	47	40
Wolves	42	13	7	1	59	28	2	3	16	18	48	40
Everton	42	12	5	4	61	31	1	8	12	28	58	39
Grimsby T	42	13	4	4	44	20	4	1	16	21	53	39
WBA	42	12	3	6	54	31	4	3	14	35	57	38
LIVERPOOL	**42**	**11**	**4**	**6**	**43**	**23**	**2**	**8**	**11**	**17**	**41**	**38**
Sheffield W	42	9	8	4	35	23	4	4	13	28	54	38
Aston Villa	42	7	6	8	47	56	6	3	12	34	54	35
Blackburn R	42	10	6	5	32	24	2	3	16	23	72	33

Reds' leading League goalscorer: Howe 17

DIVISION 1 1936-1937

	P	W	D	L	F	A	W	D	L	F	A	Pts
Manchester C	42	15	5	1	56	22	7	8	6	51	39	57
Charlton A	42	15	5	1	37	13	6	7	8	21	36	54
Arsenal	42	10	10	1	43	20	8	6	7	37	29	52
Derby Co	42	13	3	5	58	39	8	4	9	38	51	49
Wolves	42	16	2	3	63	24	5	3	13	21	43	47
Brentford	42	14	5	2	58	32	4	5	12	24	46	46
Middlesbrough	42	14	6	1	49	22	5	2	14	25	49	46
Sunderland	42	17	2	2	59	24	2	4	15	30	63	44
Portsmouth	42	13	3	5	41	29	4	7	10	21	37	44
Stoke C	42	12	6	3	52	27	3	6	12	20	30	42
Birmingham	42	9	7	5	36	24	4	8	9	28	36	41
Grimsby T	42	13	3	5	60	32	4	4	13	26	49	41
Chelsea	42	11	6	4	36	21	3	7	11	16	34	41
Preston NE	42	10	6	5	35	28	4	7	10	21	39	41
Huddersfield T	42	12	5	4	39	21	0	10	11	23	43	39
WBA	42	13	3	5	45	32	3	3	15	32	66	38
Everton	42	12	7	2	56	23	2	2	17	25	55	37
LIVERPOOL	**42**	**9**	**8**	**4**	**38**	**26**	**3**	**3**	**15**	**24**	**58**	**35**
Leeds U	42	14	3	4	44	20	1	1	19	16	60	34
Bolton W	42	6	6	9	22	33	4	8	9	21	33	34
Manchester U	42	8	9	4	29	26	2	3	16	26	52	32
Sheffield W	42	8	5	8	32	29	1	7	13	21	40	30

Reds' leading League goalscorer: Howe 16

DIVISION 1 1937-1938

	P	W	D	L	F	A	W	D	L	F	A	Pts
Arsenal	42	15	4	2	52	16	6	6	9	25	28	52
Wolves	42	11	8	2	47	21	9	3	9	25	28	51
Preston NE	42	9	9	3	34	21	7	8	6	30	23	49
Charlton A	42	14	5	2	43	14	2	9	10	22	37	46
Middlesbrough	42	12	4	5	40	26	7	4	10	32	39	46
Brentford	42	10	6	5	44	27	8	3	10	25	32	45
Bolton W	42	11	6	4	38	22	4	9	8	26	38	45
Sunderland	42	12	6	3	32	18	2	10	9	23	39	44
Leeds U	42	11	6	4	38	26	3	9	9	26	43	43
Chelsea	42	11	6	4	40	22	3	7	11	25	43	41
LIVERPOOL	**42**	**9**	**5**	**7**	**40**	**30**	**6**	**6**	**9**	**25**	**41**	**41**
Blackpool	42	10	5	6	33	26	6	3	12	28	40	40
Derby Co	42	10	5	6	42	36	5	5	11	24	51	40
Everton	42	11	5	5	54	34	5	2	14	25	41	39
Huddersfield T	42	11	3	7	29	24	6	2	13	26	44	39
Leicester C	42	9	6	6	31	26	5	5	11	23	49	39
Stoke C	42	10	7	4	42	21	3	5	13	16	38	38
Birmingham	42	7	11	3	34	28	3	7	11	24	34	38
Portsmouth	42	11	6	4	41	22	2	6	13	21	46	38
Grimsby T	42	11	5	5	29	23	2	7	12	22	45	38
Manchester C	42	12	2	7	49	33	2	6	13	31	44	36
WBA	42	10	5	6	46	36	4	3	14	28	55	36

Reds' leading League goalscorer: Hanson 14

DIVISION 1 1938-1939

	P	W	D	L	F	A	W	D	L	F	A	Pts
Everton	42	17	3	1	60	18	10	2	9	28	34	59
Wolves	42	14	6	1	55	12	8	5	8	33	27	55
Charlton A	42	16	3	2	49	24	6	3	12	26	35	50
Middlesbrough	42	13	6	2	64	27	7	3	11	29	47	49
Arsenal	42	14	3	4	34	14	5	6	10	21	27	47
Derby Co	42	12	3	6	39	22	7	5	9	27	33	46
Stoke C	42	13	6	2	50	25	4	6	11	21	43	46
Bolton W	42	10	6	5	39	25	5	9	7	28	33	45
Preston NE	42	13	7	1	44	19	3	5	13	19	40	44
Grimsby T	42	11	6	4	38	26	5	5	11	23	43	43
LIVERPOOL	**42**	**12**	**6**	**3**	**40**	**24**	**2**	**8**	**11**	**22**	**39**	**42**
Aston Villa	42	11	3	7	44	25	5	6	10	27	35	41
Leeds U	42	11	5	5	40	27	5	4	12	19	40	41
Manchester U	42	7	9	5	30	20	4	7	10	27	45	38
Blackpool	42	9	8	4	37	26	3	6	12	19	42	38
Sunderland	42	7	7	7	30	29	6	5	10	24	38	38
Portsmouth	42	10	7	4	25	15	2	6	13	22	55	37
Brentford	42	11	2	8	30	27	3	6	12	23	47	36
Huddersfield T	42	11	4	6	38	18	1	7	13	20	46	35
Chelsea	42	10	5	6	43	29	2	4	15	21	51	33
Birmingham	42	10	5	6	40	27	2	3	16	22	57	32
Leicester C	42	7	6	8	35	35	2	5	14	13	47	29

Reds' leading League goalscorers: Fagan, Nieuwenhuys & Taylor 14

DIVISION 1 1939-1940

	P	W	D	L	F	A	W	D	L	F	A	Pts
Blackpool	3	2	0	0	4	2	1	0	0	1	0	6
Sheffield U	3	1	0	0	2	1	1	1	0	1	0	5
Arsenal	3	2	0	0	6	2	0	1	0	2	2	5
LIVERPOOL	**3**	**2**	**0**	**0**	**5**	**1**	**0**	**0**	**1**	**1**	**2**	**4**
Everton	3	0	1	0	1	1	1	1	0	4	3	4
Bolton W	3	1	0	0	2	1	1	0	1	4	4	4
Derby Co	3	2	0	0	3	0	0	0	1	0	3	4
Charlton A	3	1	0	0	2	0	1	0	1	1	4	4
Stoke C	3	1	0	1	5	2	0	1	0	2	2	3
Manchester U	3	1	0	0	4	0	0	1	1	1	3	3
Brentford	3	1	0	0	1	0	0	1	1	2	3	3
Chelsea	3	1	1	0	4	3	0	0	1	0	1	3
Grimsby T	3	1	1	0	2	0	0	0	1	0	4	3
Aston Villa	3	1	0	1	3	2	0	0	1	0	1	2
Sunderland	3	1	0	1	4	2	0	0	1	2	5	2
Wolves	3	0	1	0	2	2	0	1	1	1	2	2
Huddersfield T	3	0	0	1	0	1	1	0	1	2	2	2
Portsmouth	3	1	0	0	2	1	0	0	2	1	4	2
Preston NE	3	0	2	0	0	0	0	0	1	0	2	2
Blackburn R	3	0	1	0	2	2	0	0	2	1	3	1
Middlesbrough	3	0	1	0	2	2	0	0	2	1	6	1
Leeds U	3	0	0	2	0	2	0	1	0	0	0	1

Reds' leading League goalscorer: Taylor 2

DIVISION 1 1946-1947

	P	W	D	L	F	A	W	D	L	F	A	Pts
LIVERPOOL	**42**	**13**	**3**	**5**	**42**	**24**	**12**	**4**	**5**	**42**	**28**	**57**
Manchester U	42	17	3	1	61	19	5	9	7	34	35	56
Wolves	42	15	1	5	66	31	10	5	6	32	25	56
Stoke C	42	14	5	2	52	21	10	2	9	38	32	55
Blackpool	42	14	1	6	38	32	8	5	8	33	38	50
Sheffield U	42	12	4	5	51	32	9	3	9	38	43	49
Preston NE	42	10	7	4	45	27	8	4	9	31	47	47
Aston Villa	42	9	6	6	39	24	9	3	9	28	29	45
Sunderland	42	11	3	7	33	27	7	5	9	32	39	44
Everton	42	13	5	3	40	24	4	4	13	22	43	43
Middlesbrough	42	11	3	7	46	32	6	5	10	27	36	42
Portsmouth	42	11	3	7	42	27	5	6	10	24	33	41
Arsenal	42	9	5	7	43	33	7	4	10	29	37	41
Derby Co	42	13	2	6	44	28	5	3	13	29	51	41
Chelsea	42	9	3	9	33	39	7	4	10	36	45	39
Grimsby T	42	9	6	6	37	35	4	6	11	24	47	38
Blackburn R	42	6	5	10	23	27	8	3	10	22	26	36
Bolton W	42	8	5	8	30	28	5	3	13	27	41	34
Charlton A	42	6	6	9	34	32	5	6	10	23	39	34
Huddersfield T	42	11	4	6	34	24	2	3	16	19	55	33
Brentford	42	5	5	11	19	35	4	2	15	26	53	25
Leeds U	42	6	5	10	30	30	0	1	20	15	60	18

Reds' leading League goalscorers: Balmer & Stubbins 24

DIVISION 1 1947-1948

	P	W	D	L	F	A	W	D	L	F	A	Pts
Arsenal	42	15	3	3	56	15	8	10	3	25	17	59
Manchester U	42	11	7	3	50	27	8	7	6	31	21	52
Burnley	42	12	5	4	31	12	8	7	6	25	31	52
Derby Co	42	11	6	4	38	24	8	6	7	39	33	50
Wolves	42	12	4	5	45	29	7	5	9	38	41	47
Aston Villa	42	13	5	3	42	22	6	4	11	23	35	47
Preston NE	42	13	4	4	43	35	7	3	11	24	33	47
Portsmouth	42	13	5	3	44	17	6	2	13	24	33	45
Blackpool	42	13	4	4	37	14	4	6	11	20	27	44
Manchester C	42	13	3	5	37	22	2	9	10	15	25	42
LIVERPOOL	**42**	**9**	**8**	**4**	**39**	**23**	**7**	**2**	**12**	**26**	**38**	**42**
Sheffield U	42	13	4	4	44	24	3	6	12	21	46	42
Charlton A	42	8	4	9	33	29	9	2	10	24	37	40
Everton	42	10	2	9	30	26	7	4	10	22	40	40
Stoke C	42	9	5	7	29	23	5	5	11	12	32	38
Middlesbrough	42	8	7	6	37	27	6	2	13	34	46	37
Bolton W	42	11	2	8	29	25	5	3	13	17	33	37
Chelsea	42	11	6	4	38	27	3	3	15	15	44	37
Huddersfield T	42	7	6	8	25	24	5	6	10	26	36	36
Sunderland	42	11	4	6	33	18	2	6	13	23	49	36
Blackburn R	42	8	5	8	35	30	3	5	13	19	42	32
Grimsby T	42	5	5	11	20	35	3	1	17	25	76	22

Reds' leading League goalscorer: Stubbins 24

DIVISION 1 1948-1949

	P	W	D	L	F	A	W	D	L	F	A	Pts
Portsmouth	42	18	3	0	52	12	7	5	9	32	30	58
Manchester U	42	11	7	3	40	20	10	4	7	37	24	53
Derby Co	42	17	2	2	48	22	5	7	9	26	33	53
Newcastle U	42	12	5	4	35	29	8	7	6	35	27	52
Arsenal	42	13	5	3	51	18	5	8	8	23	26	49
Wolves	42	13	5	3	48	19	4	7	10	31	47	46
Manchester C	42	10	8	3	28	21	5	7	9	19	30	45
Sunderland	42	8	10	3	27	19	5	7	9	22	39	43
Charlton A	42	10	5	6	38	31	5	7	9	25	36	42
Aston Villa	42	10	6	5	40	36	6	4	11	20	40	42
Stoke C	42	14	3	4	43	24	2	6	13	23	44	41
LIVERPOOL	**42**	**5**	**10**	**6**	**25**	**18**	**8**	**4**	**9**	**28**	**25**	**40**
Chelsea	42	10	6	5	43	27	2	8	11	26	41	38
Bolton W	42	10	4	7	43	32	4	6	11	16	36	38
Burnley	42	10	6	5	27	19	2	8	11	16	31	38
Blackpool	42	8	8	5	24	25	3	8	10	30	42	38
Birmingham C	42	9	7	5	19	10	2	8	11	17	28	37
Everton	42	12	5	4	33	25	1	6	14	8	38	37
Middlesbrough	42	10	6	5	37	23	1	6	14	9	34	34
Huddersfield T	42	6	7	8	19	24	6	3	12	21	45	34
Preston NE	42	8	6	7	36	36	3	5	13	26	39	33
Sheffield U	42	8	9	4	32	25	3	2	16	25	53	33

Reds' leading League goalscorer: Balmer 14

DIVISION 1 1949-1950

	P	W	D	L	F	A	W	D	L	F	A	Pts
Portsmouth	42	12	7	2	44	15	10	2	9	30	23	53
Wolves	42	11	8	2	47	21	9	5	7	29	28	53
Sunderland	42	14	6	1	50	23	7	4	10	33	39	52
Manchester U	42	11	5	5	42	20	7	9	5	27	24	50
Newcastle U	42	14	4	3	49	23	5	8	8	28	32	50
Arsenal	42	12	4	5	48	24	7	7	7	31	31	49
Blackpool	42	10	8	3	29	14	7	7	7	17	21	49
LIVERPOOL	**42**	**10**	**7**	**4**	**37**	**23**	**7**	**7**	**7**	**27**	**31**	**48**
Middlesbrough	42	14	2	5	37	18	6	5	10	22	30	47
Burnley	42	9	7	5	23	17	7	6	8	17	23	45
Derby Co	42	11	5	5	46	26	6	5	10	23	35	44
Aston Villa	42	10	7	4	31	19	5	5	11	30	42	42
Chelsea	42	7	7	7	31	30	5	9	7	27	35	40
WBA	42	9	7	5	28	16	5	5	11	19	37	40
Huddersfield T	42	11	4	6	34	22	3	5	13	18	51	37
Bolton W	42	10	5	6	34	22	0	9	12	11	37	34
Fulham	42	8	6	7	24	19	2	8	11	17	35	34
Everton	42	6	8	7	24	20	4	6	11	18	46	34
Stoke C	42	10	4	7	27	28	1	8	12	18	47	34
Charlton A	42	7	5	9	33	35	6	1	14	20	30	32
Manchester C	42	7	8	6	27	24	1	5	15	9	44	29
Birmingham C	42	6	8	7	19	24	1	6	14	12	43	28

Reds' leading League goalscorer: Liddell 18

DIVISION 1 1950-1951

	P	W	D	L	F	A	W	D	L	F	A	Pts
Tottenham H	42	17	2	2	54	21	8	8	5	28	23	60
Manchester U	42	14	4	3	42	16	10	4	7	32	24	56
Blackpool	42	12	6	3	43	19	8	4	9	36	34	50
Newcastle U	42	10	6	5	36	22	8	7	6	26	31	49
Arsenal	42	11	5	5	47	28	8	4	9	26	28	47
Middlesbrough	42	12	7	2	51	25	6	4	11	25	40	47
Portsmouth	42	8	10	3	39	30	8	5	8	32	38	47
Bolton W	42	11	2	8	31	20	8	5	8	33	41	45
LIVERPOOL	**42**	**11**	**5**	**5**	**28**	**25**	**5**	**6**	**10**	**25**	**34**	**43**
Burnley	42	9	7	5	27	16	5	7	9	21	27	42
Derby Co	42	10	5	6	53	33	6	3	12	28	42	40
Sunderland	42	8	9	4	30	21	4	7	10	33	52	40
Stoke C	42	10	5	6	28	19	3	9	9	22	40	40
Wolves	42	9	3	9	44	30	6	5	10	30	31	38
Aston Villa	42	9	6	6	39	29	3	7	11	27	39	37
WBA	42	7	4	10	30	27	6	7	8	23	34	37
Charlton A	42	9	4	8	35	31	5	5	11	28	49	37
Fulham	42	8	5	8	35	37	5	6	10	17	31	37
Huddersfield T	42	8	4	9	40	40	7	2	12	24	52	36
Chelsea	42	9	4	8	31	25	3	4	14	22	40	32
Sheffield W	42	9	6	6	43	32	3	2	16	21	51	32
Everton	42	7	5	9	26	35	5	3	13	22	51	32

Reds' leading League goalscorer: Liddell 15

DIVISION 1 1951-1952

	P	W	D	L	F	A	W	D	L	F	A	Pts
Manchester U	42	15	3	3	55	21	8	8	5	40	31	57
Tottenham H	42	16	1	4	45	20	6	8	7	31	31	53
Arsenal	42	13	7	1	54	30	8	4	9	26	31	53
Portsmouth	42	13	3	5	42	25	7	5	9	26	33	48
Bolton W	42	11	7	3	35	26	8	3	10	30	35	48
Aston Villa	42	13	3	5	49	28	6	6	9	30	42	47
Preston NE	42	10	5	6	39	22	7	7	7	35	32	46
Newcastle U	42	12	4	5	62	28	6	5	10	36	45	45
Blackpool	42	12	5	4	40	27	6	4	11	24	37	45
Charlton A	42	12	5	4	41	24	5	5	11	27	39	44
LIVERPOOL	**42**	**6**	**11**	**4**	**31**	**25**	**6**	**8**	**7**	**26**	**36**	**43**
Sunderland	42	8	6	7	41	28	7	6	8	29	33	42
WBA	42	8	9	4	38	29	6	4	11	36	48	41
Burnley	42	9	6	6	32	19	6	4	11	24	44	40
Manchester C	42	7	5	9	29	28	6	8	7	29	33	39
Wolves	42	8	6	7	40	33	4	8	9	33	40	38
Derby Co	42	10	4	7	43	37	5	3	13	20	43	37
Middlesbrough	42	12	4	5	37	25	3	2	16	27	63	36
Chelsea	42	10	3	8	31	29	4	5	12	21	43	36
Stoke C	42	8	6	7	34	32	4	1	16	15	56	31
Huddersfield T	42	9	3	9	32	35	1	5	15	17	47	28
Fulham	42	5	7	9	38	31	3	4	14	20	46	27

Reds' leading League goalscorer: Liddell 19

DIVISION 1 1952-1953

	P	W	D	L	F	A	W	D	L	F	A	Pts
Arsenal	42	15	3	3	60	30	6	9	6	37	34	54
Preston NE	42	15	3	3	46	25	6	9	6	39	35	54
Wolves	42	13	5	3	54	27	6	8	7	32	36	51
WBA	42	13	3	5	35	19	8	5	8	31	41	50
Charlton A	42	12	8	1	47	22	7	3	11	30	41	49
Burnley	42	11	6	4	36	20	7	6	8	31	32	48
Blackpool	42	13	5	3	45	22	6	4	11	26	48	47
Manchester U	42	11	5	5	35	30	7	5	9	34	42	46
Sunderland	42	11	9	1	42	27	4	4	13	26	55	43
Tottenham H	42	11	6	4	55	37	4	5	12	23	32	41
Aston Villa	42	9	7	5	36	23	5	6	10	27	38	41
Cardiff C	42	7	8	6	32	17	7	4	10	22	29	40
Middlesbrough	42	12	5	4	46	27	2	6	13	24	50	39
Bolton W	42	9	4	8	39	35	6	5	10	22	34	39
Portsmouth	42	10	6	5	44	34	4	4	13	30	49	38
Newcastle U	42	9	5	7	34	33	5	4	12	25	37	37
LIVERPOOL	**42**	**10**	**6**	**5**	**36**	**28**	**4**	**2**	**15**	**25**	**54**	**36**
Sheffield W	42	8	6	7	35	32	4	5	12	27	40	35
Chelsea	42	10	4	7	35	24	2	7	12	21	42	35
Manchester C	42	12	2	7	45	28	2	5	14	27	59	35
Stoke C	42	10	4	7	35	26	2	6	13	18	40	34
Derby Co	42	9	6	6	41	29	2	4	15	18	45	32

Reds' leading League goalscorer: Liddell 13

DIVISION 1 1953-1954

	P	W	D	L	F	A	W	D	L	F	A	Pts
Wolves	42	16	1	4	61	25	9	6	6	35	31	57
WBA	42	13	5	3	51	24	9	4	8	35	39	53
Huddersfield T	42	13	6	2	45	24	7	5	9	33	37	51
Manchester U	52	11	6	4	41	27	7	6	8	32	31	48
Bolton W	42	14	6	1	45	20	4	6	11	30	40	48
Blackpool	42	13	6	2	43	19	6	4	11	37	50	48
Burnley	42	16	2	3	51	23	5	2	14	27	44	46
Chelsea	42	12	3	6	45	26	4	9	8	29	42	44
Charlton A	42	14	4	3	51	26	5	2	14	24	51	44
Cardiff C	42	12	4	5	32	27	6	4	11	19	44	44
Preston NE	42	12	2	7	43	24	7	3	11	44	34	43
Arsenal	42	8	8	5	42	37	7	5	9	33	36	43
Aston Villa	42	12	5	4	50	28	4	4	13	20	40	41
Portsmouth	42	13	5	3	53	31	1	6	14	28	58	39
Newcastle U	42	9	2	10	43	40	5	8	8	29	37	38
Tottenham H	42	11	3	7	38	33	5	2	14	27	43	37
Manchester C	42	10	4	7	35	31	4	5	12	27	46	37
Sunderland	42	11	4	6	50	37	3	4	14	31	52	36
Sheffield W	42	12	4	5	43	30	3	2	16	27	61	36
Sheffield U	42	9	5	7	43	38	2	6	13	26	52	33
Middlesbrough	42	6	6	9	29	35	4	4	13	31	56	30
LIVERPOOL	**42**	**7**	**8**	**6**	**49**	**38**	**2**	**2**	**17**	**19**	**59**	**28**

Reds' leading League goalscorers: Bimpson & Smyth 13

DIVISION 2 1954-1955

	P	W	D	L	F	A	W	D	L	F	A	Pts
Birmingham C	42	14	4	3	56	22	8	6	7	36	25	54
Luton T	42	18	2	1	55	18	5	6	10	33	35	54
Rotherham U	42	17	1	3	59	22	8	3	10	35	42	54
Leeds U	42	14	4	3	43	19	9	3	9	27	34	53
Stoke C	42	12	5	4	38	17	9	5	7	31	29	52
Blackburn R	42	14	4	3	73	31	8	2	11	41	48	50
Notts Co	42	14	3	4	46	27	7	3	11	28	44	48
West Ham U	42	12	4	5	46	28	6	6	9	28	42	46
Bristol R	42	15	4	2	52	23	4	3	14	23	47	45
Swansea T	42	15	3	3	58	28	2	6	13	28	55	43
LIVERPOOL	**42**	**11**	**7**	**3**	**55**	**37**	**5**	**3**	**13**	**37**	**59**	**42**
Middlesbrough	42	13	1	7	48	31	5	5	11	25	51	42
Bury	42	10	5	6	44	35	5	6	10	33	37	41
Fulham	42	10	5	6	46	29	4	6	11	30	50	39
Nottingham F	42	8	4	9	29	29	8	3	10	29	33	39
Lincoln C	42	8	6	7	39	35	5	4	12	29	44	36
Port Vale	42	10	6	5	31	21	2	5	14	17	50	35
Doncaster R	42	10	5	6	35	34	4	2	15	23	61	35
Hull C	42	7	5	9	30	35	5	5	11	14	34	34
Plymouth A	42	10	4	7	29	26	2	3	16	28	56	31
Ipswich T	42	10	3	8	37	28	1	3	17	20	64	28
Derby Co	42	6	6	9	39	34	1	3	17	14	48	23

Reds' leading League goalscorer: Liddell 30

DIVISION 2 1955-1956

	P	W	D	L	F	A	W	D	L	F	A	Pts
Sheffield W	42	13	5	3	60	28	8	8	5	41	34	55
Leeds U	42	17	3	1	51	18	6	3	12	29	42	52
LIVERPOOL	**42**	**14**	**3**	**4**	**52**	**25**	**7**	**3**	**11**	**33**	**38**	**48**
Blackburn R	42	13	4	4	55	29	8	2	11	29	36	48
Leicester C	42	15	3	3	63	23	6	3	12	31	55	48
Bristol R	42	13	3	5	53	33	8	3	10	31	37	48
Nottingham F	42	9	5	7	30	26	10	4	7	38	37	47
Lincoln C	42	14	5	2	49	17	4	5	12	30	48	46
Fulham	42	15	2	4	59	27	5	4	12	30	52	46
Swansea T	42	14	4	3	49	23	6	2	13	34	58	46
Bristol C	42	14	4	3	49	20	5	3	13	31	44	45
Port Vale	42	12	4	5	38	21	4	9	8	22	37	45
Stoke C	42	13	2	6	47	27	7	2	12	24	35	44
Middlesbrough	42	11	4	6	46	31	5	4	12	30	47	40
Bury	42	9	5	7	44	39	7	3	11	42	51	40
West Ham U	42	12	4	5	52	27	2	7	12	22	42	39
Doncaster R	42	11	5	5	45	30	1	6	14	24	66	35
Barnsley	42	10	5	6	33	35	1	7	13	14	49	34
Rotherham U	42	7	5	9	29	34	5	4	12	27	41	33
Notts Co	42	8	5	8	39	37	3	4	14	16	45	31
Plymouth A	42	7	6	8	33	25	3	2	16	21	62	28
Hull C	42	6	4	11	32	45	4	2	15	21	52	26

Reds' leading League goalscorer: Liddell 28

DIVISION 2 1956-1957

	P	W	D	L	F	A	W	D	L	F	A	Pts
Leicester C	42	14	5	2	68	36	11	6	4	41	31	61
Nottingham F	42	13	4	4	50	29	9	6	6	44	26	54
LIVERPOOL	**42**	**16**	**1**	**4**	**53**	**26**	**5**	**10**	**6**	**29**	**28**	**53**
Blackburn R	42	12	6	3	49	32	9	4	8	34	43	52
Stoke C	42	16	2	3	64	18	4	6	11	19	40	48
Middlesbrough	42	12	5	4	51	29	7	5	9	33	31	48
Sheffield U	42	11	6	4	45	28	8	2	11	42	48	46
West Ham U	42	12	4	5	31	24	7	4	10	28	39	46
Bristol R	42	12	5	4	47	19	6	4	11	34	48	45
Swansea T	42	12	3	6	53	34	7	4	10	37	56	45
Fulham	42	13	1	7	53	32	6	3	12	31	44	42
Huddersfield T	42	10	3	8	33	27	8	3	10	35	47	42
Bristol C	42	13	2	6	49	32	3	7	11	25	47	41
Doncaster R	42	12	5	4	51	21	3	5	13	26	56	40
Leyton O	42	7	8	6	34	38	8	2	11	32	46	40
Grimsby T	42	12	4	5	41	26	5	1	15	20	36	39
Rotherham U	42	9	7	5	37	26	4	4	13	37	49	37
Lincoln C	42	9	4	8	34	27	5	2	14	20	53	34
Barnsley	42	8	7	6	39	35	4	3	14	20	54	34
Notts Co	42	7	6	8	34	32	2	6	13	24	54	30
Bury	42	5	3	13	37	47	3	6	12	23	49	25
Port Vale	42	7	4	10	31	42	1	2	18	26	59	22

Reds' leading League goalscorer: Liddell 21

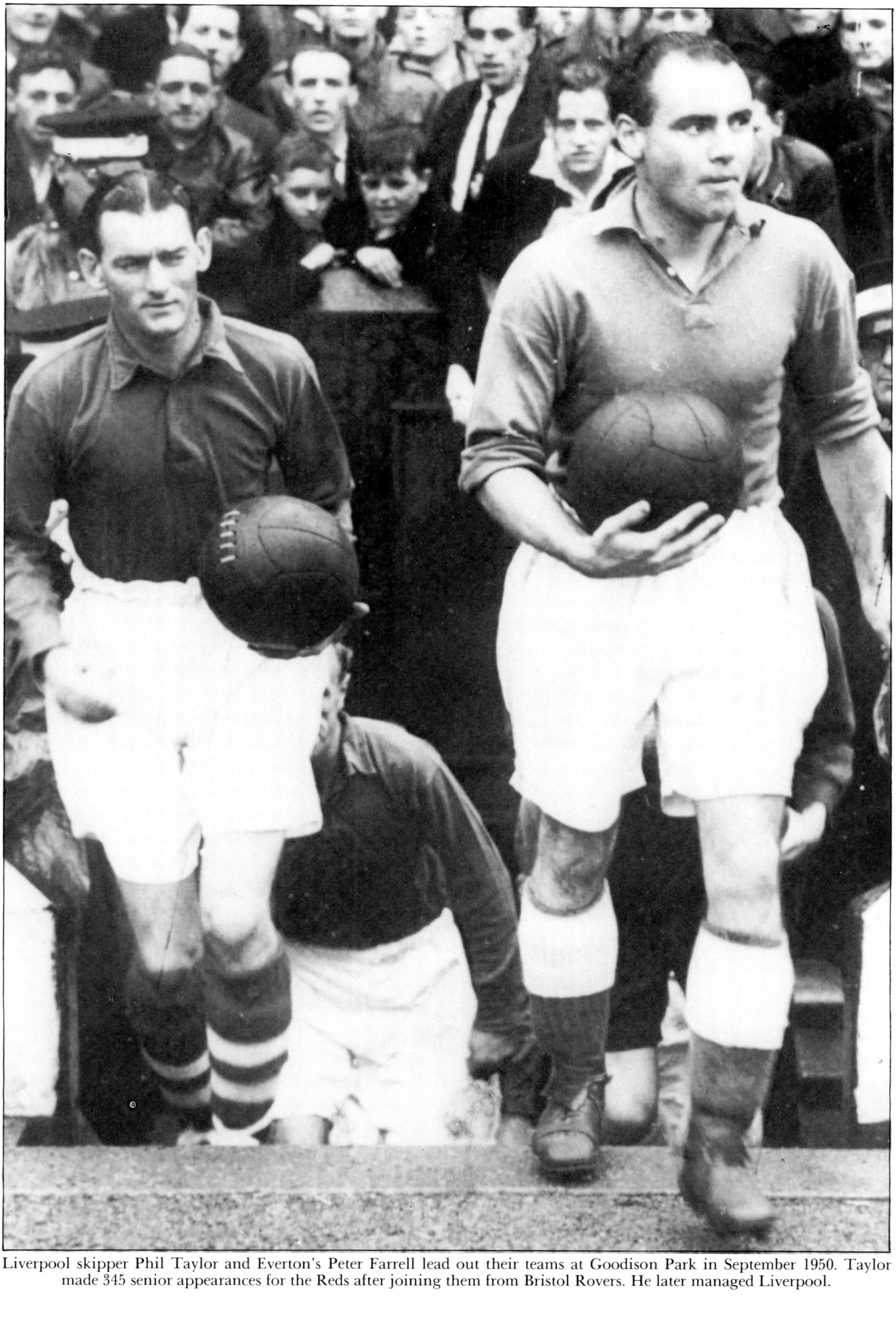

Liverpool skipper Phil Taylor and Everton's Peter Farrell lead out their teams at Goodison Park in September 1950. Taylor made 345 senior appearances for the Reds after joining them from Bristol Rovers. He later managed Liverpool.

DIVISION 2 1957-1958

	P	W	D	L	F	A	W	D	L	F	A	Pts
West Ham U	42	12	8	1	56	25	11	3	7	45	29	57
Blackburn R	42	13	7	1	50	18	9	5	7	43	39	56
Charlton A	42	15	3	3	65	33	9	4	8	42	36	55
LIVERPOOL	**42**	**17**	**3**	**1**	**50**	**13**	**5**	**7**	**9**	**29**	**41**	**54**
Fulham	42	13	5	3	53	24	7	7	7	44	35	52
Sheffield U	42	12	5	4	38	22	9	5	7	37	28	52
Middlesbrough	42	13	3	5	52	29	6	4	11	31	45	45
Ipswich T	42	13	4	4	45	29	3	8	19	23	40	44
Huddersfield T	42	9	8	4	28	24	5	8	8	35	42	44
Bristol R	42	12	5	4	52	31	5	3	13	33	49	42
Stoke C	42	9	4	8	49	36	9	2	10	26	37	42
Leyton O	42	14	2	5	53	27	4	3	14	24	52	41
Grimsby T	42	13	4	4	54	30	4	2	15	32	53	40
Barnsley	42	10	6	5	40	25	4	6	11	30	49	40
Cardiff C	42	10	5	6	44	31	4	4	13	19	46	37
Derby Co	42	11	3	7	37	36	3	5	13	23	45	36
Bristol C	42	9	5	7	35	31	4	4	13	28	57	35
Rotherham U	42	8	3	10	38	44	6	2	13	27	57	33
Swansea T	42	8	3	10	48	45	3	6	12	24	54	31
Lincoln C	42	6	6	9	33	35	5	3	13	22	47	31
Notts Co	42	9	3	9	24	31	3	3	15	20	49	30
Doncaster R	42	7	5	9	34	40	1	6	14	22	48	27

Reds' leading League goalscorer: Liddell 22

DIVISION 2 1958-1959

	P	W	D	L	F	A	W	D	L	F	A	Pts
Sheffield W	42	18	2	1	68	13	10	4	7	38	35	62
Fulham	42	18	1	2	65	26	9	5	7	31	35	60
Sheffield U	42	16	2	3	54	15	7	5	9	28	33	53
LIVERPOOL	**42**	**15**	**3**	**3**	**57**	**25**	**9**	**2**	**10**	**30**	**37**	**53**
Stoke C	42	16	2	3	48	19	5	5	11	24	39	49
Bristol R	42	13	5	3	46	23	5	7	9	34	41	48
Derby Co	42	15	1	5	46	29	5	7	9	28	42	48
Charlton A	42	13	3	5	53	33	5	4	12	39	57	43
Cardiff C	42	12	2	7	37	26	6	5	10	28	39	43
Bristol C	42	11	3	7	43	27	6	4	11	31	43	41
Swansea T	42	12	5	4	52	30	4	4	13	27	51	41
Brighton & HA	42	10	9	2	46	29	5	2	14	28	61	41
Middlesbrough	42	9	7	5	51	26	6	3	12	36	45	40
Huddersfield T	42	12	3	6	39	20	4	5	12	23	35	40
Sunderland	42	13	4	4	42	23	3	4	14	22	52	40
Ipswich T	42	12	4	5	37	27	5	2	14	25	50	40
Leyton O	42	9	4	8	43	30	5	4	12	28	48	36
Scunthorpe U	42	7	6	8	32	37	5	3	13	23	47	33
Lincoln C	42	10	5	6	45	37	1	2	18	18	56	29
Rotherham U	42	9	5	7	32	28	1	4	16	10	54	29
Grimsby T	42	7	7	7	41	36	2	3	16	21	54	28
Barnsley	42	8	4	9	34	34	2	3	16	21	57	27

Reds' leading League goalscorer: Melia 21

DIVISION 2 1959-1960

	P	W	D	L	F	A	W	D	L	F	A	Pts
Aston Villa	42	17	3	1	62	19	8	6	7	27	24	59
Cardiff C	42	15	2	4	55	36	8	10	3	35	26	58
LIVERPOOL	**42**	**15**	**3**	**3**	**59**	**28**	**5**	**7**	**9**	**31**	**38**	**50**
Sheffield U	42	12	5	4	43	22	7	7	7	25	29	50
Middlesbrough	42	14	5	2	56	21	5	5	11	34	43	48
Huddersfield T	42	13	3	5	44	20	6	6	9	29	32	47
Charlton A	42	12	7	2	55	28	5	6	10	35	59	47
Rotherham U	42	9	9	3	31	23	8	4	9	30	37	47
Bristol R	42	12	6	3	42	28	6	5	10	30	50	47
Leyton O	42	12	4	5	47	25	3	10	8	29	36	44
Ipswich T	42	12	5	4	48	24	7	1	13	30	44	44
Swansea T	42	12	6	3	54	32	3	4	14	28	52	40
Lincoln C	42	11	3	7	41	25	5	4	12	34	53	39
Brighton & HA	42	7	8	6	35	32	6	4	11	32	44	38
Scunthorpe U	42	9	7	5	38	26	4	3	14	19	45	36
Sunderland	42	8	6	7	35	29	4	6	11	17	36	36
Stoke C	42	8	3	10	40	38	6	4	11	26	45	35
Derby Co	42	9	4	8	31	28	5	3	13	30	49	35
Plymouth A	42	10	6	5	42	36	3	3	15	19	53	35
Portsmouth	42	6	6	9	36	36	4	6	11	23	41	32
Hull C	42	7	6	8	27	30	3	4	14	21	46	30
Bristol C	42	8	3	10	27	31	3	2	16	33	66	27

Reds' leading League goalscorers: Hickson & Hunt 21

DIVISION 2 1960-1961

	P	W	D	L	F	A	W	D	L	F	A	Pts
Ipswich T	42	15	3	3	55	24	11	4	6	45	31	59
Sheffield U	42	16	2	3	49	22	10	4	7	32	29	58
LIVERPOOL	**42**	**14**	**5**	**2**	**49**	**21**	**7**	**5**	**9**	**38**	**37**	**52**
Norwich C	42	15	3	3	46	20	5	6	10	24	33	49
Middlesbrough	42	13	6	2	44	20	5	6	10	39	54	48
Sunderland	42	12	5	4	47	24	5	8	8	28	36	47
Swansea T	42	14	4	3	49	26	4	7	10	28	47	47
Southampton	42	12	4	5	57	35	6	4	11	27	46	44
Scunthorpe U	42	9	8	4	39	25	5	7	9	30	39	43
Charlton A	42	12	3	6	60	42	4	8	9	37	49	43
Plymouth A	42	13	4	4	52	32	4	4	13	29	50	42
Derby Co	42	9	6	6	46	35	6	4	11	34	45	40
Luton T	42	13	5	3	48	27	2	4	15	23	52	39
Leeds U	42	7	7	7	41	38	7	3	11	34	45	38
Rotherham U	42	9	7	5	37	24	3	6	12	28	40	37
Brighton & HA	42	9	6	6	33	26	5	3	13	28	49	37
Bristol R	42	13	4	4	52	35	2	3	16	21	57	37
Stoke C	42	9	6	6	39	26	3	6	12	12	33	36
Leyton O	42	10	5	6	31	29	4	3	14	24	49	36
Huddersfield T	42	7	5	9	33	33	6	4	11	29	38	35
Portsmouth	42	10	6	5	38	27	1	5	15	26	64	33
Lincoln C	42	5	4	12	30	43	3	4	14	18	52	24

Reds' leading League goalscorer: Lewis 19

DIVISION 2 1961-1962

	P	W	D	L	F	A	W	D	L	F	A	Pts
LIVERPOOL	**42**	**18**	**3**	**0**	**68**	**19**	**9**	**5**	**7**	**31**	**24**	**62**
Leyton O	42	11	5	5	34	17	11	5	5	35	23	54
Sunderland	42	17	3	1	60	16	5	6	10	25	34	53
Scunthorpe U	42	14	4	3	52	26	7	3	11	34	45	49
Plymouth A	42	12	4	5	45	30	7	4	10	30	45	46
Southampton	42	13	3	5	53	28	5	6	10	24	34	45
Huddersfield T	42	11	5	5	39	22	5	7	9	28	37	44
Stoke C	42	13	4	4	34	17	4	4	13	21	40	42
Rotherham U	42	9	6	6	36	30	7	3	11	34	46	41
Preston NE	42	11	4	6	34	23	4	6	11	21	34	40
Newcastle U	42	10	5	6	40	27	5	4	12	24	31	39
Middlesbrough	42	11	3	7	45	29	5	4	12	31	43	39
Luton T	42	12	1	8	44	37	5	4	12	25	34	39
Walsall	42	11	7	3	42	23	3	4	14	28	52	39
Charlton A	42	10	5	6	38	30	5	4	12	31	45	39
Derby Co	42	10	7	4	42	27	4	4	13	26	48	39
Norwich C	42	10	6	5	36	28	4	5	12	25	42	39
Bury	42	9	4	8	32	36	8	1	12	20	40	39
Leeds U	42	9	6	6	24	19	3	6	12	26	42	36
Swansea T	42	10	5	6	38	30	2	7	12	23	53	36
Bristol R	42	11	3	7	36	31	2	4	15	17	50	33
Brighton & HA	42	7	7	7	24	32	3	4	14	18	54	31

Reds' leading League goalscorer: Hunt 41

DIVISION 1 1962-1963

	P	W	D	L	F	A	W	D	L	F	A	Pts
Everton	42	14	7	0	48	17	11	4	6	36	25	61
Tottenham H	42	14	6	1	72	28	9	3	9	39	34	55
Burnley	42	14	4	3	41	17	8	6	7	37	40	54
Leicester C	42	14	6	1	53	23	6	6	9	26	30	52
Wolves	42	11	6	4	51	25	9	4	8	42	40	50
Sheffield W	42	10	5	6	38	26	9	5	7	39	37	48
Arsenal	42	11	4	6	44	33	7	6	8	42	44	46
LIVERPOOL	**42**	**13**	**3**	**5**	**45**	**22**	**4**	**7**	**10**	**26**	**37**	**44**
Nottingham F	42	12	4	5	39	28	5	6	10	28	41	44
Sheffield U	42	11	7	3	33	20	5	5	11	25	40	44
Blackburn R	42	11	4	6	55	34	4	8	9	24	37	42
West Ham U	42	8	6	7	39	34	6	6	9	34	35	40
Blackpool	42	8	7	6	34	27	5	7	9	24	37	40
WBA	42	11	1	9	40	37	5	6	10	31	42	39
Aston Villa	42	12	2	7	38	23	3	6	12	24	45	38
Fulham	42	8	6	7	28	30	6	4	11	22	41	38
Ipswich T	42	5	8	8	34	39	7	3	11	25	39	35
Bolton W	42	13	3	5	35	18	2	2	17	20	57	35
Manchester U	42	6	6	9	36	38	6	4	11	31	43	34
Birmingham C	42	6	8	7	40	40	4	5	12	23	50	33
Manchester C	42	7	5	9	30	45	3	6	12	28	57	31
Leyton O	42	4	5	12	22	37	2	4	15	15	44	21

Reds' leading League goalscorer: Hunt 24

DIVISION 1 1963-1964

	P	W	D	L	F	A	W	D	L	F	A	Pts
LIVERPOOL	**42**	**16**	**0**	**5**	**60**	**18**	**10**	**5**	**6**	**32**	**27**	**57**
Manchester U	42	15	3	3	54	19	8	4	9	36	43	53
Everton	42	14	4	3	53	26	7	6	8	31	38	52
Tottenham H	42	13	3	5	54	31	9	4	8	43	50	51
Chelsea	42	12	3	6	36	24	8	7	6	36	32	50
Sheffield W	42	15	3	3	50	24	4	8	9	34	43	49
Blackburn R	42	10	4	7	44	28	8	6	7	45	37	46
Arsenal	42	10	7	4	56	37	7	4	10	34	45	45
Burnley	42	14	3	4	46	23	3	7	11	25	41	44
WBA	42	9	6	6	43	35	7	5	9	27	26	43
Leicester C	42	9	4	8	33	27	7	7	7	28	31	43
Sheffield U	42	10	6	5	35	22	6	5	10	26	42	43
Nottingham F	42	9	5	7	34	24	7	4	10	30	44	41
West Ham U	42	8	7	6	45	38	6	5	10	24	36	40
Fulham	42	11	8	2	45	23	2	5	14	13	42	39
Wolves	42	6	9	6	36	34	6	6	9	34	46	39
Stoke C	42	9	6	6	49	33	5	4	12	28	45	38
Blackpool	42	8	6	7	26	29	5	3	13	26	44	35
Aston Villa	42	8	6	7	35	29	3	6	12	27	42	34
Birmingham C	42	7	7	7	33	32	4	0	17	21	60	29
Bolton W	42	6	5	10	30	35	4	3	14	18	45	28
Ipswich T	42	9	3	9	38	45	0	4	17	18	76	25

Reds' leading League goalscorer: Hunt 31

DIVISION 1 1964-1965

	P	W	D	L	F	A	W	D	L	F	A	Pts
Manchester U	42	16	4	1	52	13	10	5	6	37	26	61
Leeds U	42	16	3	2	53	23	10	6	5	30	29	61
Chelsea	42	15	2	4	48	19	9	6	6	41	35	56
Everton	42	9	10	2	37	22	8	5	8	32	38	49
Nottingham F	42	10	7	4	45	33	7	6	8	26	34	47
Tottenham H	42	18	3	0	65	20	1	4	16	22	51	45
LIVERPOOL	**42**	**12**	**5**	**4**	**42**	**33**	**5**	**5**	**11**	**25**	**40**	**44**
Sheffield W	42	13	5	3	37	15	3	6	12	20	40	43
West Ham U	42	14	2	5	48	25	5	2	14	34	46	42
Blackburn R	42	12	2	7	46	33	4	8	9	37	46	42
Stoke C	42	11	4	6	40	27	5	6	10	27	39	42
Burnley	42	9	9	3	39	26	7	1	13	31	44	42
Arsenal	42	11	5	5	42	31	6	2	13	27	44	41
WBA	42	10	5	6	45	25	3	8	10	25	40	39
Sunderland	42	12	6	3	45	26	2	3	16	19	48	37
Aston Villa	42	14	1	6	36	24	2	4	15	21	58	37
Blackpool	42	9	7	5	41	28	3	4	14	26	50	35
Leicester C	42	9	6	6	43	36	2	7	12	26	49	35
Sheffield U	42	7	5	9	30	29	5	6	10	20	35	35
Fulham	42	10	5	6	44	32	1	7	13	16	46	34
Wolves	42	8	2	11	33	36	5	2	14	26	53	30
Birmingham C	42	6	8	7	36	40	2	3	16	28	56	27

Reds' leading League goalscorer: Hunt 25

DIVISION 1 1965-1966

	P	W	D	L	F	A	W	D	L	F	A	Pts
LIVERPOOL	**42**	**17**	**2**	**2**	**52**	**15**	**9**	**7**	**5**	**27**	**19**	**61**
Leeds U	42	14	4	3	49	15	9	5	7	30	23	55
Burnley	42	15	3	3	45	20	9	4	8	34	27	55
Manchester U	42	12	8	1	50	20	6	7	8	34	39	51
Chelsea	42	11	4	6	30	21	11	3	7	35	32	51
WBA	42	11	6	4	58	34	8	6	7	33	35	50
Leicester C	42	12	4	5	40	28	9	3	9	40	37	49
Tottenham H	42	11	6	4	55	37	5	6	10	20	29	44
Sheffield U	42	11	6	4	37	25	5	5	11	19	34	43
Stoke C	42	12	6	3	42	22	3	6	12	23	42	42
Everton	42	12	6	3	39	19	3	5	13	17	43	41
West Ham U	42	12	5	4	46	33	3	4	14	24	50	39
Blackpool	42	9	5	7	36	29	5	4	12	19	36	37
Arsenal	42	8	8	5	36	31	4	5	12	26	44	37
Newcastle U	42	10	5	6	26	20	4	4	13	24	43	37
Aston Villa	42	10	3	8	39	34	5	3	13	30	46	36
Sheffield W	42	11	6	4	35	18	3	2	16	21	48	36
Nottingham F	42	11	3	7	31	26	3	5	13	25	46	36
Sunderland	42	13	2	6	36	28	1	6	14	15	44	36
Fulham	42	9	4	8	34	37	5	3	13	33	48	35
Northampton T	42	8	6	7	31	32	2	7	12	24	60	33
Blackburn R	42	6	1	14	30	36	2	3	16	27	52	20

Reds' leading League goalscorer: Hunt 30

DIVISION 1 1966-1967

	P	W	D	L	F	A	W	D	L	F	A	Pts
Manchester U	42	17	4	0	51	13	7	8	6	33	32	60
Nottingham F	42	16	4	1	41	13	7	6	8	23	28	56
Tottenham H	42	15	3	3	44	21	9	5	7	27	27	56
Leeds U	42	15	4	2	41	17	7	7	7	21	25	55
LIVERPOOL	**42**	**12**	**7**	**2**	**36**	**17**	**7**	**6**	**8**	**28**	**30**	**51**
Everton	42	11	4	6	39	22	8	6	7	26	24	48
Arsenal	42	11	6	4	32	20	5	8	8	26	27	46
Leicester C	42	12	4	5	47	28	6	4	11	31	43	44
Chelsea	42	7	9	5	33	29	8	5	8	34	33	44
Sheffield U	42	11	5	5	34	22	5	5	11	18	37	42
Sheffield W	42	9	7	5	39	19	5	6	10	17	28	41
Stoke C	42	11	5	5	40	21	6	2	13	23	37	41
WBA	42	11	1	9	40	28	5	6	10	37	45	39
Burnley	42	11	4	6	43	28	4	5	12	23	48	39
Manchester C	42	8	9	4	27	25	4	6	11	16	27	39
West Ham U	42	8	6	7	40	31	6	2	13	40	53	36
Sunderland	42	12	3	6	39	26	2	5	14	19	46	36
Fulham	42	8	7	6	49	34	3	5	13	22	49	34
Southampton	42	10	3	8	49	41	4	3	14	25	51	34
Newcastle U	42	9	5	7	24	27	3	4	14	15	54	33
Aston Villa	42	7	5	9	30	33	4	2	15	24	52	29
Blackpool	42	1	5	15	18	36	5	4	12	23	40	21

Reds' leading League goalscorer: Hunt 14

DIVISION 1 1967-1968

	P	W	D	L	F	A	W	D	L	F	A	Pts
Manchester C	42	17	2	2	52	16	9	4	8	34	27	58
Manchester U	42	15	2	4	49	21	9	6	6	40	34	56
LIVERPOOL	**42**	**17**	**2**	**2**	**51**	**17**	**5**	**9**	**7**	**20**	**23**	**55**
Leeds U	42	17	3	1	49	14	5	6	10	22	27	53
Everton	42	18	1	2	43	13	5	5	11	24	27	52
Chelsea	42	11	7	3	34	25	7	5	9	28	43	48
Tottenham H	42	11	7	3	44	20	8	2	11	26	39	47
WBA	42	12	4	5	45	25	5	8	8	30	37	46
Arsenal	42	12	6	3	37	23	5	4	12	23	33	44
Newcastle U	42	12	7	2	38	20	1	8	12	16	47	41
Nottingham F	42	11	6	4	34	22	3	5	13	18	42	39
West Ham U	42	8	5	8	43	30	6	5	10	30	39	38
Leicester C	42	7	7	7	37	34	6	5	10	27	35	38
Burnley	42	12	7	2	38	16	2	3	16	26	55	38
Sunderland	42	8	7	6	28	28	5	4	12	23	33	37
Southampton	42	9	8	4	37	31	4	3	14	29	52	37
Wolves	42	10	4	7	45	36	4	4	13	21	39	36
Stoke C	42	10	3	8	30	29	4	4	13	20	44	35
Sheffield W	42	6	10	5	32	24	5	2	14	19	39	34
Coventry C	42	8	5	8	32	32	1	10	10	19	39	33
Sheffield U	42	7	4	10	25	31	4	6	11	24	39	32
Fulham	42	6	4	11	27	41	4	3	14	29	57	27

Reds' leading League goalscorer: Hunt 25

DIVISION 1 1968-1969

	P	W	D	L	F	A	W	D	L	F	A	Pts
Leeds U	42	18	3	0	41	9	9	10	2	25	17	67
LIVERPOOL	**42**	**16**	**4**	**1**	**36**	**10**	**9**	**7**	**5**	**27**	**14**	**61**
Everton	42	14	5	2	43	10	7	10	4	34	26	57
Arsenal	42	12	6	3	31	12	10	6	5	25	15	56
Chelsea	42	11	7	3	40	24	9	3	9	33	29	50
Tottenham H	42	10	8	3	39	22	4	9	8	22	29	45
Southampton	42	13	5	3	41	21	3	8	10	16	27	45
West Ham U	42	10	8	3	47	22	3	10	8	19	28	44
Newcastle U	42	12	7	2	40	20	3	7	11	21	35	44
WBA	42	11	7	3	43	26	5	4	12	21	41	43
Manchester U	42	13	5	3	38	18	2	7	12	19	35	42
Ipswich T	42	10	4	7	32	26	5	7	9	27	34	41
Manchester C	42	13	6	2	49	20	2	4	15	15	35	40
Burnley	42	11	6	4	36	25	4	3	14	19	57	39
Sheffield W	42	7	9	5	27	26	3	7	11	14	28	36
Wolves	42	7	10	4	26	22	3	5	13	15	36	35
Sunderland	42	10	6	5	28	18	1	6	14	15	49	34
Nottingham F	42	6	6	9	17	22	4	7	10	28	35	33
Stoke C	42	9	7	5	24	24	0	8	13	16	39	33
Coventry C	42	8	6	7	32	22	2	5	14	14	42	31
Leicester C	42	8	8	5	27	24	1	4	16	12	44	30
QPR	42	4	7	10	20	33	0	3	18	19	62	18

Reds' leading League goalscorer: Hunt 13

DIVISION 1 1969-1970

	P	W	D	L	F	A	W	D	L	F	A	Pts
Everton	42	17	3	1	46	19	12	5	4	26	15	66
Leeds U	42	15	4	2	50	19	6	11	4	34	30	57
Chelsea	42	13	7	1	36	18	8	6	7	34	32	55
Derby Co	42	15	3	3	45	14	7	6	8	19	23	53
LIVERPOOL	**42**	**10**	**7**	**4**	**34**	**20**	**10**	**4**	**7**	**31**	**22**	**51**
Coventry C	42	9	6	6	35	28	10	5	6	23	20	49
Newcastle U	42	14	2	5	42	16	3	11	7	15	19	47
Manchester U	42	8	9	4	37	27	6	8	7	29	34	45
Stoke C	42	10	7	4	31	23	5	8	8	25	29	45
Manchester C	42	8	6	7	25	22	8	5	8	30	26	43
Tottenham H	42	11	2	8	27	21	6	7	8	27	34	43
Arsenal	42	7	10	4	29	23	5	8	8	22	26	42
Wolves	42	8	8	5	30	23	4	8	9	25	34	40
Burnley	42	7	7	7	33	29	5	8	8	23	32	39
Nottingham F	42	8	9	4	28	28	2	9	10	22	43	38
WBA	42	10	6	5	39	25	4	3	14	19	41	37
West Ham U	42	8	8	5	28	21	4	4	13	23	39	36
Ipswich T	42	9	5	7	23	20	1	6	14	17	43	31
Southampton	42	3	12	6	24	27	3	5	13	22	40	29
Crystal P	42	5	6	10	20	36	1	9	11	14	32	27
Sunderland	42	4	11	6	17	24	2	3	16	13	44	26
Sheffield W	42	6	5	10	23	27	2	4	15	17	44	25

Reds' leading League goalscorer: Graham 13

DIVISION 1 1970-1971

	P	W	D	L	F	A	W	D	L	F	A	Pts
Arsenal	42	18	3	0	41	6	11	4	6	30	23	65
Leeds U	42	16	2	3	40	12	11	8	2	32	18	64
Tottenham H	42	11	5	5	33	19	8	9	4	21	14	52
Wolves	42	13	3	5	33	22	9	5	7	31	32	52
LIVERPOOL	**42**	**11**	**10**	**0**	**30**	**10**	**6**	**7**	**8**	**12**	**14**	**51**
Chelsea	42	12	6	3	34	21	6	9	6	18	21	51
Southampton	42	12	5	4	35	15	5	7	9	21	29	46
Manchester U	42	9	6	6	29	24	7	5	9	36	42	43
Derby Co	42	9	5	7	32	26	7	5	9	24	28	42
Coventry C	42	12	4	5	24	12	4	6	11	13	26	42
Manchester C	42	7	9	5	30	22	5	8	8	17	20	41
Newcastle U	42	9	9	3	27	16	5	4	12	17	30	41
Stoke C	42	10	7	4	28	11	2	6	13	16	37	37
Everton	42	10	7	4	32	16	2	6	13	22	44	37
Huddersfield T	42	7	8	6	19	16	4	6	11	21	33	36
Nottingham F	42	9	4	8	29	26	5	4	12	13	35	36
WBA	42	9	8	4	34	25	1	7	13	24	50	35
Crystal P	42	9	5	7	24	24	3	6	12	15	33	35
Ipswich T	42	9	4	8	28	22	3	6	12	14	26	34
West Ham U	42	6	8	7	28	30	4	6	11	19	30	34
Burnley	42	4	8	9	20	31	3	5	13	9	32	27
Blackpool	42	3	9	9	22	31	1	6	14	12	35	23

Reds' leading League goalscorer: A.Evans 10

DIVISION 1 1971-1972

	P	W	D	L	F	A	W	D	L	F	A	Pts
Derby Co	42	16	4	1	43	10	8	6	7	26	23	58
Leeds U	42	17	4	0	54	10	7	5	9	19	21	57
LIVERPOOL	**42**	**17**	**3**	**1**	**48**	**16**	**7**	**6**	**8**	**16**	**14**	**57**
Manchester C	42	16	3	2	48	15	7	8	6	29	30	57
Arsenal	42	15	2	4	36	13	7	6	8	22	27	52
Tottenham H	42	16	3	2	45	13	3	10	8	18	29	51
Chelsea	42	12	7	2	41	20	6	5	10	17	29	48
Manchester U	42	13	2	6	39	26	6	8	7	30	35	48
Wolves	42	10	7	4	35	23	8	4	9	30	34	47
Sheffield U	42	10	8	3	39	26	7	4	10	22	34	46
Newcastle U	42	10	6	5	30	18	5	5	11	19	34	41
Leicester C	42	9	6	6	18	11	4	7	10	23	35	39
Ipswich T	42	7	8	6	19	19	4	8	9	20	34	38
West Ham U	42	10	6	5	31	19	2	6	13	16	32	36
Everton	42	8	9	4	28	17	1	9	11	9	31	36
WBA	42	6	7	8	22	23	6	4	11	20	31	35
Stoke C	42	6	10	5	26	25	4	5	12	13	31	35
Coventry C	42	7	10	4	27	23	2	5	14	17	44	33
Southampton	42	8	5	8	31	28	4	2	15	21	52	31
Crystal P	42	4	8	9	26	31	4	5	12	13	34	29
Nottingham F	42	6	4	11	25	29	2	5	14	22	52	25
Huddersfield T	42	4	7	10	12	22	2	6	13	15	37	25

Reds' leading League goalscorer: Toshack 13

DIVISION 1 1972-1973

	P	W	D	L	F	A	W	D	L	F	A	Pts
LIVERPOOL	**42**	**17**	**3**	**1**	**45**	**19**	**8**	**7**	**6**	**27**	**23**	**60**
Arsenal	42	14	5	2	31	14	9	6	6	26	29	57
Leeds U	42	15	4	2	45	13	6	7	8	26	32	53
Ipswich T	42	10	7	4	34	20	7	7	7	21	25	48
Wolves	42	13	3	5	43	23	5	8	8	23	31	47
West Ham U	42	12	5	4	45	25	5	7	9	22	28	46
Derby Co	42	15	3	3	43	18	4	5	12	13	36	46
Tottenham H	42	10	5	6	33	23	6	8	7	25	25	45
Newcastle U	42	12	6	3	35	19	4	7	10	25	32	45
Birmingham	42	11	7	3	39	22	4	5	12	14	32	42
Manchester C	42	12	4	5	36	20	3	7	11	21	40	41
Chelsea	42	9	6	6	30	22	4	8	9	19	29	40
Southampton	42	8	11	2	26	17	3	7	11	21	35	40
Sheffield U	42	11	4	6	28	18	4	6	11	23	41	40
Stoke C	42	11	8	2	38	17	3	2	16	23	39	38
Leicester C	42	7	9	5	23	18	3	8	10	17	28	37
Everton	42	9	5	7	27	21	4	6	11	14	28	37
Manchester U	42	9	7	5	24	19	3	6	12	20	41	37
Coventry C	42	9	5	7	27	24	4	4	13	13	31	35
Norwich C	42	7	9	5	22	19	4	1	16	14	44	32
Crystal P	42	7	7	7	25	21	2	5	14	16	37	30
WBA	42	8	7	6	25	24	1	3	17	13	38	28

Reds' leading League goalscorers: Keegan & Toshack 13

DIVISION 1 1973-1974

	P	W	D	L	F	A	W	D	L	F	A	Pts
Leeds U	42	12	8	1	38	18	12	6	3	28	13	62
LIVERPOOL	**42**	**18**	**2**	**1**	**34**	**11**	**4**	**11**	**6**	**18**	**20**	**57**
Derby Co	42	13	7	1	40	16	4	7	10	12	26	48
Ipswich T	42	10	7	4	38	21	8	4	9	29	37	47
Stoke C	42	13	6	2	39	15	2	10	9	15	27	46
Burnley	42	10	9	2	29	16	6	5	10	27	37	46
Everton	42	12	7	2	29	14	4	5	12	21	34	44
QPR	42	8	10	3	30	17	5	7	9	26	35	43
Leicester C	42	10	7	4	35	17	3	9	9	16	24	42
Arsenal	42	9	7	5	23	16	5	7	9	26	35	42
Tottenham H	42	9	4	8	26	27	5	10	6	19	23	42
Wolves	42	11	6	4	30	18	2	9	10	19	31	41
Sheffield U	42	7	7	7	25	22	7	5	9	19	27	40
Manchester C	42	10	7	4	25	17	4	5	12	14	29	40
Newcastle U	42	9	6	6	28	21	4	6	11	21	27	38
Coventry C	42	10	5	6	25	18	4	5	12	18	36	38
Chelsea	42	9	4	8	36	29	3	9	9	20	31	37
West Ham U	42	7	7	7	36	32	4	8	9	19	28	37
Birmingham C	42	10	7	4	30	21	2	6	13	22	43	37
Southampton	42	8	10	3	30	20	3	4	14	17	48	36
Manchester U	42	7	7	7	23	20	3	5	13	15	28	32
Norwich C	42	6	9	6	25	27	1	6	14	12	35	29

Reds' leading League goalscorers: Keegan 12

DIVISION 1 1974-1975

	P	W	D	L	F	A	W	D	L	F	A	Pts
Derby Co	42	14	4	3	41	18	7	7	7	26	31	53
LIVERPOOL	**42**	**14**	**5**	**2**	**44**	**17**	**6**	**6**	**9**	**16**	**22**	**51**
Ipswich T	42	17	2	2	47	14	6	3	12	19	30	51
Everton	42	10	9	2	33	19	6	9	6	23	23	50
Stoke C	42	12	7	2	40	18	5	8	8	24	30	49
Sheffield U	42	12	7	2	35	20	6	6	9	23	31	49
Middlesbrough	42	11	7	3	33	14	7	5	9	21	26	48
Manchester C	42	16	3	2	40	15	2	7	12	14	39	46
Leeds U	42	10	8	3	34	20	6	5	10	23	29	45
Burnley	42	11	6	4	40	29	6	5	10	28	38	45
QPR	42	10	4	7	25	17	6	6	9	29	37	42
Wolves	42	12	5	4	43	21	2	6	13	14	33	39
West Ham U	42	10	6	5	38	22	3	7	11	20	37	39
Coventry C	42	8	9	4	31	27	4	6	11	20	35	39
Newcastle U	42	12	4	5	39	23	3	5	13	20	49	39
Arsenal	42	10	6	5	31	16	3	5	13	16	33	37
Birmingham C	42	10	4	7	34	28	4	5	12	19	33	37
Leicester C	42	8	7	6	25	17	4	5	12	21	43	36
Tottenham H	42	8	4	9	29	27	5	4	12	23	36	34
Luton T	42	8	6	7	27	26	3	5	13	20	39	33
Chelsea	42	4	9	8	22	31	5	6	10	20	41	33
Carlisle U	42	8	2	11	22	21	4	3	14	21	38	29

Reds' leading League goalscorers: Toshack 12

DIVISION 1 1975-1976

	P	W	D	L	F	A	W	D	L	F	A	Pts
LIVERPOOL	**42**	**14**	**5**	**2**	**41**	**21**	**9**	**9**	**3**	**25**	**10**	**60**
QPR	42	17	4	0	42	13	7	7	7	25	20	59
Manchester U	42	16	4	1	40	13	7	6	8	28	29	56
Derby Co	42	15	3	3	45	30	6	8	7	30	28	53
Leeds U	42	13	3	5	37	19	8	6	7	28	27	51
Ipswich T	42	11	6	4	36	23	5	8	8	18	25	46
Leicester C	42	9	9	3	29	24	4	10	7	19	27	45
Manchester C	42	14	5	2	46	18	2	6	13	18	28	43
Tottenham H	42	6	10	5	33	32	8	5	8	30	31	43
Norwich C	42	10	5	6	33	26	6	5	10	25	32	42
Everton	42	10	7	4	37	24	5	5	11	23	42	42
Stoke C	42	8	5	8	25	24	7	6	8	23	26	41
Middlesbrough	42	9	7	5	23	11	6	3	12	23	34	40
Coventry C	42	6	9	6	22	22	7	5	9	25	35	40
Newcastle U	42	11	4	6	51	26	4	5	12	20	36	39
Aston Villa	42	11	8	2	32	17	0	9	12	19	42	39
Arsenal	42	11	4	6	33	19	2	6	13	14	34	36
West Ham U	42	10	5	6	26	23	3	5	13	22	48	36
Birmingham C	42	11	5	5	36	26	2	2	17	21	49	33
Wolves	42	7	6	8	27	25	3	4	14	24	43	30
Burnley	42	6	6	9	23	26	3	4	14	20	40	28
Sheffield U	42	4	7	10	19	32	2	3	16	14	50	22

Reds' leading League goalscorer: Toshack 16

DIVISION 1 1978-1979

	P	W	D	L	F	A	W	D	L	F	A	Pts
LIVERPOOL	**42**	**19**	**2**	**0**	**51**	**4**	**11**	**6**	**4**	**34**	**12**	**68**
Nottingham F	42	11	10	0	34	10	10	8	3	27	16	60
WBA	42	13	5	3	38	15	11	6	4	34	20	59
Everton	42	12	7	2	32	17	5	10	6	20	23	51
Leeds U	42	11	4	6	41	25	7	10	4	29	27	50
Ipswich T	42	11	4	6	34	21	9	5	7	29	28	49
Arsenal	42	11	8	2	37	18	6	6	9	24	30	48
Aston Villa	42	8	9	4	37	26	7	7	7	22	23	46
Manchester U	42	9	7	5	29	25	6	8	7	31	38	45
Coventry C	42	11	7	3	41	29	3	9	9	17	39	44
Tottenham H	42	7	8	6	19	25	6	7	8	29	36	41
Middlesbrough	42	10	5	6	33	21	5	5	11	24	29	40
Bristol C	42	11	6	4	34	19	4	4	13	13	32	40
Southampton	42	9	10	2	35	20	3	6	12	12	33	40
Manchester C	42	9	5	7	34	28	4	8	9	24	28	39
Norwich C	42	7	10	4	29	19	0	13	8	22	38	37
Bolton W	42	10	5	6	36	28	2	6	13	18	47	35
Wolves	42	10	4	7	26	26	3	4	14	18	42	34
Derby Co	42	8	5	8	25	25	2	6	13	19	46	31
QPR	42	4	9	8	24	33	2	4	15	21	40	25
Birmingham C	42	5	9	7	24	25	1	1	19	13	39	22
Chelsea	42	3	5	13	23	42	2	5	14	21	50	20

Reds' leading League goalscorer: Dalglish 21

DIVISION 1 1981-1982

	P	W	D	L	F	A	W	D	L	F	A	Pts
LIVERPOOL	**42**	**14**	**3**	**4**	**39**	**14**	**12**	**6**	**3**	**41**	**18**	**87**
Ipswich T	42	17	1	3	47	25	9	4	8	28	28	83
Manchester U	42	12	6	3	27	9	10	6	5	32	20	78
Tottenham H	42	12	4	5	41	26	8	7	6	26	22	71
Arsenal	42	13	5	3	27	15	7	6	8	21	22	71
Swansea C	42	13	3	5	34	16	8	3	10	24	35	69
Southampton	42	15	2	4	49	30	4	7	10	23	37	66
Everton	42	11	7	3	33	21	6	6	9	23	29	64
West Ham U	42	9	10	2	42	29	5	6	10	24	28	58
Manchester C	42	9	7	5	32	23	6	6	9	17	27	58
Aston Villa	42	9	6	6	28	24	6	6	9	27	29	57
Nottingham F	42	7	7	7	19	20	8	5	8	23	28	57
Brighton & HA	42	8	7	6	30	24	5	6	10	13	28	52
Coventry C	42	9	4	8	31	24	4	7	10	25	38	50
Notts Co	42	8	5	8	32	33	5	3	13	29	36	47
Birmingham C	42	8	6	7	29	25	2	8	11	24	36	44
WBA	42	6	6	9	24	25	5	5	11	22	32	44
Stoke C	42	9	2	10	27	28	3	6	12	17	35	44
Sunderland	42	6	5	10	19	26	5	6	10	19	32	44
Leeds U	42	6	11	4	23	20	4	1	16	16	41	42
Wolves	42	8	5	8	19	20	2	5	14	13	43	40
Middlesbrough	42	5	9	7	20	24	3	6	12	14	28	39

Reds' leading League goalscorer: Rush 17

DIVISION 1 1976-1977

	P	W	D	L	F	A	W	D	L	F	A	Pts
LIVERPOOL	**42**	**18**	**3**	**0**	**47**	**11**	**5**	**8**	**8**	**15**	**22**	**57**
Manchester C	42	15	5	1	38	13	6	9	6	22	21	56
Ipswich T	42	15	4	2	41	11	7	4	10	25	28	52
Aston Villa	42	17	3	1	55	17	5	4	12	21	33	51
Newcastle U	42	14	6	1	40	15	4	7	10	24	34	49
Manchester U	42	12	6	3	41	22	6	5	10	30	40	47
WBA	42	10	6	5	38	22	6	7	8	24	34	45
Arsenal	42	11	6	4	37	20	5	5	11	27	39	43
Everton	42	9	7	5	35	24	5	7	9	27	40	42
Leeds U	42	8	8	5	28	26	7	4	10	20	25	42
Leicester C	42	8	9	4	30	28	4	9	8	17	32	42
Middlesbrough	42	11	6	4	25	14	3	7	11	15	31	41
Birmingham C	42	10	6	5	38	25	3	6	12	25	36	38
QPR	42	10	7	4	31	21	3	5	13	16	31	38
Derby Co	42	9	9	3	36	18	0	10	11	14	37	37
Norwich C	42	12	4	5	30	23	2	5	14	17	41	37
West Ham U	42	9	6	6	28	23	2	8	11	18	42	36
Bristol C	42	8	7	6	25	19	3	6	12	13	29	35
Coventry C	42	7	9	5	34	26	3	6	12	14	33	35
Sunderland	42	9	5	7	29	16	2	7	12	17	38	34
Stoke C	42	9	8	4	21	16	1	6	14	7	35	34
Tottenham H	42	9	7	5	26	20	3	2	16	22	52	33

Reds' leading League goalscorer: Keegan 16

DIVISION 1 1979-1980

	P	W	D	L	F	A	W	D	L	F	A	Pts
LIVERPOOL	**42**	**15**	**6**	**0**	**46**	**8**	**10**	**4**	**7**	**35**	**22**	**60**
Manchester U	42	17	3	1	43	8	7	7	7	22	27	58
Ipswich T	42	14	4	3	43	13	8	5	8	25	26	53
Arsenal	42	8	10	3	24	12	10	6	5	28	24	52
Nottingham F	42	16	4	1	44	11	4	4	13	19	32	48
Wolves	42	9	6	6	29	20	10	3	8	29	27	47
Aston Villa	42	11	5	5	29	22	5	9	7	22	28	46
Southampton	42	14	2	5	53	24	4	7	10	12	29	45
Middlesbrough	42	11	7	3	31	14	5	5	11	19	30	44
WBA	42	9	8	4	37	23	2	11	8	17	27	41
Leeds U	42	10	7	4	30	17	3	7	11	16	33	40
Norwich C	42	10	8	3	38	30	3	6	12	20	36	40
Crystal P	42	9	9	3	26	13	3	7	11	15	37	40
Tottenham H	42	11	5	5	30	22	4	5	12	22	40	40
Coventry C	42	12	2	7	34	24	4	5	12	22	42	39
Brighton & HA	42	8	8	5	25	20	3	7	11	22	37	37
Manchester C	42	8	8	5	28	25	4	5	12	15	41	37
Stoke C	42	9	4	8	27	26	4	6	11	17	32	36
Everton	42	7	7	7	28	25	2	10	9	15	26	35
Bristol C	42	6	6	9	22	30	3	7	11	15	36	31
Derby Co	42	9	4	8	36	29	2	4	15	11	38	30
Bolton W	42	5	11	5	19	21	0	4	17	19	52	25

Reds' leading League goalscorer: Johnson 21

DIVISION 1 1982-1983

	P	W	D	L	F	A	W	D	L	F	A	Pts
LIVERPOOL	**42**	**16**	**4**	**1**	**55**	**16**	**8**	**6**	**7**	**32**	**21**	**82**
Walford	42	16	2	3	49	20	6	3	12	25	37	71
Manchester U	42	14	7	0	39	10	5	6	10	17	28	70
Tottenham H	42	15	4	2	50	15	5	5	11	15	35	69
Nottingham F	42	12	5	4	34	18	8	4	9	28	32	69
Aston Villa	42	17	2	2	47	15	4	3	14	15	35	68
Everton	42	13	6	2	43	19	5	4	12	23	29	64
West Ham U	42	13	3	5	41	23	7	1	13	27	39	64
Ipswich T	42	11	3	7	39	23	4	10	7	25	27	58
Arsenal	42	11	6	4	36	19	5	4	12	22	37	58
WBA	42	11	5	5	35	20	4	7	10	16	29	57
Southampton	42	11	5	5	36	22	4	7	10	18	36	57
Stoke C	42	13	4	4	34	21	3	5	13	19	43	57
Norwich C	42	10	6	5	30	18	4	6	11	22	40	54
Notts Co	42	12	4	5	37	25	3	3	15	18	46	52
Sunderland	42	7	10	4	30	22	5	4	12	18	39	50
Birmingham C	42	9	7	5	29	24	3	7	11	11	31	50
Luton T	42	7	7	7	34	33	5	6	10	31	51	49
Coventry C	42	10	5	6	29	17	3	4	14	19	42	48
Manchester C	42	9	5	7	26	23	4	3	14	21	47	47
Swansea C	42	10	4	7	32	29	0	7	14	19	40	41
Brighton & HA	42	8	7	6	25	22	1	6	14	13	46	40

Reds' leading League goalscorer: Rush 24

DIVISION 1 1977-1978

	P	W	D	L	F	A	W	D	L	F	A	Pts
Nottingham F	42	15	6	0	37	8	10	8	3	32	16	64
LIVERPOOL	**42**	**15**	**4**	**2**	**37**	**11**	**9**	**5**	**7**	**28**	**23**	**57**
Everton	42	14	4	3	47	22	8	7	6	29	23	55
Manchester C	42	14	4	3	46	21	6	8	7	28	30	52
Arsenal	42	14	5	2	38	12	7	5	9	22	25	52
WBA	42	13	5	3	35	18	5	9	7	27	35	50
Coventry C	42	13	5	3	48	23	5	7	9	27	39	48
Aston Villa	42	11	4	6	33	18	7	6	8	24	24	46
Leeds U	42	12	4	5	39	21	6	6	9	24	32	46
Manchester U	42	9	6	6	32	23	7	4	10	35	40	42
Birmingham C	42	8	5	8	32	30	8	4	9	23	30	41
Derby Co	42	10	7	4	37	24	4	6	11	17	35	41
Norwich C	42	10	8	3	28	20	1	10	10	24	46	40
Middlesbrough	42	8	8	5	25	19	4	7	10	17	35	39
Wolves	42	7	8	6	30	27	5	4	12	21	37	36
Chelsea	42	7	11	3	28	20	4	3	14	18	49	36
Bristol C	42	9	6	6	37	26	2	7	12	12	27	35
Ipswich T	42	10	5	6	32	24	1	8	12	15	37	35
QPR	42	8	8	5	27	26	1	7	13	20	38	33
West Ham U	42	8	6	7	31	28	4	2	15	21	41	32
Newcastle U	42	4	6	11	26	37	2	4	15	16	41	22
Leicester C	42	4	7	10	16	32	1	5	15	10	38	22

Reds' leading League goalscorer: Dalglish 20

DIVISION 1 1980-1981

	P	W	D	L	F	A	W	D	L	F	A	Pts
Aston Villa	42	16	3	2	40	13	10	5	6	32	27	60
Ipswich T	42	15	4	2	45	14	8	6	7	32	29	56
Arsenal	42	13	8	0	36	17	6	7	8	25	28	53
WBA	42	15	4	2	40	15	5	8	8	20	27	52
LIVERPOOL	**42**	**13**	**5**	**3**	**38**	**15**	**4**	**12**	**5**	**24**	**27**	**51**
Southampton	42	15	4	2	47	22	5	6	10	29	34	50
Nottingham F	42	15	3	3	44	20	4	9	8	18	24	50
Manchester U	42	9	11	1	30	14	6	7	8	21	22	48
Leeds U	42	10	5	6	19	19	7	5	9	20	28	44
Tottenham H	42	9	9	3	44	31	5	6	10	26	37	43
Stoke C	42	8	9	4	31	23	4	9	8	20	37	42
Manchester C	42	10	7	4	35	25	4	4	13	21	34	39
Birmingham C	42	11	5	5	32	23	2	7	12	18	38	38
Middlesbrough	42	14	4	3	38	16	2	1	18	15	45	37
Everton	42	8	6	7	32	25	5	4	12	23	33	36
Coventry C	42	9	6	6	31	30	4	4	13	17	38	36
Sunderland	42	10	4	7	32	19	4	3	14	20	34	35
Wolves	42	11	2	8	26	20	2	7	12	17	35	35
Brighton & HA	42	10	3	8	30	26	4	4	13	24	41	35
Norwich C	42	9	7	5	34	25	4	0	17	15	48	33
Leicester C	42	7	5	9	20	23	6	1	14	20	44	32
Crystal P	42	6	4	11	32	37	0	3	18	15	46	19

Reds' leading League goalscorer: McDermott 13

DIVISION 1 1983-1984

	P	W	D	L	F	A	W	D	L	F	A	Pts
LIVERPOOL	**42**	**14**	**5**	**2**	**50**	**12**	**8**	**9**	**4**	**23**	**20**	**80**
Southampton	42	15	4	2	44	17	7	7	7	22	21	77
Nottingham F	42	14	4	3	47	17	8	4	9	29	28	74
Manchester U	42	14	3	4	43	18	6	11	4	28	23	74
QPR	42	14	4	3	37	12	8	3	10	30	25	73
Arsenal	42	10	5	6	41	29	8	4	9	33	31	63
Everton	42	9	9	3	21	12	7	5	9	23	30	62
Tottenham H	42	11	4	6	31	24	6	6	9	33	41	61
West Ham U	42	10	4	7	39	24	7	5	9	21	31	60
Aston Villa	42	14	3	4	34	22	3	6	12	25	39	60
Watford	42	9	7	5	36	31	7	2	12	32	46	57
Ipswich T	42	11	4	6	34	23	4	4	13	21	34	53
Sunderland	42	8	9	4	26	18	5	4	12	16	35	52
Norwich C	42	9	8	4	34	20	3	7	11	14	29	51
Leicester C	42	11	5	5	40	30	2	7	12	25	38	51
Luton T	42	7	5	9	30	33	7	4	10	23	33	51
WBA	42	10	4	7	30	25	4	5	12	18	37	51
Stoke C	42	11	4	6	30	23	2	7	12	14	40	50
Coventry C	42	8	5	8	33	33	5	6	10	24	44	50
Birmingham C	42	7	7	7	19	18	5	5	11	20	32	48
Notts Co	42	6	7	8	31	36	4	4	13	19	36	41
Wolves	42	4	8	9	15	28	2	3	16	12	52	29

Reds' leading League goalscorer: Rush 32

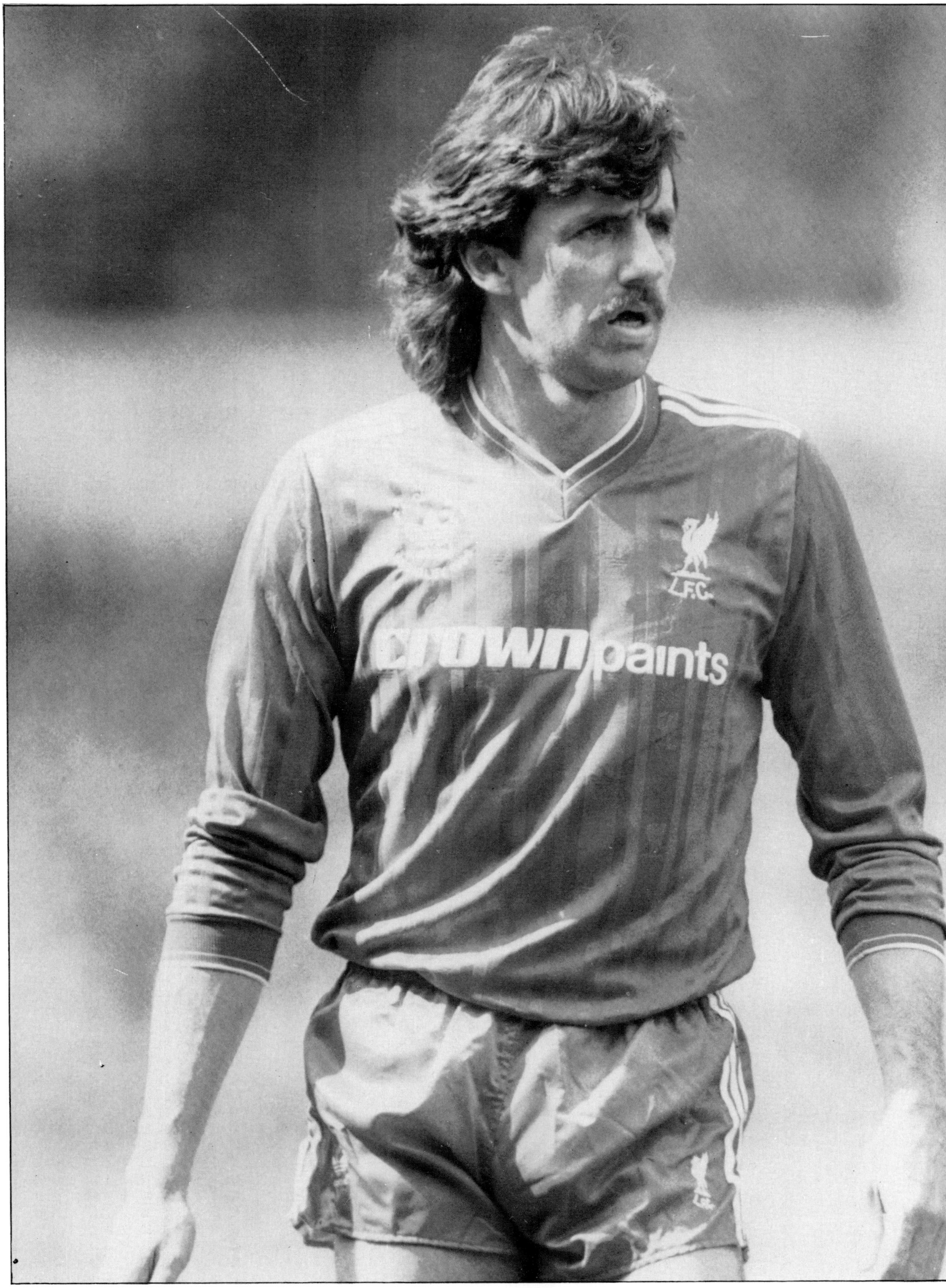

Elegant defender Mark Lawrenson joined Liverpool from Brighton for £900,000 in August 1981 and went on to make nearly 350 senior appearances for them, gaining three League Championship medals and three Milk Cup winners' medals as well as a European Cup winners' medal. A regular for the Republic of Ireland, Lawrenson retired through injury in 1988. He was appointed manager of Oxford United but subsequently lost his job after Dean Saunders was transferred to Derby over his head. Ironically, Saunders later cost Liverpool nearly £3 million.

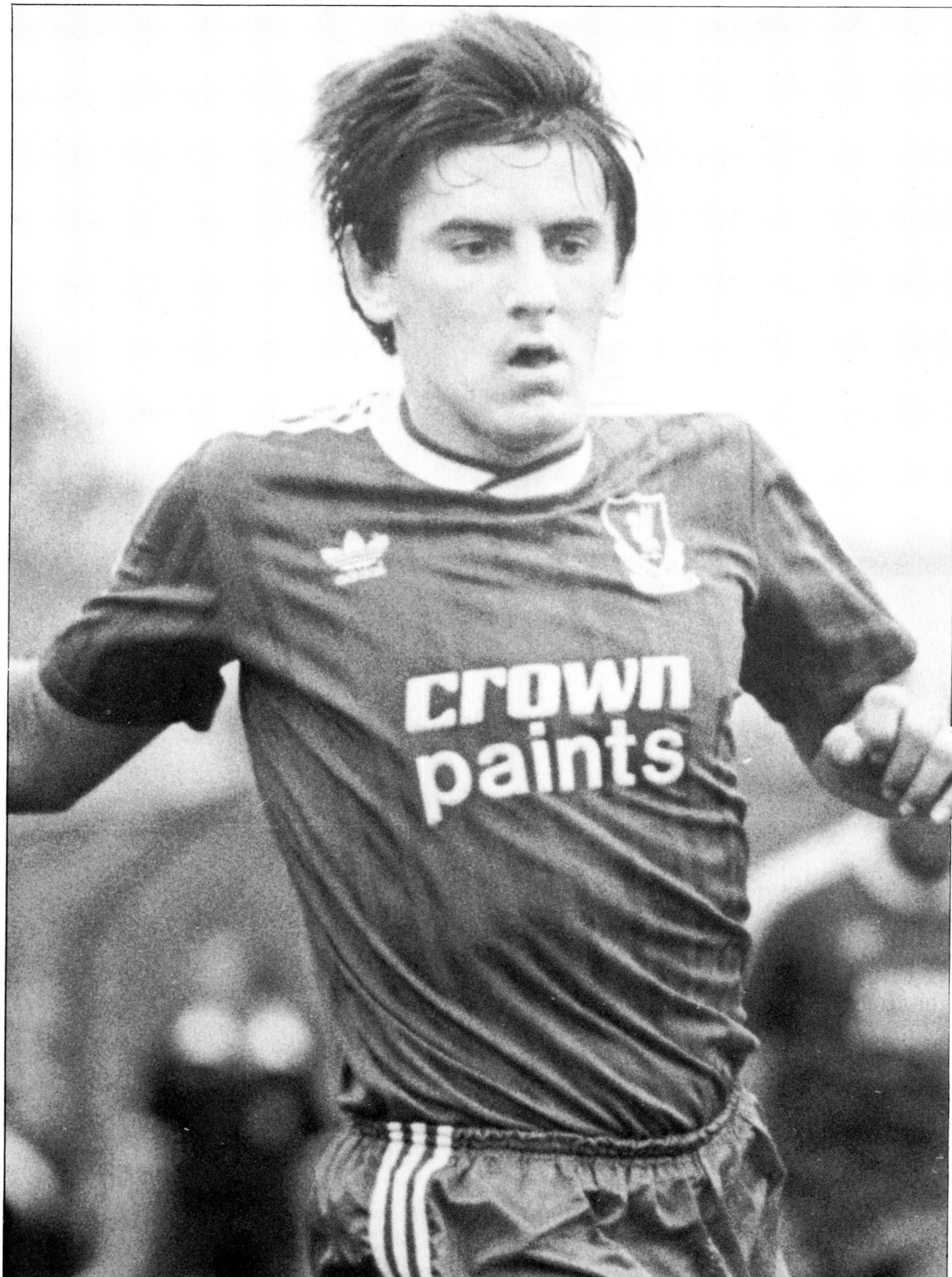

England midfielder Peter Beardsley cost Liverpool £1.9 million when he joined them from Newcastle United in the 1987 close season, a fee which made him the most expensive player to move between Football League clubs. His career had been rescued by Newcastle, when he was playing in the NASL with Vancouver Whitecaps and he played alongside Kevin Keegan for the Magpies. With Liverpool he scored 46 goals in 131 League games and gained two League Championship medals and one FA Cup winners' medal before joining Everton for £1 million in August 1991.

DIVISION 1 1984-1985

	P	W	D	L	F	A	W	D	L	F	A	Pts
Everton	42	16	3	2	58	17	12	3	6	30	26	90
LIVERPOOL	**42**	**12**	**4**	**5**	**36**	**19**	**10**	**7**	**4**	**32**	**16**	**77**
Tottenham H	42	11	3	7	46	31	12	5	4	32	20	77
Manchester U	42	13	6	2	47	13	9	4	8	30	34	76
Southampton	42	13	4	4	29	18	6	7	8	27	29	68
Chelsea	42	13	3	5	38	20	5	9	7	25	28	66
Arsenal	42	14	5	2	37	14	5	4	12	24	35	66
Sheffield W	42	12	7	2	39	21	5	7	9	19	24	65
Nottingham F	42	13	4	4	35	18	6	3	12	21	30	64
Aston Villa	42	10	7	4	34	20	5	4	12	26	40	56
Watford	42	10	5	6	48	30	4	8	9	33	41	55
WBA	42	11	4	6	36	23	5	3	13	22	39	55
Luton T	42	12	5	4	40	22	3	4	14	17	39	54
Newcastle U	42	11	4	6	33	26	2	9	10	22	44	52
Leicester C	42	10	4	7	39	25	5	2	14	26	48	51
West Ham U	42	7	8	6	27	23	6	4	11	24	45	51
Ipswich T	42	8	7	6	27	20	5	4	12	19	37	50
Coventry C	42	11	3	7	29	22	4	2	15	18	42	50
QPR	42	11	6	4	41	30	2	5	14	12	42	50
Norwich C	42	9	6	6	28	24	4	4	13	18	40	49
Sunderland	42	7	6	8	20	26	3	4	14	20	36	40
Stoke C	42	3	3	15	18	41	0	5	16	6	50	17

Reds' leading League goalscorer: Wark 18

DIVISION 1 1985-1986

	P	W	D	L	F	A	W	D	L	F	A	Pts
LIVERPOOL	**42**	**16**	**4**	**1**	**58**	**14**	**10**	**6**	**5**	**31**	**23**	**88**
Everton	42	16	3	2	54	18	10	5	6	33	23	86
West Ham U	42	17	2	2	48	16	9	4	8	26	24	84
Manchester U	42	12	5	4	35	12	10	5	6	35	24	76
Sheffield W	42	13	6	2	36	23	8	4	9	27	31	73
Chelsea	42	12	4	5	32	27	8	7	6	25	29	71
Arsenal	42	13	5	3	29	15	7	4	10	20	32	69
Nottingham F	42	11	5	5	38	25	8	6	7	31	28	68
Luton T	42	12	6	3	37	15	6	6	9	24	29	66
Tottenham H	42	12	2	7	47	25	7	6	8	27	27	65
Newcastle U	42	12	5	4	46	31	5	7	9	21	41	63
Watford	42	11	6	4	40	22	5	5	11	29	40	59
QPR	42	12	3	6	33	20	3	4	14	20	44	52
Southampton	42	10	6	5	32	18	2	4	15	19	44	46
Manchester C	42	7	7	7	25	26	4	5	12	18	31	45
Aston Villa	42	7	6	8	27	28	3	8	10	24	39	44
Coventry C	42	6	5	10	31	35	5	5	11	17	36	43
Oxford U	42	7	7	7	34	27	3	5	13	28	53	42
Leicester C	42	7	8	6	35	35	3	4	14	19	41	42
Ipswich T	42	8	5	8	20	24	3	3	15	12	31	41
Birmingham C	42	5	2	14	13	25	3	3	15	17	48	29
WBA	42	3	8	10	21	36	1	4	16	14	53	24

Reds' leading League goalscorer: Rush 22

DIVISION 1 1986-1987

	P	W	D	L	F	A	W	D	L	F	A	Pts
Everton	42	16	4	1	49	11	10	4	7	27	20	86
LIVERPOOL	**42**	**15**	**3**	**3**	**43**	**16**	**8**	**5**	**8**	**29**	**26**	**77**
Tottenham H	42	14	3	4	40	14	7	5	9	28	29	71
Arsenal	42	12	5	4	31	12	8	5	8	27	23	70
Norwich C	42	9	10	2	27	20	8	7	6	26	31	68
Wimbledon	42	11	5	5	32	22	8	4	9	25	28	66
Luton T	42	14	5	2	29	13	4	7	10	18	32	66
Nottingham F	42	12	8	1	36	14	6	3	12	28	37	65
Watford	42	12	5	4	38	20	6	4	11	29	34	63
Coventry C	42	14	4	3	35	17	3	8	10	15	28	63
Manchester U	42	13	3	5	38	18	1	11	9	14	27	56
Southampton	42	11	5	5	44	24	3	5	13	25	44	52
Sheffield W	42	9	7	5	39	24	4	6	11	19	35	52
Chelsea	42	8	6	7	30	30	5	7	9	23	34	52
West Ham U	42	10	4	7	33	28	4	6	11	19	39	52
QPR	42	9	7	5	31	27	4	4	13	17	37	50
Newcastle U	42	10	4	7	33	29	2	7	12	14	36	47
Oxford U	42	8	8	5	30	25	3	5	13	14	44	46
Charlton A	42	7	7	7	26	22	4	4	13	19	33	44
Leicester C	42	9	7	5	39	24	2	2	17	15	52	42
Manchester C	42	8	6	7	28	24	0	9	12	8	33	39
Aston Villa	42	7	7	7	25	25	1	5	15	20	54	36

Reds' leading League goalscorer: Rush 30

DIVISION 1 1987-1988

	P	W	D	L	F	A	W	D	L	F	A	Pts
LIVERPOOL	**40**	**15**	**5**	**0**	**49**	**9**	**11**	**7**	**2**	**38**	**15**	**90**
Manchester U	40	14	5	1	41	17	9	7	4	30	21	81
Nottingham F	40	11	7	2	40	17	9	6	5	27	22	73
Everton	40	14	4	2	34	11	5	9	6	19	16	70
QPR	40	12	4	4	30	14	7	6	7	18	24	67
Arsenal	40	11	4	5	35	16	7	8	5	23	23	66
Wimbledon	40	8	9	3	32	20	6	6	8	26	27	57
Newcastle U	40	9	6	5	32	23	5	8	7	23	30	56
Luton T	40	11	6	3	40	21	3	5	12	17	37	53
Coventry C	40	6	8	6	23	25	7	6	7	23	28	53
Sheffield W	40	10	2	8	27	30	5	6	9	25	36	53
Southampton	40	6	8	6	27	26	6	6	8	22	27	50
Tottenham H	40	9	5	6	26	23	3	6	11	12	25	47
Norwich C	40	7	5	8	26	26	5	4	11	14	26	45
Derby Co	40	6	7	7	18	17	4	6	10	17	28	43
West Ham U	40	6	9	5	23	21	3	6	11	17	31	42
Charlton A	40	7	7	6	23	21	2	8	10	15	31	42
Chelsea	40	7	11	2	24	17	2	4	14	26	51	42
Portsmouth	40	4	8	8	21	27	3	6	11	15	39	35
Watford	40	4	5	11	15	24	3	6	11	12	27	32
Oxford U	40	5	7	8	24	34	1	6	13	20	46	31

Reds' leading League goalscorer: Aldridge 26

DIVISION 1 1988-1989

	P	W	D	L	F	A	W	D	L	F	A	Pts
Arsenal	38	10	6	3	35	19	12	4	3	38	17	76
LIVERPOOL	**38**	**11**	**5**	**3**	**33**	**11**	**11**	**5**	**3**	**32**	**17**	**76**
Nottingham F	38	8	7	4	31	16	9	6	4	33	27	64
Norwich C	38	8	7	4	23	20	9	4	6	25	25	62
Derby Co	38	9	3	7	23	18	8	4	7	17	20	58
Tottenham H	38	8	6	5	31	24	7	6	6	29	22	57
Coventry C	38	9	4	6	28	23	5	9	5	19	19	55
Everton	38	10	7	2	33	18	4	5	10	17	27	54
QPR	38	9	5	5	23	16	5	6	8	20	21	53
Millwall	38	10	3	6	27	21	4	8	7	20	31	53
Manchester U	38	10	5	4	27	13	3	7	9	18	22	51
Wimbledon	38	10	3	6	30	19	4	6	9	20	27	51
Southampton	38	6	7	6	25	26	4	8	7	27	40	45
Charlton A	38	6	7	6	25	24	4	5	10	19	34	42
Sheffield W	38	6	6	7	21	25	4	6	9	13	26	42
Luton T	38	8	6	5	32	21	2	5	12	10	31	41
Aston Villa	38	7	6	6	25	22	2	7	10	20	34	40
Middlesbrough	38	6	7	6	28	30	3	5	11	16	31	39
West Ham U	38	3	6	10	19	30	7	2	10	18	32	38
Newcastle U	38	3	6	10	19	28	4	4	11	13	35	31

Reds' leading League goalscorer: Aldridge 21

DIVISION 1 1989-1990

	P	W	D	L	F	A	W	D	L	F	A	Pts
LIVERPOOL	**38**	**13**	**5**	**1**	**38**	**15**	**10**	**5**	**4**	**40**	**22**	**79**
Aston Villa	38	13	3	3	36	20	8	4	7	21	18	70
Tottenham H	38	12	1	6	35	24	7	5	7	24	23	63
Arsenal	38	14	3	2	38	11	4	5	10	16	27	62
Chelsea	38	8	7	4	31	24	8	5	6	27	26	60
Everton	38	14	3	2	40	16	3	5	11	17	30	59
Southampton	38	10	5	4	40	27	5	5	9	31	36	55
Wimbledon	38	5	8	6	22	23	8	8	3	25	17	55
Nottingham F	38	9	4	6	31	21	6	5	8	24	26	54
Norwich C	38	7	10	2	24	14	6	4	9	20	28	53
QPR	38	9	4	6	27	22	4	7	8	18	22	50
Coventry C	38	11	2	6	24	25	3	5	11	15	34	49
Manchester U	38	8	6	5	26	14	5	3	11	20	33	48
Manchester C	38	9	4	6	26	21	3	8	8	17	31	48
Crystal P	38	8	7	4	27	23	5	2	12	15	43	48
Derby Co	38	9	1	9	29	21	4	6	9	14	19	46
Luton T	38	8	8	3	24	18	2	5	12	19	39	43
Sheffield W	38	8	6	5	21	17	3	4	12	14	34	43
Charlton A	38	4	6	9	18	25	3	3	13	13	32	30
Millwall	38	4	6	9	23	25	1	5	13	16	40	26

Reds' leading League goalscorer: Barnes 22

DIVISION 1 1990-1991

	P	W	D	L	F	A	W	D	L	F	A	Pts
Arsenal	38	15	4	0	51	10	9	9	1	23	8	*83
LIVERPOOL	**38**	**14**	**3**	**2**	**42**	**13**	**9**	**4**	**6**	**35**	**27**	**76**
Crystal P	38	11	6	2	26	17	9	3	7	24	24	69
Leeds U	38	12	2	5	46	23	7	5	7	19	24	64
Man City	38	12	3	4	35	25	5	8	6	29	28	62
Man Utd	38	11	4	4	34	17	5	8	6	24	28	†59
Wimbledon	38	8	6	5	28	22	6	8	5	25	24	56
Nottingham F	38	11	4	4	42	21	3	8	8	23	29	54
Everton	38	9	5	5	26	15	4	7	8	24	31	51
Tottenham H	38	8	9	2	35	22	3	7	9	16	28	49
Chelsea	38	10	6	3	33	25	3	4	12	25	44	49
QPR	38	8	5	6	27	22	4	5	10	17	31	46
Sheffield U	38	9	3	7	23	23	4	4	11	13	32	46
Southampton	38	9	6	4	33	22	3	3	13	25	47	45
Norwich C	38	9	3	7	27	32	4	3	12	14	32	45
Coventry C	38	10	6	3	30	16	1	5	13	12	33	44
Aston Villa	38	7	9	3	29	25	2	5	12	17	33	41
Luton T	38	7	5	7	22	18	3	2	14	20	43	37
Sunderland	38	6	6	7	15	16	2	4	13	23	44	34
Derby Co	38	3	8	8	25	36	2	1	16	12	39	24

**Arsenal had two points deducted for disciplinary reasons. †Man United had one point deducted for disciplinary reasons.*

Reds' leading League goalscorers: Barnes & Rush 16

DIVISION 1 1991-1992

	P	W	D	L	F	A	W	D	L	F	A	Pts
Leeds U	42	13	8	0	38	13	9	8	4	36	24	82
Manchester U	42	12	7	2	34	13	9	8	4	29	20	78
Sheffield W	42	13	5	3	39	24	8	7	6	23	25	75
Arsenal	42	12	7	2	51	22	7	8	6	30	24	72
Manchester C	42	13	4	4	32	14	7	6	8	29	34	70
LIVERPOOL	**42**	**13**	**5**	**3**	**34**	**17**	**3**	**11**	**7**	**13**	**23**	**64**
Aston Villa	42	13	3	5	31	16	4	6	11	17	28	60
Nottingham F	42	10	7	4	36	27	6	4	11	24	31	59
Sheffield U	42	9	6	6	29	23	7	3	11	36	40	57
Crystal P	42	7	8	6	24	25	7	7	7	29	36	57
QPR	42	6	10	5	25	21	6	8	7	23	26	54
Everton	42	8	8	5	28	19	5	6	10	24	32	53
Wimbledon	42	10	5	6	32	20	3	9	9	21	33	53
Chelsea	42	7	8	6	31	30	6	6	9	19	30	53
Tottenham H	42	7	3	11	33	35	8	4	9	25	28	52
Southampton	42	7	5	9	17	28	7	5	9	22	27	52
Oldham A	42	11	5	5	46	36	3	4	14	17	31	51
Norwich C	42	8	6	7	29	28	3	6	12	18	35	45
Coventry C	42	6	7	8	18	15	5	4	12	17	29	44
Luton T	42	10	7	4	25	17	0	5	16	13	54	42
Notts Co	42	7	5	9	24	29	3	5	13	16	33	40
West Ham U	42	6	6	9	22	24	3	5	13	15	35	38

Reds' leading League goalscorer: Saunders 10

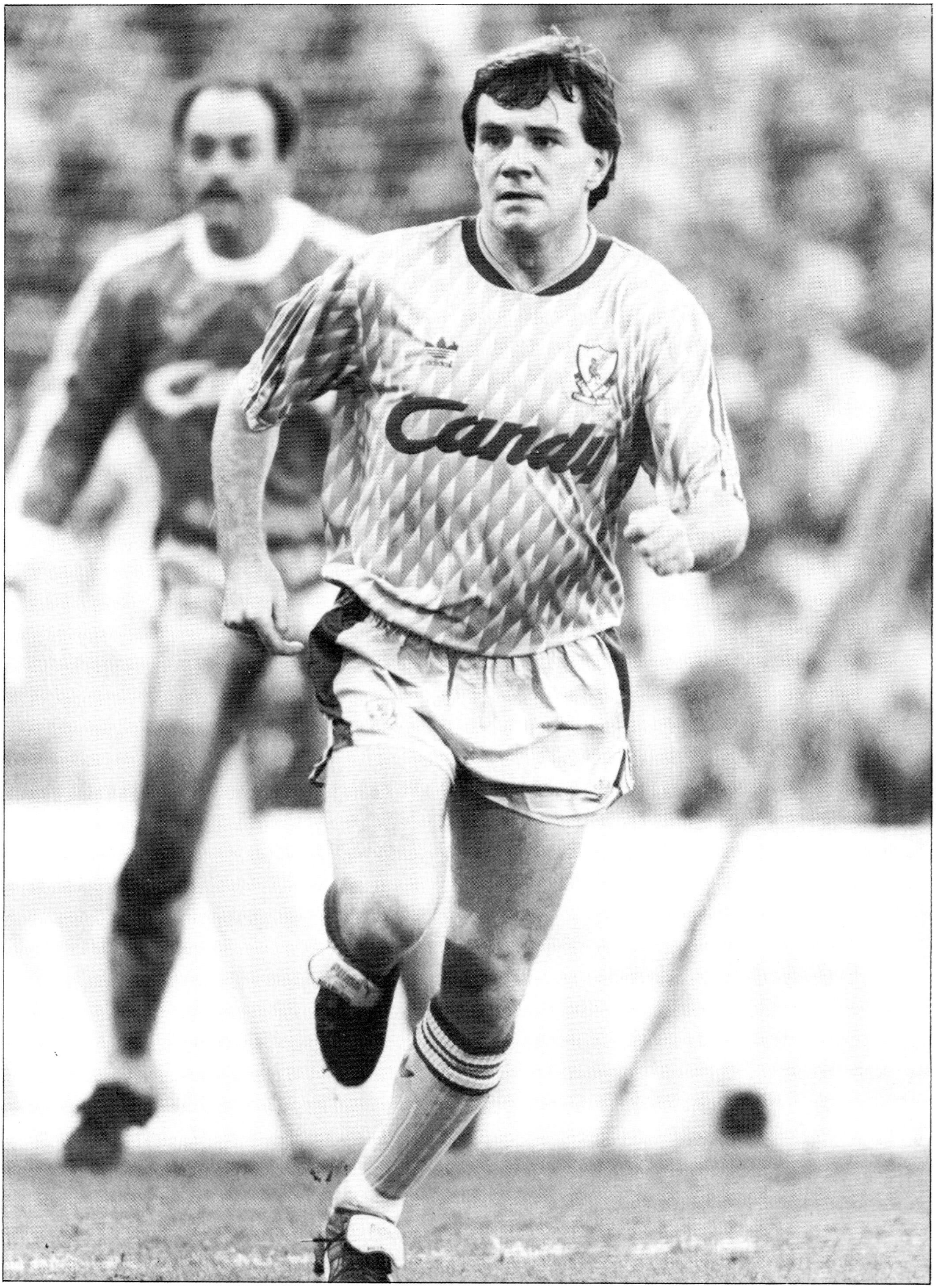

Midfielder Ray Houghton scored 28 goals in 153 League games for Liverpool after joining them from Oxford United for £800,000 in October 1987. Houghton, a Republic of Ireland international despite being born in Glasgow, gained two League Championship medals and two FA Cup winners' medals before being transferred to Aston Villa in 1992. Before Oxford he played for Fulham.